EVERYMAN, I will go with thee,

and be thy guide,

In thy most need to go by thy side

JOHN RICHARD GREEN

Born in 1837 at Oxford and educated at Jesus College there. In 1860 took Holy orders and in 1866 was appointed incumbent of St Philip's, Stepney. Retired from the Church in 1869 and became librarian at Lambeth. He died in 1883.

JOHN RICHARD GREEN

A Short History
of the
English People

IN TWO VOLUMES · VOLUME TWO

INTRODUCTION AND NOTES BY
L. CECIL JANE

WITH A SURVEY OF
THE PERIOD 1815–1960

DENT : LONDON
EVERYMAN'S LIBRARY
DUTTON: NEW YORK

© Revisions, J. M. Dent & Sons Ltd, 1960

All rights reserved
Made in Great Britain
at the
Aldine Press · Letchworth · Herts
for
J. M. DENT & SONS LTD
Aldine House · Bedford Street · London
First included in Everyman's Library 1915
Last revised 1960
Last reprinted 1968

NO. *728*

SBN: 460 00728 9

CONTENTS

VOLUME TWO

The pagination in this edition is continuous throughout the two volumes

CHAPTER VIII

PURITAN ENGLAND

CHAPTER IX

THE REVOLUTION

CHAPTER X

MODERN ENGLAND

vi

Contents

A POLITICAL AND SOCIAL SURVEY (1815—1914)

CHAPTER I

FROM WATERLOO TO THE REFORM BILL, 1815—1832

CHAPTER II

FROM THE REFORM BILL TO THE EDUCATION ACT OF 1870, 1832—1870

CHAPTER III

FROM THE EDUCATION ACT (1870) TO THE OUTBREAK OF THE EUROPEAN WAR, 1870—1914

CHAPTER IV

A SUMMARY OF EVENTS, 1914-1960

MAPS

CHAPTER VIII

PURITAN ENGLAND

Section I.—The Puritans, 1583—1603

[*Authorities.*—The chief sources are Strype's Works and Parker's Correspondence; a selection of ecclesiastical documents will be found in Prothero, " Statutes and Constitutional Documents." Other works of importance are Whittingham, " Brieff Discours of Troubles at Frankfort (1575) "; Pierce, " Historical Introduction to the Marprelate Tracts "; the " Diaries of Wallington "; the " Memoirs of Colonel Hutchinson," by his wife; and Masson, " Life of Milton." The best general Church history is that edited by Hunt and Stephens, the volume dealing with Elizabeth and James I. being by Frere. See also Hallam, " Constitutional History."]

No greater moral change ever passed over a nation than passed The over England during the years which parted the middle of the reign Bible of Elizabeth from the meeting of the Long Parliament. England became the people of a book, and that book was the Bible. It was as yet the one English book which was familiar to every Englishman; it was read at churches and read at home, and everywhere its words, as they fell on ears which custom had not deadened to their force and beauty, kindled a startling enthusiasm. When Bishop Bonner set up the first six Bibles in St. Paul's " many well-disposed people used much to resort to the hearing thereof, especially when they could get any that had an audible voice to read to them. . . . One John Porter used sometimes to be occupied in that goodly exercise, to the edifying of himself as well as others. This Porter was a fresh young man and of a big stature; and great multitudes would resort thither to hear him, because he could read well and had an audible voice." The popularity of the Bible was owing to other causes besides that of religion. The whole prose literature of England, save the forgotten tracts of Wyclif, has grown up since the translation of the Scriptures by Tyndall and Coverdale. No history, no romance, no poetry, save the little-known verse of Chaucer, existed for any practical purpose in the English tongue when the Bible was ordered to be set up in churches. Sunday after Sunday, day after day, the crowds that gathered round Bonner's Bibles in the nave of St. Paul's, or the family group that hung on the words of the Geneva Bible in the devotional exercises at home, were leavened with a new literature. Legends and annals, war song and psalm, State-rolls and biographies, the mighty voices of prophets, the parables of Evangelists, stories of mission journeys, of perils by the sea and among the heathen, philosophic arguments, apocalyptic visions, all were flung broadcast over minds unoccupied

431

for the most part by any rival learning. The disclosure of the stores of Greek literature had wrought the revolution of the Renascence. The disclosure of the older mass of Hebrew literature wrought the revolution of the Reformation. But the one revolution was far deeper and wider in its effects than the other. No version could transfer to another tongue the peculiar charm of language which gave their value to the authors of Greece and Rome. Classical letters, therefore, remained in the possession of the learned, that is of the few; and among these, with the exception of Colet and More, or of the pedants who revived a Pagan worship in the gardens of the Florentine Academy, their direct influence was purely intellectual. But the tongue of the Hebrew, the idiom of Hellenistic Greek, lent themselves with a curious felicity to the purposes of translation. As a mere literary monument, the English version of the Bible remains the noblest example of the English tongue. Its perpetual use made it from the instant of its appearance the standard of our language. But for the moment its literary effect was less than its social. The power of the book over the mass of Englishmen showed itself in a thousand superficial ways, and in none more conspicuously than in the influence it exerted on ordinary speech. It formed, we must repeat, the whole literature which was practically accessible to ordinary Englishmen; and when we recall the number of common phrases which we owe to great authors, the bits of Shakspere, or Milton, or Dickens, or Thackeray, which unconsciously interweave themselves in our ordinary talk, we shall better understand the strange mosaic of Biblical words and phrases which coloured English talk two hundred years ago. The mass of picturesque allusion and illustration which we borrow from a thousand books, our fathers were forced to borrow from one; and the borrowing was the easier and the more natural that the range of the Hebrew literature fitted it for the expression of every phase of feeling. When Spenser poured forth his warmest love-notes in the "Epithalamion," he adopted the very words of the Psalmist, as he bade the gates open for the entrance of his bride. When Cromwell saw the mists break over the hills of Dunbar, he hailed the sun burst with the cry of David: "Let God arise, and let his enemies be scattered. Like as the sun riseth, so shalt thou drive them away!" Even to common minds this familiarity with grand poetic imagery in prophet and apocalypse gave a loftiness and ardour of expression, that with all its tendency to exaggeration and bombast we may prefer to the slipshod vulgarisms of the shopkeeper of to-day.

But far greater than its effect on literature or social phrase was the effect of the Bible on the character of the people at large. Elizabeth might silence or tune the pulpits; but it was impossible for her to silence or tune the great preachers of justice, and mercy, and truth, who spoke from the book which she had again opened for her people. The whole moral effect which is produced now-a-days by the religious newspaper, the tract, the essay, the lecture, the missionary report, the sermon, was then produced by the Bible alone. And its effect in this way, however dispassionately we examine it, was simply amazing. The whole temper of the nation was changed. A new conception of life and of man superseded the old. A new moral and religious impulse spread through every class. Literature reflected the general tendency of the time; and the dumpy little quartos of controversy and piety, which still crowd our older libraries, drove before them the classical translations and Italian novelettes of the age of Elizabeth. " Theology rules there," said Grotius of England, only ten years after the Queen's death; and when Casaubon, the last of the great scholars of the sixteenth century, was invited to England by King James, he found both King and people indifferent to letters. " There is a great abundance of theologians in England," he says to a friend; " all point their studies in that direction." The study of the country gentleman pointed towards theology as much as that of the scholar. As soon as Colonel Hutchinson " had improved his natural understanding with the acquisition of learning, the first studies he exercised himself in were the principles of religion." The whole nation became, in fact, a Church. The great problems of life and death, whose " obstinate questionings " found no answer in the higher minds of Shakspere's day, pressed for an answer from the men who followed him. We must not, indeed, picture the early Puritan as a gloomy fanatic. It was long before the religious movement—which affected the noble and the squire as much as the shopkeeper or the farmer— came into conflict with general culture. With the close of the Elizabethan age, indeed, the intellectual freedom which had marked it faded insensibly away: the bold philosophical speculations which Sydney had caught from Bruno, and which had brought on Marlowe and Raleigh the charge of atheism, died, like her own religious indifference, with the Queen. But the lighter and more elegant sides of the Elizabethan culture harmonized well enough with the temper of the Puritan gentleman. The figure of Colonel Hutchinson, one of the Regicides, stands out from his wife's canvas with the grace and tenderness of a portrait by Vandyck. She dwells on the personal beauty which distinguished his youth, on " his teeth even and white as the purest ivory," " his hair of brown, very thickset in his youth, softer than the finest silk, curling with loose great rings at the ends." Serious as was his temper in graver matters, the young squire was fond of hawking, and piqued himself on his skill in dancing and fence. His artistic taste showed itself in a critical love of " gravings, sculpture, and all liberal arts," as well as in the pleasure he took in his gardens, " in the improvement of his grounds, in planting groves and walks and fruit trees." If he was " diligent in his examination of the Scriptures," " he had a great love for music, and often diverted himself with a viol, on which he played masterly." A taste for music, indeed, seems to have been common in the graver homes of the time. If we pass from Owthorpe and Colonel Hutchinson to the house of a London

scrivener in Bread Street, we find Milton's father, precisian and
man of business as he was, composing madrigals to Oriana, and
rivalling Bird and Gibbons as a writer of sacred song. We miss,
indeed, the passion of the Elizabethan time, its caprice, its largeness of feeling and sympathy, its quick pulse of delight; but, on
the other hand, life gains in moral grandeur, in a sense of the
dignity of manhood, in orderliness and equable force. The temper
of the Puritan gentleman was just, noble, and self-controlled. The
larger geniality of the age that had passed away shrank into an
intense tenderness within the narrower circle of the home. " He
was as kind a father," says Mrs. Hutchinson of her husband, " as
dear a brother, as good a master, as faithful a friend as the world
had." Passion was replaced by a manly purity. " Neither in youth
nor riper years could the most fair or enticing woman ever draw
him so much as into unnecessary familiarity or dalliance. Wise
and virtuous women he loved, and delighted in all pure and holy
and unblameable conversation with them, but so as never to excite
scandal or temptation. Scurrilous discourse even among men he
abhorred; and though he sometimes took pleasure in wit and
mirth, yet that which was mixed with impurity he never could
endure." The play and wilfulness of life, in which the Elizabethans
found its chiefest charm, the Puritan regarded as unworthy of its
character and end. His aim was to attain self-command, to be
master of himself, of his thought and speech and acts. A certain
gravity and reflectiveness gave its tone to the lightest details of
his daily converse with the world about him. His temper, quick as
it might naturally be, was kept under strict control. In his discourse
he was ever on his guard against talkativeness or frivolity, striving
to be deliberate in speech and " ranking the words beforehand."
His life was orderly and methodical, sparing of diet and of self-
indulgence; he rose early, " he never was at any time idle, and
hated to see any one else so." The new sobriety and self-restraint
marked itself even in his change of dress. The gorgeous colours
and jewels of the Renascence disappeared. Colonel Hutchinson
" left off very early the wearing of anything that was costly, yet
in his plainest negligent habit appeared very much a gentleman."
The loss of colour and variety in costume reflected no doubt a
certain loss of colour and variety in life itself; but it was a loss
compensated by solid gains. Greatest among these, perhaps, was
the new conception of social equality. Their common call, their
common brotherhood in Christ, annihilated in the mind of the
Puritans that overpowering sense of social distinctions which characterized the age of Elizabeth. The meanest peasant felt himself
ennobled as a child of God. The proudest noble recognized a spiritual
equality in the poorest " saint." The great social revolution of the
Civil Wars and the Protectorate was already felt in the demeanour
of gentlemen like Hutchinson. " He had a loving and sweet
courtesy to the poorest, and would often employ many spare hours
with the commonest soldiers and poorest labourers." " He never

disdained the meanest nor flattered the greatest." But it was felt
even more in the new dignity and self-respect with which the
consciousness of their " calling " invested the classes beneath the
rank of the gentry.   Take such a portrait as that which John
Wallington, a turner in Eastcheap, has left us of a London housewife, his mother. " She was very loving," he says, " and obedient
to her parents, loving and kind to her husband, very tender-
hearted to her children, loving all that were godly, much misliking
the wicked and profane. She was a pattern of sobriety unto many,
very seldom was seen abroad except at church; when others
recreated themselves at holidays and other times, she would take
her needle-work and say ' here is my recreation.' . . . God had
given her a pregnant wit and an excellent memory. She was very
ripe and perfect in all stories of the Bible, likewise in all the stories
of the Martyrs, and could readily turn to them; she was also
perfect and well seen in the English Chronicles, and in the descents
of the Kings of England. She lived in holy wedlock with her
husband twenty years, wanting but four days."

The strength, however, of the Puritan cause lay as yet rather in
the middle and professional class, than among the small traders or
the gentry; and it is in a Puritan of this class that we find the
fullest and noblest expression of the new influence which was
leavening the temper of the time. Milton is not only the highest,
but the completest type of Puritanism. His life is absolutely contemporary with that of his cause. He was born when it began to
exercise a direct power over English politics and English religion;
he died when its effort to mould them into its own shape was over,
and when it had again sunk into one of many influences to which
we owe our English character. His earlier verse, the pamphlets of
his riper years, the epics of his age, mark with a singular precision
the three great stages in its history. His youth shows us how
much of the gaiety, the poetic ease, the intellectual culture of the
Renascence lingered in a Puritan home. Scrivener and " precisian "
as his father was, he was a skilful musician; and the boy inherited
his father's skill on lute and organ. One of the finest outbursts in
the scheme of education which he put forth at a later time is a
passage, in which he vindicates the province of music as an agent
in moral training. His home, his tutor, his school were all rigidly
Puritan; but there was nothing narrow or illiberal in his early
training. " My father," he says, " destined me while yet a little
boy to the study of humane letters; which I seized with such
eagerness that from the twelfth year of my age I scarcely ever
went from my lessons to bed before midnight." But to the Greek,
Latin, and Hebrew he learnt at school, the scrivener advised him
to add Italian and French. Nor were English letters neglected.
Spenser gave the earliest turn to his poetic genius. In spite of the
war between playwright and precisian, a Puritan youth could stil
in Milton's days avow his love of the stage, " if Jonson's learned
sock be on, or sweetest Shakspere, Fancy's child, warble his native

woodnotes wild," and gather from the " masques and antique pageantry " of the court-revel hints for his own Comus and Arcades. Nor does any shadow of the coming struggle with the Church disturb the young scholar's reverie, as he wanders beneath " the high embowed roof, with antique pillars, massy proof, and storied windows richly dight, casting a dim religious light," or as he hears " the pealing organ blow to the full-voiced choir below, in service high and anthem clear." His enjoyment of the gaiety of life stands in bright contrast with the gloom and sternness of the later Puritanism. In spite of " a certain reservedness of natural disposition," which shrank from " festivities and jests, in which I acknowledge my faculty to be very slight," the young singer could still enjoy the " jest and youthful jollity " of the world around him, of its " quips and cranks and wanton wiles; " he could join the crew of Mirth, and look pleasantly on at the village fair, " where the jolly rebecks sound to many a youth and many a maid, dancing in the chequered shade." But his pleasures were unreproved. There was nothing ascetic in his look, in his slender, vigorous frame, his face full of a delicate yet serious beauty, the rich brown hair which clustered over his brow; and the words we have quoted show his sensitive enjoyment of all that was beautiful. But from coarse or sensual self-indulgence the young Puritan turned with disgust: " A certain reservedness of nature, an honest haughtiness and self-esteem, kept me still above those low descents of mind." He drank in an ideal chivalry from Spenser, but his religion and purity disdained the outer pledge on which chivalry built up its fabric of honour. " Every free and gentle spirit," said Milton, " without that oath, ought to be born a knight." It was with this temper that he passed from his London school, St. Paul's, to Christ's College at Cambridge, and it was this temper that he preserved throughout his University career. He left Cambridge, as he said afterwards, " free from all reproach, and approved by all honest men," with a purpose of self-dedication " to that same lot, however mean or high, towards which time leads me, and the will of Heaven."

Even in the still calm beauty of a life such as this, we catch the sterner tones of the Puritan temper. The very height of its aim, the intensity of its moral concentration, brought with them a loss of the genial delight in all that was human which distinguished the men of the Renascence. " If ever God instilled an intense love of moral beauty into the mind of any man," said Milton, " he has instilled it into mine." " Love Virtue," closed his Comus, " she alone is free! " But the love of virtue and of moral beauty, if it gave strength to human conduct, narrowed human sympathy and human intelligence. Already in Milton we note " a certain reservedness of temper," a contempt for " the false estimates of the vulgar," a proud retirement from the meaner and coarser life around him. Great as was his love for Shakspere, we can hardly fancy him delighting in Falstaff. In minds of a less cultured order, this moral

tension ended in a hard unsocial sternness of life. The ordinary
Puritan, like the housewife of Eastcheap whom we have noticed
above, " loved all that were godly, much misliking the wicked and
profane." His bond to other men was not the sense of a common
manhood, but the recognition of a brotherhood among the elect.
Without the pale of the saints lay a world which was hateful to
them, because it was the enemy of their God. It was this utter
isolation from the " ungodly " that explains the contrast which
startles us between the inner tenderness of the Puritans and the
ruthlessness of so many of their actions. Cromwell, whose son's
death (in his own words) went to his heart " like a dagger, indeed
it did! " and who rode away sad and wearied from the triumph
of Marston Moor, burst into horse-play as he signed the death-
warrant of the King. A temper which had thus lost sympathy with
the life of half the world around it could hardly sympathize with
the whole of its own life. Humour, the faculty which above all
corrects exaggeration and extravagance, died away before the new
stress and strain of existence. The absolute devotion of the Puritan
to a Supreme Will tended more and more to rob him of all sense
of measure and proportion in common matters. Little things
became great things in the glare of religious zeal; and the godly
man learnt to shrink from a surplice, or a mince-pie at Christmas,
as he shrank from impurity or a lie. Life became hard, rigid,
colourless, as it became intense. The play, the geniality, the delight
of the Elizabethan age were exchanged for a measured sobriety,
seriousness, and self-restraint. But it was a self-restraint and
sobriety which limited itself wholly to the outer life. In the inner
soul of the Puritan, sense, reason, judgment were overborne by
the terrible reality of " invisible things." Our first glimpse of
Oliver Cromwell is as a young country squire and farmer in the
marsh levels around Huntingdon and St. Ives, buried from time
to time in a deep melancholy, and haunted by fancies of coming
death. " I live in Meshac," he writes to a friend, " which they say
signifies Prolonging; in Kedar, which signifies Darkness; yet the
Lord forsaketh me not." The vivid sense of a Divine Purity close
to such men made the life of common men seem sin. " You know
what my manner of life has been," Cromwell adds. " Oh, I lived
in and loved darkness, and hated light. I hated godliness." Yet
his worst sin was probably nothing more than an enjoyment of the
natural buoyancy of youth, and a want of the deeper earnestness
which comes with riper years. In imaginative tempers, like that of
Bunyan, the struggle took a more picturesque form. John Bunyan
was the son of a poor tinker at Elstow in Bedfordshire, and even in
childhood his fancy revelled in terrible visions of Heaven and Hell.
" When I was but a child of nine or ten years old," he tells us,
" these things did so distress my soul, that then in the midst of
my merry sports and childish vanities, amidst my vain com-
panions, I was often much cast down and afflicted in my mind
therewith; yet could I not let go my sins." The sins he could not

let go were a love of hockey and of dancing on the village green; for the only real fault which his bitter self-accusation discloses, that of a habit of swearing, was put an end to at once and for ever by a rebuke from an old woman. His passion for bell-ringing clung to him even after he had broken from it as a " vain practice; " and he would go to the steeple house and look on, till the thought that a bell might fall and crush him in his sins drove him panic-stricken from the door. A sermon against dancing and games drew him for a time from these indulgences; but the temptation again overmastered his resolve. " I shook the sermon out of my mind, and to my old custom of sports and gaming I returned with great delight. But the same day, as I was in the midst of a game of cat, and having struck it one blow from the hole, just as I was about to strike it the second time, a voice did suddenly dart from heaven into my soul, which said, ' Wilt thou leave thy sins and go to Heaven, or have thy sins and go to Hell? ' At this I was put in an exceeding maze; wherefore, leaving my cat upon the ground, I looked up to heaven; and was as if I had with the eyes of my understanding seen the Lord Jesus looking down upon me, as being very hotly displeased with me, and as if He did severely threaten me with some grievous punishment for those and other ungodly practices."

The
Presby-
terians
Such was Puritanism, and it is of the highest importance to realize it thus in itself, in its greatness and its littleness, apart from the ecclesiastical system of Presbyterianism with which it is so often confounded. As we shall see in the course of our story, not one of the leading Puritans of the Long Parliament was a Presbyterian. Pym and Hampden had no sort of objection to Episcopacy, and the adoption of the Presbyterian system was only forced on the Puritan patriots in their later struggle by political considerations. But the growth of the movement, which thus influenced our history for a time, forms one of the most curious episodes in Elizabeth's reign. Her Church policy rested on the Acts of Supremacy and of Uniformity; the first of which placed all ecclesiastical jurisdiction and legislative power in the hands of the State, while the second prescribed a course of doctrine and discipline, from which no variation was legally permissible. For the nation at large, the system which was thus adopted was no doubt a wise and a healthy one. Single-handed, and unsupported by any of the statesmen or divines of their time, the Queen and the Primate forced on the warring religions a sort of armed truce. The main principles of the Reformation were accepted, but the zeal of the ultra-reformers was held at bay. The Bible was left open, private discussion was unrestrained, but the warfare of pulpit against pulpit was silenced by the licensing of preachers. An outer conformity, and attendance at public worship, was exacted from all; but the changes in ritual, by which the zealots of Geneva gave prominence to the radical features of the religious change which was passing over the country, were steadily resisted. While England was struggling for existence,

this balanced attitude of the Crown reflected faithfully enough the balanced attitude of the nation; but with the death of Mary Stuart the danger was over, and a marked change in public sentiment became at once observable. Unhappily no corresponding change took place in the Queen. With the religious enthusiasm which was growing up around her she had no sympathy whatever. Her passion was for moderation, her aim was simply civil order; and both order and moderation were threatened, as she held, by the knot of clerical bigots who gathered from this hour under the banner of Presbyterianism. Of these Thomas Cartwright was the chief. He had studied at Geneva; he returned with a fanatical faith in Calvinism, and in the system of Church government which Calvin had devised; and as Margaret Professor of Divinity at Cambridge he used to the full the opportunities which his chair gave him of propagating his opinions. No leader of a religious party ever deserved less of after sympathy than Cartwright. He was unquestionably learned and devout, but his bigotry was that of a mediæval inquisitor. The relics of the old ritual, the cross in baptism, the surplice, the giving of a ring in marriage, were to him not merely distasteful, as they were to the Puritans at large, they were idolatrous and the mark of the beast. His declamations against ceremonies and superstition however had little weight with Elizabeth or her Primates; what scared them was his reckless advocacy of a scheme of ecclesiastical government which placed the State beneath the feet of the Church. The absolute rule of bishops, indeed, he denounced as begotten of the devil; but the absolute rule of Presbyters he held to be established by the word of God. For the Church modelled after the fashion of Geneva he claimed an authority which surpassed the wildest dreams of the masters of the Vatican. All spiritual power and jurisdiction, the decreeing of doctrine, the ordering of ceremonies, lay wholly, according to his Calvinistic creed, in the hands of the ministers of the Church. To them, too, belonged the supervision of public morals. In an ordered arrangement of classes and synods, they were to govern their flocks, to regulate their own order, to decide in matters of faith, to administer " discipline." Their weapon was excommunication, and they were responsible for its use to none but Christ. The province of the civil ruler was simply " to see their decrees executed and to punish the contemners of them," for the spirit of such a system as this naturally excluded all toleration of practice or belief. With the despotism of a Hildebrand, Cartwright combined the cruelty of a Torquemada. Not only was Presbyterianism to be established as the one legal form of Church government, but all other forms, Episcopalian and Separatist, were to be ruthlessly put down. For heresy there was the punishment of death. Never had the doctrine of persecution been urged with such a blind and reckless ferocity. " I deny," wrote Cartwright, " that upon repentance there ought to follow any pardon of death. . . . Heretics ought to be put to death now. If this be bloody and extreme, I am content to be so counted with the Holy Ghost."

Opinions such as these might wisely have been left to be refuted by the good sense of the people itself. They found, in fact, a crushing answer in the "Ecclesiastical Polity" of Richard Hooker, a clergyman who had been Master of the Temple, but whose distaste for the controversies of its pulpit drove him from London to a Wiltshire vicarage at Boscombe, which he exchanged at a later time for the parsonage of Bishopsbourne, among the quiet meadows of Kent. The largeness of temper which characterized all the nobler minds of his day, the philosophic breadth which is seen as clearly in Shakspere as in Bacon, was united in Hooker with a grandeur and stateliness of style, which raised him to the highest rank among English prose writers. Divine as he was, his spirit and method were philosophical rather than theological. Against the ecclesiastical dogmatism of Cartwright he set the authority of reason. He abandoned the narrow ground of Scriptural argument to base his conclusions on the general principles of moral and political science, on the eternal obligations of natural law. The Presbyterian system rested on the assumption that an immutable rule for human action, in all matters relating to religion, to worship, and to the discipline and constitution of the Church, was laid down, and only laid down, in Scripture. Hooker urged that a Divine order exists, not in written revelation only, but in the moral relations, and the social and political institutions of men. He claimed for human reason the province of determining the laws of this order; of distinguishing between what is changeable and unchangeable in them, between what is eternal and what is temporary in Scripture itself. It was easy for him to push on to the field of theological controversy which Cartwright had chosen, to show historically that no form of Church government had ever been of indispensable obligation, and that ritual observances had in all ages been left to the discretion of Churches, and determined by the differences of times. But the truth on which he rested his argument against the dogmatism of the Presbyterian is of far higher value than his argument itself; for it is the truth against which ecclesiastical dogmatism, whether of the Presbyterian or the Catholic, must always shatter itself. The "Ecclesiastical Polity" appealed rather to the broad sense and intelligence of Englishmen than to the learning of divines, but its appeal was hardly needed. Popular as the Presbyterian system became in Scotland, it never took any popular hold on England; it remained to the last a clerical rather than a national creed, and even in the moment of its seeming triumph under the Commonwealth it was rejected by every part of England save London and Lancashire. But the bold challenge to the Government which was delivered in a daring "Admonition to the Parliament" had raised a panic among English statesmen and prelates which cut off all hopes of a quiet appeal to reason. It is probable that, but for the storm which

Cartwright raised, the steady growth of general discontent with he ceremonial usages he denounced would have brought about heir abolition. The Parliament of 1571 not only refused to bind he clergy to subscription to three articles on the Supremacy, the orm of Church government, and the power of the Church to ordain ites and ceremonies, but favoured the project of reforming the Liturgy by the omission of the superstitious practices. But with he appearance of the "Admonition" this natural progress of pinion abruptly ceased. The moderate statesmen who had pressed or a change in ritual withdrew from union with a party which evived the worst pretensions of the Papacy. Parker's hand pressed eavier than before on nonconforming ministers, while Elizabeth vas provoked to a measure which forms the worst blot on her reign.

The
Ecclesi-
astical
Com-
mission
1583

Her establishment of the Ecclesiastical Commission in fact converted the religious truce into a spiritual despotism. From being temporary board which represented the Royal Supremacy in matters ecclesiastical, the Commission was now turned into a permanent body wielding the almost unlimited powers of the Crown. All opinions or acts contrary to the Statutes of Supremacy nd Uniformity fell within its cognizance. A right of deprivation placed the clergy at its mercy. It had power to alter or amend he Statutes of Colleges or Schools. Not only heresy, and schism, nd nonconformity, but incest or aggravated adultery were held o fall within its scope: its means of enquiry were left without imit, and it might fine or imprison at its will. By the mere establishment of such a Court half the work of the Reformation was undone; but the large number of civilians on the board seemed to furnish some security against the excess of ecclesiastical tyranny. Of its forty-four commissioners however few actually took any part in its proceedings; and the powers of the Commission were practically left in the hands of the successive Primates. No Archbishop of Canterbury since the days of Augustine had wielded an authority so vast, so utterly despotic, as that of Parker and Whitgift and Bancroft and Abbot and Laud. The most terrible eature of their spiritual tyranny was its wholly personal character. The old symbols of doctrine were gone, and the lawyers had not et stept in to protect the clergy by defining the exact limits of the new. The result was that at the Commission-board at Lambeth he Primates created their own tests of doctrine with an utter indifference to those created by law. In one instance Parker eprived a vicar of his benefice for a denial of the verbal inspiration of the Bible. Nor did the successive Archbishops care greatly the test was a varying or a conflicting one. Whitgift strove to orce on the Church the Calvinistic supralapsarianism of his Lambeth Articles. Bancroft, who followed him, was as earnest in nforcing his anti-Calvinistic dogma of the Divine right of the piscopate. Abbot had no mercy for Erastians. Laud had none for nti-Erastians. It is no wonder that the Ecclesiastical Commission, which these men represented, soon stank in the nostrils of the

English clergy. Its establishment however marked the adoption of a distinct policy on the part of the Crown, and its efforts were backed by stern measures of repression. All preaching or reading in private houses was forbidden; and in spite of the refusal of Parliament to enforce the requirement of them by law, subscription to the Three Articles was exacted from every member of the clergy.

For the moment these measures were crowned with success. The movement under Cartwright was checked; Cartwright himself was driven from his Professorship; and an outer uniformity of worship was more and more brought about by the steady pressure of the Commission. The old liberty which had been allowed in London and the other Protestant parts of the kingdom was no longer permitted to exist. The leading Puritan clergy, whose nonconformity had hitherto been winked at, were called upon to submit to the surplice, and to make the sign of the cross. The remonstrances of the country gentry availed as little as the protest of Lord Burleigh himself to protect two hundred of the best ministers who were driven from their parsonages on their refusal to subscribe to the Three Articles. But the result of this persecution was simply to give a fresh life and popularity to the doctrines which it aimed at crushing, by drawing together two currents of opinion which were in themselves perfectly distinct. The Presbyterian platform of Church discipline had as yet been embraced by the clergy only and by few among the clergy. On the other hand, the wish for a reform in the Liturgy, the dislike of "superstitious usages," of the use of the surplice, the sign of the cross in baptism, the gift of the ring in marriage, the posture of kneeling at the Lord's Supper, was shared by a large number of the clergy and laity alike. At the opening of Elizabeth's reign almost all the higher Churchmen but Parker were opposed to them, and a motion for their abolition in Convocation was lost but by a single vote. The temper of the country gentlemen on this subject was indicated by that of Parliament; and it was well known that the wisest of the Queen's Councillors, Burleigh, Walsingham, and Knollys, were at one in this matter with the gentry. If their common persecution did not wholly succeed in fusing these two sections of religious opinion into one, it at any rate gained for the Presbyterians a general sympathy on the part of the Puritans, which raised them from a clerical clique into a popular party. Nor were the consequences of the persecution limited to the strengthening of the Presbyterians. The "Separatists," who were beginning to withdraw from attendance at public worship, on the ground that the very existence of a national Church was contrary to the Word of God, grew quickly from a few scattered zealots to twenty thousand souls. Congregations of these Independents—or, as they were called at this time from the name of their founder, Brownists—formed rapidly throughout England; and persecution on the part of the Bishops and the Presbyterians, to both of whom their opinions were equally hateful, drove flocks of refugees over sea. So great a future awaited one of these congregations that we may pause to get a glimpse of "a poor people" in Lincolnshire and the neighbourhood, who "being enlightened by the Word of God," and their members "urged with the yoke of subscription," had been led "to see further." They rejected ceremonies as relics of idolatry, the rule of bishops as unscriptural, and joined themselves, "as the Lord's free people," into "a church estate on the fellowship of the Gospel." Choosing John Robinson as their minister, they felt their way forward to the great principle of liberty of conscience; and asserted their Christian right "to walk in all the ways which God had made known or should make known to them." Their meetings or "conventicles" soon drew down the heavy hand of the law, and the little company resolved to seek a refuge in other lands; but their first attempt at flight was prevented, and when they made another, their wives and children were seized at the very moment of entering the ship. At last, however, the magistrates gave a contemptuous assent to their project; they were in fact "glad to be rid of them at any price;" and the fugitives found shelter at Amsterdam. "They knew they were pilgrims and looked not much on these things, but lifted up their eyes to Heaven, their dearest country, and quieted their spirits." Among this little band of exiles were those who were to become famous at a later time as the Pilgrim Fathers of the *Mayflower*.

It was easy to be "rid" of the Brownists; but the political danger of the course on which the Crown had entered was seen in the rise of a spirit of vigorous opposition, such as had not made its appearance since the accession of the Tudors. The growing power of public opinion received a striking recognition in the struggle which bears the name of the "Martin Marprelate controversy." The Puritans had from the first appealed by their pamphlets from the Crown to the people, and Whitgift bore witness to their influence on opinion by his efforts to gag the Press. The regulations of the Star-Chamber for this purpose are memorable as the first step in the long struggle of government after government to check the liberty of printing. The irregular censorship which had long existed was now finally organized. Printing was restricted to London and the two Universities, the number of printers reduced, and all candidates for license to print placed under the supervision of the Company of Stationers. Every publication too, great or small, had to receive the approbation of the Primate or the Bishop of London. The first result of this system of repression was the appearance, in the very year of the Armada, of a series of anonymous pamphlets bearing the significant name of "Martin Marprelate," and issued from a secret press which found refuge from the Royal pursuivants in the country-houses of the gentry. The press was at last seized; and the suspected authors of these scurrilous libels, Penry, a young Welshman, and a minister named Udall, died, the one in prison, the other on the scaffold. But the virulence and boldness of their language produced a powerful

effect, for it was impossible under the system of Elizabeth to
" mar " the bishops without attacking the Crown; and a new age
of political liberty was felt to be at hand when Martin Marprelate
forced the political and ecclesiastical measures of the Government
into the arena of public discussion. The suppression, indeed, of
these pamphlets was far from damping the courage of the Presbyterians. Cartwright, who had been appointed by Lord Leicester
to the mastership of an hospital at Warwick, was bold enough
to organize his system of Church discipline among the clergy of
that county and of Northamptonshire. The example was widely
followed; and the general gatherings of the whole ministerial body
of the clergy, and the smaller assemblies for each diocese or shire,
which in the Presbyterian scheme bore the name of Synods and
Classes, began to be held in many parts of England for the purposes
of debate and consultation. The new organization was quickly
suppressed indeed, but Cartwright was saved from the banishment
which Whitgift demanded by a promise of submission; and the
struggle, transferred to the higher sphere of the Parliament,
widened into the great contest for liberty under James, and the
Civil War under his successor.

SECTION II.—THE FIRST OF THE STUARTS, 1604—1623

[*Authorities.*—The various Calendars of State Papers and the " Parliamentary History of England " are the most useful sources. For James I.,
his own Works. Prothero, " Statutes and Constitutional Documents,"
contains the principal documents of the reign. For Bacon, Spedding,
" Life and Letters of Lord Bacon." Among modern historians, Gardiner,
" History of England," is a mine of information and must be regarded
as the standard work on the period. Ranke, " History of England," is
especially valuable for foreign relations, and is far more readable than
Gardiner. For Gunpowder Plot, see Gerard, " What was Gunpowder
Plot ? " and Gardiner's answer, " What Gunpowder Plot was." For the
divine right of kings, see Figgis, " Divine Right of Kings."]

To judge fairly the attitude and policy of the English Puritans,
that is of three-fourths of the Protestants of England, at this
moment, we must cursorily review the fortunes of Protestantism
during the reign of Elizabeth. At the Queen's accession, the success
of the Reformation seemed almost everywhere secure. Already
triumphant in the north of Germany, the Pacification of Passau
was the signal for a beginning of its conquest of the south. The
Emperor Maximilian was believed to be wavering in the faith.
Throughout Austria and Hungary, the nobles and burghers
abandoned Catholicism in a mass. A Venetian ambassador
estimated the German Catholics at little more than one-tenth
of the whole population of Germany. The Scandinavian kingdoms
embraced the new faith, and it mastered at once the eastern and
western States of Europe. In Poland the majority of the nobles
became Protestants. Scotland flung off Catholicism under Mary,

and England veered round again to Protestantism under Elizabeth. At the same moment, the death of Henry the Second opened a way for the rapid diffusion of the new doctrines in France. Only where the dead hand of Spain lay heavy, in Castile, in Arragon, or in Italy, was the Reformation thoroughly crushed out; and even the dead hand of Spain failed to crush heresy in the Low Countries. But at the very instant of its seeming triumph, the advance of the new religion was suddenly arrested. The first twenty years of Elizabeth's reign were a period of suspense. The progress of Protestantism gradually ceased. It wasted its strength in theological controversies and persecutions, above all in the bitter and venomous discussions between the Churches which followed Luther and the Churches which followed Calvin. It was degraded and weakened by the prostitution of the Reformation to political ends, by the greed and worthlessness of the German princes who espoused its cause, by the factious lawlessness of the nobles in Poland, and of the Huguenots in France. Meanwhile the Papacy succeeded in rallying the Catholic world round the Council of Trent. The Roman Church, enfeebled and corrupted by the triumph of ages, felt at last the uses of adversity. Her faith was settled and defined. The most crying among the ecclesiastical abuses which had provoked the movement of the Reformation were sternly put down. The enthusiasm of the Protestants roused a counter enthusiasm among their opponents; new religious orders rose to meet the wants of the day; the Capuchins became the preachers of Catholicism, the Jesuits became not only its preachers, but its directors, its schoolmasters, its missionaries, its diplomatists. Their organization, their blind obedience, their real ability, their fanatical zeal galvanized the pulpit, the school, the confessional into a new life. If the Protestants had enjoyed the profitable monopoly of martyrdom at the opening of the century, the Catholics won a fair share of it as soon as the disciples of Loyola came to the front. The tracts which pictured the tortures of Campion and Southwell roused much the same fire at Toledo or Vienna as the pages of Foxe had roused in England. Even learning passed gradually over to the side of the older faith. Bellarmine, the greatest of controversialists at this time, Baronius, the most erudite of Church historians, were both Catholics. With a growing inequality of strength such as this, we can hardly wonder that the tide was seen at last to turn. A few years before the fight with the Armada Catholicism began definitely to win ground. Southern Germany, where the Austrian House, so long lukewarm in its faith, had at last become zealots in its defence, was the first country to be re-Catholicized. The success of Socinianism in Poland severed that kingdom from any real communion with the general body of the Protestant Churches; and these again were more and more divided into two warring camps by the controversies about the Sacrament and Free Will. Everywhere the Jesuits won converts, and their peaceful victories were soon backed by the arm of Spain. In the fierce struggle which followed, Philip was undoubtedly worsted. England was saved by its defeat of the Armada; the United Provinces of the Netherlands rose into a great Protestant power through their own dogged heroism and the genius of William the Silent. France was rescued, at the moment when all hope seemed gone, by the unconquerable energy of Henry of Navarre. But even in its defeat Catholicism gained ground. In the Low Countries, the Reformation was driven from the Walloon provinces, from Brabant, and from Flanders. In France, Henry the Fourth found himself obliged to purchase Paris by a mass; and the conversion of the King was followed by a quiet dissolution of the Huguenot party. Nobles and scholars alike forsook Protestantism; and though the Reformation remained dominant south of the Loire, it lost all hope of winning the country as a whole to its side.

The Gunpowder Plot
At the death of Elizabeth, therefore, the temper of every Protestant, whether in England or abroad, was that of a man who, after cherishing the hope of a crowning victory, is forced to look on at a crushing and irremediable defeat. The dream of a reformation of the universal Church was utterly at an end. The borders of Protestantism were narrowing every day, nor was there a sign that the triumph of the Papacy was arrested. The accession of James indeed raised the hopes of the Catholics in England itself; he had intrigued for their support before the Queen's death, and their persecution was relaxed for a while after he had mounted the throne. But it soon began again with even greater severity than of old, and six thousand Catholics were presented as recusants in a single year. Hopeless of aid from abroad, or of success in an open rising at home, a small knot of desperate men, with Robert Catesby, who had been engaged in the plot of Essex, at their head, resolved to destroy at a blow both King and Parliament. Barrels of powder were placed in a cellar beneath the Parliament House; and while waiting for the fifth of November, when the Parliament was summoned to meet, the plans of the little group widened into a formidable conspiracy. Catholics of greater fortune, such as Sir Everard Digby and Francis Tresham, were admitted to their confidence, and supplied money for the larger projects they designed. Arms were bought in Flanders, horses were held in readiness, a meeting of Catholic gentlemen was brought about under show of a hunting party to serve as the beginning of a rising. The destruction of the King was to be followed by the seizure of the King's children and an open revolt, in which aid might be
1604 called for from the Spaniards in Flanders. Wonderful as was the secrecy with which the plot was concealed, the cowardice of Tresham at the last moment gave a clue to it by a letter to Lord Monteagle, his relative, which warned him to absent himself from the Parliament on the fatal day; and further information brought about the discovery of the cellar and of Guido Fawkes, a soldier of fortune, who was charged with the custody of it. The hunting party broke up in despair, the conspirators were chased from

county to county, and either killed or sent to the block, and
Garnet, the Provincial of the English Jesuits, was brought to
solemn trial. He had shrunk from all part in the plot, but its
existence had been made known to him by another Jesuit, Green-
way, and horror-stricken as he represented himself to have been
he had kept the secret and left the Parliament to its doom. We
can hardly wonder that a frenzy of horror and dread filled the
minds of English Protestants at such a discovery. What intensified
the dread was a sense of defection and uncertainty within the pale
of the Church of England itself. No men could be more opposed
in their tendencies to one another than the High Churchmen, such
as Laud, and the English Latitudinarian, such as Hales. But to the
ordinary English Protestant both Latitudinarian and High Churchmen were equally hateful. To him the struggle with the Papacy
was not one for compromise or comprehension. It was a struggle
between light and darkness, between life and death. Every Protestant doctrine, from the least to the greatest, was equally true,
and equally sacred. No innovation in faith or worship was of
small account, if it tended in the direction of Rome. Ceremonies,
which in an hour of triumph might have been allowed as solaces
to weak brethren, became insufferable when they were turned by
weak brethren into a means of drawing nearer to the enemy in the
hour of defeat. The peril was too close at hand to allow of com-
promises. Now that falsehood was gaining ground, the only
security for truth was to draw a hard and fast line between truth
and falsehood. It is a temper such as this that we trace in the
Millenary Petition (as it was called), which was presented to James
the First on his accession by nearly eight hundred clergymen, a
tenth of the whole number in his realm. Its tone was not Presbyterian, but strictly Puritan. It asked for no change in the government or organization of the Church, but for a reform in the Church
courts, the provision and training of godly ministers, and the
suppression of "Popish usages" in the Book of Common Prayer.
Even those who were most opposed to the Presbyterian scheme
agreed as to the necessity of some concession on points of this sort.
"Why," asked Bacon, "should the civil state be purged and
restored by good and wholesome laws made every three years in
Parliament assembled, devising remedies as fast as time breedeth
mischief; and contrariwise the ecclesiastical state still continue
upon the dregs of time, and receive no alteration these forty-five
years or more?" A general expectation, in fact, prevailed that,
now the Queen's opposition was removed, something would be
done. But, different as his theological temper was from the purely
secular temper of Elizabeth, her successor was equally resolute
against all changes in Church matters.

No sovereign could have jarred against the conception of an
English ruler which had grown up under the Tudors more utterly
than James the First. His big head, his slobbering tongue, his
quilted clothes, his rickety legs, his goggle eyes, stood out in as

grotesque a contrast with all that men recalled of Henry or
Elizabeth as his gabble and rodomontade, his want of personal
dignity, his vulgar buffoonery, his coarseness, his pedantry, his
contemptible cowardice. Under this ridiculous exterior however
lay a man of much natural ability, a ripe scholar, with a considerable fund of shrewdness, of mother wit, and ready repartee.
His canny humour lights up the political and theological controversies of the time with quaint incisive phrases, with puns and
epigrams and touches of irony, which still retain their savour. His
reading, especially in theological matters, was extensive; and he
was a voluminous author on subjects which ranged from Pre-
destinarianism to tobacco. But his shrewdness and learning only
left him, in the phrase of Henry the Fourth, " the wisest fool in
Christendom." He had the temper of a pedant; and with it a
pedant's love of theories, and a pedant's inability to bring his
theories into any relation with actual facts. All might have gone
well had he confined himself to speculations about witchcraft,
about predestination, about the noxiousness of smoking. Unhappily
for England and for his successor, he clung yet more passionately
to two theories which contained within them the seeds of a death-
struggle between his people and the Crown. The first was that of
a Divine right of Kings. Even before his accession to the English
throne, he had formulated the theory of an absolute royalty in
his work on " The True Law of Free Monarchy; " and announced
that, " although a good King will frame his actions to be according
to law, yet he is not bound thereto, but of his own will and for
example-giving to his subjects." The notion was a wholly new one;
and like most of James's notions was founded simply on a blunder,
or at the best on a play upon words. " An absolute King," or
" an absolute monarchy," meant, with the Tudor statesmen who
used the phrase, a sovereign or rule complete in themselves, and
independent of all foreign or Papal interference. James chose to
regard the words as implying the monarch's freedom from all
control by law, or from responsibility to anything but his own royal
will. The King's blunder however became a system of government,
a doctrine which bishops preached from the pulpit, and for which
brave men laid their heads on the block. The Church was quick to

adopt its sovereign's discovery. Convocation in its book of Canons
denounced as a fatal error the assertion that " all civil power,
jurisdiction, and authority were first derived from the people and
disordered multitude, or either is originally still in them, or else
is deduced by their consent naturally from them, and is not God's
ordinance originally descending from Him and depending upon
Him." In strict accordance with James's theory, these doctors
declared sovereignty in its origin to be the prerogative of birthright, and inculcated passive obedience to the monarch as a
religious obligation. Cowell, a civilian, followed up the discoveries
of Convocation by an announcement that " the King is above the
law by his absolute power," and that " notwithstanding his oath

he may alter and suspend any particular law that seemeth hurtful to the public estate." The book was suppressed on the remonstrance of the House of Commons, but the party of passive obedience grew fast. A few years before the King's death, the University of Oxford decreed solemnly that "it was in no case lawful for subjects to make use of force against their princes, or to appear offensively or defensively in the field against them." The King's "arrogant speeches," if they roused resentment in the Parliaments to which they were addressed, created by sheer force of repetition a certain belief in the arbitrary right they challenged for the Crown. We may give one instance of their tone from a speech delivered in the Star-Chamber. "As it is atheism and blasphemy to dispute what God can do," said James, "so it is presumption and a high contempt in a subject to dispute what a King can do, or to say that a King cannot do this or that." A few years after his accession his words had startled English ears with a sense of coming danger to the national liberty. "If the practice should follow the positions," was the comment of a thoughtful observer, "we are not likely to leave to our successors that freedom we received from our forefathers."

It is necessary to weigh, throughout the course of James's reign, this aggressive attitude of the Crown, if we would rightly judge what seems at first sight to be an aggressive tone in some of the proceedings of the Parliaments. With new claims of power such as these before them, to have stood still would have been ruin. The claim, too, was one which jarred against all that was noblest in the Puritan tone of the time. The temper of the Puritan was eminently a temper of law. The diligence with which he searched the Scriptures sprang from his earnestness to discover a Divine Will which in all things, great or small, he might implicitly obey. But this implicit obedience was reserved for the Divine Will alone; for human ordinances derived their strength only from their correspondence with the revealed law of God. The Puritan was bound by his very religion to examine every claim made on his civil and spiritual obedience by the powers that be; and to own or reject the claim, as it accorded with the higher duty which he owed to God. "In matters of faith," Mrs. Huchinson tells us of her husband, "his reason always submitted to the Word of God; but in all other things the greatest names in the world would not lead him without reason." It was plain that an impassable gulf parted such a temper as this from the temper of unquestioning devotion to the Crown which James demanded. It was a temper not only legal, but even pedantic in its legality, intolerant from its very sense of a moral order and law of the lawlessness and disorder of a personal tyranny; a temper of criticism, of judgment, and, if need be, of stubborn and unconquerable resistance; of a resistance which sprang, not from the disdain of authority, but from the Puritan's devotion to an authority higher than that of Kings. But if the theory of a Divine right of Kings was certain to rouse against it all the nobler energies of Puritanism, there was something which roused its nobler and its pettier instincts of resistance alike in James's second theory of a Divine right of Bishops. Elizabeth's conception of her Ecclesiastical Supremacy had been a sore stumbling-block to her subjects, but Elizabeth at least regarded the Supremacy simply as a branch of her ordinary prerogative. Not only were the clergy her subjects, but they were more her subjects than the laity. She treated them in fact as her predecessors had treated the Jews. If she allowed nobody else to abuse or to rob them, she robbed and abused them herself to her heart's content. But the theory which James held as to Church and State was as different from that of Elizabeth, as the theological bent of his mind was different from her secular temper. His patristic reading had left behind it the belief in a Divine right of Bishops, as sacred and as absolute as the Divine right of Kings. Unbroken episcopal succession and hereditary regal succession were with the new sovereign the inviolable bases of Church and State. The two systems confirmed and supported each other. " No bishop, no King," ran the famous formula which embodied the King's theory. But behind his intellectual convictions lay a host of prejudices derived from his youth. The Scotch Presbyters had insulted and frightened him in the early days of his reign, and he chose to confound Puritanism with Presbyterianism. No prejudice however was really required to suggest his course. In itself it was logical, and consistent with the premisses from which it started. The very ceremonies which the Puritans denounced were ceremonies which had plenty of authority in the writings of the Fathers. That they were offensive to consciences seemed to the King no reason whatever for suppressing them. It was for the Christian to submit, as it was for the subject to submit, and to leave these high matters to bishops and princes for decision. If James accepted the Millenarian Petition, and summoned a conference of prelates and Puritan divines at Hampton Court, it was not for any real discussion of the grievances alleged, but for the display of his own theological learning. The bishops had the wit to declare that the insults he showered on their opponents were dictated by the Holy Ghost. The Puritans still ventured to dispute his infallibility. James broke up the conference with a threat which revealed the policy of the Crown. " I will make them conform," he said of the remonstrants, " or I will harry them out of the land."

It is only by thoroughly realizing the temper of the nation on religious and civil subjects, and the temper of the King, that we can understand the long Parliamentary conflict which occupied the whole of James's reign. But to make its details intelligible we must briefly review the relations which existed at his accession between the two Houses and the Crown. In an earlier part of this work we have noted the contrast between Wolsey and Cromwell in their dealings with the Parliament. The wary prescience of the first had seen in it, even in its degradation under the Tudors, the memorial of an older freedom, and a centre of national resistance to the new despotism which Henry was establishing, should the nation ever rouse itself to resist. Never perhaps was English liberty in such deadly peril as when Wolsey resolved on the practical suppression of the two Houses. But the bolder genius of Cromwell set contemptuously aside the apprehensions of his predecessor. His confidence in the power of the Crown revived the Parliament as an easy and manageable instrument of tyranny. The old forms of constitutional freedom were turned to the profit of the Royal despotism, and a revolution which for the moment left England absolutely at Henry's feet was wrought out by a series of Parliamentary Statutes. Throughout Henry's reign Cromwell's confidence seemed justified by the spirit of slavish submission which pervaded the Houses. On only one occasion did the Commons refuse to pass a bill brought forward by the Crown. But the effect of the great religious change for which Cromwell's measures made room began to be felt during the minority of Edward the Sixth; and the debates and divisions on the religious reaction which Mary pressed on the Parliament were many and violent. A great step forward was marked by the effort of the Crown to neutralize by "management" an opposition which it could no longer overawe. An unscrupulous use of the Royal prerogative packed the Parliament with nominees of the Crown. Twenty-two new boroughs were created under Edward, fourteen under Mary; some, indeed, places entitled to representation by their wealth and population, but the bulk of them small towns or hamlets which lay wholly at the disposal of the Royal Council. But the increasing pressure of the two Houses was seen in the further step on which Edward's Council ventured in issuing a circular to the Sheriffs, in which they were ordered to set all freedom of election aside. Where the Council recommended " men of learning and wisdom," in other words men compliant with its will, there its directions were to be " regarded and well followed." Elizabeth, though with greater caution, adopted the system of her two predecessors, both in the creation of boroughs and the recommendation of candidates; but her keen political instinct soon perceived the uselessness of both expedients. She fell back as far as she could on Wolsey's policy of practical abolition, and summoned Parliaments at longer and longer intervals. By rigid economy, by a policy of balance and peace, she strove, and for a long time successfully strove, to avoid the necessity of assembling them at all. But Mary of Scotland and Philip of Spain proved friends to English liberty in its sorest need. The death-struggle with Catholicism forced Elizabeth to have recourse to her Parliament, and as she was driven to appeal for increasing supplies the tone of the Parliament rose higher and higher. On the question of taxation or monopolies her fierce spirit was forced to give way to its demands. On the question of religion she refused all concession, and England was driven to await a change of system from her successor. But it is clear, from the earlier acts of his reign, that

James had long before his accession been preparing for a struggle with the Houses, rather than for a policy of concession. During the Queen's reign, the power of Parliament had sprung mainly from the continuance of the war, and from the necessity under which the Crown lay of appealing to it for supplies. It is fair to the war party in Elizabeth's Council to remember that they were fighting not merely for Protestantism abroad, but for constitutional liberty at home. When Essex overrode Burleigh's counsels of peace, the old minister pointed to the words of the Bible, "a bloodthirsty man shall not live out half his days." But Essex and his friends had nobler motives for their policy of war than a thirst for blood; and James had meaner motives for his policy of peace than a hatred of bloodshedding. The peace which he hastened to conclude with Spain was intended to free the Crown from its dependence on the Parliament; and had he fallen back after the close of the war on Elizabeth's policy of economy, he might yet have succeeded in his aim. But the debt left by the war was only swollen by his profligate extravagance; and peace was hardly concluded when he was forced to appeal once more to his Parliament for supplies.

The Parliament of 1604 met in another mood from that of any Parliament which had met for a hundred years. Short as had been the time since his accession, the temper of the King had already disclosed itself; and men were dwelling ominously on the claims of absolutism in Church and State which were constantly on the Royal lips. Above all, the hopes of religious concessions to which the Puritans had clung had been dashed to the ground in the Hampton Court Conference; and of the squires and burgesses who made up the new House of Commons three-fourths were in sympathy Puritan. The energy which marked their action from the beginning shows that the insults which James had heaped on the Puritan divines had stirred the temper of the nation at large. The first step of the Commons was to name a committee to frame bills for the redress of the more crying ecclesiastical grievances; and the rejection of the measures they proposed was at once followed by an outspoken address to the King. The Parliament, it said, had come together in a spirit of peace: "Our desire was of peace only, and our device of unity." Their aim had been to extinguish the long-standing dissension among the ministers, and to preserve uniformity by the abandonment of "a few ceremonies of small importance," by the redress of some ecclesiastical abuses, and by the establishment of an efficient training for a preaching clergy. If they had waived their right to deal with these matters during the old age of Elizabeth, they asserted it now. "Let your Majesty be pleased to receive public information from your Commons in Parliament, as well of the abuses in the Church, as in the Civil State and Government." The claim of absolutism was met in words which sound like a prelude to the Petition of Right. "Your Majesty would be misinformed," said their address, "if any man should deliver that the Kings of England have any absolute power in themselves either to alter religion, or to make any laws concerning the same, otherwise than as in temporal causes, by consent of Parliament." The address was met by a petulant scolding from James; and the bishops, secure of the support of the Crown, replied by an act of bold defiance. The Canons enacted in the Convocation of 1604 bound the clergy to subscribe to the Three Articles, which Parliament had long before refused to render obligatory on them; and compelled all curates and lecturers to conform strictly to the rubrics of the prayer-book on pain of deprivation. In the following winter, three hundred of the Puritan clergy were driven from their livings for non-compliance with these requirements. The only help came from an unlooked-for quarter. The jealousy which had always prevailed between the civil and ecclesiastical courts united with the general resentment of the country at these ecclesiastical usurpations to spur the Judges to an attack on the High Commission. By a series of decisions on appeal they limited its boundless jurisdiction, and restricted its powers of imprisonment to cases of schism and heresy. But the Judges were of little avail against the Crown; and James was resolute in his support of the bishops. Fortunately his prodigality had already in a few years of peace doubled the debt which Elizabeth had left after fifteen years of war; and the course of illegal taxation on which he entered was far from supplying the deficit of the Exchequer. His first great constitutional innovation was the imposition of Customs duties on almost all kinds of merchandise, imported or exported. The imposition was not, indeed, without precedent. A duty on imports which had been introduced in one or two instances under Mary had been extended by Elizabeth to currants and wine; but the impost, trivial in itself, had been pushed no farther, nor had it ever been claimed or regarded as more than an exceptional measure of finance. Had Elizabeth cared to extend it, her course would probably have been gradual and tentative, and have aimed at escaping public observation. But James was a fanatical believer in the rights and power of his crown, and he cared quite as much to assert his absolute authority over impositions as to fill his Treasury. A case therefore was brought before the Exchequer Chamber, and the judgment of the Court asserted the King's right to levy what Customs duties he would at his pleasure. " All customs," said the Judges, " are the effects of foreign commerce, but all affairs of commerce and treaties with foreign nations belong to the King's absolute power. He therefore, who has power over the cause, must have power over the effect." The importance of a decision which freed the Crown from the necessity of resorting to Parliament was seen keenly enough by James. English commerce was growing fast, and English merchants were fighting their way to the Spice Islands, and establishing settlements in the dominions of the Mogul. The judgment gave him a revenue which was sure to grow rapidly, and he acted on it with decision. A Royal proclamation imposed a system of Customs duties on all articles of export and import. But if the new duties came in fast, the Royal debt grew faster. The peace expenditure of James exceeded the war expenditure of Elizabeth, and necessity forced on the King a fresh assembling of Parliament. He forbade the Commons to enter on the subject of the new duties, but their remonstrance was none the less vigorous. "Finding that your Majesty without advice or counsel of Parliament hath lately in time of peace set both greater impositions and more in number than any of your noble ancestors did ever in time of war," they prayed "that all impositions set without the assent

of Parliament may be quite abolished and taken away," and that "a law be made to declare that all impositions set upon your people, their goods or merchandise, save only by common consent in Parliament, are and shall be void." From the new question of illegal taxation they turned, with no less earnestness, to the older question of ecclesiastical reform. Before granting the supply which the Crown required, they demanded that the jurisdiction of the High Commission should be regulated by Statute, in other words that ecclesiastical matters should be recognized as within the cognizance of Parliament; and that the deprived ministers should again be suffered to preach. Whatever concessions James might offer on the subject of the Customs, he would allow no interference with his ecclesiastical prerogative; the Parliament was dissolved, and four years passed before the financial straits of the Government forced James to face the two Houses again. But the spirit of resistance was now fairly roused. Never had an election stirred so much popular passion as that of 1614. In every case where rejection was possible, the Court candidates were rejected. All the

leading members of the Country party, or as we should call it now the Opposition, were again returned. But three hundred of the members were wholly new men; and among these we note for the first time the names of the great leaders in the later struggle with the Crown. Somersetshire returned John Pym; Yorkshire, Thomas Wentworth; St. Germain's, John Eliot. Signs of an unprecedented excitement were seen in the vehement cheering and hissing which for the first time marked the proceedings of the Commons. But the policy of the Parliament was precisely the same as that of its predecessors. The Commons refused to grant supplies till grievances had been redressed, and fixed on that of illegal taxation as the first to be amended. Unluckily the inexperience of the bulk of the members led them into quarrelling on a point of privilege with the Lords; and the King, who had been frightened beyond his wont at the vehemence of their tone and language, seized on the quarrel as a pretext for their dissolution.

The
Royal
Despot-
ism
1614
to
1621 Four of the leading members in the dissolved Parliament were sent to the Tower; and the terror and resentment which it had roused in the King's mind were seen in the obstinacy with which he long persisted in governing without any Parliament at all. For seven years he carried out with a blind recklessness his theory of

an absolute rule, unfettered by any scruples as to the past, or any dread of the future. All the abuses which Parliament after Parliament had denounced were not only continued, but developed in a spirit of defiance. The Ecclesiastical Commission was hounded on to a fresh persecution. James had admitted the illegality of Royal proclamations, but he issued them now in greater numbers than ever. The refusal of supplies was met by persistence in the levy of imposts; and, when this proved insufficient to meet the wants of the Treasury, by falling back on a resource, which even Wolsey in the height of the Tudor power had been forced to abandon. But the letters from the Royal Council demanding benevolences or loans from every landowner remained generally unanswered. In the three years which followed the dissolution of 1614 the strenuous efforts of the Sheriffs only raised sixty thousand pounds, a sum less than two-thirds of the value of a single subsidy; and although the remonstrances of the western counties were roughly silenced by the threats of the Council, two counties, those of Hereford and Stafford, sent not a penny to the last. In his distress for money James was driven to expedients which widened the breach between the gentry and the Crown. He had refused to part with the feudal privileges which had come down to him from the Middle Ages, such as his right to the wardship of young heirs and the marriage of heiresses, and these were now recklessly used as a means of fiscal extortion. He degraded the nobility by a shameless sale of peerages. Of the ninety lay peers whom he left in the Upper House at his death, a large part had been created by sheer bargaining during his reign. By shifts such as these James put off from day to day the necessity for again encountering the one body which could permanently arrest his effort after despotic rule. But there still remained a body whose tradition was strong enough, not indeed to arrest, but to check it. The lawyers had been subservient beyond all other classes to the Crown. In the narrow pedantry with which they bent before precedents, without admitting any distinction between precedents drawn from a time of freedom and precedents drawn from the worst times of tyranny, the Judges had supported James in his claims to impose Customs duties, and even to levy benevolences. But beyond precedents even the Judges refused to go. They had done their best, when the case came before them, to restrict the jurisdiction of the ecclesiastical courts within legal and definite bounds: and when James asserted an inherent right in the King to be consulted as to the decision, whenever any case affecting the prerogative came before his courts, they timidly, but firmly, repudiated such a right as unknown to the law. James sent for them to the Royal closet, and rated them like schoolboys, till they fell on their knees, and, with a single exception, pledged themselves to obey his will. The Chief-Justice, Sir Edward Coke, a narrow-minded and bitter-tempered man, but of the highest eminence as a lawyer, and with a reverence for the law that over-rode every other instinct, alone remained firm. When any case

came before him, he answered, he would act as it became a judge
to act. The provision which then made the judicial office tenable
at the King's pleasure, but which had long been forgotten, was
revived to humble the law in the person of its chief officer; and
Coke, who had at once been dismissed from the Council, was on
the continuance of his resistance deprived of his post of Chief-
Justice. No act of James seems to have stirred a deeper horror and
resentment among Englishmen than this announcement of his will
to tamper with the course of justice. It was an outrage on the
growing sense of law, as the profusion and profligacy of the Court
were an outrage on the growing sense of morality. The Treasury
was drained to furnish masques and revels on a scale of unexampled
splendour. Lands and jewels were lavished on young adventurers,
whose fair faces caught the Royal fancy. The Court of Elizabeth
had been as immoral as that of her successor, but its immorality
had been shrouded by a veil of grace and chivalry. But no veil hid
the degrading grossness of the Court of James. The King was held,
though unjustly, to be a drunkard, and suspected of vices compared
with which drunkenness was almost a virtue. Actors in the royal
masques were seen rolling intoxicated in open Court at the King's
feet. A scandalous trial showed great nobles and officers of state
in league with cheats and astrologers and poisoners. James himself
meddled with justice to obtain a shameful divorce for Lady Essex,
the most profligate woman of her time; and her subsequent bridal
with one of his favourites was celebrated in his presence. Before
scenes such as these, the half-idolatrous reverence with which the
sovereign had been regarded throughout the period of the Tudors
died away into abhorrence and contempt. The players openly
mocked at the King on the stage. Mrs. Hutchinson denounces the
orgies of Whitehall in words as fiery as those with which Elijah
denounced the sensuality of Jezebel. But the immorality of James's
Court was hardly more despicable than the imbecility of his government. In the silence of Parliament, the Royal Council, composed
as it was not merely of the ministers, but of the higher nobles and
great officers of state, had served even under a despot like Henry
the Eighth as a check upon the purely arbitrary authority of the
Crown. But after the death of Lord Burleigh's son, Robert Cecil,
the minister whom Elizabeth had bequeathed to him, and whose
services in procuring his accession were rewarded by the Earldom
of Salisbury, all real control over affairs was withdrawn by James
from the Council, and entrusted to worthless favourites whom the
King chose to raise to honour. A Scotch page named Carr was
created Earl of Rochester, married after her divorce to Lady Essex,
and only hurled from favour and power by the discovery of a
horrible crime, the murder of Sir Thomas Overbury by poison, of
which he and his Countess were convicted of being the instigators.
But the shame of one favourite only hurried James into the choice
of another; and George Villiers, a handsome young adventurer,
was raised rapidly through every rank of the peerage, made Marquis

and Duke of Buckingham, and entrusted with the direction of
English policy. The payment of bribes to him, or marriage with
his greedy relatives, soon became the only road to political preferment. Resistance to his will was inevitably followed by dismissal from office. Even the highest and most powerful of the
nobility were made to tremble at the nod of this young upstart.
" Never any man in any age, nor, I believe, in any country," says
the astonished Clarendon, " rose in so short a time to so much
greatness of honour, power, or fortune, upon no other advantage
or recommendation than of the beauty or gracefulness of his
person." But the selfishness and recklessness of Buckingham were
equal to his beauty; and the haughty young favourite on whose
neck James loved to loll, and whose cheek he slobbered with
kisses, was destined to drag down in his fatal career the throne of
the Stuarts.

The new system was even more disastrous in its results abroad
than at home. The withdrawal of power from the Council left
James in effect his own prime minister, and master of the control
of affairs as no English sovereign had been before him. At his
accession he found the direction of foreign affairs in the hands of
Cecil, and so long as Cecil lived the Elizabethan policy was in the
main adhered to. Peace, indeed, was made with Spain; but a close
alliance with the United Provinces, and a close friendship with
France, held the ambition of Spain as effectually in check as war.
No sooner did signs of danger appear in Germany from the bigotry
of the House of Austria, than the marriage of the King's daughter,
Elizabeth, with the Elector-Palatine promised English support
to its Protestant powers. It was, indeed, mainly to the firm
direction of English policy during Cecil's ministry that the preservation of peace throughout Europe was due. But the death of
Cecil, and the dissolution of the Parliament of 1614, were quickly
followed by a disastrous change. James at once proceeded to undo
all that the struggle of Elizabeth and the triumph of the Armada
had done. He withdrew gradually from the close connexion with
France. He began a series of negotiations for the marriage of his
son with a Princess of Spain. Each of his successive favourites
supported the Spanish alliance; and after years of secret intrigue
the King's intentions were proclaimed to the world, at the moment
when the religious truce which had so long preserved the peace of
Germany was broken by the revolt of Bohemia against the Austrian
Archduke Ferdinand, who claimed its crown, and by its election
of the Elector-Palatine to the vacant throne. From whatever
quarter the first aggression had come, it was plain that a second
great struggle in arms between Protestantism and Catholicism was
now to be fought out on German soil. It was their prescience of the
coming conflict, and of the pitiful part which James would play
in it, which, on the very eve of the crisis, spurred the Protestant
party among his ministers to support an enterprise which promised
to detach the King from his new policy by entangling him in a war

1604
to
1623

The
Spanish
Policy

1617

1619

with Spain. Sir Walter Raleigh, the one great name of the Elizabethan time that still lingered on, had been imprisoned ever since the beginning of the new reign in the Tower on a charge of treason. He now offered to sail to the Orinoco, and discover a gold mine which he believed to exist on its banks. Guiana was Spanish ground; and the appeal to the King's cupidity was backed by the Protestant party with the purpose of bringing on, through Raleigh's settlement there, a contest with Spain. But though he yielded to the popular feeling in suffering Raleigh to sail, James had given previous warning of the voyage to his new ally; and the expedition had hardly landed, when it was driven back with loss from the coast. Raleigh's attempt to seize the Spanish treasure-ships on his return, with the same aim of provoking a war, was defeated by a mutiny among his crews; and the death of the broken-hearted adventurer on the scaffold atoned for the affront to Spain. But the failure of Raleigh's efforts to anticipate the crisis quickened the anxiety of the people at large when the crisis arrived. The German Protestants were divided by the fatal jealousy between their Lutheran and Calvinist princes; but it was believed that England could unite them, and it was on England's support that the Bohemians counted when they chose James's son-in-law for their king. A firm policy would at any rate have held Spain inactive, and limited the contest to Germany itself. But the "statecraft" on which James prided himself led him to count, not on Spanish fear, but on Spanish friendship. He refused aid to the Protestant union of the German Princes when they espoused the cause of Bohemia, and threatened war against Holland, the one power which was earnest in the Palatine's cause. It was in vain that both Court and people were unanimous in their cry for war; that Archbishop Abbot from his sick-bed implored the King to strike one blow for Protestantism; that Spain openly took part with the Catholic League, which had now been formed under the Duke of Bavaria, and marched an army upon the Rhine. James still pressed his son-in-law to withdraw from Bohemia, and counted on his influence with Spain to induce its armies to retire when once the Bohemian struggle was over. But a battle before the walls of Prague, which crushed the Bohemian revolt, drove Frederick back on the Rhine, to find the Spaniards encamped as its masters in the heart of the Palatinate. James had been duped, and for the moment he bent before the burst of popular fury which the danger to German Protestantism called up. A national subscription for the

defence of the Palatinate enabled its Elector to raise an army; and his army was joined by a force of English volunteers under Sir Horace Vere. The cry for a Parliament, the necessary prelude to a war, overpowered the King's secret resistance, and the warlike speech with which he opened its session roused an enthusiasm which recalled the days of Elizabeth.

The Commons answered the King's appeal by a unanimous vote —" lifting their hats as high as they could hold them "—that for the recovery of the Palatinate they would adventure their fortunes, their estates, and their lives. "Rather this declaration," cried a leader of the Country party when it was read by the Speaker, "than ten thousand men already on the march!" But it met with no corresponding pledge or announcement of policy from James; on the contrary, he gave license for the export of arms to Spain. As yet constitutional grievances had been passed by, but the Royal defiance roused the Commons to revive a Parliamentary right which had slept ever since the reign of Henry the Sixth, the right of the Lower House to impeach great offenders at the bar of the Lords. The new weapon was put to a summary use. The most crying constitutional grievance sprang from the revival of monopolies, after the pledge of Elizabeth to suppress them; and the impeachment of a host of monopolists again put an end to this attempt to raise a revenue for the Crown without a grant from Parliament. But the blow at the corruption of the Court which followed was of a far more serious order. Not only was the Chancellor, Francis Bacon, Lord Verulam and Viscount St. Albans, the most distinguished man of his time for learning and ability, but his high position as an officer of the Crown made his impeachment for bribery a direct claim on the Parliament's part to supervise the Royal administration. James was too shrewd to mistake the importance of the step; but the hostility of Buckingham to the Chancellor, and Bacon's own confession of his guilt, made it difficult to resist his condemnation. Energetic too as its measures were, the Parliament respected scrupulously the King's prejudices in other matters; and even when checked by an adjournment, resolved unanimously to support him in any earnest effort for the Protestant cause. For the moment its resolve gave vigour to the Royal policy. James had aimed throughout at the restitution of Bohemia to Ferdinand, and at inducing the Emperor, through the mediation of Spain, to abstain from any retaliation on the Palatinate. He now freed himself for a moment from the trammels of diplomacy, and enforced a cessation of the attack on his son-in-law's dominions by a threat of war. The suspension of arms lasted through the summer; but mere threats could do no more, and on the conquest of the Upper Palatinate at the close of the truce by the forces of the Catholic League, James suddenly returned to his old resolve to rely on negotiations, and on the friendly mediation of Spain. Gondomar, the Spanish ambassador, who had become all-powerful at the English Court, was assured that no effectual aid should be sent to the Palatinate. The English fleet, which was cruising by way of menace off the Spanish coast, was called home. The King dismissed those of his ministers who still opposed a Spanish policy; and threatened on trivial pretexts a war with the Dutch, the one great Protestant power that remained in alliance with England, and was ready to back the Elector. But he had still to reckon with his Parliament; and the first act of the Parliament on its re-assembling was to demand a declaration of war with Spain.

The instinct of the nation was wiser than the statecraft of the King. Ruined and enfeebled as she really was, Spain to the world at large still seemed the champion of Catholicism. It was the entry of her troops into the Palatinate which had first widened the local war in Bohemia into a great struggle for the suppression of Protestantism along the Rhine; above all it was Spanish influence, and the hopes held out of a marriage of his son with a Spanish Infanta, which were luring the King into his fatal dependence on the great enemy of the Protestant cause. In their petition the Houses coupled with their demands for war the demand of a Protestant marriage for their future King. Experience proved in later years how perilous it was for English freedom that the heir to the Crown should be brought up under a Catholic mother; but James was beside himself at their presumption in dealing with mysteries of State. "Bring stools for the Ambassadors," he cried in bitter irony as the committee of the Commons appeared before him. He refused the petition, forbade any further discussion of State policy, and threatened the speakers with the Tower. "Let us resort to our prayers," a member said calmly as the King's letter was read, "and then consider of this great business." The temper of the Commons was seen in the Protestation which met the Royal command to abstain from discussion. The House resolved "That the liberties, franchises, privileges, and jurisdictions of Parliament are the ancient and undoubted birthright and inheritance of the subjects of England; and that the arduous and urgent affairs concerning the King, State, and defence of the Realm, and of the Church of England, and the making and maintenance of laws, and redress of grievances, which daily happen within this Realm, are proper subjects and matter of Council and debate in Parliament. And that in the handling and proceeding of those businesses every member of the House hath, and of right ought to have, freedom of speech to propound, treat, reason, and bring to conclusion the same."

The King answered the Protestation by a characteristic outrage. He sent for the Journals of the House, and with his own hand tore out the pages which contained it. "I will govern," he said, "according to the common weal, but not according to the common will." A few days after he dissolved the Parliament. "It is the best thing that has happened in the interests of Spain and of the Catholic religion since Luther began preaching," wrote the Count of Gondomar to his master, in his joy that all danger of war had passed away. "I am ready to depart," Sir Henry Saville, on the other hand, murmured on his death-bed, "the rather that having lived in good times I foresee worse." Abroad indeed all was lost; and Germany plunged wildly and blindly forward into the chaos of the Thirty Years' War. But for England the victory of freedom was practically won. James had himself ruined the system of Elizabeth. In his desire for personal government he had destroyed the authority of the Council. He had accustomed men to think

lightly of the great ministers of the Crown, to see them browbeaten
by favourites, and driven from office for corruption. He had dis-
enchanted his people of their blind faith in the Crown by a policy
at home and abroad which ran counter to every national instinct.
He had quarrelled with, and insulted the Houses, as no English
sovereign had ever done before; and all the while he was conscious
that the authority he boasted of was passing, without his being
able to hinder it, to the Parliament which he outraged. There was
shrewdness as well as anger in his taunt at its "ambassadors."
A power had at last risen up in the Commons with which the
Monarchy was henceforth to reckon. In spite of the King's
petulant outbreaks, Parliament had asserted and enforced its
exclusive right to the control of taxation. It had suppressed
monopolies. It had reformed abuses in the courts of law. It had
revived the right of impeaching and removing from office even the
highest ministers of the Crown. It had asserted its privilege of free
discussion on all questions connected with the welfare of the realm.
It had claimed to deal with the question of religion. It had even
declared its will on the sacred "mystery" of foreign policy.
James might tear the Protestation from its Journals, but there
were pages in the record of the Parliament of 1621 which he never
could tear out.

SECTION III.—THE KING AND THE PARLIAMENT, 1623—1629

[*Authorities.*—To those already mentioned may be added Bulstrode
Whitelocke, " Memorials of English Affairs," and Rushworth, " Historical Collections." For constitutional documents, see Gardiner,
" Documents of the Puritan Revolution." For individuals, see the
character sketches in Clarendon's " History of the Great Rebellion," and
their lives in the " Dictionary of National Biography." For the general
religious history of the period, see the volume by Gardiner in Hunt and
Stephens, " History of the English Church."]

In the obstinacy with which he clung to his Spanish policy James
stood absolutely alone; for not only the old nobility and the statesmen who preserved the tradition of the age of Elizabeth, but even
his own ministers, with the exception of Buckingham, were at one
with the Commons. The King's aim, as we have said, was to
enforce peace on the combatants, and to bring about the restitution
of the Palatinate to the Elector, through the influence of Spain. It
was to secure this influence that he pressed for a closer union with
the great Catholic power; and of this union, and the success of the
policy which it embodied, the marriage of his son Charles with the
Infanta, which had been held out as a lure to his vanity, was to be
the sign. The more, however, James pressed for this consummation
of his projects, the more Spain held back; but so bent was the
King on its realization that, after fruitless negotiations, the Prince
quitted England in disguise, and appeared with Buckingham at
Madrid to claim his promised bride. It was in vain that the

The
Spanish
Marriage

Spanish Court rose in its demands; for every new demand was met by fresh concessions on the part of England. The abrogation of the penal laws against the Catholics, a Catholic education for the Prince's children, a Catholic household for the Infanta, all were no sooner asked than they were granted. But the marriage was still delayed, while the influence of the new policy on the war in Germany was hard to see. The Catholic League, and its army under the command of Count Tilly, won triumph after triumph over their divided foes. The reduction of Heidelberg and Mannheim completed the conquest of the Palatinate, whose Elector fled helplessly to Holland, while his Electoral dignity was transferred by the Emperor to the Duke of Bavaria. But there was still no sign of the hoped-for intervention on the part of Spain. At last the pressure of Charles himself brought about the disclosure of the secret of its policy. "It is a maxim of state with us," the Duke of Olivarez confessed, as the Prince demanded an energetic interference in Germany, "that the King of Spain must never fight against the Emperor. We cannot employ our forces against the Emperor." "If you hold to that," replied the Prince, "there is an end of all."

His return was the signal for a burst of national joy. All London was alight with bonfires, in her joy at the failure of the Spanish match, and of the collapse, humiliating as it was, of the policy which had so long trailed English honour at the chariot-wheels of Spain. Charles returned with the fixed resolve to take the direction of affairs out of his father's hands. The journey to Madrid had revealed to those around him the strange mixture of obstinacy and weakness in the Prince's character, the duplicity which lavished promises because it never purposed to be bound by any, the petty pride that subordinated every political consideration to personal vanity or personal pique. He had granted demand after demand, till the very Spaniards lost faith in his concessions. With rage in his heart at the failure of his efforts, he had renewed his betrothal on the very eve of his departure, only that he might insult the Infanta by its withdrawal when he was safe at home. But to England at large the baser features of his character were still unknown. The stately reserve, the personal dignity and decency of manners which distinguished the Prince, contrasted favourably with the gabble and indecorum of his father. The courtiers indeed who saw him in his youth, would often pray God that "he might be in the right way when he set; for if he was in the wrong he would prove the most wilful of any king that ever reigned." But the nation was willing to take his obstinacy for firmness; as it took the pique which inspired his course on his return for patriotism and for the promise of a nobler rule. His first acts were energetic

enough. The King was forced to summon a Parliament, and to concede the point on which he had broken with the last, by laying before it the whole question of the Spanish negotiations. Buckingham and the Prince personally joined the Parliament in its demand for a rupture of the treaties and a declaration of war. A subsidy was eagerly voted; the persecution of the Catholics, which had long been suspended out of deference to Spanish intervention, recommenced with vigour. The head of the Spanish party in the ministry, Cranfield, Earl of Middlesex, the Lord Treasurer, was impeached on a charge of corruption, and dismissed from office. James was swept along helplessly by the tide; but, helpless as he was, his shrewdness saw clearly enough the turn that things were really taking. " You are making a rod for your own back," he said to Buckingham, when his favourite pressed him to consent to Cranfield's disgrace. But Charles and Buckingham were still resolute in their project of war. The Spanish ambassador quitted the realm; a treaty of alliance was concluded with Holland; negotiations were begun with the Lutheran Princes of North Germany, who had looked coolly on at the ruin of the Calvinistic Elector-Palatine; and the marriage of Charles with Henrietta, a daughter of Henry the Fourth of France, and sister of its King, promised a renewal of the system of Elizabeth. At this juncture the death of the old King placed Charles upon the throne; and his first Parliament met him in a passion of loyalty. " We can hope everything from the King who now governs us," cried Sir Benjamin Rudyard in the Commons. But there were cooler heads in the Commons than Sir Benjamin Rudyard's; and, loyal as the Parliament was, enough had taken place in the short interval between the accession of the new monarch and its assembling to temper its loyalty with caution.

The war with Spain, it must be remembered, meant to common Englishmen a war with Catholicism; and the fervour against Popery without roused a corresponding fervour against Popery within the realm. Every Papist seemed to Protestant eyes an enemy at home. A Churchman who leaned to Popery was a traitor in the ranks. The temper of the Commons on these points was clear to every observer. "Whatever mention does break forth of the fears or dangers in religion, and the increase of Popery," wrote a member who was noting the proceedings of the House, " their affections are much stirred." But Charles had already renewed the toleration of the Catholics, and warned the House to leave priest and recusant to the discretion of the Crown. It was soon plain that his ecclesiastical policy would be even more hostile to the Puritans than that of his father had been. Bishop Laud was put practically at the head of ecclesiastical affairs, and Laud had at once drawn up a list of ministers divided ominously into " orthodox " and " Puritan." The most notorious among the High Church divines, Doctor Montagu, advocated in his sermons the Divine right of Kings and the Real Presence, besides slighting the Protestant churches of the Continent in favour of the Church of Rome. The first act of the Commons was to summon Montagu to their bar, and to commit him to prison. But there were other grounds for their distrust besides the King's ecclesiastical tendency. The subsidy of the last Parliament had been wasted, yet Charles still refused to declare with what power England was at war, or to avow that the great fleet he was manning was destined to act against Spain. The real part which he had played in the marriage negotiations had gradually been revealed, and the discovery had destroyed all faith in his Protestant enthusiasm. His reserve therefore was met by a corresponding caution. While voting a subsidy, the Commons restricted their grant of certain Customs duties, which had commonly been granted to the new sovereign for life, to a single year. The restriction was taken as an insult; Charles refused to accept the grant, and Buckingham resolved to break with the Parliament at any cost. He suddenly demanded a new subsidy, a demand made merely to be denied, and which died without debate. But the denial increased the King's irritation, and he marked it by drawing Montagu from the prison, by promoting him to a Royal chaplaincy, and by levying his disputed customs on his own authority. The Houses met at Oxford in a sterner temper. " England," cried Sir Robert Philips, " is the last monarchy that yet retains her liberties. Let them not perish now ! " But the Commons had no sooner announced their resolve to consider public grievances before entering on other business than they were met by a dissolution. Buckingham, who was more powerful with Charles than he had been with his father, had resolved to lure England from her constitutional struggle by a great military triumph; and staking everything on success, he sailed for the Hague to conclude a general alliance against the House of Austria, while a fleet of ninety vessels and ten thousand soldiers left Plymouth for the coast of Spain. But if the projects of Charles were bolder than those of his predecessor, his execution of them was just as incapable. The alliance broke utterly down. After an idle descent on Cadiz the Spanish expedition returned, broken with mutiny and disease. The enormous debt which had been incurred in its equipment forced the favourite to advise a new summons of the Houses; but he was keenly alive to the peril in which his failure had plunged him, and to a coalition which had been formed between his rivals at Court and the leaders of the last Parliament. His reckless daring led him to anticipate the danger, and by a series of blows to strike terror into his opponents. Lord Pembroke was forced to a humiliating submission; Lord Arundel was sent to the Tower. Sir Richard Philips, Coke, and four other leading patriots were made Sheriffs of their counties, and thus prevented from sitting in the coming Parliament. But their exclusion only left the field free for a more terrible foe.

Eliot

If Hampden and Pym are the great figures which embody the later national resistance, the earlier struggle for Parliamentary liberty centres in the figure of Sir John Eliot. Of an old family— ennobled since his time—which had settled under Elizabeth near the fishing hamlet of St. Germains, and whose stately mansion gives its name of Port Eliot to a little town on the Tamar, he had risen

to the post of Vice-Admiral of Devonshire under the patronage of
Buckingham, and had seen his activity in the suppression of piracy
in the Channel rewarded by an unjust imprisonment. He was now
in the first vigour of manhood, with a mind exquisitely cultivated
and familiar with the poetry and learning of his day, a nature
singularly lofty and devout, a fearless and vehement temper. There
was a hot impulsive element in his nature which showed itself in
youth in his drawing sword on a neighbour who denounced him to
his father, and which in later years gave its characteristic fire to
his eloquence. But his intellect was as clear and cool as his temper
was ardent. In the general enthusiasm which followed on the
failure of the Spanish Marriage, he had stood almost alone in
pressing for a recognition of the rights of Parliament, as a preliminary to any real reconciliation with the Crown. He fixed, from
the very outset of his career, on the responsibility of the royal
ministers to Parliament, as the one critical point for English liberty.
It was to enforce the demand of this that he availed himself of
Buckingham's sacrifice of the Treasurer, Cranfield, to the resentment of the Commons. "The greater the delinquent," he urged,
"the greater the delict. They are a happy thing, great men and
officers, if they be good, and one of the greatest blessings of the
land: but power converted into evil is the greatest curse that can
befall it." But the new Parliament had hardly met, when he came
to the front to threaten a greater criminal than Cranfield. So
menacing were his words, as he called for an inquiry into the failure
before Cadiz, that Charles himself stooped to answer threat with
threat. "I see," he wrote to the House, "you especially aim at
the Duke of Buckingham. I must let you know that I will not
allow any of my servants to be questioned among you, much less
such as are of eminent place and near to me." A more direct attack
on a right already acknowledged in the impeachment of Bacon and
Cranfield could hardly be imagined, but Eliot refused to move
from his constitutional ground. The King was by law irresponsible,
he "could do no wrong." If the country therefore was to be saved   1626
from a pure despotism, it must be by enforcing the responsibility
of the ministers who counselled and executed his acts. Eliot
persisted in denouncing Buckingham's incompetence and corruption, and the Commons ordered the subsidy which the Crown had
demanded to be brought in "when we shall have presented our
grievances, and received his Majesty's answer thereto." Charles
summoned them to Whitehall, and commanded them to cancel
the condition. He would grant them "liberty of counsel, but not
of control;" and he closed the interview with a significant threat.
"Remember," he said, "that Parliaments are altogether in my
power for their calling, sitting, and dissolution: and therefore, as
I find the fruits of them to be good or evil, they are to continue
or not to be." But the will of the Commons was as resolute as the
will of the King. Buckingham's impeachment was voted and
carried to the Lords. The favourite took his seat as a peer to listen

to the charge with so insolent an air of contempt that one of the managers appointed by the Commons to conduct it turned sharply on him. " Do you jeer, my Lord! " said Sir Dudley Digges. " I can show you when a greater man than your Lordship—as high as you in place and power, and as deep in the King's favour—has been hanged for as small a crime as these articles contain." The " proud carriage " of the Duke provoked an invective from Elio? which marks a new era in Parliamentary speech. From the first the vehemence and passion of his words had contrasted with the grave, colourless reasoning of older speakers. His opponents complained that Eliot aimed to " stir up affections." The quick emphatic sentences he substituted for the cumbrous periods of the day, his rapid argument, his vivacious and caustic allusions, his passionate appeals, his fearless invective, struck a new note in English eloquence. The frivolous ostentation of Buckingham, his very figure blazing with jewels and gold, gave point to the fierce attack. " He has broken those nerves and sinews of our land, the stores and treasures of the King. There needs no search for it. It is too visible. His profuse expenses, his superfluous feasts, his magnificent buildings, his riots, his excesses, what are they but the visible evidences of an express exhausting of the State, a chronicle of the immensity of his waste of the revenues of the Crown? " With the same terrible directness Eliot reviewed the Duke's greed and corruption, his insatiate ambition, his seizure of all public authority, his neglect of every public duty, his abuse for selfish ends of the powers he had accumulated. " The pleasure of his Majesty, his known directions, his public acts, his acts of council, the decrees of courts—all must be made inferior to this man's will. No right, no interest may withstand him. Through the power of state and justice he has dared ever to strike at his own ends." " My Lords," he ended, after a vivid parallel between Buckingham and Sejanus, " you see the man! What have been his actions, what he is like, you know! I leave him to your judgment. This only is conceived by us, the knights, citizens, and burgesses of the Commons House of Parliament, that by him came all our evils, in him we find the causes, and on him must be the remedies! Pereat qui perdere cuncta festinat. Opprimatur ne omnes opprimat! "

The reply of Charles was as fierce and sudden as the attack of Eliot. He hurried to the House of Peers to avow as his own the deeds with which Buckingham was charged. Eliot and Digges were called from their seats, and committed prisoners to the Tower. The Commons, however, refused to proceed with public business till their members were restored; and after a ten days' struggle Eliot was released. But his release was only a prelude to the close of the Parliament. " Not one moment," the King replied to the prayer of his Council for delay; and the final remonstrance in which the Commons begged him to dismiss Buckingham from his service for ever was met by their instant dissolution. The remonstrance was burnt by Royal order, Eliot was deprived of his Vice-Admiralty and the subsidies which the Parliament had refused to grant till their grievances were redressed were levied in the arbitrary form of benevolences. But the tide of public resistance was slowly rising. Refusals to give anything, "save by way of Parliament," came in from county after county. The arguments of the judges, who summoned the subsidy-men of Middlesex and Westminster to persuade them to comply, were met by the crowd with a tumultuous shout of "a Parliament! a Parliament! else no subsidies!" Kent stood out to a man. In Bucks the very justices neglected to ask for the "free gift." The freeholders of Cornwall only answered that, "if they had but two kine, they would sell one of them for supply to his Majesty—in a Parliamentary way." The failure of the voluntary benevolence was met by the levy of a forced loan. Commissioners were named to assess the amount which every landowner was bound to lend, and to examine on oath all who refused. Every means of persuasion, as of force, was resorted to. The High Church pulpits resounded with the cry of "passive obedience." Dr. Mainwaring preached before Charles himself, that the King needed no Parliamentary warrant foɪ taxation, and that to resist his will was to incur eternal damnation. Soldiers were quartered on recalcitrant boroughs. Poor men who refused to lend were pressed into the army or navy. Stubborn tradesmen were flung into prison. Buckingham himself undertook the task of overawing the nobles and the gentry. Among the bishops, the Primate and Bishop Williams of Lincoln alone resisted the King's will. The first was suspended on a frivolous pretext, and the second was disgraced. But in the country at large resistance was universal. The northern counties in a mass set the Crown at defiance. The Lincolnshire farmers drove the Commissioners from the town. Shropshire, Devon, and Warwickshire "refused utterly." Eight peers, with Lord Essex and Lord Warwick at their head, declined to comply with the exaction as illegal. Two hundred country gentlemen, whose obstinacy had not been subdued by their transfer from prison to prison, were summoned before the Council. John Hampden, as yet only a young Buckinghamshire squire, appeared at the board to begin that career of patriotism which has made his name dear to Englishmen. "I could be content to lend," he said, "but fear to draw on myself that curse in Magna Charta, which should be read twice a year against those who infringe it." So close an imprisonment in the Gate House rewarded his protest, "that he never afterwards did look like the same man he was before." With gathering discontent as well as bankruptcy before him, nothing could save the Duke but a great military success; and he equipped a force of seven thousand men for the maddest and most profligate of all his enterprises. In the great struggle with Catholicism the hopes of every Protestant rested on the union of England with France against the House of Austria. From causes never fully explained, but in which a personal pique against the French minister, Cardinal Richelieu, mingled with the

1623
to
1629

desire to win an easy popularity at home by supporting the French Huguenots, Buckingham at this juncture broke suddenly with France, sailed in person to the Isle of Rhé, and roused the great Huguenot city of Rochelle to revolt. The expedition was as disastrous as it was impolitic. After a useless siege of the castle of St. Martin, the English troops were forced to fall back along a narrow causeway to their ships; and in the retreat two thousand fell, without the loss of a single man to their enemies.

The
Petition
of Right

The first result of Buckingham's folly was the fall of Rochelle and the ruin of the Huguenot cause in France. Indirectly, as we have seen, it helped on the ruin of the cause of Protestantism in Germany. But in England it forced on Charles, overwhelmed as he was with debt and shame, the summoning of a new Parliament; a Parliament which met in a mood even more resolute than the last. The Court candidates were everywhere rejected. The patriot leaders were triumphantly returned. To have suffered in the recent resistance to arbitrary taxation was the sure road to a seat. In spite of Eliot's counsel, all other grievances, even that of Buckingham himself, gave place to the craving for redress of wrongs done to personal liberty. "We must vindicate our ancient liberties," said Sir Thomas Wentworth, in words soon to be remembered against himself: "we must reinforce the laws made by our ancestors. We must set such a stamp upon them, as no licentious spirit shall dare hereafter to invade them." Heedless of sharp and menacing messages from the King, of demands that they should take his "Royal word" for their liberties, the House bent itself

1628

to one great work, the drawing up a Petition of Right. The statutes that protected the subject against arbitrary taxation, against loans and benevolences, against punishment, outlawry, or deprivation of goods, otherwise than by lawful judgment of his peers, against arbitrary imprisonment without stated charge, against billeting of soldiery on the people or enactment of martial law in time of peace, were formally recited. The breaches of them under the last two sovereigns, and above all since the dissolution of the last Parliament, were recited as formally. At the close of this significant list, the Commons prayed " that no man hereafter be compelled to make or yield any gift, loan, benevolence, tax, or such like charge, without common consent by Act of Parliament. And that none be called to make answer, or to take such oaths, or to be confined or otherwise molested or disputed concerning the same, or for refusal thereof. And that no freeman may in such manner as is before mentioned be imprisoned or detained. And that your Majesty would be pleased to remove the said soldiers and mariners, and that your people may not be so burthened in time to come. And that the commissions for proceeding by martial law may be revoked and annulled, and that hereafter no commissions of like nature may issue forth to any person or persons whatsoever to be executed as aforesaid, lest by colour of them any of your Majesty's subjects be destroyed and put to death, contrary to the laws and franchises of the land. All which they humbly pray of your most excellent Majesty, as their rights and liberties, according to the laws and statutes of the realm. And that your Majesty would also vouchsafe to declare that the awards, doings, and proceedings to the prejudice of your people in any of the premises shall not be drawn hereafter into consequence or example. And that your Majesty would be pleased graciously for the further comfort and safety of your people to declare your Royal will and pleasure, that in the things aforesaid all your officers and ministers shall serve you according to the laws and statutes of this realm, as they tender the honour of your Majesty and the prosperity of the kingdom." It was in vain that the Lords desired to conciliate Charles by a reservation of his "sovereign power." "Our petition," Pym quietly replied, "is for the laws of England, and this power seems to be another power distinct from the power of the law." The Lords yielded, but Charles gave an evasive reply; and the failure of the more moderate counsels for which his own had been set aside, called Eliot again to the front. In a speech of unprecedented boldness he moved the presentation to the King of a Remonstrance on the state of the realm. But at the moment when he again touched on Buckingham's removal as the preliminary of any real improvement the Speaker of the House interposed. "There was a command laid on him," he said, "to interrupt any that should go about to lay an aspersion on the King's ministers." The breach of their privilege of free speech produced a scene in the Commons such as St. Stephen's had never witnessed before. Eliot sate abruptly down amidst the solemn silence of the House. "Then appeared such a spectacle of passions," says a letter of the time, "as the like had seldom been seen in such an assembly: some weeping, some expostulating, some prophecying of the fatal ruin of our kingdom, some playing the divines in confessing their sins and country's sins which drew these judgments upon us, some finding, as it were, fault with those that wept. There were above an hundred weeping eyes, many who offered to speak being interrupted and silenced by their own passions." Pym himself rose only to sit down choked with tears. At last Sir Edward Coke found words to blame himself for the timid counsels which had checked Eliot at the beginning of the Session, and to protest "that the author and source of all those miseries was the Duke of Buckingham."

Shouts of assent greeted the resolution to insert the Duke's name in their Remonstrance. But the danger to his favourite overcame the King's obstinacy, and to avert it he suddenly offered to consent to the Petition of Right. His consent won a grant of subsidy from the Parliament, and such a ringing of bells and lighting of bonfires from the people "as were never seen but upon his Majesty's return from Spain." But, like all Charles's concessions, it came too late to effect the end at which he aimed. The Commons persisted in presenting their Remonstrance. Charles received it coldly and ungraciously; while Buckingham, who had stood defiantly at his master's side as he was denounced, fell on his knees to speak. " No, George! " said the King as he raised him; and his demeanour gave emphatic proof that the Duke's favour remained undiminished. " We will perish together, George," he added at a later time, " if thou dost." No shadow of his doom, in fact, had fallen over the brilliant favourite, when, after the prorogation of the Parliament, he set out to take command of a new expedition for the relief of Rochelle. But a lieutenant in the army, John Felton, soured by neglect and wrongs, had found in the Remonstrance some fancied sanction for the revenge he plotted, and, mixing with the throng which crowded the hall at Portsmouth, he stabbed Buckingham to the heart. Charles flung himself on his bed in a passion of tears when the news reached him; but outside the Court it was welcomed with a burst of joy. Young Oxford bachelors, grave London aldermen, vied with each other in drinking healths to Felton. " God bless thee, little David," cried an old woman, as the murderer passed manacled by; " the Lord comfort thee," shouted the crowd, as the Tower gates closed on him. The very crews of the Duke's armament at Portsmouth shouted to the King, as he witnessed their departure, a prayer that he would " spare John Felton, their sometime fellow soldier." But whatever national hopes the fall of Buckingham had aroused were quickly dispelled. Weston, a creature of the Duke, became Lord Treasurer, and his system remained unchanged. " Though our Achan is cut off," said Eliot, " the accursed thing remains."

The Quarrel of Religion It seemed as if no act of Charles could widen the breach which his reckless lawlessness had made between himself and his subjects. But there was one thing dearer to England than free speech in Parliament, than security for property, or even personal liberty; and that one thing was, in the phrase of the day, " the Gospel." The gloom which at the outset of this reign we saw settling down on every Puritan heart had deepened with each succeeding year. The great struggle abroad had gone more and more against Protestantism, and at this moment the end of the cause seemed to have come. In Germany Lutheran and Calvinist alike lay at last beneath the heel of the Catholic House of Austria. The fall of Rochelle left the Huguenots of France at the feet of a Roman Cardinal. While England was thrilling with excitement at the thought that her own hour of deadly peril might come again, as it had come in the year of the Armada, Charles raised Laud to the Bishopric of London, and entrusted him with the direction of ecclesiastical affairs. To the excited Protestantism of the country, Laud, and the High Churchmen whom he headed, seemed a danger more really formidable than the Popery which was making such mighty strides abroad. They were traitors at home, traitors to God and their country at once. Their aim was to draw the Church of England farther away from the Protestant Churches, and nearer to the Church which Protestants regarded as Babylon. They aped Roman ceremonies. Cautiously and tentatively they were intro-

ducing Roman doctrine. But they had none of the sacerdotal
independence which Rome had at any rate preserved. They were
abject in their dependence on the Crown. Their gratitude for the
Royal protection which enabled them to defy the religious instincts
of the realm showed itself in their erection of the most dangerous
pretensions of the monarchy into religious dogmas. Their model,
Bishop Andrewes, declared James to have been inspired by God.
They preached passive obedience to the worst tyranny. They
declared the person and goods of the subject to be at the King's
absolute disposal. They turned religion into a systematic attack
on English liberty. Up to this time, however, they had been little
more than a knot of courtly parsons—for the mass of the clergy,
like their flocks, were steady Puritans—but the well-known energy
of Laud promised a speedy increase of their numbers and their
power. Sober men looked forward to a day when every pulpit
would be ringing with exhortations to passive obedience, with
denunciations of Calvinism and apologies for Rome. Of all the
members of the House of Commons Eliot was least fanatical in his
natural bent, but the religious crisis swept away for the moment
all other thoughts from his mind. " Danger enlarges itself in so
great a measure," he wrote from the country, " that nothing but
Heaven shrouds us from despair." The House met in the same
temper. The first business it called up was that of religion. " The
Gospel," Eliot burst forth, " is that Truth in which this kingdom
has been happy through a long and rare prosperity. This ground,
therefore, let us lay for a foundation of our building, that that
Truth, not with words, but with actions we will maintain! "
" There is a ceremony," he went on, " used in the Eastern Churches,
of standing at the repetition of the Creed, to testify their purpose
to maintain it, not only with their bodies upright, but with their
swords drawn. Give me leave to call that a custom very com-
mendable! " The Commons answered their leader's challenge by
a solemn vow. They avowed that they held for truth that sense of
the Articles as established by Parliament, which by the public act
of the Church, and the general and current exposition of the
writers of their Church, had been delivered unto them. But the
debates over religion were suddenly interrupted. The Commons,
who had deferred all grant of customs till the wrong done in the
illegal levy of them was redressed, had summoned the farmers of
those dues to the bar; but though they appeared, they pleaded the
King's command as a ground for their refusal to answer. The
House was proceeding to a protest, when the Speaker signified that
he had received a Royal order to adjourn. Dissolution was clearly
at hand, and the long-suppressed indignation broke out in a scene
of strange disorder. The Speaker was held down in the chair, while
Eliot, still clinging to his great principle of ministerial responsibility,
denounced the new Treasurer as the adviser of the measure. " None
have gone about to break Parliaments," he added in words to
which after events gave a terrible significance, " but in the end

Parliaments have broken them." The doors were locked, and in spite of the Speaker's protests, of the repeated knocking of the usher sent by Charles to summon the Commons to his presence in the Lords' chamber, and of the gathering tumult within the House itself, the loud " Aye, Aye " of the bulk of the members supported Eliot in his last vindication of English liberty. By successive resolutions the Commons declared whosoever should bring in innovations in religion, or whatever minister advised the levy of subsidies not granted in Parliament, " a capital enemy to the Kingdom and Commonwealth," and every subject voluntarily complying with illegal acts and demands " a betrayer of the liberty of England, and an enemy of the same."

SECTION IV.—NEW ENGLAND

[*Authorities.*—Documents are calendared in the Colonial Calendar. The best account of the English settlements during the period is Doyle, " History of the English in America." For Laud, see his Diary; Heylyn's " Life of Laud "; and Prynne, " Canterbury's Doom."]

England and the New World
The dissolution of the Parliament of 1629 marked the darkest hour of Protestantism, whether in England or in the world at large. But it was in this hour of despair that the Puritans won their noblest triumph. They " turned," to use Canning's words in a far truer and grander sense than that which he gave to them, they " turned to the New World to redress the balance of the Old." It was during the years of tyranny which followed the close of the third Parliament of Charles that the great Puritan emigration founded the States of New England.

The Puritans were far from being the earliest among the English colonists of North America. There was little in the circumstances which attended the first discovery of the Western world which promised well for freedom; its earliest result, indeed, was to give an enormous impulse to the most bigoted and tyrannical of the Continental powers, and to pour the wealth of Mexico and Peru into the treasury of Spain. But while the Spanish galleons traversed the Southern seas, and Spanish settlers claimed the southern part of the great continent for the Catholic crown, the truer instinct of Englishmen drew them to the ruder and more barren districts along the shore of Northern America. Long before the time of Columbus the fisheries of the North Sea had made the merchants of Bristol familiar with the coasts of Greenland; and two years before the great navigator reached the actual mainland of America, a Venetian merchant, John Cabot, who dwelt at Bristol, had landed with a crew of English sailors among the icy solitudes of Labrador. A year later his son, Sebastian Cabot, sailing from the same English port to the same point on the American coast, pushed south as far as Maryland, and north as high as Hudson's Bay. For a long time, however, no one followed in the track of these bold adventurers. While France settled its Canadian colonists along the St. Lawrence, and Spain—already mistress of the South—extended its dominions as far northwards as Florida, the attention of English-men limited itself to the fisheries of Newfoundland. It was only in the reign of Elizabeth that men's thoughts turned again to the discoveries of Cabot. Frobisher, in a vessel no bigger than a man-of-war's barge, made his way to the coast of Labrador; and the false news which he brought back of the existence of gold mines there drew adventurer after adventurer among the icebergs of Hudson's Straits. Luckily the quest of gold proved a vain one; and the nobler spirits among those who had engaged in it turned to plans of colonization. But the country, vexed by long winters, and thinly peopled by warlike tribes of Indians, gave a rough welcome to the earlier colonists. After a fruitless attempt to form a settlement, Sir Humphry Gilbert, one of the noblest spirits of his time, turned homewards again, to find his fate in the stormy seas. "We are as near to Heaven by sea as by land," were the famous words he was heard to utter, ere the light of his little bark was lost for ever in the darkness of the night. An expedition sent by his brother-in-law, Sir Walter Raleigh, explored Pamlico Sound; and the country they discovered, a country where, in their poetic fancy, "men lived after the manner of the Golden Age," received from Elizabeth, the Virgin Queen, the name of Virginia. The introduction of tobacco and of the potato into Europe dates from Raleigh's discovery; but the energy of his settlers was distracted by the delusive dream of gold, the hostility of the native tribes drove them from the coast, and it is through the gratitude of later times for what he strove to do, rather than for what he did, that Raleigh, the capital of North Carolina, preserves his name. The first permanent settlement on the Chesapeake was effected in the beginning of the reign of James the First, and its success was due to the conviction of the settlers that the secret of the New World's conquest lay simply in labour. Among the hundred and five colonists who originally landed, forty-eight were gentlemen, and only twelve were tillers of the soil. Their leader, John Smith, however, not only explored the vast bay of Chesapeake and dis-covered the Potomac and the Susquehannah, but held the little company together in the face of famine and desertion till the colonists had learnt the lesson of toil. In his letters to the colonizers at home he set resolutely aside the dream of gold. "Nothing is to be expected thence," he wrote of the new country, "but by labour;" and supplies of labourers, aided by a wise allotment of lands to each colonist, secured after five years of struggle the fortunes of Virginia. "Men fell to building houses and planting corn;" the very streets of Jamestown, as their capital was called from the reigning sovereign, were sown with tobacco; and in fifteen years the colony numbered five thousand souls.

The laws and representative institutions of England were first introduced into the New World in the settlement of Virginia:

1576

1584

1606

some years later a principle as unknown to England as it was to
the greater part of Europe found its home in another colony, which
received its name of Maryland from Henrietta Maria, the queen of
Charles the First. Calvert, Lord Baltimore, one of the best of the
Stuart counsellors, was forced by his conversion to Catholicism to
seek a shelter for himself and colonists of his new faith in the
district across the Potomac, and round the head of the Chesapeake.
As a purely Catholic settlement was impossible, he resolved to
1634 open the new colony to men of every faith. " No person within this
province," ran the earliest law of Maryland, " professing to believe
in Jesus Christ, shall be in any ways troubled, molested, or dis-
countenanced for his or her religion, or in the free exercise thereof."
Long however before Lord Baltimore's settlement in Maryland,
only a few years indeed after the settlement of Smith in Virginia,
the little church of Brownist or Independent refugees, whom we
saw driven in Elizabeth's reign to Amsterdam, had resolved to quit
Holland and find a home in the wilds of the New World. They
were little disheartened by the tidings of suffering which came
from the Virginian settlement. " We are well weaned," wrote
their minister, John Robinson, " from the delicate milk of the
mother-country, and inured to the difficulties of a strange land:
the people are industrious and frugal. We are knit together as a
body in a most sacred covenant of the Lord, of the violation
whereof we make great conscience, and by virtue whereof we hold
ourselves strictly tied to all care of each other's good and of the
whole. It is not with us as with men whom small things can discourage." Returning from Holland to Southampton, they started
in two small vessels for the new land: but one of these soon put
back, and only its companion, the *Mayflower*, a bark of a hundred
and eighty tons, with forty-one emigrants and their families on
board, persisted in prosecuting its voyage. The little company of
1620 the " Pilgrim Fathers," as after-times loved to call them, landed
on the barren coast of Massachusetts at a spot to which they gave
the name of Plymouth, in memory of the last English port at which
they touched. They had soon to face the long hard winter of the
north, to bear sickness and famine: even when these years of toil
and suffering had passed there was a time when " they knew not
at night where to have a bit in the morning." Resolute and
industrious as they were, their progress was very slow; and at the
end of ten years they numbered only three hundred souls. But
small as it was, the colony was now firmly established and the
struggle for mere existence was over. " Let it not be grievous unto
you," some of their brethren had written from England to the
poor emigrants in the midst of their sufferings, " that you have
been instrumental to break the ice for others. The honour shall be
yours to the world's end."

From the moment of their establishment the eyes of the English
Puritans were fixed on the little Puritan settlement in North
America. The sanction of the Crown was necessary to raise it into

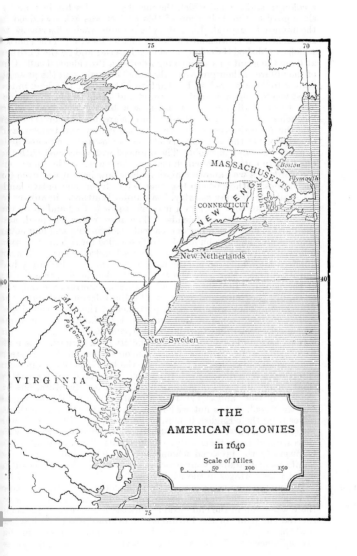

THE
AMERICAN COLONIES
in 1640

Scale of Miles
0   50   100   150

a colony; and the aid which the merchants of Boston in Lincoln
shire gave to the realization of this project was acknowledged in
the name of its capital. Eight days before announcing his resolve to
govern henceforth without Parliaments, Charles granted the charter
which established the colony of Massachusetts; and by the Puritans
at large the grant was at once regarded as a Providential call. Out
of the failure of their great constitutional struggle, and the pressing
danger to " godliness " in England, rose the dream of a land in the
West where religion and liberty could find a safe and lasting home.
The third Parliament of Charles was hardly dissolved, when
" conclusions " for the establishment of a great colony on the other
side the Atlantic were circulating among gentry and traders, and
descriptions of the new country of Massachusetts were talked over
in every Puritan household. The proposal was welcomed with the
quiet, stern enthusiasm which marked the temper of the time; but
the words of a well-known emigrant show how hard it was even for
the sternest enthusiasts to tear themselves from their native land.
" I shall call that my country," said John Winthrop, in answer to
feelings of this sort, " where I may most glorify God and enjoy the
presence of my dearest friends." The answer was accepted, and
the Puritan emigration began on a scale such as England had never
before seen. The two hundred who first sailed for Salem were soon
followed by Winthrop himself with eight hundred men; and seven
hundred more followed ere the first year of the Royal tyranny had
run its course. Nor were the emigrants, like the earlier colonists
of the South, " broken men," adventurers, bankrupts, criminals,
or simply poor men and artisans, like the Pilgrim Fathers of the
Mayflower. They were in great part men of the professional and
middle classes; some of them men of large landed estate, some
zealous clergymen like Cotton, Hooker, and Roger Williams, some
shrewd London lawyers, or young scholars from Oxford. The bulk
were god-fearing farmers from Lincolnshire and the Eastern
counties. They desired in fact " only the best " as sharers in their
enterprise; men driven forth from their fatherland not by earthly
want, or by the greed of gold, or by the lust of adventure, but by
the fear of God, and the zeal for a godly worship. But strong as
was their zeal, it was not without a wrench that they tore them
selves from their English homes. " Farewell, dear England! " was
the cry which burst from the first little company of emigrants as its
shores faded from their sight. " Our hearts," wrote Winthrop's
followers to the brethren whom they had left behind, " shall be
fountains of tears for your everlasting welfare, when we shall be
in our poor cottages in the wilderness."

During the next two years, as the sudden terror which had found
so violent an outlet in Eliot's warnings died for the moment away,
there was a lull in the emigration. But the measures of Laud soon
revived the panic of the Puritans. The shrewdness of James had
read the very heart of the man, when Buckingham pressed for his
first advancement to the see of St. David's. " He hath a restless

1629

1630

Laud
and the
Puritans

spirit," said the old King, " which cannot see when things are well, but loves to toss and change, and to bring matters to a pitch of reformation floating in his own brain. Take him with you, but by my soul you will repent it." Cold, pedantic, ridiculous, super-stitious as he was (he notes in his diary the entry of a robin-red-breast into his study as a matter of grave moment), William Laud rose out of the mass of court-prelates by his industry, his personal unselfishness, his remarkable capacity for administration. At a later period, when immersed in State-business, he found time to acquire so complete a knowledge of commercial affairs that the London merchants themselves owned him a master in matters of trade. But his real influence was derived from the unity of his purpose. He directed all the power of a clear, narrow mind, and a dogged will, to the realization of a single aim. His resolve was to raise the Church of England to what he conceived to be its real position as a branch, though a reformed branch, of the great Catholic Church throughout the world; protesting alike against the innovations of Rome and the innovations of Calvin, and basing its doctrines and usages on those of the Christian communion in the centuries which preceded the Council of Nicæa. The first step in the realization of such a theory was the severance of whatever ties had hitherto united the English Church to the Reformed Churches of the Continent. In Laud's view episcopal succession was of the essence of a Church, and by their rejection of bishops, the Lutheran and Calvinistic Churches of Germany and Switzerland had ceased to be Churches at all. The freedom of worship therefore which had been allowed to the Huguenot refugees from France, or the Walloons from Flanders, was suddenly withdrawn; and the requirement of conformity with the Anglican ritual drove them in crowds from the southern ports to seek toleration in Holland. The same conformity was required from the English soldiers and merchants abroad, who had hitherto attended without scruple the services of the Calvinistic churches. The English ambassador in Paris was forbidden to visit the Huguenot conventicle at Charenton. As Laud drew further from the Protestants of the Continent, he drew, consciously or unconsciously, nearer to Rome. His theory owned Rome as a true branch of the Church, though severed from that of England by errors and innovations against which Laud vigorously protested. But with the removal of these obstacles reunion would naturally follow, and his dream was that of bridging over the gulf which ever since the Reformation had parted the two Churches. The secret offer of a cardinal's hat proved Rome's sense that Laud was doing her work for her; while his rejection of it, and his own reiterated protestations, prove equally that he was doing it unconsciously. Union with the great body of Catholicism, indeed, he regarded as a work which only time could bring about, but for which he could prepare the Church of England by raising it to a higher standard of Catholic feeling and Catholic practice. The great obstacle in his way was the Puritanism of nine-tenths of the

English people, and on Puritanism he made war without mercy. No sooner had his elevation to the see of Canterbury placed him at the head of the English Church, than he turned the High Commission into a standing attack on the Puritan ministers. Rectors and vicars were scolded, suspended, deprived for " Gospel preaching." The use of the surplice, and the ceremonies most offensive to Puritan feeling, were enforced in every parish. The lectures founded in towns, which were the favourite posts of Puritan preachers, were rigorously suppressed. They found a refuge among the country gentlemen, and the Archbishop withdrew from the country gentlemen the privilege of keeping chaplains, which they had till then enjoyed. As parishes became vacant the High Church bishops filled them with men who denounced Calvinism, and declared passive obedience to the sovereign to be part of the law of God. The Puritans soon felt the stress of this process, and endeavoured to meet it by buying up the appropriations of livings, and securing through feeoffees a succession of Protestant ministers in the parishes of which they were patrons: but Laud cited the feeoffees into the Star Chamber, and roughly put an end to them. Nor was the persecution confined to the clergy. Under the two last reigns the small pocket-Bibles called the Geneva Bibles had become universally popular amongst English laymen; but their marginal notes were found to savour of Calvinism, and their importation was prohibited. The habit of receiving the communion in a sitting posture had become common, but kneeling was now enforced, and hundreds were excommunicated for refusing to comply with the injunction. A more galling means of annoyance was found in the different views of the two religious parties on the subject of Sunday. The Puritans identified the Lord's day with the Jewish Sabbath, and transferred to the one the strict observances which were required for the other. The Laudian clergy, on the other hand, regarded it simply as one among the holidays of the Church, and encouraged their flocks in the pastimes and recreations after service which had been common before the Reformation. The Crown under James had taken part with the High Churchmen, and had issued a " Book of Sports " which recommended certain games as lawful and desirable on the Lord's day. The Parliament, as might be expected, was stoutly on the other side, and had forbidden Sunday pastimes by statute. The general religious sense of the country was undoubtedly tending to a stricter observance of the day, when Laud brought the contest to a sudden issue. He summoned the Chief-Justice, Richardson, who had enforced the statute in the western shires, to the Council-table, and rated him so violently that the old man came out complaining he had been all but choked by a pair of lawn sleeves. He then ordered every minister to read the Royal declaration in favour of Sunday pastimes from the pulpit. One Puritan minister had the wit to obey, and to close the reading with the significant hint, " you have heard read, good people, both the commandment of God and the commandment of man! Obey which you please." But the bulk refused to comply with the Archbishop's will. The result followed at which Laud no doubt had aimed. Hundreds of Puritan ministers were cited before the High Commission, and silenced or deprived. In the diocese of Norwich alone thirty parochial ministers were expelled from their cures.

The suppression of Puritanism in the ranks of the clergy was only a preliminary to the real work on which the Archbishop's mind was set, the preparation for Catholic reunion by the elevation of the clergy to a Catholic standard in doctrine and ritual. Laud publicly avowed his preference of an unmarried to a married priesthood. Some of the bishops, and a large part of the new clergy who occupied the posts from which the Puritan ministers had been driven, advocated doctrines and customs which the Reformers had denounced as sheer Papistry; the practice, for instance, of auricular confession, a real presence in the Sacrament, or prayers for the dead. One prelate, Montagu, was in heart a convert to Rome. Another, Goodman, died acknowledging himself a Papist. Meanwhile Laud was indefatigable in his efforts to raise the civil and political status of the clergy to the point which it had reached ere the fatal blow of the Reformation fell on the priesthood. Among the archives of his see lies a large and costly volume in vellum, containing a copy of such records in the Tower as concerned the privileges of the clergy. Its compilation was entered in the Archbishop's diary as one among the " twenty-one things which I have projected to do if God bless me in them," and as among the fifteen to which before his fall he had been enabled to add his emphatic " done." The power of the Bishops' Courts, which had long fallen into decay, revived under his patronage. In 1636 he was able to induce the King to raise a prelate, Juxon, Bishop of London, to the highest civil post in the realm, that of Lord High Treasurer. " No Churchman had it since Henry the Seventh's time," Laud comments proudly. " I pray God bless him to carry it so that the Church may have honour, and the State service and content by it. And now, if the Church will not hold up themselves, under God I can do no more." As he aimed at a higher standard of Catholicism in the clergy, so he aimed at a nearer approach to the pomp of Catholicism in public worship. His conduct in his own house at Lambeth brings out with singular vividness the reckless courage with which he threw himself across the religious instincts of a time when the spiritual aspect of worship was overpowering in most men's minds its æsthetic and devotional sides. Men noted as a fatal omen the accident which marked his first entry into Lambeth; for the overladen ferry-boat upset in the passage of the river, and though the horses and servants were saved, the Archbishop's coach remained at the bottom of the Thames. But no omen, carefully as he might note it, brought a moment's hesitation to the bold, narrow mind of the new Primate. His first act, he boasted, was the setting about a restoration of his chapel; and, as

Laud and the Clergy

Laud managed it, his restoration was the simple undoing of all that
had been done there by his predecessors since the Reformation. In
Edward's time iconoclasm had dashed the stained glass from its
windows, in Elizabeth's time the communion table had been moved
into the middle of the chapel. It was probably Abbot who had
abolished the organ and choir. Abbot, indeed, had put the finishing stroke on all attempts at a higher ceremonial. Neither he nor
his household would bow at the name of Christ. The credence table
had disappeared. Copes, still in use at the Communion in Parker's
day, had ceased to be used in Laud's. Bare as its worship was,
however, the chapel of Lambeth House was one of the most conspicuous among the ecclesiastical buildings of the time; it had seen
the daily worship of every Primate since Cranmer, and was a place
" whither many of the nobility, judges, clergy, and persons of all
sorts, as well strangers as natives, usually resorted." But to Laud
its state seemed intolerable. With characteristic energy he aided
with his own hands in the replacement of the painted glass in its
windows, and racked his wits in piecing the fragments together.
The glazier was scandalized by the Primate's express command to
repair and set up again the " broken crucifix " in the east window.
The holy table was removed from the centre, and set altarwise
against the eastern wall, with a cloth of arras behind it, on which
was embroidered the history of the Last Supper. The elaborate
woodwork of the screen, the rich copes of the chaplain, the silver
candlesticks, the credence table, the organ and the choir, the
stately ritual, the bowings at the sacred name, the genuflexions to
the altar, made the chapel at last such a model of worship as Laud
desired. If he could not exact an equal pomp of devotion in other
quarters, he exacted as much as he could. Bowing to the altar was
introduced into all cathedral churches. A royal injunction ordered
the removal of the communion table, which for the last half-century
or more had in almost every parish church stood in the middle of
the nave, back to its pre-Reformation position in the chancel, and
secured it from profanation by a rail. The removal implied, and
was understood to imply, a recognition of the Real Presence, and
a denial of the doctrine which Englishmen generally held about
the Lord's Supper. But, strenuous as was the resistance Laud
encountered, his pertinacity and severity warred it down. Vicars
who denounced the change from their pulpits were fined, imprisoned, and deprived of their benefices. Churchwardens who
refused or delayed to obey the injunction were rated at the
Commission-table, and frightened into compliance.

The
Puritan
Colonies
　　In their last Remonstrance to the King the Commons had
denounced Laud as the chief assailant of the Protestant character
of the Church of England; and every year of his Primacy showed
him bent upon justifying the accusation. His policy was no longer
the purely conservative policy of Parker or Whitgift; it was
aggressive and revolutionary. His " new counsels " threw whatever force there was in the feeling of conservatism into the hands

f the Puritan, for it was the Puritan who now seemed to be defending the old character of the Church of England against its Primate's attacks. But backed as Laud was by the power of the Crown, the struggle became more hopeless every day. The Puritan saw his ministers silenced or deprived, his Sabbath profaned, the most sacred act of his worship brought near, as he fancied, to the Roman mass. Roman doctrine met him from the pulpit, Roman practices met him in the Church. We can hardly wonder that with such a world around them " godly people in England began to apprehend a special hand of Providence in raising this plantation " in Massachusetts; " and their hearts were generally stirred to come over." It was in vain that weaker men returned to bring news of hardships and dangers, and told how two hundred of the new comers had perished with their first winter. A letter from Winthrop told how the rest toiled manfully on. " We now enjoy God and Jesus Christ," he wrote to those at home, " and is not that enough? I thank God I like so well to be here as I do not repent my coming. I would not have altered my course though I had foreseen all these afflictions. I never had more content of mind." With the strength and manliness of Puritanism, its bigotry and narrowness had crossed the Atlantic too. Roger Williams, a young minister who held the doctrine of freedom of conscience, was driven from the new settlement, to become a preacher among the settlers of Rhode Island. The bitter resentment stirred in the emigrants by persecution at home was seen in their abolition of Episcopacy and their prohibition of the use of the Book of Common Prayer. The intensity of its religious sentiments turned the colony into a theocracy. " To the end that the body of the Commons may be preserved of honest and good men, it was ordered and agreed that for the time to come no man shall be admitted to the freedom of the body politic but such as are members of some of the churches within the bounds of the same." As Laud's hands grew heavier the number of Puritan emigrants rose fast. Three thousand new colonists arrived from England in a single year. The landing of Harry Vane, the son of a Secretary of State, and destined to play one of the first parts in the coming revolution, seemed to herald the coming of the very heads of the Puritan movement. The story that a royal embargo alone prevented Cromwell from crossing the seas is probably unfounded, but it is certain that nothing but the great change which followed on the Scotch rising prevented the flight of men of the highest rank. Lord Warwick secured the proprietorship of the Connecticut valley. Lord Saye and Sele and Lord Brooke began negotiations for transferring themselves to the New World. Hampden purchased a tract of land on the Narragansett. The growing stream of meaner emigrants marks the terrible pressure of the time. Between the sailing of Winthrop's expedition and the assembly of the Long Parliament, in the space, that is, of ten or eleven years, two hundred emigrant ships had crossed the Atlantic, and twenty thousand Englishmen had found a refuge in the West.

1636

SECTION V.—THE TYRANNY, 1629—1640

[*Authorities.*—To those already mentioned may be added the " Strafford Letters and Despatches "; the " Autobiography of Sir Simonds d'Ewes "; Baillie's " Letters and Journals," for the relations between England and Scotland under Charles I. Among modern works may be mentioned, in addition to those already mentioned, Hume Brown, " History of Scotland," and Andrew Lang, " History of Scotland "; and Traill, " Strafford."]

The
Suspension
of Parliament

At the opening of his Third Parliament Charles had hinted in ominous words that the continuance of Parliament at all depended on its compliance with his will. " If you do not your duty," said the King, " mine would then order me to use those other means which God has put into my hand." The threat, however, failed to break the resistance of the Commons, and the ominous words passed into a settled policy. " We have showed," said a Proclamation which followed on the dissolution of the Houses, " by our frequent meeting our people, our love to the use of Parliament; yet, the late abuse having for the present driven us unwillingly out of that course, we shall account it presumption for any to prescribe any time unto us for Parliament."

No Parliament in fact met for eleven years. But it would be unjust to charge the King at the outset of this period with any definite scheme of establishing a tyranny, or of changing what he conceived to be the older constitution of the realm. He " hated the very name of Parliaments," but in spite of his hate he had no settled purpose of abolishing them. His belief was that England would in time recover its senses, and that then Parliament might re-assemble without inconvenience to the Crown. In the interval, however long it might be, he proposed to govern single-handed by the use of " those means which God had put into his hands." Resistance, indeed, he was resolved to put down. The leaders of the country party in the last Parliament were thrown into prison; and Eliot died, the first martyr of English liberty, in the Tower. Men were forbidden to speak of the re-assembling of a Parliament. Laud was encouraged to break the obstinate opposition of the Puritans by the enforcement of religious uniformity. But here the King stopped. The opportunity which might have suggested dreams of organized despotism to a Richelieu, suggested only means of filling the Exchequer to Charles. He had in truth neither the grander nor the meaner instincts of the born tyrant. He did not seek to gain an absolute power over his people, because he believed that his absolute power was already a part of the constitution of the country. He set up no standing army to secure it, partly because he was poor, but yet more because his faith in his position was such that he never dreamt of any effectual resistance. His expedients for freeing the Crown from that dependence on Parliaments against which his pride as a sovereign revolted were simply peace and economy. To secure the first he sacrificed an opportunity greater than ever his father had trodden under foot. The fortunes of the great struggle in Germany were suddenly reversed at this juncture by the appearance of Gustavus Adolphus, with a Swedish army, in the heart of Germany. Tilly was defeated and slain; the Catholic League humbled in the dust; Munich, the capital of its Bavarian leader, occupied by the Swedish army, and the Lutheran princes of North Germany freed from the pressure of the Imperial soldiery; while the Emperor himself, trembling within the walls of Vienna, was driven to call for aid from Wallenstein, an adventurer whose ambition he dreaded, but whose army could alone arrest the progress of the Protestant conqueror. The ruin that James had wrought was suddenly averted; but the victories of Protestantism had no more power to draw Charles out of the petty circle of his politics at home than its defeats had had power to draw James out of the circle of his imbecile diplomacy. To support Gustavus by arms, or even by an imposing neutrality, meant a charge on the Royal Treasury which necessitated a fresh appeal to the Commons; and this appeal Charles was resolved never to make. At the very crisis of the struggle therefore he patched up a hasty peace with both the two great Catholic powers of France and Spain, and fell back from any interference with the affairs of the Continent. His whole attention was absorbed by the pressing question of revenue. The debt was a large one; and the ordinary income of the Crown, unaided by parliamentary supplies, was utterly inadequate to meet its ordinary expenditure. Charles was himself frugal and laborious; and the administration of Weston, the new Lord Treasurer, whom he created Earl of Portland, contrasted advantageously with the waste and extravagance of the government under Buckingham. But economy failed to close the yawning gulf of the Treasury, and the course into which Charles was driven by the financial pressure showed with how wise a prescience the Commons had fixed on the point of arbitrary taxation as the chief danger to constitutional freedom.

It is curious to see to what shifts the Royal pride was driven in his effort at once to fill the Exchequer, and yet to avoid, as far as he could, any direct breach of constitutional law in the imposition of taxes by the sole authority of the Crown. The dormant powers of the prerogative were strained to their utmost. The right of the Crown to force knighthood on the landed gentry was revived, in order to squeeze them into composition for the refusal of it. Fines were levied on them for the redress of defects in their title-deeds. Commission of the Forests exacted large sums from the neighbouring landowners for their encroachments on Crown lands. London, the special object of courtly dislike, on account of its stubborn Puritanism. was brought within the sweep of Royal extortion by the enforcement of an illegal proclamation which James had issued, prohibiting its extension. Every house throughout the large suburban districts in which the prohibition had been

disregarded was only saved from demolition by the payment
three years' rental to the Crown. The Treasury gained a hundre
thousand pounds by this clever stroke, and Charles gained t
bitter enmity of the great city whose strength and resources we
fatal to him in the coming war. Though the Catholics were
longer troubled by any active persecution, and the Lord Treasur
was in heart a Papist, the penury of the Exchequer forced t
Crown to maintain the old system of fines for "recusancy
Vexatious measures of extortion such as these were far less hurtf
to the State than the conversion of justice into a means of suppl
ing the Royal necessities by means of the Star Chamber. T
jurisdiction of the King's Council had been revived, as we ha
seen, by Wolsey as a check on the nobles; and it had receive
great development, especially on the side of criminal law, durir
the Tudor reigns. Forgery, perjury, riot, maintenance, fraud, libe
and conspiracy, were the chief offences cognizable in this Cour
but its scope extended to every misdemeanor, and especially
charges where, from the imperfection of the common law, or t
power of offenders, justice was baffled in the lower Courts. I
process resembled that of Chancery: it usually acted on an i
formation laid before it by the King's Attorney. Both witness
and accused were examined on oath by special interrogatorie
and the Court was at liberty to adjudge any punishment short
death. The possession of such a weapon would have been fatal
liberty under a great tyrant; under Charles it was turned simp
to the profit of the Exchequer. Large numbers of cases whi
would ordinarily have come before the Courts of Common La
were called before the Star Chamber, simply for the purpose
levying fines for the Crown. The same motive accounts for t
enormous penalties which were exacted for offences of a trivi
character. The marriage of a gentleman with his niece was punish
by the forfeiture of twelve thousand pounds, and fines of four a
five thousand pounds were awarded for brawls between lords
the Court. Money for the fleet was procured by a stretch of t
prerogative which led afterwards to the great contest over shi
money. The legal research of Noy, one of the law officers of t
Crown, found precedents among the records in the Tower for t
provision of ships for the King's use by the port-towns of t
kingdom, and for the furnishing of their equipment by the maritir
counties. The precedents dated from times when no permane
fleet existed, and when sea warfare was waged by vessels lent f
the moment by the various ports. But they were seized as a mea
of equipping a permanent navy without cost to the Exchequ
and the writs which were issued to London and the chief Engli
ports were enforced by fine and imprisonment. Shifts of this kin
however, did little to fill the Treasury, great as was the annoyan
they caused. Charles was driven from courses of doubtful legali
to a more open defiance of law. Monopolies, abandoned
Elizabeth, extinguished by Act of Parliament under James, a

denounced with his own assent in the Petition of Right, were revived on a scale far more gigantic than had been seen before, the companies who undertook them paying a fixed duty on their profits as well as a large sum for the original concession of the monopoly. Wine, soap, salt, and almost every article of domestic consumption fell into the hands of monopolists, and rose in price out of all proportion to the profit gained by the Crown. " They sup in our cup," Colepepper said afterwards in the Long Parliament, " they dip in our dish, they sit by our fire; we find them in the dye-fat, the wash bowls, and the powdering tub. They share with the cutler in his box. They have marked and sealed us from head to foot." Nothing, indeed, better marks the character of Charles than his conduct as to the Petition of Right. He had given his assent to it, he was fond of bidding Parliament rely on his " Royal word," but the thought of his pledge seems never to have troubled him for an instant. From the moment he began his career of government without a Parliament every one of the abuses he had promised to abolish, such as illegal imprisonment, or tampering with the judges, was resorted to as a matter of course. His penury, in spite of the financial expedients we have described, drove him inevitably on to the fatal rock of illegal taxation. The exaction of Customs duties went on as of old at the ports. Writs were issued for the levy of " benevolences " from the shires. The resistance of the London merchants was roughly put down by the Star Chamber. Chambers, an alderman of London, who complained bitterly that men were worse off in England than in Turkey, was ruined by a fine of two thousand pounds, and died broken-hearted in prison. The freeholders of the counties were more difficult to deal with. When those of Cornwall were called together at Bodmin to contribute to a voluntary loan, half the hundreds refused, and the yield of the rest came to little more than two thousand pounds. One of the Cornishmen has left an amusing record of the scene before the Commissioners appointed for assessment of the loan. " Some with great words and threatenings, some with persuasions," he says, " were drawn to it. I was like to have been complimented out of my money; but knowing with whom I had to deal, I held, when I talked with them, my hands fast in my pockets."

Vexatious indeed and illegal as were the proceedings of the Crown, **Strafford** there seems to have been little apprehension of any permanent danger to freedom in the country at large. To those who read the letters of the time there is something inexpressibly touching in the general faith of their writers in the ultimate victory of the Law. Charles was obstinate, but obstinacy was too common a foible amongst Englishmen to rouse any vehement resentment. The people were as stubborn as their King, and their political sense told them that the slightest disturbance of affairs must shake down the financial fabric which Charles was slowly building up, and force him back on subsidies and a Parliament. Meanwhile they would wait for better days, and their patience was aided by the general prosperity of the country. The long peace was producing its inevitable results in a vast extension of commerce and a rise of manufactures in the towns of the West Riding of Yorkshire. Fresh land was being brought into cultivation, and a great scheme was set on foot for reclaiming the Fens. The new wealth of the country gentry, through the increase of rent, was seen in the splendour of the houses which they were raising. The contrast of this peace and prosperity with the ruin and bloodshed of the Continent afforded a ready argument to the friends of the King's system. So tranquil was the outer appearance of the country that in Court circles all sense of danger had disappeared. "Some of the greatest statesmen and privy councillors," says May, "would ordinarily laugh when the word, 'liberty of the subject,' was named." There were courtiers bold enough to express their hope that "the King would never need any more Parliaments." But beneath this outer calm "the country," Clarendon honestly tells us while eulogizing the Peace, "was full of pride and mutiny and discontent." Thousands, as we have seen, were quitting England for America. The gentry held aloof from the Court. "The common people in the generality and the country freeholders would rationally argue of their own rights and the oppressions which were laid upon them." If Charles was content to deceive himself, there was one man among his ministers who saw that the people were right in their policy of patience, and that unless other measures were taken the fabric of Royal despotism would fall at the first breath of adverse fortune. Sir Thomas Wentworth, a great Yorkshire land-owner and one of the representatives of his county in Parliament, had stood for years past among the more prominent members of the Country party in the Commons. But from the first moment of his appearance in public his passionate desire had been to find employment in the service of the Crown. At the close of the preceding reign he was already connected with the Court, he had secured a seat in Yorkshire for one of the Royal ministers, and was believed to be on the high road to a peerage. But the con-sciousness of political ability which spurred his ambition roused the jealousy of Buckingham; and the haughty pride of Wentworth was flung by repeated slights into an attitude of opposition, which his eloquence—grander in its sudden outbursts, though less earnest and sustained, than that of Eliot—soon rendered formidable. But his patriotism was still little more than hostility to the favourite, and his intrigues at Court roused Buckingham to crush, by a signal insult, the rival whose genius he instinctively dreaded. While sitting in his court as sheriff of Yorkshire, Wentworth received the announcement of his dismissal from office, and of the gift of his post to Sir John Savile, his rival in the county. "Since they will thus weakly breathe on me a seeming disgrace in the public face of my country," he said with a characteristic outburst of con-temptuous pride, "I shall crave leave to wipe it away as openly, as easily!" He sprang at once to the front of the Commons in urging

he Petition of Right. Whether in that crisis of Wentworth's life
ome nobler impulse, some true passion for the freedom he was
o betray mingled with his thirst for revenge, it is hard to tell.
But his words were words of fire. "If he did not faithfully insist
or the common liberty of the subject to be preserved whole and
ntire," it was thus he closed one of his speeches on the Petition,
"it was his desire that he might be set as a beacon on a hill for all
men else to wonder at."

It is as such a beacon that his name has stood from that time to
this. The death of Buckingham had no sooner removed the obstacle
that stood between his ambition and the end at which it had aimed
throughout, than the cloak of patriotism was flung by. Wentworth
was admitted to the Royal Council, and as he took his seat at the
board he promised to "vindicate the Monarchy for ever from the
conditions and restraints of subjects." So great was the faith in
his zeal and power which he knew how to breathe into his Royal
master, that he was at once raised to the peerage, and rewarded
with the high post of Lord President of the North. Charles had
good ground for this rapid confidence in his new minister. In
Wentworth, or as we may call him from the title he assumed at
the close of his life, in the Earl of Strafford, the very genius of
tyranny was embodied. He was far too clear-sighted to share his
master's belief that the arbitrary power which Charles was wielding formed any part of the old constitution of the country, or to
believe that the mere lapse of time would so change the temper
of Englishmen as to reconcile them to despotism. He knew that
absolute rule was a new thing in England, and that the only way of
permanently establishing it was not by reasoning, or by the force
of custom, but by the force of fear. His system was the expression
of his own inner temper; and the dark gloomy countenance, the
dull heavy eye, which meet us in Strafford's portrait are the best
commentary on his policy of "Thorough." It was by the sheer
strength of his genius, by the terror his violence inspired amid the
meaner men whom Buckingham had left, by the general sense of
his power, that he had forced himself upon the Court. He had
none of the small arts of a courtier. His air was that of a silent,
proud, passionate man; when he first appeared at Whitehall his
rough uncourtly manners provoked a smile in the Royal circle, but
the smile soon died into a general hate. The Queen, frivolous and
meddlesome as she was, detested him; his fellow-ministers intrigued
against him, and seized on his hot speeches against the great lords,
his quarrels with the Royal household, his transports of passion
at the very Council-table, to ruin him in his master's favour. The
King himself, while steadily supporting him against his rivals, was
utterly unable to understand his drift. Charles valued him as an
administrator, disdainful of private ends, crushing great and small
with the same haughty indifference to men's love or hate, and
devoted to the one aim of building up the power of the Crown.
But in his purpose of preparing for the great struggle with freedom

which he saw before him, of building up by force such a despotism in England as Richelieu was building up in France, and of thus making England as great in Europe as France had been made by Richelieu, he could look for little sympathy and less help from the King.

Wentworth's genius turned impatiently to a sphere where it could act alone, untrammelled by the hindrances it encountered at home. His purpose was to prepare for the coming contest by the provision of a fixed revenue, arsenals, fortresses, and a standing army, and it was in Ireland that he resolved to find them. He saw in the miserable country which had hitherto been a drain upon the resources of the Crown the lever he needed for the overthrow of English freedom. It was easy by the balance of Catholic against Protestant to make both parties dependent on the Royal authority; the rights of conquest, which in Strafford's theory vested the whole land in the absolute possession of the Crown, gave him a large field for his administrative ability; and for the rest he trusted, and trusted justly, to the force of his genius and of his will. In 1632 he was made Lord Deputy, and five years later his aim seemed all but realized. "The King," he wrote to Laud, " is as absolute here as any prince in the world can be." Wentworth's government indeed was a mere rule of terror. Archbishop Usher, with almost every name which we can respect in the island, was the object of his insult and oppression. His tyranny strode over all legal bounds. A few insolent words, construed as mutiny, were enough to bring Lord Mountnorris before a council of war, and to inflict on him a sentence of death. In one instance Wentworth, it is said, used his power for the basest personal ends: an adulterous passion for the Chancellor's daughter-in-law led him to order that peer to settle his estate in her favour, and, on his refusal, to deprive him of office. But such instances were rare. His tyranny aimed at public ends, and in Ireland the heavy hand of a single despot delivered the mass of the people at any rate from the local despotism of a hundred masters. The Irish landowners were for the first time made to feel themselves amenable to the law. Justice was enforced, outrage was repressed, the condition of the clergy was to some extent raised, the sea was cleared of the pirates who infested it. The foundation of the linen manufacture which was to bring wealth to Ulster, and the first development of Irish commerce, date from the Lieutenancy of Wentworth. But good government was only a means with him for further ends. The noblest work to be done in Ireland was the bringing about a reconciliation between Catholic and Protestant, and an obliteration of the anger and thirst for vengeance which had been raised by the Ulster Plantation. Strafford, on the other hand, angered the Protestants by a toleration of Catholic worship and a suspension of the persecution which had feebly begun against the priesthood, while he fed the irritation of the Catholics by schemes for a Plantation of Connaught. His whole aim was to

encourage a disunion which left both parties dependent for support
and protection on the Crown. It was a policy which was to end in
bringing about the horrors of the Irish Massacre, the vengeance of
Cromwell, and the long series of atrocities on both sides which
make the story of the country he ruined so terrible to tell. But
for the hour it left Ireland helpless in his hands. He had doubled
the revenue. He had raised an army. He felt himself strong
enough at last, in spite of the panic with which Charles heard his
project, to summon an Irish Parliament. His aim was to read a
lesson to England and the King, by showing how completely that
dreaded thing, a Parliament, could be made the organ of the
Royal will; and his success was complete. Two-thirds, indeed,
of an Irish House of Commons consisted of the representatives of
wretched villages, the pocket-boroughs of the Crown; while absent
peers were forced to send in their proxies to the Council to be used
at its pleasure. But precautions were hardly needed. The two
Houses trembled at the stern master who bade their members not
let the King "find them muttering, or, to speak it more truly,
mutinying in corners," and voted with a perfect docility the means
of maintaining an army of five thousand foot and five hundred
horse. Even had the subsidy been refused, the result would have
been the same. "I would undertake," wrote Strafford, "upon
the peril of my head, to make the King's army able to subsist and
to provide for itself among them without their help."

While Strafford was thus working out his system of "Thorough"
on one side of St. George's Channel, it was being carried out on the
other by a mind inferior, indeed, to his own in genius, but almost
equal to it in courage and tenacity. On the death of Weston, Laud
became virtually first minister of the Crown at the English Council-
board. We have already seen with what a reckless and unscrupulous activity he was crushing Puritanism in the English Church,
and driving Puritan ministers from English pulpits; and in this
work his new position enabled him to back the authority of the
High Commission by the terrors of the Star Chamber. It was a

work, indeed, which to Laud's mind was at once civil and religious:
he had allied the cause of ecclesiastical dogmatism with that of
absolutism in the State; and, while borrowing the power of the
Crown to crush ecclesiastical liberty, he brought the influence of
the Church to bear on the ruin of civil freedom. But his power
stopped at the Scotch frontier. Across the Border stood a Church
with bishops indeed, but without a ritual, modelled on the doctrine
and system of Geneva, Calvinist in teaching and in government.
The mere existence of such a Church gave countenance to English
Puritanism, and threatened in any hour of ecclesiastical weakness
to bring a Presbyterian influence to bear on the Church of England.
With Scotland, indeed, Laud could only deal indirectly through
Charles, for the King was jealous of any interference of his English
ministers or Parliament with his Northern Kingdom. But Charles
was himself earnest to deal with it. He had imbibed his father's

hatred of the Presbyterian system, and from the outset of hi
reign he had been making advance after advance towards th
re-establishment of Episcopacy. To understand, however, wha
had been done, and the relations which had by this time grown u
between Scotland and its King, we must take up again the brie
thread of its history which we broke at the moment when Mary
fled for refuge over the English border.

After a few years of wise and able rule, the triumph of Pro
testantism under the Earl of Murray had been interrupted by hi
assassination, by the revival of the Queen's faction, and by th
renewal of civil war. The reaction, however, was a brief one, an
the general horror excited by the Massacre of St. Bartholomew
completed the ruin of the Catholic cause. Edinburgh, the las
fortress held in Mary's name, surrendered to an English force sen
by Elizabeth; and its captain, the chivalrous Kirkcaldy of Grange
was hung for treason at the market-cross. The people of the Low
lands, indeed, were now stanch for the new faith; and the Pro
testant Church rose rapidly after the death of Knox into a powe
which appealed at every critical juncture to the deeper feeling
of the nation at large. In the battle with Catholicism the bishop
had clung to the old religion; and the new faith, left withou
episcopal interference, and influenced by the Genevan training o
Knox, borrowed from Calvin its model of Church government, as i
borrowed from Calvin its theology. The system of Presbyterianism, as it grew
up at the outset without direct recognition from the law, boun
Scotland together by its administrative organization, its church
synods and general assemblies, while it called the people at large
by the power it conferred upon the lay elders in each congregation
to a voice, and, as it proved, a decisive voice, in the administration
of affairs. Its government by ministers gave it the look of a
ecclesiastical despotism, but no Church constitution has proved in
practice so democratic as that of Scotland. Its influence in raising
the nation at large to a consciousness of its own power is shown
by the change which passes, from the moment of its final establish
ment, over the face of Scotch history. The country ceases to belong
to the great nobles, who had turned it into their battle ground
ever since the death of Bruce. After the death of the Earl o

Morton, who had put an end to the civil war, and ruled the country
for five years with a wise and steady hand, the possession of the
young sovereign, James the Sixth, was disputed indeed by one
noble and another; but the power of the Church was felt more
and more over nobles and King. Melville, who had succeeded to
much of Knox's authority, claimed for the ecclesiastical body an
independence of the State which James hardly dared to resent
while he writhed helplessly beneath the sway which public opinion
expressed through the General Assembly of the Church, exercised
over the civil government. In the great crisis of the Armada hi
hands were fettered by the league with England which it forced
upon him. The democratic boldness of Calvinism allied itself with

he spiritual pride of the Presbyterian ministers in their dealings with the Crown. Melville in open Council took James by the sleeve, and called him "God's silly vassal!" "There are two Kings," he told him, when James extolled his Royal authority, "and two kingdoms in Scotland. There is Christ Jesus the King, and His Kingdom the Kirk, whose subject King James the Sixth is, and of whose kingdom not a king, nor a lord, nor a head, but a member." The words and tone of the great preacher were bitterly remembered when James mounted the English throne. "A Scottish Presbytery," he said at the Hampton Court Conference, "as well fitteth with Monarchy as God and the Devil! No Bishop, no King!" But Scotland was resolved on "no bishop." Episcopacy had become identified among the more zealous Scotchmen with the old Catholicism they had shaken off. When he appeared at a later time before the English Council-table, Melville took the Archbishop of Canterbury by the sleeves of his rochet, and, shaking them in his manner, called them Romish rags, and the mark of the Beast.

Four years, therefore, after the ruin of the Armada, Episcopacy was formally abolished, and the Presbyterian system established by law as the mode of government of the Church of Scotland. The rule of the Church was placed in a General Assembly, with subordinate Provincial Synods, Presbyteries, and Kirk Sessions, by which its discipline was carried down to every member of a congregation. As yet, however, the authority of the Assembly was hardly felt north of the Tay, while the system of Presbytery had by no means won the hold it afterwards gained over the people, even to the south of that river; and James had no sooner succeeded to the English throne than he used his new power in a struggle to undo the work which had been done. Melville, after his scornful protest at the Council-table, was banished from Scotland, and died in exile at Sedan. The old sees were restored, and three of the new bishops were consecrated in England, and returned to communicate the gift of Apostolical succession to their colleagues.

But Episcopacy remained simply a name. The Presbyterian organization remained untouched in doctrine or discipline. All that James could do was to set his prelates to preside as permanent moderators in the provincial synods, and to prevent the Assembly from meeting without a summons from the Crown. The struggle, however, went on throughout his reign with varying success. An attempt to vest the government of the Church in the King and Bishops was foiled by the protest of the Presbyterian party; but a General Assembly, gathered at Perth, was induced to adopt some of the ecclesiastical practices most distasteful to them. The earlier policy of Charles, though it followed his father's line of action, effected little save a partial restoration of Church-lands, which the lords were forced to surrender. But Laud had no sooner become minister than his vigorous action made itself felt. The King's first acts were directed rather to points of outer observance than to any attack on the actual fabric of Presbyterian organiza-

tion. The Estates were induced to withdraw the control of ecclesi
astical apparel from the Assembly, and to commit it to the Crown
a step soon followed by a resumption of their episcopal costum
on the part of the Scotch bishops. When the Bishop of Moray
preached before Charles in his rochet, on the King's visit to Edin
burgh, it was the first instance of its use since the Reformation
The innovation was followed by the issue of a Royal warrant which
directed all ministers to use the surplice in divine worship. From
costume, however, the busy minister soon passed to weightier
matters. Many years had gone by since he had vainly invited
James to draw his Scotch " subjects to a nearer conjunction with
the liturgy and canons of this nation." " I sent him back again,"
said the shrewd old King, " with the frivolous draft he had drawn
For all that, he feared not my anger, but assaulted me again
with another ill-fangled platform to make that stubborn Kirk
stoop more to the English platform, but I durst not play fast and
loose with my word. He knows not the stomach of that people."
But Laud had known how to wait, and his time had come at last
A new diocese, that of Edinburgh, was created, and the Archbishop
of St. Andrews was named chancellor of the realm. A book of

Canons, issued by the sole authority of the King, ignored Assembly
and Kirk Session, and practically abolished the whole Presbyterian
system. As daring a stretch of the prerogative superseded what
was known as Knox's Liturgy—the book of Common Order drawn
up on the Genevan model by that Reformer, and generally used
throughout Scotland—by a new Liturgy based on the English
Book of Common Prayer. The Liturgy and Canons had been
Laud's own handiwork; in their composition the General Assembly
had neither been consulted nor recognized, and to enforce them on
Scotland was to effect an ecclesiastical revolution of the most
serious kind. The books, however, were backed by a Royal
Injunction, and Laud flattered himself that the revolution had
been wrought.

Triumphant in Scotland, with Scotch Presbyterianism—as he
fancied—at his feet, Laud's hand fell heavier than ever on the
English Puritans. There were signs of a change of temper which
might have made even a bolder man pause. Thousands, as we have
seen, of " the best " scholars, merchants, lawyers, farmers, were
flying over the Atlantic to seek freedom and purity of religion
in the wilderness. Great landowners and nobles were preparing to
follow. Hundreds of ministers had quitted their parsonages rather
than abet the Royal insult to the sanctity of the Sabbath. The
Puritans who remained among the clergy were giving up their
homes rather than consent to the change of the Sacred table into
an altar, or to silence in their protests against the new Popery
The noblest of living Englishmen refused to become the priest of
a Church whose ministry could only be " bought with servitude
and forswearing." We have seen John Milton leave Cambridge,
self-dedicated " to that same lot, however mean or high, to which

time leads me and the will of Heaven." But the lot to which these called him was not the ministerial office to which he had been destined from his childhood. In later life he told bitterly the story, how he had been "Church-outed by the prelates." "Coming to some maturity of years, and perceiving what tyranny had invaded in the Church, that he who would take orders must subscribe slave, and take an oath withal, which unless he took with a conscience that would retch he must either straight perjure or split his faith, I thought it better to prefer a blameless silence before the sacred office of speaking, bought and begun with servitude and forswearing." In spite therefore of his father's regrets, he retired to a new home which the scrivener had found at Horton, a village in the neighbourhood of Windsor, and quietly busied himself with study and poetry. The poetic impulse of the Renascence had been slowly dying away under the Stuarts. The stage was falling into mere coarseness and horror; Shakspere had died quietly at Stratford in Milton's childhood; the last and worst play of Ben Jonson appeared in the year of his settlement at Horton; and though Ford and Massinger still lingered on, there were no successors for them but Shirley and Davenant. The philosophic and meditative taste of the age had produced indeed poetic schools of its own: poetic satire had become fashionable in Hall, better known afterwards as a bishop, and had been carried on vigorously by George Wither; the so-called "metaphysical" poetry, the vigorous and pithy expression of a cold and prosaic good sense, began with Sir John Davies, and buried itself in fantastic affectations in Donne; religious verse had become popular in the gloomy allegories of Quarles and the tender refinement which struggles through a jungle of puns and extravagances in George Herbert. But what poetic life really remained was to be found only in the caressing fancy and lively badinage of lyric singers like Herrick, whose grace is untouched by passion and often disfigured by coarseness, and pedantry; or in the school of Spenser's more direct successors where Brown, in his pastorals, and the two Fletchers, Phineas and Giles, in their unreadable allegories, still preserved something of their master's sweetness, if they preserved nothing of his power. Milton was himself a Spenserian; he owned to Dryden in later years that "Spenser was his original," and in some of his earliest lines at Horton he dwells lovingly on "the sage and solemn tunes" of the "Faerie Queen," its "forests and enchantments drear, where more is meant than meets the ear." But of the weakness and affectation which characterized Spenser's successors he had not a trace. In the "Allegro" and "Penseroso," the first results of his retirement at Horton, we catch again the fancy and melody of the Elizabethan verse, the wealth of its imagery, its wide sympathy with nature and man. There is a loss, perhaps, of the older freedom and spontaneity of the Renascence, a rhetorical rather than passionate turn in the young poet, a striking absence of dramatic power, and a want of precision and exactness even in

1629
to
1640
his picturesque touches. Milton's imagination is not strong enough
to identify him with the world which he imagines; he stands apart
from it, and looks at it as from a distance, ordering it and arranging
it at his will. But if in this respect he falls, both in his earlier and
later poems, far below Shakspere or Spenser, the deficiency is all
but compensated by his nobleness of feeling and expression, the
severity of his taste, his sustained dignity, and the perfectness and
completeness of his work. The moral grandeur of the Puritan
breathes, even in these lighter pieces of his youth, through every
line. The " Comus " planned as a masque for the festivities which
the Earl of Bridgewater was holding at Ludlow Castle, rises into
an almost impassioned pleading for the love of virtue.

Hamp-
den and
Ship-
money
The historic interest of Milton's " Comus " lies in its forming
part of a protest made by the more cultured Puritans at this time
against the gloomier bigotry which persecution was fostering in
the party at large. The patience of Englishmen, in fact, was slowly
wearing out. There was a sudden upgrowth of virulent pamphlets
of the old Martin Marprelate type. Men, whose names no one asked,
hawked libels, whose authorship no one knew, from the door of the
tradesman to the door of the squire. As the hopes of a Parliament
grew fainter, and men despaired of any legal remedy, violent and
weak-headed fanatics came, as at such times they always come
to the front. Leighton, the father of the saintly Archbishop of that
name, had given a specimen of their tone at the outset of this
period, by denouncing the prelates as men of blood, Episcopacy
as Antichrist, and the Popish queen as a daughter of Heth. The
1633
" Histrio-mastix " of Prynne, a lawyer distinguished for his constitutional knowledge, but the most obstinate and narrow-minded
of men, marked the deepening of Puritan bigotry under the fostering warmth of Laud's persecution. The book was an attack on
players as the ministers of Satan, on theatres as the Devil's chapels,
on hunting, on maypoles, the decking of houses at Christmas with
evergreens, on cards, music, and false hair. The attack on the stage
was as offensive to the more cultured minds among the Puritan
party as to the Court itself; Selden and Whitelock took a prominent part in preparing the grand masque by which the Inns of
Court resolved to answer its challenge, and in the following year
Milton wrote his masque of " Comus " for Ludlow Castle. To leave
Prynne, however, simply to the censure of wiser men than himself
was too sensible a course for the angry Primate. No man was ever
sent to prison before or since for such a sheer mass of nonsense; but
the prison with which Laud rewarded Prynne's enormous folly
tamed his spirit so little that a new tract written within its walls
attacked the bishops as devouring wolves and lords of Lucifer.
A fellow-prisoner, John Bastwick, declared in his " Litany " that
" Hell was broke loose, and the Devils in surplices, hoods, copes,
and rochets, were come among us." Burton, a London clergyman
silenced by the High Commission, called on all Christians to resist
the bishops as " robbers of souls, limbs of the Beast, and factors of

Antichrist." Raving of this sort, however, though it showed how fast the storm of popular passion was gathering, was not so pressing a difficulty to the Royal ministers at this time as the old difficulty of the Exchequer. The ingenious devices of the Court lawyers, the revived prerogatives, the illegal customs, the fines and confiscations which were alienating one class after another and sowing in home after home the seeds of a bitter hatred to the Crown, had failed to recruit the Treasury. In spite of the severe economy of Charles and his ministers new exactions were necessary, at a time when the rising discontent made every new exaction a challenge to revolt. But danger and difficulty were lost on the temper of the two men who really governed England. To Laud and Strafford, indeed, the King seemed over-cautious, the Star Chamber feeble, the Judges over-scrupulous. "I am for Thorough," the one writes to the other in alternate fits of impatience at the slow progress they are making. Strafford was anxious that his good work might not " be spoiled on that side." Laud echoed the wish, while he envied the free course of the Lord Lieutenant. " You have a good deal of humour here," he writes, " for your proceeding. Go on a' God's name. I have done with expecting of Thorough on this side." The financial pressure was seized by both to force the King on to a bolder course. " The debt of the Crown being taken off," Strafford urged, " you may govern at your will." All pretence of precedents was thrown aside, and Laud resolved to find a permanent revenue in the conversion of the " ship-money " levied on ports and the maritime counties into a general tax imposed by the Royal will upon the whole country. The sum expected from the tax was no less than a quarter of a million a year. " I know no reason," Strafford had written significantly, " but you may as well rule the common lawyers in England as I, poor beagle, do here; " and a bench of Judges, remodelled on his hint for the occasion, no sooner declared the new impost to be legal than he drew the logical deduction from their decision. " Since it is lawful for the King to impose a tax for the equipment of the navy, it must be equally so for the levy of an army: and the same reason which authorizes him to levy an army to resist, will authorize him to carry that army abroad that he may prevent invasion. Moreover what is law in England is law also in Scotland and Ireland. The decision of the judges will therefore make the King absolute at home and formid- able abroad. Let him only abstain from war for a few years that he may habituate his subjects to the payment of that tax, and in the end he will find himself more powerful and respected than any of his predecessors." But there were men who saw the danger to freedom in this levy of ship-money as clearly as Strafford himself. John Hampden, a friend of Eliot's, a man of consummate ability, of unequalled power of persuasion, of a keen intelligence, ripe learning, and a character singularly pure and loveable, had already shown the firmness of his temper in his refusal to contribute to the forced loan of 1626. He now repeated his refusal, declared ship-

1629
to
1640
—
The
Resist-
ance

July,
1637

money an illegal impost, and resolved to rouse the spirit of the country by an appeal for protection to the law.

The news of Hampden's resistance thrilled through England at the very moment when men were roused by the news of resistance in the north. The submission with which Scotland had bent to aggression after aggression found an end at last. The Dean of Edinburgh had no sooner opened the new Prayer Book than a murmur ran through the congregation, and the murmur soon grew into a formidable riot. The Church was cleared, the service read, but the rising discontent frightened the judges into a decision that the Royal writ enjoined the purchase, and not the use, of the Prayer Book. Its use was at once discontinued, and the angry orders which came from England for its restoration were met by a shower of protests from every part of Scotland. The Duke of Lennox alone took sixty-eight petitions with him to the Court; while ministers, nobles, and gentry poured into Edinburgh to organize the national resistance. The effect of these events in Scotland was at once seen in the open demonstration of discontent south of the border. Prynne and his fellow pamphleteers, when Laud dragged them before the Star Chamber as " trumpets of sedition," listened with defiance to their sentence of exposure in the pillory and imprisonment for life; and the crowd who filled Palace Yard to witness their punishment groaned at the cutting off of their ears, and " gave a great shout " when Prynne urged that the sentence on him was contrary to the law. A hundred thousand Londoners lined the road as they passed on the way to prison; and the journey of these " Martyrs," as the spectators called them, was like a triumphal progress. Startled as he was at the sudden burst of popular feeling, Laud was dauntless as ever; and Prynne's entertainers, as he passed through the country, were summoned before the Star Chamber, while the censorship struck fiercer blows at the Puritan press. But the real danger lay not in the libels of silly zealots but in the attitude of Scotland, and in the effect which was being produced in England at large by the trial of Hampden. For twelve days the cause of ship-money was solemnly argued before the full bench of Judges. It was proved that the tax in past times had been levied only in cases of sudden emergency, and confined to the coast and port towns alone, and that even the show of legality had been taken from it by formal Statute and by the Petition of Right. The case was adjourned, but the discussion told not merely on England but on the temper of the Scots. Charles had replied to their petitions by a simple order to all strangers to leave the capital. But the Council was unable to enforce his order; and the nobles and gentry before dispersing to their homes named a body of delegates, under the odd title of " the Tables," who carried on through the winter a series of negotiations with the Crown. The negotiations were interrupted in the following spring by a renewed order for their dispersion, and for the acceptance of a Prayer Book; while the

Nov.
1637

1638

judges in England delivered at last their long-delayed decision on Hampden's case. All save two laid down the broad principle that no Statute prohibiting arbitrary taxation could be pleaded against the King's will. "I never read or heard," said Judge Berkley, "that lex was rex, but it is common and most true that rex is lex." Finch, the Chief-Justice, summed up the opinions of his fellow judges. "Acts of Parliament to take away the King's Royal power in the defence of his kingdom are void," he said: "they are void Acts of Parliament to bind the King not to command the subjects, their persons, and goods, and I say their money too, for no Acts of Parliament made any difference."

"I wish Mr. Hampden and others to his likeness," the Lord Lieutenant wrote bitterly from Ireland, "were well whipt into their right senses." Amidst the exultation of the Court over the decision of the judges, Wentworth saw clearly that Hampden's work had been done. His resistance had roused England to a sense of the danger to her freedom, and forced into light the real character of the Royal claims. How stern and bitter the temper even of the noblest Puritans had become at last we see in the poem which Milton produced at this time, his elegy of "Lycidas." Its grave and tender lament is broken by a sudden flash of indignation at the dangers around the Church, at the "blind mouths that scarce themselves know how to hold a sheep-hook," and to whom "the hungry sheep look up, and are not fed," while "the grim wolf" of Rome "with privy paw daily devours apace, and nothing said!" The stern resolve of the people to demand justice on their tyrants spoke in his threat of the axe. Strafford and Laud, and Charles himself, had yet to reckon with "that two-handed engine at the door" which stood "ready to smite once, and smite no more." But stern as was the general resolve, there was no need for immediate action, for the difficulties which were gathering in the north were certain to bring a strain on the Government which would force it to seek support from the people. The King's demand for immediate submission, which reached Edinburgh with the significant comment of the Hampden judgment, at once gathered the whole body of remonstrants together round "the Tables" at Stirling; and a protestation, read at Edinburgh, was followed, on Archibald Johnston of Warriston's suggestion, by the renewal of the Covenant with God which had been drawn up and sworn to in a previous hour of peril, when Mary was still plotting against Protestantism, and Spain was preparing its Armada. "We promise and swear," ran the solemn engagement at its close, "by the great name of the Lord our God, to continue in the profession and obedience of the said Religion, and that we shall defend the same, and resist all their contrary errors and corruptions, according to our vocation and the utmost of that power which God has put into our hands all the days of our life." The Covenant was signed in the churchyard of the Grey Friars at Edinburgh, in a tumult of enthusiasm, "with such content and joy as those who, having long before been outlaws and rebels, are admitted again into covenant with God." Gentlemen and nobles rode with the documents in their pockets over the country, gathering subscriptions to it, while the ministers pressed for a general consent to it from the pulpit. But pressure was needless. " Such was the zeal of subscribers that for a while many subscribed with tears on their cheeks; " some were indeed reputed to have " drawn their own blood and used it in place of ink to underwrite their names." The force given to Scottish freedom by this revival of religious fervour was seen in the new tone adopted by the Covenanters. The Marquis of Hamilton, who had come as Royal Commissioner to put an end to the quarrel, was at once met by demands for an abolition of the Court of High Commission, and withdrawal of the Books of Canons and Common Prayer, a free Parliament, and a free General Assembly. It was in vain that he threatened war; even the Council pressed Charles to give fuller satisfaction to the people. " I will rather die," the King wrote to Hamilton, " than yield to these impertinent and damnable demands; " but it was needful to gain time. " The discontents at home," wrote Lord Northumberland to Strafford, " do rather increase than lessen: " and Charles was without money or men. It was in vain that he begged for a loan from Spain on promise of declaring war against Holland, or that he tried to procure ten thousand troops from Flanders who might be useful in England after their victory over Scottish freedom. The loan and troops were both refused, and the contributions offered by the English Catholics did little to recruit the Exchequer. Charles had directed the Marquis to delay any decisive breach till the Royal fleet appeared in the Forth; but it was hard to equip a fleet at all. Scotland indeed was sooner ready for war than the King. The volunteers who had been serving in the Thirty Years' War streamed home at the call of their brethren. General Leslie, a veteran trained under Gustavus, came from Sweden to take the command of the new forces. A voluntary war tax was levied in every shire. The danger at last forced the King to yield to the Scotch demands; but he had no sooner yielded than the concession was withdrawn, and the Assembly hardly met before it was called upon to disperse. The order however was disregarded till it had abolished the innovations in worship and discipline, deposed the bishops, and formally set the Presbyterian Church courts up again. The news that Charles was gathering an army at York, and reckoning for support on the clans of the north, was answered by the

seizure of Edinburgh, Dumbarton, and Stirling; while ten thousand well-equipped troops under Leslie and the Earl of Montrose seized Aberdeen, and brought the Catholic Earl of Huntly a prisoner to the south. Instead of overawing the country, the appearance of the Royal fleet in the Forth was the signal for Leslie's march on the Border. Charles had hardly pushed across the Tweed, when the " old little crooked soldier," encamping on the hill of Dunse Law, fairly offered him battle.

Charles however was not strong enough to fight, and the two armies returned home on his consent to the gathering of a free Assembly and Parliament. But the pacification at Berwick was a mere suspension of arms; the King's summons of Wentworth, now created Earl of Strafford, from Ireland was a proof that violent measures were in preparation, and the Scots met the challenge by demands for the convocation of triennial Parliaments, for freedom of elections and of debate. Strafford counselled that they should be whipped back into their senses; and the discovery of a correspondence which was being carried on between some of the Covenanter leaders and the French Court raised hopes in the King that an appeal to the country for aid against " Scotch treason " would still find an answer in English loyalty. While Strafford hurried to Ireland to levy forces, Charles summoned what from its brief duration is known as the Short Parliament. The Houses met in a mood which gave hopes of an accommodation with the Crown, but all hope of bringing them into an attack on Scotland proved fruitless. The intercepted letters were quietly set aside, and the Commons declared as of old that redress of grievances must precede the grant of supplies. Even an offer to relinquish ship-money failed to draw Parliament from its resolve, and after three weeks' sitting it was roughly dissolved. " Things must go worse before they go better " was the cool comment of St. John, one of the patriot leaders. But the country was strangely moved. " So great a defection in the kingdom," wrote Lord Northumberland, " hath not been known in the memory of man." Strafford alone stood undaunted. He had returned from Ireland, where he had easily obtained money and men from his servile Parliament, to pour fresh vigour into the Royal counsels, and to urge that, by the refusal of the Parliament to supply the King's wants, Charles was freed from all rule of government, and entitled to supply himself at his will. The Earl was bent upon war, and took command of the Royal army, which again advanced to the north. But the Scots were already across the Border; forcing the passage of the Tyne in the face of an English detachment, they occupied Newcastle, and despatched from that town their proposals of peace. They prayed the King to consider their grievances, and, " with the advice and consent of the Estates of England convened in Parliament, to settle a firm and desirable peace." The prayer was backed by preparations for a march upon York, where Charles had already abandoned himself to despair. Behind him in fact England was all but in revolt. The London apprentices mobbed Laud at Lambeth, and broke up the sittings of the High Commission at St. Paul's. The war was denounced everywhere as " the Bishops' War," and the new levies murdered officers whom they suspected of Papistry, broke down altar-rails in every church they passed, and deserted to their homes. Even in the camp itself neither the threats nor prayers of Strafford could recall the troops to their duty, and he was forced to own that two months were required before they could

1629
to
1640
—
The
Bishops'
War

1640

be fit for the field. The success of the Scots emboldened two peers, Lord Wharton and Lord Howard, to present a petition for peace to the King himself; and though Strafford arrested and proposed to shoot them, the Council shrank from desperate courses. The threat of a Scotch advance forced Charles at last to give way, and after endeavouring to evade the necessity of convoking a Parliament by summoning a " Great Council of the Peers " at York, the general repudiation of his project drove him to summon the Houses once more to Westminster.

Section VI.—The Long Parliament, 1640—1644

[*Authorities.*—Clarendon, " History of the Rebellion " (edited Macray), is the most valuable authority for the period, despite the fact that it must be used with caution owing to the bias of the author; for its general character see the articles by Firth in the " English Historical Review," 1904, and the comments of Ranke in the appendix to his " History of England." Other sources, in addition to those already mentioned under previous sections, are May, " History of the Long Parliament "; the notes of proceedings by Verney (Camden Society), and the " Old Parliamentary History." Further details may be drawn from the Clarendon and Ormond Papers. Among modern works, Gardiner and Ranke are the most important; for Pym, see the " Dictionary of National Biography."]

Pym   If Strafford embodied the spirit of tyranny, John Pym, the leader of the Commons from the first meeting of the new Houses at Westminster, stands out for all after time as the embodiment of law. A Somersetshire gentleman of good birth and competent fortune, he entered on public life in the Parliament of 1614, and was imprisoned for his patriotism at its close. He had been a leading member in that of 1620, and one of the " twelve ambassadors " for whom James ordered chairs to be set at Whitehall. Of the band of patriots with whom he had stood side by side in the constitutional struggle against the earlier despotism of Charles he was the sole survivor. Coke had died of old age; Cotton's heart was broken by oppression; Eliot had perished in the Tower; Wentworth had apostatized. Pym alone remained, resolute, patient as of old; and as the sense of his greatness grew silently during the eleven years of deepening tyranny, the hope and faith of better things clung almost passionately to the man who never doubted of the final triumph of freedom and the law. At their close, Clarendon tells us, in words all the more notable for their bitter tone of hate, " he was the most popular man, and the most able to do hurt, that have lived at any time." He had shown he knew how to wait, and when waiting was over he showed he knew how to act. On the eve of the Long Parliament he rode through England to quicken the electors to a sense of the crisis which had come at last; and on the assembling of the Commons he took his place, not merely as member for Tavistock, but as their acknowledged head. Few of the country gentlemen, indeed, who formed the bulk of the members, had sat in any previous House; and of the few, none represented in so eminent a way the Parliamentary tradition on which the coming struggle was to turn. Pym's eloquence, inferior in boldness and originality to that of Eliot or Wentworth, was better suited by its massive and logical force to convince and guide a great party; and it was backed by a calmness of temper, a dexterity and order in the management of public business, and a practical power of shaping the course of debate, which gave a form and method to Parliamentary proceedings such as they had never had before. Valuable, however, as these qualities were, it was a yet higher quality which raised Pym into the greatest, as he was the first, of Parliamentary leaders. Of the five hundred members who sate round him at St. Stephen's, he was the one man who had clearly foreseen, and as clearly resolved how to meet, the difficulties which lay before them. It was certain that Parliament would be drawn into a struggle with the Crown. It was probable that in such a struggle the House of Commons would be hampered, as it had been hampered before, by the House of Lords. The legal antiquarians of the older constitutional school stood helpless before such a conflict of co-ordinate powers, a conflict for which no provision had been made by the law, and on which precedents threw only a doubtful and conflicting light. But with a knowledge of precedent as great as their own, Pym rose high above them in his grasp of constitutional principles. He was the first English statesman who discovered, and applied to the political circumstances around him, what may be called the doctrine of constitutional proportion. He saw that as an element of constitutional life Parliament was of higher value than the Crown; he saw, too, that in Parliament itself the one essential part was the House of Commons. On these two facts he based his whole policy in the contest which followed. When Charles refused to act with the Parliament, Pym treated the refusal as a temporary abdication on the part of the sovereign, which vested the executive power in the two Houses, until new arrangements were made. When the Lords obstructed public business, he warned them that obstruction would only force the Commons " to save the kingdom alone." Revolutionary as these principles seemed at the time, they have both been recognized as bases of our constitution since the days of Pym. The first principle was established by the Convention and Parliament which followed on the departure of James the Second; the second by the acknowledgement on all sides since the Reform Bill of 1832 that the government of the country is really in the hands of the House of Commons, and can only be carried on by ministers who represent the majority of that House. Pym's temper, indeed, was the very opposite of the temper of a revolutionist. Few natures have ever been wider in their range of sympathy or action. Serious as his purpose was, his manners were genial, and even courtly: he turned easily from an invective against Strafford to a chat with Lady Carlisle; and the grace and gaiety of his social tone, even when the care and weight of public affairs were bringing him to his grave, gave rise to a hundred silly scandals among the prurient Royalists. It was this striking combination of genial versatility with a massive force in his nature which marked him out from the first moment of power as a born ruler of men. He proved himself at once the subtlest of diplomatists and the grandest of demagogues. He was equally at home in tracking the subtle intricacies of the Army Plot, or in kindling popular passion with words of fire. Though past middle life when his work really began, for he was born in 1584, four years before the coming of the Armada, he displayed from the first meeting of the Long Parliament the qualities of a great administrator, an immense faculty for labour, a genius for organization, patience, tact, a power of inspiring confidence in all whom he touched, calmness and moderation under good fortune or ill, an immovable courage, an iron will. No English ruler has ever shown greater nobleness of natural temper or a wider capacity for government than the Somersetshire squire whom his enemies, made clear-sighted by their hate, greeted truly enough as " King Pym."

His ride over England on the eve of the elections had been hardly needed, for the summons of a Parliament at once woke the kingdom to a fresh life. The Puritan emigration to New England was suddenly and utterly suspended; "the change," said Winthrop, " made all men to stay in England in expectation of a new world." The public discontent spoke from every Puritan pulpit, and expressed itself in a sudden burst of pamphlets, the first-fruits of the thirty thousand which were issued before the Restoration, and which turned England at large into a school of political discussion. The resolute looks of the members as they gathered at Westminster contrasted with the hesitating words of the King, and each brought from borough or county a petition of grievances. Fresh petitions were brought every day by bands of citizens or farmers. Forty committees were appointed to examine and report on them, and their reports formed the grounds on which the Commons acted. One by one the illegal acts of the Tyranny were annulled. Prynne and his fellow " martyrs," recalled from their prisons, entered London in triumph amidst the shouts of a great multitude who strewed laurel in their path. The civil and criminal jurisdiction of the Privy Council, the Star Chamber, the court of High Commission, the irregular jurisdictions of the Council of the North, of the Duchy of Lancaster, the County of Chester, and a crowd of lesser tribunals were summarily abolished. Ship-money was declared illegal, and the judgment in Hampden's case annulled. A statute declaring "the ancient right of the subjects of this kingdom that no subsidy, custom, import, or any charge whatsoever, ought or may be laid or imposed upon any merchandize exported or imported by subjects, denizens, or aliens, without common consent in Parliament," put an end for ever to all preensions to a right of arbitrary taxation on the part of the Crown. Triennial Bill enforced the assembly of the Houses every three ears and bound the returning officers to proceed to election if the oyal writ failed to summon them. Charles protested, but gave ay. He was forced to look helplessly on at the wreck of his yranny, for the Scotch army was still encamped in the north; nd the Parliament, which saw in the presence of the Scots a ecurity against its own dissolution, was in no hurry to vote the oney necessary for their withdrawal. "We cannot do without hem," Strode honestly confessed, "the Philistines are still too trong for us." Meanwhile the Commons were dealing roughly with he agents of the Royal system. In every county a list of the Royal fficers, under the name of "delinquents," was ordered to be repared and laid before the Houses. Windebank, the Secretary f State, with the Chancellor, Finch, fled in terror over sea. Laud imself was flung into prison. The shadow perhaps of what was o come falls across the pages of his Diary, and softens the hard emper of the man into a strange tenderness. "I stayed at Lambeth ill the evening," writes the Archbishop, "to avoid the gaze of he people. I went to evening prayer in my chapel. The Psalms f the day, and chapter fifty of Isaiah, gave me great comfort. od make me worthy of it and fit to receive it. As I went to my arge hundreds of my poor neighbours stood there, and prayed for y safety and return to my house. For which I bless God and hem."

But even Laud, hateful as he was to all but the poor neighbours hose prayers his alms had won, was not the centre of so great and niversal a hatred as the Earl of Strafford. Strafford's guilt was ore than the guilt of a servile instrument of tyranny, it was the uilt of "that grand apostate to the Commonwealth who," in the errible words which closed Lord Digby's invective, "must not xpect to be pardoned in this world till he be despatched to the ther." He was conscious of his danger, but Charles forced him o attend the Court; and with characteristic boldness he resolved o anticipate attack by charging the Parliamentary leaders with a reasonable correspondence with the Scots. He was just laying is scheme before Charles when the news reached him that Pym as at the bar of the Lords with his impeachment for High Treason. "With speed," writes an eye-witness, "he comes to the House: e calls rudely at the door," and, "with a proud glooming look, akes towards his place at the board-head. But at once many bid im void the House, so he is forced in confusion to go to the door ll he was called." He was only recalled to hear his committal to he Tower. He was still resolute to retort the charge of treason on is foes, and "offered to speak, but was commanded to be gone ithout a word." The keeper of the Black rod demanded his sword s he took him in charge. "This done, he makes through a number f people towards his coach, no man capping to him, before whom hat morning the greatest of all England would have stood

uncovered." The effect of the blow was seen in the cessation on th
King's part of his old tone of command, and in the attempt h
made to construct a ministry from among the patriots, with Lor
Bedford at their head, on condition that Strafford's life should b
spared. But the price was too high to pay; the negotiations wer
interrupted by Bedford's death, and by the discovery that Charl
had been listening all the while to a knot of adventurers wh
proposed to bring about his end by stirring the army to an attac
on the Parliament. The discovery of the Army Plot sealed Stra
ford's fate. The trial of his Impeachment began in Westminste
Hall, and the whole of the House of Commons appeared to suppo
it. The passion which the cause excited was seen in the loud cri
of sympathy or hatred which burst from the crowded benches o
either side. For fifteen days Strafford struggled with a remarkab
courage and ingenuity against the list of charges, and he ha
melted his audience to tears by the pathos of his defence when th
trial was suddenly interrupted. Though tyranny and misgover
ment had been conclusively proved against him, the technic
proof of treason was weak. "The law of England," to use Hallam
words, "is silent as to conspiracies against itself," and treason b
the Statute of Edward the Third was restricted to a levying of wa
against the King or a compassing of his death. The Commor
endeavoured to strengthen their case by bringing forward the not
of a meeting of the Council in which Strafford had urged the use o
his Irish troops "to reduce this kingdom to obedience;" but th
words were still technically doubtful, and the Lords would onl
admit the evidence on condition of wholly reopening the cas
Pym and Hampden remained convinced of the sufficiency of th
impeachment; but the House broke loose from their control, an
guided by St. John and Lord Falkland, resolved to abandon thes
judicial proceedings, and fall back on the resource of a Bill o
Attainder. Their course has been bitterly censured by some whos
opinion in such a matter is entitled to respect. But the crime o
Strafford was none the less a crime that it did not fall within th
scope of the Statute of Treasons. It is impossible indeed to provid
for some of the greatest dangers which can happen to nation
freedom by any formal statute. Even now a minister might ava
himself of the temper of a Parliament elected in some moment o
popular panic, and, though the nation returned to its senses, migl
simply by refusing to appeal to the country govern in defianc
of its will. Such a course would be technically legal, but such
minister would be none the less a criminal. Strafford's cours
whether it fell within the Statute of Treasons or no, was fro
beginning to end an attack on the freedom of the whole natio
In the last resort a nation retains the right of self-defence, and th
Bill of Attainder is the assertion of such a right for the punishme
of a public enemy who falls within the scope of no written law
The chance of the offender's escape roused the Londoners to frenzy
and crowds surrounded the Houses, with cries of "Justice," whi

ᴛʜᴇ Lords passed the Bill. The Earl's one hope was in the King, ʙᴜt three days later the royal sanction was given, and he passed ᴛᴏ his doom. Strafford died as he had lived. His friends warned ʜɪm of the vast multitude gathered before the Tower to witness his ᴅᴏʟʟ. "I know how to look death in the face, and the people too," ʜᴇ answered proudly. "I thank God I am no more afraid of death, ʙᴜt as cheerfully put off my doublet at this time as ever I did ᴡʜᴇn I went to bed." As the axe fell, the silence of the great ᴍᴜltitude was broken by a universal shout of joy. The streets ʙlazed with bonfires. The bells clashed out from every steeple. "Many," says an observer, "that came to town to see the execuᴛɪon rode in triumph back, waving their hats, and with all expresꜱɪons of joy through every town they went, crying, 'His head is ᴏff! His head is off!'"

Great as were the changes which had been wrought in the first ꜱɪx months of the Long Parliament, they had been based strictly ᴏn precedent, and had, in fact, been simply a restoration of the ᴏlder English constitution as it existed at the close of the Wars of ᴛʜe Roses. But every day made it harder to remain quietly in this ᴘᴏsition. On the one hand, the air, since the army conspiracy, was ꜰᴜll of rumours and panic; the creak of a few boards revived the ᴍᴇmory of the Gunpowder Plot, and the members rushed out of ᴛʜe House of Commons in the full belief that it was undermined. ᴏn the other hand, Charles regarded his consent to the new ᴍᴇasures as having been extorted by force, and to be retracted ᴀt the first opportunity. Both Houses, in their terror, swore to ᴅefend the Protestant religion and the public liberties, an oath ᴡʜich was subsequently exacted from every one engaged in civil ᴇmployment, and voluntarily taken by the great mass of the ᴘᴇople. The same terror of a counter-revolution induced Hyde ᴀnd the "moderate men" in the Commons to bring in a bill ᴘroviding that the present Parliament should not be dissolved but ʙy its own consent. Charles signed the bill without protest, but ʜe was already seeking aid from France, and preparing for the ᴄᴏunter-revolution it was meant to meet. Hitherto, the Scotch ᴀrmy had held him down, but its payment and withdrawal could ᴏ longer be delayed, and it was no sooner on its way homeward ᴛʜan the King resolved to prevent its return. In spite of prayers ꜰrom the Parliament he left London for Edinburgh, yielded to ᴇvery demand of the Assembly and the Scotch Estates, attended ᴛʜe Presbyterian worship, lavished titles and favours on the Earl ᴏf Argyle and the patriot leaders, and gained for a few months a ᴘopularity which spread dismay in the English Parliament. Their ᴅread of his designs was increased when he was found to have ʙᴇen intriguing all the while with the Earl of Montrose—who had ꜱᴇceded from the patriot party before his coming, and been ꜱewarded for his secession with imprisonment in the castle of ᴇdinburgh—and when Hamilton and Argyle withdrew suddenly ꜰrom the capital, and charged the King with a treacherous plot

to seize and carry them out of the realm. The popular fright wa
fanned to frenzy by news which came suddenly from Ireland
where the fall of Strafford had put an end to all semblance of rule
The disbanded soldiers of the army he had raised spread over th
country, and stirred the smouldering disaffection into a flame.
conspiracy, organized with wonderful power and secrecy, burs
forth in Ulster, where the confiscation of the Settlement had neve
been forgiven, and spread like wildfire over the centre and west o
the island. Dublin was saved by a mere chance; but in the ope
country the work of murder went on unchecked. Fifty thousan
English people perished in a few days, and rumour doubled an
trebled the number. Tales of horror and outrage, such as maddene
our own England when they reached us from Cawnpore, came da
after day over the Irish Channel. Sworn depositions told ho
husbands were cut to pieces in presence of their wives, thei

children's brains dashed out before their faces, their daughter
brutally violated and driven out naked to perish frozen in th
woods. " Some," says May, " were burned on set purpose, other
drowned for sport or pastime, and if they swam kept from landin
with poles, or shot, or murdered in the water; many were burie
quick, and some set into the earth breast-high and there left t
famish." The new feature of the revolt, beside the massacre wit
which it opened, was its religious character. It was no longer
struggle, as of old, of Celt against Saxon, but of Catholic agains
Protestant. The Papists within the Pale joined hands in it wit
the wild kernes outside the Pale. The rebels called themselve
" Confederate Catholics," resolved to defend " the public and fre
exercise of the true and Catholic Roman religion." The pani
waxed greater when it was found that they claimed to be acting b
the King's commission, and in aid of his authority. They professe
to stand by Charles and his heirs against all that should " directl
and indirectly endeavour to suppress their Royal prerogatives.
They showed a Commission, purporting to have been issued b
Royal command at Edinburgh, and styled themselves " the King'
army." The Commission was a forgery, but belief in it was quickene
by the want of all sympathy with the national honour which Charle
displayed. To him the revolt seemed a useful check on his opponent
" I hope," he wrote coolly, when the news reached him, " this i
news of Ireland may hinder some of these follies in England.
Above all, it would necessitate the raising of an army, and with a
army at his command he would again be the master of the Parlia
ment. The Parliament, on the other hand, saw in the Irish revol
the disclosure of a vast scheme for a counter-revolution, of whic
the withdrawal of the Scotch army, the reconciliation of Scotland
the intrigues at Edinburgh, the exultation of the royalists at th
King's return, and the appearance of a royalist party in the Hous
itself, were all parts. At the head of the new party stood Lor
Falkland, a man learned and accomplished, the centre of a circl
which embraced the most liberal thinkers of his day, a kee

asoner and able speaker, whose convictions still went with the
arliament, while his wavering and impulsive temper, his love of
ie Church, which was now being threatened, his passionate long-
gs for peace, his sympathy for the fallen, led him to struggle for
King whom he distrusted, and to die in a cause that was not his
wn. Behind him clustered intriguers like Hyde, chivalrous soldiers
ke Sir Edmund Verney ("I have eaten the King's bread and
rved him now thirty years, and I will not do so base a thing as
distrust him"), men frightened at the rapid march of change,
by the dangers which threatened Episcopacy. With a broken
arliament, and perils gathering without, Pym resolved to appeal
r aid to the nation itself. The Solemn Remonstrance which he
id before the House was a detailed narrative of the work which
ie Parliament had done, the difficulties it had surmounted, and
ie new dangers which lay in its path. The Parliament had been
narged with a design to abolish Episcopacy, it declared its purpose
be simply that of reducing the power of Bishops. Politically it
pudiated the taunt of revolutionary aims. It demanded only
ie observance of the existing laws against Papistry, securities
r the due administration of justice, and the employment of
inisters who possessed the confidence of Parliament. The new

ing's party fought fiercely, debate followed debate, the sittings
ere prolonged till, for the first time in the history of the House,
ghts had to be brought in; and it was only at midnight, and by
majority of eleven, that the Remonstrance was finally adopted,
ter a scene of unexampled violence. On an attempt of the
inority to offer a formal protest the slumbering passion burst
ito a flame. "Some waved their hats over their heads, and others
ok their swords in their scabbards out of their belts, and held
iem by the pommels in their hands, setting the lower part on the
round." Only Hampden's coolness and tact averted a conflict.
he Remonstrance was felt on both sides to be a crisis in the
ruggle. "Had it been rejected," said Cromwell, as he left the
ouse, "I would have sold to-morrow all I possess, and left
ngland for ever." Listened to sullenly by the King, it kindled
fresh the spirit of the country: London swore to live and die with
ie Parliament; associations were formed in every county for the
efence of the Houses; and when the guard which Lord Essex
ad given them was withdrawn by the King, the populace crowded
own to Westminster to take its place.

The question which had above all broken the unity of the Parlia-
ient had been the question of the Church. All were agreed on the
ecessity of its reform, for the Laudian party of High Churchmen
ere rendered powerless by the course of events; and one of the
rst acts of the Parliament had been to appoint a Committee of
eligion for this purpose. Within, as without the House, the general
pinion was in favour of a reduction of the power and wealth of the
hurch, without any radical change in its constitution. Even
mong the bishops themselves, the more prominent saw the need

for consenting to the abolition of Chapters and Bishops' Cour
as well as to the creation of a council of ministers in each dioce
which had been suggested by Archbishop Usher as a check
episcopal autocracy. A scheme to this effect was drawn up
Bishop Williams of Lincoln; but it was far from meeting the wish
of the general body of the Commons. Pym and Lord Falkla
demanded, in addition to these changes, a severance of the cler
from all secular or state offices, and an expulsion of the bisho
from the House of Lords. The last demand was backed by
petition from seven hundred ministers of the Church; but t
strife between the two sections of episcopal reformers gave streng
to the growing party who demanded the abolition of Episcopa
altogether. The doctrines of Cartwright had risen into populari
under the persecution of Laud, and Presbyterianism was now
formidable force among the middle classes. Its chief strength l
in the eastern counties and in London, where a few ministers su
as Calamy and Marshall had formed a committee for its diffusio
while in Parliament it was represented by Lord Brooke, Lo
Mandeville, and Lord Saye and Sele. In the Commons Sir Har
Vane represented a more extreme party of reformers, the Ind
pendents of the future, whose sentiments were little less host
to Presbyterianism than to Episcopacy, but who acted with t
Presbyterians for the present, and formed a part of what becar
known as the "Root and Branch party," from its demand for t
extirpation of prelacy. The attitude of Scotland in the gre
struggle with tyranny, and the political advantage of a religio
union between the two kingdoms, as well as the desire to knit t
English Church more closely to the general body of Protestantis
gave fresh force to the Presbyterian scheme. Milton, who after t
composition of his "Lycidas," had spent a year in foreign trav
but had been called home from Italy by the opening of the Parli
ment, threw himself hotly into the theological strife. He held
"an unjust thing that the English should differ from all Church
as many as be reformed." In spite of this pressure however, ar
of a Petition from London with fifteen thousand signatures to t
same purport, the Committee of Religion reported in favour of t
moderate reforms suggested by Falkland and Pym; and the fir
of these was embodied by the former in a bill for the expulsion
bishops from the House of Peers, which passed the Commo
almost unanimously. Rejected by the Lords on the eve of t
King's journey to Scotland, it was again introduced on his retur
but, in spite of violent remonstrances from the Commons, the b
still hung fire among the Peers. The delay roused the excit
crowd of Londoners who gathered round Whitehall; the bishop
carriages were stopped; and the prelates themselves rabbled o
their way to the House. The angry pride of Williams induced te
of his fellow bishops to declare themselves prevented from atten
ance in Parliament, and to protest against all acts done in the
absence as null and void. The Protest was met at once on t

rt of the Peers by the committal of the prelates who had signed
to the Tower. But the contest gave a powerful aid to the projects
the King. The courtiers declared openly that the rabbling of
e bishops proved that there was "no free Parliament," and
rove to bring about fresh outrages by gathering troops of officers
d soldiers of fortune, who were seeking for employment in the
ish war, and pitting them against the crowds at Whitehall. The
rawls of the two parties, who gave each other the nicknames of
Round-heads" and "Cavaliers," created fresh alarm in the
arliament; but Charles persisted in refusing it a guard. "On
e honour of a King," he engaged to defend them from violence as
mpletely as his own children, but the answer had hardly been
ven when his Attorney appeared at the bar of the Lords, and
cused Hampden, Pym, Hollis, Strode, and Haselrig of high
eason in their correspondence with the Scots. A herald-at-arms
peared at the bar of the Commons, and demanded the surrender
the five members. All constitutional law was set aside by a
arge which proceeded personally from the King, which deprived
e accused of their legal right to a trial by their peers, and
mmoned them before a tribunal which had no pretence to a
risdiction over them. The Commons simply promised to take
e demand into consideration, and again requested a guard. "I
ll reply to-morrow," said the King. On the morrow he summoned
ree hundred gentlemen to follow him, and, embracing the Queen,
omised her that in an hour he would return master of his king-
m. A mob of Cavaliers joined him as he left the palace, and
mained in Westminster Hall as Charles, accompanied by his
phew, the Elector-Palatine, entered the House of Commons.
Mr. Speaker," he said, "I must for a time borrow your chair!"
e paused with a sudden confusion as his eye fell on the vacant
ot where Pym commonly sate: for at the news of his approach
e House had ordered the five members to withdraw. "Gentle-
en," he began in slow broken sentences, "I am sorry for this
casion of coming unto you. Yesterday I sent a Sergeant-at-arms
on a very important occasion, to apprehend some that by my
mmand were accused of high treason, whereunto I did expect
edience, and not a message." Treason, he went on, had no
ivilege, "and therefore I am come to know if any of these
rsons that were accused are here." There was a dead silence,
ly broken by his reiterated "I must have them wheresoever I
d them." He again paused, but the stillness was unbroken.
en he called out, "Is Mr. Pym here?" There was no answer;
d Charles, turning to the Speaker, asked him whether the five
embers were there. Lenthall fell on his knees, and replied that
had neither eyes nor tongue to see or say anything save what
e House commanded him. "Well, well," Charles angrily retorted,
'tis no matter. I think my eyes are as good as another's!"
here was another long pause, while he looked carefully over the
nks of members. "I see," he said at last, "my birds are flown,

but I do expect you will send them to me." If they did not, ▮ added, he would seek them himself; and with a closing prote▮ that he never intended any force, " he went out of the House says an eye-witness, " in a more discontented and angry passio than he came in."

The Eve of the War

Nothing but the absence of the five members, and the cal▮ dignity of the Commons, had prevented the King's outrage fro▮ ending in bloodshed. " It was believed," says Whitelocke, wh▮ was present at the scene, " that if the King had found them ther▮ and called in his guards to have seized them, the members of t▮ House would have endeavoured the defence of them, which mig▮ have proved a very unhappy and sad business." Five hundr▮ gentlemen of the best blood in England would hardly have stoc tamely by while the bravoes of Whitehall laid hands on their leaders in the midst of the Parliament. But Charles was blin▮ to the danger of his new course. The five members had take▮ refuge in the city, and it was there that on the next day the Kir▮ himself demanded their surrender from the aldermen at Guildha▮ Cries of " Privilege " rang round him as he returned through t▮ streets: the writs issued for the arrest of the five were disregarde▮ by the Sheriffs, and a proclamation issued four days later, declarir▮ them traitors, was answered by their triumphant return to S▮ Stephen's. The Trained Bands of London and Southwark were c▮ foot, and the London watermen, sworn " to guard the Parliamen▮ the Kingdom, and the King," escorted the five members as the▮ passed along the river to Westminster. Terror drove the Cavalie▮ from Whitehall, and Charles stood absolutely alone; for the outra▮ had severed him for the moment from his new friends in t▮ Parliament, and from the ministers, Falkland and Colepeppe▮ whom he had chosen among them. But lonely as he was, Charl▮ had resolved on war. The Earl of Newcastle was despatched ▮ muster a Royal force in the north; and as the five membe▮

re-entered the House, Charles withdrew from Whitehall. Bot▮ sides prepared for the coming struggle. The Queen sailed fro▮ Dover with the crown jewels to buy munitions of war. The Cavalie▮ again gathered round the King, and the Royalist press flooded t▮ country with State papers drawn up by Hyde. On the other han▮ mounted processions of freeholders from Buckinghamshire an▮ Kent traversed London on their way to St. Stephen's, vowing ▮ live and die with the Parliament. The Tower was blockaded, an▮ the two great arsenals, Portsmouth and Hull, secured by Pym▮ forethought. The Lords were scared out of their policy of obstru▮ tion by his bold announcement of the new position taken by t▮ House of Commons. " The Commons," said their leader, " will ▮ glad to have your concurrence and help in saving the kingdon▮ but if they fail of it, it should not discourage them in doing the▮ duty. And whether the kingdom be lost or saved, they shall ▮ sorry that the story of this present Parliament should tell posterit▮ that in so great a danger and extremity the House of Commo▮

hould be enforced to save the kingdom alone." The effect of
ʼym's words was seen in the passing of the bill for excluding
ishops from the House of Lords. The great point, however, was
o secure armed support from the nation at large, and here both
ides were in a difficulty. Previous to the innovations introduced
·y the Tudors, and which had been taken away by the bill against
·ressing soldiers, the King in himself had no power of calling on
is subjects generally to bear arms, save for purposes of restoring
·rder or meeting foreign invasion. On the other hand, no one
ontended that such a power had ever been exercised by the two
Iouses without the King; and Charles steadily refused to consent
o the Militia bill, in which the command of the national force was
iven in every county to men devoted to the Parliamentary cause.
ᵒoth parties therefore broke through constitutional precedent,
he Parliament in appointing Lord Lieutenants of the Militia by
·rdinance of the two Houses, Charles in levying forces by Royal
ommissions of array. The King's great difficulty lay in procuring
·rms, and at the end of April he suddenly appeared before Hull,
he magazine of the north, and demanded admission. The new
ᵍovernor, Sir John Hotham, fell on his knees, but refused to open
he gates: and the avowal of his act by the Parliament was
ollowed by the withdrawal of the new Royalist party among its
nembers from their seats at Westminster. Falkland, Colepepper,
nd Hyde, with thirty-two peers and sixty members of the House
·f Commons, joined Charles at York; and Lyttelton, the Lord
Keeper, followed with the Great Seal. But the King's warlike
·rojects were still checked by the general opposition of the country.
ᴬ great meeting of the Yorkshire freeholders which he convened
·n Heyworth Moor ended in a petition praying him to be reconciled
o the Parliament, and in spite of gifts of plate from the Universities
nd nobles of his party arms and money were still wanting for his
ew levies. The two Houses, on the other hand, gained in unity
nd vigour by the withdrawal of the Royalists. The Militia was
apidly enrolled, Lord Warwick named to the command of the
leet, and a loan opened in the city to which the women brought
·ven their wedding rings. The tone of the two Houses had risen
vith the threat of force: and their last proposals demanded the
·owers of appointing and dismissing the Royal ministers, naming
ᵍuardians for the Royal children, and of virtually controlling
nilitary, civil, and religious affairs. "If I granted your demands,"
eplied Charles, "I should be no more than the mere phantom of
king."

The most probable estimate of the number of victims in the Irish
· massacre " is some five thousand, though many more perished later
·y indirect means; see Gardiner, " History of England," and Lecky,
· History of England." The most moderate contemporary estimate
·laced the number at 37,000. Commissions of array had been used to
aise men for foreign service under Edward I. and other kings. This was
leclared illegal by various statutes. Commissions of array to raise men

1642
to
1646

for home defence, or on the excuse of danger of invasion, had been use
by the Tudors, and their issue was regarded by them as a royal prerog
tive; for the popular idea of the right of impressment for the army, se
" Henry IV.," Part I., Act IV., Scene 2. A statute of Charles I., howeve
had declared it to be illegal to impress men except to repel invasion
unless they were bound to serve by tenure.

Section VII.—The Civil War, July 1642—August 1646

[*Authorities.*—Clarendon's " History " is the main authority. Se
also Ludlow's " Memoirs " (edited Firth); Mrs. Hutchinson's memoir
of her husband, Colonel Hutchinson (edited Firth); the Clarke Paper
(edited Firth); the " Diary of Sir Henry Slingsby " for the views of a
ordinary cavalier; and the " Memoirs of Captain Hodgson " for thou
of an ordinary Puritan. For Cromwell, see Carlyle's " Letters an
Speeches of Oliver Cromwell," and Firth, " Cromwell." Various colle
tions of contemporary pamphlets have been printed, *e.g.*, those in tl
"Harleian Miscellany" and the "Somers Tracts"; see also Maseres, "Sele
Tracts Relating to the Civil Wars." For the army, Firth, " Cromwell
Army." For Fairfax, see Sprigge, " Anglia Rediviva," an account of tl
operations of the New Model by Fairfax's chaplain; the " Fairfax Corre
spondence "; and Clements Markham, " Life of Fairfax." For parlia
mentary proceedings, in addition to the sources already mentione
Vicars, " England's Parliamentary Chronicle." Also of value are tl
various papers connected with the Verney Family; *i.e.*, " Memoirs «
the Verney Family," the " Verney Papers " (Camden Society), an
" Verney's Notes of the Long Parliament " (Camden Society). Fe
Montrose, Napier, " Memoirs of the Marquis of Montrose."]

Edgehill

The breaking off of negotiations was followed on both sides b
preparations for immediate war. Hampden, Pym, and Holli
became the guiding spirits of a Committee of Public Safety whic
was created by Parliament as its administrative organ; Englis
and Scotch officers were drawn from the Low Countries, and Lor
Essex named commander of an army of twenty thousand foot an
four thousand horse. The confidence on the Parliamentary sid
was great; " we all thought one battle would decide," Baxte
confessed after the first encounter; for the King was almo
destitute of money and arms, and in spite of his strenuous effor
to raise recruits he was embarrassed by the reluctance of his ow
adherents to begin the struggle. Resolved, however, to force on
contest, he raised the Royal Standard at Nottingham " on tl

Aug. 23

evening of a very stormy and tempestuous day," but the countr
made no answer to his appeal; while Essex, who had quitte
London amidst the shouts of a great multitude, with orders fro
the Parliament to follow the King, " and by battle or other wa
rescue him from his perfidious councillors and restore him t
Parliament," mustered his army at Northampton. Charles ha
but a handful of men, and the dash of a few regiments of hors
would have ended the war; but Essex shrank from a decisiv
stroke, and trusted to reduce Charles to submission by a show «
force. No sooner, however, had the King fallen back on Shrewsbur
than the whole face of affairs suddenly changed. Catholics an

Royalists rallied fast to his standard, and a bold march on London drew Essex from his inactivity at Worcester to protect the capital. The two armies fell in with one another on the field of Edgehill, near Banbury. The encounter was a surprise, and the battle which followed was little more than a confused combat of horse. At its outset the desertion of Sir Faithful Fortescue, with a whole regiment, threw the Parliamentary forces into disorder, while the Royalist horse on either wing drove their opponents from the field; but the reserve of Lord Essex broke the Royalist foot, which formed the centre of the King's line, and though his nephew, Prince Rupert, brought back his squadrons in time to save Charles from capture or flight, the night fell on a drawn battle. The moral advantage, however, rested with the King. Essex had learned that his troopers were no match for the Cavaliers, and his withdrawal to Warwick left open the road to the capital. Rupert pressed for an instant march on London, but the proposal found stubborn opponents among the moderate Royalists, who dreaded the complete triumph of Charles as much as his defeat. The King therefore paused for the time at Oxford, where he was received with uproarious welcome; and when the cowardice of its garrison delivered Reading to Rupert's horse, and his daring capture of Brentford drew the Royal army in his support almost to the walls of the capital, the panic of the Londoners was already over, and the junction of their trainbands with the army of Essex forced Charles to fall back again on his old quarters. But though the Parliament rallied quickly from the blow of Edgehill, the war, as its area widened through the winter, went steadily for the King. The fortification of Oxford gave him a firm hold on the midland counties; while the balance of the two parties in the north was overthrown by the march of the Earl of Newcastle, with the force he had raised in Northumberland, upon York. Lord Fairfax, the Parliamentary leader in that county, was thrown back on the manufacturing towns of the West Riding, where Puritanism found its stronghold; and the arrival of the Queen with arms from Holland encouraged the Royal army to push its scouts across the Trent, and threaten the eastern counties, which held firmly for the Parliament. The stress of the war was shown by the vigorous exertions of the two Houses. The negotiations which had gone on into the spring were broken off by the old demand that the King should return to his Parliament; London was fortified; and a tax of two millions a year was laid on the districts which adhered to the Parliamentary cause. Essex, whose army had been freshly equipped, was ordered to advance upon Oxford; but though the King held himself ready to fall back on the west, the Earl shrank from again risking his raw army in an encounter. He confined himself to the recapture of Reading, and to a month of idle encampment round Brill, while disease thinned his ranks and the Royalists beat up his quarters.

While Essex lingered and manœuvred, Charles boldly detached part of his small force at Oxford to strengthen a Royalist rising

1642
to
1646
—
The
Cornish
rising

May,
1643
in the west. Nowhere was the Royal cause to take so brave o
noble a form as among the Cornishmen. Cornwall stood apart fron
the general life of England: cut off from it not only by difference
of blood and speech, but by the feudal tendencies of its people, wh
clung with a Celtic loyalty to their local chieftains, and suffere
their fidelity to the Crown to determine their own. They had a
yet done little more than keep the war out of their own county
but the march of a small Parliamentary force under Lord Stamfor
upon Launceston forced them into action. A little band of Cornish
men gathered round the chivalrous Sir Bevil Greenvil, " so destitut
of provisions that the best officers had but a biscuit a day," an
with only a handful of powder for the whole force; but starvin
and outnumbered as they were, they scaled the steep rise o
Stratton Hill, sword in hand, and drove Stamford back on Exeter
with a loss of two thousand men, his ordnance and baggage train
Sir Ralph Hopton, the best of the Royalist generals, took th
command of their army as it advanced into Somerset, and dre
the stress of the war into the west. Essex despatched a picke
force under Sir William Waller to check their advance; bu
Somerset was already lost ere he reached Bath, and the Cornish
men stormed his strong position on Lansdowne Hill in the teet
of his guns. But the stubborn fight robbed the victors of thei
leaders; Hopton was wounded, Greenvil slain, and with them fel
the two heroes of the little army, Sir Nicholas Slanning and Si
John Trevanion, " both young, neither of them above eight an
twenty, of entire friendship to one another, and to Sir Bev
Greenvil." Waller, beaten as he was, hung on their weakened forc
as it moved for aid upon Oxford, and succeeded in cooping up th
foot in Devizes. But the horse broke through, and joining an arm
which had been sent to their relief under Wilmot, afterwards Lor
Rochester, turned back, and dashed Waller's army to pieces in
fresh victory on Roundway Down. The Cornish rising seemed t
have turned the tide of the war. Strengthened by their earlie
successes, and by the succours which his Queen brought from th
north, Charles had already prepared to advance, when Ruper
in a daring raid upon Wycombe, met a party of Parliamentar
horse, with Hampden at its head, on Chalgrove field. The skirmis
ended in the success of the Royalists, and Hampden was see
riding off the field " before the action was done, which he neve
used to do, and with his head hanging down, and resting his hand
upon the neck of his horse." He was mortally wounded, and h
death seemed an omen of the ruin of the cause he loved. Disaste
followed disaster. Essex, more and more anxious for a peace, fe
back on Uxbridge; while a cowardly surrender of Bristol to Princ
Rupert gave Charles the second city of the kingdom, and th
mastery of the west. The news fell on the Parliament " like
sentence of death." The Lords debated nothing but proposals c
peace. London itself was divided; " a great multitude of the wive
of substantial citizens " clamoured at the door of the Commons fc

eace; and a flight of six of the few peers who remained at West-
inster to the camp at Oxford proved the general despair of the
arliament's success.

From this moment, however, the firmness of the Parliamentary
aders began slowly to reverse the fortunes of the war. Waller was
eceived on his return from Roundway Hill " as if he had brought
he King prisoner with him." A new army was placed under the
ommand of Lord Manchester to check the progress of Newcastle.
n the west, indeed, things still went badly. Prince Maurice con-
nued Rupert's career of success, and the conquest of Barnstaple
nd Exeter secured Devon for the King. Gloucester alone inter-
pted the communications between his forces in Bristol and in
ne north; and Charles moved against the city, with hope of a
peedy surrender. But the gallant resistance of the town called
ssex to its relief. It was reduced to a single barrel of powder
hen the Earl's approach forced Charles to raise the siege; and
ne Puritan army fell steadily back again on London, after an
ndecisive engagement near Newbury, in which Lord Falkland
ll, " ingeminating ' Peace, peace! ' " and the London trainbands
ung Rupert's horsemen roughly off their front of pikes. In this
osture of his affairs nothing but a great victory could have saved
ne King, for the day which witnessed the triumphant return of
ssex witnessed the solemn taking of the Covenant. Pym had
solved, at last, to fling the Scotch sword into the wavering
alance; and in the darkest hour of the Parliament's cause Sir
arry Vane had been despatched to Edinburgh to arrange the
rms on which the aid of Scotland would be given. First amongst
nem stood the demand of a " unity in Religion; " an adoption, in
ther words, of the Presbyterian system by the Church of England.
vents had moved so rapidly since the earlier debates on Church
overnment in the Commons that some arrangement of this kind
ad become a necessity. The bishops to a man, and the bulk of
ne clergy whose bent was purely episcopal, had joined the Royal
use, and were being expelled from their livings as " delinquents."
ome new system of Church government was imperatively called
r by the religious necessities of the country; and, though Pym
nd the leading statesmen were still in opinion moderate Episco-
alians, the growing force of Presbyterianism, as well as the needs
f the war, forced them to seek such a system in the adoption of
ne Scotch discipline. Scotland, for its part, saw that the triumph
f the Parliament was necessary for its own security; and what-
ver difficulties stood in the way of Vane's wary and rapid negotia-
ons were removed by the policy of the King. While the
arliament looked for aid to the north, Charles had long been
eeking assistance from the Irish rebels. The Massacre had left
nem the objects of a vengeful hate such as England had hardly
nown before, but with Charles they were simply counters in his
me of king-craft. The conclusion of a truce with them left the
rmy under Lord Ormond, which had hitherto held their revolt in

check, at the King's disposal for service in England; and at th
same moment he secured a force of Irish Catholics to support b
their landing in Argyleshire a rising of the Highlands unde
Montrose, which aimed at the overthrow of the government a
Edinburgh. None of the King's schemes proved so fatal to hi
cause as these. On their discovery officer after officer in his ow
army flung down their commissions, the peers who had fled t
Oxford fled back again to London, and the Royalist reaction i
the Parliament itself came utterly to an end. Scotland, anxiou
for its own safety, hastened to sign the Covenant; and th
Commons, " with uplifted hands," swore in St. Margaret's churc
to observe it. They pledged themselves to " bring the Churches o
God in the three Kingdoms to the nearest conjunction and un
formity in religion, confession of faith, form of Church governmen
direction for worship, and catechizing; that we, and our posterit
after us, may as brethren live in faith and love, and the Lord ma
delight to live in the midst of us : " to extirpate Popery, prelacy
superstition, schism, and profaneness; to " preserve the rights an
privileges of the Parliament, and the liberties of the Kingdom;
to punish malignants and opponents of reformation in Church an
State; to " unite the two Kingdoms in a firm peace and union t
all posterity." The Covenant ended with a solemn acknowledg
ment of national sin, and a vow of reformation. " Our true, un
feigned purpose, desire, and endeavour for ourselves and all othe
under our power and charge, both in public and private, in a
duties we owe to God and man, is to amend our lives, and each on
to go before another in the example of a real reformation."

The conclusion of the Covenant had been the last work of Pym
but it was only a part of the great plan which he had formed, an
which was carried out by the " Committee of the Two Kingdoms,
entrusted after his death (Dec. 1643) with the conduct of the wa
and of foreign affairs. Three strong armies, comprising a force o
fifty thousand men, had been raised for the coming campaign
Essex, with the army of the centre, was charged with the duty o
watching the King at Oxford, and following him if he moved, a
was expected, to the north against the Scots. Waller, with th
army of the west, was ordered to check Prince Maurice, in Dorse
and Devon. The force of fourteen thousand men which had bee
raised by the zeal of the eastern counties, and in which Cromwell
name was becoming famous as a leader, was raised into a thir
army under Lord Manchester, and directed to co-operate in Yor
shire with Sir Thomas Fairfax and the Scots. Charles was at one
thrown on the defensive. The Irish troops whose aid he ha
secured by his truce with the rebels were cut to pieces soon afte
their arrival in England, those who landed in the south by Walle
and their fellows in Cheshire by Sir Thomas Fairfax. The hand
of the last commander had been freed by the march of Newcastl
to the Border, which the Scots were crossing " in a great frost an
snow; " but after his dispersion of the Irish troops, he at one

alled back his opponent to York by a victory on his return over the
rces which the Marquis had left to protect that capital. The plan
f Pym was now rapidly developed. Essex and Waller joined in
he blockade of Oxford, while Manchester and Fairfax united with
he Scots under the walls of York. Newcastle's cry for aid had
lready been answered by the despatch of Prince Rupert from
xford to gather forces on the Welsh border; and the brilliant
artizan, after breaking the sieges of Newark and Latham House,
urst over the Lancashire Hills into Yorkshire, slipped by the
arliamentary army, and made his way untouched into York.
ut the success of his feat of arms tempted him to a fresh act of
aring; he resolved on a decisive battle, and a discharge of

usketry from the two armies as they faced each other on Marston
oor brought on, as evening gathered, a disorderly engagement.
n the one flank a charge of the King's horse broke that of the
cotch; on the other, Cromwell's brigade of "Ironsides" won as
omplete a success over Rupert's troopers. "God made them as
tubble to our swords," wrote the general at the close of the day;
ut in the heat of victory he called back his men from the chase
back Manchester in his attack on the Royalist foot, and to rout
heir other wing of horse as it returned breathless from pursuing
ne Scots. Nowhere had the fighting been so fierce. A young
uritan who lay dying on the field told Cromwell as he bent over
im that one thing lay on his spirit. "I asked him what it was,"
romwell wrote afterwards. "He told me it was that God had not
uffered him to be any more the executioner of his enemies." At
ight-fall all was over; and the Royalist cause in the north had
erished at a single blow. Newcastle fled over sea: York sur-
endered, and Rupert, with hardly a man at his back, rode south-
ard to Oxford. The blow was the more terrible that it fell on
harles at a moment when his triumph in every other quarter was
eing secured by a series of brilliant and unexpected successes.
fter a month's siege the King had escaped from Oxford; had
aited till Essex marched into the west; and then, turning fiercely
n Waller at Cropredy Bridge, had driven him back broken to
ondon, two days before the battle at Marston Moor. Charles
llowed up his success by hurrying in the track of Essex, whom
e hoped to crush between his own force and that under Prince
laurice which the Earl had marched to attack. By a fatal error,
ssex plunged into Cornwall, where the country was hostile, and
here the King hemmed him in among the hills, drew his lines
ghtly round his army, and forced the whole body of the foot to
urrender at his mercy, while the horse cut their way through the
esiegers, and Essex himself fled by sea to London. The day of
e surrender was signalized by a Royalist triumph in Scotland
hich promised to undo what Marston Moor had done. The plot
hich had long since been formed for the conquest of Scotland
as revived by the landing of Irish soldiers in Argyle. Montrose,
rowing himself into the Highlands, called the clans to arms;

1642
to
1646

and flinging his new force on that of the Covenanters at Tipper
muir, gained a victory which enabled him to occupy Perth, t
sack Aberdeen, and to spread terror to Edinburgh. The news fire
Charles, as he came up from the west, to venture on a march upo
London; but though the Scots were detained by the siege of New
castle, the rest of the victors at Marston Moor lay in his path a
Newbury, and their force was strengthened by the army which ha
surrendered in Cornwall, and was again brought into the field
The furious charges of the Royalists failed to break the Parlia

Oct. 1644

mentary squadrons, and the soldiers of Essex wiped away the sham
of their defeat by flinging themselves on the cannon they had lost
and bringing them back in triumph to their lines. Cromwell seize
the moment of victory, and begged hard to be suffered to charg
with his single brigade. But Manchester, like Essex, shrank from
a crowning victory over the King. Charles was allowed to with
draw his army to Oxford, and even to reappear unchecked in th
field of his defeat.

Crom-
well

The quarrel of Cromwell with Lord Manchester at Newbury wa
destined to give a new colour and direction to the war. Pym, i
fact, had hardly been borne to his grave in Westminster Abbe
before England instinctively recognized a successor of yet greate

1599

genius in the victor of Marston Moor. Born in the closing years o
Elizabeth's reign, the child of a cadet of the great house of th
Cromwells of Hinchinbrook, and connected by their mothers wit
Hampden and St. John, Oliver had been recalled by his father'
death from a short stay at Cambridge to the little family estate a
Huntingdon, which he quitted for a farm at St. Ives. We hav
already seen his mood during the years of Tyranny, as he dwel
in " prolonging " and " blackness "amidst fancies of coming death
the melancholy which formed the ground of his nature feedin
itself on the inaction of the time. But his energy made itself fe
the moment the Tyranny was over. His father had sat, with thre
of his uncles, in the later Parliaments of Elizabeth. Oliver ha
himself been returned to that of 1628, and the town of Cambridg
sent him as its representative to the Short Parliament as to th
Long. It is in the latter that a courtier, Sir Philip Warwick, give
us our first glimpse of his actual appearance. " I came into th
House one morning, well clad, and perceived a gentleman speakin
whom I knew not, very ordinarily apparelled, for it was a plai
cloth-suit, which seemed to have been made by an ill countr
tailor. His linen was plain, and not very clean; and I remember
speck or two of blood upon his little band, which was not muc
larger than his collar. His hat was without a hat-band. His statur
was of a good size; his sword stuck close to his side; his counten
ance swoln and reddish; his voice sharp and untuneable, and hi
eloquence full of fervour." He was already " much hearkene
unto," but his power was to assert itself in deeds rather than i
words. He appeared at the head of a troop of his own raising a
Edgehill; but with the eye of a born soldier he at once saw th

lot in the army of Essex. "A set of poor tapsters and town
pprentices," he warned Hampden, "would never fight against
nen of honour;" and he pointed to religious enthusiasm as the
ne weapon which could meet and turn the chivalry of the Cavalier.
Even to Hampden the plan seemed impracticable; but the regiment of a thousand men which Cromwell raised for the Association
f the Eastern Counties, and which soon became known as his
ronsides, was formed strictly of "men of religion." He spent his
ortune freely on the task he set himself. "The business . . .
ath had of me in money between eleven and twelve hundred
ounds, therefore my private estate can do little to help the
ublic. . . . I have little money of my own (left) to help my
oldiers." But they were "a lovely company," he tells his friends
vith soldierly pride. No blasphemy, drinking, disorder, or impiety
vere suffered in their ranks. "Not a man swears but he pays his
welve pence." Nor was his choice of "men of religion" the only
nnovation Cromwell introduced into his new regiment. The social
raditions which restricted command to men of birth were dis-
egarded. "It may be," he wrote, in answer to complaints from
he committee of the Association, "it provokes your spirit to see
uch plain men made captains of horse. It had been well that men
f honour and birth had entered into their employments; but
vhy do they not appear? But seeing it is necessary the work must
go on, better plain men than none: but best to have men patient
of wants, faithful and conscientious in their employment, and such,
I hope, these will approve themselves." The words paint Cromwell's temper accurately enough: he is far more of the practical
soldier than of the theological reformer; though his genius already
breaks in upon his aristocratic and conservative sympathies, and
catches glimpses of the social revolution to which the war was
drifting. "I had rather," he once burst out impatiently, "have
a plain russet-coated captain, that knows what he fights for and
loves what he knows, than what you call a gentleman, and is
nothing else. I honour a gentleman that is so indeed!" he ends
with a characteristic return to his more common mood of feeling.
The same practical temper broke out in an innovation which had
more immediate results. Bitter as had been his hatred of the
bishops, and strenuously as he had worked to bring about a change
in Church government, Cromwell, like most of the Parliamentary
leaders, seems to have been content with the new Presbyterianism,
and the Presbyterians were more than content with him. Lord
Manchester "suffered him to guide the army at his pleasure."
"The man, Cromwell," writes the Scotchman Baillie, "is a very
wise and active head, universally well beloved as religious and
stout." But against dissidents from their own system, the Presbyterians were as bitter as Laud himself; and, as we shall see, Nonconformity was now rising every day into larger proportions, while
the new claim of liberty of worship was becoming one of the problems of the time. Cromwell met the problem in his unspeculative

fashion. He wanted good soldiers and good men; and, if the
were these, the Independent, the Baptist, the Leveller, found ent
among his Ironsides. "You would respect them, did you s
them," he answered the panic-stricken Presbyterians who charge
them with "Anabaptistry" and revolutionary aims: "they a
no Anabaptists: they are honest, sober Christians; they expe
to be used as men." He was soon to be driven—as in the soci
change we noticed before—to a far larger and grander point
view. "The State," he boldly laid down at last, "in choosing me
to serve it, takes no notice of their opinions. If they be willi
faithfully to serve it, that satisfies." But as yet he was busier wi
his new regiment than with theories; and the Ironsides were i
sooner in action than they proved themselves such soldiers as th
war had never seen yet. "Truly they were never beaten at all
their leader said proudly at its close. At Winceby fight the
charged "singing psalms," cleared Lincolnshire of the Cavendishe
and freed the eastern counties from all danger from Newcastle
part. At Marston Moor they faced and routed Rupert's chivalr
At Newbury it was only Manchester's reluctance that hindere
them from completing the ruin of Charles.

Cromwell had shown his capacity for organization in the creatio
of the Ironsides; his military genius had displayed itself at Marsto
Moor. Newbury first raised him into a political leader. "Withou
a more speedy, vigorous, and effective prosecution of the war," h
said to the Commons after his quarrel with Manchester, "castin
off all lingering proceedings, like those of soldiers of fortune beyon
sea to spin out a war, we shall make the kingdom weary of us, an
hate the name of a Parliament." But under the leaders who a
present conducted it a vigorous conduct of the war was hopeles
They were, in Cromwell's plain words, "afraid to conquer." The
desired not to crush Charles, but to force him back, with as muc
of his old strength remaining as might be, to the position of
constitutional King. The old loyalty, too, clogged their enterprise
they shrank from the taint of treason. "If the King be beaten,
Manchester urged at Newbury, "he will still be king; if he bea
us he will hang us all for traitors." To a mood like this Cromwell'
reply seemed horrible. "If I met the King in battle I would fir
my pistol at the King as at another." The army, too, as he lon
ago urged at Edgehill, was not an army to conquer with. Now
as then, he urged that till the whole force was new modelled, an
placed under a stricter discipline, "they must not expect an
notable success in anything they went about." But the first ste
in such a re-organization must be a change of officers. The arm
was led and officered by members of the two Houses, and th
Self-renouncing Ordinance, which was introduced by Cromwel
and Vane, declared the tenure of military or civil offices incom
patible with a seat in either. In spite of a long and bitter resistance
which was justified at a later time by the political results which
followed this rupture of the tie which had hitherto bound the Army

to the Parliament, the drift of public opinion was too strong to be withstood. The passage of the Ordinance brought about the retirement of Essex, Manchester, and Waller; and the new organization of the army went rapidly on under a new commander-in-chief, Sir Thomas Fairfax, the hero of the long contest in Yorkshire, and who had been raised into fame by his victory at Nantwich, and his bravery at Marston Moor. The principles on which Cromwell had formed his Ironsides were carried out on a larger scale in the " New Model." The one aim was to get together twenty thousand " honest " men. " Be careful," Cromwell wrote, " what captains of horse you choose, what men be mounted. A few honest men are better than numbers. If you choose godly honest men to be captains of horse, honest men will follow them." The result was a curious medley of men of different ranks among the officers of the New Model. The bulk of those in high command remained men of noble or gentle blood, Montagues, Pickerings, Fortescues, Sheffields, Sidneys, and the like. But side by side with these, though in far smaller proportion, were seen officers like Ewer, who had been a serving-man, like Okey, who had been a drayman, or Rainsborough, who had been a " skipper at sea." Equally strange was the mixture of religions in its ranks. A clause in the Act for new modelling the army had enabled Fairfax to dispense with the signature of the Covenant in the case of " godly men; " and among the farmers from the eastern counties, who formed the bulk of its privates, dissidence of every type had gained a firm foothold. A result hardly less notable, though less foreseen, was the youth of the officers. Among those in high command there were few who, like Cromwell, had passed middle age. Fairfax was but thirty-three, and most of his colonels were even younger. Of the political aspect of the New Model we shall have to speak at a later time; but as yet its energy was directed solely to " the speedy and vigorous prosecution of the war." The efforts of the peace party were frustrated at the very moment when Fairfax was ready for action by the policy of the King. From the moment when Newbury marked the breach between the peace and war parties in the Parliament, the Scotch Commissioners had been backed by the former in pressing for fresh negotiations with Charles. These were opened at Uxbridge, and prolonged for six months; but the hopes of concession which Charles had held out through the winter were suddenly withdrawn in the spring. He saw, as he thought, the Parliamentary army dissolved and ruined by the new modelling, at the instant when news came from Scotland of fresh successes on the part of Montrose, and of his overthrow of the Marquis of Argyle's troops in the victory of Inverlochy. " Before the end of the summer," wrote the conqueror, " I shall be in a position to come to your Majesty's aid with a brave army." The negotiations at Uxbridge were at once broken off, and a few months later the King opened his campaign by a march to the north where he hoped to form a junction with Montrose. Leicester was stormed, the blockade of Chester

raised, and the eastern counties threatened, until Fairfax, who
had hoped to draw Charles back again by a blockade of Oxford,
hurried at last on his track. Cromwell, who had been suffered by
the House to retain his command for a few days, joined Fairfax
as he drew near the King, and his arrival was greeted by loud
shouts of welcome from the troops. The two armies met near
Naseby, to the north-west of Northampton. The King was eager
to fight. " Never have my affairs been in as good a state," he cried;
and Prince Rupert was as impatient as his uncle. On the other
side, even Cromwell doubted the success of the new experiment.
" I can say this of Naseby," he wrote soon after, " that when I saw
the enemy draw up and march in gallant order towards us, and we
a company of poor ignorant men, to seek to order our battle, the
general having commanded me to order all the horse, I could not,
riding alone about my business, but smile out to God in praises, in
assurance of victory, because God would by things that are not
bring to nought things that are. Of which I had great assurance,
and God did it." The battle began with a furious charge of Rupert
uphill, which routed the wing opposed to him under Ireton; while
the Royalist foot, after a single discharge, clubbed their muskets
and fell on the centre under Fairfax so hotly that it slowly and
stubbornly gave way. But the Ironsides were conquerors on the
left. A single charge broke the northern horse under Langdale, who
had already fled before them at Marston Moor; and holding his
troops firmly in hand, Cromwell fell with them on the flank of the
Royalist foot in the very crisis of its success. A panic of the Royal
reserve, and its flight from the field, aided his efforts: it was in
vain that Rupert returned with forces exhausted by pursuit, that
Charles, in a passion of despair, called on his troopers for " one
charge more." The battle was over: artillery, baggage, even the
Royal papers, fell into the conquerors' hands: five thousand men
surrendered; only two thousand followed the King in his headlong
flight upon the west. The war was ended at a blow. While Charles
wandered helplessly in search of fresh forces, Fairfax marched
rapidly into Somersetshire, routed the Royal forces at Langport,
and in three weeks was master of the west. A victory at Kilsyth,
which gave Scotland for the moment to Montrose, threw a transient
gleam over the darkening fortunes of his master's cause; but the
surrender of Bristol, and the dispersion of the last force Charles
could collect in an attempt to relieve Chester, was followed by
news of the crushing and irretrievable defeat of the " Great
Marquis " at Philiphaugh. In the wreck of the Royal cause we
may pause for a moment over an incident which brings out in
relief the best temper of both sides. Cromwell " spent much time
with God in prayer before the storm " of Basing House, where the
Marquis of Winchester had held stoutly out through the war for
the King. The storm ended its resistance, and the brave old
Royalist was brought in a prisoner with his house flaming around
him. He " broke out," reports a Puritan bystander, " and said,

that if the King had no more ground in England but Basing
House he would adventure it as he did, and so maintain it to the
uttermost,' comforting himself in this matter ' that Basing House
was called Loyalty.' " Of loyalty such as this Charles was utterly
unworthy. The seizure of his papers at Naseby had hardly disclosed
his intrigues with the Irish Catholics when the Parliament was able
to reveal to England a fresh treaty with them, which purchased
no longer their neutrality, but their aid, by the simple concession
of every demand they had made. The shame was without profit,
for whatever aid Ireland might have given came too late to be of
service. The spring of the following year saw the few troops who
still clung to Charles surrounded and routed at Stow. " You have
done your work now," their leader, Sir Jacob Astley, said bitterly
to his conquerors, " and may go to play, unless you fall out among
yourselves."

SECTION VIII.—THE ARMY AND THE PARLIAMENT, 1646—1649

[*Authorities.*—To those already mentioned may be added Herbert's
" Memoirs," and the " Eikon Basilike." For Scottish history, Burnet,
" Lives of the Hamiltons." For the Independents, Masson, " Life of
Milton."]

With the close of the Civil War we enter on a short period of
confused struggles, tedious and uninteresting in its outer details,
but of far higher interest than even the War itself in its bearing on
our after history. Modern England, the England among whose
thoughts and sentiments we actually live, began with the triumph
of Naseby. Old things passed suddenly away. When Astley gave
up his sword the " work " of the generations which had struggled
for Protestantism against Catholicism, for public liberty against
absolute rule, in his own emphatic phrase, was " done." So far as
these contests were concerned, however, the later Stuarts might
strive to revive them, England could safely " go to play." But
with the end of this older work a new work at once began. The
constitutional and ecclesiastical problems which still in one shape
or another beset us started to the front as subjects of national
debate in the years between the close of the Civil War and the
death of the King. The two great parties which have ever since
divided the social, the political, and the religious life of England,
whether as Independents and Presbyterians, as Whigs and Tories,
or as Conservatives and Liberals, sprang into organized existence
in the contest between the Army and the Parliament. Then for the
first time began the struggle between political tradition and political
progress, between the principle of religious conformity and the
principle of religious freedom, which is far from having ended yet.

It was the religious struggle which drew the political in its train.
We have already witnessed the rise under Elizabeth of sects who
did not aim, like the Presbyterians, at a change in Church govern-

The
Indepen-
dents

ment, but rejected the notion of a national Church at all, and insisted on the right of each congregation to perfect independence of faith and worship. At the close of the Queen's reign, however these "Brownists," as they were called from one Brown, a clergyman who maintained their tenets, had almost entirely disappeared. Some, as we saw in the notable instance of the congregation which produced the Pilgrim Fathers, had found a refuge in Holland, but the bulk had been driven to a fresh conformity with the Established Church. "As for those which we call Brownists," says Bacon " being when they were at the best a very small number of very silly and base people, here and there in corners dispersed, they are now (thanks be to God) by the good remedies that have been used suppressed and worn out so as there is scarce any news of them." As soon, however, as Abbot's primacy promised a milder rule, the Separatist refugees began to venture timidly back again to England. During their exile in Holland the main body, under Robinson, had contented themselves with the free development of their system of independent congregations, each forming in itself a complete Church, and to them the name of Independents at a later time attached itself. A small part, however, had drifted into a more marked severance in doctrine from the Established Church, especially in their belief of the necessity of adult baptism, a belief from which their obscure congregation at Leyden became known as that of the Baptists. Both of these sects gathered a church in London in the middle of James's reign, but the persecuting zeal of Laud prevented any spread of their opinions under that of his successor; and it was not till their numbers were suddenly increased by the return of a host of emigrants from New England, with Hugh Peters at their head, on the opening of the Long Parliament, that the Congregational or Independent body began to attract attention. Lilburne and Burton soon declared themselves adherents of what was called "the New England way;" and a year later saw in London alone the rise of "four score congregations of several sectaries," as Bishop Hall scornfully tells us, "instructed by guides fit for them, cobblers, tailors, felt-makers, and such-like trash." But little religious weight however could be attributed as yet to the Congregational movement. Baxter at this time had not heard of the existence of any Independents. Milton in his earlier pamphlets shows no sign of their influence. Of the hundred and five ministers present in the Westminster Assembly only five were Congregational in sympathy, and these were all returned refugees from Holland. Among the one hundred and twenty London ministers in 1643, only three were suspected of leaning towards the Sectaries.

Presby-
terian
England
The struggle with Charles in fact at its outset only threw new difficulties in the way of religious freedom. It was with strictly conservative aims in ecclesiastical as in political matters that Pym and his colleagues began the strife. Their avowed purpose was simply to restore the Church of England to its state under Eliza-

ɔeth, and to free it from " innovations," from the changes intro-
luced by Laud and his fellow prelates. The great majority of the
Parliament were averse to any alterations in the constitution or
loctrine of the Church itself; and it was only the refusal of the
ɔishops to accept any diminution of their power and revenues, the
growth of a party hostile to Episcopalian Government, the necessity
or purchasing the aid of the Scots by a union in religion as in
ɔolitics, and above all the urgent need of constructing some new
ɔcclesiastical organization in the place of the older organization
which had become impossible from the Royalist attitude of the
ɔishops, that forced on the two Houses the adoption of the
Ƈovenant. But the change to a Presbyterian system of Church
government seemed at that time of little import to the bulk of
Englishmen. The Laudian dogma of the necessity of bishops was
held by few; and the change was generally regarded with approval
as one which brought the Church of England nearer to that of
Scotland, and to the reformed Churches of the continent. But
whatever might be the change in its administration, no one
imagined that it had ceased to be the Church of England. The
Tudor theory of its relation to the State, of its right to embrace all
Englishmen within its pale, and to dictate what should be their
faith and form of worship, remained utterly unquestioned by any
man of note. The sentiments on which such a theory rested indeed
for its main support, the power of historical tradition, the association of " dissidence " with danger to the state, the strong English
instinct of order, the as strong English dislike of " innovations,"
with the abhorrence of "indifference," as a sign of luke-warmness
in matters of religion, had only been intensified by the earlier
incidents of the struggle with the King. The Parliament therefore
had steadily pressed on the new system of ecclesiastical government
in the midst of the troubles of the war. An Assembly of Divines
assembled at Westminster received orders to revise the Articles,
to draw up a Confession of Faith, and a Directory of Public
Worship, and these, with their scheme of Church government, a
scheme only distinguished from that of Scotland by the significant
addition of a lay court of superior appeal set by Parliament over
the whole system of Church courts and assemblies, were accepted
by the Houses and embodied in a series of Ordinances.

Had the change been made at the moment when " with uplifted
hands " the Commons swore to the Covenant in St. Margaret's it
would probably have been accepted by the country at large. But
it met with a very different welcome when it came at the end of
the war. In spite of repeated votes of Parliament for its establishment, the pure Presbyterian system took root only in London and
Lancashire. While the Divines, indeed, were drawing up their
platform of uniform belief and worship in the Jerusalem Chamber
dissidence had grown into a religious power. In the terrible agony
of the long struggle against Charles, individual conviction became
a stronger force than religious tradition. Theological speculation

took an unprecedented boldness from the temper of the times
Four years after the war had begun a horror-stricken pamphletee
numbered sixteen religious sects as existing in defiance of the law
and, widely as these bodies differed among themselves, all at one
in repudiating any right of control in faith or worship by the
Church or its clergy. Milton, who had left his Presbyterian stand
point, saw at last that "new Presbyter is but old Priest wri
large." The question of sectarianism soon grew into a practica
one from its bearing on the war: for the class specially infected
with the new spirit of religious freedom was just the class to whose
zeal and vigour the Parliament was forced to look for success in
its struggle. We have seen the prevalence of this spirit among the
farmers from whom Cromwell drew his Ironsides, and his enlist
ment of these "sectaries" was the first direct breach in the ole
system of conformity. Cromwell had signed the Covenant, and
there is no reason for crediting him with any aversion to Presby
terianism as a system of doctrine or of Church organization. His
first step, indeed, was a purely practical one, a step dictated by
military necessities, and excused in his mind by a sympathy with
"honest" men, as well as by the growing but still vague notion
of a communion among Christians wider than that of outer con
formity in worship or belief. But the alarm and remonstrances of
the Presbyterians forced his mind rapidly forward. "The State in
choosing men to serve it," Cromwell wrote before Marston Moor
"takes no notice of their opinions. If they be willing faithfully
to serve it, that satisfies." Marston Moor encouraged him to press
on the Parliament the necessity of at least "tolerating" dissi
dents, and he succeeded in procuring the appointment of a com
mittee to find some means of effecting this. But the conservative
temper of the Presbyterian Churchmen was fairly roused by his
act, and by the growth of sectarianism. "We detest and abhor,"
wrote the London clergy in 1645, "the much endeavoured Tolera
tion." The corporation of London petitioned Parliament to
suppress "all sects without toleration." The Parliament itself
was steadily on the conservative side, but the fortunes of the war
told as steadily against conservatism. Essex and the Presbyterians
marched from defeat to defeat. It was necessary to new mode
the army, and to raise the New Model it was found necessary to
give Fairfax power to dispense with any signatures to the Covenant.
The victory of Naseby raised a far wider question than that of
mere toleration. "Honest men served you faithfully in this action,"
Cromwell wrote to the Speaker of the House of Commons from
the very field. "Sir, they are trusty: I beseech you in the name
of God not to discourage them. He that ventures his life for the
liberty of his country, I wish he trust God for the liberty of his
conscience." The storm of Bristol encouraged him to proclaim the
new principles yet more distinctly. "Presbyterians, Independents,
all here have the same spirit of faith and prayer, the same presence
and answer. They agree here, have no names of difference; pity

t is it should be otherwise anywhere. All that believe have the real unity, which is the most glorious, being the inward and spiritual, in the body and in the head. For being united in forms (commonly called uniformity), every Christian will for peace' sake study and do as far as conscience will permit. And from brethren in things of the mind we look for no compulsion but that of light and reason.''

The increasing firmness of Cromwell's language was due to the growing irritation of his Presbyterian opponents. The two parties became every day more clearly defined. The Presbyterian ministers complained bitterly of the increase of the sectaries, and denounced the existing toleration. Scotland, whose army was still before Newark, pressed for the execution of the Covenant and the universal enforcement of a Presbyterian uniformity. Sir Harry Vane, on the other hand, was striving to bring the Parliament round to less rigid courses by the introduction of two hundred and thirty new members, who filled the seats left vacant by Royalist secessions, and the more eminent of whom, such as Ireton and Algernon Sidney, were inclined to the Independents. The pressure of the New Model, and the remonstrances of Cromwell as its mouthpiece, hindered any effective movement towards persecution. Amidst the wreck of his fortunes Charles intrigued busily with both parties, and promised liberty of worship to Vane and the Independents, at the moment when he was negotiating for a refuge with the Presbyterian Scots. His negotiations were quickened by the march of Fairfax upon Oxford. Driven from his last refuge, the King after some aimless wanderings made his appearance in the camp of the Scots. Lord Leven at once fell back with his Royal prize on Newcastle. The new aspect of affairs threatened the party of religious freedom with ruin. Hated as they were, by the Scots, by the Lords, by the city of London, the apparent junction of Charles with their enemies destroyed their growing hopes in the Commons, where the prospects of a speedy peace on Presbyterian terms at once swelled the majority of their opponents. The two Houses laid their conditions of peace before the King without a dream of resistance from one who seemed to have placed himself at their mercy. They required for the Parliament the command of the army and fleet for twenty years; the exclusion of all "Malignants," or Royalists who had taken part in the war, from civil and military office; the abolition of Episcopacy; and the establishment of a Presbyterian Church. Of toleration or liberty of conscience they said not a word. The Scots pressed these terms on the King "with tears;" his Royalist friends, and even the Queen, urged their acceptance. But the aim of Charles was simply delay. Time and the dissensions of his enemies, as he believed, were fighting for him. "I am not without hope," he wrote coolly, "that I shall be able to draw either the Presbyterians or the Independents to side with me for extirpating one another, so that I shall be really King again." His refusal of the terms offered by the Houses was a defeat for the Presbyterians. "What will become

*D 728

**1646
to
1649**

of us," asked one of them, " now that the King has rejected our
proposals? " " What would have become of us," retorted an Inde
pendent, " had he accepted them ? " The vigour of Holles and the
Conservative leaders in the Parliament rallied however to a bolder
effort. While the Scotch army lay at Newcastle they could not
insist on dismissing their own. But the withdrawal of the Scots
from England would not only place the King's person in the hands
of the Houses, but enable them to free themselves from the pressure
of their own soldiers by disbanding the New Model. Hopeless of
success with the King, and unable to bring him into Scotland in
face of the refusal of the General Assembly to receive a sovereign
who would not swear to the Covenant, the Scottish army accepted
£400,000 in discharge of its claims, handed Charles over to a com
mittee of the Houses, and marched back over the Border. Masters

*Jan.
1647*

of the King, the Presbyterian leaders at once moved boldly to
their attack on the Sectaries. They voted that the army should be
disbanded, and that a new army should be raised for the suppres
sion of the Irish rebellion with strictly Presbyterian officers at its
head. It was in vain that the men protested against being severed
from " officers that we love," and that the Council of Officers strove
to gain time by pressing on the Parliament the danger of mutiny.
Holles and his fellow leaders were resolute, and their ecclesiastical
legislation showed the end at which their resolution aimed. Direct
enforcement of conformity was impossible till the New Model was
disbanded; but the Parliament pressed on in the work of providing
the machinery for enforcing it as soon as the army was gone. Vote
after vote ordered the setting up of Presbyteries throughout the
country, and the first fruits of these efforts were seen in the
Presbyterian organization of London, and in the first meeting of
its Synod at St. Paul's. Even the officers on Fairfax's staff were
ordered to take the Covenant.

**The
Army
and the
Parlia-
ment**

All hung however on the disbanding of the New Model, and the
New Model showed no will to disband itself. Its new attitude can
only fairly be judged by remembering what the conquerors of
Naseby really were. They were soldiers of a different class and of
a different temper from the soldiers of any other army that the
world has seen. Their ranks were filled for the most part with
young farmers and tradesmen of the lower sort, maintaining them
selves, for their pay was twelvemonths in arrear, mainly at their
own cost. They had been specially picked as " honest " or religious
men, and, whatever enthusiasm or fanaticism they may have
shown, their very enemies acknowledged the order and piety of
their camp. They looked on themselves not as swordsmen, to be
caught up and flung away at the will of a paymaster, but as men
who had left farm and merchandise at a direct call from God. A
great work had been given them to do, and the call bound them
till it was done. Kingcraft, as Charles was hoping, might yet restore
tyranny to the throne. A more immediate danger threatened that
liberty of conscience which was to them " the ground of the quarrel,

and for which so many of their friends' lives had been lost, and so much of their own blood has been spilt.' They would wait before disbanding till these liberties were secured, and if need came they would again act to secure them. But their resolve sprang from no pride in the brute force of the sword they wielded. On the contrary, as they pleaded passionately at the bar of the Commons, " on becoming soldiers we have not ceased to be citizens." Their aims and proposals throughout were purely those of citizens, and of citizens who were ready the moment their aim was won to return peacefully to their homes. Thought and discussion had turned the army into a vast Parliament, a Parliament which regarded itself as the representatives of " godly " men in as high a degree as the Parliament at Westminster, and which must have become every day more conscious of its superiority in political capacity to its rival. Ireton, the moving spirit of the New Model, had no equal as a statesman in St. Stephen's: nor is it possible to compare the large and far-sighted proposals of the army with the blind and narrow policy of the two Houses. Whatever we may think of the means by which the New Model sought its aims, we must in justice remember that, so far as those aims went, the New Model was in the right. For the last two hundred years England has been doing little more than carrying out in a slow and tentative way the scheme of political and religious reform which the army propounded at the close of the Civil War. It was not till the rejection of the officers' proposals had left little hope of conciliation that the army acted, but its action was quick and decisive. It set aside for all political purposes the Council of Officers, and elected a new Council of Adjutators or Assistants, two members being named by each regiment, which summoned a general meeting of the army at Triploe Heath, where the proposals of pay and disbanding made by the Parliament were rejected with cries of " Justice." While the army was gathering, in fact, the Adjutators had taken a step which put submission out of the question. A rumour that the King was to be removed to London, a new army raised, a new civil war begun, roused the soldiers to madness. Five hundred troopers suddenly appeared before Holmby House, where the King was residing in charge of the Parliamentary Commissioners, and displaced its guards. " Where is your commission for this act?" Charles asked the cornet who commanded them. " It is behind me," said Joyce, pointing to his soldiers. " It is written in very fine and legible characters," laughed the King. The seizure had in fact been previously concerted between Charles and the Adjutators. " I will part willingly," he told Joyce, " if the soldiers confirm all that you have promised me. You will exact from me nothing that offends my conscience or my honour." " It is not our maxim," replied the cornet, " to constrain the conscience of anyone, still less that of our King." After a first burst of terror at the news, the Parliament fell furiously on Cromwell, who had relinquished his command and quitted the army before the close of the war, and had ever since been employed as a mediator between the two parties. The charge of having incited the mutiny fell before his vehement protest, but he was driven to seek refuge with the army, and in three days it was in full march upon London. Its demands were expressed with perfect clearness in an " Humble Representation " which it addressed to the Houses. " We desire a settlement of the Peace of the kingdom and of the liberties of the subject according to the votes and declarations of Parliament. We desire no alteration in the civil government: as little do we desire to interrupt or in the least to intermeddle with the settling of the Presbyterial government." They demanded toleration; but " not to open a way to licentious living under pretence of obtaining ease for tender consciences, we profess, as ever, in these things when the state has made a settlement we have nothing to say, but to submit or suffer." It was with a view to such a settlement that they demanded the expulsion of eleven members from the Commons with Holles at their head, whom the soldiers charged with stirring up strife between the army and the Parliament, and with a design of renewing the civil war. After fruitless negotiations the terror of the Londoners forced the eleven to withdraw; and the House named Commissioners to treat on the questions at issue.

The
Army
and the
King
Though Fairfax and Cromwell had at last been forced from their position as mediators into a hearty co-operation with the army, its political direction rested at this moment with Cromwell's son-in-law, Henry Ireton, and Ireton looked for a real settlement, not to the Parliament, but to the King. " There must be some difference," he urged bluntly, " between conquerors and conquered; " but the terms which he laid before Charles were terms of studied moderation. The vindictive spirit which the Parliament had shown against the Royalists and the Church disappeared in the terms he laid before the King; and the army contented itself with the banishment of seven leading " delinquents," a general Act of Oblivion for the rest, the withdrawal of all coercive power from the clergy, the control of Parliament over the military and naval forces for ten years, and its nomination of the great officers of State. Behind these demands however came the masterly and comprehensive plan of political reform which had already been sketched by the army in the " Humble Representation," with which it had begun its march on London. Belief and worship were to be free to all. Acts enforcing the use of the Prayer-book, or attendance at Church, or the enforcement of the Covenant were to be repealed. Even Papists, whatever other restraints might be imposed, were to be freed from the bondage of compulsory worship. Parliaments were to be triennial, and the House of Commons to be reformed by a fairer distribution of seats and of electoral rights; taxation was to be readjusted; legal procedure simplified; a crowd of political, commercial, and judicial privileges abolished. Ireton believed that Charles could be " so managed " (says Mrs. Hutchinson) " as to comply with the public good of his people after he could no longer

phold his violent will." But Charles was equally dead to the
moderation and to the wisdom of this great Act of Settlement.
He saw in the crisis nothing but an opportunity of balancing one
party against another; and believed that the army had more need
of his aid than he of the army's. "You cannot do without me—
you are lost if I do not support you," he said to Ireton as he
pressed his proposals. "You have an intention to be the arbitrator
between us and the Parliament," Ireton quietly replied, "and we
mean to be so between the Parliament and your Majesty." But
the King's tone was soon explained by a rising of the London mob
which broke into the House of Commons, and forced its members
to recall the eleven. While fourteen peers and a hundred Commoners
fled to the army, those who remained at Westminster prepared for
an open struggle with it, and invited Charles to return to London.
But the army was again on the march. "In two days," Cromwell
said coolly, "the city will be in our hands." The soldiers entered
London in triumph, and restored the fugitive members; the
eleven were again expelled, and the army leaders resumed negotiations with the King. The indignation of the soldiers at his delays
and intrigues made the task hourly more difficult; but Cromwell,
who now threw his whole weight on Ireton's side, clung to the hope
of accommodation with a passionate tenacity. His mind, conservative by tradition, and above all practical in temper, saw the
political difficulties which would follow on the abolition of Royalty,
and in spite of the King's evasions he persisted in negotiating with
him. But Cromwell stood almost alone; the Parliament refused to
accept Ireton's proposals as a basis of peace, Charles still evaded,
and the army then grew restless and suspicious. There were cries
for a wide reform, for the abolition of the House of Peers, for a new
House of Commons; and the Adjutators called on the Council of
Officers to discuss the question of abolishing Royalty itself. Cromwell was never braver than when he faced the gathering storm,
forbade the discussion, adjourned the Council, and sent the officers
to their regiments. But the strain was too great to last long, and
Charles was still resolute to "play his game." He was in fact so *Nov.*
far from being in earnest in his negotiations with Cromwell and *1647*
Ireton, that at the moment they were risking their lives for him
he was conducting another and equally delusive negotiation with
the Parliament, fomenting the discontent in London, preparing for
a fresh Royalist rising, and for an invasion of the Scots in his
favour. "The two nations," he wrote joyously, "will soon be at
war." All that was needed for the success of his schemes was his
own liberty; and in the midst of his hopes of an accommodation
Cromwell found with astonishment that he had been duped
throughout, and that the King had fled.

The flight fanned the excitement of the army into frenzy, and The
only the courage of Cromwell averted an open mutiny in its gather- Second
ing at Ware. But even Cromwell was powerless to break the spirit Civil
which now pervaded the soldiers, and the King's perfidy left him War

without resource. "The King is a man of great parts and great understanding," he said at last, "but so great a dissembler and so false a man that he is not to be trusted." By a strange error Charles had made his way from Hampton Court to the Isle of Wight perhaps with some hope from the sympathy of Colonel Hammond, the Governor of Carisbrook Castle, and again found himself a prisoner. Foiled in his effort to put himself at the head of the new civil war, he set himself to organize it from his prison; and while again opening delusive negotiations with the Parliament, he signed a secret treaty with the Scots for the invasion of the realm. The rise of Independency, and the practical suspension of the Covenant, had produced a violent reaction in his favour north of the Tweed. The nobles gathered round the Duke of Hamilton, and carried the elections against Argyle and the adherents of the Parliament; and on the King's consenting to a stipulation for the re-establishment of Presbytery in England, they ordered an army to be levied for his support. In England the whole of the conservative party, with many of the most conspicuous members of the Long Parliament at its head, was drifting, in its horror of the religious and political changes which seemed impending, towards the King; and the news from Scotland gave the signal for fitful insurrections in almost every quarter. London was only held down by main force, old officers of the Parliament unfurled the Royal flag in South Wales, and surprised Pembroke. The seizure of Berwick and Carlisle opened a way for the Scotch invasion. Kent, Essex, and Hertford broke out in revolt. The fleet in the Downs sent their captains on shore, hoisted the King's pennon, and blockaded the Thames. "The hour is come for the Parliament to save the kingdom and to govern alone," cried Cromwell; but the Parliament only showed itself eager to take advantage of the crisis to profess its adherence to Royalty, to re-open the negotiations it had broken off with the King, and to deal the fiercest blow at religious freedom which it had ever received. The Presbyterians flocked back to their seats; and an "Ordinance for the suppression of Blasphemies and Heresies," which Vane and Cromwell had long held at bay, was passed by triumphant majorities. Any man—runs this terrible statute—denying the doctrine of the Trinity or of the Divinity of Christ, or that the books of Scripture are not "the Word of God," or the resurrection of the body, or a future day of judgment, and refusing on trial to abjure his heresy, "shall suffer the pain of death." Any man declaring (amidst a long list of other errors) "that man by nature hath free will to turn to God," that there is a Purgatory, that images are lawful, that infant baptism is unlawful; any one denying the obligation of observing the Lord's day, or asserting "that the Church government by Presbytery is anti-Christian or unlawful," shall on a refusal to renounce his errors "be commanded to prison." It was plain that the Presbyterian party counted on the King's success to resume its policy of conformity, and had Charles been free, or the New Model disbanded, ts hopes would probably have been realized. But Charles, though ager to escape, was still safe at Carisbrook; and the New Model vas facing fiercely the danger which surrounded it. The wanton enewal of the war at a moment when all tended to peace swept rom the mind of Fairfax and Cromwell, as from that of the army t large, every thought of reconciliation with the King. Soldiers nd generals were at last bound together again in a stern resolve. On the eve of their march against the revolt all gathered in a olemn prayer-meeting, and came " to a very clear and joint esolution, ' That it was our duty, if ever the Lord brought us ack again in peace, to call Charles Stuart, that man of blood, to ccount for the blood he has shed and mischief he has done to his tmost against the Lord's cause and people in this poor nation.' " n three days Fairfax had trampled down the Kentish insurgents, nd had prisoned those of the eastern counties within the walls of Colchester, while Cromwell drove the Welsh insurgents within hose of Pembroke. Both the towns however held stubbornly out; nd though a Royalist rising under Lord Holland in the neighbour- hood of London was easily put down, there was no force left to tem the inroad of the Scots, who were pouring over the Border ome twenty thousand strong. Luckily the surrender of Pembroke t the critical moment set Cromwell free. Pushing rapidly north- ward with five thousand men, he called in the force under Lambert vhich had been gallantly hanging on the Scottish flank, and pushed over the Yorkshire hills into the valley of the Ribble. The Duke of Hamilton, reinforced by three thousand Royalists of the north, had advanced as far as Preston. With an army which now numbered ten thousand men, Cromwell poured down on the flank of the Duke's straggling line of march, attacked the Scots as they retired behind the Ribble, passed the river with them, cut their rearguard to pieces at Wigan, forced the defile at Warrington, where the flying enemy made a last and desperate stand, and forced their foot to surrender, while Lambert hunted down Hamilton and the horse. Fresh from its victory, the New Model pushed over the Border, while the peasants of Ayrshire and the west rose in the " Whiggamore raid " (notable as the first event in which we find the name " Whig," which possibly the same as our " Whey," and conveys a taunt against the " sour-milk " faces of the fanatical Ayrshiremen), and, marching upon Edinburgh, dis- persed the Royalist party and again installed Argyle in power.

Argyle welcomed Cromwell as a deliverer, but the victorious general had hardly entered Edinburgh when he was recalled by pressing news from the south. The temper with which the Parlia- ment had met the Royalist revolt was, as we have seen, widely different from that of the army. It had recalled the eleven members, and had passed the Ordinance against heresy. At the moment of the victory at Preston the Lords were discussing charges of treason against Cromwell, while commissioners had again been sent to the Isle of Wight, in spite of the resistance of the Independents, to conclude peace with the King. Royalists and Presbyterians alike pressed Charles to grasp the easy terms which were now offered him. But his hopes from Scotland had only broken down to give place to hopes of a new war with the aid of an army from Ireland and the negotiation saw forty days wasted in useless chicanery "Nothing," Charles wrote to his friends, "is changed in my designs." But at this moment the surrender of Colchester and the convention with Argyle set free the army, and petitions from its regiments at once demanded "justice on the King." A fresh "Remonstrance" from the Council of Officers called for the election of a new Parliament; for electoral reform; for the recognition of the supremacy of the Parliament "in all things;" for the change of kingship, should it be retained, into a magistracy elected by the Parliament, and without veto on its proceedings; and demanded above all "that the capital and grand author of our troubles, by whose commissions, commands, and procurements, and in whose behalf and for whose interest only, of will and power, all our wars and troubles have been, with all the miseries attending them, may be specially brought to justice for the treason, blood, and mischief he is therein guilty of." The reply of the Parliament to this Remonstrance was to accept the King's concessions, unimportant as they were, as a basis of peace. The step was accepted by the soldiers as a defiance: Charles was again seized by a troop of horse, and carried off to Hurst Castle; while a letter from Fairfax announced the march of his army upon London. "We shall know now," said Vane, as the troops took their post round the Houses of Parliament, "who is on the side of the King, and who on the side of the people." But the terror of the army proved weaker among their members than the agonized loyalty which strove to save Charles, and an immense majority in both Houses still voted for the acceptance of the terms he had offered. The next morning saw Colonel Pride at the door of the House of Commons with a list of forty members of the majority in his hands. The Council of Officers had resolved to exclude them, and as each member made his appearance he was arrested, and put in confinement. "By what right do you act?" a member asked. "By the right of the sword," Hugh Peters is said to have replied. The House was still resolute, but on the following morning forty more members were excluded, and the rest gave way. The formal expulsion of one hundred and forty members left the Independents, who alone remained, free to co-operate with the army which had delivered them; the peace votes were at once rescinded; the removal of Charles to Windsor was followed by an instant resolution for his trial, and by the nomination of a Court of one hundred and fifty Commissioners to conduct it, with John Bradshaw, a lawyer of eminence, at their head. The rejection of this Ordinance by the few peers who remained brought about a fresh resolution from the lower House, "that the People are, under God, the original of all just power; that the Commons of England in arliament assembled—being chosen by, and representing, the eople—have the supreme power in this nation; and that what-ever is enacted and declared for law by the Commons in Parlia-ient assembled hath the force of a law, and all the people of this ation are concluded thereby, although the consent and con-urrence of the King or House of Peers be not had thereunto."

Charles appeared before the Court only to deny its competence nd to refuse to plead; but thirty-two witnesses were examined ɔ satisfy the consciences of his judges, and it was not till the fifth ay of the trial that he was condemned to death as a tyrant, traitor, urderer, and enemy of his country. The popular excitement had ented itself in cries of "Justice," or "God save your Majesty," s the trial went on, but all save the loud outcries of the soldiers as hushed as Charles passed to receive his doom. The dignity hich he had failed to preserve in his long jangling with Bradshaw nd the judges returned at the call of death. Whatever had been ie faults and follies of his life, "he nothing common did, or mean, pon that memorable scene." Two masked executioners awaited ie King as he mounted the scaffold, which had been erected utside one of the windows of the Banqueting House at Whitehall; ie streets and roofs were thronged with spectators; and a strong ɔdy of soldiers stood drawn up beneath. His head fell at the first low, and as the executioner lifted it to the sight of all a groan of ity and horror burst from the silent crowd.

Section IX.—The Commonwealth, 1649—1653

[*Authorities.*—The Thurloe Papers are the most important source for is period; Whitelocke, "Ludlow and the Parliamentary History," is ' value. For Scotland, see Firth, "Scotland under the Commonwealth" ıd "Scotland under the Protectorate." For Ireland, Carte, "History ' James, Duke of Ormond"; the Ormond Papers; and Prendergast, Cromwellian Settlement." For foreign affairs, see Ranke and Gar-iner, whose histories are also the best general accounts of the period. or Cromwell, see Carlyle, and Firth's "Cromwell."]

The news of the King's death was received throughout Europe ith a thrill of horror. The Czar of Russia chased the English nvoy from his court. The ambassador of France was withdrawn n the proclamation of the Republic. The Protestant powers of ıe Continent seemed more anxious than any to disavow all con-ection with the Protestant people who had brought a King to the lock. Holland took the lead in acts of open hostility to the new ower as soon as the news of the execution reached the Hague; he States-General waited solemnly on the Prince of Wales, who ɔok the title of Charles the Second, and recognized him as Majesty," while they refused an audience to the English envoys. 'heir Stadtholder, his brother-in-law, the Prince of Orange, was ıpported by popular sympathy in the aid and encouragement he

afforded to Charles; and the eleven ships of the English fleet, which
had found a refuge at the Hague ever since their revolt from the
Parliament, were suffered to sail under Rupert's command on an
errand of sheer piracy, though with a Royal commission, and to
render the seas unsafe for English traders. The danger, however,
was far greater nearer home. The Scots proclaimed Charles the
Second as their King on the news of his father's death, and at once
despatched an embassy to the Hague to invite him to ascend the
throne. Ormond, who had at last succeeded in uniting the countless
factions who ever since the Rebellion had turned Ireland into
chaos, the old Irish Catholics or native party under Owen Roe
O'Neil, the Catholics of the English Pale, the Episcopalian Royalists,
the Presbyterial Royalists of the north, called on Charles to land
at once in a country where he would find three-fourths of its people
devoted to his cause. Nor was the danger from without met by
resolution and energy on the part of the diminished Parliament
which remained the sole depositary of legal powers. The Commons
entered on their new task with hesitation and delay. More than a
month passed after the King's execution before the Monarchy was
formally abolished, and the government of the nation provided
for by the creation of a Council of State consisting of forty-one
members selected from the Commons, who were entrusted with full
executive power at home or abroad. Two months more elapsed
before the passing of the memorable Act which declared " that the
People of England and of all the dominions and territories thereunto belonging are, and shall be, and are hereby constituted, made,
established, and confirmed to be a Commonwealth and Free State,
and shall henceforward be governed as a Commonwealth and Free
State by the supreme authority of this nation, the Representatives
of the People in Parliament, and by such as they shall appoint
and constitute officers and ministers for the good of the people,
and that without any King or House of Lords."

Of the dangers which threatened the new Commonwealth some
were more apparent than real. The rivalry of France and Spain,
both anxious for its friendship, secured it from the hostility of the
greater powers of the Continent, and the ill-will of Holland could
be delayed, if not averted, by negotiations. The acceptance of the
Covenant was insisted on by Scotland before it would formally
receive Charles as its ruler, and nothing but necessity would induce
him to comply with such a demand. On the side of Ireland the
danger was more pressing, and an army of twelve thousand men
was set apart for a vigorous prosecution of the Irish war. The
Commonwealth found considerable difficulties at home. The death
of Charles gave fresh vigour to the Royalist cause, and the new
loyalty was stirred to enthusiasm by the publication of the " Eikon
Basilike," a work really due to the ingenuity of Dr. Gauden, a
Presbyterian minister, but which was believed to have been composed by the King himself in his later hours of captivity, and
which reflected with admirable skill the hopes, the suffering, and

he piety of the Royal "martyr." The dreams of a rising were
oughly checked by the execution of the Duke of Hamilton and
ords Holland and Capell, who had till now been confined in the
'ower. But the popular disaffection told even on the Council of
tate. A majority of its members declined the oath offered to them
t their earliest meeting, pledging them to an approval of the
king's death and the establishment of the Commonwealth. Half
he judges retired from the bench. Thousands of refusals met the
emand of an engagement to be faithful to the Republic which
vas made from all beneficed clergymen and public functionaries.
t was not till May, and even then in spite of the ill-will of the
itizens, that the Council ventured to proclaim the Commonwealth
a London. A yet more formidable peril lay in the selfishness of
he Parliament itself. It was now a mere fragment of the House
f Commons; the members of the Rump—as it was contemptu-
usly called—numbered hardly a hundred, and of those the average
ttendance was little more than fifty. In reducing it by "Pride's
'urge" to the mere shadow of a House the army had never dreamt
f its continuance as a permanent assembly: it had, in fact,
isisted as a condition of even its temporary continuance that it
hould prepare a bill for the summoning of a fresh Parliament.
'he plan put forward by the Council of Officers is still interesting
s the base of many later efforts towards parliamentary reform;
t advised a dissolution in the spring, the assembling every two
ears of a new Parliament consisting of four hundred members,
lected by all householders rateable to the poor, and a redistribu-
ion of seats which would have given the privilege of representation
o all places of importance. Paid military officers and civil officials
vere excluded from election. The plan was apparently accepted
y the Commons, and a bill based on it was again and again
iscussed; but there was a suspicion that no serious purpose of its
wn dissolution was entertained by the House. The popular dis-
ontent at once found a mouthpiece in John Lilburne, a brave,
ot-headed soldier, and the excitement of the army appeared
iddenly in a formidable mutiny. "You must cut these people
a pieces," Cromwell burst out in the Council of State, "or they
ill cut you in pieces;" and a forced march of fifty miles to
urford enabled him to burst on the mutinous regiments at mid-
ight, and to stamp out the revolt. But resolute as he was against
isorder, Cromwell went honestly with the army in its demand of a
ew Parliament; he believed, and in his harangue to the mutineers
e pledged himself to the assertion, that the House purposed to
issolve itself. Within the House, however, a vigorous knot of
oliticians was resolved to prolong its existence; and in a witty
araphrase of the story of Moses, Henry Martyn had already
ictured the Commonwealth as a new-born and delicate babe, and
inted that "no one is so proper to bring it up as the mother who
as brought it into the world." As yet, however, their intentions
ere kept secret, and in spite of the delays thrown in the way of

the bill for a new Representative body Cromwell entertained no
serious suspicion of such a design, when he was summoned to
Ireland by a series of Royalist successes which left only Dublin
in the hands of the Parliamentary forces.

With Scotland threatening war, and a naval struggle impending
with Holland, it was necessary that the work of the army in Ireland
should be done quickly. The temper, too, of Cromwell and his
soldiers was one of vengeance, for the horror of the Irish Massacre
remained living in every English breast, and the revolt was looked
upon as a continuance of the Massacre. "We are come," he said
on his landing, "to ask an account of the innocent blood that hath
been shed, and to endeavour to bring to an account all who by
appearing in arms shall justify the same." A sortie from Dublin
had already broken up Ormond's siege of the capital; and feeling
himself powerless to keep the field before the new army, the
Marquess had thrown his best troops, three thousand Englishmen
under Sir Arthur Aston, as a garrison into Drogheda. The storm

of Drogheda was the first of a series of awful massacres. The
garrison fought bravely, and repulsed the first attack; but a
second drove Aston and his force back to the Mill-Mount. "Our
men getting up to them," ran Cromwell's terrible despatch, "were
ordered by me to put them all to the sword. And indeed, being in
the heat of action, I forbade them to spare any that were in arms
in the town, and I think that night they put to death about two
thousand men." A few fled to St. Peter's church, "whereupon I
ordered the steeple to be burned, where one of them was heard
to say in the midst of the flames: 'God damn me, I burn, I burn.' "
"In the church itself nearly one thousand were put to the sword.
I believe all their friars were knocked on the head promiscuously
but two," but these were the sole exceptions to the rule of killing
the soldiers only. At a later time Cromwell challenged his enemies
to give "an instance of one man since my coming into Ireland
not in arms, massacred, destroyed, or burnt." But for soldier
there was no mercy. Of the remnant who surrendered through
hunger, "when they submitted, their officers were knocked on the
head, every tenth man of the soldiers killed, and the rest shipped
for the Barbadoes." "I am persuaded," the despatch ends, "that
this is a righteous judgment of God upon these barbarous wretches
who have imbrued their hands in so much innocent blood, and
that it will tend to prevent the effusion of blood for the future."
A detachment sufficed to relieve Derry, and to quiet Ulster; and
Cromwell turned to the south, where as stout a defence was followed
by as terrible a massacre at Wexford. Fresh successes at Ross
and Carrick brought him to Waterford; but the city held stubbornly out, disease thinned his army, where there was scarce an
officer who had not been sick, and the general himself was arrested
by illness, and at last the tempestuous weather drove him into
winter quarters at Cork with his work half done. The winter was
one of terrible anxiety. The Parliament showed less and le

inclination to dissolve itself, and met the growing discontent by a stricter censorship of the press and a fruitless prosecution of John Lilburne. English commerce was ruined by the piracies of Rupert's fleet, which now anchored at Kinsale to support the Royalist cause in Ireland. The energy of Vane indeed had already re-created a navy, squadrons were being despatched into the British seas, the Mediterranean, and the Levant, and Colonel Blake, who had distinguished himself by his heroic defence of Taunton during the war, was placed at the head of a fleet which drove Rupert from the Irish coast, and finally blockaded him in the Tagus. But even the energy of Vane quailed before the danger from the Scots. "One must go and die there," the young King cried at the news of Ormond's defeat before Dublin, "for it is shameful for me to live elsewhere." But his ardour for an Irish campaign cooled as Cromwell marched from victory to victory; and from the isle of Jersey, which alone remained faithful to him of all his southern dominions, Charles renewed the negotiations with Scotland which his hopes from Ireland had broken. They were again delayed by a proposal on the part of Montrose to attack the very Government with whom his master was negotiating; but the failure and death of the Marquis in the spring forced Charles to accept the Presbyterian conditions. The news of the negotiations at Breda filled the Parliament with dismay, for Scotland was raising an army, and Fairfax, while willing to defend England against a Scotch invasion, scrupled to take the lead in an invasion of Scotland. The Council recalled Cromwell from Ireland, but his cooler head saw that there was yet time to finish his work in the west. During the winter he had been busily preparing for a new campaign, and it was only after the storm of Clonmell, and the overthrow of the Irish army under Hugh O'Neile in the hottest fight the army had yet fought, that he embarked again for England.

1650

Cromwell entered London amidst the shouts of a great multitude; and a month later, as Charles landed on the shores of Scotland, the English army started for the north. It crossed the Tweed, fifteen thousand men strong; but the terror of the Irish massacres hung round its leader, the country was deserted as he advanced, and he was forced to cling for provisions to the fleet which sailed along the coast. Leslie, with a larger force, refused battle and lay obstinately in his lines between Edinburgh and Leith; a march of the English army round his position to the slopes of the Pentlands only brought about a change of the Scottish front; and as Cromwell fell back baffled upon Dunbar, Leslie encamped upon the heights above the town, and cut off the English retreat along the coast by the seizure of Cockburnspath. His post was almost unassailable, while the soldiers of Cromwell fell fast with disease; and their general had resolved on an embarcation of his forces, when he saw in the dusk of evening signs of movement in the Scottish camp. Leslie's caution had at last been overpowered by the zeal of the preachers, and his army moved down

Dunbar
and
Worcester

to the lower ground between the hillside on which it was encampe
and a little brook which covered the English front. His horse wa
far in advance of the main body, and it had hardly reached th
level ground when Cromwell in the dim dawn flung his whole forc
upon it. " They run, I profess they run! " he cried as the Scotc
horse broke after a desperate resistance, and threw into confusio
the foot who were hurrying to their aid. Then, as the sun rose ove
the mist of the morning, he added in nobler words: " Let God arise
and let his enemies be scattered! Like as the mist vanisheth, s
shalt Thou drive them away! " In less than an hour the victor
was complete. The defeat at once became a rout; ten thousan
prisoners were taken, with all the baggage and guns; thre
thousand were slain, with scarce any loss on the part of th
conquerors. Leslie reached Edinburgh, a general without an army

The effect of Dunbar was at once seen in the attitude of th
Continental powers. Spain hastened to recognize the Republic
and Holland offered its alliance. But Cromwell was watching wit
anxiety the growing discontent at home. The general amnest
claimed by Ireton and the bill for the Parliament's dissolution sti
hung on hand; the reform of the courts of justice, which had bee
pressed by the army, failed before the obstacles thrown in its wa
by the lawyers in the Commons. " Relieve the oppressed," Crom
well wrote from Dunbar, " hear the groans of poor prisoners. B
pleased to reform the abuses of all professions. If there be any on
that makes many poor to make a few rich, that suits not a Commor
wealth." But the Parliament was seeking to turn the current c
public opinion in favour of its own continuance by a great diplo
matic triumph. It resolved secretly on the wild project of bringin
about a union between England and Holland, and it took advantag
of Cromwell's victory to despatch Oliver St. John with a statel
embassy to the Hague. His rejection of the alliance and Treaty c
Commerce which the Dutch offered were followed by the disclosur
of the English proposal of union; but the proposal was at onc
rejected. The envoys, who returned angrily to the Parliamen
attributed their failure to the posture of affairs in Scotland, wher
Charles was preparing for a new campaign. " I believe the Kin
will set up on his own score now," Cromwell had written afte
Dunbar. Humiliation after humiliation had been heaped o
Charles since he landed in his northern realm. He had subscribe
to the Covenant; he had listened to sermons and scoldings fro
the ministers; he had been called on to sign a declaration tha
acknowledged the tyranny of his father and the idolatry of hi
mother. Hardened and shameless as he was, the young King for
moment recoiled. " I could never look my mother in the fac
again," he cried, " after signing such a paper; " but he signed. H
was still, however, a King only in name, shut out from the Counc
and the army, with his friends excluded from all part in goverr
ment or the war. But he was at once freed by the victory of Dunba
With the overthrow of Leslie fell the power of Argyle and th

arrow Presbyterians whom he led. Hamilton, the brother and
successor of the Duke who had been captured at Preston, brought
back the Royalists to the camp, and Charles insisted on taking
art in the Council and on being crowned at Scone. Master of
Edinburgh, but foiled in an attack on Stirling, Cromwell waited
through the winter and the long spring, while intestine feuds broke
up the nation opposed to him, and while the stricter Covenanters
retired sulkily from the Royal army on the return of the
"Malignants," the "Royalists" of the earlier war, to its ranks.
With summer the campaign recommenced, but Leslie again fell
back on his system of positions, and Cromwell, finding his camp
at Stirling unassailable, crossed into Fife and left the road open
to the south. The bait was taken. In spite of Leslie's counsels
Charles resolved to invade England, and was soon in full march
through Lancashire upon the Severn, with the English horse under
Lambert hanging on his rear, and the English foot hastening to
close the road to London by York and Coventry. "We have done
to the best of our judgment," Cromwell replied to the angry alarm
of the Parliament, "knowing that if some issue were not put to
this business it would occasion another winter's war." At Coventry
he learnt Charles's position, and swept round by Evesham upon
Worcester, where the Scotch King was encamped. Throwing half
his force across the river, Cromwell attacked the town on both
sides on the anniversary of his victory at Dunbar. He led the van
in person, and was "the first to set foot on the enemy's ground."
When Charles descended from the Cathedral Tower to fling himself
on the eastern division, Cromwell hurried over the river, and was
soon "riding in the midst of the fire." For four or five hours, he
told the Parliament, "it was as stiff a contest as ever I have seen;"
the Scots outnumbered and beaten into the city gave no answer
but shot to offers of quarter, and it was not till nightfall that all
was over. The loss of the victors was as usual inconsiderable. The
conquered lost six thousand men, and all their baggage and
artillery. Leslie was among the prisoners: Hamilton among the
dead.

"Now that the King is dead and his son defeated," Cromwell
said gravely to the Parliament, "I think it necessary to come to a
settlement." But the settlement which had been promised after
Naseby was still as distant as ever after Worcester. The bill for
dissolving the present Parliament, though Cromwell pressed it in
person, was only passed, after bitter opposition, by a majority of
two; and even this success had been purchased by a compromise
which permitted the House to sit for three years more. Internal
affairs were simply at a dead lock. The Parliament appointed
committees to prepare plans for legal reforms, or for ecclesiastical
reforms, but it did nothing to carry them into effect. It was overpowered by the crowd of affairs which the confusion of the war
had thrown into its hands, by confiscations, sequestrations, appointments to civil and military offices, the whole administration

in fact of the state; and there were times when it was driven
to a resolve not to take any private affairs for weeks together in
order that it might make some progress with public business. To
add to this confusion and muddle there were the inevitable scandals
which arose from it; charges of malversation and corruption were
hurled at the members of the House; and some, like Haselrig, were
accused with justice of using their power to further their own
interests. The one remedy for all this was, as the army saw, the
assembly of a new and complete Parliament in place of the mere
" rump " of the old; but this was the one measure which the House
was resolute to avert. Vane spurred it to a new activity. The
Amnesty Bill was forced through after fifteen divisions. A Grand
Committee, with Sir Matthew Hale at its head, was appointed to
consider the reform of the law. The union with Scotland was
pushed resolutely forward; eight English Commissioners convoked
a Convention of delegates from its counties and boroughs at
Edinburgh, and in spite of dogged opposition procured a vote in
favour of union. A bill was introduced ratifying the measure, and
admitting representatives from Scotland into the next Parliament.
A similar plan was soon proposed for a union with Ireland. But it
was necessary for Vane's purposes not only to show the energy of
the Parliament, but to free it from the control of the army. His
aim was to raise in the navy a force devoted to the House and to
eclipse the glories of Dunbar and Worcester by yet greater triumphs
at sea. With this view the quarrel with Holland had been carefully nursed; a " Navigation Act " prohibiting the importation of
foreign vessels of any but the products of the countries to which
they belonged struck a fatal blow at the carrying trade from which
the Dutch drew their wealth; and fresh debates arose from the
English claim to salutes from all vessels in the Channel. The two

fleets met before Dover, and a summons from Blake to lower the
Dutch flag was met by the Dutch admiral, Van Tromp, with a
broadside. The States-General attributed the collision to accident
and offered to recall Van Tromp; but the English demands rose
at each step in the negotiations till war became inevitable. The
army hardly needed the warning conveyed by the introduction of
a bill for its disbanding to understand the new policy of the Parliament. It was significant that while accepting the bill for its own
dissolution the House had as yet prepared no plan for the assembly
which was to follow it; and the Dutch war had hardly been
declared when, abandoning the attitude of inaction which it had
observed since the beginning of the Commonwealth, the army
petitioned, not only for reform in Church and State, but for an
explicit declaration that the House would bring its proceedings to
a close. The Petition forced the House to discuss a bill for " a New
Representative," but the discussion soon brought out the resolve
of the sitting members to continue as a part of the coming Parliament without re-election. The officers, irritated by such a claim,
demanded in conference after conference an immediate dissolution

and the House as resolutely refused. In ominous words Cromwell supported the demand of the army. " As for the members of this Parliament, the army begins to take them in disgust. I would it did so with less reason." There was just ground, he urged, for discontent in their selfish greed of houses and lands, the scandalous lives of many, their partiality as judges, their interference with the ordinary course of law in matters of private interest, their delay of law reform, above all in their manifest design of perpetuating their own power. " There is little to hope for from such men," he ended with a return to his predominant thought, " for a settlement of the nation."

The crisis was averted for a moment by the events of the war. A terrible storm had separated the two fleets when on the point of engaging in the Orkneys, but Ruyter and Blake met again in the Channel, and after a fierce struggle the Dutch were forced to retire under cover of night. Since the downfall of Spain Holland had been the first naval power in the world, and the spirit of the nation rose gallantly with its earliest defeat. Immense efforts were made to strengthen the fleet, and the veteran, Van Tromp, who was replaced at its head, appeared in the Channel with seventy-three ships of war. Blake had but half the number, but he at once accepted the challenge, and the unequal fight went on doggedly till nightfall, when the English fleet withdrew shattered into the Thames. Tromp swept the Channel in triumph, with a broom at his masthead; and the tone of the House lowered with the defeat of their favourite force. A compromise seems to have been arranged between the two parties, for the bill providing a new Representative was again pushed on; and the Parliament agreed to retire in the coming November, while Cromwell offered no opposition to a reduction of the Army. But the courage of the House rose again with a turn of fortune. The strenuous efforts of Blake enabled him again to put to sea in a few months after his defeat, and a running fight through four days ended at last in an English victory, though Tromp's fine seamanship enabled him to save the convoy he was guarding. The House at once insisted on the retention of its power. Not only were the existing members to continue as members of the New Parliament, depriving the places they represented of their right of choosing representatives, but they were to constitute a Committee of Revision, to determine the validity of each election, and the fitness of the members returned. A conference took place between the leaders of the Commons and the Officers of the Army, who resolutely demanded not only the omission of these clauses, but that the Parliament should at once dissolve itself, and commit the new elections to the Council of State. " Our charge," retorted Haselrig, " cannot be transferred to any one." The conference was adjourned till the next morning, on an understanding that no decisive step should be taken; but it had no sooner re-assembled, than the absence of the leading members confirmed the news that Vane was fast pressing the bill for a new Representative through

the House. "It is contrary to common honesty," Cromwell angril[y]
broke out; and, quitting Whitehall, he summoned a company o[f]
musketeers to follow him as far as the door of the Commons. H[e]
sate down quietly in his place, " clad in plain grey clothes and gre[y]
worsted stockings," and listened to Vane's passionate argument[s]
"I am come to do what grieves me to the heart," he said to hi[s]
neighbour, St. John, but he still remained quiet, till Vane presse[d]
the House to waive its usual forms and pass the bill at onc[e]
"The time has come," he said to Harrison. "Think well," replie[d]
Harrison, "it is a dangerous work!" and Cromwell listened fo[r]
another quarter of an hour. At the question " that this Bill d[o]
pass," he at length rose, and his tone grew higher as he repeate[d]
his former charges of injustice, self-interest, and delay. " You[r]
hour is come," he ended, "the Lord hath done with you!" [A]
crowd of members started to their feet in angry protest. " Com[e,]
come," replied Cromwell, " we have had enough of this; " an[d]
striding into the midst of the chamber, he clapt his hat on his hea[d]
and exclaimed, " I will put an end to your prating! " In the di[n]
that followed his voice was heard in broken sentences—" It is n[o]
fit that you should sit here any longer! You should give place t[o]
better men! You are no Parliament." Thirty musketeers entere[d]
at a sign from their General, and the fifty members present crowde[d]
to the door. "Drunkard!" Cromwell broke out as Wentwort[h]
passed him; and Martin was taunted with a yet coarser nam[e.]
Vane, fearless to the last, told him his act was " against all righ[t]
and all honour." "Ah, Sir Harry Vane, Sir Harry Vane," Crom[-]
well retorted in bitter indignation at the trick he had been playe[d.]
"You might have prevented all this, but you are a juggler, an[d]
have no common honesty! The Lord deliver me from Sir Harr[y]
Vane!" The Speaker refused to quit his seat, till Harrison offere[d]
to "lend him a hand to come down." Cromwell lifted the mac[e]
from the table. "What shall we do with this bauble?" he sai[d]
"Take it away!" The door of the house was locked at last, an[d]
the dispersion of the Parliament was followed a few hours after b[y]
that of its executive committee, the Council of State. Cromwe[ll]
himself summoned them to withdraw. "We have heard," replie[d]
a member, John Bradshaw, " what you have done this morning a[t]
the House, and in some hours all England will hear it. But yo[u]
mistake, sir, if you think the Parliament dissolved. No power o[f]
earth can dissolve the Parliament but itself, be sure of that!"

SECTION X.—THE FALL OF PURITANISM, 1653—1660

[*Authorities.*—Thurloe's State Papers, the Calendar of State Papers,
.rlyle's " Letters and Speeches of Oliver Cromwell," Ludlow's
Memoirs," the Clarke Papers, and Whitelocke's " Memorials " are the
ief sources. For the proceedings of the Commonwealth and Pro-
:torate parliaments, see Husband and Scobell's collections of ordin-
.ces. For the restoration, see Clarendon's account; Pepys' " Diary "
d Evelyn's " Diary." The Instrument of Government, the Humble
titition and Advice, and the Declaration of Breda will be found in
.rdiner's " Documents of the Puritan Revolution." For general
story, see Gardiner, " History of the Commonwealth and Protec-
·ate," and Firth's continuation; Ranke, " History of England," and
rth, " Cromwell."]

The dispersion both of the Parliament and of its executive com-
ission left England without a government, for the authority of
ery official ended with that of the body from which his power
is derived. Cromwell, in fact, as Captain-General of the forces,
und himself left solely responsible for the maintenance of public
der. But no thought of military despotism can be fairly traced
the acts of the general or the army. They were in fact far
om regarding their position as a revolutionary one. Though
capable of justification on any formal ground, their proceedings
.d as yet been substantially in vindication of the older constitu-
on, and the opinion of the nation had gone fully with the army
its demand for a full and efficient body of representatives, as
ell as in its resistance to the project by which the Rump would
ive deprived half England of its rights of election. It was only
hen no other means existed of preventing such a wrong that the
ldiers had driven out the wrongdoers. " It is you that have
rced me to this," Cromwell exclaimed, as he drove the members
om the House; " I have sought the Lord night and day that He
ould rather slay me than put me upon the doing of this work."
he act was one of violence to the members of the House, but the
t which it aimed at preventing was one of violence on their part
the constitutional rights of the whole nation. The people had
fact been " dissatisfied in every corner of the realm " at the
ate of public affairs: and the expulsion of the members was
tified by a general assent. " We did not hear a dog bark at their
·ing," the Protector said years afterwards. Whatever anxiety
ay have been felt at the use which was like to be made of " the
wer of the sword," was at once dispelled by a proclamation of
e officers. Their one anxiety was " not to grasp the power
urselves nor to keep it in military hands, no not for a day," and
.eir promise to " call to the government men of approved fidelity
d honesty " was redeemed by the nomination of a new Council
State, consisting of eight officers of high rank and four civilians,
.th Cromwell as their head, and a seat in which was offered,
.ough fruitlessly, to Vane. The first business of such a body was

The
Puritan
Conven-
tion

clearly to summon a new Parliament and to resign its trust int
its hands: but the bill for Parliamentary reform had dropped wit
the expulsion: and reluctant as the Council was to summon th
new Parliament on the old basis of election, it shrank from th
responsibility of effecting so fundamental a change as the creatic
of a new basis by its own authority. It was this difficulty whic
led to the expedient of a Constituent Convention. Cromwell tol
the story of this unlucky assembly some years after with a
amusing frankness. " I will come and tell you a story of my ow
weakness and folly. And yet it was done in my simplicity—I da
avow it was. . . . It was thought then that men of our ow
judgment, who had fought in the wars, and were all of a pie
on that account—why, surely, these men will hit it, and these me
will do it to the purpose, whatever can be desired! And surely w
did think, and I did think so—the more blame to me!" Of th
hundred and fifty-six men, " faithful, fearing God, and hatin
covetousness," whose names were selected for this purpose by th
Council of State, from lists furnished by the congregation
churches, the bulk were men, like Ashley Cooper, of good bloc
and " free estates; " and the proportion of burgesses, such as th
leather-merchant, Praise-God Barebones, whose name was eager
seized on as a nickname for the body to which he belonged, seen
to have been much the same as in earlier Parliaments. But th
circumstances of their choice told fatally on the temper of i
members. Cromwell himself, in the burst of rugged eloquence wit
which he welcomed their assembling, was carried away by
strange enthusiasm. " Convince the nation," he said, "that
men fearing God have fought them out of their bondage under th
regal power, so men fearing God do now rule them in the fea
of God. . . . Own your call, for it is of God: indeed, it is marve
lous, and it hath been unprojected. . . . Never was a suprem
power under such a way of owning God and being owned by Him.
A spirit yet more enthusiastic at once appeared in the proceedin
of the Convention. The resignation of their powers by Cromwe
and the Council into its hands left it the one supreme authorit
but by the instrument which convoked it provision had been mac
that this authority should be transferred in fifteen months t
another assembly elected according to its directions. Its work wa
in fact, to be that of a constituent assembly, paving the way for
Parliament on a really national basis; but the Convention put th
largest construction on its commission, and boldly undertook th
whole task of constitutional reform. Committees were appointe
to consider the needs of the Church and the nation. The spirit o
economy and honesty which pervaded the assembly appeared i
its redress of the extravagance which prevailed in the civil servic
and of the inequality of taxation. With a remarkable energy
undertook a host of reforms, for whose execution England has ha
to wait to our own day. The Long Parliament had shrunk fro
any reform of the Court of Chancery, where twenty-three thousan

ases were waiting unheard. The Convention proposed its abolition. The work of compiling a single code of laws, begun under the Long Parliament by a committee with Sir Matthew Hale at its head, was again pushed forward. The frenzied alarm which these bold measures aroused among the lawyer class was soon backed by that of the clergy, who saw their wealth menaced by the establishment of civil marriage and by proposals to substitute the free contributions of congregations for the payment of tithes. The landed proprietors too rose against the scheme for the abolition of lay-patronage, which was favoured by the Convention, and predicted an age of confiscation. The "Barebones Parliament," as the assembly was styled in derision, was charged with a design to ruin property, the Church, and the law, with enmity to knowledge, and blind and ignorant fanaticism. Cromwell himself shared the general uneasiness at its proceedings. His mind was that of an administrator, rather than that of a statesman, unspeculative, deficient in foresight, conservative, and eminently practical. He saw the need of administrative reform in Church and State; but he had no sympathy whatever with the revolutionary theories which were filling the air around him. His desire was for "a settlement" which should be accompanied with as little disturbance of the old state of things as possible. If Monarchy had vanished in the turmoil of war, his experience of the Long Parliament only confirmed him in his belief of the need of establishing an executive power of a similar kind, apart from the power of the legislature, as a condition of civil liberty. His sword had won "liberty of conscience;" but passionately as he clung to it, he was still for an established Church, for a parochial system, and a ministry maintained by tithes. His social tendencies were simply those of the class to which he belonged. "I was by birth a gentleman," he told a later Parliament, and in the old social arrangement of "a nobleman, a gentleman, a yeoman," he saw "a good interest of the nation and a great one." He hated "that levelling principle" which tended to the reducing of all to one equality. "What was the purport of it," he asks with an amusing simplicity, "but to make the tenant as liberal a fortune as the landlord?"

To a practical temper such as this the speculative reforms of the Convention were as distasteful as to the lawyers and clergy whom they attacked. "Nothing," said Cromwell, "was in the hearts of these men but 'overturn, overturn.'" But he was delivered from his embarrassment by the internal dissensions of the Assembly itself. The day after the decision against tithes the more conservative members snatched a vote by surprise "that the sitting of this Parliament any longer, as now constituted, will not be for the good of the Commonwealth, and that it is requisite to deliver up unto the Lord-General the powers we received from him." The Speaker placed their abdication in Cromwell's hands, and the act was confirmed by the subsequent adhesion of a majority of the members. The dissolution of the Convention replaced matters in

the state in which its assembly had found them; but there was
still the same general anxiety to substitute some sort of legal rule
for the power of the sword. The Convention had named during its
session a fresh Council of State, and this body at once drew up,
under the name of the Instrument of Government, a remarkable
Constitution, which was adopted by the Council of Officers. They
were driven by necessity to the step from which they had shrunk
before, that of convening a Parliament on the reformed basis of
representation. The House was to consist of four hundred members
from England, thirty from Scotland, and thirty from Ireland. The
seats hitherto assigned to small and rotten boroughs were transferred to larger constituencies, and for the most part to counties.
All special rights of voting in the election of members was abolished
and replaced by a general right of suffrage, based on the possession
of real or personal property to the value of two hundred pounds.
Catholics and " Malignants," as those who had fought for the King,
were called, were alone excluded from the franchise. Constitu-
tionally, all further organization of the form of government should
have been left to this Assembly; but the dread of disorder during
the interval of its election, as well as a longing for " settlement,"
drove the Council to complete their work by pressing the office of
" Protector " upon Cromwell. " They told me that except I would
undertake the government they thought things would hardly come
to a composure or settlement, but blood and confusion would
break in as before." If we follow, however, his own statement, it
was when they urged that the acceptance of such a Protectorate
actually limited his power as Lord-General, and " bound his hand
to act nothing without the consent of a Council until the Parliament," that the post was accepted. The powers of the new Protector indeed were strictly limited. Though the members of the
Council were originally named by him, each member was irre-
movable save by consent of the rest: their advice was necessary
in all foreign affairs, their consent in matters of peace and war,
their approval in nominations to the great offices of state, or the
disposal of the military or civil power. With this body too lay the
choice of all future Protectors. To the administrative check of the
Council was added the political check of the Parliament. Three
years at the most were to elapse between the assembling of one
Parliament and another. Laws could not be made, nor taxes
imposed but by its authority, and after the lapse of twenty days
the statutes it passed became laws even if the Protector's assent
was refused to them. The new Constitution was undoubtedly
popular; and the promise of a real Parliament in a few months
covered the want of any legal character in the new rule. The
Government was generally accepted as a provisional one, which
could only acquire legal authority from the ratification of its acts

in the coming session; and the desire to settle it on such a Parliamentary basis was universal among the members of the new
Assembly which met in the autumn at Westminster.

Few Parliaments have ever been more memorable, or more truly
representative of the English people, than the Parliament of 1654.
It was the first Parliament in our history where members from
Scotland and Ireland sate by side with those from England, as
they sit in the Parliament of to-day. The members for rotten
boroughs and pocket-boroughs had disappeared. In spite of the
exclusion of the Royalists from the polling-booths, and the
arbitrary erasure of the names of a few ultra-republican members
by the Council, the House had a better title to the name of a " free
Parliament " than any which had sat before. The freedom with
which the electors had exercised their right of voting was seen
indeed in the large number of Presbyterian members who were
returned, and in the reappearance of Haselrig and Bradshaw, with
many members of the Long Parliament, side by side with Lord
Herbert and the older Sir Harry Vane. The first business of the
House was clearly to consider the question of government; and
Haselrig, with the fiercer republicans, at once denied the legal
existence of either Council or Protector, on the ground that the
Long Parliament had never been dissolved. Such an argument,
however, told as much against the Parliament in which they sate
as against the administration itself, and the bulk of the Assembly
contented themselves with declining to recognize the Constitution
of Protectorate as of more than provisional validity. They proceeded at once to settle the government on a Parliamentary basis.
The " Instrument " was taken as the groundwork of the new
Constitution, and carried clause by clause. That Cromwell should
retain his rule as Protector was unanimously agreed; that he
should possess the right of veto or a co-ordinate legislative power
with the Parliament was hotly debated, though the violent
language of Haselrig did little to disturb the general tone of
moderation. Suddenly, however, Cromwell interposed. If he had
undertaken the duties of Protector with reluctance, he looked on
all legal defects in his title as more than supplied by the general
acceptance of the nation. " I called not myself to this place," he
urged, " God and the people of these kingdoms have borne testimony to it." His rule had been accepted by London, by the army,
by the solemn decision of the judges, by addresses from every shire,
by the very appearance of the members of the Parliament in answer
to his writ. " Why may I not balance this Providence," he asked,
" with any hereditary interest ? " In this national approval he saw
a call from God, a Divine Right of a higher order than that of the
kings who had gone before. But there was another ground for the
anxiety with which he watched the proceedings of the Commons.
His passion for administration had far overstepped the bounds of
a merely provisional rule in the interval before the assembling of
the Parliament. His desire for " settlement " had been strengthened
not only by the drift of public opinion, but by the urgent need of
every day; and the power reserved by the " Instrument " to issue
temporary Ordinances, " until further order in such matters, to be

taken by the Parliament," gave a scope to his marvellous activity of which he at once took advantage. Sixty-four Ordinances had been issued in the nine months before the meeting of the Parliament. Peace had been concluded with Holland. The Church had been set in order. The law itself had been minutely regulated. The union with Scotland had been brought to completion. So far was Cromwell from dreaming that these measures, or the authority which enacted them, would be questioned, that he looked to Parliament simply to complete his work. "The great end of your meeting," he said at the first assembly of its members, "is healing and settling." Though he had himself done much, he added "there was still much to be done." Peace had to be made with Portugal, and alliance with Spain. Bills were laid before the House for the codification of the law. The plantation and settlement of Ireland had still to be completed. He resented the setting these projects aside for constitutional questions which, as he held, a Divine call had decided, but he resented yet more the renewed claim advanced by Parliament to the sole power of legislation. As we have seen, his experience of the evils which had arisen from the concentration of legislative and executive power in the Long Parliament had convinced Cromwell of the danger to public liberty which lay in such a union. He saw in the joint government of "a single person and a Parliament" the only assurance "that Parliaments should not make themselves perpetual," or that their power should not be perverted to public wrong. But whatever strength there may have been in the Protector's arguments, the act by which he proceeded to enforce them was fatal to liberty and in the end to Puritanism. "If my calling be from God," he ended, "and my testimony from the People, God and the People shall take it from me, else I will not part from it." And he announced that no member would be suffered to enter the House without signing an engagement "not to alter the Government as it is settled in a single person and a Parliament." No act of the Stuarts had been a bolder defiance of constitutional law; and the act was as needless as it was illegal. One hundred members alone refused to take the engagement, and the signatures of three-fourths of the House proved that the security Cromwell desired might have been easily procured by a vote of Parliament. But those who remained resumed their constitutional task with unbroken firmness. They quietly asserted their sole title to government by referring the Protector's Ordinances to Committees for revision, and for conversion into laws. The "Instrument of Government" was turned into a bill, debated, and read a third time. Money votes, as in previous Parliaments, were deferred till "grievances" had been settled. But Cromwell once more intervened. The Royalists were astir again; and he attributed their renewed hopes to the hostile attitude which he attributed to the Parliament. The army which remained unpaid while the supplies were delayed, was seething with discontent. "It looks," said the Protector, "as if the

ying grounds for a quarrel had rather been designed than to
ve the people settlement. Judge yourselves whether the con-
sting of things that were provided for by this government hath
en profitable expense of time for the good of this nation." In
ords of angry reproach he declared the Parliament dissolved.

With the dissolution of the Parliament of 1654 ended all show of The
gal rule. The Protectorate, deprived by its own act of all chance New
legal sanction, became a simple tyranny. Cromwell professed, Tyranny
deed, to be restrained by the " Instrument; " but the one great
straint on his power which the Instrument provided, the inability
levy taxes save by consent of Parliament, was set aside on the
ea of necessity. " The People," said the Protector in words which
trafford might have uttered, " will prefer their real security to
rms." That a danger of Royalist revolt existed was undeniable,
ut the danger was at once doubled by the general discontent.
rom this moment, Whitelock tells us, " many sober and noble
atriots," in despair of public liberty, " did begin to incline to the
ing's restoration." In the mass of the population the reaction
as far more rapid. " Charles Stuart," writes a Cheshire corre-
ondent to the Secretary of State, " hath five hundred friends in
ese adjacent counties for every one friend to you among them."
ut before the overpowering strength of the army even this general
iscontent was powerless. Yorkshire, where the Royalist insur-
ction was expected to be most formidable, never ventured to
se at all. There were risings in Devon, Dorset, and the Welsh
larches, but they were quickly put down, and their leaders brought
the scaffold. Easily however as the revolt was suppressed, the
rror of the Government was seen in the energetic measures to
hich Cromwell resorted in the hope of securing order. The
ountry was divided into ten military governments, each with a
ajor-general at its head, who was empowered to disarm all Papists
nd Royalists, and to arrest suspected persons. Funds for the sup-
ort of this military despotism were provided by an Ordinance of the
ouncil of State, which enacted that all who had at any time borne
rms for the King should pay every year a tenth part of their
ncome, in spite of the Act of Oblivion, as a fine for their Royalist
endencies. The despotism of the major-generals was seconded by
he older expedients of tyranny. The Episcopalian clergy had been
ealous in promoting the insurrection, and they were forbidden in
evenge to act as ministers or as tutors. The press was placed
nder a strict censorship. The payment of taxes levied by the sole
uthority of the Protector was enforced by distraint; and when a
ollector was sued in the courts for redress, the counsel for the
rosecution were sent to the Tower.

If pardon, indeed, could ever be won for a tyranny, the wisdom Scotland
nd grandeur with which he used the power he had usurped would and
vin pardon for the Protector. The greatest among the many great Ireland
nterprises undertaken by the Long Parliament had been the
Jnion of the three Kingdoms: and that of Scotland with England

had been brought about, at the very end of its career, by the tac
and vigour of Sir Harry Vane. But its practical realization wa
left to Cromwell. In four months of hard fighting General Mon
brought the Highlands to a new tranquillity; and the presence o
an army of seven thousand men, backed by a line of forts, kept th
most restless of the clans in good order. The settlement of th
country was brought about by the temperance and sagacity o
Monk's successor, General Deane. No further interference with th
Presbyterian system was attempted beyond the suppression of th
General Assembly. But religious liberty was resolutely protected
and Deane ventured even to interfere on behalf of the miserabl
victims whom Scotch bigotry was torturing and burning on th
charge of witchcraft. Even steady Royalists acknowledged th
justice of the Government and the wonderful discipline of i
troops. " We always reckon those eight years of the usurpation,
said Burnet afterwards, " a time of great peace and prosperity.
Sterner work had to be done before Ireland could be brought int
real union with its sister kingdoms. The work of conquest had bee
continued by Ireton, and completed after his death by Genera
Ludlow, as mercilessly as it had begun. Thousands perished b
famine or the sword. Shipload after shipload of those who sur
rendered were sent over sea for sale into forced labour in Jamaic
and the West Indies. More than forty thousand of the beate
Catholics were permitted to enlist for foreign service, and found
refuge in exile under the banners of France and Spain. The wor
of settlement, which was undertaken by Henry Cromwell, th
younger and abler of the Protector's sons, turned out to be eve
more terrible than the work of the sword. It took as its model th
Colonization of Ulster, the fatal measure which had destroyed a
hope of a united Ireland and had brought inevitably in its trai
the massacre and the war. The people were divided into classe
in the order of their assumed guilt. All who after fair trial wer
proved to have personally taken part in the massacre wer
sentenced to banishment or death. The general amnesty whic
freed " those of the meaner sort " from all question on other score
was far from extending to the landowners. Catholic proprietor
who had shown no goodwill to the Parliament, even though the
had taken no part in the war, were punished by the forfeiture of
third of their estates. All who had borne arms were held to hav
forfeited the whole, and driven into Connaught, where fresh estate
were carved out for them from the lands of the native clans. N
such doom had ever fallen on a nation in modern times as fell upo
Ireland in its new settlement. Among the bitter memories whic
part Ireland from England the memory of the bloodshed and con
fiscation which the Puritans wrought remains the bitterest; an
the worst curse an Irish peasant can hurl at his enemy is " th
curse of Cromwell." But pitiless as the Protector's policy was, i
was successful in the ends at which it aimed. The whole nativ
population lay helpless and crushed. Peace and order were restored

d a large incoming of Protestant settlers from England and otland brought a new prosperity to the wasted country. Above , the legislative union which had been brought about with otland was now carried out with Ireland, and thirty seats were otted to its representatives in the general Parliament.

In England Cromwell dealt with the Royalists as irreconcilable emies; but in every other respect he carried fairly out his pledge " healing and settling." The series of administrative reforms nned by the Convention had been partially carried into effect fore the meeting of Parliament in 1654; but the work was pushed . after the dissolution of the House with yet greater energy. arly a hundred Ordinances showed the industry of the Govern- ent. Police, public amusements, roads, finances, the condition of isons, the imprisonment of debtors, were a few among the subjects ich claimed Cromwell's attention. An Ordinance of more than ty clauses reformed the Court of Chancery. The anarchy which d reigned in the Church since the break down of Episcopacy and e failure of the Presbyterian system to supply its place, was put end to by a series of wise and temperate measures for its rganization. Rights of patronage were left untouched; but a ard of Triers, a fourth of whom were laymen, was appointed to amine the fitness of ministers presented to livings; and a Church ard of gentry and clergy was set up in every county to exercise supervision over ecclesiastical affairs, and to detect and remove ndalous and ineffectual ministers. Even by the confession of omwell's opponents, the plan worked well. It furnished the untry with " able, serious preachers," Baxter tells us, " who lived godly life, of what tolerable opinion soever they were," and, both Presbyterian and Independent ministers were presented livings at the will of their patrons, it solved so far as prac- al working was concerned the problem of a religious union nong Protestants on the base of a wide variety of Christian inion. From the Church which was thus reorganized all power interference with faiths differing from its own was resolutely thheld. Cromwell remained true throughout to his great cause religious liberty. Even the Quaker, rejected by all other Christian dies as an anarchist and blasphemer, found sympathy and pro- ction in Cromwell. The Jews had been excluded from England ce the reign of Edward the First; and a prayer which they now esented for leave to return was refused by the commission of erchants and divines to whom the Protector referred it for con- leration. But the refusal was quietly passed over, and the nnivance of Cromwell in the settlement of a few Hebrews in ndon and Oxford was so clearly understood that no one ventured interfere with them.

No part of his policy is more characteristic of Cromwell's mind, ether in its strength or in its weakness, than his management of eign affairs. While England had been absorbed in her long and stinate struggle for freedom the whole face of the world around her had changed. The Thirty Years' War was over. The victorie of Gustavus, and of the Swedish generals who followed him, had been seconded by the policy of Richelieu and the intervention of France. Protestantism in Germany was no longer in peril from the bigotry or ambition of the House of Austria; and the Treaty of Westphalia had drawn a permanent line between the territorie belonging to the adherents of the old religion and the new. There was little danger, indeed, now to Europe from the great Catholic House which had threatened its freedom ever since Charles the Fifth. Its Austrian branch was called away from dreams of aggression in the west to a desperate struggle with the Turk for the possession of Hungary and the security of Austria itself. Spain from causes which it is no part of our present story to detail, was falling into a state of strange decrepitude. So far from aiming to be mistress of Europe, she was rapidly sinking into the almost helpless prey of France. It was France which had become the dominant power in Christendom, though her position was far from being as commanding as it was to become under Lewis the Fourteenth. The peace and order which prevailed after the cessation of the religious troubles throughout her compact and fertile territory gave scope at last to the quick and industrious temper of the French people; while her wealth and energy was placed by the centralizing administration of Henry the Fourth, of Richelieu, and of Mazarin almost absolutely in the hands of the Crown. Under the three great rulers who have just been named her ambition was steadily directed to the same purpose of territorial aggrandizement, and though limited as yet to the annexation of the Spanish and Imperial territories, which still parted her frontier from the Pyrenees, the Alps, and the Rhine, a statesman of wise political genius would have discerned the beginning of that great struggle for supremacy over Europe at large which was only foiled by the genius of Marlborough and the victories of the Grand Alliance. But in his view of European politics Cromwell was misled by the conservative and unspeculative temper of his mind as well as by the strength of his religious enthusiasm. Of the change in the world around him he seems to have discerned nothing. He brought to the Europe of Mazarin simply the hopes and ideas with which all England was thrilling in his youth at the outbreak of the Thirty Years' War. Spain was still to him " the head of the Papal Interest," whether at home or abroad. " The Papists in England," he said to the Parliament of 1656, " have been accounted, ever since I was born, Spaniolized; they never regarded France, or any other Papist state, but Spain only." The old English hatred of Spain, the old English resentment at the shameful part which the nation had been forced to play in the great German struggle by the policy of James and of Charles, lived on in Cromwell, and was only strengthened by the religious enthusiasm which the success of Puritanism had kindled within him. " The Lord Himself," he wrote to his admirals as they sailed to the West Indies, " hath

ntroversy with your enemies; even with that Romish Babylon
which the Spaniard is the great underpropper. In that respect
e fight the Lord's battles." What Sweden had been under
ustavus, England, Cromwell dreamt, might be now—the head of
great Protestant League in the struggle against Catholic aggres-
on. "You have on your shoulders," he said to the Parliament of
54, "the interest of all the Christian people of the world. I wish
may be written on our hearts to be zealous for that interest."
he first step in such a struggle would necessarily be to league the
rotestant powers together, and Cromwell's earliest efforts were
rected to bring the ruinous and indecisive quarrel with Holland
an end. The fierceness of the strife had grown with each engage-
ent; but the hopes of Holland fell with her admiral, Tromp,
ho received a mortal wound at the moment when he had succeeded
forcing the English line; and the skill and energy of his suc-
ssor, De Ruyter, struggled in vain to restore her waning fortunes.
he was saved by the expulsion of the Long Parliament, which
d persisted in its demand of a political union of the two countries;
d the new policy of Cromwell was seen in the conclusion of
eace on a simple pledge from the Dutch to compensate English
erchants for their losses in the war. The peace with Holland
as followed by the conclusion of like treaties with Sweden and
ith Denmark; and on the arrival of a Swedish envoy with offers
a league of friendship, Cromwell endeavoured to bring the Dutch,
e Brandenburgers, and the Danes into the same confederation of
e Protestant powers. His efforts in this direction, though they
ever wholly ceased, were foiled for the moment; but Cromwell
as resolute to kindle again the religious strife which had been
osed by the treaty of Westphalia, and he seized on a quarrel
etween the Duke of Savoy and his Protestant subjects in the
alleys of Piedmont as a means of kindling it. A ruthless massacre
these Vaudois by the Duke's troops had roused deep resentment
roughout England, a resentment which still breathes in the
oblest of Milton's sonnets. While the poet called on God to avenge
is "slaughtered saints whose bones lie scattered on the Alpine
ountains cold," Cromwell was already busy with the work of
rthly vengeance. An English envoy appeared at the Duke's
urt with haughty demands of redress. Their refusal would have
een followed by instant war, for the Protestant Cantons of
witzerland were bribed into promising a force of ten thousand
en for an attack on Savoy; and how far Cromwell expected the
ame to spread was seen in his attitude towards Spain. He had
lready demanded freedom of trade and worship for English
erchants in Spanish America; and a fleet with three thousand
en on board was now secretly dispatched against San Domingo.
As though to announce the outbreak of a world-wide struggle,
lake appeared in the Mediterranean, bombarded Algiers, and
estroyed the fleet with which its pirates had ventured through
he reign of Charles to insult the English coast. The thunder of his

1653
to
1660

1653

1654

1655

1653
to
1660
guns, every Puritan believed, would be heard in the castle of S
Angelo, and Rome itself would have to bow to the greatness
Cromwell. But the vast schemes of the Protector everywhere brok
down. The cool Italian who ruled France, Cardinal Mazarin, foile
his projects in Piedmont by forcing the Duke of Savoy to gra
the English demands. Blake, who had sailed to the Spanish coas
failed to intercept the treasure fleet from America, and the We
Indian expedition was foiled in its descent on San Domingo. I
conquest of Jamaica, important as it really was in breaking throug
the monopoly of the New World in the South which Spain had t
now enjoyed, seemed at the time but a poor result for the va
expenditure of money and blood. The war which the attack o
San Domingo necessarily brought on saw the last and grandest
the triumphs of England's first great admiral. Blake found th

1657
Plata fleet guarded by galleons in the strongly armed harbour
Santa Cruz. He forced an entrance into the harbour, sunk
burnt every ship in it, and worked his fleet out again in the mid
of a gale. His death, as the fleet touched at Plymouth on i
return, alone damped the joy at this great victory. But Cromw
desired triumphs on land as on sea; and his desire threw hi
blindfold into the hands of Mazarin, who was engaged on h
part in the war with Spain which was brought afterwards to a clo
in the Treaty of the Pyrenees. Cromwell's demand of Dunkir
which had long stood in the way of any acceptance of his offers
aid, was at last conceded; and a detachment of the Puritan arm
joined the French troops who were attacking Flanders under th
1658
command of Turenne. Their valour and discipline was shown b
the part they took in the victory of the Dunes, a victory whic
forced the Flemish towns to open their gates to the French, an
gave Dunkirk to Cromwell.

The
Parlia-
ment of
1657
Never had the fame of England stood higher; and yet never ha
any English ruler committed so fatal a blunder as that of Cromw
in aiding the ambition of France. But the errors of his forei
policy were small in comparison with the errors of his policy
home. The government of the Protector had become a simp
tyranny, but it was impossible for him to remain content with t
position of a tyrant. He was as anxious as ever to give a legal bas
to his administration; and he seized on the war as a pretext f
again summoning a Parliament. But he no longer trusted, as
the Parliament of 1654, to perfect freedom of election. The sixt
members sent from Ireland and Scotland were simply nominees
the Government. Its whole influence was exerted to secure t
return of the more conspicuous members of the Council. A
Catholics, and all Royalists who had actually fought for the Kin
were still disqualified from voting. It was calculated that of t
members returned one-half were bound to the Government by ti
Sep.
1656
of profit or place. But Cromwell was still unsatisfied. A certifica
of the Council was required from each member before admission
the House; and a fourth of the whole number returned—o

undred in all, with Haselrig at their head—were by this means
excluded on grounds of disaffection or want of religion. To these
arbitrary acts of violence the House replied only by a course of
singular moderation and wisdom. From the first it disclaimed any
purpose of opposing the Government. One of its earliest acts
provided securities for Cromwell's person, which was threatened
by constant plots of assassination. It supported him in his war
policy, and voted supplies of unprecedented extent for the maintenance of the struggle. It was this attitude of loyalty which gave
force to its steady refusal to sanction the system of tyranny
which had practically placed England under martial law. In his
opening address Cromwell boldly took his stand in support of the
military despotism wielded by the major-generals. " It hath been
more effectual towards the discountenancing of vice and settling
religion than anything done these fifty years. I will abide by it,"
he said, with singular vehemence, " notwithstanding the envy and
slander of foolish men. I could as soon venture my life with it as
with anything I ever undertook. If it were to be done again, I
would do it." But no sooner had a bill been introduced into Parliament to confirm the proceedings of the major-generals than a long
debate showed the temper of the Commons. They had resolved to
acquiesce in the Protectorate, but they were equally resolved to
bring it again to a legal mode of government. This indeed was the
aim of even Cromwell's wiser adherents. " What makes me fear
the passing of this Act," one of them wrote to his son Henry, " is
that thereby His Highness' government will be more founded in
force, and more removed from that natural foundation which the
people in Parliament are desirous to give him, supposing that he
will become more theirs than now he is." The bill was rejected,
and Cromwell bowed to the feeling of the nation by withdrawing
the powers of the major-generals. But the defeat of the tyranny
of the sword was only a step towards a far bolder effort for the
restoration of the power of the law. It was no mere pedantry, still
less was it vulgar flattery, which influenced the Parliament in their
offer to Cromwell of the title of King. The experience of the last
few years had taught the nation the value of the traditional forms
under which its liberties had grown up. A king was limited by
constitutional precedents. " The king's prerogative," it was well
urged, " is under the courts of justice, and is bounded as well as
any acre of land, or anything a man hath." A Protector, on the
other hand, was new in our history, and there were no traditional
means of limiting his power. " The one office being lawful in its
nature," said Glynne, " known to the nation, certain in itself, and
confined and regulated by the law, and the other not so—that was
the great ground why the Parliament did so much insist on this
office and title." Under the name of Monarchy, indeed, the question
really at issue between the party headed by the officers and the
party led by the lawyers in the Commons was that of the restoration of constitutional and legal rule. The proposal was carried by

an overwhelming majority, but a month passed in endless con
sultations between the Parliament and the Protector. His good
sense, his knowledge of the general feeling of the nation, his rea
desire to obtain a settlement which should secure the ends for which
Puritanism had fought, political and religious liberty, broke, i
conference after conference, through a mist of words. But his re
concern throughout was with the temper of the army. To Cromwe
his soldiers were no common swordsmen. They were "godly men
men that will not be beaten down by a worldly and carnal spir
while they keep their integrity;" men in whose general voice h
recognized the voice of God. "They are honest and faithful men,
he urged, "true to the great things of the Government. An
though it really is no part of their goodness to be unwilling t
submit to what a Parliament shall settle over them, yet it is m
duty and conscience to beg of you that there may be no hard thing
put upon them which they cannot swallow. I cannot think Go
would bless an undertaking of anything which would justly an
with cause grieve them." The temper of the army was soon show
Its leaders, with Lambert, Fleetwood, and Desborough at the
head, placed their commands in Cromwell's hands. A petition fro
the officers to Parliament demanded the withdrawal of the propos
to restore the Monarchy, "in the name of the old cause for which
they had bled." Cromwell at once anticipated the coming deba
on this petition, a debate which might have led to an open breac
between the army and the Commons, by a refusal of the Crow
"I cannot undertake this Government," he said, "with that tit
of King; and that is my answer to this great and weighty business

Disappointed as it was, the Parliament with singular self-restrai
turned to other modes of bringing about its purpose. The offer
the Crown had been coupled with the condition of accepting
Constitution, which was a modification of the Instrument
Government adopted by the Parliament of 1654, and this Co
stitution Cromwell emphatically approved. "The things provid
by this Act of Government," he owned, "do secure the liberti
of the people of God as they never before have had them." Wi
a change of the title of King into that of Protector, the Act
Government now became law: and the solemn inauguration
the Protector by the Parliament was a practical acknowledgme
on the part of Cromwell of the illegality of his former rule. In t
name of the Commons the Speaker invested him with a mantle
State, placed the sceptre in his hand, and girt the sword of justi
by his side. By the new Act of Government Cromwell was allow
to name his own successor, but in all after cases the office was
be an elective one. In every other respect the forms of the old
Constitution were carefully restored. Parliament was again
consist of two Houses, the seventy members of "the other House
being named by the Protector. The Commons regained their o
right of exclusively deciding on the qualification of their membe
Parliamentary restrictions were imposed on the choice of membe

the Council, and officers of State or of the army. A fixed revenue was voted to the Protector, and it was provided that no moneys would be raised but by assent of Parliament. Liberty of worship was secured for all but Papists, Prelatists, Socinians, or those who denied the inspiration of the Scriptures; and liberty of conscience was secured for all.

The excluded members were again admitted when the Parlia- Death of Cromwell ment reassembled after an adjournment of six months; and the hasty act of Cromwell in giving his nominees in " the other House " the title of Lords kindled a quarrel which was busily fanned by Haselrig. But while the Houses were busy with their squabble the hand of death was falling on the Protector. He had long been weary of his task. " God knows," he burst out a little time before to the Parliament, " I would have been glad to have lived under my woodside, and to have kept a flock of sheep, rather than to have undertaken this government." And now to the weariness of power was added the weakness and feverish impatience of disease. Vigorous and energetic as his life had seemed, his health was by no means as strong as his will; he had been struck down by intermittent fever in the midst of his triumphs both in Scotland and in Ireland, and during the past year he had suffered from repeated attacks of it. " I have some infirmities upon me," he owned twice over in his speech at the opening of the Parliament; and his feverish irritability was quickened by the public danger. No supplies had been voted, and the pay of the army was heavily in arrear, while its temper grew more and more sullen at the appearance of the new Constitution and the reawakening of the Royalist intrigues. The continuance of the Parliamentary strife threw Cromwell at last, says an observer at this court, " into a rage and passion like unto madness." Summoning his coach, by a sudden impulse, the Protector drove with a few guards to Westminster; and, setting aside the remonstrances of Fleetwood, summoned the two Houses to his presence. " I do dissolve this Parliament," he Feb. 1658 ended a speech of angry rebuke, " and let God be judge between you and me." Fatal as was the error, for the moment all went well. The army was reconciled by the blow levelled at its opponents, and the few murmurers were weeded from its ranks by a careful remodelling. The triumphant officers vowed to stand or fall with his Highness. The danger of a Royalist rising vanished before a host of addresses from the counties. Great news too came from abroad, where victory in Flanders, and the cession of Dunkirk, set the seal on Cromwell's glory. But the fever crept steadily on, and his looks told the tale of death to the Quaker, Fox, who met him riding in Hampton Court Park. " Before I came to him," he says, " as he rode at the head of his Life Guards, I saw and felt a waft of death go forth against him, and when I came to him he looked like a dead man." In the midst of his triumph Cromwell's heart was in fact heavy with the sense of failure. He had no desire to play the tyrant; nor had he any belief in the permanence of a

1653
to
1660

mere tyranny. He had hardly dissolved the Parliament before h
was planning the summons of another, and angry at the oppositi
which his Council offered to the project. " I will take my ov
resolutions," he said gloomily to his household; " I can no long
satisfy myself to sit still, and make myself guilty of the loss of a
the honest party and of the nation itself." But before his pla
could be realized the overtaxed strength of the Protector sudden
gave way. He saw too clearly the chaos into which his dea
would plunge England to be willing to die. " Do not think I sh
die," he burst out with feverish energy to the physicians wl
gathered round him; " say not I have lost my reason! I tell yo
the truth. I know it from better authority than any you can hav
from Galen or Hippocrates. It is the answer of God himself to ou
prayers ! " Prayer indeed rose from every side for his recovery, b
death drew steadily nearer, till even Cromwell felt that his hou
was come. " I would be willing to live," the dying man murmure
" to be further serviceable to God and his people, but my work
done! Yet God will be with his people ! " A storm which tore roo
from houses, and levelled huge trees in every forest, seemed
fitting prelude to the passing away of his mighty spirit. Three day
later, on the third of September, the day which had witnessed h
victories of Worcester and Dunbar, Cromwell quietly breathe
his last.

The
Fall of
Puri-
tanism

So absolute even in death was his sway over the minds of men
that, to the wonder of the excited Royalists, even a doubtfu
nomination on his death-bed was enough to secure the peacefu
succession of his son, Richard Cromwell. Many, in fact, who ha
rejected the authority of his father submitted peaceably to the ne
Protector. Their motives were explained by Baxter, the mos
eminent among the Presbyterian ministers, in the address t
Richard which announced his adhesion. " I observe," he says
" that the nation generally rejoice in your peaceable entrance upo
the Government. Many are persuaded that you have been strangel
kept from participating in any of our late bloody contentions, tha
God might make you the healer of our breaches, and employ yo
in that Temple work which David himself might not be honoure
with, though it was in his mind, because he shed blood abundantl
and made great wars." The new Protector was a weak and worth
less man, but the bulk of the nation were content to be ruled by
one who was at any rate no soldier, no Puritan, and no innovator
Richard was known to be lax and godless in his conduct, and he
was believed to be conservative and even Royalist in heart. The
tide of reaction was felt even in his Council. Their first act was to
throw aside one of the greatest of Cromwell's reforms, and to fal
back in the summons which they issued for the new Parliament on
the old system of election. It was felt far more keenly in the tone
of the new House of Commons. The republicans under Vane,
backed adroitly by the Royalists, fell hotly on Cromwell's system.
The fiercest attack of all came from Sir Ashley Cooper, a Dorset-

re gentleman who had changed sides in the civil war, had fought
the King and then for the Parliament, had been a member of
omwell's Council, and had of late ceased to be a member of it.
s virulent invective on " his Highness of deplorable memory,
o with fraud and force deprived you of your liberty when living
d entailed slavery on you at his death," was followed by an
ually virulent invective against the army. " They have not only
bdued their enemies," said Cooper, " but the masters who raised
d maintained them! They have not only conquered Scotland
d Ireland, but rebellious England too; and there suppressed a
alignant party of magistrates and laws." The army was quick
th its reply. The Council of its officers demanded the appoint-
ent of a soldier as their General in the place of the new Protector,
o had assumed the command. The Commons at once ordered
e dismissal of all officers who refused to engage " not to disturb
interrupt the free meetings of Parliament; " and Richard
dered the Council of Officers to dissolve. Their reply was a
mand for the dissolution of the Parliament, a demand with
hich Richard was forced to comply. The great work of the army
wever was still to secure a settled government, and setting aside
e new Protector, whose weakness was now evident, they resolved
fall back on the Parliament they had expelled from St. Stephen's,
tt which remained the one body that could put forward a legiti-
ate claim to power. Of the one hundred and sixty members who
d continued to sit after the King's death, about ninety returned
their seats, and resumed the administration of affairs. But the
emory of the Expulsion made any trust in or reconciliation with
e army impossible. In spite of Vane's counsels a reform of the
fficers was at once proposed, and though a Royalist rising in
heshire under Sir George Booth threw the disputants for a moment
gether, the struggle revived as the danger passed away. A new
pe indeed filled men's minds. Not only was the nation sick of
ilitary rule, but the army, unconquerable so long as it held
gether, at last showed signs of division; and Haselrig was en-
uraged by the temper of the troops in Scotland and Ireland to
emand the dismissal of Fleetwood and Lambert from their com-
ands. They answered by driving the Parliament again from
Vestminster, and by marching to meet the army under Monk
hich was threatening to advance from Scotland to the South.
egotiation gave Monk time to gather a Convention at Edinburgh,
nd to strengthen himself with money and recruits. Then he
dvanced rapidly to Coldstream, and the cry of " a free Parlia-
ent " ran like fire through the country. Not only Fairfax, who
ppeared in arms in Yorkshire, but the ships on the Thames, and
ie mob which thronged the streets of London caught up the cry;
ie army, thrown into confusion by its own divisions, strove to
heck the tide of feeling by recalling the Commons; and Monk,
ho lavished protestations of loyalty to that assembly, while
e accepted petitions for a " Free Parliament," entered London

1653
to
1660

1659

1660

1653
to
1660

unopposed. From the moment of his entry the restoration of the Stuarts became inevitable. The army, resolute as it still remained for the maintenance of " the Cause," was deceived by Monk's declarations of loyalty to it, and rendered powerless by an adroit dispersion of the troops over the country. At the instigation of Ashley Cooper those who remained of the members who had been excluded from the House of Commons by Pride's Purge again forced their way into Parliament, and at once resolved on a dissolution and the election of a new House of Commons. The new House, which bears the name of the Convention, had hardly taken the solemn League and Covenant which showed its Presbyterian temper, and its leaders had only begun to draw up terms on which a Royal restoration might be assented to, when they found that Monk had betrayed them, and was already in negotiation with the exiled Court. All exaction of terms was now impossible; the Declaration of Breda, in which Charles promised a general pardon, religious toleration, and satisfaction to the army, was received with a burst of national enthusiasm; and the old Constitution was restored by a solemn vote of the Convention, " that according to the ancient and fundamental laws of this Kingdom, the government is, and ought to be, by King, Lords, and Commons." The

May,
1660

vote was hardly passed when Charles landed at Dover, and made his way amidst the shouts of a great multitude to Whitehall. " It is my own fault," laughed the new King, with characteristic irony, " that I had not come back sooner; for I find nobody who does not tell me he has always longed for my return."

Milton

Puritanism, so men believed, had fallen never to rise again. As a political experiment it had ended in utter failure and disgust. As a religious system of national life it brought about the wildest outbreak of moral revolt that England has ever witnessed. And yet Puritanism was far from being dead; it drew indeed a nobler life from its very fall. Nothing aids us better to trace the real course of Puritan influence since the fall of Puritanism than the thought of the two great works which have handed down from one generation to another its highest and noblest spirit. From that time to this the most popular of all religious books has been the Puritan allegory of the " Pilgrim's Progress." The most popular of all English poems has been the Puritan epic of the " Paradise Lost." Milton had been engaged during the civil war in strife with Presbyterians and with Royalists, pleading for civil and religious freedom, for freedom of social life, and freedom of the press. At a later time he became Latin Secretary to the Protector, in spite of a blindness which had been brought on by the intensity of his study. The Restoration found him of all living men the most hateful to the Royalists; for it was his " Defence of the English People " which had justified throughout Europe the execution of the King. Parliament ordered his book to be burnt by the common hangman, he was for a time imprisoned, and even when released he had to live amidst threats of assassination from fanatical Cavaliers. To

he ruin of his cause were added personal misfortunes in the bankruptcy of the scrivener who held the bulk of his property, and in
the Fire of London, which deprived him of much of what was left.
As age drew on, he found himself reduced to comparative poverty,
and driven to sell his library for subsistence. Even among the
sectaries who shared his political opinions Milton stood in religious
opinion alone, for he had gradually severed himself from every
accepted form of faith, had embraced Arianism, and had ceased
to attend at any place of worship. Nor was his home a happy one.
The grace and geniality of his youth disappeared in the drudgery of
a schoolmaster's life and amongst the invectives of controversy.
In age his temper became stern and exacting. His daughters, who
were forced to read to their blind father in languages which they
could not understand, revolted utterly against their bondage. But
solitude and misfortune only brought out into bolder relief Milton's
inner greatness. There was a grand simplicity in the life of his later
years. He listened every morning to a chapter of the Hebrew
Bible, and after musing in silence for a while pursued his studies
till mid-day. Then he took exercise for an hour, played for another
hour on the organ or viol, and renewed his studies. The evening
was spent in converse with visitors and friends. For lonely and
unpopular as Milton was, there was one thing about him which
made his house in Bunhill Fields a place of pilgrimage to the wits
of the Restoration. He was the last of the Elizabethans. He had
possibly seen Shakspere, as on his visits to London after his retirement to Stratford the playwright passed along Bread Street to his
wit combats at the Mermaid. He had been the contemporary of
Webster and Massinger, of Herrick and Crashaw. His "Comus"
and "Arcades" had rivalled the masques of Ben Jonson. It was
with a reverence drawn from thoughts like these that Dryden
looked on the blind poet as he sate, clad in black, in his chamber
hung with rusty green tapestry, his fair brown hair falling as of
old over a calm, serene face that still retained much of its youthful
beauty, his cheeks delicately coloured, his clear grey eyes showing
no trace of their blindness. But famous, whether for good or ill, as
his prose writings had made him, during fifteen years only a few
sonnets had broken his silence as a singer. It was now, in his
blindness and old age, with the cause he loved trodden under foot
by men as vile as the rabble in "Comus," that the genius of Milton
took refuge in the great poem on which through years of silence
his imagination had still been brooding.

　　On his return from his travels in Italy, Milton spoke of himself　The
as musing on "a work not to be raised from the heat of youth or　Paradise
the vapours of wine, like that which flows as waste from the pen　Lost
of some vulgar amourist or the trencher fury of a rhyming parasite,
nor to be obtained by the invocation of Dame Memory and her
Siren daughters; but by devout prayer to that Eternal Spirit who
can enrich with all utterance and knowledge, and sends out his
Seraphim, with the hallowed fire of his altar, to touch and purify

the lips of whom He pleases." His lips were touched at last. Sev
years after the Restoration appeared the " Paradise Lost," a
four years later the " Paradise Regained " and " Samson Agonistes
in the severe grandeur of whose verse we see the poet hims
" fallen," like Samson, " on evil days and evil tongues, with dar
ness and with danger compassed round." But great as the two la
works were, their greatness was eclipsed by that of their pr
decessor. The whole genius of Milton expressed itself in t
" Paradise Lost." The romance, the gorgeous fancy, the dari
imagination which he shared with the Elizabethan poets, the lar
but ordered beauty of form which he had drunk in from t
literature of Greece and Rome, the sublimity of conception, t
loftiness of phrase which he owed to the Bible, blended in th
story " of man's first disobedience, and the fruit of that forbidd
tree, whose mortal taste brought death into the world and all o
woe." It is only when we review the strangely mingled elemen
which make up the poem, that we realize the genius which fuse
them into such a perfect whole. The meagre outline of the Hebre
legend is lost in the splendour and music of Milton's verse. Th
stern idealism of Geneva is clothed in the gorgeous robes of th
Renascence. If we miss something of the free play of Spenser
fancy, and yet more of the imaginative delight in their ow
creations which gives so exquisite a life to the poetry of the ear
dramatists, we find in place of these the noblest example whic
our literature affords of the ordered majesty of classic form. B
it is not with the literary value of the " Paradise Lost " that we a
here concerned. Its historic importance lies in this, that it is th
Epic of Puritanism. Its scheme is the problem with which th
Puritan wrestled in hours of gloom and darkness, the problem
sin and redemption, of the world-wide struggle of evil against goo
The intense moral concentration of the Puritan had given a
almost bodily shape to spiritual abstractions before Milton gav
life and being to the forms of Sin and Death. It was the Purita
tendency to mass into one vast " body of sin " the various form
of human evil, and by the very force of a passionate hatred t
exaggerate their magnitude and their power, to which we owe th
conception of Milton's Satan. The greatness of the Puritan ai
in the long and wavering struggle for justice and law and a high
good; the grandeur of character which the contest develope
the colossal forms of good and evil which moved over its stag
the debates and conspiracies and battles which had been men
life for twenty years; the mighty eloquence and mightier ambitio
which the war had roused into being—all left their mark on th
" Paradise Lost." Whatever was highest and best in the Purita
temper spoke in the nobleness and elevation of the poem, in it
purity of tone, in its grandeur of conception, in its ordered an
equable realization of a great purpose. Even in his boldest flight
Milton is calm and master of himself. His touch is always sur
Whether he passes from Heaven to Hell, or from the council ha

Satan to the sweet conference of Adam and Eve, his tread is
eady and unfaltering. But if the poem expresses the higher
ualities of the Puritan temper, it expresses no less exactly its
efects. Throughout it we feel almost painfully a want of the finer
nd subtler sympathies, of a large and genial humanity, of a sense
spiritual mystery. Dealing as Milton does with subjects the
ost awful and mysterious that poet ever chose, he is never
oubled by the obstinate questionings of invisible things which
unted the imagination of Shakspere. We look in vain for any
schylean background of the vast unknown. "Man's dis-
edience" and the scheme for man's redemption are laid down
clearly and with just as little mystery as in a Puritan discourse.
n topics such as these, even God the Father (to borrow Pope's
eer) "turns a school divine." As in his earlier poems he had
dered and arranged nature, so in the "Paradise Lost" Milton
ders and arranges Heaven and Hell. His mightiest figures, Angel
Archangel, Satan or Belial, stand out colossal but distinct.
here is just as little of the wide sympathy with all that is human
hich is so loveable in Chaucer and Shakspere. On the contrary
e Puritan individuality is nowhere so overpowering as in Milton.
e leaves the stamp of himself deeply graven on all he creates. We
ar his voice in every line of his poem. The cold, severe con-
ption of moral virtue which reigns throughout it, the intellectual
ay in which he paints and regards beauty (for the beauty of Eve
a beauty which no mortal man may love) are Milton's own. We
el his inmost temper in the stoical self-repression which gives
s dignity to his figures. Adam utters no cry of agony when he
driven from Paradise. Satan suffers in a defiant silence. It is
this intense self-concentration that we must attribute the
range deficiency of humour which Milton shared with the
uritans generally, and which here and there breaks the sublimity
his poem with strange slips into the grotesque. But it is above
l to this Puritan deficiency in human sympathy that we must
tribute his wonderful want of dramatic genius. Of the power
hich creates a thousand different characters, which endows each
ith its appropriate act and word, which loses itself in its own
eations, no great poet ever had less.

The poem of Milton was the epic of a fallen cause. The broken
ope, which had seen the Kingdom of the Saints pass like a dream
vay, spoke in its very name. Paradise was lost once more, when
e New Model, which embodied the courage and the hope of Puri-
nism, laid down its arms. In his progress to the capital Charles
assed in review the soldiers assembled on Blackheath. Betrayed
y their general, abandoned by their leaders, surrounded as they
ere by a nation in arms, the gloomy silence of their ranks awed
ven the careless King with a sense of danger. But none of the
ictories of the New Model were so glorious as the victory which
won over itself. Quietly, and without a struggle, as men who
owed to the inscrutable will of God, the farmers and traders who

had dashed Rupert's chivalry to pieces on Naseby field, who had scattered at Worcester the " army of the aliens," and driven into helpless flight the sovereign that now came " to enjoy his own again," who had renewed beyond sea the glories of Cressy and Agincourt, had mastered the Parliament, had brought a King to justice and the block, had given laws to England, and held even Cromwell in awe, became farmers and traders again, and were known among their fellow-men by no other sign than their greater soberness and industry. And, with them, Puritanism laid down the sword. It ceased from the long attempt to build up a kingdom of God by force and violence, and fell back on its truer work of building up a kingdom of righteousness in the hearts and consciences of men. It was from the moment of its seeming fall that its real victory began. As soon as the wild orgy of the Restoration was over, men began to see that nothing that was really worth in the work of Puritanism had been undone. The revels of Whitehall, the scepticism and debauchery of courtiers, the corruption of statesmen, left the mass of Englishmen what Puritanism had made them, serious, earnest, sober in life and conduct, firm in their love of Protestantism and of freedom. In the Revolution of 1688 Puritanism did the work of civil liberty which it had failed to do in that of 1642. It wrought out through Wesley and the revival of the eighteenth century the work of religious reform which its earlier efforts had only thrown back for a hundred years. Slowly but steadily it introduced its own seriousness and purity into English society, English literature, English politics. The whole history of English progress since the Restoration, on its moral and spiritual sides, has been the history of Puritanism.

CHAPTER IX

THE REVOLUTION

Section I.—England and the Revolution

[*Authorities.*—For social conditions, see the diaries of Pepys and Evelyn, and the Restoration Dramatists, with Macaulay's essay. For Bacon, see Spedding, " Life and Letters of Lord Bacon," and the edition of his works. For Hobbes, see his " Leviathan," and Leslie Stephen, History of Eighteenth-Century Thought." For the Royal Society, Sprat, " History of the Royal Society."]

No event ever marked a deeper or a more lasting change in the Modern temper of the English people than the entry of Charles the Second England into Whitehall. With it modern England begins. Influences which had up to this time moulded our history, the theological influence of the Reformation, the monarchical influence of the new kingship, the feudal influence of the Middle Ages, the yet earlier influence of tradition and custom, suddenly lost power over the minds of men. We find ourselves all at once among the great currents of thought and activity which have gone on widening and deepening from that time to this. The England around us is our own England, an England whose chief forces are industry and science, the love of popular freedom and of law, an England which presses steadily forward to a larger social justice and equality, and which tends more and more to bring every custom and tradition, religious, intellectual, and political, to the test of pure reason. Between modern thought, on some at least of its more important sides, and the thought of men before the Restoration there is a great gulf fixed. A political thinker in the present day would find it equally hard to discuss any point of statesmanship with Lord Burleigh or with Oliver Cromwell. He would find no point of contact between their ideas of national life or national welfare, their conception of government or the ends of government, their mode of regarding economical and social questions, and his own. But no gulf of this sort parts us from the men who followed the Restoration. From that time to this, whatever differences there may have been as to practical conclusions drawn from them, there has been a substantial agreement as to the grounds of our political, our social, our intellectual and religious life. Paley would have found no difficulty in understanding Tillotson: Newton and Sir Humphry Davy could have talked without a sense of severance. There would have been nothing to hinder a perfectly clear discussion on government or law between John Locke and Jeremy Bentham. The change from the old England to the new is so startling that

567

The
Puritan
Ideal

we are apt to look on it as a more sudden change than it really was, and the outer aspect of the Restoration does much to strengthen this impression of suddenness. The aim of the Puritan had been to set up a visible Kingdom of God upon earth. He had wrought out his aim by reversing the policy of the Stuarts and the Tudors. From the time of Henry the Eighth to the time of Charles the First, the Church had been looked upon primarily as an instrument for securing, by moral and religious influences, the social and political ends of the State. Under the Commonwealth, the State, in its turn, was regarded primarily as an instrument for securing through its political and social influences the moral and religious ends of the Church. In the Puritan theory, Englishmen were " the Lord's people; " a people dedicated to Him by a solemn Covenant, and whose end as a nation was to carry out His will. For such an end it was needful that rulers, as well as people, should be " godly men." Godliness became necessarily the chief qualification for public employment. The new modelling of the army filled its ranks with " saints." Parliament resolved to employ no man " but such as the House shall be satisfied of his real godliness." The Covenant which bound the nation to God bound it to enforce God's laws even more earnestly than its own. The Bible lay on the table of the House of Commons; and its prohibition of swearing, of drunkenness, of fornication became part of the law of the land. Adultery was made felony without the benefit of clergy. Pictures whose subjects jarred with the new decorum were ordered to be burnt, and statues were chipped ruthlessly into decency. It was in the same temper that Puritanism turned from public life to private. The Covenant bound not the whole nation only, but every individual member of the nation, to " a jealous God," a God jealous of any superstition that robbed him of the worship which was exclusively his due, jealous of the distraction and frivolity which robbed him of the entire devotion of man to his service. The want of poetry, of fancy, in the common Puritan temper condemned half the popular observances of England as superstitions. It was superstitious to keep Christmas, or to deck the house with holly and ivy. It was superstitious to dance round the village maypole. It was flat Popery to eat a mince-pie. The rough sport, the mirth and fun of " merry England," were out of place in an England called with so great a calling. Bull-baiting, bear-baiting, horse-racing, cock-fighting, the village revel, the dance on the village green, were put down with the same indiscriminating severity. The long struggle between the Puritans and the playwrights ended in the closing of every theatre.

The
Revolt
of the
Restora-
tion

The Restoration brought Charles to Whitehall: and in an instant the whole face of England was changed. All that was noblest and best in Puritanism was whirled away with its pettiness and its tyranny in the current of the nation's hate. Religion had been turned into a political and a social tyranny, and it fell with their fall. Godliness became a by-word of scorn; sobriety in dress, in speech, in manners was flouted as a mark of the detested Puritanism. Butler, in his "Hudibras," poured insult on the past with a pedantic buffoonery for which the general hatred, far more than its humour, secured a hearing. Archbishop Sheldon listened to the mock sermon of a Cavalier who held up the Puritan phrase and the Puritan twang to ridicule in his hall at Lambeth. Duelling and raking became the marks of a fine gentleman; and grave divines winked at the follies of "honest fellows," who fought, gambled, swore, drank, and ended a day of debauchery by a night in the gutter. The life of a man of fashion vibrated between frivolity and excess. One of the comedies of the time tells the courtier that "he must dress well, dance well, fence well, have a talent for love letters, an agreeable voice, be amorous and discreet—but not too constant." But to graces such as these the rakes of the Restoration added a shamelessness and a brutality which passes belief. Lord Rochester was a fashionable poet, and the titles of some of his poems are such as no pen of our day could copy. Sir Charles Sedley was a fashionable wit, and the foulness of his words made even the porters of Covent Garden pelt him from the balcony when he ventured to address them. The truest type of the time is the Duke of Buckingham, and the most characteristic event in the Duke's life was a duel in which he consummated his seduction of Lady Shrewsbury by killing her husband, while the Countess in disguise as a page held his horse for him and looked on at the murder. Vicious as the stage was, it only reflected the general vice of the time. The Comedy of the Restoration borrowed everything from the Comedy of France save the poetry, the delicacy, and good taste which veiled its grossness. Seduction, intrigue, brutality, cynicism, debauchery, found fitting expression in dialogue of a studied and deliberate foulness, which even its wit fails to redeem from disgust. Wycherley, the first dramatist of the time, remains the most brutal among all writers for the stage; and nothing gives so damning an impression of his day as the fact that he found actors to repeat his words and audiences to applaud them. In men such as Wycherley Milton found types for the Belial of his great poem, "than whom a spirit more lewd fell not from Heaven, or more gross to love vice for itself." He piques himself on the frankness and "plain dealing" which painted the world as he saw it, a world of brawls and assignations, of orgies at Vauxhall, and fights with the watch, of lies and double-entendres, of knaves and dupes, of men who sold their daughters, and women who cheated their husbands. But the cynicism of Wycherley was no greater than that of the men about him; and in mere love of what was vile, in contempt of virtue and disbelief in purity or honesty, the King himself stood ahead of any of his subjects.

It is easy however to exaggerate the extent of this reaction. So far as we can judge from the memoirs of the time, its more violent forms were practically confined to the capital and the Court. The mass of Englishmen were satisfied with getting back their may-

The Earlier Change

poles and mince-pies; and a large part of the people remained
Puritan in life and belief, though they threw aside many of the
outer characteristics of Puritanism. Nor was the revolution in
feeling as sudden as it seemed. Even if the political strength of
Puritanism had remained unbroken, its social influence must soon
have ceased. The young Englishmen who grew up in the midst of
civil war knew nothing of the bitter tyranny which gave its zeal
and fire to the religion of their fathers. From the social and religious
anarchy around them, from the endless controversies and dis
cussions of the time, they drank in the spirit of scepticism, of
doubt, of free inquiry. If religious enthusiasm had broken the spell
of ecclesiastical tradition, its own extravagance broke the spell of
religious enthusiasm; and the new generation turned in disgust
to try forms of political government and spiritual belief by the
cooler and less fallible test of reason. It is easy to see the rapid
spread of such a tendency even in the families of the leading
Puritans. Neither of Cromwell's sons made any pretensions to
religion. Cromwell himself in his later years felt bitterly that
Puritanism had missed its aim. He saw the country gentleman
alienated from it by the despotism it had brought in its train,
alienated perhaps even more by the appearance of a religious
freedom for which he was unprepared, drifting into a love of the
older Church that he had once opposed. He saw the growth of
a dogged resistance in the people at large. The attempt to secure
spiritual results by material force had failed, as it always fails.
It broke down before the indifference and resentment of the great
mass of the people, of men who were neither lawless nor enthusiasts
but who clung to the older traditions of social order, and whose
humour and good sense revolted alike from the artificial conception
of human life which Puritanism had formed and from its effort
to force such a conception on a people by law. It broke down, too,
before the corruption of the Puritans themselves. It was impossible
to distinguish between the saint and the hypocrite as soon as
godliness became profitable. Ashley Cooper, a sceptic in religion
and a profligate in morals, was among "the loudest bagpipes of
the squeaking train." Even amongst the really earnest Puritans
prosperity disclosed a pride, a worldliness, a selfish hardness which
had been hidden in the hour of persecution. The tone of Cromwell's
later speeches shows his consciousness that the ground was slipping
from under his feet. He no longer dwells on the dream of a Puritan
England, of a nation rising as a whole into a People of God. He
falls back on the phrases of his youth, and the saints become again
a "peculiar people," a remnant, a fragment among the nation at
large. But the influences which were really foiling Cromwell's aim
and forming beneath his eyes the new England from which he
turned in despair, were influences whose power he can hardly have
recognized. Even before the outburst of the Civil War a small
group of theological Latitudinarians had gathered round Lord
Falkland at Great Tew. In the very year when the King's standard

was set up at Nottingham, Hobbes published the first of his works on Government. The last Royalist had only just laid down his arms when the little company who were at a later time to be known as the Royal Society gathered round Wilkins at Oxford. It is in this group of scientific observers that we catch the secret of the coming generation. From the spiritual problems with which it had so long wrestled in vain, England turned at last to the physical world around it, to the observation of its phenomena, to the discovery of the laws which govern them. The pursuit of Physical Science became a passion; and its method of research, by observation, comparison, and experiment, transformed the older methods of inquiry in matters without its pale. In religion, in politics, in the study of man and of nature, not faith but reason, not tradition but inquiry, were to be the watchwords of the coming time. The dead-weight of the past was suddenly rolled away, and the new England heard at last and understood the call of Francis Bacon.

If in our notice of the Elizabethan literature we omitted all mention of Lord Bacon, it is because the scientific influence of Bacon told not on the age of Elizabeth but on the age of the Restoration. "For my name and memory," he said at the close of his life, "I leave it to men's charitable speeches, and to foreign nations, and the next age." It was to the "next age" too that, in spite of the general sense of his wisdom and ability, the scientific method of Bacon really made its first appeal. What belonged to his own time was the poorest and meanest part of him. Francis Bacon was born at the opening of Elizabeth's reign, three years before the birth of Shakspere. He was the younger son of a Lord Keeper, as well as the nephew of Lord Burleigh, and even in boyhood his quickness and sagacity won the favour of the Queen. Elizabeth "delighted much to confer with him, and to prove him with questions: unto which he delivered himself with that gravity and maturity above his years that her Majesty would often term him 'the young Lord Keeper.' " His earlier hopes of Court success, however, were soon dashed to the ground. He was left poor by his father's death; the ill-will of the Cecils barred his advancement with the Queen: and a few years before Shakspere's arrival in London he entered at Gray's Inn, and soon became one of the most successful lawyers of the time. At twenty-three he was a member of the House of Commons, and his judgment and eloquence at once brought him to the front. "The fear of every man that heard him was lest he should make an end," Ben Jonson tells us. The steady growth of his reputation was quickened by the appearance of his "Essays," a work remarkable, not merely for the condensation of its thought and its felicity and exactness of expression, but for the power with which it applied to human life that experimental analysis which Bacon was at a later time to make the key of Science. His fame at once became great at home and abroad, but with this nobler fame Bacon could not content himself. He was conscious of great powers, as well as great aims for the public

Marginal notes:

Lord Bacon

1561

1597

good; and it was a time when such aims could hardly be realized
save through the means of the Crown. But political employment
seemed farther off than ever. At the outset of his career in Parlia
ment he had irritated Elizabeth by a free opposition to her demand
of a subsidy; and though the offence was atoned for by profuse
apologies, and by the cessation of all further resistance to the
policy of the Court, the law offices of the Crown were more than
once refused to him, and it was only after the publication of his
" Essays " that he could obtain some slight promotion as a Queen's
Counsel. The moral weakness which at once disclosed itself is
perhaps the best justification of the Queen in her reluctance—a
reluctance so strangely in contrast with her ordinary course—to
bring the wisest head in her realm to her Council-board. The men
whom Elizabeth employed were for the most part men whose
intellect was directed by a strong sense of public duty. Their
reverence for the Queen, strangely exaggerated as it may seem to us
was guided and controlled by an ardent patriotism and an earnest
sense of religion; and with all their regard for the Royal pre
rogative, they never lost their regard for the law. The grandeur
and originality of Bacon's intellect parted him from men like these
quite as much as the bluntness of his moral perceptions. In politics
as in science, he had little reverence for the past. Law, constitu
tional privileges, or religion, were to him simply means of bringing
about certain ends of good government; and if these ends could
be brought about in shorter fashion he saw only pedantry in
insisting on more cumbrous means. He had great social and political
ideas to realize, the reform and codification of the law, the civiliza
tion of Ireland, the purification of the Church, the union—at a
later time—of Scotland and England, educational projects, projects
of material improvement, and the like; and the direct and shortest
way of realizing these ends was in Bacon's eyes the use of the
power of the Crown. But whatever charm such a conception of the
Royal power might have for her successor, it seems to have had
little charm for Elizabeth; nor was her nature likely to be won by
the servility with which Bacon strove to improve his new oppor
tunity of advancement. Partly, perhaps, from rivalry with the
Cecils, but certainly in great part from his appreciation of Bacon's
power, Lord Essex had steadily backed his efforts after promotion
and his disappointment in them had been alleviated by the Earl's
generous present of an estate worth (in our money) some twelve
thousand pounds. Bacon showed a true friendship for Essex by
dissuading him from the career of opposition which at last brought
him to the block; but every tie of friendship and gratitude was
forgotten when he appeared as Queen's Counsel to support the
charge of treason at the Earl's trial. He aggravated and pressed
home the charge with his whole energy and skill; and accepted a
large gift from the court for his later service in publishing a garbled
account of the " practices and treasons " of his friend. But
Elizabeth still remained cold to his advances; and it was not til

he accession of James that the rays of Royal favour broke slowly
pon him. He became successively Solicitor and Attorney-General;
he year of Shakspere's death saw him called to the Privy Council;
e verified Elizabeth's prediction by becoming Lord Keeper. At
st the goal of his ambition was reached. He had attached himself
o the rising fortunes of Buckingham, and the favour of Buckingham
ade him Lord Chancellor. He was raised to the peerage as Baron
erulam, and created, at a later time, Viscount St. Albans. But
he nobler dreams for which these meaner honours had been sought
scaped his grasp. His projects still remained projects, while Bacon
o retain his hold on office was stooping to a miserable compliance
ith the worst excesses of Buckingham and his Royal master. The
ears during which he held the Chancellorship were the most dis-
raceful years of a disgraceful reign. They saw the execution of
aleigh, the sacrifice of the Palatinate, the exaction of benevolences,
he multiplication of monopolies, the supremacy of Buckingham.
gainst none of the acts of folly and wickedness which distinguished
ames's government did Bacon do more than protest; in some of
he worst, and above all in the attempt to coerce the judges into
rostrating law at the King's feet, he took a personal part. But
en his remonstrances were too much for the young favourite,
ho regarded him as the mere creature of his will. It was in vain
at Bacon flung himself at the Duke's feet, and begged him to
ardon a single instance of opposition to his caprice. A Parliament
as impending, and Buckingham resolved to avert from himself
e storm which was gathering by sacrificing to it his meaner
ependants. To ordinary eyes the Chancellor was at the summit
f human success. Jonson had just sung of him as one "whose
en thread the Fates spin round and full out of their choicest
d their whitest wool," when the storm burst. The great Parlia-
ent of 1620 met after a silence of six disgraceful years, and one
f its first acts was to charge Bacon with corruption in the exercise
f his office. He at once pleaded guilty to the charge. "I do
ainly and ingenuously confess that I am guilty of corruption,
d do renounce all defence." "I beseech your Lordships," he
lded, "to be merciful to a broken reed." The heavy fine imposed
n him was remitted by the Crown; but the Great Seal was taken
om him, and he was declared incapable of holding office in the
ate or of sitting in Parliament.

Bacon's fall restored him to that position of real greatness from
hich his ambition had so long torn him away. "My conceit of his
erson," said Ben Jonson, "was never increased towards him by
s place or honours. But I have and do reverence him for his
eatness that was only proper to himself, in that he seemed to me
er by his work one of the greatest men, and most worthy of
dmiration, that had been in many ages. In his adversity I ever
ayed that God would give him strength: for greatness he could
t want." His intellectual activity was never more conspicuous
an in the last four years of his life. He began a digest of the laws,

1618

The
Novum
Orga-
num

and a " History of England under the Tudors," revised ar
expanded his " Essays," dictated a jest book, and busied himse
with experiments in physics. It was while studying the effect
cold in preventing animal putrefaction that he stopped his coa
to stuff a fowl with snow and caught the fever which ended in h

1626 death. The great work of his life remained a fragment to the las
Even as a boy at College he had expressed his dislike of t
Aristotelean philosophy, as " a philosophy only strong for disput
tions and contentions, but barren of the production of works f
the benefit of the life of man." As a law-student of twenty-one l
sketched in a tract on the " Greatest Birth of Time " the syste
of inductive inquiry he was already prepared to substitute for

1605 At forty-four, after the final disappointment of his political hop
from Elizabeth, the publication of the " Advancement of Lear
ing " marked the first decisive appearance of the new philosoph
The close of this work was, in his own words, " a general a
faithful perambulation of learning, with an inquiry what par
thereof lie fresh and waste, and not improved and converted l
the industry of man; to the end that such a plot, made a
recorded to memory, may both minister light to any public design
tion and also serve to excite voluntary endeavours." It was on
by such a survey, he held, that men could be turned from usele
studies, or ineffectual means of pursuing more useful ones, a
directed to the true end of knowledge as " a rich storehouse f
the glory of the Creator and the relief of man's estate." Two yea
later appeared his " Cogitata et Visa," a first sketch of the " Novu
Organum," which in its complete form was presented to Jam
immediately before Bacon's fall. The year after his fall he p
duced his " Natural and Experimental History." This, with t
" Novum Organum " and the " Advancement of Learning," w
all of his projected " Instauratio Magna " which he was destin
to complete—and even of this portion we have only part of t

1620 last two divisions. The " Ladder of the Understanding," whi
was to have followed these and led up from experience to scien
the " Anticipations," or provisional hypotheses for the inquir
of the new philosophy, and the closing account of " Science
Practice " were left for posterity to bring to completion. " V
may, as we trust," said Bacon, " make no despicable beginnin
The destinies of the human race must complete it, in such a mann
perhaps as men looking only at the present world would not read
conceive. For upon this will depend, not only a speculative goc
but all the fortunes of mankind, and all their power." When
turn from words like these to the actual work which Bacon d
it is hard not to feel a certain disappointment. He did r
thoroughly understand the older philosophy which he attacke
His revolt from the waste of human intelligence which he conceiv
to be owing to the adoption of a false method of investigati
blinded him to the real value of deduction as an instrument
discovery; and he was encouraged in his contempt for it as mu

y his own ignorance of mathematics as by the non-existence in s day of the great deductive sciences of physics and astronomy. or had he a more accurate prevision of the method of modern ience. The inductive process to which he exclusively directed en's attention bore no fruit in Bacon's hands. The "art of vestigating nature" on which he prided himself has proved seless for scientific purposes, and would be rejected by modern vestigators. Where he was on a more correct track he can hardly e regarded as original. "It may be doubted," says Dugald tewart, "whether any one important rule with regard to the ue method of investigation be contained in his works of which no int can be traced in those of his predecessors." Not only indeed id Bacon fail to anticipate the methods of modern science, but e even rejected the great scientific discoveries of his own day. [e set aside with the same scorn the astronomical theory of opernicus and the magnetic investigations of Gilbert, and the ontempt seems to have been fully returned. "The Lord Chan- ellor wrote on science," said Harvey, the discoverer of the irculation of the blood, "like a Lord Chancellor."

In spite however of his inadequate appreciation either of the old hilosophy or the new, the almost unanimous voice of later ages as attributed, and justly attributed, to the "Novum Organum" decisive influence on the development of modern science. If he ailed in revealing the method of experimental research, Bacon as the first to proclaim the existence of a Philosophy of Science, o insist on the unity of knowledge and inquiry throughout the hysical world, to give dignity by the large and noble temper in which he treated them to the petty details of experiment in which cience had to begin, to clear a way for it by setting scornfully side the traditions of the past, to claim for it its true rank and alue, and to point to the enormous results which its culture would ring in increasing the power and happiness of mankind. In one espect his attitude was in the highest degree significant. The age n which he lived was one in which theology was absorbing the ntellectual energy of the world. He was the servant, too, of a king ith whom theological studies superseded all others. But if he owed in all else to James, Bacon would not, like Casaubon, bow n this. He would not even, like Descartes, attempt to transform heology by turning reason into a mode of theological demon- tration. He stood absolutely aloof from it. Though as a politician e did not shrink from dealing with such subjects as Church Reform, e dealt with them simply as matters of civil polity. But from his xhaustive enumeration of the branches of human knowledge he xcluded theology, and theology alone. His method was of itself napplicable to a subject, where the premises were assumed to be ertain, and the results known. His aim was to seek for unknown esults by simple experiment. It was against received authority nd accepted tradition in matters of inquiry that his whole system protested; what he urged was the need of making belief rest strictly on proof, and proof rest on the conclusions drawn from evidence by reason. But in theology—all theologians asserted—reason played but a subordinate part. " If I proceed to treat of it," said Bacon, " I shall step out of the bark of human reason and enter into the ship of the Church. Neither will the stars of philosophy, which have hitherto so nobly shone on us, any longer give us their light." The certainty indeed of conclusions on such subjects was out of harmony with the grandest feature of Bacon's work, his noble confession of the liability of every inquirer to error. It was his especial task to warn men against the " vain shows " of knowledge which had so long hindered any real advance in it, the " idols " of the Tribe, the Den, the Forum, and the Theatre, the errors which spring from the systematizing spirit which pervades all masses of men, or from individual idiosyncrasies, or from the strange power of words and phrases over the mind, or from the traditions of the past. Nor were the claims of theology easily to be reconciled with the position which he was resolute to assign to natural science. " Through all those ages," Bacon says, " wherein men of genius or learning principally or ever moderately flourished the smallest part of human industry has been spent on natural philosophy, though this ought to be esteemed as the great mother of the sciences: for all the rest, if torn from this root, may perhaps be polished and formed for use, but can receive little increase.' It was by the adoption of the method of inductive inquiry which physical science was to make its own, and by basing inquiry on the ground which physical science could supply, that the moral sciences, ethics and politics, could alone make any real advance. " Let none expect any great promotion of the sciences, especially in their effective part, unless natural philosophy be drawn out to particular sciences; and, again, unless these particular sciences be brought back again to natural philosophy. From this defect it is that astronomy, optics, music, many mechanical arts, and (what seems stranger) even moral and civil philosophy and logic rise but little above the foundations, and only skim over the varieties and surfaces of things."

Begin-
nings of
English
Science

It was this lofty conception of the position and destiny of natural science which Bacon was the first to impress upon mankind at large. The age was one in which knowledge, as we have seen, was passing to fields of inquiry which had till then been unknown, in which Kepler and Galileo were creating modern astronomy, in which Descartes was revealing the laws of motion, and Harvey the circulation of the blood. But to the mass of men this great change was all but imperceptible; and it was the energy, the profound conviction, the eloquence of Bacon which first called the attention of mankind as a whole to the power and importance of physical research. It was he who by his lofty faith in the results and victories of the new philosophy nerved its followers to a zeal and confidence equal to his own. It was he who above all gave dignity to the slow and patient processes of investigation, of experiment, of comparison, to the sacrificing of hypothesis to fact, to the single aim after truth, which was to be the law of modern science. But, in England at least, Bacon stood—as we have said—before his age. The beginnings of physical science were more slow and timid there than in any country of Europe. Only two discoveries of any real value came from English research before the Restoration; the first, Gilbert's discovery of terrestrial magnetism in the close of Elizabeth's reign; the next, the great discovery of the circulation of the blood, which was taught by Harvey in the reign of James. But apart from these illustrious names England took little share in the scientific movement of the continent; and her whole energies seemed to be whirled into the vortex of theology and politics by the Civil War. But the war had not reached its end when a little group of students were to be seen in London, men "inquisitive," says one of them, "into natural philosophy and other parts of human learning, and particularly of what hath been called the New Philosophy . . . which from the times of Galileo at Florence, and Sir Francis Bacon (Lord Verulam) in England, hath been much cultivated in Italy, France, Germany, and other parts abroad, as well as with us in England." The strife of the time indeed aided in directing the minds of men to natural inquiries. "To have been always tossing about some theological question," says the first historian of the Royal Society, Bishop Sprat, " would have been to have made that their private diversion, the excess of which they disliked in the public. To have been eternally musing on civil business and the distresses of the country was too melancholy a reflection. It was nature alone which could pleasantly entertain them in that estate." Foremost in the group stood Doctors Wallis and Wilkins, whose removal to Oxford, which had just been reorganized by the Puritan Visitors, divided the little company into two societies. The Oxford society, which was the more important of the two, held its meetings at the lodgings of Dr. Wilkins, who had become Warden of Wadham College, and added to the names of its members that of the eminent mathematician Dr. Ward, and that of the first of English economists, Sir William Petty. " Our business," Wallis tells us, " was (precluding matters of theology and State affairs) to discourse and consider of philosophical inquiries and such as related thereunto, as Physick, Anatomy, Geometry, Astronomy, Navigation, Statics, Magnetics, Chymicks, Mechanicks, and Natural Experiments: with the state of these studies, as then cultivated at home and abroad. We then discoursed of the circulation of the blood, the valves in the *venæ lacteæ*, the lymphatic vessels, the Copernican hypothesis, the nature of comets and new stars, the satellites of Jupiter, the oval shape of Saturn, the spots in the sun and its turning on its own axis, the inequalities and selenography of the moon, the several phases of Venus and Mercury, the improvement of telescopes, the grinding of glasses for that purpose, the weight of air, the possibility or impossibility of vacuities, and nature's

1645

1643

abhorrence thereof, the Torricellian experiment in quicksilver, the descent of heavy bodies and the degree of acceleration therein and divers other things of like nature."

The Royal Society
The other little company of inquirers, who remained in London was at last broken up by the troubles of the Second Protectorate but it was revived at the Restoration by the return to London of the more eminent members of the Oxford group. Science suddenly became the fashion of the day. Charles was himself a fair chemist and took a keen interest in the problems of navigation. The Duke of Buckingham varied his freaks of rhyming, drinking, and fiddling by fits of devotion to his laboratory. Poets like Denham and Cowley, courtiers like Sir Robert Murray and Sir Kenelm Digby, joined the scientific company to which in token of his sympathy

1662
with it the King gave the title of "The Royal Society." The curious glass toys called Prince Rupert's drops recall the scientific inquiries which amused the old age of the great cavalry-leader of the Civil War. Wits and fops crowded to the meetings of the new Society. Statesmen like Lord Somers felt honoured at being chosen its presidents. Its definite establishment marks the opening of a great age of scientific discovery in England. Almost every year of the half-century which followed saw some step made to a wider and truer knowledge. Our first national observatory rose at Greenwich, and modern astronomy began with the long series of astronomical observations which immortalized the name of Flamsteed. His successor, Halley, undertook the investigation of the tides, of comets, and of terrestrial magnetism. Hooke improved the microscope, and gave a fresh impulse to microscopical research. Boyle made the air-pump a means of advancing the science of pneumatics, and became the founder of experimental chemistry. Wilkins pointed forward to the science of philology in his scheme of a universal language. Sydenham introduced a careful observation of nature and facts which changed the whole face of medicine. The physiological researches of Willis first threw light upon the structure of the brain. Woodward was the founder of mineralogy. In his edition of Willoughby's " Ornithology," and in his own " History of Fishes," John Ray was the first to raise zoology to the rank of a science; and the first scientific classification of animals was attempted in his " Synopsis of Quadrupeds." Modern botany began with his " History of Plants," and the researches of an Oxford professor, Robert Morrison; while Grow divided with Malpighi the credit of founding the study of vegetable physiology. But great as some of these names undoubtedly are, they are lost in

1642
the lustre of Isaac Newton. Newton was born at Woolsthorpe in Lincolnshire, on Christmas-day, in the memorable year which saw the outbreak of the Civil War. In the year of the Restoration he entered Cambridge, where the teaching of Isaac Barrow quickened his genius for mathematics, and where the method of Descartes had superseded the older modes of study. From the close of his Cambridge career his life became a series of great physical dis-

veries. At twenty-three he facilitated the calculation of planetary
ovements by his theory of Fluxions. The optical discoveries to **1665**
hich he was led by his experiments with the prism, and which
e partly disclosed in the lectures which he delivered as Mathe-
atical Professor at Cambridge, were embodied in the theory of
ght which he laid before the Royal Society on becoming a Fellow **1671**
it. His discovery of the law of gravitation had been made as
rly as 1666; but the erroneous estimate which was then generally
ceived of the earth's diameter prevented him from disclosing it
r sixteen years; and it was not till the eve of the Revolution
at the " Principia " revealed to the world his new theory of the **1687**
niverse.

It is impossible to do more than indicate, in such a summary as The
e have given, the wonderful activity of directly scientific thought Latitudi-
hich distinguished the age of the Restoration. But the sceptical narians
d experimental temper of mind which this activity disclosed
ld on every phase of the world around it. We see the attempt to
ing religious speculation into harmony with the conclusions of
ason and experience in the school of Latitudinarian theologians
ho sprang from the group of thinkers which gathered on the eve
f the Civil War round Lord Falkland at Great Tew. Whatever
erdict history may pronounce on Falkland's political career, his
ame must ever remain memorable in the history of religious
ought. A new era in English religion began with the speculations
f the men he gathered round him. Their work was above all to
eny the authority of tradition in matters of faith, as Bacon had
enied it in matters of physical research; and to assert in the one
eld as in the other the supremacy of reason as a test of truth. Of
e authority of the Church, its Fathers, and its Councils, John
ales, a Canon of Windsor, and a friend of Laud, said briefly " it is
one." He dismissed with contempt the accepted test of uni-
ersality. " Universality is such a proof of truth as truth itself is
shamed of. The most singular and strongest part of human
uthority is properly in the wisest and the most virtuous, and these,
trow, are not the most universal." William Chillingworth, a man
f larger if not keener mind, had been taught by an early con-
ersion to Catholicism, and by a speedy return, the insecurity of
ny basis for belief but that of private judgment. In his " Religion
f Protestants " he set aside ecclesiastical tradition or Church
uthority as grounds of faith in favour of the Bible, but only of
e Bible as interpreted by the common reason of men. Jeremy
aylor, the most brilliant of English preachers, a sufferer like
hillingworth on the Royalist side during the troubles, and who
as rewarded at the Restoration with the bishopric of Down,
mited even the authority of the Scriptures themselves. Reason
as the one means which Taylor approved of in interpreting the
ible; but the certainty of the conclusions which reason drew
om the Bible varied, as he held, with the conditions of reason
self. In all but the simplest truths of natural religion " we are

not sure not to be deceived." The deduction of points of belief from the words of the Scriptures was attended with all the uncertainty and liability to error which sprang from the infinite variety of human understandings, the difficulties which hinder the discovery of truth, and the influences which divert the mind from accepting or rightly estimating it. It was plain to a mind like Chillingworth's that this denial of authority, this perception of the imperfection of reason in the discovery of absolute truth, struck as directly at the root of Protestant dogmatism, as at the root of Catholic infallibility. "If Protestants are faulty in this matter [of claiming authority] it is for doing it too much and not too little. This presumptuous imposing of the senses of man upon the words of God, of the special senses of man upon the general words of God, and laying them upon men's consciences together under the equal penalty of death and damnation, this vain conceit that we can speak of the things of God better than in the words of God, this deifying our own interpretations and tyrannous enforcing them upon others, this restraining of the word of God from that latitude and generality, and the understandings of men from that liberty wherein Christ and His apostles left them, is and hath been the only foundation of all the schisms of the Church, and that which makes them immortal." In his "Liberty of Prophecying" Jeremy Taylor pleaded the cause of toleration with a weight of argument which hardly required the triumph of the Independents and the shock of Naseby to drive it home. But the freedom of conscience which the Independent founded on the personal communion of each soul with God, the Latitudinarian founded on the weakness of authority and the imperfection of human reason. Taylor pleads even for the Anabaptist and the Romanist. He only gives place to the action of the civil magistrate in "those religions whose principles destroy government," and "those religions—if there be any such—which teach ill life." Hales openly professed that he would quit the Church to-morrow if it required him to believe that all that dissented from it must be damned. Chillingworth denounced persecution in words of fire. "Take away this persecution, burning, cursing, damning of men for not subscribing the words of men as the words of God; require of Christians only to believe Christ and to call no man master but Him; let them leave claiming infallibility that have no title to it, and let them that in their own words disclaim it, disclaim it also in their actions. . . . Protestants are inexcusable if they do offer violence to other men's consciences." From the denunciation of intolerance the Latitudinarians passed easily to the dream of comprehension which had haunted every nobler soul since the "Utopia" of More. Hales based his loyalty to the Church of England on the fact that it was the largest and the most tolerant Church in Christendom. Chillingworth pointed out how many obstacles to comprehension were removed by such a simplification of belief as flowed from a rational theology. Like More, he asked for "such an ordering of the public service of God

s that all who believe the Scripture and live according to it might
ithout scruple or hypocrisy or protestation in any part join in
." Taylor, like Chillingworth, rested his hope of union on the
implification of belief. He saw a probability of error in all the
reeds and confessions adopted by Christian Churches. "Such
odies of confessions and articles," he said, "must do much hurt."
He is rather the schismatic who makes unnecessary and incon-
enient impositions, than he who disobeys them because he cannot
o otherwise without violating his conscience." The Apostles'
reed in its literal meaning seemed to him the one term of Christian
nion which the Church had any right to impose.

With the Restoration the Latitudinarians came at once to the
ront. They were soon distinguished from both Puritans and High
hurchmen by their opposition to dogma, by their preference of
eason to tradition whether of the Bible or the Church, by their
asing religion on a natural theology, by their aiming at rightness
f life rather than at correctness of opinion, by their advocacy of
oleration and comprehension as the grounds of Christian unity.
hillingworth and Taylor found successors in the restless elo-
ense of Burnet, the enlightened piety of Tillotson, and the calm
hilosophy of Bishop Butler. Meanwhile the impulse which such
en were giving to religious speculation was being given to
olitical and social inquiry by a mind of far greater keenness and
ower.

Bacon's favourite secretary was Thomas Hobbes. "He was Hobbes
eloved by his Lordship," Aubrey tells us, "who was wont to have
im walk in his delicate groves, where he did meditate; and when
notion darted into his mind, Mr. Hobbes was presently to write
down. And his Lordship was wont to say that he did it better
han anyone else about him; for that many times when he read
heir notes he scarce understood what they writ, because they
nderstood it not clearly themselves." The long life of Hobbes   1588
overs a memorable space in our history. He was born in the year   to
f the victory over the Armada; he died, at the age of ninety-two,   1679
nly nine years before the Revolution. His ability soon made itself
elt, and in his earlier days he was the secretary of Bacon, and the
iend of Ben Jonson and Lord Herbert of Cherbury. But it was
ot till the age of fifty-four, when he withdrew to France on the   1642
ve of the Great Rebellion, that his speculations were made known
o the world in his treatise "De Cive." He joined the exiled Court
t Paris, and became mathematical tutor to Charles the Second,
hose love and regard for him seems to have been real to the
nd. But his post was soon forfeited by the appearance of his
Leviathan;" he was forbidden to approach the Court, and   1651
eturned to England, where he seems to have acquiesced in the
ule of Cromwell. The Restoration brought him a pension; but his
wo great works were condemned by Parliament, and "Hobbism"
ecame, ere he died, the popular synonym for irreligion and
nmorality. Prejudice of this kind sounded oddly in the case of a

writer who had laid down, as the two things necessary to salvation
Faith in Christ and obedience to the law. But the prejudice sprang
from a true sense of the effect which the Hobbist philosophy must
necessarily have on the current religion and the current notion
of political and social morality. Hobbes was the first great English
writer who dealt with the science of government from the ground
not of tradition, but of reason. It was in his treatment of man in
the stage of human development which he supposed to precede
that of society that he came most roughly into conflict with the
accepted beliefs. Men, in his theory, were by nature equal, and
their only natural relation was a state of war. It was no innate
virtue of man himself which created human society out of the
chaos of warring strengths. Hobbes in fact denied the existence
of the more spiritual sides of man's nature. His hard and narrow
logic dissected every human custom and desire, and reduced even
the most sacred to demonstrations of a prudent selfishness. Friendship was simply a sense of social utility to one another. The so
called laws of nature, such as gratitude or the love of our neighbour
were in fact contrary to the natural passions of man, and powerless
to restrain them. Nor had religion rescued man by the interposi-
tion of a Divine will. Nothing better illustrates the daring with
which the new scepticism was to break through the theological
traditions of the older world than the pitiless logic with which
Hobbes assailed the very theory of revelation. "To say God hath
spoken to man in a dream, is no more than to say man dreamed
that God hath spoken to him." "To say one hath seen a vision
or heard a voice, is to say he hath dreamed between sleeping and
waking." Religion, in fact, was nothing more than "the fear of
invisible powers;" and here, as in all other branches of human
science, knowledge dealt with words and not with things. It was
man himself who for his own profit created society, by laying down
certain of his natural rights and retaining only those of self
preservation. A Covenant between man and man originally created
"that great Leviathan called the Commonwealth or State, which
is but an artificial man, though of greater stature and strength
than the natural, for whose protection and defence it was intended.
The fiction of such an "original contract" has long been dismissed
from political speculation, but its effect at the time of its first
appearance was immense. Its almost universal acceptance put an
end to the religious and patriarchal theories of society, on which
Kingship had till now founded its claim of a Divine right to
authority which no subject might question. But if Hobbes destroyed
the old ground of Royal despotism, he laid a new and a firmer one.
To create a society at all, he held that the whole body of the
governed must have resigned all rights save that of self-preserva-
tion into the hands of a single ruler, who was the representative of
all. Such a ruler was absolute, for to make terms with him implied
a man making terms with himself. The transfer of rights was
inalienable, and after generations were as much bound by it as

he generation which made the transfer. As the head of the whole
ody, the ruler judged every question, settled the laws of civil
ustice or injustice, or decided between religion and superstition.
Iis was a Divine Right, and the only Divine Right, because in
im were absorbed all the rights of each of his subjects. It was not
n any constitutional check that Hobbes looked for the prevention
f tyranny, but in the common education and enlightenment as
o their real end and the best mode of reaching it on the part of
oth subjects and Prince. And the real end of both was the weal
f the Commonwealth at large. It was in laying boldly down this
nd of government, as well as in the basis of contract on which he
nade government repose, that Hobbes really influenced all later
olitics. Locke, like his master, derived political authority from
he consent of the governed, and adopted the common weal as its
nd. But in the theory of Locke the people remain passively in
ossession of the power which they have delegated to the Prince,
nd have the right to withdraw it if it be used for purposes incon-
istent with the end which society was formed to promote. To the
rigin of all power in the people, and the end of all power for the
eople's good—the two great doctrines of Hobbes—Locke added
he right of resistance, the responsibility of princes to their subjects
or a due execution of their trust, and the supremacy of legislative
ssemblies as the voice of the people itself. It was in this modified
nd enlarged form that the new political philosophy revealed itself
n the Revolution of 1688.

Section II.—The Restoration, 1660—1667

[*Authorities.*—For Clarendon's ministry, see his Life. For the period
n general, see Burnet, " History of his Own Time," with Foxcroft's
upplement ; Clarke, " Life of James II. "; Macpherson, " Original
'apers "; the diaries of Pepys and Evelyn; Temple's Works; and
he works of Andrew Marvel. The " Parliamentary History " and the
alendar of State Papers, Domestic (to 1676) must be added. Among
nodern historians, Ranke, " History of England," is the most important;
ee also Hallam, " Constitutional History "; Osmund Airy, " Charles
I."; and Macaulay's " Essays." For the Nonconformists, see Baxter's
Autobiography "; Bunyan's works ; and Hutton's volume in Hunt
nd Stephens, " History of the English Church." For documents, see
obertson, " Select Statutes, Cases, and Documents."]

It is only by a survey of the larger tendencies of English thought   The
hat we can understand the course of English history in the years   Restora-
hich followed the Restoration. When Charles the Second entered   tion
Vhitehall, the work of the Long Parliament seemed undone. Not
nly was the Monarchy restored, but it was restored without
estriction or condition; and of the two great influences which had
itherto served as checks on its power, the first, that of Puritanism,
ad become hateful to the nation at large, while the second, the
radition of constitutional liberty, was discredited by the issue of

the Civil War. But amidst all the tumult of demonstrative loyalty
the great " revolution of the seventeenth century," as it has justly
been styled, went steadily on. The supreme power was gradually
transferred from the Crown to the House of Commons. Step by
step, Parliament drew nearer to a solution of the political problem
which had so long foiled its efforts, the problem how to make it
will the law of administrative action without itself undertaking
the task of administration. It is only by carefully fixing our eye
on this transfer of power, and by noting the successive steps toward
its realization, that we can understand the complex history of the
Restoration and the Revolution.

The first acts of the new Government showed a sense that, loyal
as was the temper of the nation, its loyalty was by no means the
blind devotion of the Cavalier. The chief part in the Restoration
had in fact been played by the Presbyterians; and the Presbyterians were still powerful from their exclusive possession of the
magistracy and all local authority. The first ministry, therefore,
which Charles ventured to form, bore on it the marks of a compromise. Its most influential member was Sir Edward Hyde, the
adviser of the King during his exile, who now became Earl of
Clarendon and Lord Chancellor. Lord Southampton, a steady
Royalist, accepted the post of Lord Treasurer; and the devotion
of Ormond was rewarded with a dukedom and the dignity of Lord
Steward. But the Presbyterian interest was even more powerfully
represented. Monk remained Lord-General with the title of Duke
of Albemarle. The King's brother, James, Duke of York, was
made Lord Admiral; but the administration of the fleet was
virtually in the hands of one of Cromwell's followers, Montagu,
the new Earl of Sandwich. Lord Saye and Sele was made Lord
Privy Seal. Sir Ashley Cooper was soon rewarded for his services
by a barony and the office of Chancellor of the Exchequer. Of the
two Secretaries of State, the one, Nicholas, was a devoted Royalist,
the other, Morice, was a steady Presbyterian. Of the thirty
members of the Privy Council, twelve had borne arms against the
King. It was clear that such a ministry was hardly likely to lend
itself to a mere policy of reaction; and even its most Royalist
members, Clarendon and Southampton, were Royalists of a
constitutional type.

The
Conven-
tion
The policy of the new Government, therefore, fell fairly in with
the temper of the Convention, which, after declaring itself a Parliament, proceeded to consider the measures which were requisite for
a settlement of the nation. The Convention had been chosen under
the ordinances which excluded Royalist " Malignants " from the
right of voting; and the bulk of its members were men of Presbyterian sympathies, loyalist to the core, but as averse to despotism
as the Long Parliament itself. In its earlier days a member who
asserted that those who had fought against the King were as guilty
as those who cut off his head was sternly rebuked from the Chair.
The first measure which was undertaken by the House, the Bill of

Indemnity and Oblivion for all offences committed during the recent troubles, showed at once the moderate character of the Commons. In the punishment of the Regicides indeed, a Presbyterian might well be as zealous as a Cavalier. In spite of a Proclamation he had issued in the first days of his return, in which mercy was virtually promised to all the judges of the late King who surrendered themselves to justice, Charles pressed for revenge on those whom he regarded as his father's murderers, and the Lords went hotly with the King. It is to the credit of the Commons that they steadily resisted the cry for blood. By the original provisions of the Bill of Oblivion and Indemnity only seven of the living Regicides were excluded from pardon; and though the rise of Royalist fervour during the three months in which the bill was under discussion forced the House in the end to leave almost all to the course of justice, the requirement of a special Act of Parliament for the execution of those who had surrendered under the Proclamation protected the lives of most of them. Twenty-eight of the King's Judges were in the end arraigned at the bar, but only thirteen were executed, and only one of these, General Harrison, had played any conspicuous part in the rebellion. Twenty others, who had been prominent in what were now called " the troubles " of the past twenty years, were declared incapable of holding office under the State: and by an unjustifiable clause which was introduced into the Act before its final adoption, Sir Harry Vane and General Lambert, though they had taken no part in the King's death, were specially exempted from the general pardon. In dealing with the questions of property which arose from the confiscations and transfers of estates during the Civil Wars the Convention met yet greater difficulties. No opposition was made to the resumption of all Crown-lands by the State, but the Convention desired to protect the rights of those who had purchased Church property, and of those who were in actual possession of private estates which had been confiscated by the Long Parliament, and by the government which succeeded it. The bills however which they prepared for this purpose were delayed by the artifices of Hyde; and at the close of the session the bishops and the evicted Royalists quietly re-entered into the occupation of their old possessions. The Royalists indeed were far from being satisfied with this summary confiscation. Fines and sequestrations had impoverished all the steady adherents of the Royal cause, and had driven many of them to forced sales of their estates; and a demand was made for compensation for their losses and the cancelling of such sales. Without such provisions, said the frenzied Cavaliers, the bill would be " a Bill of Indemnity for the King's enemies, and of Oblivion for his friends." But here the Convention stood firm. All transfers of property by sale were recognized as valid, and all claims of compensation for losses by sequestration were barred by the Act. From the settlement of the nation the Convention passed to the settlement of the relations between the nation and the

Crown. So far was the constitutional work of the Long Parliament from being undone, that its more important measures were silently accepted as the base of future government. Not a voice demanded the restoration of the Star Chamber, or of monopolies, or of the Court of High Commission; no one disputed the justice of the condemnation of Ship-money, or the assertion of the sole right of Parliament to grant supplies to the Crown. The Militia, indeed, was placed in the King's hands; but the army was disbanded, though Charles was permitted to keep a few regiments for his guard. The revenue was fixed at £1,200,000; and this sum was granted to the King for life, a grant which might have been perilous for freedom had not the taxes provided to supply the sum fallen constantly below this estimate, while the current expenses of the Crown, even in time of peace, greatly exceeded it. But even for this grant a heavy price was exacted. Though the rights of the Crown over lands held, as the bulk of English estates were held, in military tenure, had ceased to be of any great pecuniary value, they were indirectly a source of considerable power. The right of wardship and of marriage, above all, enabled the sovereign to exercise a galling pressure on every landed proprietor in his social and domestic concerns. Under Elizabeth, the right of wardship had been used to secure the education of all Catholic minors in the Protestant faith; and under James and his successor minors and heiresses had been granted to Court favourites or sold in open market to the highest bidder. But the real value of these rights to the Crown lay in the political pressure which it was able to exert through them on the country gentry. A squire was naturally eager to buy the good will of a sovereign who might soon be the guardian of his daughter and the administrator of his estate. But the same motives which made the Crown cling to this prerogative made the Parliament anxious to do away with it. Its efforts to bring this about under James the First had been foiled by the King's stubborn resistance; but the long interruption of these rights during the wars made their revival almost impossible at the Restoration, and one of the first acts therefore of the Convention was to free the country gentry by abolishing the claims of the Crown to reliefs and wardship, purveyance, and pre-emption, and by the conversion of lands held till then in chivalry into lands held in common socage. In lieu of his rights, Charles accepted a grant of £100,000 a year; a sum which it was originally purposed to raise by a tax on the lands thus exempted from feudal exactions; but which was provided for in the end, with less justice, by a general excise.

The Cavalier Parliament Successful as the Convention had been in effecting the settlement of political matters, it failed in bringing about a settlement of the Church. In his proclamation from Breda, Charles had promised to respect liberty of conscience, and to assent to any Acts of Parliament which should be presented to him for its security. The Convention was in the main Presbyterian; but it soon became plain that the continuance of a purely Presbyterian system was im possible. " The generality of the people," wrote a shrewd Scotch observer from London, " are doting after Prelacy and the Service-book." The Convention, however, still hoped for some modified form of Episcopalian government which would enable the bulk of the Puritan party to remain within the Church. A large part of the existing clergy, indeed, were Independents, and for these no compromise with Episcopacy was possible: but the greater number were moderate Presbyterians, who were ready " for fear of worse " to submit to such a plan of Church government as Archbishop Usher had proposed, a plan in which the bishop was only the president of a diocesan board of presbyters, and to accept the Liturgy with a few amendments and the omission of the " super-stitious practices." It was to a compromise of this kind that the King himself leant at the beginning, and a Royal proclamation declared his approval of the Puritan demands; but a bill intro-duced by Sir Matthew Hale to turn this proclamation into law was foiled by the opposition of Hyde, and by the promise of a Con-ference. The ejected Episcopalian clergy who still remained alive entered again into their livings; the bishops returned to their sees; and the dissolution of the Convention-Parliament destroyed the last hope of an ecclesiastical compromise. The tide of loyalty had, in fact, been rising fast during its session, and the influence of this was seen in one of the latest resolutions of the Convention itself. The bodies of Cromwell, Bradshaw, and Ireton were torn by its order from their graves and hung on gibbets at Tyburn, while those of Pym and Blake were cast out of Westminster Abbey into St. Margaret's churchyard. But in the elections for the new Parliament the zeal for Church and King swept all hope of modera-tion and compromise before it. The new members were for the most part young men, and " the most profane, swearing fellows," wrote a Puritan, Samuel Pepys, " that ever I heard in my life." The Presbyterians sank to a handful of fifty members. The loyalty of the Parliament far outran that of Clarendon himself. Though it confirmed the acts of the Convention, it could with difficulty be brought to assent to the Act of Indemnity. The Commons pressed for the prosecution of Vane. Vane was protected alike by the spirit of the law and by the King's pledge to the Convention that, even if convicted of treason, he would not suffer him to be brought to the block. But he was now brought to trial on the charge of treason against a King " kept out of his Royal authority by traitors and rebels," and his spirited defence served as an excuse for his execution. " He is too dangerous a man to let live," Charles wrote with characteristic coolness, " if we can safely put him out of the way." But the new members were yet better Churchmen than loyalists. A common suffering had thrown the gentry and the Episcopalian clergy together, and for the first time in our history the country squires were zealous for the Church. At the opening of their session they ordered every member to receive the communion, and the League and Covenant to be solemnly burnt by the common

1660
to
1667

hangman in Palace Yard. The bishops were restored to their seats in the House of Lords. The conference at the Savoy between the Episcopalians and Presbyterians broke up in anger, and the few alterations made in the Liturgy were made with a view to disgust rather than to conciliate the Puritan party. The strongholds of this party were the corporations of the boroughs; and an attempt was made to drive them from these by a severe Corporation Act, which required a reception of the communion according to the rites of the Anglican Church, a renunciation of the League and Covenant, and a declaration that it was unlawful on any grounds to take up arms against the King, before admission to municipal offices. A more deadly blow was dealt at the Puritans in the renewal of the Act of Uniformity. Not only was the use of the Prayer-book, and the Prayer-book only, enforced in all public worship, but an unfeigned consent and assent was demanded from every minister of the Church to all which was contained in it; while, for the first time since the Reformation, all orders save those conferred by the hands of bishops were legally disallowed. It was in vain that Ashley opposed the bill fiercely in the Lords, and that even Clarendon, who felt that the King's word was at stake, pressed for the insertion of clauses enabling the Crown to grant dispensations from its provisions. Charles, whose aim was to procure a toleration for the Catholics by allowing the Presbyterians to feel the pressure of persecution, assented to the bill while he promised to suspend its execution by the exercise of his prerogative.

St. Bartholomew's Day 1662

The bishops however were resolute to enforce the law; and on St. Bartholomew's day, the last day allowed for compliance with its requirements, nearly two thousand rectors and vicars, or about a fifth of the English clergy, were driven from their parishes as Nonconformists. No such sweeping change in the religious aspect of the Church had ever been seen before. The changes of the Reformation had been brought about with little change in the clergy itself. Even the severities of the High Commission under Elizabeth ended in the expulsion of a few hundreds. If Laud had gone zealously to work in emptying Puritan pulpits, his zeal had been to a great extent foiled by the restrictions of the law and by the growth of Puritan sentiment in the clergy as a whole. A far wider change had been brought about by the Civil War; but the change had been gradual, and had been wrought for the most part on political or moral rather than on religious grounds. The parsons expelled were expelled as royalists or as unfitted for their office by idleness or vice or inability to preach. The change wrought by St. Bartholomew's day was a distinctly religious change, and it was a change which in its suddenness and completeness stood utterly alone. The rectors and vicars who were driven out were the most learned and the most active of their order. The bulk of the great livings throughout the country were in their hands. They stood at the head of the London clergy, as the London clergy stood in general repute at the head of their class throughout

England. They occupied the higher posts at the two Universities. No English divine, save Jeremy Taylor, rivalled Howe as a preacher. No parson was so renowned a controversialist, or so indefatigable a parish priest, as Baxter. And behind these men stood a fifth of the whole body of the clergy, men whose zeal and labour had diffused throughout the country a greater appearance of piety and religion than it had ever displayed before. But the expulsion of these men was far more to the Church of England than the loss of their individual services. It was the definite expulsion of a great party which from the time of the Reformation had played the most active and popular part in the life of the Church. It was the close of an effort which had been going on ever since Elizabeth's accession to bring the English Communion into closer relations with the Reformed Communions of the Continent, and into greater harmony with the religious instincts of the nation at large. The Church of England stood from that moment isolated and alone among all the churches of the Christian world. The Reformation had severed it irretrievably from those which still clung to the obedience of the Papacy. By its rejection of all but episcopal orders, the Act of Uniformity severed it as irretrievably from the general body of the Protestant Churches, whether Lutheran or Reformed. And while thus cut off from all healthy religious communion with the world without, it sank into immobility within. With the expulsion of the Puritan clergy, all change, all efforts after reform, all national development, suddenly stopped. From that time to this the Episcopal Church has been unable to meet the varying spiritual needs of its adherents by any modification of its government or its worship. It stands alone among all the religious bodies of Western Christendom in its failure through two hundred years to devise a single new service of prayer or of praise. But if the issues of St. Bartholomew's day have been harmful to the spiritual life of the English Church, they have been in the highest degree advantageous to the cause of religious liberty. At the Restoration religious freedom seemed again to have been lost. Only the Independents and a few despised sects, such as the Quakers, upheld the right of every man to worship God according to the bidding of his own conscience. The great bulk of the Puritan party, with the Presbyterians at its head, were at one with their opponents in desiring a uniformity of worship, if not of belief, throughout the land; and, had the two great parties within the Church held together, their weight would have been almost irresistible. Fortunately the great severance of St. Bartholomew's day drove out the Presbyterians from the Church to which they clung, and forced them into a general union with sects which they had hated till then almost as bitterly as the bishops themselves. A common persecution soon blended the Nonconformists into one. Persecution broke down before the numbers, the wealth, and the political weight of the new sectarians; and the Church, for the first time in its history, found itself confronted with an organized

**1660
to
1667**

body of Dissenters without its pale. The impossibility of crushing such a body as this wrested from English statesmen the first legal recognition of freedom of worship in the Toleration Act; their rapid growth in later times has by degrees stripped the Church of almost all the exclusive privileges which it enjoyed as a religious body, and now threatens what remains of its official connection with the State. With these remoter consequences however we are not as yet concerned. It is enough to note here that with the Act of Uniformity and the expulsion of the Puritan clergy a new element in our religious and political history, the element of Dissent, the influence of the Nonconformist churches, comes first into play.

The Persecution

The immediate effect of their expulsion on the Puritans was to beget a feeling of despair. Many were for retiring to Holland others proposed flight to New England and the American colonies Charles however was anxious to make use of them in carrying out his schemes for a toleration of the Catholics; and fresh hopes of protection were raised by a Royal proclamation, which expressed the King's wish to exempt from the penalties of the Act " those who, living peaceably, do not conform themselves thereunto, through scruple and tenderness of misguided conscience, but modestly and without scandal perform their devotions in their own way." Charles promised to bring a measure to this effect before Parliament in its coming session. The bill which was thus introduced would have enabled the King to dispense, not only with the provisions of the Act of Uniformity, but with all laws and statutes enforcing conformity in worship, or imposing religious

1663

tests. Its aim was so obvious, and its unconstitutional character so clear, that even the Nonconformists withdrew from supporting it; and Ashley alone among the Puritan leaders undertook its defence. The threatening attitude of the Commons soon forced the King to withdraw it; but the temper of the Church was now roused, and the hatred of the Nonconformists was embittered by

1664

suspicions of the King's secret designs. The Houses extorted from Charles a proclamation for the banishment of Roman Catholic priests; and by their Conventicle Act of the following year, they punished by fine, imprisonment, and transportation, all meetings of more than five persons for any religious worship but that of the

1665

Common Prayer. The Five Mile Act, a year later, completed the code of persecution. By its provisions, every clergyman who had been driven out by the Act of Uniformity was called on to swear that he held it unlawful under any pretext to take up arms against the King, and that he would at no time " endeavour any alteration of government in Church or State." In case of refusal, he was forbidden to go within five miles of any borough, or of any place where he had been wont to minister. As the main body of the Non conformists belonged to the city and trading classes, the effect of this measure was to rob them of any religious teaching at all. But the tide of religious intolerance was now slowly ebbing, and a motion to impose the oath of the Five Mile Act on every person the nation was rejected in the same session by a majority of six. The sufferings of the Nonconformists indeed could hardly fail to tell on the sympathies of the people. The thirst for revenge, which had been roused by the tyranny of the Presbyterians in their hour of triumph, was satisfied by their humiliation in the hour of defeat. The sight of pious and learned clergymen driven from their homes and their flocks, of religious meetings broken up by the constables, of preachers set side by side with thieves and outcasts in the dock, of gaols crammed with honest enthusiasts whose piety was their only crime, pleaded more eloquently for toleration than all the reasoning in the world. We have a clue to the extent of the persecution from what we know to have been its effect on a single sect. The Quakers had excited alarm by their extravagances of manner, their refusal to bear arms or to take oaths; and a special act was passed for their repression. They were one of the smallest of the Nonconformist bodies, but more than four thousand were soon in prison, and of these five hundred were imprisoned in London alone. Large as it was, the number rapidly increased: and the King's Declaration of Indulgence, twelve years later, set free twelve thousand Quakers who had found their way to the gaols. Of the sufferings of the expelled clergy one of their own number, Richard Baxter, has given us an account. " Many hundreds of these, with their wives and children, had neither house nor bread. . . Their congregations had enough to do, besides a small maintenance, to help them out of prisons, or to maintain them there. Though they were as frugal as possible they could hardly live; some lived on little more than brown bread and water, many had but eight or ten pounds a year to maintain a family, so that a piece of flesh has not come to one of their tables in six weeks' time; their allowance could scarce afford them bread and cheese. One went to plow six days and preached on the Lord's Day. Another was forced to cut tobacco for a livelihood." But poverty was the least of their sufferings. They were jeered at by the players. They were hooted through the streets by the mob. " Many of the ministers, being afraid to lay down their ministry after they had been ordained to it, preached to such as would hear them in fields and private houses, till they were apprehended and cast into gaols, where many of them perished." They were excommunicated in the Bishops' Court, or fined for non-attendance at church; and a crowd of informers grew up who made a trade of detecting the meetings they held at midnight. Alleyn, the author of the well-known " Alarm to the Unconverted," died at thirty-six from the sufferings he endured in Taunton Gaol. Vavasour Powell, the apostle of Wales, spent the eleven years which followed the Restoration in prisons at Shrewsbury, Southsea, and Cardiff, till he perished in the Fleet. John Bunyan was for twelve years a prisoner at Bedford.

We have already seen the atmosphere of excited feeling in which the youth of Bunyan had been spent. From his childhood he heard

1660 to 1667

The Pilgrim's Progress

1645

1653

heavenly voices, and saw visions of heaven; from his childhood too, he had been wrestling with an overpowering sense of sin, which sickness and repeated escapes from death did much as he grew up to deepen. But in spite of his self-reproaches his life was a religious one; and the purity and sobriety of his youth was shown by his admission at seventeen into the ranks of the " New Model." Two years later the war was over, and Bunyan found himself married before he was twenty to a " godly " wife, as young and as poor as himself. So poor were the young couple that they could hardly muster a spoon and a plate between them; and the poverty of their home deepened, perhaps, the gloom of the young tinker's restlessness and religious depression. His wife did what she could to comfort him, teaching him again to read and write, for he had forgotten his school-learning, and reading with him in two little " godly " books which formed his library. But the darkness only gathered the thicker round his imaginative soul. " I walked," he tells us of this time, " to a neighbouring town; and sate down upon a settle in the street, and fell into a very deep pause about the most fearful state my sin had brought me to; and after long musing lifted up my head; but methought I saw as if the sun that shineth in the heavens did grudge to give me light; and as if the very stones in the street and tiles upon the houses did band themselves against me. Methought that they all combined together to banish me out of the world. I was abhorred of them, and wept to dwell among them, because I had sinned against the Saviour. Oh, how happy now was every creature over I! for they stood fast and kept their station. But I was gone and lost." At last, after more than two years of this struggle, the darkness broke. Bunyan felt himself " converted," and freed from the burthen of his sin. He joined a Baptist church at Bedford, and a few years later he became famous as a preacher. As he held no formal post of minister in the congregation, his preaching even under the Protectorate was illegal and " gave great offence," he tells us, " to the doctors and priests of that county," but he persisted with little real molestation until the Restoration. Six months after the King's return he was committed to Bedford Gaol on a charge of preaching in unlicensed conventicles; and his refusal to promise to abstain from preaching kept him there eleven years. The gaol was crowded with prisoners like himself, and amongst them he continued his ministry, supporting himself by making tagged thread laces, and finding some comfort in the Bible, the " Book of Martyrs," and the writing materials which he was suffered to have with him in his prison. But he was in the prime of life; his age was thirty-two when he was imprisoned; and the inactivity and severance from his wife and little children was hard to bear. " The parting with my wife and poor children," he says in words of simple pathos, " hath often been to me in this place as the pulling of the flesh from the bones; and that not only because I am somewhat too fond of those great mercies, but also because I should have often brought to my mind the many hardships, miseries, and wants that my poor family was like to meet with should I be taken from them, especially my poor blind child, who lay nearer to my heart than all besides. Oh, the thoughts of the hardships I thought my poor blind one might go under would break my heart to pieces. ' Poor child,' thought I, ' what sorrow art thou like to have for thy portion in this world! Thou must be beaten, must beg, suffer hunger, cold, nakedness, and a thousand calamities, though I cannot now endure the wind should blow upon thee.' " But suffering could not break his purpose, and Bunyan found compensation for the narrow bounds of his prison in the wonderful activity of his pen. Tracts, controversial treatises, poems, meditations, his " Grace Abounding," and his " Holy City," followed each other in quick succession. It was in his gaol that he wrote the first and greatest part of his " Pilgrim's Progress." In no book do we see more clearly the new imaginative force which had been given to the common life of Englishmen by their study of the Bible. Its English is the simplest and the homeliest English which has ever been used by any great English writer; but it is the English of the Bible. The images of the " Pilgrim's Progress " are the images of prophet and evangelist; it borrows for its tenderer outbursts the very verse of the Song of Songs, and pictures the Heavenly City in the words of the Apocalypse. But so completely has the Bible become Bunyan's life that one feels its phrases as the natural expression of his thoughts. He has lived in the Bible till its words have become his own. He has lived among its visions and voices of heaven till all sense of possible unreality has died away. He tells his tale with such a perfect naturalness that allegories become living things, that the Slough of Despond and Doubting Castle are as real to us as places we see every day, that we know Mr. Legality and Mr. Worldly Wiseman as if we had met them in the street. It is in this amazing reality of impersonation that Bunyan's imaginative genius specially displays itself. But this is far from being his only excellence. In its range, in its directness, in its simple grace, in the ease with which it changes from lively dialogue to dramatic action, from simple pathos to passionate earnestness, in the subtle and delicate fancy which often suffuses its childlike words, in its playful humour, its bold character-painting, in the even and balanced power which passes without effort from the Valley of the Shadow of Death to the land " where the Shining Ones commonly walked, because it was on the borders of heaven," in its sunny kindliness, unbroken by one bitter word, the " Pilgrim's Progress " is among the noblest of English poems. For if Puritanism had first discovered the poetry which contact with the spiritual world awakes in the meanest souls, Bunyan was the first of the Puritans who revealed this poetry to the outer world. The journey of Christian from the City of Destruction to the Heavenly City is simply a record of the life of such a Puritan as Bunyan himself, seen through an imaginative haze of spiritual idealism in which its commonest incidents are heightened and glorified. He is himself the Pilgrim who flies from the City of Destruction, who climbs the hill Difficulty, who faces Apollyon, who sees his loved ones cross the river of Death towards the Heavenly City, and how, because " the hill on which the City was framed was higher than the clouds, they therefore went up through the region of the air, sweetly talking as they went."

The popularity which the " Pilgrim's Progress " enjoyed from the first proves that the religious sympathies of the English people were still mainly Puritan. Before Bunyan's death in 1688 ten editions of the book had already been sold, and though even Cowper hardly dared to quote it for fear of moving a sneer in the polite world of his day, its favour among the middle classes and the poor has grown steadily from its author's day to our own. It is probably the most popular and the most widely known of all English books. But the inner current of the national life had little relation to the outer history of the Restoration. While Bunyan was lying in Bedford Gaol, and the Church was carrying on its bitter persecution of the Nonconformists, England was plunging into a series of humiliations and losses without example in its history. The fatal strife with Holland which had been closed by the wisdom of Cromwell was renewed. The quarrel of the Dutch and English merchants on the Guinea coast, where both sought a monopoly of the trade in gold dust and slaves, was fanned by the ambition of the Duke of York and by the resentment of Charles himself at the insults he had suffered from Holland in his exile into a war. An obstinate battle off Lowestoft ended in a victory for the English fleet; but in a subsequent encounter with De Ruyter off the North Foreland Monk and his fleet were only saved from destruction by the arrival of a reinforcement under Prince Rupert. " They may be killed," said De Witt, " but they cannot be conquered; " and the saying was as true of one side as of the other. A third battle, as hard-fought as its predecessors, ended in the triumph of the English, and their fleet sailed along the coast of Holland, burning ships and towns. But the thought of triumph was soon forgotten in the terrible calamities which fell on the capital. In six months a hundred thousand Londoners died of the Plague which broke out in its crowded streets; and the Plague was followed by a fire, which beginning near Fish Street reduced the whole city to ashes from the Tower to the Temple. Thirteen hundred houses and ninety churches were destroyed. The loss of merchandise and property was beyond count. The Treasury was empty, and neither ships nor forts were manned, when the Dutch fleet appeared in the Nore, advanced unopposed up the Thames to Gravesend, forced the boom which protected the Medway, burnt three men-of-war which lay anchored in the river, and for six weeks sailed proudly along the southern coast, the masters of the Channel.

The
War
with
Holland

1664

1665

1666

1667

Charles appears to have exercised his influence generally rather on the side of moderation than of revenge; the House of Lords was anxious to adopt more severe measures than were actually taken.

Section III.—Charles the Second, 1667—1673

[*Authorities.*—To those mentioned under the previous section may
be added the " Grammont Memoirs," for the court scandal of the
period; Kennet's " Register," and his anonymous " Complete History
of England "; North's " Examen, an answer to Kennet " ; and the
appendices to Dalrymple's " Memoirs." For foreign policy, Mignet,
" Négociations relatives à la Succession d'Espagne," and Lefèvre-
Pontalis, " Jean de Witt." Lingard's " History of England " is specially
valuable for this period; see also Macaulay's " History of England."
Christie, " Life of Shaftesbury," is the most complete biography of that
statesman.]

The thunder of the Dutch guns in the Medway and the Thames Charles
woke England to a bitter sense of its degradation. The dream of the
Second
loyalty was over.   " Everybody now-a-days," Pepys tells us,
" reflect upon Oliver and commend him, what brave things he
did, and made all the neighbour princes fear him."   But Oliver's
successor was coolly watching this shame and discontent of his
people with the one aim of turning it to his own advantage.   To
Charles the Second the degradation of England was only a move
in the political game which he was playing, a game played with so
consummate a secrecy and skill that it deceived not only the
closest observers of his own day but still misleads historians of
ours. What his subjects saw in their King was a pleasant, brown-
faced gentleman playing with his spaniels, or drawing caricatures
of his ministers, or flinging cakes to the water-fowl in the park.
To all outer seeming Charles was the most consummate of idlers.
" He delighted," says one of his courtiers, " in a bewitching kind
of pleasure called sauntering."   The business-like Pepys soon discovered that " the King do mind nothing but pleasures, and hates
the very sight or thoughts of business."   He only laughed when
Tom Killigrew frankly told him that badly as things were going
there was one man whose employment would soon set them right,
" and this is one Charles Stuart, who now spends his time in employing his lips about the Court, and hath no other employment."
That Charles had great natural parts no one doubted. In his earlier
days of defeat and danger he showed a cool courage and presence of
mind which never failed him in the many perilous moments of his
reign.   His temper was pleasant and social, his manners perfect,
and there was a careless freedom and courtesy in his address which
won over everybody who came into his presence.   His education
indeed had been so grossly neglected that he could hardly read a
plain Latin book; but his natural quickness and intelligence
showed itself in his pursuit of chemistry and anatomy, and in the
interest he showed in the scientific inquiries of the Royal Society.
Like Peter the Great, his favourite study was that of naval archi-
tecture, and he piqued himself on being a clever ship-builder. He
had some little love too for art and poetry, and a taste for music.
But his shrewdness and vivacity showed itself most in his endless

talk. He was fond of telling stories, and he told them with a good deal of grace and humour. His humour indeed never forsook him: even on his death-bed he turned to the weeping courtiers around and whispered an apology for having been so unconscionable a time in dying. He held his own fairly with the wits of his Court, and bandied repartees on equal terms with Sedley or Buckingham. Even Rochester in his merciless epigram was forced to own that " Charles never said a foolish thing." He had inherited in fact his grandfather's gift of pithy sayings, and his cynical irony often gave an amusing turn to them. When his brother, the most unpopular man in England, solemnly warned him of plots against his life, Charles laughingly bid him set all fear aside. " They will never kill me, James," he said, " to make you king." But courage and wit and ability seemed to have been bestowed on him in vain. Charles hated business. He gave no sign of ambition. The one thing he seemed in earnest about was sensual pleasure, and he took his pleasure with a cynical shamelessness which roused the disgust even of his shameless courtiers. Mistress followed mistress, and the guilt of a troop of profligate women was blazoned to the world by the gift of titles and estates. The Royal bastards were set amongst English nobles. The Ducal house of Grafton springs from the King's adultery with Barbara Palmer, whom he created Duchess of Cleveland. The Dukes of St. Albans owe their origin to his intrigue with Nell Gwynn, a player and a courtezan. Louise de Querouaille, a mistress sent by France to win him to its interests, became Duchess of Portsmouth, and ancestress of the house of Richmond. An earlier mistress, Lucy Walters, had made him father in younger days of the boy whom he raised to the Dukedom of Monmouth, and to whom the Dukes of Buccleugh trace their line. But Charles was far from being content with these recognized mistresses, or with a single form of self-indulgence. Gambling and drinking helped to fill up the vacant moments when he could no longer toy with his favourites or bet at Newmarket. No thought of remorse or of shame seems ever to have crossed his mind. " He could not think God would make a man miserable," he said once, " only for taking a little pleasure out of the way." From shame indeed he was shielded by his cynical disbelief in human virtue. Virtue he regarded simply as a trick by which clever hypocrites imposed upon fools. Honour among men seemed to him as mere a pretence as chastity among women. Gratitude he had none, for he looked upon self-interest as the only motive of men's actions, and though soldiers had died and women had risked their lives for him, he " loved others as little as he thought they loved him." But if he felt no gratitude for benefits he felt no resentment for wrongs. He was incapable either of love or of hate. The only feeling he retained for his fellow-men was that of an amused contempt.

The King's Policy

It was difficult for Englishmen to believe that any real danger to liberty could come from an idler and a voluptuary such as Charles the Second. But in the very difficulty of believing this lay half the

King's strength. He had in fact no taste whatever for the despotism of the Stuarts who had gone before him. His shrewdness laughed his grandfather's theories of Divine Right down the wind. His indolence made such a personal administration as that which his father delighted in burthensome to him: he was too humorous a man to care for the pomp and show of power, and too good-natured a man to play the tyrant. "He told Lord Essex," Burnet says, "that he did not wish to be like a Grand Signior, with some mutes about him, and bags of bowstrings to strangle men; but he did not think he was a king so long as a company of fellows were looking into his actions, and examining his ministers as well as his accounts." "A king," he thought, "who might be checked, and have his ministers called to an account, was but a king in name." In other words, he had no settled plan of tyranny, but he meant to rule as independently as he could, and from the beginning to the end of his reign there never was a moment when he was not doing something to carry out his aim. But he carried it out in a tentative, irregular fashion which it was as hard to detect as to meet. Whenever there was any strong opposition he gave way. If popular feeling demanded the dismissal of his ministers, he dismissed them. If it protested against his declaration of Indulgence, he recalled it. If it cried for victims in the frenzy of the Popish Plot, he gave it victims till the frenzy was at an end. It was easy for Charles to yield and to wait, and just as easy for him to take up the thread of his purpose again the moment the pressure was over. The one fixed resolve which overrode every other thought in the King's mind was a resolve "not to set out on his travels again." His father had fallen through a quarrel with the two Houses, and Charles was determined to remain on good terms with the Parliament till he was strong enough to pick a quarrel to his profit. He treated the Lords with an easy familiarity which robbed opposition of its seriousness. "Their debates amused him," he said in his indolent way; and he stood chatting before the fire while peer after peer poured invectives on his ministers, and laughed louder than the rest when Shaftesbury directed his coarsest taunts at the barrenness of the Queen. Courtiers were entrusted with the secret "management" of the Commons: obstinate country gentlemen were brought to the Royal closet to kiss the King's hand and listen to the King's pleasant stories of his escape after Worcester; and yet more obstinate country gentlemen were bribed. Where bribes, flattery, and management failed, Charles was content to yield and to wait till his time came again. Meanwhile he went on patiently gathering up what fragments of the old Royal power still survived, and availing himself of whatever new resources offered themselves. If he could not undo what Puritanism had done in England, he could undo its work in Scotland and in Ireland. Before the Civil War these kingdoms had served as useful checks on English liberty, and by simply regarding the Union which the Long Parliament and the Protector had brought about as a nullity in law it was possible they might become checks again. In his undoing the Union Charles was supported by Clarendon and the Constitutional loyalists, partly from sheer abhorrence of changes wrought by their political opponents, and partly from a dread that the Scotch and Irish members would form a party in the English Parliament which would always be at the service of the Crown. In both the lesser kingdoms too a measure which seemed to restore somewhat of their independence was for the moment popular. But the results of this step were quick in developing themselves. In Scotland the Covenant was at once abolished. The new Scotch Parliament at Edinburgh, which soon won the name of the Drunken Parliament, outdid the wildest loyalty of the English Cavaliers by annulling in a single Act all the proceedings of its predecessors during the last eight-and-twenty years. By this measure the whole Church system of Scotland fell legally to the ground. The General Assembly had already been prohibited from meeting by Cromwell; the kirk-sessions and ministers' synods were now suspended. The bishops were again restored to their spiritual pre-eminence, and to their seats in Parliament. An iniquitous trial sent the Earl of Argyle, the only noble strong enough to oppose the Royal will, to the block. The government was entrusted to a knot of profligate statesmen who were directed by Lord Lauderdale, one of the ablest and most unscrupulous of the King's ministers; and their policy was steadily directed to the two purposes of humbling Presbyterianism—as the force which could alone restore Scotland to freedom and enable her to lend aid as before to English liberty in any struggle with the Crown—and of raising a Royal army which might be ready in case of trial to march over the border to the King's support. In Ireland the dissolution of the Union brought back the bishops to their sees; but whatever wish Charles may have had to restore the balance of Catholic and Protestant as a source of power to the Crown was baffled by the obstinate resistance of the Protestant settlers to any plans for redressing the confiscations of Cromwell. Five years of bitter struggle between the dispossessed loyalists and the new occupants left the Protestant ascendency unimpaired; and in spite of a nominal surrender of one-third of the confiscated estates to their old possessors, hardly a sixth of the profitable land in the island remained in Catholic holding. The claims of the Duke of Ormond too made it necessary to leave the government in his hands, and Ormond's loyalty was too moderate and constitutional to lend itself to any of the schemes of absolute rule which under Tyrconnell played so great a part in the next reign. But the severance of the two kingdoms from England was in itself a gain to the Royal authority; and Charles turned quickly to the building up of a Royal army at home. A standing army had become so hateful a thing to the body of the nation, and above all to the Royalists whom the New Model had trodden under foot, that it was impossible to propose its establishment. But in the mind of h the Royal brothers their father's downfall had been owing to want of a disciplined force which would have trampled out the t efforts of national resistance; and while disbanding the New del, Charles availed himself of the alarm created by a mad ng of some Fifth-Monarchy men in London under an old soldier led Venner to retain five thousand horse and foot in his service ler the name of his guards. A body of "gentlemen of quality l veteran soldiers, excellently clad, mounted, and ordered," was is kept ready for service near the Royal person; and in spite the scandal which it aroused the King persisted, steadily but tiously, in gradually increasing its numbers. Twenty years er it had grown to a force of seven thousand foot and one usand seven hundred horse and dragoons at home, with a erve of six fine regiments abroad in the service of the United ovinces.

But Charles was too quick-witted a man to believe, as his brother nes believed, that it was possible to break down English freedom the Royal power or by a few thousand men in arms. It was still s possible by such means to break down, as he wished to break wn, English Protestantism. In heart, whether the story of his unciation of Protestantism during his exile be true or no, he had g ceased to be a Protestant. Whatever religious feeling he had s on the side of Catholicism; he encouraged conversions among courtiers, and the last act of his life was to seek formal admission o the Roman Church. But his feelings were rather political n religious. He saw that despotism in the State could hardly co-st with free inquiry and free action in matters of the conscience, l that government, in his own words, "was a safer and easier ng where the authority was believed infallible and the faith and omission of the people were implicit." The difficulties of a change religion probably seemed the less to him that he had long lived road, where the sight of a people changing its belief with a change its sovereign's faith was not a very rare one. But though he inted much on the dissensions between Protestant Churchmen d Protestant Dissenters, and two years after his accession spatched a secret agent to Rome to arrange a reconciliation with e Papacy, he saw that for any real success in his political or igious aims he must seek resources elsewhere than at home. this moment France was the dominant power in Europe. Its ung King, Lewis the Fourteenth, avowed himself the champion Catholicism and despotism against civil and religious liberty roughout the world. France was the wealthiest of European wers, and her subsidies could free Charles from dependence on s Parliament. Her army was the finest in the world, and French diers could put down any resistance from English patriots. The l of Lewis could alone realize the aims of Charles, and Charles is freed by nature from any shame or reluctance to pay the price ich Lewis demanded for his aid. The price was that of a silent ncurrence in his designs on Spain. Robbed of its chief source of

Charles and France

**1667
to
1673**

wealth by the revolt of the United Provinces and the decay
Flanders, enfeebled within by the persecution of the Inquisiti
by the suppression of civil freedom, and by a ruinous financ
oppression, Spain had not only ceased to threaten Europe b
herself trembled at the threats of France. The aim of Lewis was
rob it of the Low Countries, but the presence of the French
Flanders was equally distasteful to England and to Holland, a
in such a contest Spain was sure of the aid both of these states a
of the Empire. For some years Lewis contented himself w
perfecting his army and preparing by skilful negotiations to ma
such a league of the great powers against him impossible. I
first success in England was in the marriage of the King. Portug
which had only just shaken off the rule of Spain, was rea
dependent upon France; and in accepting the hand of Cathari
of Braganza in spite of the protests of Spain, Charles announced
adhesion to the alliance of Lewis. Already English opinion saw t
danger of such a course, and veered round to the Spanish side
early as 1661 the London mob backed the Spanish ambassador
a street squabble for precedence with the ambassador of Fran
"We do all naturally love the Spanish," says Pepys, " and ha
the French." The sale of Dunkirk, the one result of Cromwe
victories, to France fanned the national irritation to frenzy; a
the war with Holland seemed at one time likely to end in a w
with Lewis. The war was in itself a serious stumbling-block in t
way of his projects. To aid either side was to throw the other
the aid of Austria and Spain, and to build up a league which wou
check France in its aims; and yet the peace which could alo
enable Lewis to seize Flanders by keeping the states of Europe d
united was impossible without some sort of intervention. He w
forced therefore to give aid to Holland, and the news of his purpo
at once roused England to a hope of war. When Charles announc
it to the Houses, " there was a great noise," says Louvois, " in t
Parliament to show the joy of the two Houses at the prospect ol
fight with us." But the dexterous delays of Charles were second
by the skill with which Lewis limited his aid to the exact for
which was needful to bring about a close of the war, and the sudd
conclusion of peace again left the ground clear for his diplomati
intrigues.

**The
Fall of
Claren-
don.**

In England the irritation was great and universal, but it took
turn which helped to carry out the plans of the King. From t
moment when his bill to vest a dispensing power in the Crown ha
been defeated by Clarendon's stubborn opposition, Charles h
resolved to rid himself of the Chancellor. The Presbyterian part
represented by Ashley, united with Arlington and the ministe

1663

who were really in favour of Catholicism to bring about his ove
throw. But Clarendon was still strong in the support of the Hou
of Commons, whose Churchmanship was as resolute as his ow
Foiled in their efforts to displace him, his rivals availed themselv
of the jealousy of the merchant-class to drive him against his w

o the war with Holland; and though the Chancellor succeeded
forcing the Five Mile Act through the two Houses in the teeth
Ashley's protests, the calculations of his enemies were soon
rified.   The failures and shame of the war broke the union
tween Clarendon and Parliament; his pride and venality had
de him unpopular with the nation at large; and the threat of an
peachment enabled Charles to gratify his long-hoarded revenge
the dismissal of the Chancellor from his office, and by an order
quit the realm. By the exile of Clarendon, the death of South-
pton, and the retirement of Ormond and Nicholas, the Cavalier
rty in the Council ceased to exist; and the section which had
ginally represented the Presbyterians, and which under the
idance of Ashley had struggled in vain for toleration against the
urchmen and the Parliament, came to the front of affairs. The
igious policy of Charles had as yet been defeated by the sturdy
urchmanship of the Parliament, the influence of Clarendon, and
e reluctance of the Presbyterians as a body to accept the Royal
ndulgence " at the price of a toleration of Catholicism and a
cognition of the King's power to dispense with Parliamentary
tutes. But there were signs in the recent conduct of the Parlia-
ent and in its break with the Chancellor that the policy of
rsecution had been overdone. Charles trusted that the pressure
t on the Nonconformists by the Conventicle Act and the Five
le Act would drive them to seek relief at almost any cost, and he
ain proposed a general toleration. He looked to Ashley and his
rty for support. But their temper was already changed. Instead
toleration they pressed for a union of Protestants which would
ve utterly foiled the King's projects; and a scheme of Protestant
mprehension, which had been approved by the moderate divines
both sides, by Tillotson and Stillingfleet on the part of the
urch, as well as by Manton and Baxter on the part of the Non-
nformists, was laid by the new Minister before the House of
mmons. Even its rejection failed to bring Ashley and his party
ck to their old position. They were still for toleration, but only
r a toleration the benefit of which did not extend to Catholics,
in respect the laws have determined the principles of the Romish
ligion to be inconsistent with the safety of your Majesty's person
d government." The policy of the Council at home was deter-
ined, indeed, by the look of public affairs abroad. Lewis had
ickly shown the real cause of the eagerness with which he had
essed on the Peace of Breda between England and the Dutch.
e had secured the non-interference of the Emperor by a secret
eaty which shared the Spanish dominions between the two
onarchs in case the King of Spain died without an heir. England,
he believed, was held in check by Charles, and Holland was too
chausted by the late war to interfere alone. On the very day
erefore on which the treaty was signed he sent in his formal
aims on the Low Countries; his army at once took the field, and
e fall of six fortresses without resistance left Turenne master of

1667
to
1673
—
1665

1667

1669

1667

1667 to 1673

Flanders. Holland at once protested and armed; but it co
do nothing without aid, and its appeal to England remain
unanswered. Lewis was ready to pay a high price for English n
trality. He offered to admit England to a share in the event
partition of the Spanish monarchy, and to assign to her t
American possessions of the Spanish crown, if she would assent
his schemes on the Low Countries. Charles was already, in fa
engaged in secret negotiations on this basis, but the projects
the King were soon checked by the threatening tone of the Parl
ment, and by the attitude of his own ministers. To Ashley a
his followers an increase of the French power seemed dangero
to English Protestantism. Even Arlington, Catholic as in he
he was, thought more of the political interests of England, a
of the invariable resolve of its statesmen since Elizabeth's day
keep the French out of Flanders, than of the interests of Catholicis.
Lewis, warned of his danger, still strove to win over English opini
by offers of peace on moderate terms, while he was writing
Turenne, " I am turning over in my head things that are far fr
impossible, and go to carry them into execution whatever they m

1668 cost." Three armies were, in fact, ready to march on Spa
Germany, and Flanders, when Arlington despatched Sir Willia
Temple to the Hague, and the signature of a Triple Alliance betwe
England, Holland, and Sweden bound Lewis to the terms he h
offered as a blind, and forced on him the Peace of Aix-la-Chapel

The Treaty of Dover

Few measures have won a greater popularity than the Trip
Alliance. " It is the only good public thing," says Pepys, " th
hath been done since the King came to England." Even the To
Dryden counted among the worst of Shaftesbury's crimes th
" the Triple Bond he broke." In form indeed the Alliance simp
bound Lewis to adhere to terms of peace proposed by himself, a
those advantageous terms. But, in fact, as we have seen, it utter
ruined his plans. It brought about that union of the powers
Europe against which, as he felt instinctively, his ambition wou
dash itself in vain. It was Arlington's aim to make the Allian
the nucleus of a greater confederation; and he tried not only
perpetuate it, but to include within it the Swiss Cantons, t
Empire, and the House of Austria. His efforts were foiled; b
the " Triple Bond " bore within it the germs of the Grand Allian
which at last saved Europe. To England it at once brought ba
the reputation which she had lost since the death of Cromwell.
was, in fact, a return to the Protector's policy of a league with t
Protestant powers of the North as a security against the aggressi
of the Catholic powers of the South. But it was not so much t
action of England which had galled the pride of Lewis, as t
energy and success of Holland. That " a nation of shopkeepers
(for Lewis applied the phrase to Holland long before Napole
applied it to England) should have foiled his plans at the ve
momont of their realization, " stung him," he owned, " to t
quick." If he refrained from an instant attack it was to nurse

er revenge. His steady aim during the three years which
owed the Peace of Aix-la-Chapelle was to isolate the United
ovinces, to bring about again the neutrality of the Empire, to
eak the Triple Alliance by detaching Sweden and by securing
arles, and to leave his prey without help, save from the idle
odwill of Brandenburg and Spain. His diplomacy was every-
ere successful, but it was nowhere so successful as with England.
arles had been stirred to a momentary pride by the success of
e Triple Alliance, but he had never seriously abandoned his
licy, and he was resolute at last to play an active part in realizing

It was clear that little was to be hoped for from his old plans
uniting the Catholics and the Nonconformists, and from this
oment he surrendered himself utterly to France. The Triple
liance was hardly concluded when he declared to Lewis his
rpose of entering into an alliance with him, offensive and de-
sive. He owned to being the only man in his kingdom who
sired such a league, but he was determined to realize his desire,
atever might be the sentiments of his ministers. His ministers,
leed, he meant either to bring over to his schemes or to outwit.
vo of them, Arlington and Sir Thomas Clifford, were Catholics in
art like the King; and they were summoned, with the Duke of
ork, who had already secretly embraced Catholicism, to a con-
ence in which Charles, after pledging them to secresy, declared
mself a Catholic, and asked their counsel as to the means of
tablishing the Catholic religion in his realm. It was resolved by
e four to apply to Lewis for aid in this purpose; and Charles
oceeded to seek from the King a " protection," to use the words
the French ambassador, " of which he has always hoped to feel
e powerful effects in the execution of his design of changing the
esent state of religion in England for a better, and of establishing
s authority so as to be able to retain his subjects in the obedience
ey owe him." He offered to declare his religion, and to join
ance in an attack on Holland, if Lewis would grant him a subsidy
ual to a million a year. On this basis a secret treaty was negotiated
the year 1670 at Dover between Charles and his sister Henrietta,
e Duchess of Orleans. It provided that Charles should announce
s conversion, and that in case of any disturbance arising from
ch a step he should be supported by a French army and a French
bsidy. War was to be declared by both powers against Holland,
igland furnishing a small land force, but bearing the chief burthen
the contest at sea, on condition of an annual subsidy of three
llions of francs. In the event of the King of Spain's death
thout a son, Charles promised to support France in her claims
on Flanders.

Nothing marks better the political profligacy of the age than
at Arlington, the author of the Triple Alliance, should have been
osen as the confidant of Charles in his Treaty of Dover. But to
l save Arlington and Clifford the King's change of religion or his
litical aims remained utterly unknown. It would have been

1669

1670

The De-
clara-
tion of
Indul-
gence

1667
to
1673

impossible to obtain the consent of the party in the Royal Cou
which represented the old Presbyterians, of Ashley or Lauderd
or the Duke of Buckingham, to the Treaty of Dover. But it v
possible to trick them into approval of a war with Holland by pl
ing on their desire for a toleration of the Nonconformists.
announcement of the King's Catholicism was therefore deferr
and a series of mock negotiations, carried on through Buckingha
ended in the conclusion of a sham treaty which was communica
to Lauderdale and to Ashley, a treaty which suppressed all menti
of the religious changes or of the promise of French aid in bring
them about, and simply stipulated for a joint war against
Dutch. In such a war there was no formal breach of the Tri
Alliance, for the Triple Alliance only provided against an atta
on the dominions of Spain, and Ashley and his colleagues w

1671

lured into assent to it in 1671 by the promise of a toleration
their own terms. Charles in fact yielded the point to which he h
hitherto clung, and, as Ashley demanded, promised that no Catho
should be benefited by the Indulgence. The bargain once stru
and his ministers outwitted, it only remained for Charles to outv
his Parliament. A large subsidy was demanded for the fleet, und
the pretext of upholding the Triple Alliance, and the subsidy w
no sooner granted than the two Houses were adjourned. Fre
supplies were obtained by closing the Exchequer and suspendi
—under Clifford's advice—the payment of either principal
interest on loans advanced to the public Treasury. The measu
spread bankruptcy among half the goldsmiths of London; but

1672

was followed in 1672 by one yet more startling, the Declaration
Indulgence. By virtue of his ecclesiastical powers the King order
"that all manner of penal laws on matters ecclesiastical again
whatever sort of Nonconformists or recusants should be from th
day suspended," and gave liberty of public worship to all d
sidents save Catholics, who were allowed to practise their religi
only in private houses. The effect of the Declaration went far
justify Ashley and his colleagues (if anything could justify th
course) in the bargain by which they purchased toleration. Ministe
returned, after years of banishment, to their homes and their flock
Chapels were reopened. The gaols were emptied. Bunyan left
prison at Bedford; and thousands of Quakers, who had been t
especial objects of persecution, were set free to worship God aft
their own fashion.

The War
with
Holland

The Declaration of Indulgence was at once followed by a declar
tion of war against the Dutch on the part of both England a
France; and the success of the Allies seemed at first complete. T
French army passed the Rhine, overran three of the States witho
opposition, and pushed its outposts to within sight of Amsterda
It was only by skill and desperate courage that the Dutch shi
under De Ruyter held the English fleet under the Duke of York
bay in an obstinate battle off the coast of Suffolk. The triumph
the English cabinet was shown in the elevation of the leaders

th its parties. Ashley was made Chancellor and Earl of Shaftesry, and Clifford became Lord Treasurer. But the Dutch were
ved by the pride with which Lewis rejected their offers of subission, and by the approach of winter which suspended his
erations. The plot of the two Courts hung for success on the
ances of a rapid surprise; and with the appointment of the
ung Prince of Orange to the command of the Dutch army all
ance of a surprise was over. Young as he was, William of Orange
once displayed the cool courage and tenacity of his race. " Do
u not see your country is lost ? " asked the Duke of Buckingham,
ho had been sent to negotiate at the Hague. " There is a sure
ay never to see it lost," replied William, " and that is, to die in
e last ditch." The unexpected delay forced on Charles a fresh
sembly of the Parliament; for the supplies which he had so
scrupulously procured were already exhausted, while the closing
the Treasury had shaken all credit and rendered it impossible
raise a loan. It was necessary in 1673 to appeal to the Commons,
it the Commons met in a mood of angry distrust. The war,
popular as it was, they left alone. What overpowered all other
elings was a vague sense, which we know now to have been
stified by the facts, that liberty and religion were being unrupulously betrayed. There was a suspicion that the whole
rmed force of the nation was in Catholic hands. The Duke of
ork was believed to be in heart a Papist, and he was in command
 the fleet. Catholics had been placed as officers in the force which
as being raised for the war in Holland, and a French general, the
ount of Schomberg, had been sent to take command of it. Lady
astlemaine, the King's mistress, paraded her conversion; and
oubts were fast gathering over the Protestantism of the King.
here was a general suspicion that a plot was on foot for the
stablishment of Catholicism and despotism, and that the war and
ie Indulgence were parts of the plot. The change of temper in
ie Commons was marked by the appearance of what was from
iat time called the Country party, with Lords Russell and
avendish and Sir William Coventry at its head, a party which
ympathized with the Nonconformists but looked on it as its first
uty to guard against the designs of the Court. As to the Declaraon of Indulgence however, all parties in the House were at one.
'he Commons resolved " that penal statutes in matters ecclesistical cannot be suspended but by consent of Parliament," and
efused supplies till the Declaration was recalled. The King yielded;
ut the Declaration was no sooner recalled than a Test Act was
assed through both Houses without opposition, which required
rom everyone in the civil and military employment of the State
he oaths of allegiance and supremacy, a declaration against tran
ıbstantiation, and a reception of the sacrament according to the
ites of the Church of England. Clifford at once counselled resistnce, and Buckingham talked flightily about bringing the army to
ondon, but Arlington saw that all hope of carrying the " great

1673
to
1678

plan " through was at an end, and pressed Charles to yield.
dissolution was the King's only resource, but in the temper of t
nation a new Parliament would have been yet more violent th
the present one; and Charles sullenly gave way. No measure h
ever brought about more startling results. The Duke of Yo
owned himself a Catholic, and resigned his office as Lord Hi
Admiral. Throngs of excited people gathered round the Lo
Treasurer's house at the news that Clifford, too, had owned
being a Catholic and had laid down his staff of office. The
resignation was followed by that of hundreds of others in the arr
and the civil service of the Crown. On public opinion the effect w
wonderful. " I dare not write all the strange talk of the town
says Evelyn. The resignations were held to have proved t
existence of the dangers which the Test Act had been passed
meet. From this moment all trust in Charles was at an end. " T
King," Shaftesbury said bitterly, " who if he had been so hap
as to have been born a private gentleman had certainly passed f
a man of good parts, excellent breeding, and well natured, ha
now, being a Prince, brought his affairs to that pass that there
not a person in the world, man or woman, that dares rely up
him or put any confidence in his word or friendship."

Section IV.—Danby, 1673—1678

[*Authorities.*—As under the previous section, with the addition
the " Memoirs of Sir John Reresby," and Danby's " Letters."]

Shaftes-
bury

The one man in England on whom the discovery of the King
perfidy fell with the most crushing effect was the Chancellor, Lo
Shaftesbury. Throughout his life Ashley Cooper had piqued hims
on a penetration which read the characters of men around him, a
on a political instinct which discerned every coming change. H
self-reliance was wonderful. In mere boyhood he saved his esta
from the greed of his guardians by boldly appealing in person
Noy, who was then Attorney-General. As an undergraduate
Oxford he organized a rebellion of the freshmen against the oppre
sive customs which were enforced by the senior men of his colleg
and succeeded in abolishing them. At eighteen he was a memb
of the Short Parliament. On the outbreak of the Civil War he to
part with the King; but in the midst of the Royal successes
foresaw the ruin of the Royal cause, passed to the Parliamen
attached himself to the fortunes of Cromwell, and became memb
of the Council of State. A temporary disgrace during the last yea
of the Protectorate only quickened him to a restless hatred whic
did much to bring about its fall. We have already seen his bitt
invectives against the dead Protector, his intrigues with Mon
and the active part which he took, as member of the Council
State, in the King's recall. Charles rewarded his services with
peerage, and with promotion to a foremost share in the Roy

uncils. Ashley was then a man of forty, and under the Common-
alth he had been famous, in Dryden's contemptuous phrase, as
he loudest bagpipe of the squeaking train"; but he was no
oner a minister of Charles than he flung himself into the de-
uchery of the Court with an ardour which surprised even his
ster. "You are the wickedest dog in England!" laughed Charles
some unscrupulous jest of his councillor's. "Of a subject, Sir,
elieve I am!" was the unabashed reply. But the debauchery of
hley was simply a mask. He was, in fact, temperate by nature
d habit, and his ill-health rendered any great excess impossible.
n soon found that the courtier who lounged in Lady Castle-
ine's boudoir, or drank and jested with Sedley and Buckingham,
s a diligent and able man of business. "He is a man," says
e puzzled Pepys, three years after the Restoration, "of great
siness, and yet of pleasure and dissipation too." His rivals were
envious of the ease and mastery with which he dealt with
estions of finance, as of the "nimble wit" which won the favour
the King. Even in later years his industry earned the grudging
aise of his enemies. Dryden owned that as Chancellor he was
swift to despatch and easy of access," and wondered at the rest-
s activity which "refused his age the needful hours of rest."
s activity indeed was the more wonderful that his health was
terly broken. An accident in early days left behind it an abiding
eakness, whose traces were seen in the furrows which seared his
ng pale face, in the feebleness of his health, and the nervous
emor which shook his puny frame. The "pigmy body" seemed
fretted to decay" by the "fiery soul" within it. But pain and
eakness brought with them no sourness of spirit. Ashley was
tacked more unscrupulously than any statesman save Walpole;
t Burnet, who did not love him, owns that he was never bitter
angry in speaking of his assailants. Even the wit with which he
ushed them was commonly good-humoured. "When will you
ve done preaching?" a bishop murmured testily, as Shaftesbury
s speaking in the House of Peers. "When I am a bishop, my
rd!" was the laughing reply.

As a statesman Ashley not only stood high among his con-
mporaries from his wonderful readiness and industry, but he
ood far above them in his scorn of personal profit. Even Dryden,
hile raking together every fault in the Chancellor, owns that his
nds were clean. As a political leader his position was to modern
es odd enough. In religion he was at best a Deist, with some
nciful notions "that after death our souls lived in stars," and
s life was that of a debauchee. But, Deist and debauchee as he
as, he represented, as we have seen, the Presbyterian and Non-
nformist party in the Royal Council. He was the steady and
hement advocate of toleration, but his advocacy was based on
rely political grounds. He saw that persecution would fail to
ing back the Dissenters to the Church, and that the effort to
call them only left Protestants disunited and at the mercy of

Shaftes-
bury's
Policy

their enemies. But in the temper of England after the Restorati
he saw no hope of obtaining toleration save from the policy of th
King. Wit, debauchery, rapidity in the despatch of business, we
all used as means to keep Charles firm in his plans of toleratio
and to secure him as a friend in the struggle which Ashley carri
on against the intolerance of Clarendon. Charles, as we have see
had his own game to play and his own reasons for protecti
Ashley during his vehement but fruitless struggle against the Te
and Corporation Act, the Act of Uniformity, and the persecutio
of the dissidents. Fortune at last smiled on the unscrupulo
ability with which he entangled Clarendon in the embarrassmen
of the Dutch war of 1664, and took advantage of the alienation
the Parliament to ensure his fall. Of the yet more unscrupulo
bargain which followed we have already spoken. Ashley bough
as he believed, the Declaration of Indulgence, the release of th
imprisoned Nonconformists, and freedom of worship for all diss
dents, at the price of a consent to the second attack on Hollan
and he was looked on by the public at large as the minister mo
responsible both for the measures he advised and the measures
had nothing to do with. But while facing the gathering storm
unpopularity Ashley learnt in a moment of drunken confidenc
the secret of the King's religion. He owned to a friend " his troub
at the black cloud which was gathering over England; " bu
troubled as he was, he still believed himself strong enough to us
Charles for his own purposes. His acceptance of the Chancellorshi
and of the Earldom of Shaftesbury, as well as his violent defenc
of the war on opening the Parliament, identified him yet mor
with the Royal policy. It was at this moment, if we credit a state
ment of doubtful authority in itself but which squares with th
sudden change in his course, that he learnt from Arlington th
secret of the Treaty of Dover. Whether this were so, or whethe
suspicion, as in the people at large, deepened into certainty
Shaftesbury saw he had been duped. To the bitterness of such
discovery was added the bitterness of having aided in scheme
which he abhorred. His change of policy was rapid and complete
He suddenly pressed for the withdrawal of the Declaration
Indulgence. Alone among his fellow-ministers he supported th
Test Act with extraordinary vehemence. His success in displacin
James and Clifford, and in creating a barrier against any futur
Catholic projects, gave him hopes of revenging the deceit whic
had been practised on him by forcing his policy on the King. Fo
the moment indeed Charles was helpless. He found himself, as h
had told Lewis long before, alone in his realm. The Test Act ha
been passed unanimously by both Houses. Even the Noncon
formists deserted him, and preferred persecution to the support o
his plans. The dismissal of the Catholic officers made the employ
ment of force, if he ever contemplated it, impossible, while the i
success of the Dutch war robbed him of all hope of aid from France
The firmness of the Prince of Orange had at last roused the stubbor

ergy of his countrymen. The French conquests on land were
wly won back, and at sea the fleet of the allies was still held in
eck by the fine seamanship of De Ruyter. Nor was William less
ccessful in diplomacy than in war. The House of Austria was at
st roused to action by the danger which threatened Europe, and
s union with the United Provinces laid the foundation of the
and Alliance. Shaftesbury resolved to put an end to the war;
d for this purpose he threw himself into hearty alliance with
e Country party in the Commons, and welcomed the Duke of
mond and Prince Rupert, who were looked upon as " great
rliament men," back to the Royal Council. It was to Shaftesry's influence that Charles attributed the dislike which the
mmons displayed to the war, and their refusal of a grant of
pplies for it until fresh religious securities were devised. It was

his instigation that an address was presented by both Houses
ainst the plan of marrying James to a Catholic princess, Mary of
odena. But the projects of Shaftesbury were suddenly interrupted
 an unexpected act of vigour on the part of the King. The
ouses were no sooner prorogued in November than the Chancellor
as ordered to deliver up the Seals.

" It is only laying down my gown and buckling on my sword,"
aftesbury is said to have replied to the Royal bidding; and,
ough the words were innocent enough, for the sword was part of
e usual dress of a gentleman which he must necessarily resume
hen he laid aside the gown of the Chancellor, they were taken as
nveying a covert threat. He was still determined to force on the
ing a peace with the States. But he looked forward to the dangers
 the future with even greater anxiety than to those of the present.
he Duke of York, the successor to the throne, had owned himself a
atholic, and almost everyone agreed that securities for the national
ligion would be necessary in the case of his accession. But Shaftesry saw, and it is his especial merit that he did see, that with a
ng like James, convinced of his Divine Right and bigoted in his
ligious fervour, securities were valueless. From the first he
etermined to force on Charles his brother's exclusion from the
rone, and his resolve was justified by the Revolution which finally
d the work he proposed to do. Unhappily he was equally deter-
ined to fight Charles with weapons as vile as his own. The result
 Clifford's resignation, of James's acknowledgment of his con-
ersion, had been to destroy all belief in the honesty of public men.
 panic of distrust had begun. The fatal truth was whispered that
harles himself was a Catholic. In spite of the Test Act, it was
ispected that men Catholics in heart still held high office in the
tate, and we know that in Arlington's case the suspicion was just.
haftesbury seized on this public alarm, stirred above all by a
nse of inability to meet the secret dangers which day after day
as disclosing, as the means of carrying out his plans. He began
nning the panic by tales of a Papist rising in London, and of a
oming Irish revolt with a French army to back it. He retired to

1673 to 1678

his house in the City to find security against a conspiracy wh
had been formed, he said, to cut his throat. Meanwhile he rapi
organized the Country party in the Parliament, and placed hims
openly at its head. An address for the removal of minist
"popishly affected or otherwise obnoxious or dangerous" v
presented on the reassembling of the Houses in 1674, and t
refusal of supplies made a continuance of the war impossible.

1674

bill was brought in to prevent all Catholics from approaching t
Court, in other words for removing James from the King's Counc
A far more important bill was that of the Protestant Securiti
which was pressed by Shaftesbury, Halifax, and Carlisle, the lead
of the new Opposition in the House of Lords, a bill which enact
that any prince of the blood should forfeit his right to the Crow
on his marriage with a Catholic. The bill, which was the fi
sketch of the later Exclusion Bill, failed to pass, but its failure l
the Houses excited and alarmed. Shaftesbury was busy intrigui
in the City, corresponding with William of Orange, and pressi
for a war with France which Charles could only avert by an appe
to Lewis, a subsidy from whom enabled him to prorogue the Parli
ment. But Charles saw that the time had come to give wa
"Things have turned out ill," he said to Temple with a burst
unusual petulance, "but had I been well served I might have ma
a good business of it." His concessions however were as usu
complete. He dismissed Buckingham and Arlington. He ma
peace with the Dutch. But Charles was never more formidab
than in the moment of defeat, and he had already resolved on
new policy by which the efforts of Shaftesbury might be held
bay. Ever since the opening of his reign he had clung to a syste
of balance, had pitted Churchman against Nonconformist, a
Ashley against Clarendon, partly to preserve his own independenc
and partly with a view of winning some advantage to the Catholi
from the political strife. The temper of the Commons had enabl
Clarendon to baffle the King's attempts; and on his fall Charl
felt strong enough to abandon the attempt to preserve a politic
balance, and had thrown himself on the support of Lewis and t
Nonconformists in his new designs. But the new policy bro
down like the old. The Nonconformists refused to betray the cau
of Protestantism, and Shaftesbury, their leader, was pressing
measures which would rob Catholicism of the hopes it had gain
from the conversion of James. In straits like these Charles resolv
to win back the Commons by boldly adopting the policy on whi
the House was set. The majority of its members were still a ma
of Cavalier Churchmen, who regarded Sir Thomas Osborne,
dependant of Arlington's, as their representative in the Roy
Councils. The King had already created Osborne Earl of Danb
and raised him to the post of Lord Treasurer in Clifford's roor
In 1674 he frankly adopted the policy of his party in the Parliamen

Danby   The policy of Danby was simply that of Clarendon. He had
Clarendon's love of the Church, his equal hatred of Popery an

ssent, his high notions of the prerogative tempered by a faith in rliament and the law. The union between the Church and the own was ratified in a conference between Danby and the bishops Lambeth; and its first fruits were seen in the rigorous enforcement of the law against conventicles, and the exclusion of all atholics from Court. The Lady Mary, the eldest child of James, as confirmed by the King's orders as a Protestant, while the rliament which was assembled in 1675 was assured that the Test ct should be rigorously enforced. The change in the Royal policy me not a moment too soon. As it was, the aid of the Cavalier rty which rallied round Danby hardly saved the King from the miliation of being forced to recall the troops he still maintained the French service. To gain a majority on this point Danby was rced to avail himself of a resource which from this time played r nearly a hundred years an important part in English politics. e bribed lavishly. He was more successful in winning back the ajority of the Commons from their alliance with the Country rty by reviving the old spirit of religious persecution. He oposed that the test which had been imposed by Clarendon on unicipal officers should be extended to all functionaries of the ate; that every member of either House, every magistrate and blic officer, should swear never to take arms against the King to "endeavour any alteration of the Protestant religion now tablished by law in the Church of England, or any alteration in e Government in Church and State as it is by law established." he Bill was forced through the Lords by the bishops and the valier party, and its passage through the Commons was only erted by a quarrel on privilege between the two Houses which aftesbury dexterously fanned into flame. On the other hand the untry party remained strong enough to refuse supplies. Eager they were for the war with France which Danby promised, the ommons could not trust the King; and Danby was soon to discver how wise their distrust had been. For the Houses were no oner prorogued than Charles revealed to him the negotiations he d been all the while carrying on with Lewis, and required him sign a treaty by which, on consideration of a yearly pension aranteed on the part of France, the two sovereigns bound themlves to enter into no engagements with other powers, and to lend ch other aid in case of rebellion in their dominions. Such a treaty t only bound England to dependence on France, but freed the ing from all Parliamentary control. But his minister pleaded in ain for delay and for the advice of the Council. Charles answered is entreaties by signing the treaty with his own hand. Danby und himself duped by the King as Shaftesbury had found himlf duped; but his bold temper was only spurred to fresh plans r rescuing the King from his bondage to Lewis. To do this the rst step was to reconcile the King and the Parliament, which met 1676 after a prorogation of fifteen months. The Country party ood in the way of such a reconciliation, but Danby resolved to

1673
to
1678

break its strength by measures of unscrupulous vigour, for whic
a blunder of Shaftesbury's gave an opportunity. Shaftesbur
despaired of bringing the House of Commons, elected as it had bee
fifteen years before in a moment of religious and political reactio
to any steady opposition to the Crown. He had already moved a
address for a dissolution; and he now urged that as a statute
Edward the Third ordained that Parliaments should be held " on
a year or oftener if need be," the Parliament by the recent pr
rogation of a year and a half had ceased legally to exist. T
Triennial Act deprived such an argument of any force. But Dan
represented it as a contempt of the House, and the Lords at h
bidding committed its supporters, Shaftesbury, Buckinghar

1677

Salisbury, and Wharton, to the Tower in 1677. While the Oppos
tion cowered under the blow, Danby pushed on a measure whic
was designed to win back alarmed Churchmen to confidence in t
Crown. By the bill for the Security of the Church it was provide
that on the succession of a king not a member of the Establishe
Church the appointment of bishops should be vested in the existi
prelates, and that the King's children should be placed in t
guardianship of the Archbishop of Canterbury.

Treaty
of Nime-
guen

The bill however failed in the Commons; and a grant of suppl
was only obtained by Danby's profuse bribery. The progress of t
war abroad, indeed, was rousing panic in England faster tha
Danby could allay it. The successes of the French arms in Flander
and a defeat of the Prince of Orange at Cassel stirred the who
country to a cry for war. The House of Commons echoed the cry i
an address to the Crown; but Charles parried the blow by deman
ing a supply before the war was declared, and on the refusal of t
still suspicious House prorogued the Parliament. Fresh and larg
subsidies from France enabled him to continue this prorogation f
seven months. But the silence of the Parliament did little to silen
the country; and Danby took advantage of the popular cry for wa
to press an energetic course of action on the King. In its will
check French aggression the Cavalier party was as earnest as t
Puritan, and Danby aimed at redeeming his failure at home b
uniting the Parliament through a vigorous policy abroad. A
usual, Charles gave way. He was himself for the moment uneas
at the appearance of the French on the Flemish coast, and he owne
that " he could never live at ease with his subjects " if Flande
were abandoned. He allowed Danby, therefore, to press on bot
parties the necessity for mutual concessions, and to define the ne
attitude of England by a step which was to produce results fa
more momentous than any of which either Charles or his minist
dreamed. The Prince of Orange was suddenly invited to Englan
and wedded to Mary, the eldest child of the Duke of York. As t
King was childless, and James had no son, Mary was presumptiv
heiress of the Crown. The marriage therefore promised a clos
political union in the future with Holland, and a correspondin
opposition to the ambition of France. With the country it wa

popular as a Protestant match, and as ensuring a Protestant
successor to James. Lewis was bitterly angered; he rejected the
English propositions of peace, and again set his army in the field.
Danby was ready to accept the challenge, and the withdrawal of
the English ambassador from Paris was followed in 1678 by an
assembly of the Parliament. A warlike speech from the throne was
answered by a warlike address from the House, supplies were voted,
and an army raised. But the actual declaration of war still failed
to appear. While Danby threatened war, Charles was busy turning
the threat to his own profit, and gaining time by prorogations for
a series of base negotiations. At one stage he demanded from
Lewis a fresh pension for the next three years as the price of his
good offices with the allies. Danby stooped to write the demand,
and Charles added, "This letter is written by my order, C.R."
A force of three thousand English soldiers were landed at Ostend;
but the allies were already broken by their suspicions of the King's
real policy, and Charles soon agreed for a fresh pension to recall
the brigade. The bargain was hardly struck when Lewis withdrew
the terms of peace he had himself offered, and on the faith of which
England had ostensibly retired from the scene. Danby at once
offered fresh aid to the allies, but all faith in England was lost. One
power after another gave way to the new French demands, and
the virtual victory of Lewis was secured in July, 1678, by the
Peace of Nimeguen.

The Treaty of Nimeguen not only left France the arbiter of
Europe, but it left Charles the master of a force of twenty thousand
men levied for the war he refused to declare, and with nearly a
million of French money in his pocket. His course had roused into
fresh life the old suspicions of his perfidy, and of a secret plot with
Lewis for the ruin of English freedom and of English religion. That
there was such a plot we know; and the hopes of the Catholic party
mounted as fast as the panic of the Protestants. Coleman, the
secretary of the Duchess of York, and a busy intriguer, had gained
sufficient knowledge of the real plans of the King and of his brother
to induce him to beg for money from Lewis in the work of further-
ing them by intrigues in the Parliament. A passage from his letter
gives us a glimpse of the wild hopes which were stirring among
the hotter Catholics of the time. "They had a mighty work on
their hands," he wrote, "no less than the conversion of three
kingdoms, and by that perhaps the utter subduing of a pestilent
heresy which had so long domineered over a great part of the
northern world. Success would give the greatest blow to the
Protestant religion that it had received since its birth." The letter
was secret; but the hopes of the Catholics were known, and the
alarm grew fast. Meanwhile one of the vile impostors who are
always thrown to the surface at times of great public agitation was
ready to take advantage of the general alarm by the invention of a
Popish plot. Titus Oates, a Baptist minister before the Restoration,
a curate and navy chaplain after it, but left penniless by his

infamous character, had sought bread in a conversion to Catholicism, and had been received into Jesuit houses at Valladolid and St. Omer. While he remained there, he learnt the fact of a secret meeting of the Jesuits in London, which was probably nothing but the usual congregation of the order. On his expulsion for mis conduct this single fact widened in his fertile brain into a plot for the subversion of Protestantism and the death of the King. His story was laid before Charles, and received with cool incredulity but Oates made affidavit of its truth before a London magistrate Sir Edmondsbury Godfrey, and at last managed to appear before the Council. He declared that he had been trusted with letters which disclosed the Jesuit plans. They were stirring rebellion in Ireland; in Scotland they disguised themselves as Cameronians in England their aim was to assassinate the King, and to leave the throne open to the Papist Duke of York. But no letters appeared to support these monstrous charges, and Oates would have been dismissed with contempt but for the seizure of Coleman's correspondence. His letters gave a new colour to the plot. Danby himself, conscious of the truth that there were designs which Charles dared not avow, was shaken in his rejection of the disclosures, and inclined to use them as weapons to check the King in his Catholic policy. But a more unscrupulous hand had already seized on the growing panic. Shaftesbury, released after a long imprisonment and desperate of other courses, threw himself into the plot. " Let the Treasurer cry as loud as he pleases against Popery," he laughed " I will cry a note louder." But no cry was needed to heighten the popular frenzy from the moment when Sir Edmondsbury Godfrey a magistrate before whom Oates had laid his information, was found in a field near London with his sword run through his heart His death was assumed to be murder, and the murder to be an attempt of the Jesuits to " stifle the plot." A solemn funeral added to public agitation; and the two Houses named committees to investigate the charges made by Oates.

The fall of Danby In this investigation Shaftesbury took the lead. Whatever his personal ambition may have been, his public aims in all that followed were wise and far-sighted. He aimed at forcing Charles to dissolve the Parliament and appeal again to the nation. He aimed at forcing on Charles a ministry which should break his dependence on France and give a constitutional turn to his policy. He saw that no guaranty would really avail to meet the danger of a Catholic sovereign, and he aimed at excluding James from the throne. But in pursuing these aims he rested wholly on the plot. He fanned the popular panic by accepting without question some fresh depositions in which Oates charged five Catholic peers with part in the Jesuit conspiracy. The peers were sent to the Tower and two thousand suspected persons were hurried to prison. A proclamation ordered every Catholic to leave London. The train bands were called to arms, and patrols paraded through the streets to guard against the Catholic rising which Oates declared to be at

and. Meanwhile Shaftesbury turned the panic to political account
y forcing through Parliament against the fierce opposition of the
ourt party a bill which excluded Catholics from a seat in either
ouse. The exclusion remained in force for a century and a half;
ut it had really been aimed against the Duke of York, and Shaftes-
ury was defeated by a proviso which exempted James from the
peration of the bill. The plot too which had been supported for
ur months by the sole evidence of Oates, began to hang fire; but
promise of reward brought forward a villain, named Bedloe, with
les beside which those of Oates seemed tame. The two informers
ere now pressed forward by an infamous rivalry to stranger and
ranger revelations. Bedloe swore to the existence of a plot for
e landing of a Papist army and a general massacre of the Pro-
stants. Oates capped the revelations of Bedloe by charging the
ueen herself, at the bar of the Lords, with knowledge of the plot
murder her husband. Monstrous as such charges were, they
vived the waning frenzy of the people and of the two Houses.
he peers under arrest were ordered to be impeached. A new
roclamation enjoined the arrest of every Catholic in the realm.
series of judicial murders began with the trial and execution of
leman, which even now can only be remembered with horror.
ut the alarm must soon have worn out had it only been supported
y perjury. What gave force to the false plot was the existence of
true one. Coleman's letters had won credit for the perjuries of
ates, and a fresh discovery now won credit for the perjuries of
edloe. The English ambassador at Paris, Edward Montagu,
turned home on a quarrel with Danby, obtained a seat in the
ouse of Commons, and in spite of the seizure of his papers laid
n the table of the House the despatch which had been forwarded
Lewis, demanding payment of the King's services to France
ring the late negotiations. The House was thunderstruck; for,
rong as had been the general suspicion, the fact of the dependence
England on a foreign power had never before been proved.
anby's name was signed to the despatch, and he was at once
npeached on a charge of high treason. But Shaftesbury was more
ger to secure the election of a new Parliament than to punish his
val, and Charles was resolved to prevent at any price a trial which
uld not fail to reveal the disgraceful secret of his foreign policy.
harles was in fact at Shaftesbury's mercy, and the bargain for
hich Shaftesbury had been playing had to be struck. The Earl
reed that the impeachment should be dropped, and the King
omised that a new Parliament should be summoned, and a new
inistry called into office.

SECTION V.—SHAFTESBURY, 1679—1682

[Authorities.—As before, with the addition of Russell's "Life of William Lord Russell," Foxcroft, "Life of Halifax," and Pollock, "The Popish Plot."]

Sir
William
Temple

When the Parliament met in March, 1679, the King's pledge was redeemed by the dismissal of Danby from his post of Treasurer, and the constitution of a new ministry. Shaftesbury, as its most important member, became President of the Council. The chiefs of the Country party, Lord Russell and Lord Cavendish, took their seats at the board with Lords Holles and Roberts, the older representatives of the Presbyterian party which had merged in the general Opposition. Savile, Lord Halifax, as yet known only as a keen and ingenious speaker, entered the ministry in the train of his own connection, Lord Shaftesbury, while Lord Essex and Lord Capel, two of the most popular among the Country leaders, went to the Treasury. The recall of Sir William Temple, the negotiator of the Triple Alliance, from his embassy at the Hague to fill the post of Secretary of State, promised a foreign policy which would again place England high among the European powers. Temple returned with a plan of administration which, fruitless as it directly proved, is of great importance as marking the silent change which was passing over the Constitution. Like many men of his time, he was equally alarmed at the power both of the Crown and of the Parliament. In moments of national excitement the power of the Houses seemed irresistible. They had overthrown Clarendon. They had overthrown Clifford and the Cabal. They had just overthrown Danby. But though they were strong enough in the end to punish ill government, they showed no power of securing good government or of permanently influencing the policy of the Crown. For nineteen years, in fact, with a Parliament always sitting, Charles had had it all his own way. He had made war against the will of the nation, and he had refused to make war when the nation demanded it. While every Englishman hated France, he had made England a mere dependency of the French King. The remedy for this state of things, as it was afterwards found, was a very simple one. By a change which we shall have to trace, the Ministry has now become a Committee of State-officers, named by the majority of the House of Commons from amongst the more prominent of its representatives in either House, whose object in accepting office is to do the will of that majority. So long as the majority of the House of Commons itself represents the more powerful current of public opinion it is clear that such an arrangement makes government an accurate reflection of the national will. But obvious as such a plan may seem to us, it had as yet occurred to no English statesman. Even to Temple the one remedy seemed to lie in the restoration of the Royal Council to its older powers. This body, composed as it was of the great officers of the Court, the Royal

Treasurer and Secretaries, and a few nobles specially summoned
to it by the sovereign, formed up to the close of Elizabeth's reign
a sort of deliberative assembly to which the graver matters of
public administration were commonly submitted by the Crown.
A practice, however, of previously submitting such measures to a
smaller body of the more important councillors must always have
existed; and under James this secret committee, which was then
known as the Cabala or Cabal, began almost wholly to supersede
the Council itself. In the large and balanced Council which was
formed after the Restoration all real power rested with the
" Cabala " of Clarendon, Southampton, Ormond, Monk, and the
two Secretaries; and on Clarendon's fall these were succeeded by
Clifford, Arlington, Buckingham, Ashley, and Lauderdale. By a
mere coincidence the initials of the latter names formed the word
" Cabal," which has ever since retained the sinister meaning their
unpopularity gave to it. The effect of these smaller committees
had undoubtedly been to remove the check which the larger
numbers and the more popular composition of the Royal Council
laid upon the Crown. The unscrupulous projects which made the
Cabal of Clifford and his fellows a by-word among Englishmen
could never have been laid before a Council of great peers and
hereditary officers of State. To Temple therefore the organization
of the Council seemed to furnish a check on mere personal government which Parliament was unable to supply. For this purpose
the Cabala, or Cabinet, as it was now becoming the fashion to term
the confidential committee of the Council, was abolished. The
Council itself was restricted to thirty members, and their joint
income was not to fall below £300,000, a sum little less than what
was estimated as the income of the whole House of Commons. A
body of great nobles and proprietors, not too numerous for secret
deliberation, and wealthy enough to counterbalance either the
Commons or the Crown, would form, Temple hoped, a barrier
against the violence and aggression of the one power, and a check
on the mere despotism of the other.

The new Council and the new ministry gave fair hope of a wise The Ex-
and patriotic government. But the difficulties were still great. The clusion
nation was frenzied with suspicion and panic. The elections to the
new Parliament had taken place amidst a whirl of excitement
which left no place for candidates of the Court; and so un-
manageable was the temper of the Commons that Shaftesbury was
unable to carry out his part of the bargain with Charles. The
Commons insisted on carrying the impeachment of Danby to the
bar of the Lords. The appointment of the new ministry, indeed,
was welcomed with a burst of general joy; but the disbanding of
the army and the withdrawal of the Duke of York to Holland at
the King's command failed to restore public confidence. At the
bottom of the panic lay the dread of a Catholic successor to the
throne, a dread which the after history of James fully justified.
Shaftesbury was earnest for the exclusion of James, but as yet the

majority of the Council shrank from the step, and supported plan which Charles brought forward for restraining the powers of his successor. By this project the presentation to Church living was to be taken out of the new monarch's hands. The last Parlia ment of the preceding reign was to continue to sit; and th appointment of all Councillors, Judges, Lord-Lieutenants, an officers in the fleet, was vested in the two Houses so long as Catholic sovereign was on the throne. The extent of these pro visions showed the pressure which Charles felt, but Shaftesbury wa undoubtedly right in setting the plan aside as at once insufficien and impracticable. He continued to advocate the Exclusion in th Royal Council; and a bill for depriving James of his right to th Crown, and for devolving it on the next Protestant in the line of succession was introduced into the Commons by his adherents an passed the House by a large majority. It was known that Charle would use his influence with the Peers for its rejection. The Ea therefore fell back on the tactics of Pym. A bold Remonstranc was prepared in the Commons. The City of London was read with an address to the two Houses in favour of the bill. All Charle could do was to gain time by the prorogation of the Parliamen for a few months.

But delay would have been useless had the Country part remained at one. The temper of the nation and of the House o Commons was so hotly pronounced in favour of the Exclusion of the Duke that union among the patriot ministers must in the en have secured it and spared England the necessity for the Revolu tion of 1688. The wiser leaders among them, indeed, were alread leaning to the very change which that Revolution brought about If James were passed over, his daughter Mary, the wife of th Prince of Orange, stood next in the order of succession; and th plan of Temple, Essex, and Halifax was to bring the Prince ove to England during the prorogation, to introduce him into th Council, and to pave his way to the throne. Unhappily Shaftes bury was contemplating a very different course. For reasons whic still remain obscure, he distrusted the Prince of Orange. His desir for a more radical change may have been prompted by the maxir ascribed to him that " a bad title makes a good king." But what ever were his motives, he had resolved to set aside the claim of both James and his children, and to place the Duke of Monmout on the throne. Monmouth was the eldest of the King's bastards a weak and worthless profligate in temper, but popular throug his personal beauty and his reputation for bravery. He had jus returned in triumph from suppressing a revolt which had broke out among the Scotch Covenanters in the western shires; and th tale was at once set about of a secret marriage between the Kin and his mother which would have made him lawful heir to th throne. Shaftesbury almost openly espoused his cause. He presse the King to give him the command of the Guards, which woul have put the only military force in Monmouth's hands. Left a

lone in this course by the opposition of his colleagues, the Earl
ᴜrew himself more and more on the support of the Plot. The
ᴘrosecution of its victims was pushed recklessly on. Three Catholics
ᴡere hanged in London. Eight priests were put to death in the
ᴄᴏuntry. Pursuivants and informers spread terror through every
ᴘopish household. Shaftesbury counted on the reassembling of the
ᴘarliament to bring all this terror to bear upon the King. But
ᴄharles had already seized on the breach which the Earl's policy
ᴜad made in the ranks of the Country party. He saw that Shaftes-
ᴜury was unsupported by any of his colleagues save Russell. To
ᴛemple, Essex, or Halifax it seemed possible to bring about the
ᴀccession of Mary without any violent revolution; but to set
ᴀside, not only the right of James, but the right of his Protestant
ᴄhildren, was to ensure a civil war. The influence, however, of
ᴘhaftesbury over the Commons promised a speedy recognition of
ᴍonmouth, and Temple could only meet this by advising Charles
ᴛᴏ dissolve the Parliament.

Shaftesbury's anger vented itself in threats that the advisers of Shaftesbury's
Dis-
missal ᴛhis dissolution should pay for it with their heads. The danger was
ᴡrought home to them by a sudden illness of the King; and the
ᴘrospect of ruin if Monmouth should succeed in his design drew the
ᴍoderate party in the Council, whether they would or no, to the
ᴅuke of York. It was the alarm which Essex and Halifax felt at the
ᴛhreats of Shaftesbury which made them advise the recall of James
ᴇn the King's illness; and though the Duke again withdrew to
ᴇdinburgh on his brother's recovery, the same ministers encouraged
ᴄharles to send Monmouth out of the country and to dismiss
ᴘhaftesbury himself from the Council. The dismissal was the signal
ᴏr a struggle to whose danger Charles was far from blinding him-
ᴇlf. What had saved him till now was his cynical courage. In the
ᴍidst of the terror and panic of the Plot men " wondered to see
ᴇim quite cheerful amidst such an intricacy of troubles," says the
ᴄourtly Reresby, " but it was not in his nature to think or perplex
ᴇimself much about anything." Even in the heat of the tumult
ᴡhich followed on Shaftesbury's dismissal, Charles was seen fishing
ᴀnd sauntering as usual in Windsor Park. But closer observers
ᴛhan Reresby saw beneath this veil of indolent unconcern a con-
ᴇiousness of new danger. " From this time," says Burnet, " his
ᴇmper was observed to change very visibly." He became in fact
ᴇsullen and thoughtful; he saw that he had to do with a strange
ᴇort of people, that could neither be managed nor frightened." But
ᴇe faced the danger with his old unscrupulous coolness. He re-
ᴏpened secret negotiations with France. Lewis was as alarmed as
ᴄharles himself at the warlike temper of the nation, and as anxious
ᴛᴏ prevent the assembly of a Parliament; but the terms on which
ᴇe offered a subsidy were too humiliating even for the King's
ᴀcceptance. The failure forced him to summon a new Parliament:
ᴀnd the terror, which Shaftesbury was busily feeding with new tales
ᴏf massacre and invasion, returned members even more violent

than the members of the House he had just dismissed. Even the
Council shrank from the King's proposal to prorogue this Parlia
ment at its first meeting in 1680, but Charles persisted. Alone as
he stood, he was firm in his resolve to gain time, for Time, as he
saw, was working in his favour. The tide of public sympathy was
beginning to turn. The perjury of Oates proved too much at last
for the credulity of juries; and the acquittal of four of his victims
was a sign that the panic was beginning to ebb. A far stronger
proof of this was seen in the immense efforts which Shaftesbury
made to maintain it. Fresh informers were brought forward to
swear a plot for the assassination of the Earl himself, and to the
share of the Duke of York in the conspiracies of his fellow Papists.
A paper found in a meal-tub was produced as evidence of the new
danger. Gigantic torch-light processions paraded the streets of
London, and the effigy of the Pope was burnt amidst the wild
outcry of a vast multitude.

Peti-
tioners
and Ab-
horrers
     Acts of yet greater daring showed the lengths to which Shaftes
bury was now ready to go. He had grown up amidst the tumult
of civil war, and, greyheaded as he was, the fire and vehemence of
his early days seemed to wake again in the singular recklessness
with which he drove on the nation to a new struggle in arms. In
1680 he formed a committee for promoting agitation throughout
the country; and the petitions which it drew up for the assembly
of the Parliament were sent to every town and grand jury, and
sent back again with thousands of signatures. Monmouth, in spite
of the King's orders, returned at Shaftesbury's call to London,
and a daring pamphlet pointed him out as the nation's leader in
the coming struggle against Popery and tyranny. So great was the
alarm of the Council that the garrison in every fortress was held
in readiness for instant war. But the danger was really over. The
tide of opinion had fairly turned. Acquittal followed acquittal.
A reaction of horror and remorse at the cruelty which had hurried
victim after victim to the gallows succeeded to the pitiless frenzy
which Shaftesbury had fanned into a flame. Anxious as the nation
was for a Protestant sovereign, its sense of justice revolted against
the wrong threatened to James' Protestant children; and every
gentleman in the realm felt insulted at the project of setting Mary
aside to put the crown of England on the head of a Royal bastard.
The memory too of the Civil War was still fresh and keen, and the
rumour of an outbreak of revolt rallied every loyalist round the
King. The host of petitions which Shaftesbury procured from the
counties was answered by a counter host of addresses from thou
sands who declared their " abhorrence " of the plans against the
Crown. The country was divided into two great factions of
" petitioners " and " abhorrers," the germs of the two great parties
of " Whigs " and " Tories " which have played so prominent a part
in our political history from the time of the Exclusion Bill. Charles
at once took advantage of this turn of affairs. He recalled the Duke
of York to the Court. He received the resignations of Russell and

avendish, who alone in the Council still supported Shaftesbury's
projects, "with all his heart." Shaftesbury met defiance with
efiance. Followed by a crowd of his adherents he attended before
he Grand Jury of Middlesex, to present the Duke of York as a
atholic recusant, and the King's mistress, the Duchess of Ports-
nouth, as a national nuisance, while Monmouth returned to make
progress through the country, and won favour everywhere by his
vinning demeanour. Above all, Shaftesbury relied on the temper
f the Commons, elected as they had been in the very heat of the
anic and irritated by the long prorogation; and the first act of
he House on meeting in October was to vote that their care should
e "to suppress Popery and prevent a Popish successor." Rumours
f a Catholic plot in Ireland were hardly needed to push the
xclusion Bill through the Commons without a division; and even
he Council wavered before the resolute temper of their opponents.
emple and Essex both declared themselves in favour of the
xclusion. Of all the leaders of the Country party, only Lord
Ialifax now remained opposed to it, and his opposition simply
imed at securing its object by less violent means. "My Lord
alifax is entirely in the interest of the Prince of Orange," the
rench ambassador, Barillon, wrote to his master, "and what he
eems to be doing for the Duke of York is really in order to make
n opening for a compromise by which the Prince of Orange may
enefit." But Charles eagerly seized on this fatal disunion in the
nly party which could effectively check his designs. He dismissed
ssex and Temple and backed by his personal influence the
loquence of Halifax in bringing about the rejection of the Ex-
lusion Bill in the Lords. The same fate awaited Shaftesbury's
espairing efforts to pass a Bill of Divorce, which would have
nabled Charles to put away his queen on the ground of barrenness,
nd by a fresh marriage to give a Protestant heir to the throne.

Bold as the King's action had been, it rested for support simply
n the change in public feeling, and this Shaftesbury resolved to
heck and turn by a great public impeachment which would revive
nd establish the general belief in the Plot. Lord Stafford, who
om his age and rank was looked on as the leader of the Catholic
arty, had lain a prisoner in the Tower since the first outburst of
opular frenzy. He was now solemnly impeached; and his trial in
ecember 1680 mustered the whole force of informers to prove the
ruth of a Catholic conspiracy against the King and the realm. The
vidence was worthless; but the trial revived, as Shaftesbury had
oped, much of the old panic, and the condemnation of the prisoner
y a majority of his peers was followed by his death on the scaffold.
he blow produced its effect on all but Charles. Even Lord
underland, the ablest of the new ministers who had succeeded
emple and his friends, pressed the King to give way. Halifax,
hile still firm against the Exclusion Bill, took advantage of the
opular pressure to introduce a measure which would with less
now of violence have as completely accomplished the ends of an

exclusion as the bill itself, a measure which would have taken from James on his accession the right of veto on any bill passed by the two Houses, the right of negotiating with foreign states, or of appointing either civil or military officers save with the consent of Parliament. The plan was no doubt prompted by the Prince of Orange; and the States of Holland supported it by pressing Charles to come to an accommodation with his subjects which would enable them to check the perpetual aggressions which France had been making on her neighbours since the Peace of Nimeguen. But deserted as he was by his ministers, and even by his mistress, for the Duchess of Portsmouth had been cowed into supporting the exclusion by the threats of Shaftesbury, Charles was determined to resist every project whether of exclusion or limitation. On refusal of supplies he dissolved the Parliament. The truth was that he had at last succeeded in procuring the aid of France. Without the knowledge of his ministers he had renewed his secret negotiations, had pledged himself to withdraw from alliance with all the opponents of French policy, and in return had been promised a subsidy which recruited his Treasury and again rendered him independent of Parliaments. With characteristic subtilty however he summoned, in March 1681, a new Parliament. The summons was a mere blind. The King's one aim was to frighten the country into reaction by the dread of civil strife; and his summons of the Parliament to Oxford was an appeal to the country against the disloyalty of the capital, and an adroit means of reviving the memories of the Civil War. With the same end he ordered his guards to accompany him, on the pretext of anticipated disorder; and Shaftesbury, himself terrified at the projects of the Court, aided the King's designs by appearing with his followers in arms on the plea of self-protection. The violence of the Parliament played yet more effectually into the King's hands. Its members were the same as those who had been returned to the Parliament he had just dissolved, and their temper was more vehement than ever. The rejection of a new Limitation Bill brought forward by Halifax, which while conceding to James the title of King would have vested the actual functions of government in the Prince of Orange, alienated the more moderate and sensible of the Country party. Their attempt to revive the panic by impeaching an informer FitzHarris, before the House of Lords in defiance of the constitutional rule which entitled him as a commoner to a trial by his peers in the course of common law, did still more to throw public opinion on the side of the Crown. Shaftesbury's course rested wholly on the belief that the penury of the Treasury left Charles at his mercy and that a refusal of supplies must wring from the King his assent to the exclusion. But the gold of France had freed the King from his thraldom. He had used the Parliament simply to exhibit himself as a sovereign whose patience and conciliatory temper was rewarded with insult and violence; and now that he saw his end accomplished, he suddenly dissolved the Houses in April, and pealed in a Royal declaration to the justice of the nation at rge.

The appeal was met by an almost universal burst of loyalty. The hurch rallied to the King; his declaration was read from every ulpit; and the Universities solemnly decided that " no religion, o law, no fault, no forfeiture," could avail to bar the sacred right hereditary succession. The arrest of Shaftesbury on a charge of uborning false witnesses to the Plot marked the new strength of ue Crown. London indeed was still true to him; the Middlesex rand Jury ignored the bill of his indictment; and his discharge om the Tower was welcomed in every street with bonfires and nging of bells. But a fresh impulse was given to the loyal enthu- asm of the country at large by the publication of a plan found mong his papers, the plan of a secret association for the furtherance f the exclusion, whose members bound themselves to obey the rders of Parliament even after its prorogation or dissolution by ue Crown. Charles pushed boldly on in his new course. He con- rmed the loyalty of the Church by renewing the persecution of the onconformists. The Duke of York returned in triumph to St. ames's, and the turn of the tide was so manifest that Lord underland and the ministers, who had wavered till now, openly ought the Duke's favour. Monmouth, who had resumed his rogresses through the country as a means of checking the tide of eaction, was at once arrested. A daring breach of custom placed ories in 1682 as sheriffs of the City of London, and the packed iries they nominated left the life of every exclusionist at the mercy f the Crown. Shaftesbury, alive to the new danger, plunged esperately into conspiracies with a handful of adventurers as esperate as himself, hid himself in the City, where he boasted that en thousand " brisk boys " were ready to appear at his call, and rged his friends to rise in arms. But their delays drove him to ight; and in January 1683, two months after his arrival in Iolland, the soul of the great leader, great from his immense nergy and the wonderful versatility of his genius, but whose genius nd energy had ended in wrecking for the time the fortunes of English freedom and in associating the noblest of causes with the ilest of crimes, found its first quiet in death.

1682
to
1688

SECTION VI.—THE SECOND STUART TYRANNY, 1682—1688

[*Authorities.*—For the closing years of Charles II. and the reign o
James II., in addition to Burnet, may be mentioned Dalrymple'
" Memoirs," especially valuable for the appendices in the third volume
Bramston's " Autobiography "; the " Diary of Henry Hyde, Earl o
Clarendon," and the " Diary of Thomas Cartwright." Clarke's " Lif
of James II." contains the king's autobiographical remains. Lutterell
" Brief Historical Relation of State Affairs " is valuable for Londor
The Ellis Correspondence and the Clarendon Correspondence are usefu
for James II. Wellwood, " Memoirs," is valuable for the Revolution fror
a Whig standpoint. Macaulay's " History " is the most famous moder.
account; Lingard and Ranke must also be consulted.]

The
Royal
Triumph

The flight of Shaftesbury proclaimed the triumph of the King
His wonderful sagacity had told him when the struggle was ove
and further resistance useless. But the Whig leaders, who ha
delayed to answer the Earl's call, still nursed projects of rising i
arms; and the more desperate spirits who had clustered round hir
as he lay hidden to the City took refuge in plots of assassinatio
and in a plan for murdering Charles and his brother as they passe
the Rye-house on their road from London to Newmarket. Both th
conspiracies were betrayed, and though they were wholly distinc
from one another the cruel ingenuity of the Crown lawyers blende
them into one. Lord Essex, the last of an ill-fated race, saved him
self from a traitor's death by suicide in the Tower. Lord Russell

1683

convicted on a charge of sharing in the Rye-house plot, wa
beheaded in Lincoln Inn Fields. The same fate awaited Algerno
Sidney. Monmouth fled in terror over sea, and his flight wa
followed by a series of prosecutions for sedition directed agains
his followers. In 1683 the Constitutional opposition which had hel
Charles so long in check lay crushed at his feet. A weaker ma
might easily have been led into a wild tyranny by the mad out
burst of loyalty which greeted his triumph. On the very day whe
the crowd around Russell's scaffold were dipping their hand
kerchiefs in his blood, as in the blood of a martyr, the Universit
of Oxford solemnly declared that the doctrine of passive obedience
even to the worst of rulers, was a part of religion. But Charles sav
that immense obstacles still lay in the road of a mere tyranny
The Church was as powerful as ever, and the mention of a renewa
of the Indulgence to Nonconformists had to be withdrawn befor
the opposition of the bishops. He was careful therefore during th
few years which remained to him to avoid the appearance of an
open violation of public law. He suspended no statute. He impose
no tax by Royal authority. He generally enforced the Test Act
Nothing indeed shows more completely how great a work the Lon
Parliament had done than a survey of the reign of Charles th
Second. " The King," Hallam says very truly, " was restored t
nothing but what the law had preserved to him." No attempt wa
made to restore the abuses which the patriots of 1641 had swept

away. Parliament was continually summoned. In spite of its frequent refusal of supplies, no attempt was ever made to raise money by unconstitutional means. The few illegal proclamations issued under Clarendon ceased with his fall. No effort was made to revive the Star Chamber and the Court of High Commission; and if judges were servile and juries sometimes packed, there was no open interference with the course of justice. In two remarkable points freedom had made an advance even on 1641. From the moment when printing began to tell on public opinion, it had been gagged by a system of licences. The regulations framed under Henry the Eighth subjected the press to the control of the Star Chamber, and the Martin Marprelate libels brought about a yet more stringent control under Elizabeth. Even the Long Parliament laid a heavy hand on the press, and the great remonstrance of Milton in his " Areopagitica " fell dead on the ears of his Puritan associates. But the statute for the regulation of printing which was passed immediately after the Restoration expired finally in 1679, and the temper of the Parliament gave no hope of any successful attempt to re-establish the censorship. To the freedom of the press the Habeas Corpus Act added a new security for the personal freedom of every Englishman. Against arbitrary imprisonment provision had been made in the earliest ages by a famous clause in the Great Charter. No free man could be held in prison save on charge or conviction of crime or for debt; and every prisoner on a criminal charge could demand as a right from the court of King's Bench the issue of a writ of " habeas corpus," which bound his gaoler to produce both the prisoner and the warrant on which he was imprisoned, that the court might judge whether he was imprisoned according to law. In cases however of imprisonment on a warrant of the Royal Council it had been sometimes held by judges that the writ could not be issued, and under Clarendon's administration instances had in this way occurred of imprisonment without legal remedy. But his fall was quickly followed by the introduction of a bill to secure this right of the subject, and after a long struggle the Act which is known as the Habeas Corpus Act passed finally in 1679. By this great statute the old practice of the law was freed from all difficulties and exceptions. Every prisoner committed for any crime save treason or felony was declared entitled to his writ even in the vacations of the courts, and heavy penalties were enforced on judges or gaolers who refused him this right. Every person committed for felony or treason was entitled to be released on bail, unless indicted at the next session of gaol delivery after his commitment, and to be discharged if not indicted at the sessions which followed. It was forbidden under the heaviest penalties to send a prisoner into any places or fortresses beyond the seas.

Galling to the Crown as the freedom of the press and the Habeas Corpus Act were soon found to be, Charles made no attempt to curtail the one or to infringe the other. But while cautious to avoid rousing popular resistance, he moved coolly and resolutely forward on the path of despotism. It was in vain that Halifax pressed for energetic resistance to the aggressions of France, for the recall of Monmouth, or for the calling of a fresh Parliament. Like every other English statesman he found he had been duped, and that now his work was done he was suffered to remain in office but left without any influence in the government. In spite of his remonstrances the Test Act was violated by the readmission of James to a seat in the Council, and by his restoration to the office of Lord High Admiral. Parliament, in defiance of the Triennial Act, remained unassembled during the remainder of the King's reign. His secret alliance with France furnished Charles with the funds he immediately required, and the rapid growth of the customs through the increase of English commerce promised to give him a revenue which, if peace were preserved, would save him from the need of a fresh appeal to the Commons. All opposition was at an end. The strength of the Country party had been broken by the reaction against Shaftesbury's projects, and by the flight and death of its more prominent leaders. Whatever strength it retained lay chiefly in the towns, and these were now attacked by writs of " quo warranto," which called on them to show cause why their charters should not be declared forfeited on the ground of abuse of their privileges. A few verdicts on the side of the Crown brought about a general surrender of municipal liberties; and the grant of fresh charters, in which all but ultra-loyalists were carefully excluded from their corporations, placed the representation of the boroughs in the hands of the Crown. Against active discontent Charles had long been quietly providing by the gradual increase of his Guards. The withdrawal of its garrison from Tangier enabled him to raise their force to nine thousand well-equipped soldiers, and to supplement this force, the nucleus of our present standing army, by a reserve of six regiments, which were maintained, till they should be needed at home, in the service of the United Provinces. But great as the danger really was, it lay not so much in isolated acts of tyranny as in the character and purpose of Charles himself. His death at the very moment of his triumph saved English freedom. He had regained his old popularity, and at the news of his danger in the spring of 1685 crowds thronged the churches, praying that God would raise him up again to be a father to his people. The bishops around his bed fell on their knees and implored his blessing, and Charles with outstretched hands solemnly gave it to them. But while his subjects were praying, and his bishops seeking a blessing, the one anxiety of the King was to die reconciled to the Catholic Church. When his chamber was cleared a priest named Huddleston, who had saved his life after the battle of Worcester, received his confession and administered the last sacraments. Charles died as he had lived: brave, witty, cynical, even in the presence of death. Tortured as he was with pain, he begged the bystanders to forgive him for being so unconscionable a time in lying. One mistress, the Duchess of Portsmouth, hung weeping over his bed. His last thought was of another mistress, Nell Gwynn. ' Do not," he whispered to his successor ere he sank into a fatal stupor, " do not let poor Nelly starve! "

The first words of James on his accession in February 1685 were a pledge to preserve the laws inviolate, and to protect the Church. The pledge was welcomed by the whole country with enthusiasm. All the suspicions of a Catholic sovereign seemed to have disappeared. " We have the word of a King! " ran the general cry, " and of a King who was never worse than his word." The conviction of his brother's faithlessness stood James in good stead. He was looked upon as narrow, impetuous, stubborn, and despotic in heart, but even his enemies did not accuse him of being false. Above all he was believed to be keenly alive to the honour of his country, and resolute to free it from foreign dependence. It was necessary to summon a Parliament, for the Royal revenue ceased with the death of the King; but the elections, swayed at once by the tide of loyalty and by the command of the boroughs which the surrender of their charters had given to the Crown, sent up a House of Commons in which James found few members who were not to his mind. The question of religious security was waived at a hint of the Royal displeasure. A revenue of nearly two millions was granted to the King for life. All that was wanted to rouse the loyalty of the country into fanaticism was supplied by a rebellion in the north, and by another under Monmouth in the west. The hopes of Scotch freedom had clung ever since the Restoration to the house of Argyle. The great Marquis, as we have seen, had been brought to the block at the Restoration. His son, the Earl of Argyle, had been unable to save himself even by a life of singular caution and obedience from the ill-will of the vile politicians who governed Scotland. He was at last convicted of treason on grounds at which every English statesman stood aghast. " We should not hang a dog here," Halifax protested, " on the grounds on which my lord Argyle has been sentenced to death." The Earl escaped however to Holland, and lived peaceably there during the six last years of the reign of Charles. Monmouth found the same refuge at the Hague, where a belief in his father's love and purpose to recall him secured him a kindly reception from William of Orange. But the accession of James was a death-blow to the hopes of the Duke, while it stirred the fanaticism of Argyle to a resolve of wresting Scotland from the rule of a Popish king. The two leaders determined to appear in arms in England and the North, and the two expeditions sailed within a few days of each other. Argyle's attempt was soon over. His clan of the Campbells rose on his landing in Cantyre, but the country had been occupied for the King, and quarrels among the exiles who accompanied him robbed his effort of every chance of success. His force scattered without a fight; and Argyle, arrested in an attempt to escape, was hurried to a traitor's death. Monmouth for a time found brighter fortune. His

popularity in the west was great, and though the gentry held aloof
when he landed at Lyme, the farmers and traders of Devonshire
and Dorset flocked to his standard. The clothier-towns of Somerset
were still true to the Whig cause, and on the entrance of the Duke
into Taunton the popular enthusiasm showed itself in flowers
which wreathed every door, as well as in a train of young girls who
presented Monmouth with a Bible and a flag. His forces now
amounted to six thousand men, but whatever chance of success
he might have had was lost by his assumption of the title of King.
The gentry, still true to the cause of Mary and of William, held
stubbornly aloof, while the Guards hurried to the scene of the
revolt, and the militia gathered to the Royal standard. Foiled in
an attempt on Bristol and Bath, Monmouth fell back on Bridgewater, and flung himself in the night of the sixth of July, 1685, on
the King's forces, which lay encamped on Sedgemoor. The surprise
failed; and the brave peasants and miners who followed the Duke,
checked in their advance by a deep drain which crossed the moor,
were broken after a short resistance by the Royal horse. Their
leader fled from the field, and after a vain effort to escape from the
realm, was captured and sent pitilessly to the block.

**The
Bloody
Assize**
Never had England shown a firmer loyalty; but its loyalty was
changed into horror by the terrible measures of repression which
followed on the victory of Sedgemoor. Even North, the Lord
Keeper, a servile tool of the Crown, protested against the license
and bloodshed in which the troops were suffered to indulge after
the battle. His protest however was disregarded, and he withdrew
broken-hearted from the Court to die. James was, in fact, resolved
on a far more terrible vengeance; and the Chief-Justice Jeffreys,
a man of great natural powers but of violent temper, was sent to
earn the Seals by a series of judicial murders which have left his
name a byword for cruelty. Three hundred and fifty rebels were
hanged in the " Bloody Circuit," as Jeffreys made his way through
Dorset and Somerset. More than eight hundred were sold into
slavery beyond sea. A yet larger number were whipped and
imprisoned. The Queen, the maids of honour, the courtiers, even
the Judge himself, made shameless profit from the sale of pardons.
What roused pity above all were the cruelties wreaked upon
women. Some were scourged from market-town to market-town.
Mrs. Lisle, the wife of one of the Regicides, was sent to the block
at Winchester for harbouring a rebel. Elizabeth Gaunt, for the
same act of womanly charity, was burned at Tyburn. Pity turned
into horror when it was found that cruelty such as this was avowed
and sanctioned by the King. Even the cold heart of General
Churchill, to whose energy the victory at Sedgemoor had mainly
been owing, revolted at the ruthlessness with which James turned
away from all appeals for mercy. " This marble," he cried as he
struck the chimney-piece on which he leant, " is not harder than
the King's heart." But it was soon plain that the terror which the
butchery was meant to strike into the people was part of a larger

purpose. The revolt was made a pretext for a vast increase of the standing army. Charles, as we have seen, had silently and cautiously raised it to nearly ten thousand men; James raised it at one sweep to twenty thousand. The employment of this force was to be at home, not abroad, for the hope of an English policy in foreign affairs had already faded away. In the design which James had at heart he could look for no consent from Parliament; and however his pride revolted against a dependence on France, it was only by French gold and French soldiers that he could hope to hold the Parliament permanently at bay. A week therefore after his accession he assured Lewis that his gratitude and devotion to him equalled that of Charles himself. " Tell your master," he said to the French ambassador, " that without his protection I can do nothing. He has a right to be consulted, and it is my wish to consult him, about everything." The pledge of subservience was rewarded with the promise of a subsidy, and the promise was received with expressions of delight and servility which Charles would have mocked at.

Never had the secret league with France seemed so full of danger to English religion. Europe had long been trembling at the ambition of Lewis; it was trembling now at his bigotry. He had proclaimed warfare against civil liberty in his attack upon Holland; he declared war at this moment upon religious freedom by revoking the Edict of Nantes, the measure by which Henry the Fourth, after his abandonment of Protestantism, secured toleration and the free exercise of their worship for his Protestant subjects. It had been respected by Richelieu even in his victory over the Huguenots, and only lightly tampered with by Mazarin. But from the beginning of his reign Lewis had resolved to set aside its provisions, and his revocation of it in 1685 was only the natural close of a progressive system of persecution. The Revocation was followed by outrages more cruel than even the bloodshed of Alva. Dragoons were quartered on Protestant families, women were flung from their sick-beds into the streets, children were torn from their mothers' arms to be brought up in Catholicism, ministers were sent to the galleys. In spite of the royal edicts, which forbade even flight to the victims of these horrible atrocities, a hundred thousand Protestants fled over the borders, and Holland, Switzerland, the Palatinate, were filled with French exiles. Thousands found refuge in England, and their industry founded in the fields east of London the silk trade of Spitalfields. But while Englishmen were quivering with horror at the news from France, James in defiance of the law was filling his new army with Catholic officers. He dismissed Halifax on his refusal to consent to a plan for repealing the Test Act, and met the Parliament in 1686 with a haughty declaration that whether legal or no his grant of commissions to Catholics must not be questioned, and a demand of supplies for his new troops. Loyal as was the temper of the Houses, their alarm at Popery and at a standing army was yet stronger than their loyalty. The

Commons by the majority of a single vote deferred the grant of supplies till grievances were redressed, and demanded in their address the recall of the illegal commissions. The Lords took a bolder tone; and the protest of the bishops against any infringement of the Test Act was backed by the eloquence of Halifax. But both Houses were at once prorogued. The King resolved to obtain from the judges what he could not obtain from Parliament. He remodelled the bench by dismissing four judges who refused to lend themselves to his plans; and their successors decided in the case of Sir Edward Hales, a Catholic officer in the Royal army, that a Royal dispensation could be pleaded in bar of the Test Act. The principle laid down by the judges asserted the right of the Crown to override the laws; and it was applied by James with a reckless impatience of all decency and self-restraint. Catholics were admitted into civil and military offices without stint, and four Roman Catholic peers were sworn as members of the Privy Council. The laws which forbade the presence of Catholic priests in the realm or the open exercise of Catholic worship were set at nought. A gorgeous chapel was opened in the Palace of St. James for the worship of the King. Carmelites, Benedictines, Franciscans, appeared in their religious garb in the streets of London, and the Jesuits set up a crowded school in the Savoy.

The quick growth of discontent at these acts would have startled a wiser man into prudence, but James prided himself on the reckless violence of his procedure. A riot which took place on the opening of a fresh Catholic chapel in the City was followed by the establishment of a camp of thirteen thousand men at Hounslow to overawe the capital. The course which James intended to follow in England was shown by the course he was following in the sister kingdoms. In Scotland he acted as a pure despot. He placed its government in the hands of two lords, Melfort and Perth, who had embraced his own religion, and put a Catholic in command of the Castle of Edinburgh. Under Charles the Scotch Parliament had been the mere creature of the Crown, but servile as were its members, there was a point at which their servility stopped. When James boldly required from them the toleration of Catholics, they refused to pass such an Act. It was in vain that the King tempted them to consent by the offer of a free trade with England. " Shall we sell our God ? " was the indignant reply. James at once ordered the Scotch judges to treat all laws against Catholics as null and void, and his orders were obeyed. In Ireland his policy threw off even the disguise of law. Papists were admitted by the King's command to the Council and to civil offices. A Catholic, Lord Tyrconnell, was put at the head of the army, and set instantly about its reorganization by cashiering Protestant officers and by admitting two thousand Catholic natives into its ranks. Meanwhile James had begun in England a bold and systematic attack upon the Church. He regarded his ecclesiastical supremacy as a weapon providentially left to him for undoing the work which it had

abled his predecessors to do. Under Henry and Elizabeth it had
been used to turn the Church of England from Catholic to Pro-
stant. Under James it should be used to turn it back again from
rotestant to Catholic. The High Commission indeed had been
eclared illegal by an Act of the Long Parliament, and this Act
ad been confirmed by the Parliament of the Restoration. But
ae statute was roughly set aside. Seven Commissioners were
ppointed in 1686 for the government of the Church, with Jeffreys
their head; and the first blow of the Commission was at the
ishop of London. James had forbidden the clergy to preach
gainst Popery, and ordered Bishop Compton to suspend a London
car who set this order at defiance. The Bishop's refusal was
unished by his own suspension. But the pressure of the Com-
ission only drove the clergy to a bolder defiance of the Royal will.
rmons against superstition were preached from every pulpit;
ad the two most famous divines of the day, Tillotson and Stilling-
et, put themselves at the head of a host of controversialists who
attered pamphlets and tracts from every printing press.

Foiled in his direct efforts to overawe the Church, James resolved
attack it in the great institutions which had till now been its
ronghold. To secure the Universities for Catholicism was to seize
ae only training schools which the clergy possessed. Cambridge
deed escaped easily. A Benedictine monk who presented himself
ith Royal letters recommending him for the degree of a master
arts was rejected on his refusal to sign the Articles: and the
ice-Chancellor paid for the rejection by dismissal from his office.
ut a far more violent and obstinate attack was directed against
xford. The Master of University College, who declared himself
convert, was authorized to retain his post in defiance of the law.
assey, a Roman Catholic, was presented by the Crown to the
eanery of Christ Church. Magdalen was the wealthiest Oxford
ollege, and James in 1687 recommended one Farmer, a Catholic
infamous life and not even qualified by statute for the office,
its vacant headship. The Fellows remonstrated, and on the
jection of their remonstrance chose Hough, one of their own
amber, as their President. The Commission declared the election
oid; and James, shamed out of his first candidate, recommended
second, Parker, Bishop of Oxford, a Catholic in heart and the
eanest of his courtiers. But the Fellows held stubbornly to their
gal head. It was in vain that the King visited Oxford, summoned
em to his presence, and rated them as they knelt before him like
hoolboys. "I am King," he said, "I will be obeyed! Go to your
aapel, this instant, and elect the Bishop! Let those who refuse
ok to it, for they shall feel the whole weight of my hand!" It
as felt that to give Magdalen as well as Christ Church into Catholic
ands was to turn Oxford into a Catholic seminary, and the King's
areats were calmly disregarded. But they were soon carried out.
special Commission visited the University, pronounced Hough
a intruder, set aside his appeal to the law, burst open the door of

James
and the
Universi-
ties

1682
to
1688

his President's house to install Parker in his place, and on the
refusal to submit deprived the Fellows of their fellowships. T
expulsion of the Fellows was followed on a like refusal by that
the Demies. Parker, who died immediately after his installatic
was succeeded by a Roman Catholic bishop in partibus, Bon
venture Giffard, and twelve Catholics were admitted to fellowshi
in a single day.

Declara-
tion of
Indul-
gence

The work James was doing in the Church he was doing with
mad a recklessness in the State. Parliament, which had been ke
silent by prorogation after prorogation, was finally dissolved; an
the King was left without a check in his defiance of the law. It w
in vain that the bulk of the Catholic gentry stood aloof and p
dicted the inevitable reaction his course must bring about, or th
Rome itself counselled greater moderation. James was infatuat
with the success of his enterprises. He resolved to show the wor
that even the closest ties of blood were as nothing to him if th
conflicted with the demands of his faith. His marriage with An
Hyde, the daughter of Clarendon, bound both the Chancellor's so
to his fortunes; and on his accession he had sent his elder brothe
in-law, Edward, Earl of Clarendon, as Lord Lieutenant to Irelan
and raised the younger, Laurence, Earl of Rochester, to the po
of Lord Treasurer. But Rochester was now told that the Ki
could not safely entrust so great a charge to anyone who did n
share his sentiments on religion, and on his refusal to abandon
faith he was driven from office. His brother, Clarendon, shared
fall. A Catholic, Lord Bellasys, became First Lord of the Treasur
which was put into commission after Rochester's removal; an
another Catholic, Lord Arundell, became Lord Privy Seal. Pet
a Jesuit, was called to the Privy Council. The Nuncio of the Po
was received in state at Windsor. But even James could hardly f
to perceive the growth of public discontent. The great Tory nobl
if they were staunch for the Crown, were as resolute Englishmen
their hatred of mere tyranny as the Whigs themselves. James ga
the Duke of Norfolk the sword of State to carry before him as
went to Mass. The Duke stopped at the Chapel door. "Yo
father would have gone further," said the King. "Your Majesty
father was the better man," replied the Duke, "and he would n
have gone so far." The young Duke of Somerset was ordered
introduce the Nuncio into the Presence Chamber. "I am advised
he answered, "that I cannot obey your Majesty without breaki
the law." "Do you not know that I am above the law?" Jam
asked angrily. "Your Majesty may be, but I am not," retort
the Duke. He was dismissed from his post; but the spirit
resistance spread fast. In spite of the King's letters, the govern
of the Charter House, who numbered among them some of t
greatest English nobles, refused to admit a Catholic to the benef
of the foundation. The most devoted loyalists began to murm
when James demanded apostasy as a proof of their loyalty.
had soon in fact to abandon all hope of bringing the Church or t

1687

ries over to his will. He turned, as Charles had turned, to the onconformists, and published in 1687 a Declaration of Indulnce which annulled the penal laws against Nonconformists and .tholics alike, and abrogated every Act which imposed a test as qualification for office in Church or State. The temptation to cept such an offer was great, for, since the fall of Shaftesbury, rsecution had fallen heavily on the Protestant dissidents, and e can hardly wonder that the Nonconformists wavered for a ne. But the great body of them, and all the more venerable mes among them, remained true to the cause of freedom. Baxter, owe, Bunyan, all refused an Indulgence which could only be irchased by the violent overthrow of the law. A mere handful of ldresses could be procured by the utmost pressure, and it was on plain that the attempt to divide the forces of Protestantism d utterly failed.

The failure of his Declaration only spurred James to an attempt procure a repeal of the Test Act from Parliament itself. But no ee Parliament could be brought, as he knew, to consent to its peal. The Lords indeed could be swamped by lavish creations of w peers. "Your troop of horse," his minister, Lord Sunderland, ld Churchill, " shall be called up into the House of Lords." But was a harder matter to secure a compliant House of Commons. ie Lord Lieutenants were directed to bring about such a " regula- n " of the governing body in boroughs as would ensure the turn of candidates pledged to the repeal of the Test, and to iestion every magistrate in their county as to his vote. Half of em at once refused, and a long list of great nobles—the Earls of xford, Shrewsbury, Dorset, Derby, Pembroke, Rutland, Aber- venny, Thanet, Northampton, and Abingdon—were at once smissed from their Lord Lieutenancies. The justices when iestioned simply replied that they would vote according to their nsciences, and send members to Parliament who would protect e Protestant religion. After repeated " regulations " it was found possible to form a corporate body which would return repre- ntatives willing to comply with the Royal will. All thought of a irliament had to be abandoned; and even the most bigoted urtiers counselled moderation at this proof of the stubborn position which James must prepare to encounter from the peers, e gentry, and the trading classes. The clergy alone still hesitated any open act of resistance. Even the tyranny of the Commission d the attack on the Universities failed to rouse into open dis- rection men who had been preaching Sunday after Sunday the ictrine of passive obedience to the worst of kings. But James emed resolved to rouse them. On the twenty-seventh of April, 88, he issued a fresh Declaration of Indulgence, and ordered ery clergyman to read it during divine service on two successive indays. Little time was given for deliberation, but little time is needed. The clergy refused almost to a man to be the instru- ents of their own humiliation. The Declaration was read in only

four of the London churches, and in these the congregation flocke
out of church at the first words of it. Nearly all of the countr
clergy refused to obey the Royal orders. The Bishops went wit
the rest of the clergy. A few days before the appointed Sunda
Archbishop Sancroft called his suffragans together, and the si
who were able to appear at Lambeth signed a temperate protest t
the King, in which they declined to publish an illegal Declaratio
"It is a standard of rebellion," James exclaimed as the Prima
presented the paper; and the resistance of the clergy was no soon
announced to him than he determined to wreak his vengeance o
the Prelates who had signed the protest. He ordered the Eccles
astical Commissioners to deprive them of their sees, but in th
matter even the Commissioners shrank from obeying him. Th
Chancellor, Lord Jeffreys, advised a prosecution for libel as a
easier mode of punishment; and the Bishops, who refused to giv
bail, were committed on this charge to the Tower. They passed t
their prison amidst the shouts of a great multitude, the sentine
knelt for their blessing as they entered its gates, and the soldie
of the garrison drank their healths. So threatening was the temp
of the nation that his ministers pressed James to give way. B
his obstinacy grew with the danger. "Indulgence," he sai
"ruined my father;" and on June the 29th the Bishops appeare
as criminals at the bar of the King's Bench. The jury had bee
packed, the judges were mere tools of the Crown, but judges an
jury were alike overawed by the indignation of the people at larg
No sooner had the foreman of the jury uttered the words "N
guilty" than a roar of applause burst from the crowd, and hors
men spurred along every road to carry over the country the new
of the acquittal.

SECTION VII.—WILLIAM OF ORANGE

[*Authorities.*—As under the previous section. For the documents
this and the succeeding periods, see Robertson, "Select Statutes, Case
and Documents."]

**The
Great-
ness of
France**

Amidst the tumult of the Plot and the Exclusion Bill the wis
among English statesmen had fixed their hopes steadily on th
succession of Mary, the elder daughter and heiress of James. Th
tyranny of her father's reign made this succession the hope of th
people at large. But to Europe the importance of the change, when
ever it should come about, lay not so much in the succession o
Mary, as in the new power which such an event would give to he
husband, William Prince of Orange. We have come in fact to
moment when the struggle of England against the aggression of it
King blends with the larger struggle of Europe against the aggre
sion of Lewis the Fourteenth, and it is only by a rapid glance at th
political state of the Continent that we can understand the re

ture and results of the Revolution which drove James from the
rone.

At this moment France was the dominant power in Christendom.
he religious wars which began with the Reformation broke the
ength of the nations around her. Spain was no longer able to
ht the battle of Catholicism. The Peace of Westphalia, by the
dependence it gave to the German princes and the jealousy it left
ve between the Protestant and Catholic powers, destroyed the
ength of the Empire. The German branch of the House of
stria, spent with the long struggle of the Thirty Years' War,
d enough to do in battling hard against the advance of the
rks from Hungary on Vienna. The victories of Gustavus and
the generals whom he formed had been dearly purchased by the
haustion of Sweden. The United Provinces were as yet hardly
garded as a great power, and were trammelled by their contest
th England for the empire of the seas. England, which under
omwell promised for a moment to take the lead in Europe, sank
der Charles and James into a dependency of France. France
one profited by the general wreck. The wise policy of Henry the
urth in securing religious peace by a toleration to the Protestants
d undone the ill effects of its religious wars. The Huguenots were
ll numerous south of the Loire, but the loss of their fortresses
d turned their energies into the peaceful channels of industry
d trade. Feudal disorder was roughly put down by Richelieu,
d the policy by which he gathered all local power into the hands
the crown, though fatal in the end to the real welfare of France,
ve it for the moment an air of good government and a command
er its internal resources which no other country could boast.
compact and fertile territory, the natural activity and enterprise
its people, and the rapid growth of its commerce and of manu-
ttures were sources of natural wealth which even its heavy
xation failed to check. In the latter half of the seventeenth
ntury France was looked upon as the wealthiest power in Europe.
he yearly income of the French crown was double that of England,
d even Lewis the Fourteenth trusted as much to the credit of his
asury as to the glory of his arms. "After all," he said, when
e fortunes of war began to turn against him, "it is the last
vereign which must win!" It was in fact this superiority in
alth which enabled France to set on foot forces such as had never
en seen in Europe since the downfall of Rome. At the opening
the reign of Lewis the Fourteenth its army mustered a hundred
ousand men. With the war against Holland it rose to nearly two
ndred thousand. In the last struggle against the Grand Alliance
ere was a time when it counted nearly half a million of men in
ms. Nor was France content with these enormous land forces.
nce the ruin of Spain the fleets of Holland and of England had
one disputed the empire of the seas. Under Richelieu and Mazarin
ance could hardly be looked upon as a naval power. But the
rly years of Lewis saw the creation of a navy of 100 men-of-war,

and the fleets of France soon held their own against England the Dutch.

Such a power would have been formidable at any time; but was doubly formidable when directed by statesmen who in kno ledge and ability were without rivals in Europe. No diplomat could compare with Lionne, no war minister with Louvois, financier with Colbert. Their young master, Lewis the Fourteen bigoted, narrow-minded, commonplace as he was, without person honour or personal courage, without gratitude and without pit insane in his pride, insatiable in his vanity, brutal in his selfishne had still many of the qualities of a great ruler: industry, patienc quickness of resolve, firmness of purpose, a capacity for discerni greatness and using it, an immense self-belief and self-confiden and a temper utterly destitute indeed of real greatness, but wi a dramatic turn for seeming to be great. As a politician Lewis h simply to reap the harvest which the two great Cardinals who we before him had sown. Both had used to the profit of France t exhaustion and dissension which the wars of religion had broug upon Europe. Richelieu turned the scale against the House Austria by his alliance with Sweden, with the United Provinc and with the Protestant princes of Germany; and the two gre treaties by which Mazarin ended the Thirty Years' War, t Treaty of Westphalia and the Treaty of the Pyrenees, left t Empire disorganized and Spain powerless. From that mome indeed Spain had sunk into a strange decrepitude. Robbed of t chief source of her wealth by the independence of Holland, weaken at home by the revolt of Portugal, her infantry annihilated Condé in his victory of Rocroi, her fleet ruined by the Dutch, l best blood drained away to the Indies, the energies of her peo destroyed by the suppression of all liberty, civil or religious, l intellectual life crushed by the Inquisition, her industry cripp by the expulsion of the Moors, by financial oppression, and by t folly of her colonial system, the kingdom which under Philip t Second had aimed at the empire of the world lay helpless a exhausted under Philip the Fourth. The aim of Lewis from 16 the year when he really became master of France, was to carry the policy of his predecessors, and above all to complete the ruin Spain. The conquest of the Spanish provinces in the Netherlan would carry his border to the Scheldt. A more distant hope lay the probable extinction of the Austrian line which now sat on t throne of Spain. By securing the succession to their throne fo French prince, not only Castile and Arragon with the Span dependencies in Italy and the Netherlands, but the Spanish emp in the New World would be added to the dominions of Fran Nothing could save Spain but a union of the European powe and to prevent this union by his negotiations was a work at whi Lewis toiled for years. The intervention of the Empire was p vented by a renewal of the old alliances between France and t lesser German princes. A league with the Turks gave Aust

ough to do on her eastern border. The policy of Charles the
cond bound England to inaction. Spain was at last completely
lated, and the death of Philip the Fourth gave a pretence for
ar of which Lewis availed himself in 1667. Flanders was occupied
two months. Franche-Comté was seized in seventeen days. But
e suddenness and completeness of the French success awoke a
neral terror before which the King's skilful diplomacy gave way.
olland was roused to a sense of danger at home by the appearance
French arms on the Rhine. England woke from her lethargy on
e French seizure of the coast-towns of Flanders. Sweden joined
e two Protestant powers in the Triple Alliance; and the dread of
wider league forced Lewis to content himself with the southern
lf of Flanders and the possession of a string of fortresses which
actically left him master of the Netherlands.

Lewis was maddened by the check. He not only hated the Dutch
Protestants and Republicans; but he saw in them an obstacle
hich had to be taken out of the way ere he could resume his
tack on Spain. Four years were spent in preparations for a
cisive blow at this new enemy. The French army was raised to a
ndred and eighty thousand men. Colbert created a fleet which
valled that of Holland in number and equipment. Sweden was
ain won over. England was again secured by the Treaty of Dover.
eanwhile Holland lay wrapt in a false security. The alliance with
ance had been its traditional policy, and it was especially dear
the party of the great merchant class which had mounted to
wer on the fall of the House of Orange. John de Witt, the leader
this party, though he had been forced to conclude the Triple
liance by the advance of Lewis to the Rhine, still clung blindly
the friendship of France. His trust only broke down when the
ench army crossed the Dutch border in 1672 and the glare of its
tch-fires was seen from the walls of Amsterdam. For the moment
olland lay crushed at the feet of Lewis, but the arrogance of the
nqueror roused again the stubborn courage which had wrung
ctory from Alva and worn out the pride of Philip the Second.
e fall of De Witt raised the Orange party again to power, and
lled the Prince of Orange to the head of the Republic. Though
e young Stadholder had hardly reached manhood, his great
alities at once made themselves felt. His earlier life had schooled
m in a wonderful self-control. He had been left fatherless and
but friendless in childhood, he had been bred among men who
ked on his very existence as a danger to the State, his words
d been watched, his looks noted, his friends jealously withdrawn.
such an atmosphere the boy grew up silent, wary, self-contained,
ave in temper, cold in demeanour, blunt and even repulsive in
dress. He was weak and sickly from his cradle, and manhood
ought with it an asthma and consumption which shook his frame
th a constant cough; his face was sullen and bloodless and
ored with deep lines which told of ceaseless pain. But beneath
is cold and sickly presence lay a fiery and commanding temper,

William
of
Orange

an immoveable courage, and a political ability of the highest orde
William was a born statesman. Neglected as his education ha
been in other ways, for he knew nothing of letters or of art, ╵
had been carefully trained in politics by John de Witt; and t╵
wide knowledge with which in his first address to the States-Gener
the young Stadholder reviewed the general state of Europe, t╵
cool courage with which he calculated the chances of the strugg╵
at once won him the trust of his countrymen. Their trust was so╵
rewarded. Holland was saved, and province after province w╵
back from the arms of France, by William's dauntless resolv
Like his great ancestor, William the Silent, he was a luckless cor
mander, and no general had to bear more frequent defeats. B╵
he profited by defeat as other men profit by victory. His brave╵
indeed was of that nobler cast which rises to its height in momen
of ruin and dismay. The coolness with which, boy-general as ╵
was, he rallied his broken squadrons amidst the rout of Seneff ar
wrested from Condé at the last the fruits of his victory, mov╵
his veteran opponent to a generous admiration. It was in su╵
moments indeed that the real temper of the man broke throug
the veil of his usual reserve. A strange light flashed from his ey
as soon as he was under fire, and in the terror and confusion ╵
defeat his manners took an ease and gaiety that charmed eve╵
soldier around him.

William and Charles II. The political ability of William was seen in the skill with whic
he drew Spain and the Empire into a coalition against France. B╵
France was still matchless in arms, and the effect of her victori
was seconded by the selfishness of the allies, and above all by t╵
treacherous diplomacy of Charles the Second. William was forc╵
to consent in 1679 to the Treaty of Nimeguen, which left Fran╵
dominant over Europe as she had never been before. Hollar
indeed was saved from the revenge of Lewis, but fresh spoils ha
been wrested from Spain, and Franche-Comté, which had bee
restored at the close of the former war, was retained at the end ╵
this. Above all France overawed Europe by the daring and succe
with which she had faced, single-handed, the wide coalition again
her. Her King's arrogance became unbounded. Lorraine w╵
turned into a subject-state. Genoa was bombarded, and its Do╵
forced to seek pardon in the antechambers of Versailles. The Po╵
was humiliated by the march of an army upon Rome to avenge
slight offered to the French ambassador. The Empire was outrag╵
by a shameless seizure of Imperial fiefs in Elsass and elsewher
The whole Protestant world was defied by the horrible cruelti
which followed the Revocation of the Edict of Nantes. In t╵
mind of Lewis peace meant a series of outrages on the powe
around him, but every outrage helped the cool and silent adversa╵
who was looking on from the Hague to build up the Great Allian╵
of all Europe, from which alone he looked for any effectual che╵
to the ambition of France. The experience of the last war ha
taught William that of such an alliance England must form a par

ᵭd we have already seen how much English politics were influenced
ᵭuring the reign of Charles by the struggle between William and
ᴸewis to secure English aid. A reconciliation of the King with his
ᵭarliament was an indispensable step towards freeing Charles
ᵭom his dependence on France, and it was to such a reconciliation
ᵭat William at first bent his efforts, but he was foiled by the
ᵭeadiness with which Charles clung to the power whose aid was
ᵭeedful to carry out the schemes which he was contemplating. In
ᵭis leaning towards France however Charles stood utterly alone.
ᵭis most devoted ministers foiled their sovereign's efforts as far
ᵭs they could. Even Arlington, Catholic as at heart he was, refused
ᵭ look on while France made the Flemish coast its own, and
ᵭespatched Temple to frame the Triple Alliance which defeated its
ᵭopes. Danby was even more hostile to France, and in wresting
ᵭom his master permission to offer William the hand of Mary he
ᵭealt Lewis what proved to be a fatal blow. James was without a
ᵭon, and the marriage with Mary secured to William on his father-
ᵭ-law's death the aid of England in his great enterprise. But it
ᵭas impossible to wait for that event, and though William used
ᵭis new position to bring Charles round to a more patriotic policy,
ᵭis efforts were still fruitless. The storm of the Popish Plot com-
ᵭlicated his position. In the earlier stages of the Exclusion Bill,
ᵭhen the Parliament seemed resolved simply to pass over James
ᵭnd to seat Mary at once on the throne after her uncle's death,
ᵭilliam stood apart from the struggle, doubtful of its issue, though
ᵭrepared to accept the good luck if it came to him. The fatal error
ᵭf Shaftesbury in advancing the claims of Monmouth forced him
ᵭnto activity. To preserve his wife's right of succession, with all
ᵭhe great issues which were to come of it, no other course was left
ᵭhan to adopt the cause of the Duke of York. In the crisis of the
ᵭtruggle, therefore, William threw his whole weight on the side of
ᵭames. The eloquence of Halifax secured the rejection of the
ᵭxclusion Bill, and Halifax (as we know now) was the mouthpiece
ᵭf William.

But while England was seething with the madness of the Popish **William**
ᵭlot and of the royalist reaction, the great European struggle was **and**
ᵭrawing nearer and nearer. The patience of Germany was worn out, **James**
ᵭnd in 1686 its princes bound themselves in the Treaty of Augs- **II.**
ᵭurg to resist further aggressions on the part of France. From that
ᵭoment a fresh war became inevitable, and William watched the
ᵭourse of his father-in-law with redoubled anxiety. His efforts in
ᴱngland had utterly failed. James had renewed his brother's secret
ᵭreaty with France, and plunged into a quarrel with his people
ᵭhich of itself would have prevented him from giving any aid in a
ᵭtruggle abroad. The Prince could only silently look on, with a
ᵭesperate hope that James might yet be brought to a nobler policy.
ᵭe refused all encouragement to the leading malcontents who were
ᵭlready calling on him to interfere in arms. On the other hand he
ᵭeclined to support the King in his schemes for the abolition of the

Test. "You ask me," he said to his father-in-law, "to countenance an attack on my religion. That I cannot do!" If he still cherished hopes of bringing about a peace between the King and people which might enable him to enlist England in the Grand Alliance, they vanished in 1687 before the Declaration of Indulgence. In union with Mary he addressed a temperate protest against this measure to the King. But the discovery of the plans which James was now forming, plans which were intended to rob Mary of a part of her future dominions as well as to cripple for ever the power of England, forced him at last into earnest action. The King felt strong enough to carry through his system of government during his own lifetime; but the protest of Mary and William left little doubt that the changes he had made would be overthrown at his death. He resolved therefore (if we trust the statement of the French ambassador) to place Ireland in such a position of independence that she might serve as a refuge for his Catholic subjects from any Protestant successor. Clarendon was succeeded in the charge of the island by the Catholic Lord Tyrconnell, and the new governor went roughly to work. Every Englishman was turned out of office. Every Judge, every Privy Councillor, every Mayor and Alderman of a borough, was soon a Catholic and an Irishman. In a few months the English ascendency was overthrown, and the life and fortune of every English settler were at the mercy of the natives on whom they had trampled since Cromwell's day. The Irish army, purged of its Protestant soldiers, was entrusted to Catholic officers, and the dread of another massacre spread panic through the island. Fifteen hundred Protestant families fled terror-stricken across the Channel. The rest of the Protestants gathered together and prepared for self-defence. William had a right on Mary's behalf to guard against such a plan of dismembering her inheritance; and Dykvelt, who was despatched as his ambassador to England, organized with wonderful ability the various elements of disaffection into a compact opposition. Danby and Bishop Compton answered for the Church. The Nonconformists were won by a promise of toleration. A regular correspondence was established between the Prince and some of the great nobles. But William still shrank from the plan of an intervention in arms. General as the disaffection undoubtedly was, the position of James seemed to be secure. He counted on the aid of France. He had an army of twenty thousand men. Scotland, crushed by the failure of Argyle's rising, could give no such aid as it gave to the Long Parliament. Ireland was ready to rise for the Catholic cause and to throw, if needed, its soldiers on the western coast. Above all it was doubtful if in England itself disaffection would turn into actual rebellion. The "Bloody Assize" had left its terror on the Whigs. The Tories and the Churchmen, angered as they were, were still hampered by their doctrine of non-resistance. It was still therefore the aim of William to discourage all violent counsels, and to confine himself to organizing such a general opposition as would force ames by legal means to reconcile himself to the country, to abandon his policy at home and abroad, and to join the alliance against France.

But at this moment the whole course of William's policy was changed by an unforeseen event. His own patience and that of the nation rested on the certainty of Mary's succession; for James was without a son, and five years had passed since the last pregnancy of his second wife, Mary of Modena. But in the midst of the King's struggle with the Church it was announced that the Queen was again with child. Though the news was received with general unbelief, it at once forced on the crisis which William had hoped to defer. If, as the Catholics joyously foretold, the child were a boy, and, as was certain, brought up a Catholic, the highest Tory had to resolve at last whether the tyranny under which England lay would go on for ever. William could no longer blind himself to the need of a struggle and a speedy one. "It is now or never," he said to Dykvelt. The hesitation of England was indeed at an end. Danby, loyal above all to the Church and firm in his hatred of France, answered for the Tories; Compton for the High Churchmen, goaded at last into rebellion by the Declaration of Indulgence. The Earl of Devonshire, the Lord Cavendish of the Exclusion struggle, answered for the Whigs. A formal invitation to William to intervene in arms for the restoration of English liberty and the protection of the Protestant religion was signed by these leaders and carried in June to the Hague by Herbert, the most popular of English seamen, who had been deprived of his command for a refusal to vote against the Test. The nobles who signed it called on William to appear with an army, and pledged themselves to rise in arms on his landing. Whatever lingering hesitation remained was swept away by the Trial of the Bishops and the birth of a Prince of Wales. The invitation was sent from London on the very day of the Acquittal. The general excitement, the shouts of the boats which covered the river, the bonfires in every street, showed indeed that the country was on the eve of revolt. The army itself, on which James had implicitly relied, suddenly showed its sympathy with the people. James was at Hounslow when the news of the Acquittal reached him, and as he rode from the camp he heard a great shout behind him. "What is that?" he asked. "It is nothing," was the reply, "only the soldiers are glad that the Bishops are acquitted!" "Do you call that nothing?" grumbled the King. The shout told him that he stood utterly alone in his realm. The peerage, the gentry, the bishops, the clergy, the Universities, every lawyer, every trader, every farmer, stood aloof from him. His very soldiers forsook him. The most devoted Catholics pressed him to give way. But to give way was to reverse every act he had done since his accession, and to change the whole nature of his government. All show of legal rule had disappeared. Sheriffs, mayors, magistrates, appointed by the Crown in defiance of a parliamentary statute, were no real officers

The Invitation

in the eye of the law. Even if the Houses were summoned, membe
returned by officers such as these could form no legal Parliamen
Hardly a Minister of the Crown or a Privy Councillor exercise
any lawful authority. James had brought things to such a pa
that the restoration of legal government meant the absolu
reversal of every act he had done. But he was in no mood
reverse his acts. His temper was only spurred to a more dogge
obstinacy by danger and remonstrance. He broke up the camp
Hounslow and dispersed its troops in distant cantonments. F
dismissed the two judges who had favoured the acquittal of t
Bishops. He ordered the chancellor of each diocese to report t
names of the clergy who had not read the Declaration of Indulgenc
But his will broke fruitlessly against the sullen resistance whic
met him on every side. Not a chancellor made a return to t
Commissioners, and the Commissioners were cowed into inactio
by the temper of the nation. When the judges who had displaye
their servility to the Crown went on circuit the gentry refused
meet them. A yet fiercer irritation was kindled by the King
resolve to supply the place of the English troops, whose temp
proved unserviceable for his purposes, by draughts from t
Catholic army which Tyrconnell had raised in Ireland. Even th
Roman Catholic peers at the Council table protested against th
measure; and six officers in a single regiment laid down the
commissions rather than enroll the Irish recruits among their me
The ballad of "Lillibullero," a scurrilous attack on the Irish Papist
was sung from one end of England to the other.

Wil-
liam's
Landing   What prevented revolt was the general resolve to wait for th
appearance of the Prince of Orange. William was gathering force
and transports with wonderful rapidity and secresy, while nob
after noble made their way to the Hague. The Earl of Shrewsbur
arrived with an offer of £12,000 towards the expedition. Edwar
Russell, the brother of Lord Russell, appeared as the representativ
of the House of Bedford. They were followed by the representa
tives of great Tory houses, by the sons of the Marquis of Wincheste
of Lord Danby, of Lord Peterborough, and by the High Churc
Lord Macclesfield. At home the Earls of Danby and Devonshir
prepared silently with Lord Lumley for a rising in the North. I
spite of the profound secresy with which all was conducted, th
keen instinct of Sunderland, who had stooped to purchase con
tinuance in office at the price of an apostasy to Catholicisn
detected the preparations of William; and the sense that h
master's ruin was at hand encouraged him to tell every secret c
James on the promise of a pardon for the crimes to which he ha
lent himself. James alone remained stubborn and insensate as c
old. He had no fear of a revolt unaided by the Prince of Orang
and he believed that the threat of a French attack on Hollan
would render William's aid impossible. But in September the long
delayed war began, and by the greatest political error of his reig
Lewis threw his forces not on Holland, but on Germany. Th

utch at once felt themselves secure; the States-General gave
eir sanction to William's project, and the armament he had
epared gathered rapidly in the Scheldt. The news no sooner
ached England than the King passed from obstinacy to panic.
y draughts from Scotland and Ireland he had mustered forty
ousand men, but the temper of the troops robbed him of all trust
them. He dissolved the Ecclesiastical Commission. He replaced
e magistrates he had driven from office. He restored their
anchises to the towns. The Chancellor carried back the Charter
London in state into the City. James dismissed Sunderland from
fice, and produced before the peers who were in London proofs
the birth of his child, which was almost universally believed to
a Catholic imposture. But concession and proof came too late.
etained by ill winds, beaten back on its first venture by a violent
orm, William's fleet of six hundred transports, escorted by fifty
en-of-war, anchored on the fifth of November in Torbay; and
s army, thirteen thousand men strong, entered Exeter amidst
e shouts of its citizens. His coming had not been looked for in
e West, and for a week no great landowner joined him. But
bles and squires soon flocked to his camp, and the adhesion of
ymouth secured his rear. Meanwhile Danby, dashing at the head
a hundred horsemen into York, gave the signal for a rising in
e North. The militia gave back his shout of " A free Parliament
d the Protestant Religion!" Peers and gentry flocked to his
andard; and a march on Nottingham united his forces to those
der Devonshire, who had mustered at Derby the great lords of
e midland and eastern counties. Everywhere the revolt was
iumphant. The garrison of Hull declared for a free Parliament.
he Duke of Norfolk appeared at the head of three hundred
ntlemen in the market-place at Norwich. Townsmen and gowns-
en greeted Lord Lovelace at Oxford with uproarious welcome.
ristol threw open its gates to the Prince of Orange, who advanced
eadily on Salisbury, where James had mustered his forces. But
e Royal army fell back in disorder. Its very leaders were secretly
edged to William, and the desertion of Lord Churchill was
llowed by that of so many other officers that James abandoned
e struggle in despair. He fled to London to hear that his daughter
nne had left St. James' to join Danby at Nottingham. " God help
e," cried the wretched King, " for my own children have forsaken
e!" His spirit was utterly broken; and though he promised to
ll the Houses together, and despatched commissioners to Hunger-
rd to treat with William on the terms of a free Parliament, in his
art he had resolved on flight. Parliament, he said to the few
ho still clung to him, would force on him concessions he could
t endure; and he only waited for news of the escape of his wife
d child to make his way to the Isle of Sheppey, where a hoy lay
ady to carry him to France. Some rough fishermen, who took
m for a Jesuit, prevented his escape, and a troop of Life Guards
rought him back in safety to London; but it was the policy of

Nov.
1688

William and his advisers to further a flight which removed the
chief difficulty out of the way. It would have been hard to depos
James had he remained, and perilous to keep him prisoner: b
the entry of the Dutch troops into London, the silence of the Princ
and an order to leave St. James', filled the King with fresh terror
and taking advantage of the means of escape which were almo
openly placed at his disposal, James a second time quitted Lond
and embarked on the 23rd of December unhindered for France.

The Re-
volution
Before flying James had burnt most of the writs convoking t
new Parliament, had disbanded his army, and destroyed so far
he could all means of government. For a few days there was a w
burst of panic and outrage in London, but the orderly instinct
the people soon reasserted itself. The Lords who were at t
moment in London provided on their own authority as Priv
Councillors for the more pressing needs of administration, a
resigned their authority into William's hands on his arrival in t
capital. The difficulty which arose from the absence of any pers
legally authorized to call Parliament together was got over
convoking the House of Peers, and forming a second body of
members who had sat in the Commons in the reign of Charles t
Second, with the Aldermen and Common Councillors of Londo
Both bodies requested William to take on himself the provision
government of the kingdom, and to issue circular letters invitin
the electors of every town and county to send up representativ

1689
to a Convention which met in January, 1689. Both Houses we
found equally resolved against any recall of or negotiation with t
fallen King. But with this step their unanimity ended. The Whig
who formed a majority in the Commons, voted a resolution whic
illogical and inconsistent as it seemed, was well adapted to uni
in its favour every element of the opposition to James: the Churc
man who was simply scared by his bigotry, the Tory who doubt
the right of a nation to depose its King, the Whig who held t
theory of a contract between King and People. They voted th
King James, " having endeavoured to subvert the constitution
this kingdom by breaking the original contract between King a
People, and by the advice of Jesuits and other wicked perso
having violated the fundamental laws, and having withdrawn hi
self out of the kingdom, has abdicated the Government, and th
the throne is thereby vacant." But in the Lords the Tories we
still in the ascendant, and the resolution was fiercely debate
Archbishop Sancroft with the High Tories held that no crime cou
bring about a forfeiture of the crown, and that James still remain
King, but that his tyranny had given the nation a right to wit
draw from him the actual exercise of government and to entru
its functions to a Regency. The moderate Tories under Danby
guidance admitted that James had ceased to be King, but deni
that the throne could be vacant, and contended that from t
moment of his abdication the sovereignty vested in his daught
Mary. It was in vain that the eloquence of Halifax backed the Wh

ers in struggling for the resolution of the Commons as it stood.
he plan of a Regency was lost by a single vote, and Danby's
heme was adopted by a large majority. But both the Tory
urses found a sudden obstacle in William. He declined to be
egent. He had no mind, he said to Danby, to be his wife's
ntleman-usher. Mary, on the other hand, refused to accept the
own save in conjunction with her husband. The two declarations
it an end to the question. It was agreed that William and Mary
ould be acknowledged as joint sovereigns, but that the actual
lministration should rest with William alone. Somers, a young
wyer who had just distinguished himself in the trial of the
ishops, and who was destined to play a great part in later history,
ew up a Declaration of Rights which was presented on February
th to William and Mary by the two Houses in the banqueting-
om at Whitehall. It recited the misgovernment of James, his
dication, and the resolve of the Lords and Commons to assert
e ancient rights and liberties of English subjects. It denied the
ght of any king to exercise a dispensing power, or to exact money
to maintain an army save by consent of Parliament. It asserted
r the subject a right to petition, to a free choice of representatives
Parliament, and a pure and merciful administration of justice.
declared the right of both Houses to liberty of debate. In full
ith that these principles would be accepted and maintained by
illiam and Mary, it ended with declaring the Prince and Princess
Orange King and Queen of England. At the close of the Declaraon, Halifax, in the name of the Estates of the Realm, prayed them
receive the crown. William accepted the offer in his own name
d his wife's, and declared in a few words the resolve of both to
aintain the laws and to govern by advice of Parliament.

Section VIII.—The Grand Alliance, 1689—1694

[*Authorities.*—As under previous sections, with the addition of the
xtracts from Bonnet's " Reports," printed in the appendix to Ranke's
History of England." For Scotland, the Leven and Melville Papers,
d Balcarres, " Memoirs Touching the Revolution in Scotland." For
eland, the anonymous " Light to the Blind," edited by Gilbert as
A Jacobite Narrative of the War in Ireland "; Plunket and Hogan,
The Jacobite War in Ireland"; Storey's " True and Impartial History";
d Mackay's " Memoirs." The Shrewsbury Correspondence is important
r this period. Texts of treaties may be found in Vast, " Grands
raités du Règne de Louis XIV."]

The blunder of Lewis in choosing Germany instead of Holland   The
r his point of attack was all but atoned for by the brilliant   Grand
ccesses with which he opened the war. The whole country west   Alliance
f the Rhine was soon in his hands; his armies were master of the
alatinate, and penetrated even to Würtemberg. His hopes had
ever been higher than at the moment when the arrival of James
t St. Germains dashed all hope to the ground. Lewis was at once

thrown back on a war of defence, and the brutal ravages whic[h]
marked the retreat of his armies from the Rhine revealed th[e]
bitterness with which his pride stooped to the necessity. Th[e]
Palatinate was turned into a desert. The same ruin fell on th[e]
stately palace of the Elector at Heidelberg, on the venerable tom[b]
of the Emperors at Speyer, on the town of the trader, on the h[ut]
of the vine-dresser. Outrages such as these only hastened the wor[k]
of his great rival. In accepting the English throne William had kn[it]
together England and Holland, the two great Protestant powe[rs]
whose fleets had the mastery of the sea, as his diplomacy had kn[it]
all Germany together a year before in the Treaty of Augsbur[g.]
But the formation of the Grand Alliance might still have bee[n]
delayed by the reluctance of the Emperor to league with Protesta[nt]
States against a Catholic King, when the ravage of the Palatina[te]
woke a thirst for vengeance in every German heart before which a[ll]
hesitation passed away. The reception of James as still King [of]
England at St. Germains gave England just ground for a declar[a]
tion of war, a step in which it was soon followed by Holland, an[d]
the two countries at once agreed to stand by one another in the
struggle against France. The adhesion of the Empire and of th[e]
two branches of the House of Austria to this agreement complete[d]
the Grand Alliance which William had designed. When Savo[y]
joined the allies in May 1689, France found herself girt in on ever[y]
side save Switzerland with a ring of foes. The Scandinavian kin[g]
doms alone stood aloof from the confederacy of Europe, and the[ir]
neutrality was unfriendly to France. Lewis was left without a sing[le]
ally save the Turk: but the energy and quickness of moveme[nt]
which sprang from the concentration of the power of France in
single hand still left the contest an equal one. The Empire wa[s]
slow; Austria was distracted by the war with the Turks; Spai[n]
was all but powerless; Holland and England were alone earne[st]
in the struggle, and England could as yet give little aid in the wa[r.]
An English brigade, formed from the regiments raised by Jame[s]
joined the Dutch army on the Sambre, and distinguished itse[lf]
under Churchill, who had been rewarded for his treason by th[e]
title of Earl of Marlborough, in a brisk skirmish with the enem[y]
at Walcourt. But William had as yet grave work to do at hom[e.]

William
and
Scotland

In England not a sword had been drawn for James. In Scotlan[d]
his tyranny had been yet greater than in England, and so far as th[e]
Lowlands went the fall of his tyranny was as rapid and complet[e.]
No sooner had he called his troops southward to meet William[']s
invasion than Edinburgh rose in revolt. The western peasants we[re]
at once up in arms, and the Episcopalian clergy who had been th[e]
instruments of the Stuart misgovernment ever since the Restor[a]
tion were rabbled and driven from their parsonages in every paris[h.]
The news of these disorders forced William to act, though he wa[s]
without a show of legal authority over Scotland; and, on th[e]
advice of the Scotch Lords present in London, he ventured [to]
summon a Convention similar to that which had been summone[d]

in England, and on his own responsibility to set aside the laws which excluded Presbyterians from the Scotch Parliament. This Convention resolved that James had forfeited the crown by misgovernment, and offered it to William and Mary. The offer was accompanied by a Claim of Right framed on the model of the Declaration of Rights to which they had consented in England, but closing with a demand for the abolition of Prelacy. Both crown and claim were accepted, and the arrival of the Scotch regiments which William had brought from Holland gave strength to the new Government. Its strength was to be roughly tested. John Graham of Claverhouse, whose cruelties in the persecution of the Western Covenanters had been rewarded by the title of Viscount Dundee, withdrew with a few troopers from Edinburgh to the Highlands, and appealed to the clans. In the Highlands nothing was known of English government or misgovernment: all that the Revolution meant to a Highlander was the restoration of the House of Argyle. The Macdonalds, the Macleans, the Camerons, were as ready to join Dundee in fighting their old oppressors, the Campbells, and the Government which upheld them, as they had been ready to join Montrose in the same cause forty years before. As William's Scotch regiments under General Mackay climbed the pass of Killiecrankie (July 27, 1689), Dundee charged them at the head of three thousand clansmen and swept them in headlong rout down the glen. But his death in the moment of victory broke the only bond which held the Highlanders together, and in a few weeks the host which had spread terror through the Lowlands melted helplessly away. In the next summer Mackay was able to build the strong post of Fort William in the very heart of the disaffected country, and his offers of money and pardon brought about the submission of the clans. Sir John Dalrymple, the Master of Stair, in whose hands the government of Scotland at this time mainly rested, had hoped that a refusal of the oath of allegiance would give grounds for a war of extermination and free Scotland for ever from its terror of the Highlanders. He had provided for the expected refusal by orders of a ruthless severity. "Your troops," he wrote to the officer in command, "will destroy entirely the country of Lochaber, Locheil's lands, Keppoch's, Glengarry's, and Glencoe's. Your powers shall be large enough. I hope the soldiers will not trouble the Government with prisoners." But his hopes were disappointed by the readiness with which the clans accepted the offers of the Government. All submitted in good time save Macdonald of Glencoe, whose pride delayed his taking of the oath till six days after the latest date fixed by the proclamation. Foiled in his larger hopes of destruction, Dalrymple seized eagerly on the pretext given by Macdonald, and an order "for the extirpation of that sect of robbers" was laid before William and received the royal signature. "The work," wrote the Master of Stair to Colonel Hamilton who undertook it, "must be secret and sudden." The troops were chosen from among the Campbells, the deadly foes of

the clansmen of Glencoe, and quartered peacefully among the
Macdonalds for twelve days, till all suspicion of their errand disappeared. At daybreak (Feb. 13, 1692) they fell on their hosts, and
in a few moments thirty of the clansfolk lay dead on the snow.
The rest, sheltered by a storm, escaped to the mountains to perish
for the most part of cold and hunger. "The only thing I regret,"
said the Master of Stair when the news reached him, "is that any
got away." Whatever horror the Massacre of Glencoe has roused
in later days, few save Dalrymple knew of it at the time. The peace
of the Highlands enabled the work of reorganization to go on
quietly at Edinburgh. In accepting the Claim of Right with its
repudiation of Prelacy, William had in effect restored the Presbyterian Church, and its restoration was accompanied by the revival
of the Westminster Confession as a standard of faith, and by the
passing of an Act which abolished lay patronage. Against the
Toleration Act which the King proposed, the Scotch Parliament
stood firm. But the King was as firm in his purpose as the Parliament. So long as he reigned, William declared in memorable words
there should be no persecution for conscience sake. "We never
could be of that mind that violence was suited to the advancing of
true religion, nor do we intend that our authority shall ever be a
tool to the irregular passions of any party."

The
Irish
Revolt
It was not in Scotland, however, but in Ireland that James and
Lewis hoped to arrest William's progress. As we have noticed
before, James had resolved soon after his accession to make Ireland
a refuge for himself and his Catholic subjects in case of mishap. As
we have seen, Lord Tyrconnell had been made general, and then
raised to the post of Lord Deputy, with a view to the carrying
out of this purpose; the army had been remodelled, by the disbanding its Protestant soldiers and filling the ranks with Papists; a
similar process had "purified" the bench of judges; the town
charters had been seized into the King's hands, and Catholic
Mayors and Catholic Sheriffs set at the head of every city and
county. With power thus placed in the hands of their bitter
enemies, the terror of a new Irish massacre spread fast among the
humbled Protestants. Those of the south for the most part forsook
their homes and fled over sea, while those of the north drew
together at Enniskillen and Londonderry. The news of the King's
fall intensified the panic. For two months Tyrconnell intrigued
with William's Government, but his aim was simply to gain time,
and at the opening of 1689 a flag was hoisted over Dublin Castle,
with the words embroidered on its folds "Now or Never." The
signal called every Catholic to arms. The maddened natives flung
themselves on the plunder which their masters had left, and in a
few weeks havoc was done, the French envoy told Lewis, which
it would take years to repair. Meanwhile James sailed from France
to Kinsale. His first work was to crush the Protestants who stood
in arms in the north. Fifty thousand men had gathered to Tyrconnell's standard, and about half the number were sent against

Londonderry, where the bulk of the fugitives found shelter behind a weak wall, manned by a few old guns, and destitute even of a ditch. But the seven thousand desperate Englishmen behind the wall made up for its weakness. So fierce were their sallies, so crushing the repulse of his attack, that the King's general, Hamilton, at last turned the siege into a blockade. The Protestants died of hunger in the streets, and of the fever which comes of hunger, but the cry of the town was still " No Surrender." The siege had lasted a hundred and five days, and only two days' food remained in Londonderry, when on the 28th of July an English ship broke the boom across the river, and the besiegers sullenly withdrew. Their defeat was turned into a rout by the men of Enniskillen, who struggled through a bog to charge an Irish force of double their number at Newtown Butler, and drove horse and foot before them in a panic which soon spread through Hamilton's whole army. The routed soldiers fell back on Dublin, where James lay helpless in the hands of the frenzied Catholics. In the Parliament he had summoned every member returned was an Irishman and a Papist, and its one aim was the ruin of the English settlers. The Act of Settlement, on which all title to property rested, was at once repealed. Three thousand Protestants of name and fortune were massed together in the hugest Bill of Attainder which the world has seen. In spite of the love which James professed for religious freedom, the Protestant clergy were driven from their parsonages, Fellows and scholars were turned out of Trinity College, and the French envoy, the Count of Avaux, dared even to propose a general massacre of the Protestants who still lingered in the districts which had submitted to James. To his credit the King shrank horror-struck from the proposal. " I cannot be so cruel," he said, " as to cut their throats while they live peaceably under my government." " Mercy to Protestants," was the cold reply, " is cruelty to Catholics."

Through the long agony of Londonderry, through the proscription and bloodshed of the new Irish rule, William was forced to look helplessly on. The best troops in the army which had been mustered at Hounslow followed Marlborough to the Sambre; and with the political embarrassments which grew up around the Government it was unable to spare a man of those who remained. The great ends of the Revolution were indeed secured, even amidst the confusion and intrigue which we shall have to describe, by the common consent of all. On the great questions of civil liberty Whig and Tory were now at one. The Declaration of Right was turned into the Bill of Rights, and the passing of this measure in 1689 restored to the monarchy the character which it had lost under the Tudors and the Stuarts. The right of the people through its representatives to depose the King, to change the order of succession, and to set on the throne whom they would, was now established. All claim of Divine Right, or hereditary right independent of the law, was formally put an end to by the election of William and

Mary. Since their day no English sovereign has been able to advance any claim to the crown save a claim which rested on a particular clause in a particular Act of Parliament. William, Mary, and Anne, were sovereigns simply by virtue of the Bill of Rights. George the First and his successors have been sovereigns solely by virtue of the Act of Settlement. An English monarch is now as much the creature of an Act of Parliament as the pettiest tax-gatherer in his realm. A limitation of the right of succession which expressed this parliamentary origin of the sovereign's right in the strongest possible way was found in the provision " that whosoever shall hereafter come to the possession of this crown shall join in communion with the Church of England as by law established." Nor was the older character of the kingship alone restored. The older constitution returned with it. Bitter experience had taught England the need of restoring to the Parliament its absolute power over taxation. The grant of revenue for life to the last two kings had been the secret of their anti-national policy, and the first act of the new legislature was to restrict the grant of the royal revenue to a term of four years. William was bitterly galled by the provision. " The gentlemen of England trusted King James," he said, " who was an enemy of their religion and their laws, and they will not trust me, by whom their religion and their laws have been preserved." But the only change brought about in the Parliament by this burst of royal anger was a resolve henceforth to make the vote of supplies an annual one, and this resolve has been adhered to ever since. A change of almost as great importance established the control of Parliament over the army. The hatred to a standing army which had begun under Cromwell had only deepened under James; but with the continental war the existence of an army was a necessity. As yet, however, it was a force which had no legal existence. The soldier was simply an ordinary subject; there were no legal means of punishing strictly military offences or of providing for military discipline: and the assumed power of billeting soldiers in private houses had been taken away by the law. The difficulty both of Parliament and the army was met by the Mutiny Act. The powers requisite for discipline in the army were conferred by Parliament on its officers, and provision was made for the pay of the force, but both pay and disciplinary powers were granted only for a few months. The Mutiny Act, like the grant of supplies, has remained annual ever since the Revolution; and as it is impossible for the State to exist without supplies, or for the army to exist without discipline and pay, the annual assembly of Parliament has become a matter of absolute necessity, and the greatest constitutional change which our history has witnessed was thus brought about in an indirect but perfectly efficient way. The dangers which experience had lately shown lay in the Parliament itself were met with far less skill. Under Charles, England had seen a Parliament, which had been returned in a moment of reaction, maintained without fresh election for eighteen years. A Triennial

Bill, which limited the duration of a Parliament to three, was passed with little opposition, but fell before the dislike and veto of William. To counteract the influence which a king might obtain by crowding the Commons with officials proved a yet harder task. A Place Bill, which excluded all persons in the employment of the State from a seat in Parliament, was defeated, and wisely defeated, in the Lords. The modern course of excluding all minor officials, but of preserving the hold of Parliament over the great officers of State by admitting them into its body, seems as yet to have occurred to nobody. It is equally strange that while vindicating its right of Parliamentary control over the public revenue and the army, the Bill of Rights should have left by its silence the control of trade to the Crown. It was only a few years later, in the discussions on the charter granted to the East India Company, that the Houses silently claimed and obtained the right of regulating English commerce.

The religious results of the Revolution were hardly less weighty than the political. In the common struggle against Catholicism, Churchman and Nonconformist had found themselves, as we have seen, strangely at one; and schemes of Comprehension became suddenly popular. But with the fall of James the union of the two bodies abruptly ceased: and the establishment of a Presbyterian Church in Scotland, together with the "rabbling" of the Episcopalian clergy in its western shires, revived the old bitterness of the clergy towards the dissidents. The Convocation rejected the scheme of the Latitudinarians for such modifications of the Prayer-book as would render possible a return of the Nonconformists, and a Comprehension Bill which was introduced into Parliament failed to pass in spite of the King's strenuous support. William's attempt to admit Dissenters to civil equality by a repeal of the Test and Corporation Acts proved equally fruitless. Active persecution, however, had now become impossible, and the passing of a Toleration Act in 1689 practically secured freedom of worship. Whatever the religious effect of the failure of the Latitudinarian schemes may have been, its political effect has been of the highest value. At no time had the Church been so strong or so popular as at the Revolution, and the reconciliation of the Nonconformists would have doubled its strength. It is doubtful whether the disinclination to all political change which has characterized it during the last two hundred years would have been affected by such a change; but it is certain that the power of opposition which it has wielded would have been enormously increased. As it was, the Toleration Act established a group of religious bodies, whose religious opposition to the Church forced them to support the measures of progress which the Church opposed. With religious forces on the one side and on the other, England has escaped the great stumbling-block in the way of nations where the cause of religion has become identified with that of political reaction. A secession from within its own ranks weakened the Church still more. The doctrine of

**1689
to
1694**

Divine Right had a strong hold on the body of the clergy, though they had been driven from their other favourite doctrine of passive obedience, and the requirement of the oath of allegiance to the new sovereigns from all persons in public functions was resented as an intolerable wrong by almost every parson. Sancroft, the Archbishop of Canterbury, with a few prelates and a large number of the higher clergy, absolutely refused the oath, treated all who took it as schismatics, and on their deprivation by Act of Parliament regarded themselves and their adherents, who were known as Nonjurors, as the only members of the true Church of England. The bulk of the clergy bowed to necessity, but their bitterness against the new Government was fanned by the expulsion of the Nonjurors into a flame, and added to the difficulties which William had to encounter.

**The
Act of
Grace**

Not the least of his difficulties arose from the temper of his Parliaments. In 1689 the Convention declared itself a Parliament. In the Commons the bulk of the members were Whigs, and their first acts were to redress the wrongs which the Whig party had suffered during the last two reigns. The attainder of Lord Russell was reversed. The judgments against Sidney, Cornish, and Alice Lisle were annulled. In spite of the opinion of the judges that the sentence on Titus Oates had been against law, the Lords refused to reverse it, but even Oates received a pardon and a pension. The Whigs however wanted, not only the redress of wrongs, but the punishment of the wrong-doers. Whig and Tory had been united, indeed, by the tyranny of James; both parties had shared in the Revolution, and William had striven to prolong their union by joining the leaders of both in his first Ministry. He named the Tory Danby Lord President, made the Whig Shrewsbury Secretary of State, and gave the Privy Seal to Halifax, a trimmer between the one party and the other. But save in a moment of common oppression or common danger union was impossible. The Whigs clamoured for the punishment of Tories who had joined in the illegal acts of Charles and of James. They refused to pass the Bill of General Indemnity which William laid before them. William on the other hand was resolved that no bloodshed or proscription should follow the revolution which had placed him on the throne. His temper was averse to persecution; he had no great love for either of the battling parties; and above all he saw that internal strife would be fatal to the effective prosecution of the war. While the cares of his new throne were chaining him to England, the confederacy of which he was the guiding spirit was proving too slow and too loosely compacted to cope with the swift and resolute movements of France. The armies of Lewis had fallen back within their own borders, but only to turn fiercely at bay. The junction of the English and Dutch fleets failed to assure them the mastery of the seas. The English navy was paralysed by the corruption which prevailed in the public service, as well as by the sloth and incapacity of its commander. The services of Admiral Herbert at the Revolution had been rewarded by the earldom of Torrington and the command of the fleet; but his indolence suffered the seas to be swept by French privateers, and his want of seamanship was shown in an indecisive engagement with a French squadron in Bantry Bay. Meanwhile Lewis was straining every nerve to win the command of the Channel; the French dockyards were turning out ship after ship, and the galleys of the Mediterranean fleet were brought round to reinforce the fleet at Brest. A French victory off the English coast would have brought serious political danger, for the reaction of popular feeling which had begun in favour of James had been increased by the pressure of the war, by the taxation, by the expulsion of the Non-jurors and the discontent of the clergy, by the panic of the Tories at the spirit of vengeance which broke out among the triumphant Whigs, and above all by the presence of James in Ireland. A new party, that of the Jacobites or adherents of King James, was just forming; and it was feared that a Jacobite rising would follow the appearance of a French fleet on the coast. In such a state of affairs William judged rightly that to yield to the Whig thirst for vengeance would have been to ruin his cause. He dissolved the Parliament after sending down to it a general pardon for all political offences, under the title of an Act of Grace, and accepted the resignations of the more violent Whigs among his counsellors. Danby was entrusted with the chief administration of affairs; for Danby had power over the Tories, and in the new Parliament which was called in 1690 the bulk of the members proved Tories. William's aim in this sudden change of front was to secure a momentary lull in English faction which would suffer him to strike at the rebellion in Ireland. While James was King in Dublin it was hopeless to crush treason at home; and so urgent was the danger, so precious every moment in the present juncture of affairs, that William could trust no one to bring the work as sharply to an end as was needful save himself.

1689
to
1694

In the autumn of the year 1689 the Duke of Schomberg had been sent with a small force to Ulster, but his landing had only roused Ireland to a fresh enthusiasm. The ranks of the Irish army were filled up at once, and James was able to face the duke at Drogheda with a force double that of his opponent. Schomberg, whose forces were all raw recruits whom it was hardly possible to trust at such odds in the field, entrenched himself at Dundalk, in a camp where pestilence soon swept off half his men, till winter parted the two armies. During the next six months James, whose treasury was utterly exhausted, strove to fill it by a coinage of brass money, while his soldiers subsisted by sheer plunder. William meanwhile was toiling hard on the other side of the Channel to bring the war to an end. Schomberg was strengthened during the winter with men and stores, and when the spring came his force reached thirty thousand men. Lewis, too, felt the importance of the coming struggle; and seven thousand picked Frenchmen, under the Count of Lauzun, were despatched to reinforce the army of James. They

The
Battle
of the
Boyne

had hardly arrived when William himself landed at Carrickfergus and pushed rapidly to the south. His columns soon caught sight of the Irish army, posted strongly behind the Boyne. "I am glad to see you, gentlemen," William cried with a burst of delight "and if you escape me now the fault will be mine." Early next morning, the First of July, 1690, the whole English army plunged into the river. The Irish foot broke in a shameful panic, but the horse made so gallant a stand that Schomberg fell in repulsing its charge, and for a time the English centre was held in check. With the arrival of William, however, at the head of the left wing, all was over. James, who had looked helplessly on, fled to Dublin and took ship at Kinsale for France, while the capital threw open its gates to the conqueror. The cowardice of the Stuart sovereign moved the scorn even of his followers. "Change kings with us," an Irish officer replied to an Englishman who taunted him with the panic of the Boyne, "change kings with us, and we will fight you again." They did better in fighting without a king. The French, indeed, withdrew scornfully from the routed army as it stood at bay beneath the walls of Limerick. "Do you call these ramparts?" sneered Lauzun: "the English will need no cannon; they may batter them down with roasted apples." But twenty thousand men remained with Sarsfield, a brave and skilful officer who had seen service in England and abroad; and his daring surprise of the English ammunition train, his repulse of a desperate attempt to storm the town, and the approach of the winter, forced William to raise the siege. The turn of the war abroad recalled him to England, and he left his work to one who was quietly proving himself a master in the art of war. Lord Marlborough had been recalled from Flanders to command a division which had landed in the south of Ireland. Only a few days remained before winter would come to break off operations, but the few days were turned to good account. Cork, with five thousand men behind its walls, was taken in forty-eight hours. Kinsale a few days later shared the fate of Cork. Winter indeed left Connaught and the greater part of Munster in Irish hands; the French force remained untouched, and the coming of a new French general, St. Ruth, with arms and supplies, encouraged the insurgents. But the spring of 1691 had hardly opened when Ginkell, the new English general, by his seizure of Athlone forced on a battle with the combined French and Irish forces at Aughrim, in which St. Ruth fell on the field and his army was utterly broken. The defeat left Limerick alone in its revolt, and even Sarsfield bowed to the necessity of a surrender Two treaties were drawn up between the Irish and English generals. By the first it was stipulated that the Catholics of Ireland should enjoy such privileges in the exercise of their religion as were consistent with law, or as they had enjoyed in the reign of Charles the Second. Both sides were, of course, well aware that such a treaty was merely waste paper, for Ginkell had no power to conclude it nor had the Irish Lords Justices. The latter, indeed, only promised to do all they could to bring about its ratification by Parliament, and this ratification was never granted. By the military treaty, those of Sarsfield's soldiers who would were suffered to follow him to France; and ten thousand men, the whole of his force, chose exile rather than life in a land where all hope of national freedom was lost. When the wild cry of the women who stood watching their departure was hushed, the silence of death settled down upon Ireland. For a hundred years the country remained at peace, but the peace was a peace of despair. The most terrible legal tyranny under which a nation has ever groaned avenged the rising under Tyrconnell. The conquered people, in Swift's bitter words of contempt, became " hewers of wood and drawers of water " to their conquerors; but till the very eve of the French Revolution Ireland ceased to be a source of terror and anxiety to England.

1689
to
1694

Short as the struggle of Ireland had been, it had served Lewis well, for while William was busy at the Boyne a series of brilliant successes restored the fortunes of France. In Flanders the Duke of Luxembourg won the victory of Fleurus. In Italy Marshal Catinat defeated the Duke of Savoy. A success of even greater moment, the last victory which France was fated to win at sea, placed for an instant the very throne of William in peril. William never showed a cooler courage than in quitting England to fight James in Ireland at a moment when the Jacobites were only looking for the appearance of a French fleet on the coast to rise in revolt. He was hardly on his way in fact when Tourville, the French admiral, put to sea with strict orders to fight. He was met by the English and Dutch fleet at Beachy Head, and the Dutch division at once engaged. Though utterly outnumbered, it fought stubbornly in hope of Herbert's aid; but Herbert, whether from cowardice or treason, looked idly on while his allies were crushed, and withdrew at nightfall to seek shelter in the Thames. The danger was as great as the shame, for Tourville's victory left him master of the Channel, and his presence off the coast of Devon invited the Jacobites to revolt. But whatever the discontent of Tories and Non-jurors against William might be, all signs of it vanished with the landing of the French. The burning of Teignmouth by Tourville's sailors called the whole coast to arms; and the news of the Boyne put an end to all dreams of a rising in favour of James. The natural reaction against a cause which looked for foreign aid gave a new strength for the moment to William in England; but ill luck still hung around the Grand Alliance. So urgent was the need for his presence abroad that William left as we have seen his work in Ireland undone, and crossed in the spring of 1691 to Flanders. It was the first time since the days of Henry the Eighth that an English king had appeared on the Continent at the head of an English army. But the slowness of the allies again baffled William's hopes. He was forced to look on with a small army while a hundred thousand Frenchmen closed suddenly around Mons, the strongest fortress of the Netherlands, and made themselves master of it in the presence

The
Jacobite
Plots

July,
1690

1691

of Lewis. The humiliation was great, and for the moment all trust in William's fortune faded away. In England the blow was felt more heavily than elsewhere. The treason which had been crushed by the indignation at Tourville's descent woke up to a fresh life. Leading Tories, such as Lord Clarendon and Lord Dartmouth, opened communications with James; and some of the leading Whigs, with the Earl of Shrewsbury at their head, angered at what they regarded as William's ingratitude, followed them in their course. In Lord Marlborough's mind the state of affairs raised hopes of a double treason. His design was to bring about a revolt which would drive William from the throne without replacing James, and give the crown to his daughter Anne, whose affection for Marlborough's wife would place the real government of England in his hands. A yet greater danger lay in the treason of Admiral Russell, who had succeeded Torrington in command of the fleet. Russell's defection would have removed the one obstacle to a new attempt which James was resolved to make for the recovery of his throne, and which Lewis had been brought to support. In the

beginning of 1692 an army of thirty thousand troops was quartered in Normandy in readiness for a descent on the English coast. Transports were provided for their passage, and Tourville was ordered to cover it with the French fleet at Brest. Though Russell had twice as many ships as his opponent, the belief in his purpose of betraying William's cause was so strong that Lewis ordered Tourville to engage the allied fleets at any disadvantage. But whatever Russell's intrigues may have meant, he was no Herbert. " Do not think I will let the French triumph over us in our own seas," he warned his Jacobite correspondents. " If I meet them I will fight them, even though King James were on board." When the two fleets met off the Norman coast his fierce attack proved Russell true to his word. Tourville's fifty vessels proved no match for the ninety ships of the allies, and after five hours of a brave struggle the French were forced to fly along the rocky coast of the Cotentin. Twenty-two of their vessels reached St. Malo; thirteen anchored with Tourville in the bays of Cherbourg and La Hogue; but their pursuers were soon upon them, and a bold attack of the English boats burnt ship after ship under the eyes of the French army. All dread of the invasion was at once at an end; and the throne of William was secured by the detection and suppression of the Jacobite conspiracy at home which the invasion was intended to support. But the overthrow of the Jacobite hopes was the least result of the victory of La Hogue. France ceased from that moment to exist as a great naval power; for though her fleet was soon recruited to its former strength, the confidence of her sailors was lost, and not even Tourville ventured again to tempt in battle the fortune of the seas. A new hope, too, broke on the Grand Alliance. The spell of French triumph was broken. The Duke of Luxembourg strove to restore the glory of the French arms by his victories over William in the two following years (1693-1694) at Steinkirk and

Neerwinden; but the battles were useless butcheries, in which the conquerors lost as many men as the conquered. From that moment France felt herself disheartened and exhausted by the vastness of her efforts. The public misery was extreme. "The country," Fénelon wrote frankly to Lewis, "is a vast hospital." For the first time in his long career of prosperity Lewis bent his pride to seek peace at the sacrifice of his conquests, and though the effort was a vain one it told that the daring hopes of French ambition were at an end, and that the work of the Grand Alliance was practically done.

In outer seeming, the Revolution of 1688 had only transferred the sovereignty over England from James to William and Mary. In actual fact, it was transferring the sovereignty from the King to the House of Commons. From the moment when its sole right to tax the nation was established by the Bill of Rights, and when its own resolve settled the practice of granting none but annual supplies to the Crown, the House of Commons became the supreme power in the State. It was impossible permanently to suspend its sittings, or, in the long run, to oppose its will, when either course must end in leaving the Government penniless, in breaking up the army and navy, and in rendering the public service impossible. But though the constitutional change was complete, the machinery of government was far from having adapted itself to the new conditions of political life which such a change brought about. However powerful the will of the House of Commons might be, it had no means of bringing its will directly to bear upon the conduct of public affairs. The Ministers who had charge of them were not its servants, but the servants of the Crown; it was from the King that they looked for direction, and to the King that they held themselves responsible. By impeachment or more indirect means the Commons could force a King to remove a Minister who contradicted their will; but they had no constitutional power to replace the fallen statesman by a Minister who would carry out their will. The result was the growth of a temper in the Lower House which drove William and his Ministers to despair. It became as corrupt, as jealous of power, as fickle in its resolves, as factious in spirit, as bodies always become whose consciousness of the possession of power is untempered by a corresponding consciousness of the practical difficulties or the moral reponsibilities of the power which they possess. It grumbled at the ill-success of the war, at the suffering of the merchants, at the discontent of the Churchmen; and it blamed the Crown and its Ministers for all at which it grumbled. But it was hard to find out what policy or measures it would have preferred. Its mood changed, as William bitterly complained, with every hour. It was, in fact, without the guidance of recognized leaders, without adequate information, and destitute of that organization out of which alone a definite policy can come. Nothing better proves the inborn political capacity of the English mind than that it should at once have found a simple and effective solution of such a difficulty as this. The credit of the solution belongs to a man whose political character was of the lowest type. Robert, Earl of Sunderland, had been a Minister in the later days of Charles the Second; and he had remained Minister through almost all the reign of James. He had held office at last only by compliance with the worst tyranny of his master, and by a feigned conversion to the Roman Catholic faith. But the ruin of James was no sooner certain than he had secured pardon and protection from William by the betrayal of the master to whom he had sacrificed his conscience and his honour. Since the Revolution, Sunderland had striven only to escape public observation in a country retirement, but at this crisis he came secretly forward to bring his unequalled sagacity to the aid of the King. His counsel was to recognize practically the new power of the Commons by choosing the Ministers of the Crown exclusively from among the members of the party which was strongest in the Lower House. As yet no Ministry, in the modern sense of the term, had existed. Each great officer of state, Treasurer, or Secretary, or Lord Privy Seal, had in theory been independent of his fellow-officers; each was the "King's servant" and responsible for the discharge of his special duties to the King alone. From time to time one Minister, like Clarendon, might tower above the rest and give a general direction to the whole course of government, but the predominance was merely personal and never permanent; and even in such a case there were colleagues who were ready to oppose or even impeach the statesman who overshadowed them. It was common for a King to choose or dismiss a single Minister without any communication with the rest; and so far from aiming at ministerial unity, even William had striven to reproduce in the Cabinet itself the balance of parties which prevailed outside it. Sunderland's plan aimed at replacing these independent Ministers by a homogeneous Ministry, chosen from the same party, representing the same sentiments, and bound together for common action by a sense of responsibility and loyalty to the party to which it belonged. Not only would such a plan secure a unity of administration which had been unknown till then, but it gave an organization to the House of Commons which it had never had before. The Ministers who were representatives of the majority of its members became the natural leaders of the House. Small factions were drawn together into the two great parties which supported or opposed the Ministry of the Crown. Above all it brought about in the simplest possible way the solution of the problem which had so long vexed both King and Commons. The new Ministers ceased in all but name to be the King's servants. They became simply an Executive Committee representing the will of the majority of the House of Commons, and capable of being easily set aside by it and replaced by a similar Committee whenever the balance of power shifted from one side of the House to the other.

Such was the origin of that system of representative government which has gone on from Sunderland's day to our own. But though William showed his own political genius in understanding and adopting Sunderland's plan, it was only slowly and tentatively that he ventured to carry it out in practice. In spite of the temporary reaction Sunderland believed that the balance of political power was really on the side of the Whigs. Not only were they the natural representatives of the principles of the Revolution, and the supporters of the war, but they stood far above their opponents in parliamentary and administrative talent. At their head stood a group of statesmen, whose close union in thought and action gained them the name of the Junto. Russell, as yet the most prominent of these, was the victor of La Hogue; Somers was a young advocate who had sprung into fame by his defence of the Seven Bishops; Lord Wharton was known as the most dexterous and unscrupulous of party managers; and Montague was fast making a reputation as the ablest of English financiers. In spite of such considerations, however, it is doubtful whether William would have thrown himself into the hands of a purely Whig Ministry but for the attitude which the Tories took towards the war. In spite of the exhaustion of France the war still languished and the allies still failed to win a single victory. Meanwhile English trade was all but ruined by the French privateers, and the nation stood aghast at the growth of taxation. The Tories, always cold in their support of the Grand Alliance, now became eager for peace. The Whigs, on the other hand, remained resolute in their support of the war. William, in whose mind the contest with France was the first object, was thus driven slowly to follow Sunderland's advice. In 1695 he dissolved Parliament, and the Whig tone of the new House of Commons enabled him to replace his Tory Ministers by the members of the Junto. Russell went to the Admiralty, Somers was named Lord Keeper, Montague Chancellor of the Exchequer, Shrewsbury Secretary of State. The changes were gradually made, but they had hardly begun when their effect was felt. The House of Commons took a new tone. The Whig majority of its members, united and disciplined, moved quietly under the direction of their leaders, the new Ministers of the Crown. Great measures, financial and constitutional, passed rapidly through Parliament. The Triennial Bill became law. In spite of the efforts of the Lords, the Commons refused to renew the bill for the censorship of the press, and its liberty was no sooner thus recognized as legal (1695), than the recognition was at once followed by the appearance of a crowd of public prints. To meet the financial strain of the war Montague established the Bank of England (1694) by adopting the plan which Paterson, a Scotch adventurer, had brought forward for the creation of a National Bank. The subscribers to a loan of £1,200,000 were formed into a Company, with no exclusive privileges, and restricted by law from lending money to the Crown without consent of Parliament; but so great had been the growth of the national wealth that in ten days the list of subscribers was full. A new source of power revealed itself in the discovery of the resources afforded by the national credit; and the rapid growth of the National Debt gave a new security against the return of the Stuarts whose first work would have been the repudiation of it. With ever greater courage and hardly less originality Montague faced the great difficulty of the debasement of the coinage and carried out its reform. The power of the new administration, the evidence of the public credit, gave strength to William abroad as at home. In 1695 the Alliance succeeded for the first time in winning a great triumph over France in the capture of Namur. Even in the troubled year which followed and amidst the distress created by the reform of the currency, William was able to hold the French at bay. But the war was fast drawing to a close. Lewis was simply fighting to secure more favourable terms, and William, though he held that " the only way of treating with France is with our swords in our hands," was almost as eager as Lewis for a peace which would leave him free to deal with a question which the health of the King of Spain now brought every day closer, the question of the succession to the Spanish throne. The obstacles which were thrown in the way of an accommodation by Spain and the Empire were set aside by a private negotiation between William and Lewis, and the year

1697 saw the conclusion of the Peace of Ryswick. In spite of failure and defeat in the field William's policy had won. The victories of France remained barren in the face of a united Europe; and her exhaustion forced her, for the first time since Richelieu's day, to consent to a disadvantageous peace. The Empire was satisfied by the withdrawal of France from every annexation, save that of Strasbourg, which she had made since the Treaty of Nimeguen. To Spain Lewis restored Luxembourg and all the conquests he had made during the war in the Netherlands. The Duke of Lorraine was replaced in his dominions. What was a far heavier humiliation to Lewis personally was his abandonment of the Stuart cause and his recognition of William as King of England. The Peace of Ryswick was thus the final and decisive defeat of the conspiracy which had gone on between Lewis and the Stuarts ever since the Treaty of Dover, the conspiracy to turn England into a Roman Catholic country and into a dependency of France.

Section IX.—Marlborough, 1698—1712

1698
to
1712

[*Authorities.*—Burnet's " Own Times " and Boyer's " Political State of Great Britain " are important; the latter was expanded into a history of Queen Anne. Swift's Works and Defoe's " History of the Union " are very valuable. For Marlborough, his Correspondence, and Coxe's Life. For Bolingbroke, his Letters and Correspondence, and Macknight's Life. For the general history of the reign, Stanhope's " Reign of Queen Anne "; Wyon's " History of Great Britain during the Reign of Queen Anne "; and Lecky's " History of England in the Eighteenth Century."]

What had bowed the pride of Lewis to the humiliating terms of the Peace of Ryswick was not so much the exhaustion of France as the need of preparing for a new and greater struggle. The death of the King of Spain, Charles the Second, was known to be at hand; and with him ended the male line of the Austrian princes, who for two hundred years had occupied the Spanish throne. How strangely Spain had fallen from its high estate in Europe the wars of Lewis had abundantly shown, but so vast was the extent of its empire, so enormous the resources which still remained to it, that under a vigorous ruler men believed its old power would at once return. Its sovereign was still master of some of the noblest provinces of the Old World and the New, of Spain itself, of the Milanese, of Naples and Sicily, of the Netherlands, of Southern America, of the noble islands of the Spanish Main. To add such a dominion as this to the dominion either of Lewis or of the Emperor would be to undo at a blow the work of European independence which William had wrought; and it was with a view to prevent either of these results that William freed his hands by the Peace of Ryswick. At this moment the claimants of the Spanish succession were three: the Dauphin, a son of the Spanish King's elder sister; the Electoral Prince of Bavaria, a grandson of his younger sister; and the Emperor, who was a son of Charles's aunt. In strict law—if there had been any law really applicable to the matter—the claim of the last was the stronger of the three; for the claim of the Dauphin was barred by an express renunciation of all right to the succession at his mother's marriage with Lewis XIV., a renunciation which had been ratified at the Treaty of the Pyrenees; and a similar renunciation barred the claim of the Bavarian candidate. The claim of the Emperor was more remote in blood, but it was barred by no renunciation at all. William however was as resolute in the interests of Europe to repulse the claim of the Emperor as to repulse that of Lewis; and it was the consciousness that the Austrian succession was inevitable if the war continued and Spain remained a member of the Grand Alliance, in arms against France and leagued with the Emperor, which made him suddenly conclude the Peace of Ryswick. Had England and Holland shared William's temper he would have insisted on the succession of the Electoral Prince to the whole Spanish dominions. But both were weary of war. In England the peace was at once followed by the reduction

The
Spanish
Succes-
sion

1698
to
1712
of the army at the demand of the House of Commons to ten thousand men; and a clamour had already begun for the disbanding even of these. It was necessary to bribe the two rival claimants to a waiver of their claims, and by the First Partition Treaty, concluded in 1698, between England, Holland, and France, the succession of the Electoral Prince was recognized on condition of the cession by Spain of its Italian possessions to his two rivals. The Milanese would thus pass to the Emperor, the Two Sicilies with the border province of Guipuscoa to France. But the arrangement was hardly concluded when the death of the Bavarian prince made the Treaty waste paper. Austria and France were left face to face, and a terrible struggle, in which the success of either would be equally fatal to the independence of Europe, seemed unavoidable. The peril was greater that the temper of England left William without the means of backing his policy by arms. The suffering which the war had caused to the merchant class and the pressure of the debt and taxation it entailed were waking every day a more bitter resentment in the people, and the general discontent avenged itself on William and the party who had backed his policy. The King's prodigal grants of crown lands to his Dutch favourites, his cold and sullen demeanour, his endeavour to maintain the standing army, robbed him of whatever popularity he still retained. The Whig Junto lost hold on the Commons. Montague was driven from his post, Somers was unscrupulously attacked, and even the boldest Whigs shrank from accepting office. William's earnest entreaty could not turn the Parliament from its resolve to send his Dutch guards out of the country, and to reduce the army from ten thousand men to seven. The navy, which had numbered forty thousand sailors during the war, was at the same time cut down to eight. How much William's hands were weakened by this peace-temper of England was shown by the Second Partition Treaty which was concluded in 1700 between the three powers. By this, in spite of the protests of the Emperor, who refused to join in the Treaty or to surrender his claim to the whole Spanish monarchy, Spain, the Netherlands, and the Indies were assigned to his second son the Archduke Charles of Austria. But the compensation granted to France was now increased. To the Two Sicilies was added the Duchy of Lorraine, whose Duke was transferred to the Milanese. If the Emperor still persisted in his refusal to come into the Treaty, his share was to pass to another unnamed prince, who was probably the Duke of Savoy.

The
Second
Grand
Alliance
The Emperor still protested, but his protest was of little moment so long as Lewis and the two maritime powers held firmly together. Nor was the bitter resentment of Spain of more avail. The Spaniards cared little whether a French or an Austrian prince sat on the throne of Charles the Second, but their pride revolted against the dismemberment of the monarchy by the loss of its Italian dependencies. Even the miserable King shared the anger of his subjects, and a will wrested from him by the factions which wrangled

er his death-bed bequeathed the whole monarchy of Spain to a
ndson of Lewis, the Duke of Anjou, the second son of the
uphin. The Treaty of Partition was so recent, and the risk of
cepting this bequest so great, that Lewis would hardly have
olved on it but for his belief that the temper of England must
cessarily render William's opposition a fruitless one. Never in
t had England been so averse from war. So strong was the
tipathy to William's foreign policy that men openly approved
what Lewis had done. Hardly anyone in England dreaded the
ccession of a boy who, French as he was, would as they believed
on be turned into a Spaniard by the natural course of events.
e succession of the Duke of Anjou was generally looked upon as
better than the increase of power which France would have
rived from the cessions of the last Treaty of Partition, cessions
ich would have turned the Mediterranean, it was said, into a
ench lake. " It grieves me to the heart," William wrote bitterly,
that almost everyone rejoices that France has preferred the will
the Treaty." Astonished and angered as he was at his rival's
each of faith, he had no means of punishing it. In 1701 the Duke
Anjou peaceably entered Madrid, and Lewis proudly boasted
at henceforth there were no Pyrenees. The life-work of William
emed undone. He knew himself to be dying. His cough was
cessant, his eyes sunk and dead, his frame so weak that he could
rdly get into his coach. But never had he shown himself so great.
is courage rose with every difficulty. His temper grew cooler and
ore serene with every insult. His large and clear-sighted intellect
oked through the temporary embarrassments of French diplomacy
d English faction to the great interests which would in the end
termine the course of European politics. Abroad and at home
l seemed to go against him. For the moment he had no ally save
olland, for Spain was now united with Lewis, and the Elector of
avaria, who held charge of the Spanish Netherlands and on whom
illiam had counted, joined the French side and proclaimed the
uke of Anjou as King in Brussels. The attitude of Bavaria
vided Germany and held the House of Austria in check. In
ngland the new Parliament was crowded with Tories who were
solute against war, and William was forced in 1701 to name a
ory Ministry with Lord Godolphin at its head, which pressed him
acknowledge the new King of Spain. As even Holland did this,
illiam was forced to submit. He could only count on France to
lp him, and he did not count in vain. Bitter as the strife of Whig
d Tory might be in England, there were two things on which
hig and Tory were agreed. Neither would suffer France to
cupy the Netherlands. Neither would endure a French attack
the Protestant succession which the Revolution of 1688 had
tablished. But the greed of Lewis blinded him to the need of
oderation in this hour of good-luck. The Spanish garrisons in the
etherlands were weak, and in the name of his grandson he intro-
uced French troops into town after town. The English Parliament

at once acquiesced in William's demand for their withdraw
but the demand was haughtily rejected. Holland, fearful
invasion as the French troops gathered on her frontier, appeal
to England for aid, and the Tory party in the Parliament saw w.
helpless rage that they were silently drifting into war. Th
impeached the leading members of the Junto for their share
the Partition Treaties; they insulted William, and delayed t
supplies. But outside the House of Commons the tide of natio
feeling rose as the designs of Lewis grew clearer and a great Fren
fleet gathered in the Channel. Its aim was revealed by the d
closure of a fresh Jacobite Plot, the proofs of which were laid bef
Parliament. Even the House of Commons took fire. The fleet w
raised to thirty thousand men, the army to ten thousand, and Ke
sent up a remonstrance against the factious measures by which t
Tories still struggled against the King's policy, and a prayer " th
addresses might be turned into Bills of Supply." William w
encouraged by these signs of a change of temper to despatch
English force to Holland, and to conclude a secret treaty wi
Holland and the Empire for the recovery of the Netherlands fro
France, and of the Sicilies and Milanese from Spain. But Engla
at large was still clinging desperately to peace, when Lewis by
sudden act forced it into war. He had acknowledged William
King in the Peace of Ryswick, and pledged himself to oppose
attacks on his throne. He now entered the bed-chamber at S
Germains where James was breathing his last, and promised
acknowledge his son at his death as King of England, Scotlan
and Ireland. The promise was in fact a declaration of war, and
a moment all England was at one in accepting the challenge. T
issue Lewis had raised was no longer a matter of European politi
but the question whether the work of the Revolution should
undone, and whether Catholicism and despotism should be replac
on the throne of England by the arms of France. On such a questi
as this there was no difference between Tory and Whig. Not a wo
of protest had been uttered when the death of the last living chi
of the Princess Anne was followed in 1701 by the passing of a
Act of Settlement which, setting aside not only the pretend
Prince of Wales and a younger daughter of James the Second, b
the Duchess of Savoy, a daughter of Henrietta of Orleans, a
other claimants nearer in blood, as disqualified by their professi
of the Catholic religion, vested the right to the crown in Sophi
Electress-Dowager of Hanover, a child of the Queen of Bohem
and a granddaughter of James the First, and the heirs of her bod
being Protestants. The same national union showed itself in t
King's welcome on his return from the Hague, where the conclusi
of a new Grand Alliance between the Empire, Holland, and th
United Provinces, had rewarded William's patience and skill. Th
Alliance was soon joined by Denmark, Sweden, the Palatinate, ar
the bulk of the German States. The Parliament which Willia
summoned in 1702, though still Tory in the main, replied

stirring appeal by voting forty thousand men for the
r.
But the King's weakness was already too great to allow of his
king the field; and he was forced to entrust the war in the
therlands to the one Englishman who had shown himself capable
a great command. John Churchill, Earl of Marlborough, was
rn in 1650, the son of a Devonshire Cavalier, whose daughter
came at the Restoration mistress of the Duke of York. The
ame of Arabella did more perhaps than her father's loyalty to
n for her brother a commission in the Royal Guards; and after
e years' service abroad under Turenne the young captain became
lonel of an English regiment which was retained in the service
France. He had already shown some of the qualities of a great
dier, an unruffled courage, a bold and venturous temper held in
eck by a cool and serene judgment, a vigilance and capacity for
during fatigue which never forsook him. In later years he was
own to spend a whole day in reconnoitring, and at Blenheim he
mained on horseback for fifteen hours. But courage and skill in
ms did less for Churchill on his return to the English court than
personal beauty. In the French camp he had been known as
the handsome Englishman;" and his manners were as winning
his person. Even in age his address was almost irresistible:
he engrossed the graces," says Chesterfield; and his air never
it the indolent sweetness which won the favour of Lady Castle-
aine. A present of £5000 from the King's mistress laid the
undation of a fortune which grew rapidly to greatness, as the
udent forethought of the handsome young soldier hardened into
e avarice of age. But it was to the Duke of York that Churchill
oked for advancement, and he earned it by the fidelity with
nich as a member of his household he clung to the Duke's fortunes
ring the dark days of the Plot. He followed James to Edinburgh
d the Hague, and was raised to the peerage on his return and
warded with the colonelcy of the Royal Life Guards. The service
rendered his master after his accession by saving the Royal
my from a surprise at Sedgemoor would have been yet more
lendidly acknowledged but for the King's bigotry. In spite of
s master's personal solicitations Churchill remained true to
rotestantism. But he knew James too well to count on further
vour; and no sentiment of gratitude hindered him from corre-
onding with the Prince of Orange, and planning a mutiny in the
my gathered to oppose him which would have brought the King
prisoner into the Prince's camp. His plot broke down, but his
sertion proved fatal to the Royal cause; and the service which
had rendered to William, base as it was, was too priceless to
iss its reward. Churchill became Earl of Marlborough; he was
it at the head of a force during the Irish war, where his rapid
ccesses at once won William's regard; and he was given high
mmand in the army of Flanders. But the treason which Marl-
rough had plotted against James was as nothing when compared

to the treason which he soon plotted against William. Great as
his greed of gold, he had married Sarah Jennings, a penni
beauty of Charles's court, in whom a violent and malignant tem
was strangely combined with a power of winning and retaining lo
Marlborough's affection for her ran like a thread of gold throu
the dark web of his career. In the midst of his marches and fr
the very battle-field he writes to his wife with the same passion
tenderness. The composure which no danger or hatred could ru
broke down into almost womanish depression at the thought of
coldness or at any burst of her violent humour. He never left
without a pang. "I did for a great while with a perspective gl
look upon the cliffs," he once wrote to her after setting out o
campaign, "in hopes that I might have had one sight of you."
was no wonder that the woman who inspired Marlborough wit
love like this bound to her the weak and feeble nature of
Princess Anne. The two friends threw off the restraints of sta
and addressed each other as "Mrs. Freeman" and "Mrs. Morle
It was through the influence of his wife that Churchill induced A
to desert her father at the Revolution; and it was on the sa
influence that his ambition counted in its designs against Willia
His plan was simply to drive the King from the throne by back
the Tories in their opposition to the war as well as by stirring
frenzy the English hatred of foreigners, and to seat Anne in
place. The discovery of his designs roused the King to a burst
unusual resentment. "Were I and my Lord Marlborough priv
persons," William exclaimed, "the sword would have to set
between us." As it was, he could only strip the Earl of his offi
and command, and drive his wife from St. James's. Anne follow
her favourite, and the court of the Princess became the centre
the Tory opposition: while Marlborough opened a corresponde
with James, and went far beyond his fellow-traitors in baseness
revealing to him, and through him to France, the war-projects
the English Cabinet.

The death of Mary forced William to recall Anne, who had n
become his successor; and with Anne the Marlboroughs returr
to court. The King could not bend himself to trust the Earl aga
but as death drew near he saw in him the one man whose splen
talents fitted him, in spite of the baseness and treason of his li
to rule England and direct the Grand Alliance in his stead. He p
Marlborough at the head of the army in Flanders, but the Earl h
only just taken the command when, on the 20th of February, 17
a fall from his horse proved fatal to the broken frame of the Ki
"There was a time when I should have been glad to have be
delivered out of my troubles," the dying man whispered to Po
land, "but I own I see another scene, and could wish to live
little longer." He knew, however, that the wish was vain, a
commended Marlborough to Anne as the fittest person to lead
armies and guide her counsels. Anne's zeal needed no quickeni
Three days after her accession on the 8th of March, the Earl w

med Captain-General of the English forces at home and abroad,
d entrusted with the entire direction of the war. His supremacy
er home affairs was secured by the elevation of Lord Godolphin,
killed financier, and a close friend of Marlborough's, to the post
Lord Treasurer. The Queen's affection for his wife ensured him
e support of the Crown at a moment when Anne's personal
pularity gave the Crown a new weight with the nation. In
gland, indeed, party feeling for the moment died away. The
ries were won over to the war now that it was waged by a Tory
neral, and the Whigs were ready to back even a Tory general
waging a Whig war. Abroad William's death shook the Grand
liance to its base; and even Holland wavered in dread of being
serted by England in the coming struggle. But the decision of
arlborough soon did away with this distrust. Anne was made to
clare from the throne her resolve to pursue with energy the
licy of her predecessor. The Tory Parliament was brought to
nction vigorous measures for the prosecution of the war. The
w general hastened to the Hague, received the command of the
utch as well as of the English forces, and drew the German
wers into the Confederacy with a skill and adroitness which even
illiam might have envied. Never was greatness more quickly
cognized than in the case of Marlborough. In a few months he
as regarded by all as the guiding spirit of the Alliance, and
inces whose jealousy had worn out the patience of William
elded without a struggle to the counsels of his successor. The
mper, indeed, of Marlborough fitted him in an especial way to be
e head of a great confederacy. Like William, he owed little of
s power to any early training. The trace of his neglected educa-
on was seen to the last in his reluctance to write. " Of all things,"
said to his wife, " I do not love writing." To pen a despatch
deed was a far greater trouble to him than to plan a campaign.
it nature had given him qualities which in other men spring
ecially from culture. His capacity for business was immense.
uring the next ten years he assumed the general direction of the
ar in Flanders and in Spain. He managed every negotiation with
e courts of the allies. He watched over the shifting phases of
nglish politics. He had to cross the Channel to win over Anne to
change in the Cabinet, or to hurry to Berlin to secure the due
ntingent of Electoral troops from Brandenburg. At the same
oment he was reconciling the Emperor with the Protestants of
ungary, stirring the Calvinists of the Cevennes into revolt,
ranging the affairs of Portugal, and providing for the protection
the Duke of Savoy. But his air showed no trace of fatigue or
ste or vexation. He retained to the last the indolent grace of
s youth. His natural dignity was never ruffled by an outbreak of
mper. Amidst the storm of battle men saw him, " without fear
danger or in the least hurry, giving his orders with all the
lmness imaginable." In the cabinet he was as cool as on the
ttle-field. He met with the same equable serenity the pettiness

of the German princes, the phlegm of the Dutch, the ignora
opposition of his officers, the libels of his political opponents. Th
was a touch of irony in the simple expedients by which he son
times solved problems which had baffled Cabinets. The King
Prussia was one of the most vexatious among the allies, but
difficulty with him ceased when Marlborough rose at a sta
banquet and handed to him a napkin. Churchill's composure rest
partly indeed on a pride which could not stoop to bare the real s
within to the eyes of meaner men. In the bitter moments befc
his fall he bade Godolphin burn some querulous letters which t
persecution of his opponents had wrung from him. " My desire
that the world may continue in their error of thinking me a hap
man, for I think it better to be envied than pitied." But in gre
measure it sprang from the purely intellectual temper of his min
His passion for his wife was the one sentiment which tinged t
colourless light in which his understanding moved. In all else
was without love or hate, he knew neither doubt nor regret.
private life he was a humane and compassionate man; but if h
position required it he could betray Englishmen to death in h
negotiations with St. Germains, or lead his army to a butchery su
as that of Malplaquet. Of honour or the finer sentiments of ma
kind he knew nothing; and he turned without a shock from gui
ing Europe and winning great victories to heap up a matchle
fortune by peculation and greed. He is perhaps the only instan
of a man of real greatness who loved money for money's sake. T
passions which stirred the men around him, whether noble
ignoble, were to him simply elements in an intellectual proble
which had to be solved by patience. " Patience will overcome a
things," he writes again and again. " As I think most things a
governed by destiny, having done all things we should subm
with patience."

Marl-
borough
and the
War

As a statesman the high qualities of Marlborough were owned l
his bitterest foes. " Over the Confederacy," says Bolingbrok
" he, a new, a private man, acquired by merit and management
more decided influence than high birth, confirmed authority, a
even the crown of Great Britain, had given to King William
But great as he was in the council, he was even greater in the fiel
He stands alone amongst the masters of the art of war as a capta
whose victories began at an age when the work of most men
done. Though he served as a young officer under Turenne and f
a few months in Ireland and the Netherlands, he had held no gre
command till he took the field in Flanders at the age of fifty-tw
He stands alone, too, in his unbroken good fortune. Voltaire not
that he never besieged a fortress which he did not take, or foug
a battle which he did not win. His difficulties came not from t
enemy, but from the ignorance and timidity of his own allies. I
was never defeated in the field, but victory after victory w
snatched from him by the incapacity of his officers or the stubbor
ness of the Dutch. What startled the cautious strategists of h

y was the vigour and audacity of his plans. Old as he was,
rlborough's designs had from the first all the dash and boldness
youth. On taking the field in 1702 he at once resolved to force
battle in the heart of Brabant. The plan was foiled by the
midity of the Dutch deputies, but his resolute advance across
e Meuse drew the French forces from that river and enabled him
reduce fortress after fortress in a series of sieges. The surrender
Liége closed a campaign which cut off the French from the Lower
ine and freed Holland from all danger of an invasion. The
ccesses of Marlborough had been brought into bolder relief by
e fortunes of the war in other quarters. In Italy Prince Eugene
Savoy showed his powers by a surprise of the French army at
emona, but no real successes had been won. An English descent
the Spanish coast ended in failure. In Germany the Bavarians
ned the French, and the united armies defeated the forces of the
npire. It was in this quarter that Lewis resolved to push his
tunes. In the spring of 1703 a fresh army under Marshal Villars
ain relieved the Elector from the pressure of the Imperial armies,
d only a strife which arose between the two commanders
dered the joint armies from marching on Vienna. Meanwhile
e timidity of the Dutch deputies served Lewis well in the Low
untries. Marlborough had been created Duke, and munificently
warded for his services in the previous year, but his hopes in this
ond campaign were foiled by the deputies of the States-General.
rene as his temper was, it broke down before their refusal to
-operate in an attack on Antwerp and French Flanders; and the
ayers of Godolphin and of the pensionary Heinsius alone induced
m to withdraw his offer of resignation. But in spite of victories
the Danube, the blunders of his adversaries on the Rhine, and
e sudden aid of an insurrection which broke out in Hungary, the
ficulties of Lewis were hourly increasing. The accession of Savoy
the Grand Alliance threatened his armies in Italy with destruc-
n. That of Portugal gave the allies a base of operations against
ain. His energy however rose with the pressure, and while the
ke of Berwick, a natural son of James the Second, was despatched
ainst Portugal, three small armies closed round Savoy. The
wer of the French troops joined the army of Bavaria on the
nube, for the bold plan of Lewis was to decide the fortunes of
e war by a victory which would wrest peace from the Empire
der the walls of Vienna.

The master-stroke of Lewis roused Marlborough at the opening **Blen-**
1704 to a master-stroke in return; but the secresy and boldness **heim**
the Duke's plans deceived both his enemies and his allies. The
ench army in Flanders saw in his march upon Maintz only a
nsfer of the war into Elsass. The Dutch were lured into suffering
eir troops to be drawn as far from Flanders as Coblentz by
oposals of a campaign on the Moselle. It was only when Marl-
rough crossed the Neckar and struck through the heart of
rmany for the Danube that the true aim of his operations was

revealed. After struggling through the hill country of Würtembe[r]
he joined the Imperial army under the Prince of Baden, storm
the heights of Donauwörth, crossed the Danube and the Le[ch]
and penetrated into the heart of Bavaria. The crisis drew the t[wo]
armies which were facing one another on the Upper Rhine to [the]
scene. The arrival of Marshal Tallard with thirty thousand Fre[nch]
troops saved the Elector of Bavaria for the moment from the ne[cessity]
of submission; but the junction of his opponent, Prince Euge[ne]
with Marlborough raised the contending forces again to an equali[ty]
and after a few marches the armies met on the north bank of [the]
Danube, near the little town of Hochstädt and the village [of]
Blindheim or Blenheim, which have given their names to the batt[le]
In one respect the struggle which followed stands almost unrival[led]
in history, for the whole of the Teutonic race was represented [in]
the strange medley of Englishmen, Dutchmen, Hanoverians, Dan[es]
Würtembergers and Austrians who followed Marlborough a[nd]
Eugene. The French and Bavarians, who numbered like th[eir]
opponents some fifty thousand men, lay behind a little stre[am]
which ran through swampy ground to the Danube. The positi[on]
was a strong one, for its front was covered by the swamp, its ri[ght]
by the Danube, its left by the hill-country in which the stre[am]
rose, and Tallard had not only entrenched himself, but was [far]
superior to his rival in artillery. But for once Marlborough's ha[nds]
were free. " I have great reason," he wrote calmly home, " to ho[pe]
that everything will go well, for I have the pleasure to find all [the]
officers willing to obey without knowing any other reason th[an]
that it is my desire, which is very different from what it was [in]
Flanders, where I was obliged to have the consent of a counci[l of]
war for everything I undertook." So formidable were the obstacl[es]
however, that though the allies were in motion at sunrise on [the]
13th of August, it was not till midday that Eugene, who co[m]
manded on the right, succeeded in crossing the stream. [The]
English foot at once forded it on the left and attacked the vill[age]
of Blindheim in which the bulk of the French infantry w[as]
entrenched, but after a furious struggle the attack was repuls[ed]
while as gallant a resistance at the other end of the line held Euge[ne]
in check. The centre, however, which the French believed to [be]
unassailable, had been chosen by Marlborough for the chief po[int]
of attack, and by making an artificial road across the morass [he]
was at last enabled to throw his eight thousand horsemen on [the]
French horse which lay covered by it. Two desperate char[ges]
which the Duke headed in person decided the day. The Fre[nch]
centre was flung back on the Danube and forced to surrend[er]
Their left fell back in confusion on Hochstädt: their right, coo[ped]
up in Blindheim and cut off from retreat, became prisoners of w[ar]
Of the defeated army only twenty thousand escaped. Twe[lve]
thousand were slain, fourteen thousand were captured. Germa[ny]
was finally freed from the French; and Marlborough, who follow[ed]
the wreck of the French host in its flight to Elsass, soon made hi[s]

f master of the Lower Moselle. But the loss of France could not   **1698**
measured by men or fortresses.   A hundred victories since   **to**
croi had taught the world to regard the French army as in-   **1712**
cible, when Blenheim and the surrender of the flower of the
ench soldiery broke the spell.   From that moment the terror of
tory passed to the side of the allies, and " Malbrook " became
ame of fear to every child in France.

In England itself the victory of Blenheim aided to bring about a   Ramil-
eat change in the political aspect of affairs. With the progress of   lies
e struggle the Tory party had slowly drifted back again into its
antipathy to a " Whig war." Marlborough strove to bind them
his policy by supporting in 1702 and 1703 a bill against occa-
nal conformity, which excluded the Nonconformists yet more
idly from all municipal rights, and by allowing the Queen to set
de the tenths and first-fruits hitherto paid by the clergy to the
own as a fund for the augmentation of small benefices. The fund
ll bears the name of Queen Anne's Bounty. But the bill against
casional conformity was steadily resisted by the Lords, and
arlborough's efforts to bend the Tory Ministers to a support of
e war were every day more fruitless. The higher Tories with Lord
ttingham at their head, who had thrown every obstacle they
uld in the way of its continuance, at last quitted office in 1704,
d Marlborough replaced them by Tories of a more moderate
mp who were still in favour of the war: by Robert Harley, who
came Secretary of State, and Henry St. John, a man of splendid
ents, who was named Secretary at War. The Duke's march into
rmany embittered the political strife. The Tories and Jacobites
reatened, if Marlborough failed, to bring his head to the block,
d only the victory of Blenheim saved him from political ruin.
wly and against his will the Duke drifted from his own party
the party which really backed his policy. He availed himself of
e national triumph over Blenheim to dissolve Parliament; the
ctions of 1705, as he hoped, returned a majority in favour of the
ar, and the efforts of Marlborough brought about a coalition
tween the Whig Junto and the moderate Tories who still clung
him, which foiled the bitter attacks of the peace party. The
pport of the Whigs was purchased by making a Whig, William
wper, Lord Keeper, and sending Lord Sunderland as Envoy to
enna Marlborough at last felt secure at home. But he had to
ar disappointment abroad. His plan of attack along the line of   **in 1705**
e Moselle was defeated by the refusal of the Imperial army to
in him. When he entered the French lines across the Dyle, the
utch generals withdrew their troops; and his proposal to attack
e Duke of Villeroy in the field of Waterloo was rejected in full
uncil of war by the deputies of the States with cries of " murder "
d " massacre."   Even Marlborough's composure broke into
tterness at the blow. " Had I had the same power I had last
ar," he wrote home, " I could have won a greater victory than
at of Blenheim." On his complaint the States recalled their

1698 to 1712

commissaries, but the year was lost; nor had greater results be brought about in Italy or on the Rhine. The spirits of the alli were only sustained by the romantic exploits of Lord Peterborou, in Spain. Profligate, unprincipled, flighty as he was, Peterborou, had a genius for war, and his seizure of Barcelona with a handful men, his recognition of the old liberties of Arragon, roused th province to support the cause of the second son of the Emper who had been acknowledged as King of Spain by the allies und the title of Charles the Third. Catalonia and Valentia soon join Arragon in declaring for Charles: while Marlborough spent t winter of 1705 in negotiations at Vienna, Berlin, Hanover, and t Hague, and in preparations for the coming campaign. Eager f freedom of action and sick of the Imperial generals as of the Dutc he planned a march over the Alps and a campaign in Italy; a though his designs were defeated by the opposition of the alli he found himself unfettered when he again appeared in Flande in 1706. Villeroy was as eager as Marlborough for an engagemen and the two armies met on the 23rd of May at the village Ramillies on the undulating plain which forms the highest grou in Brabant. The French were drawn up in a wide curve wi morasses covering their front. After a feint on their left, Ma borough flung himself on their right wing at Ramillies, crush it in a brilliant charge that he led in person, and swept along the whole line till it broke in a rout which only ended beneath the wa of Louvain. In an hour and a half the French had lost fiftee thousand men, their baggage, and their guns, and the line of t Scheldt, Brussels, Antwerp and Bruges were the prize of the victo It only needed the four successful sieges which followed the batt of Ramillies to complete the deliverance of Flanders.

The Union

The year which witnessed the victory of Ramillies remains y more memorable as the year which witnessed the final Union England with Scotland. As the undoing of the earlier union ha been the first work of the Government of the Restoration, its reviv was one of the first aims of the Government which followed t Revolution. But the project was long held in check by religio and commercial jealousies. Scotland refused to bear any part the English debt. England would not yield any share in h monopoly of trade with the Colonies. The English Churchme longed for a restoration of Episcopacy north of the border, whi the Scotch Presbyterians would not hear even of the legal toleratio of Episcopalians. In 1703, however, the Act of Security whic passed through the Scotch Parliament at last brought home English statesmen the dangers of further delay. In dealing wit this measure the Scotch Whigs, who cared only for the independen of their country, joined hand in hand with the Scotch Jacobite who looked only to the interests of the Pretender. The Jacobit excluded from the Act the name of the Princess Sophia; the Whi introduced a provision that no sovereign of England should b recognized as sovereign of Scotland save upon security given to th

ligion, freedom, and trade of the Scottish people. Great as the
nger arising from such a measure undoubtedly was, for it pointed
a recognition of the Pretender in Scotland on the Queen's death,
d such a recognition meant war between Scotland and England,
was only after three years' delay that the wisdom and resolution
Lord Somers brought the question to an issue. The Scotch
oposals of a federative rather than a legislative union were set
de by his firmness; the commercial jealousies of the English
aders were put by; and the Act of Union as finally passed in 1707
ovided that the two kingdoms should be united into one under
e name of Great Britain, and that the succession to the crown of
is United Kingdom should be ruled by the provisions of the
aglish Act of Settlement. The Scotch Church and the Scotch Law
ere left untouched: but all rights of trade were thrown open,
d a uniform system of coinage adopted. A single Parliament was
nceforth to represent the United Kingdom, and for this purpose
rty-five Scotch members were added to the five hundred and
irteen English members of the House of Commons, and sixteen
presentative peers to the one hundred and eight who formed the
nglish House of Lords. In Scotland the opposition was bitter and
most universal. The terror of the Presbyterians indeed was met
v an Act of Security which became part of the Treaty of Union,
d which required an oath to support the Presbyterian Church
om every sovereign on his accession. But no securities could satisfy
e enthusiastic patriots or the fanatical Cameronians. The
acobites sought troops from France and plotted a Stuart restora-
on. The nationalists talked of seceding from the Assembly which
ited for the Union, and of establishing a rival Parliament. In
e end, however, good sense and the loyalty of the trading classes
the cause of the Protestant succession won their way. The
easure was adopted by the Scotch Parliament, and the Treaty of
nion became in 1707 a legislative Act to which Anne gave her
ssent in noble words. "I desire," said the Queen, "and expect
om my subjects of both nations that from henceforth they act
ith all possible respect and kindness to one another, that so it
ay appear to all the world they have hearts disposed to become
ne people." Time has more than answered these hopes. The two
ations whom the Union brought together have ever since remained
ne. England gained in the removal of a constant danger of treason
nd war. To Scotland the Union opened up new avenues of wealth
hich the energy of its people turned to wonderful account. The
rms of Lothian have become models of agricultural skill. A fish-
g town on the Clyde has grown into the rich and populous
lasgow. Peace and culture have changed the wild clansmen of
e Highlands into herdsmen and farmers. Nor was the change
llowed by any loss of national spirit. The world has hardly seen
mightier and more rapid development of national energy than
at of Scotland after the Union. All that passed away was the
ealousy which had parted since the days of Edward the First two

peoples whom a common blood and common speech proclaimed to
one. The Union between Scotland and England has been real a
stable simply because it was the legislative acknowledgment a
enforcement of a national fact.

With the defeat of Ramillies the fortunes of France reached th
lowest ebb. The loss of Flanders was followed by the loss of It.
after a victory by which Eugene relieved Turin; and not only
Peterborough hold his ground in Spain, but Charles the Third w
an army of English and Portuguese entered Madrid. Marlborou
was at the height of his renown. Ramillies gave him streng
enough to force Anne, in spite of her hatred of the Whigs, to fu
his compact with them by admitting Lord Sunderland, the bitter
leader of their party, to office. But the system of political balar
which he had maintained till now was fast breaking down. Co
stitutionally, Marlborough's was the last attempt to govern Engla
on other terms than those of party government, and the union
parties to which he had clung ever since his severance from t
extreme Tories soon became impossible. The growing opposition
the Tories to the war threw the Duke more and more on the suppe
of the Whigs, and the Whigs sold their support dearly. Sunderla
was resolved to drive the moderate Tories from the Administrati
in spite of Marlborough's desire to retain them. "England," t
Duke wrote hotly, "will not be ruined because a few men are n
pleased," but the opposition of the Tories to the war left hi
helpless in the hands of the only party who steadily supported
A factious union of the Whigs with their opponents roused Ma
borough to a burst of unusual passion in Parliament, but it effect
its end by convincing him of the impossibility of further resistan
The resistance of the Queen indeed was stubborn and bitter. An
was at heart a Tory, and her old trust in Marlborough died with l
acceptance of the Whig demands. It was only by the threat
resignation that he had forced her to admit Sunderland to offic
The violent outbreak of temper with which the Duchess enforc
her husband's will changed the Queen's friendship for her into
bitter resentment. Marlborough however was forced to increa
this resentment by fresh compliances with the Whig demands, l
removing Peterborough from his command as a Tory general, ar
by wresting from Anne her consent in 1708 to the dismissal
Harley and St. John from office, and the admission of Lord Some
and Wharton into the Ministry. Somers became President of t
Council, Wharton Lord-Lieutenant of Ireland, and the Wh
victory was complete. Meanwhile, the great struggle abroad w
going on, with striking alternations of success. France rose wit
singular rapidity from the crushing blow of Ramillies. Spain w.
recovered for Philip by the victory of Marshal Berwick at Almanz
Villars won fresh triumphs on the Rhine, and Eugene, who ha
penetrated into Provence, was driven back into Italy. In Flander
the plans of Marlborough were foiled by the strategy of the Dul
of Vendôme and by the reluctance of the Dutch, who were no

,vering towards peace. In the campaign of 1708 however, ,ndôme, though superior in force, was attacked and defeated at ,denarde, and though Marlborough was hindered from striking the heart of France by the timidity of the English and Dutch ,tesmen, he reduced Lille, the strongest of the frontier fortresses, ,the face of an army of relief which numbered a hundred thousand ,n. The pride of Lewis was at last broken by defeat and by the ,rible suffering of France. He offered terms of peace which yielded that the allies had fought for. He consented to withdraw his aid ,m Philip of Spain, to give up ten Flemish fortresses to the Dutch, ,d to surrender to the Empire all that France had gained since , treaty of Westphalia. He offered to acknowledge Anne, to ,nish the Pretender from his dominions, and to demolish the ,tifications of Dunkirk, a port hateful to England as the home of , French privateers.

To Marlborough peace now seemed secure, but in spite of his England and the War ,nsels, the allies and the Whig Ministers in England demanded ,at Lewis should with his own troops compel his grandson to give the crown of Spain. " If I must wage war," replied the King, ,I had rather wage it against my enemies than against my ,ildren." At the opening of the campaign of 1709 he appealed , France, and France, exhausted as it was, answered nobly to his ,peal. The terrible slaughter which bears the name of the battle , Malplaquet showed a new temper in the French soldiery. ,arving as they were, they flung away their rations in their eager-,ss for the fight, and fell back at its close in serried masses that , efforts of Marlborough could break. They had lost twelve ,ousand men, but they had inflicted on the allies a loss of double ,at number. A " deluge of blood " such as that of Malplaquet ,creased the growing weariness of the war, and the rejection of , French offers was unjustly attributed to a desire on the part , Marlborough of lengthening out a contest which brought him ,ofit and power. The expulsion of Harley and St. John from the ,nistry had given the Tories leaders of a more vigorous stamp, ,d St. John brought into play a new engine of political attack ,nose powers soon made themselves felt. In the *Examiner* and in , crowd of pamphlets and periodicals which followed in its train, ,e humour of Prior, the bitter irony of Swift, and St. John's own ,illiant sophistry spent themselves on the abuse of the war and , its general. " Six millions of supplies and almost fifty millions , debt! " Swift wrote bitterly, " The High Allies have been the ,in of us!" Marlborough was ridiculed and reviled, he was accused , insolence, cruelty and ambition, of corruption and greed. Even ,s courage was called in question. A sudden storm of popular ,ssion showed the way in which public opinion responded to ,ese efforts. A High Church divine, Dr. Sacheverell, maintained ,e doctrine of non-resistance in a sermon at St. Paul's with a ,ldness which deserved prosecution; but in spite of the warning , Marlborough and of Somers the Whig Ministers resolved on his

1698 to 1712

impeachment. His trial in 1710 at once widened into a great par struggle, and the popular enthusiasm in Sacheverell's favour show the gathering hatred of the Whigs and the war. The most emine of the Tory Churchmen stood by his side at the bar, crowds escort him to the court and back again, while the streets rang with cr of "The Church and Dr. Sacheverell." A small majority of t peers found him guilty, but the light sentence they inflicted was effect an acquittal, and bonfires and illuminations over the wh country welcomed it as a Tory triumph.

Fall of Marlborough

The turn of popular feeling freed Anne at once from the pressu beneath which she had bent: and the skill of Harley, whose cous Mrs. Masham, had succeeded the Duchess of Marlborough in t Queen's favour, was employed in bringing about the fall both Marlborough and the Whig Ministers by playing the one off agai the other. The Whigs, who knew the Duke's alliance with th had simply been forced on him by the war, and were persuad that the Queen had no aim but to humble him, looked coolly at the dismissal of his son-in-law, Sunderland, and his frier Godolphin. Marlborough, who leaned towards a reconciliati with his old party, looked on in return while Anne dismissed t Whig Ministers in the autumn of 1710 and appointed a To Ministry in their place with Harley and St. John at its head. the face of these changes, however, the Duke did not dare encounter the risks of any decisive enterprise; and his reducti of a few sea-board towns failed to win back English feeling to t continuance of so costly a struggle. The return of a Tory House Commons sealed his fate. His wife was dismissed from court. masterly plan for a march into the heart of France in the openi of 1711 was foiled by the withdrawal of a part of his forces, and t negotiations which had for some time been conducted between t French and English Ministers without his knowledge march rapidly to a close. The sense of approaching ruin forced Marlborou at last to break with the Tory Ministry, and his efforts induced t House of Lords to denounce the contemplated peace; but t support of the Commons and the Queen, and the general hatred the war among the people, enabled Harley to ride down all resi ance. At the opening of 1712 the Whig majority in the House Lords was swamped by the creation of twelve Tory peers. Ma borough was dismissed from his command, charged with peculati and condemned as guilty by a vote of the House of Commons. I at once withdrew from England, and with his withdrawal opposition to the peace was at an end.

As to the claim to the Spanish throne, Louis XIV. contended that wife's renunciation was invalidated by the non-payment of her dov and the absence of ratification by the Cortes. The renunciation which w held to bar the claim of the Electoral Prince of Bavaria was mer private and invalid in Spanish law.

Section X.—Walpole, 1712—1742

[*Authorities.*—Coxe's " Memoirs of Sir R. Walpole " is the standard work on Walpole. Other works of importance are Horace Walpole's ' Memoirs "; Hervey's " Memoirs "; Bolingbroke's Works, especially he " Patriot King " and the " Letter to Sir William Wyndham "; Swift's Works; and Horace Walpole's Letters. The best modern history of the period is Lecky, " History of England in the Eighteenth Century."]

The struggle of the House of Lords under Marlborough's guidance Walpole against Harley and the Peace marks the close of the constitutional evolution which had been silently going on since the Restoration of the Stuarts. The defeat of the Peers and the fall of Marlborough which followed it announced that the transfer of political power to the House of Commons was complete. The machinery by which Sunderland had enabled it to direct the actual government of the country had been strengthened by the failure of Marlborough to restore the older system of administration: and the Ministers of the Crown have remained ever since an Executive Committee whose work is to carry out the will of the majority of its members. A recognition of this great change was seen in the series of " Great Commoners " who from this time became the rulers of England. The influence of political tradition, of wealth, and of the administrative training which their position often secures them, has at all times given places in the Ministry to members of the House of Lords, and a peer has sometimes figured as its nominal head. But the more natural arrangement has been the more common one; and all the greater statesmen who have guided the fortunes of England since Harley's day have been found in the Commons. Of these Great Commoners Robert Walpole was the first. Born in 1676, he entered Parliament two years before William's death as a young Norfolk landowner of fair fortune, with the tastes and air of the class from which he sprang. His big square figure, his vulgar good-humoured face were those of a common country squire. And in Walpole the squire underlay the statesman to the last. He was ignorant of books, he " loved neither writing nor reading," and if he had a taste for art, his real love was for the table, the bottle, and the chase. He rode as hard as he drank. Even in moments of political peril, the first despatch he would open was the letter from his gamekeeper. There was the temper of the Norfolk fox-hunter in the " doggedness " which Marlborough noted as his characteristic, in the burly self-confidence which declared " If I had not been Prime Minister I should have been Archbishop of Canterbury," in the stubborn courage which conquered the awkwardness of his earlier efforts to speak or met single-handed at the last the bitter attacks of a host of enemies, and above all in the genial good-humour which became with him a new force in politics. Walpole was the first Minister—it has been finely said— who gave our government that character of lenity which it has since generally deserved." No man was ever more fiercely attacked by speakers and writers, but he brought in no " gagging Act " for the press; and though the lives of most of his assailants were in his hands through their intrigues with the Pretender, he made no use of his power over them. Where his country breeding showed itself most, however, was in the shrewd, narrow, honest character of his mind. He saw very clearly, but he could not see far, and he would not believe what he could not see. He was thoroughly straightforward and true to his own convictions, so far as they went. " Robin and I are two honest men," the Jacobite Shippen owned in later years, when contrasting him with his factious opponents: " he is for King George, and I am for King James; but those men with long cravats only desire place, either under King George or King James." He saw the value of the political results which the Revolution had won, and he carried out his " Revolution principles " with a rare fidelity through years of unquestioned power. But his prosaic good sense turned sceptically away from the poetic and passionate sides of human feeling. Appeals to the loftier or purer motives of action he laughed at as " school-boy flights." For young members who talked of public virtue or patriotism he had one good-natured answer: " You will soon come off that and grow wiser."

How great a part Walpole was to play no one could as yet foresee. But even under Marlborough his practical abilities had brought him to the front. At the moment when the House of Commons was recognized as supreme, Walpole showed himself its ablest debater. Commerce promised to become the main interest of England, and the merchants were already beginning to trust to his skill in finance. As a subordinate member of the Whig Ministry at the close of the war he gave signs of that administrative ability which forced his enemies to acknowledge that " he does everything with the same ease and tranquillity as if he were doing nothing." How great was the sense of his power was seen in the action of the triumphant Tories on Marlborough's fall in 1712. Walpole alone of their Whig opponents was singled out for persecution; and a groundless charge of peculation sent him for a time to the Tower. The great work of the new Tory Ministry was to bring about a peace, and by the conclusion of a separate truce with France it at last forced all the members of the Alliance save the Emperor, who required the pressure of defeat, to consent in 1713 to the Treaty of Utrecht. this treaty the original aim of the war was silently abandoned, and the principle of the earlier Treaties of Partition adopted in its stead; but with a provision that the crowns of France and Spain should never be united. Philip remained on the Spanish throne; Spain ceded her possessions in Italy and the Netherlands to Charles, who had now become Emperor, in satisfaction of his claims; and handed over Sicily to the Duke of Savoy. Holland regained the right of placing garrisons in the strongest towns of the Netherlands as a barrier against France. England retained her conquests of Minorca

nd Gibraltar, which gave her command of the Mediterranean; her
resentment against the French privateers was satisfied by the dis-
mantling of Dunkirk; and Lewis recognized the right of Anne and
the Protestant succession in the House of Hanover. The failure of
the Queen's health made the succession the real question of the
day, and it was a question which turned all politics into faction and
intrigue. The Whigs, to secure the succession of the House of
Hanover by the overthrow of the Tories, defeated a Treaty of
Commerce in which Bolinbroke anticipated the greatest financial
triumph of William Pitt by securing freedom of trade between
England and France. The Ministry, on the other hand, in their
anxiety to strengthen themselves by binding the Church to their
side, pushed through the Houses a Schism Act, which forbade Dissenters to act as schoolmasters and tutors. But on the question of
the Succession their course was as hesitating as that of the Queen,
who hated the House of Hanover and hindered the Electoral Prince
from coming over to secure the rights of his grandmother Sophia
by taking his seat among the peers as Duke of Cambridge, but who
was too loyal to the Church to be brought into any real support of
the Pretender. Harley, who had become Earl of Oxford, intrigued
with both Hanover and St. Germains. St. John, however, who was
raised to the peerage as Viscount Bolinbroke, saw that hesitation
was no longer possible, and flung himself hotly, though secretly,
into the Jacobite cause. As the crisis grew nearer, both parties
prepared for civil war. In the beginning of 1714 the Whigs made
ready for a rising on the Queen's death, and invited Marlborough
from Flanders to head them, in the hope that his name would rally
the army to their cause. Bolinbroke on the other hand ousted
Harley from office, made the Jacobite Duke of Ormond Warden
of the Cinque Ports, the district in which either claimant of the
Crown must land, and gave Scotland in charge to the Jacobite Earl
of Mar. But events moved faster than his plans. On the 30th of
July Anne was suddenly struck with apoplexy; and at the news
the Whig Dukes of Argyll and Somerset entered the Privy Council
without summons, and found their cause supported by the Duke
of Shrewsbury, a member of the Tory Ministry, but an adherent of
the House of Hanover. Shrewsbury was suggested by the Council
and accepted by the dying Queen as Lord Treasurer. Four regiments were summoned to the capital, but the Jacobites were
hopeless and unprepared, and the Elector George of Hanover, who
had become heir to the throne on the death of the Princess Sophia,
was proclaimed as King without opposition.

The accession of George I. in August 1714 was followed by two
striking political results. Under Anne the throne had regained
much of the older influence which it lost through William's unpopularity. Under the two sovereigns who followed Anne the power
of the Crown lay absolutely dormant. They were strangers, to
whom loyalty in its personal sense was impossible ; and their
character as nearly approached insignificance as it is possible for

I 728

human character to approach it. Both were honest and straigh
forward men, who frankly accepted the irksome position of cor
stitutional kings. But neither had any qualities which could mal
their honesty attractive to the people at large. The temper of th
first was that of a gentleman usher; and his one care was to ge
money for his favourites and himself. The temper of the second wa
that of a drill-sergeant, who believed himself master of his real
while he repeated the lessons he had learnt from his wife and whic
his wife had learnt from the Minister. Their court is familiar enoug
in the witty memoirs of the time; but as political figures the tw
Georges are simply absent from our history. England was governe
by the Ministers of the Crown, and throughout the whole perio
these were mere representatives of a single political party. " Th
Tory party," Bolinbroke wrote immediately after Anne's deat
" is gone." It was Bolinbroke more than any other man who ha
ruined the Tories by diverting them from any practical part
English politics to dreams of a Stuart restoration. The discover
of the Jacobite plots which had been nursed by the late Ministe
of the Queen alienated the bulk of the landed gentry, who we
still loyal to the Revolution, of the clergy, who dreaded a Cathol
King, and of the trading classes, who shrank from the blow
public credit which a Jacobite repudiation of the debt would brin
about. The cry of the York mob at the King's accession expresse
tersely the creed of the English trader; it shouted, " Libert
Property, and No Pretender." The policy of Harley and Bolinbro
left the Whigs the only representatives of Revolution principle
of constitutional liberty and religious toleration, and when th
was fairly seen, not only merchant and squire but the nation
large went with the Whigs. In the House of Commons after Geor,
the First's accession the Tory members hardly numbered fifty, ar
their Jacobite leanings left them powerless over English politi
The King's Ministry was wholly drawn from the Whig part
though Marlborough and the leaders of the Junto were to the
surprise set aside, and the chief offices given to younger men. T
direction of affairs was really entrusted to Lord Townshend, wh
became Secretary of State, and his brother-in-law, Walpole, wh
successively occupied the posts of Paymaster of the Force
Chancellor of the Exchequer, and First Lord of the Treasury. T
Townshend Administration was the first of a series of Wh
Ministries which ruled England for half a century without ar
serious opposition. The length of their rule was due partly r
doubt to an excellent organization. While their adversaries we
divided by differences of principle and without leaders of re
eminence, the Whigs stood as one man on the principles of t
Revolution and produced great leaders who carried them in
effect. They submitted with admirable discipline to the guidan
of a knot of great landed proprietors, to the houses of Bentinc
Manners, Campbell, and Cavendish, to the Fitzroys and Lennox
the Russells and Grenvilles, families whose resistance to the Stuar

...ose share in the Revolution, whose energy in setting the line of ...anover on the throne, gave them a claim to power which their ...ber use of it long maintained without dispute. They devoted ...emselves with immense activity to the gaining and preserving ...ascendency in the House of Commons. The wealth of the Whig ...uses was ungrudgingly spent in securing a monopoly of the small ...d corrupt constituencies which formed a large part of the borough ...presentation. Of the county members, who were the weightier ...d more active part of the House, nine-tenths were for a long ...ne relatives and dependants of the Whig families. The support ...the commercial classes and of the great towns was won not only ...the resolute maintenance of public credit, but by the devotion ...a special attention to questions of trade and finance. But ...xterous as was their management and compact as was their ...ganization, it was to nobler qualities than these that the Whigs ...ved their long rule over England. They were true throughout to ...e principles on which they had risen into power, and their un...oken administration converted those principles into national ...bits. Before the fifty years of their rule had passed, Englishmen ...d forgotten that it was possible to persecute for differences of ...igion, or to put down the liberty of the press, or to tamper with ...e administration of justice, or to rule without a Parliament. ...ith the steadiness of a great oligarchy, the Whigs combined, no ...ubt, its characteristic immobility. The tone of their adminis...tion was conservative, cautious, and inactive. They were firm ...ainst any return to the past, but they shrank from any advance ...wards a new and more liberal future. " I am no reformer," ...alpole used to say, and the years of his power are years without ...rallel in our history for political stagnation. But for the time ...is inactivity not only saved them from great dangers, but fell ...with the temper of the nation at large. Their great stumbling...ocks as a party since the Revolution had been the War and the ...urch. But they had learnt to leave the Church alone, and their ...reign policy became a policy of peace. At home their inaction ...s especially popular with the one class who commonly press for ...litical activity. The energy of the trading class was absorbed ...t the time in the rapid extension of commerce and the rapid ...cumulation of wealth. So long as the country was justly and ...nstitutionally governed they were content to leave government ...the hands that held it. They wished only to be let alone to enjoy ...eir new freedom, to develop their new industries. And the Whigs ...them alone. Progress became material rather than political, ...t the material progress of the country was such as England had ...ver seen before.

The conversion of England to the Whigs was hastened by a ...sperate attempt of the Pretender to gain the throne. There was ...real hope of success, for the Jacobites in England were few, and ...e Tories were broken and dispirited by the fall of their leaders. ...rd Oxford was impeached and sent to the Tower; while Bolin-

broke fled over-sea at the threat of impeachment, and was follow
by the Duke of Ormond, the great hope of the Jacobite party. B
James Stuart was as inaccessible to reason as his father had bee
and in spite of Bolinbroke's counsels he ordered the Earl of Mar
give the signal for revolt in the North. In Scotland the triumph
the Whigs meant the continuance of the House of Argyll in pow
and the rival Highland clans were as ready for a blow at t
Campbells under Mar as they had been ready for a blow at the
under Dundee or Montrose. But Mar was a leader of differe
stamp from these. Six thousand Highlanders joined him at Pert
but his cowardice and want of conduct kept his army idle t
Argyll had gathered forces to meet it in an indecisive engageme
at Sheriffmuir. The Pretender, who arrived too late for the actio
proved a yet more sluggish and incapable leader than Mar: a
at the close of 1715 the advance of fresh forces drove James ove
sea again, and dispersed the clans to their hills. In England, t
danger passed away like a dream. A few of the Catholic gent
rose in Northumberland, under Lord Derwentwater and M
Forster; and the arrival of two thousand Highlanders who h
been sent to join them by Mar spurred them to a march in
Lancashire, where the Catholic party was strongest. But they we
soon cooped up in Preston, and driven to a cowardly surrend
The leaders paid for their treason with their heads; but no serio
steps were taken to put an end to the danger from the north
bringing the clans into order. The Ministry, which was reconstitut
at the end of 1716 by the withdrawal of Townshend and Walpo
and now acknowledged Lord Stanhope as its head, availed its
of the Whig triumph to bring about a repeal of the Schism a
the Occasional Conformity Acts, and to venture with varying succe
on two constitutional changes. Under the Triennial Bill of Willia
reign the duration of a Parliament was limited to three years. N
that the House of Commons, however, was become the ruli
power in the State, a change was absolutely required to secu
steadiness and fixity of political action; and in 1716 the durati
of Parliament was extended to seven years by the Septennial B
The power which Harley's creation of twelve peers showed t
Crown to possess of swamping the majority in the House of Pee
prompted the Ministry in 1720 to introduce a bill, whose origin w
attributed to Lord Sunderland, and which professed to secure t
liberty of that House by limiting the Peerage to its present numb
in England and substituting twenty-five hereditary for the sixte
elected Peers from Scotland. The bill was strenuously opposed
Walpole, who had withdrawn from the Ministry on the expulsi
of his friend Lord Townshend from office; and to Walpole's oppo
tion it mainly owed its defeat. It would, in fact, have render
representative government impossible; for representative gover
ment, as we have seen, had come to mean government by the w
of the House of Commons, and had Sunderland's bill passed
power would have been left which could have forced the Peers

1712
to
1742
—
The
Whigs
and
Europe

w to the will of the Lower House in matters where their opinion
s adverse to it.

Abroad the Whigs aimed strictly at the maintenance of peace
a faithful adhesion to the Treaty of Utrecht. The one obstacle
peace was Spain. Its King, Philip of Anjou, had ceded the
alian possessions of his crown and renounced his own rights of
ccession to the throne of France, but his constant dream was to
cover all he had given up. To attempt this was to defy Europe;
r Austria held the late possessions of Spain in Italy, the Milanese
d Naples, while France, since the death of Lewis the Fourteenth
ept. 1715), was ruled by the Regent Duke of Orleans, who stood
xt under the treaty in succession to the French throne through
ilip's renunciation. But the boldness of Cardinal Alberoni, who
s now the Spanish Minister, accepted the risk. He began to
trigue against the Regent in France, and supported the Jacobite
use as a means of preventing the interference of England with
s designs. He gained the aid of Sweden through the resentment
Charles the Twelfth at the cession to Hanover of the Swedish
ssessions of Bremen and Verden by the King of Denmark, who
d seized them while Charles was absent in Turkey, a cession of
e highest importance to the Electoral dominions, which were
us brought into contact with the sea, and of hardly less value to
gland, as it secured the mouths of the Elbe and the Weser, the
ief inlets for British commerce into Germany, to a friendly state.
t the efforts of Alberoni were foiled by the union of his opponents.
is first attempt was to recover the Italian provinces which Philip
d lost, and armaments greater than Spain had seen for a century
duced Sardinia in 1716, and attacked Sicily. England and France
once drew together, and were joined by Holland in a Triple
lliance, concluded in the opening of 1717, and which guaranteed
e succession of the House of Hanover in England, as well as of
e House of Orleans in France, should its boy king, Lewis XV.,
e without issue. The Triple Alliance became a Quadruple Alliance
1718 by the accession of the Emperor, whose Italian possessions
e three Powers had guaranteed; and the appearance of an
nglish squadron in the Straits of Messina was followed by an
gagement in which the Spanish fleet was all but destroyed.
lberoni strove to avenge the blow by fitting out an armament
hich the Duke of Ormond was to command for the revival of the
cobite rising in Scotland, but his fleet was wrecked in the Bay
Biscay; and the progress of the French armies in the north of
ain forced Philip at last to dismiss his Minister, to renew his
nunciation of the French throne, and to withdraw from Sardinia
d Sicily, on condition that the reversion of Parma and Tuscany
ould be secured to his son, the Infante Don Carlos. Sicily now
ssed to the Emperor, and Savoy was recompensed for its loss by
e acquisition of Sardinia, from which its Duke took the title of
ing. At the same moment the schemes of Charles the Twelfth,
ho had concluded an alliance with the Czar, Peter the Great, for

a restoration of the Stuarts, were brought to an end by his deat at the siege of Frederickshall. But the ability and sense whic Stanhope and his fellow Ministers showed in their foreign polic utterly failed them in dealing with the power of speculation whic the sudden increase of commerce was rousing at home. The un known wealth of South America had acted ever since the days of the Buccaneers like a spell on the imagination of Englishmen; an Harley gave countenance to a South Sea Company, which promise a reduction of the public debt as the price of a monopoly of th Spanish trade. Spain however clung jealously to her old pro hibitions of all foreign commerce; the Treaty of Utrecht only wo for England the right of engaging in the negro slave-trade, and of despatching a single ship to the coast; but in spite of all thi the Company again came forward, offering in exchange for ne privileges to pay off national burdens which amounted to nearly million a year. It was in vain that Walpole warned the Ministr and the country against this " dream." Both went mad; and i 1720 bubble Company followed bubble Company, till the inevitab reaction brought a general ruin in its train.

The crash brought Stanhope to the grave. Of his colleague many were found to have received bribes from the South Se Company to back its frauds. Craggs, the Secretary of State, die of terror at the investigation; Aislabie, the Chancellor of th Exchequer, was sent to the Tower; and in the general wreck of h rivals Walpole mounted again into power. His factious condu when out of office had been redeemed by his opposition to th Peerage Bill: his weight with the country dates from his prescien warnings against the South Sea speculation. In 1721 he agai became First Lord of the Treasury, while Townshend returned t his post of Secretary of State. But there was nothing to promi the longest tenure of power which any English Minister since th Revolution has ever enjoyed, for Walpole remained at the hea of affairs for twenty-one years. But his long administration almost without a history. All legislative and political activit abruptly ceased with his entry into office. Year after year passe by without a change. In the third year of his Ministry there wa but one division in the House of Commons. The Tory membe were so few that for a time they hardly cared to attend its sitting and in 1722 the loss of Bishop Atterbury of Rochester, who wa convicted of correspondence with the Pretender, deprived of h bishopric, and banished by Act of Parliament, deprived th Jacobite party of their only remaining leader. But quiet as wa the air of English politics under Walpole, his policy was in th main a large and noble one. He was the first and greatest of ou Peace Ministers. " The most pernicious circumstances," he sai " in which this country can be are those of war; as we mu be losers while it lasts and cannot be great gainers when it ends. In spite of the complications of foreign affairs and the pressure fro the Court and Opposition, he resolutely kept England at peace.

as not that the honour or influence of England suffered in Walpole's hands, for he won victories by the firmness of his policy and the skill of his negotiations as effectual as those which are won by arms. The most pressing danger to European tranquillity lay in the fact that the Emperor Charles the Sixth was without a son. He had issued a Pragmatic Sanction, by which he provided that his hereditary dominions in Austria, Hungary, and Bohemia should descend unbroken to his daughter, Maria Theresa; but the European powers had as yet declined to guarantee her succession. Spain, however, anxious as of old to recover Gibraltar and Minorca from England, and still irritated against France, offered not only to waive her own claims and guarantee the Pragmatic Sanction, but to grant the highest trading privileges in her American dominions to a commercial trading company which the Emperor had established at Ostend in defiance of the Treaty of Westphalia and the remonstrances of England and Holland, on condition that the Emperor secured the succession of Carlos, Philip's second son, to the Duchies of Parma and Tuscany. At the same time Russia, which was now governed by Catherine, the wife of Peter the Great, forced Sweden into an alliance for an attack upon Denmark, and secretly negotiated with Spain and the Emperor. Townshend met the last danger by a defensive treaty between France, England, and Prussia, which he concluded at Hanover, by a subsidy which detached Sweden from her ally, and by the despatch of a squadron to the Baltic. But the withdrawal of Prussia from the Treaty of Hanover gave fresh courage to the Emperor, and in 1727 Charles withdrew his ambassador from England, while Philip began the siege of Gibraltar. The Emperor, however, was held in check by the death of the Russian Empress and the firm attitude of England, France, and Holland; and Spain, finding herself too weak to wage war alone, concluded in 1729 the Treaty of Seville with the three powers. The Emperor still held aloof till 1731, when the five States united in the Treaty of Vienna, which satisfied Spain by giving the Italian Duchies to Don Carlos, while the maritime powers contented Charles by guaranteeing the Pragmatic Sanction.

Walpole was not only the first English Peace Minister; he was the first English Minister who was a great financier, and who regarded the development of national wealth and the adjustment of national burdens as the business of a statesman. His time of power was a time of great material prosperity. In 1724 the King could congratulate the country on its possession of " peace with all powers abroad, at home perfect tranquillity, plenty, and an uninterrupted enjoyment of all civil and religious rights." Population was growing fast. That of Manchester and Birmingham doubled in thirty years. The rise of manufactures was accompanied by a sudden increase of commerce, which was due mainly to the rapid development of our colonies. Liverpool, which owes its creation to the new trade with the West, sprang up from a little country town into the third port in the kingdom. With peace and

Walpole's Finance

security, the value of land, and with it the rental of every countr
gentleman, tripled; while the introduction of winter roots, ι
artificial grasses, of the system of a rotation of crops, changed th
whole character of agriculture, and spread wealth through th
farming classes. The wealth around him never made Walpol
swerve from a rigid economy, from the steady reduction of th
debt, or the diminution of fiscal duties. Even before the death ι
George the First the public burdens were reduced by twent
millions. But he had the sense to see that the wisest course
statesman can take in presence of a great increase in nation
industry and national wealth is to look quietly on and let it alon
What he did do however was wise, and what he strove to do wɛ
yet wiser. As early as 1720 he declared in a speech from the Thror
that nothing would more conduce to the extension of commerc
" than to make the exportation of our own manufactures, and th
importation of the commodities used in the manufacturing of then
as practicable and easy as may be." The first act of his financi
administration was to take off the duties from more than a hundre
British exports, and nearly forty articles of importation. In 173
he broke in the same enlightened spirit through the prejudic
which restricted the commerce of the colonies to the mothe
country alone, by allowing Georgia and the Carolinas to export the
rice directly to any part of Europe. The result was that the rice ·
America soon drove that of Italy and Egypt from the market. H
Excise Bill, defective as it was, was the first measure in which a
English Minister showed any real grasp of the principles of taxatior
No tax had from the first moment of its introduction been mor
unpopular than the Excise. Its origin was due to Pym and th
Long Parliament, who imposed duties on beer, cider, and perr
which at the Restoration produced an annual income of more tha
six hundred thousand pounds. The war with France brought wi
it the malt-tax and additional duties on spirits, wine, tobacc
and other articles. So great had been the increase in the publ
wealth that the return from the Excise amounted at the death
George the First to nearly two millions and a half a year. But
unpopularity remained unabated, and even philosophers like Loc
contended that the whole public revenue should be drawn fro
direct taxes upon the land. Walpole, on the other hand, saw in th
growth of indirect taxation a means of freeing the land from ɛ
burdens whatever. Smuggling and fraud diminished the reven
by immense sums. The loss on tobacco alone amounted to a thir
of the whole duty. The Excise Bill of 1733 met this evil by th
establishment of bonded warehouses, and by the collection of th
duties from the inland dealers in the form of Excise and not
Customs. The first measure would have made London a free por
and doubled English trade. The second would have so large
increased the revenue, without any loss to the consumer, as
enable Walpole to repeal the land-tax. In the case of tea an
coffee alone, the change in the mode of levying the duty brought

1712
to
1742

n additional hundred thousand pounds a year. The necessaries f life and the raw materials of manufacture were in Walpole's lan to remain absolutely untaxed. Every part of Walpole's ᶜheme has since been carried into effect; but in 1733 he stood efore his time. An agitation of unprecedented violence forced im to withdraw the bill.

But if Walpole's aims were wise and statesmanlike, he was un-ᶜrupulous in the means by which he realized them. Personally he ᵥas free from corruption; and he is perhaps the first great English ᵗatesman who left office poorer than when he entered it. But he ᵥas certainly the first who made parliamentary corruption a ᵉgular part of his system of government. Corruption was older ᵗhan Walpole, for it sprang out of the very transfer of power to ᵗhe House of Commons which had begun with the Restoration. ᵀhe transfer was complete, and the House was supreme in the ᵗtate; but while freeing itself from the control of the Crown, it ᵥas as yet only imperfectly responsible to the people. It was only ᵗ election time that a member felt the pressure of public opinion. ᵀhe secresy of parliamentary proceedings, which had been needful ᵗs a safeguard against royal interference with debate, served as a ᵗafeguard against interference on the part of constituencies. This ᵗtrange union of immense power with absolute freedom from ᵉsponsibility brought about its natural results in the bulk of ᵗembers. A vote was too valuable to be given without recompense. ᵖarliamentary support had to be bought by places, pensions, and ᵗribes in hard cash. Walpole was probably less corrupt than Danby ᵥho preceded or the Pelhams who followed him, but he was far more ᵧnical in his avowal of corruption. Even if he was falsely credited ᵥith the saying that "every man has his price," he was always ᵉady to pay the price of any man who was worth having. And he ᵥas driven to employ corruption lavishly by the very character ᵗf his rule. In the absence of a strong opposition and of great ᵗmpulses to enthusiasm a party breaks readily into factions; and ᵗhe weakness of the Tories joined with the stagnation of public ᵗffairs to beget faction among the Whigs. Walpole, too, was ᵉalous of power: and as his jealousy drove colleague after colleague ᵗut of office, they became leaders of a party of so-called "Patriots" ᵥhose whole end was to drive the Minister from his post. This ᵥhig faction, which was headed by Pulteney and Lord Chesterfield, ᵗoon rallied to it the fragment of the Tory party which remained, ᵗnd which was now guided by the virulent ability of Bolin-ᵗroke, whom Walpole had suffered to return from exile, but to ᵥhom he had refused the restoration of his seat in the House ᵗf Lords.

Through the reign of George the First these "Patriots" increased ᵗn numbers, and at the accession of his son George the Second ᵗn 1727 they counted on their enemy's fall; for the new King hated ᵗis father and his father's counsellors, and had spoken of Walpole ᵗs "a rogue." But jealous of authority as he was, George the

Walpole
and the
Parlia-
ment

Walpole
and
Queen
Caroline

*ᵢ 728

Second was absolutely guided by the adroitness of his wife, Caroline
of Anspach, and Caroline had resolved that there should be no
change in the Ministry. The ten years which followed were in fact
the years during which Walpole's power was at its highest. The
Jacobites refused to stir. The Church was quiet. The Dissenters
pressed for a repeal of the Test and Corporation Acts, but Walpole
was resolved not to rouse passions of religious hate which only
slumbered, and satisfied them by an annual Act of Indemnity for
any breach of these penal statutes. A few trade measures and
social reforms crept quietly through the Houses. An inquiry into
the state of the gaols showed that social thought was not utterly
dead. A bill of great value enacted that all proceedings in courts of
justice should henceforth be in the English language. Walpole's
chief effort at financial reform, the Excise Bill of 1733, was foiled
as we have seen by the factious ignorance of the " Patriots." The
violence of his opponents was backed by an outburst of popular
prejudice; riots almost grew into revolt; and in spite of the
Queen's wish to put down resistance by force, Walpole withdrew
the bill. " I will not be the minister," he said with noble self-
command, " to enforce taxes at the expense of blood." He showed
equal wisdom and courage in the difficulties which again rose
abroad. In 1733 the peace of Europe was broken afresh by disputes
which rose out of a contested election to the throne of Poland. The
King was eager to fight, and even Caroline's German sympathies
inclined her to join in the fray; but Walpole stood firm for the
observance of neutrality. " There are fifty thousand men slain this
year in Europe," he was able to say as the war went on, " and not
one Englishman." The intervention of England and Holland
succeeded in 1736 in restoring peace at the cost of the cession of
Naples to Don Carlos and of Lorraine to France.

The
Spanish
War

Walpole's defeat on the Excise Bill had done little to shake his
power, and Bolinbroke withdrew to France in despair at the failure
of his efforts. But the Queen's death in 1737, and the violent
support which the Prince of Wales gave the " Patriots " from hatred
to his father, were more serious blows. The country, too, wearied
at last of its monotonous prosperity and of its monotonous peace.
It was hard to keep from war in the Southern Seas. The merchant
class were determined to carry on their trade with Spanish America,
a trade which rested indeed on no legal right, but had grown largely
through the connivance of the Spanish officers during the long
alliance with England from 1670 to the War of Succession. But the
accession of a French prince to the Spanish throne had brought
about a cessation of this connivance. Philip of Anjou was hostile
to English trade with his American dominions; and the efforts of
Spain to preserve its own monopoly, to put down the vast system
of smuggling which rendered it valueless, and to restrict English
commerce to the negro slave-trade and the single ship stipulated
by the Treaty of Utrecht, brought about collisions which made it
hard to keep the peace. Walpole, who strove to do justice to both

parties in the matter, was abused as " the cur-dog of England and spaniel of France." The ill-humour of the trading classes rose to madness in 1738 when a merchant captain named Jenkins told at the bar of the House of Commons the tale of his torture by the Spaniards, and produced an ear which he said they had cut off with taunts at the English king. It was in vain that Walpole battled stubbornly against the cry for war. His negotiations were foiled by the frenzy of the one country and the pride of the other. He stood alone in his desire for peace. His peace policy rested on the alliance with Holland and France; but the temporary hostility excited by the disputes over the succession between Philip and the House of Orleans had passed away with the birth of children to Lewis the Fifteenth, and the Bourbon Courts were again united by family sympathies. He foresaw therefore that a Spanish war would probably bring with it the rupture of the French alliance at the very moment when the approaching death of the Emperor made the union of the western powers essential to the peace of Europe. Against a war which undid all that he had laboured for twenty years to do Walpole struggled hard. But the instinct of the nation was in fact wiser than the policy of the Minister. Although neither England nor Walpole knew it, a Family Compact had been concluded between France and Spain as long before as 1733, on the outbreak of the war of the Polish Succession, for the ruin of the maritime supremacy of England. Spain bound herself to deprive England gradually of her commercial privileges in America, and to transfer her trade to France. France in return engaged to support Spain at sea and to aid her in the recovery of Gibraltar. The caution with which Walpole held aloof from the Polish war rendered the Compact inoperative at the time, but neither country ceased to look forward to its future execution. France since the peace had strained every nerve to prepare a fleet; while Spain had steadily increased the restrictions on British commerce. Both were in fact watching for the opportunity of war which the Emperor's death was sure to afford, and in forcing on the struggle England only anticipated a danger which she could not escape.

The Compact however, though suspected, was still unknown, and the perils of a contest with Spain were clear enough to justify Walpole in struggling hard for peace. But he struggled single-handed. His greed of power had mastered his strong common sense; Lord Townshend had been driven from office in 1730, Lord Chesterfield dismissed in 1733; and though he started with the ablest administration ever known, Walpole was left after twenty years of administration with but a single man of ability, the Chancellor, Lord Hardwicke, in his cabinet. The colleagues whom, one by one, his jealousy had dismissed had plunged, with the exception of Townshend, into an opposition more factious and unprincipled than had ever disgraced English politics; and these " Patriots " were now reinforced by a band of younger Whigs—the " Boys,"

1712 to 1742

Fall of Walpole

as Walpole called them—whose temper revolted alike against the
peace and corruption of his policy, and at whose head stood a
young cornet of horse, William Pitt. Baffled as this opposition had
been for so many years, the sudden rush of popular passion gave
it a new strength, and in 1739 Walpole bowed to its will in declaring
war. "They may ring their bells now," the Minister said bitterly
as peals and bonfires welcomed his defeat, "but they will soon be
wringing their hands." His foresight was quickly justified. No
sooner had Admiral Vernon with an English fleet bombarded and
taken Portobello than France refused to suffer England to settle on
the mainland of South America, and despatched two squadrons to
the West Indies. At this crisis the death of Charles the Sixth (Oct.
1740) forced on the European struggle which Walpole had dreaded.
France saw in this event and the disunion which it at once brought
about an opportunity of finishing the work begun by Henry the
Second, and which Richelieu, Lewis the Fourteenth, and Cardinal
Fleury had carried on—the work of breaking up the Empire into
a group of powers too weak to resist French ambition. In union
therefore with Spain, which aimed at the annexation of the
Milanese, and the King of Prussia, Frederick the Second, who at
once occupied Silesia, France backed the Elector of Bavaria in his
claim on the Duchy of Austria, which passed with the other
hereditary dominions, by the Pragmatic Sanction, to the Queen
of Hungary, Maria Theresa. Sweden and Sardinia allied themselves
to France. England alone showed herself true to her guaranty of
the Austrian Succession. In the summer of 1741 two French armies
entered Germany, and the Elector of Bavaria appeared unopposed
before Vienna. Never had the House of Austria stood in such utter
peril. Its opponents counted on a division of its dominions. France
claimed the Netherlands, Spain the Milanese, Bavaria the kingdom
of Bohemia, Frederick the Second Silesia. Hungary and the Duchy
of Austria alone were to be left to Maria Theresa. Even England
though still true to her cause, advised her to purchase Frederick's
aid by the cession of Silesia. But the Queen refused to despair.
She won the support of Hungary by restoring its constitutional
rights; and the subsidies of England enabled her to march at the
head of a Hungarian army to the rescue of Vienna, to overrun
Bavaria, and repulse an attack of Frederick on Moravia in the
spring of 1742. But on England's part the contest went on feebly
and ineffectively. Admiral Vernon was beaten before Carthagena,
and Walpole was charged with thwarting and starving the war.
He still repelled the attacks of the "Patriots" with wonderful
spirit; but in a new Parliament his majority dropped to sixteen,
and in his own cabinet he became almost powerless. The buoyant
temper which had carried him through so many storms broke down
at last. "He who was asleep as soon as his head touched the
pillow," writes his son, "now never sleeps above an hour without
waking: and he who at dinner always forgot his own anxieties, and
was more gay and thoughtless than all the company, now sits

without speaking, and with his eyes fixed for an hour together." The end was in fact near; and the dwindling of his majority to three forced Walpole in the opening of 1742 to resign.

The attitude of Bolingbroke at the close of the reign of Anne must always remain a matter of some doubt. It is by no means certain that he desired a Jacobite restoration; it is certain that Swift, his intimate friend, did not. Perhaps the most probable conclusion is that Bolingbroke wished to be in a position of such supremacy that he might dictate to both parties and award the crown upon his own terms.

The alliance, negotiated by Ripperdà, between Spain and Austria provided that the trading privileges conceded to England by the Treaty of Utrecht should be transferred to Austria; that a double marriage alliance should be concluded, Maria Theresa and Don Carlos succeeding to the Austrian dominions, other than those in Italy, which were to pass to Don Philip and the Archduchess Maria Amelia; and that Gibraltar should be restored to Spain.

CHAPTER X

MODERN ENGLAND

Section I.—William Pitt, 1742—1762

[*Authorities.* — Horace Walpole's and Hervey's "Memoirs" an Horace Walpole's Letters are valuable sources. Lecky's "History England in the Eighteenth Century" is the best general history of the period. For Pitt, the Chatham Correspondence and the biography b Ruville. For Frederic the Great, see Carlyle's "Frederic the Great. For Clive, see Malcolm's biography, and Mill's "British India." Fe Wesley, see lives by Southey and Tyerman. Macaulay's essays o Chatham and Clive are illuminating.]

The
Church
and the
Georges
THE fall of Walpole revealed a change in the temper of Englan which was to influence from that time to this its social and politic history. New forces, new cravings, new aims, which had bee silently gathering beneath the crust of inaction, burst suddenly int view. The first of these embodied itself in the religious and philan thropic movement which bears the name of Wesley. Never ha religion seemed at a lower ebb. The progress of free inquiry, th aversion from theological strife which had been left by the Civ War, the new intellectual and material channels opened to huma energy, had produced a general indifference to the great question of religious speculation which occupied an earlier age. The Churcl predominant as its influence seemed at the close of the Revolutior had sunk into political insignificance. By a suspension of th sittings of Convocation Walpole deprived the clergy of their chie means of agitation, while he carefully abstained from all measure which could arouse the prejudices of their flocks. The bishops, wh were exclusively chosen from among the small number of Whi ecclesiastics, were rendered powerless by the Toryism and estrange ment of their clergy, while the clergy themselves stood apart fror all active interference in public affairs. Nor was their politic repose compensated by any religious activity. A large number c prelates were mere Whig partizans with no higher aim than tha of promotion. The levees of the Ministers were crowded with law sleeves. A Welsh bishop avowed that he had seen his diocese bu once, and habitually resided at the lakes of Westmoreland. Th system of pluralities turned the wealthier and more learned of th priesthood into absentees, while the bulk of them were indolen poor, and without social consideration. A shrewd, if prejudice observer brands the English clergy of the day as the most lifeles in Europe, " the most remiss of their labours in private, and th least severe in their lives." The decay of the great dissentin bodies went hand in hand with that of the Church, and during th

arly part of the century the Nonconformists declined in number
s in energy. But it would be rash to conclude from this outer
cclesiastical paralysis that the religious sentiment was dead in
ꞑe people at large. There was, no doubt, a revolt against religion
ꞑd against churches in both the extremes of English society. In
ꞑe higher circles "everyone laughs," said Montesquieu on his
isit to England, "if one talks of religion." Of the prominent states-
ꞑen of the time the greater part were unbelievers in any form of
ꞇhristianity, and distinguished for the grossness and immorality of
ꞇheir lives. Drunkenness and foul talk were thought no discredit
ꞇo Walpole. A later prime minister, the Duke of Grafton, was in
ꞑe habit of appearing with his mistress at the play. Purity and
ꞇidelity to the marriage vow were sneered out of fashion; and
ꞃord Chesterfield, in his letters to his son, instructs him in the art
ꞇ seduction as part of a polite education. At the other end of the
ꞇocial scale lay the masses of the poor. They were ignorant and
ꞃrutal to a degree which it is hard to conceive, for the vast increase
ꞇ population which followed on the growth of towns and the
ꞇevelopment of manufactures had been met by no effort for their
ꞃeligious or educational improvement. Not a new parish had been
ꞃreated. Hardly a single new church had been built. Schools there
ꞃere none, save the grammar schools of Edward and Elizabeth.
ꞇhe rural peasantry, who were fast being reduced to pauperism by
ꞑe abuse of the poor-laws, were left without moral or religious
ꞇraining of any sort. "We saw but one Bible in the parish of
ꞇheddar," said Hannah More at a far later time, "and that was
ꞇsed to prop a flower-pot." Within the towns things were worse.
ꞇhere was no effective police; and in great outbreaks the mob of
ꞃondon or Birmingham burnt houses, flung open prisons, and
ꞇcked and pillaged at their will. The criminal class gathered
ꞇoldness and numbers in the face of ruthless laws which only
ꞇstified to the terror of society, laws which made it a capital crime
ꞇ cut down a cherry tree, and which strung up twenty young
ꞇhieves of a morning in front of Newgate; while the introduction
ꞇ gin gave a new impetus to drunkenness. In the streets of London
ꞇin-shops invited every passer-by to get drunk for a penny, or
ꞇead drunk for twopence.

In spite however of scenes such as this, England as a whole The Re-
ꞇemained at heart religious. Even the apathy of the clergy was ligious
ꞑingled with a new spirit of charity and good sense, a tendency to Revival
ꞇbordinate ecclesiastical differences to the thought of a common
ꞇhristianity, and to substitute a rational theology for the worn-out
ꞇaditions of the past. In the middle class the old piety lived on
ꞇnchanged, and it was from this class that a religious revival burst
ꞇrth at the close of Walpole's ministry, which changed in a few
ꞇears the whole temper of English society. The Church was restored
ꞇo life and activity. Religion carried to the hearts of the poor
ꞇ fresh spirit of moral zeal, while it purified our literature and
ꞇur manners. A new philanthropy reformed our prisons, infused

clemency and wisdom into our penal laws, abolished the slave trade and gave the first impulse to popular education. The revival began in a small knot of Oxford students, whose revolt against the religious deadness of their times showed itself in ascetic observances an enthusiastic devotion, and a methodical regularity of life which gained them the nickname of " Methodists." Three figures detached themselves from the group as soon as, on its transfer to London in 1738, it attracted public attention by the fervour and even extravagance of its piety; and each found his special work in the great task to which the instinct of the new movement led it from the first, that of carrying religion and morality to the vast masses of population which lay concentrated in the towns or around the mines and collieries of Cornwall and the north. Whitfield, a servitor of Pembroke College, was above all the preacher of the revival Speech was governing English politics; and the religious power of speech was shown when a dread of " enthusiasm " closed against the new apostles the pulpits of the Established Church, and forced them to preach in the fields. Their voice was soon heard in the wildest and most barbarous corners of the land, among the bleak moors of Northumberland, or in the dens of London, or in the long galleries where the Cornish miner hears in the pauses of his labour the sobbing of the sea. Whitfield's preaching was such as England had never heard before, theatrical, extravagant, often common place, but hushing all criticism by its intense reality, its earnestness of belief, its deep tremulous sympathy with the sin and sorrow of mankind. It was no common enthusiast who could wring gold from the close-fisted Franklin and admiration from the fastidious Horace Walpole, or who could look down from the top of a green knoll at Kingswood on twenty thousand colliers, grimy from the Bristol coalpits, and see as he preached the tears " making white channels down their blackened cheeks." On the rough and ignorant masses to whom they spoke the effect of Whitfield and his fellow Methodists was terrible both for good and ill. Their preaching stirred a passionate hatred in their opponents. Their lives were often in danger, they were mobbed, they were ducked, they were stoned, they were smothered with filth. But the enthusiasm they aroused was equally passionate. Women fell down in convulsions strong men were smitten suddenly to the earth; the preacher was interrupted by bursts of hysteric laughter or of hysteric sobbing All the phenomena of strong spiritual excitement, so familiar now but at that time strange and unknown, followed on their sermons and the terrible sense of a conviction of sin, a new dread of hell a new hope of heaven, took forms at once grotesque and sublime Charles Wesley, a Christ Church student, came to add sweetness to this sudden and startling light. He was the " sweet singer " of the movement. His hymns expressed the fiery conviction of its converts in lines so chaste and beautiful that its more extravagant features disappeared. The wild throes of hysteric enthusiasm passed into a passion for hymn-singing, and a new musical impulse

as aroused in the people which gradually changed the face of
public devotion throughout England.

But it was his elder brother, John Wesley, who embodied in
himself not this or that side of the vast movement, but the very
movement itself. Even at Oxford, where he resided as a fellow
of Lincoln, he had been looked upon as head of the group of
Methodists, and after his return from a quixotic mission to the
Indians of Georgia he again took the lead of the little society, which
had removed in the interval to London. In power as a preacher he
stood next to Whitfield; as a hymn-writer he stood second to his
brother Charles. But while combining in some degree the excellences of either, he possessed qualities in which both were utterly
deficient; an indefatigable industry, a cool judgment, a command
over others, a faculty of organization, a singular union of patience
and moderation with an imperious ambition, which marked him
as a ruler of men. He had, besides, a learning and skill in writing
which no other of the Methodists possessed; he was older than any
of his colleagues at the start of the movement, and he outlived
them all. His life indeed from 1703 to 1791 almost covers the
century, and the Methodist body had passed through every phase
of its history before he sank into the grave at the age of eighty-
eight. It would have been impossible for Wesley to have wielded
the power he did had he not shared the follies and extravagances
as well as the enthusiasm of his disciples. Throughout his life his
asceticism was that of a monk. At times he lived on bread only,
and often slept on the bare boards. He lived in a world of wonders
and divine interpositions. It was a miracle if the rain stopped and
allowed him to set forward on a journey. It was a judgment of
Heaven if a hailstorm burst over a town which had been deaf to
his preaching. One day, he tells us, when he was tired and his
horse fell lame, " I thought—cannot God heal either man or beast
by any means or without any ?—immediately my headache ceased
and my horse's lameness in the same instant." With a still more
childish fanaticism he guided his conduct, whether in ordinary
events or in the great crises of his life, by drawing lots or watching
the particular texts at which his Bible opened. But with all this
extravagance and superstition, Wesley's mind was essentially
practical, orderly, and conservative. No man ever stood at the
head of a great revolution whose temper was so anti-revolutionary.
In his earlier days the bishops had been forced to rebuke him for
the narrowness and intolerance of his churchmanship. When
Whitfield began his sermons in the fields, Wesley " could not at
first reconcile himself to that strange way." He condemned and
fought against the admission of laymen as preachers till he found
himself left with none but laymen to preach. To the last he clung
passionately to the Church of England, and looked on the body he
had formed as but a lay society in full communion with it. He
broke with the Moravians, who had been the earliest friends of the
new movement, when they endangered its safe conduct by their

contempt of religious forms. He broke with Whitfield when th
great preacher plunged into an extravagant Calvinism. But th
same practical temper of mind which led him to reject what wa
unmeasured, and to be the last to adopt what was new, enable
him at once to grasp and organize the novelties he adopted. H
became himself the most unwearied of field preachers, and hi
journal for half a century is little more than a record of fres
journeys and fresh sermons. When once driven to employ la
helpers in his ministry he made their work a new and attractiv
feature in his system. His earlier asceticism only lingered in
dread of social enjoyments and an aversion from the gayer an
sunnier side of life which links the Methodist movement with tha
of the Puritans. As the fervour of his superstition died down int
the calm of age, his cool common sense discouraged in his follower
the enthusiastic outbursts which marked the opening of the reviva
His powers were bent to the building up of a great religious societ
which might give to the new enthusiasm a lasting and practica
form. The Methodists were grouped into classes, gathered in love
feasts, purified by the expulsion of unworthy members, an
furnished with an alternation of settled ministers and wanderin
preachers; while the whole body was placed under the absolut
government of a Conference of ministers. But so long as he live
the direction of the new religious society remained with Wesley
alone. "If by arbitrary power," he replied with a charming
simplicity to objectors, "you mean a power which I exercise simply
without any colleagues therein, this is certainly true, but I see n
hurt in it."

The new
Philan-
thropy

The great body which he thus founded—a body which numbere
a hundred thousand members at his death, and which now count
its members in England and America by millions—bears the stamp
of Wesley in more than its name. Of all Protestant Churches it i
the most rigid in its organization and the most despotic in it
government. But the Methodists themselves were the least resul
of the Methodist revival. Its action upon the Church broke th
lethargy of the clergy, and the "Evangelical" movement, which
found representatives like Newton and Cecil within the pale of th
Establishment, made the fox-hunting parson and the absente
rector at last impossible. In Walpole's day the English clergy wer
the idlest and most lifeless in the world. In our own time no body
of religious ministers surpasses them in piety, in philanthropic
energy, or in popular regard. In the nation at large appeared a new
moral enthusiasm which, rigid and pedantic as it often seemed, was
still healthy in its social tone, and whose power was seen in the
disappearance of the profligacy which had disgraced the upper
classes, and the foulness which had infested literature, ever since
the Restoration. But the noblest result of the religious reviva
was the steady attempt, which has never ceased from that day to
this, to remedy the guilt, the ignorance, the physical suffering, the
social degradation of the profligate and the poor. It was not til

e Wesleyan movement had done its work that the philanthropic
ovement began. The Sunday Schools established by Mr. Raikes
Gloucester at the close of the century were the beginnings of
pular education. By writings and by her own personal example
annah More drew the sympathy of England to the poverty and
ime of the agricultural labourer. The passionate impulse of
uman sympathy with the wronged and afflicted raised hospitals,
dowed charities, built churches, sent missionaries to the heathen,
pported Burke in his plea for the Hindoo, and Clarkson and
ilberforce in their crusade against the iniquity of the slave-trade.
is only the moral chivalry of his labours that amongst a crowd of
hilanthropists draws us most, perhaps, to the work and character
f John Howard. The sympathy which all were feeling for the
ifferings of mankind he felt for the sufferings of the worst and
ost hapless of men. With wonderful ardour and perseverance he
evoted himself to the cause of the debtor, the felon, and the
urderer. His appointment to the office of High Sheriff of Bedford-
ire drew his attention in 1774 to the state of the prisons which
ere placed in his care; and from that time the quiet country
entleman, whose only occupation had been reading his Bible and
udying his thermometer, became the most energetic and zealous
f reformers. Before a year was over he had personally visited
lmost every English gaol, and he found in nearly all of them
rightful abuses which had been noticed half a century before, but
eft unredressed by Parliament. Gaolers, who bought their places,
ere paid by fees, and suffered to extort what they could. Even
when acquitted men were dragged back to their cells for want of
unds to discharge the sums they owed to their keepers. Debtors
nd felons were huddled together in the prisons, which Howard
ound crowded by the cruel legislation of the day. No separation
as preserved between different sexes, no criminal discipline
nforced. Every gaol was a chaos of cruelty and the foulest
mmorality, from which the prisoner could only escape by sheer
tarvation or by the gaol-fever that festered without ceasing in
hese haunts of wretchedness. He saw everything with his own
yes, he tested every suffering by his own experience. In one gaol
e found a cell so narrow and noisome that the poor wretch who
nhabited it begged as a mercy for hanging. Howard shut himself
p in the cell and bore its darkness and foulness till nature could
ear no more. But it was by work of this sort, and by the faithful
pictures of such scenes which it enabled him to give, that he
brought about their reform. The work in which he recorded his
terrible experience, and the plans which he submitted for the
reformation of criminals, make him the father, so far as England
s concerned, of prison discipline. But his labours were far from
being confined to England. In journey after journey he visited the
prisons of Holland and Germany, till his longing to discover some
means of checking the fatal progress of the Plague led him to
examine the lazarettos of Europe and the East. He was still

engaged in this work of charity when he was seized by a malignant fever at Cherson in Southern Russia, and "laid quietly in the earth," as he desired.

While the revival of the Wesleys was stirring the very heart of England, its political stagnation was unbroken. The triumph of Walpole's opponents ended with their victory. Retiring to the Peers as Earl of Orford, he devoted himself to breaking up the opposition and restoring the union of the Whigs, while he remained the confidential counsellor of the King. Pulteney accepted the Earldom of Bath and at once lost much of his political weight, while his more prominent followers were admitted to office. But when on the death of their nominal leader, Lord Wilmington, Pulteney claimed the post of First Minister in 1743, Walpole quietly interfered and induced the King to raise Henry Pelham, the brother of the Duke of Newcastle, and one of his own most faithful adherents, to the head of the administration. The temper of Henry Pelham, as well as a consciousness of his own mediocrity, disposed him to a policy of conciliation which reunited the Whigs and included every man of ability in his new Ministry. The union of the party was aided by the reappearance of a danger which seemed to have passed away. The foreign policy of Walpole triumphed at the moment of his fall. The pressure of England, aided by a victory of Frederick at Chotusitz, forced Maria Theresa to consent to a peace with Prussia on the terms of the cession of Silesia; and this peace enabled the Austrian army to drive the French from Bohemia at the close of 1742. Meanwhile one English fleet blockaded Cadiz; another anchored in the bay of Naples and forced Don Carlos by a threat of bombarding his capital to conclude a treaty of neutrality, while English subsidies detached Sardinia from the French alliance. But at this point the loss of Walpole made itself felt. The foreign policy of the weak Ministry which succeeded him was chiefly directed by Lord Carteret; and Carteret, who, like the bulk of the Whig party, had long been opposed in heart to Walpole's system, resolved to change the whole character of the war. While Walpole limited his efforts to the preservation of the House of Austria as a European power, Carteret joined Maria Theresa in aiming at the ruin of the House of Bourbon. In the dreams of the statesmen of Vienna, the whole face of Europe was to be changed. Naples and Sicily were to be taken back from Spain, Elsass and Lorraine from France; and the Imperial dignity which had passed to the Elector of Bavaria, the Emperor Charles VII., was to be restored to the Austrian House. To carry out these schemes an Austrian army drove the Emperor from Bavaria in the spring of 1743; while George the Second, who warmly supported the policy of Carteret, put himself at the head of a force of forty thousand men, the bulk of whom were English and Hanoverians, and marched from the Netherlands to the Main. His advance was checked and finally turned into a retreat by the Duc de Noailles, who appeared with a superior army on the south bank of the river.

and finally throwing thirty-one thousand men across it threatened to compel the King to surrender. In the battle of Dettingen which followed (June 27, 1743) the allied army was in fact only saved from destruction by the impetuosity of the French horse and the dogged obstinacy with which the English held their ground and at last forced their opponents to recross the Main. But small as was the victory, it produced amazing results. The French evacuated Germany. The English and Austrian armies appeared on the Rhine. In the spring of 1744 an Austrian army marched upon Naples, with the purpose of transferring it after its conquest to the Emperor, whose hereditary dominions in Bavaria were to pass in return to Maria Theresa.

1742 to 1762

But if Frederick of Prussia had withdrawn from the war on the cession of Silesia, he was resolute to take up arms again rather than suffer this great aggrandisement of the House of Austria. His sudden alliance with France failed at first to change the course of the war, for though he was successful in seizing Prague and drawing the Austrian army from the Rhine he was soon driven from Bohemia, while the death of the Emperor forced Bavaria to lay down its arms and to ally itself with Maria Theresa. So high were the Queen's hopes at this moment that she formed a secret alliance with Russia for the division of the Prussian monarchy. But in 1745 the tide turned. Marshal Saxe established the superiority of the French army in Flanders by his defeat of the Duke of Cumberland. Advancing with a force of English, Dutch, and Hanoverians to the relief of Tournay, the Duke on the 31st of May 1745 found the French covered by a line of fortified villages and redoubts with but a single narrow gap near the hamlet of Fontenoy. Into this gap, however, the English troops, formed in a dense column, doggedly thrust themselves in spite of a terrible fire; but at the moment when the day seemed won the French guns, rapidly concentrated in their front, tore the column in pieces and drove it back in a slow and orderly retreat. The blow was quickly followed up in June by a victory of Frederick at Hohenfriedburg which drove the Austrians from Silesia, and by a landing of Charles Edward, the son of the Old Pretender as James Stuart was called, on the coast of Scotland at the close of July. But defeat abroad and danger at home only quickened a political reaction which had begun long before in England. Even Carteret had been startled by the plan for a dismemberment of Prussia; and as early as 1744 the bulk of the Whig party had learnt the wisdom of the more temperate policy of Walpole, and had opened the way for an accommodation with Frederick by compelling Carteret to resign. The Pelhams, who represented Walpole's system, were now supreme, and their work was aided by the disasters of 1745. When England was threatened by a Catholic Pretender, it was no time for weakening the chief Protestant power in Germany. On the refusal therefore of Maria Theresa to join in a general peace, England concluded the Convention of Hanover with Prussia at the close of August,

Fonte-noy

and withdrew so far as Germany was concerned from the war.

The danger at home indeed had already vindicated Walpole's prudence in foiling the hopes of the Pretender by his steady friendship with France. It was only from France that aid could reach the Jacobites, and the war with France at once revived their hopes. Charles Edward, the grandson of James the Second, was placed by the French Government at the head of a formidable armament in 1744; but his plan of a descent on Scotland was defeated by a storm which wrecked his fleet, and by the march of the French troops which had embarked in it to the war in Flanders. In 1745, however, the young adventurer again embarked with but seven friends in a small vessel and landed on a little island of the Hebrides. For three weeks he stood almost alone; but on the 29th of August the clans rallied to his standard in Glenfinnan, and Charles found himself at the head of fifteen hundred men. His force swelled to an army as he marched through Blair Athol on Perth, entered Edinburgh in triumph, and proclaimed " James the Eighth " at the Town Cross. Two thousand English troops who marched against him under Sir John Cope were broken and cut to pieces on the 21st of September by a single charge of the clansmen at Preston Pans, and victory at once doubled the forces of the conqueror. The Prince was now at the head of six thousand men, but all were still Highlanders, for the people of the Lowlands held aloof from his standard. It was with the utmost difficulty that he could induce them to follow him to the south. His tact and energy however at last conquered all obstacles, and after skilfully evading an army gathered at Newcastle he marched through Lancashire and pushed on the 4th of December as far as Derby. But all hope of success was at an end. Hardly a man rose in his support as he passed through the districts where Jacobitism boasted of its strength. The people flocked to see his march as if to see a show. Catholics and Tories abounded in Lancashire, but only a single squire took up arms. Manchester was looked on as the most Jacobite of English towns, but all the aid it gave was an illumination and two thousand pounds. From Carlisle to Derby he had been joined by hardly two hundred men. The policy of Walpole had in fact secured England for the House of Hanover. The long peace, the prosperity of the country, and the clemency of the Government, had done their work. Jacobitism as a fighting force was dead, and even Charles Edward saw that it was hopeless to conquer England with five thousand Highlanders. He soon learnt too that forces of double his own strength were closing on either side of him, while a third army under the King and Lord Stair covered London. Scotland itself, now that the Highlanders were away, quietly renewed in all the districts of the Lowlands its allegiance to the House of Hanover. Even in the Highlands the Macleods rose in arms for King George while the Gordons refused to stir, though roused by a small French force which landed at Montrose. To advance further south was

npossible, and Charles fell rapidly back on Glasgow; but the rein-
orcements which he found there raised his army to nine thousand
nen, and he marched on the 23rd of January, 1746, on the English
rmy under General Hawley which had followed his retreat and
ncamped near Falkirk. Again the wild charge of his Highlanders
on victory for the Prince, but victory was as fatal as defeat. The
ulk of his forces dispersed with their booty to the mountains,
nd Charles fell sullenly back to the north before the Duke of
umberland. On the 16th of April, the two armies faced one another
n Culloden Moor, a few miles eastward of Inverness. The High-
nders still numbered six thousand men, but they were starving
nd dispirited. Cumberland's force was nearly double that of the
rince. Torn by the Duke's guns, the clansmen flung themselves
a their old fashion on the English front; but they were received
ith a terrible fire of musketry, and the few that broke through
he first line found themselves fronted by a second. In a few
noments all was over, and the Highlanders a mass of hunted
igitives. Charles himself after strange adventures escaped to
'rance. In England fifty of his followers were hanged, three Scotch
rds, Lovat, Balmerino, and Kilmarnock, brought to the block,
nd forty persons of rank attainted by Act of Parliament. More
xtensive measures of repression were needful in the Highlands.
'he feudal tenures were abolished. The hereditary jurisdictions
f the chiefs were bought up and transferred to the Crown. The
rtan, or garb of the clansmen, was forbidden by law. These
neasures, followed by a general Act of Indemnity, proved effective
or their purpose. The dread of the clansmen passed away, and the
heriff's writ soon ran through the Highlands with as little resistnce as in the streets of Edinburgh.

On the Continent the war still lingered on, though its original **Peace**
urpose had disappeared. The victories of Maria Theresa in Italy **of Aix-**
vere balanced by those of France in the Netherlands, where Marshal **elle** **la-Chap-**
axe inflicted on the English and Dutch the defeats of Roucoux
nd Lauffeld. The danger of Holland and the financial exhaustion
f France at last brought about in 1748 the conclusion of a Peace at
Aix-la-Chapelle, by which both parties restored their conquests;
nd with this peace the active work of the Pelham Ministry came
o an end. Utter inaction settled down over political life, and turn-
pike bills or acts for the furtherance of trade engaged the attention
f Parliament till the death of Henry Pelham in 1754. But abroad
hings were less quiet. The Peace of Aix-la-Chapelle was in fact a
nere truce forced on the contending powers by sheer exhaustion.
'rance was dreaming of far wider schemes for the humiliation of
ingland. The troubled question of the trade with America had
nly been waived by Spain. The two powers of the House of
3ourbon were still united by the Family Compact, and as early as
752 the Queen of Hungary by a startling change of policy had
ecretly drawn to their alliance. Neither Maria Theresa nor Saxony
n fact had ever really abandoned the design for the recovery of

Silesia and for a partition of Prussia. The jealousy which Russ
entertained of the growth of a strong power in North German
brought the Czarina Elizabeth to promise aid to their scheme; an
in 1755 the league of these three powers with France and Spain wa
silently completed. So secret were these negotiations that they ha
utterly escaped the notice of the Duke of Newcastle, the broth
of Henry Pelham, and his successor in the direction of Englis
affairs; but they were detected from the first by the keen eye
Frederick of Prussia, who found himself face to face with a line
foes which stretched from Paris to St. Petersburg.

The danger to England was hardly less. France appeared agai
on the stage with a vigour and audacity which recalled the days
Lewis the Fourteenth. The weakness and corruption of its goverr
ment were hidden for the time by the daring scope of its plans an
the ability of the agents it found to carry them out. The aims
France spread far beyond Europe. In India, a French adventure
was founding a French Empire, and planning the expulsion of th
English merchants from their settlements along the coast. I
America, France not only claimed the valleys of the St. Lawrenc
and the Mississippi, but forbade the English Colonists to cross th
Alleghanies, and planted Fort Duquesne on the waters of the Ohi
The disastrous repulse of General Braddock, who had marched o
this fort in 1755 with a small force of regulars and Colonial Militia
awoke even Newcastle to his danger; and the alliance betwee
England and Prussia at the close of the year gave the signal fo
the Seven Years' War. No war has had greater results on th
history of the world or brought greater triumphs to England; bu
few have had more disastrous beginnings. Newcastle was too wea
and ignorant to rule without aid, and yet too greedy of power t
purchase aid by sharing it with more capable men. His preparation
for the gigantic struggle before him may be guessed from the fac
that there were but three regiments fit for service in England a
the opening of 1756. France on the other hand was quick in he
attack. Port Mahon in Minorca, the key of the Mediterranean, wa
besieged by the Duke of Richelieu and forced to capitulate. T
complete the shame of England, a fleet sent to its relief unde
Admiral Byng retreated before the French. In Germany Frederic
had seized Dresden at the outset of the war, and forced the Saxo
army to surrender; and in 1757 his victory at Prague made hir
master of Bohemia; but a defeat at Kolin drove him to retrea
again into Saxony. In the same year the Duke of Cumberland, wh
had taken post on the Weser with an army of fifty thousand me
for the defence of Hanover, fell back before a French army to th
mouth of the Elbe, and engaged by the Convention of Closter
Seven to disband his forces. A despondency without parallel in ou
history took possession of our coolest statesmen, and even th
impassive Chesterfield cried in despair, "We are no longer
nation."

But the nation of which Chesterfield despaired was really on th

ve of its greatest triumphs, and the miserable incapacity of the
Duke of Newcastle only called to the front the genius of William
Pitt. Pitt was the grandson of a governor of Madras, who had
entered Parliament in 1734 as member for one of his father's pocket
boroughs, and had at once headed the younger " Patriots " in their
attack on Walpole. His fiery spirit had been hushed in office during
the " broad-bottom administration " which followed the Minister's
fall, but the death of Henry Pelham again replaced him at the head
of the opposition. The first disaster of the war drove Newcastle
from office, and in November 1756 Pitt became Secretary of State;
but in four months he was forced to resign, and Newcastle re-
appointed. In July 1757 however, it was necessary to recall him.
The failure of Newcastle's administration forced the Duke to a
junction with his rival; and fortunately for their country, the
character of the two statesmen made the compromise an easy one.
For all that Pitt coveted, for the general direction of public affairs,
the control of foreign policy, the administration of the war, Newcastle had neither capacity nor inclination. On the other hand, his
skill in parliamentary management was unrivalled. If he knew
little else, he knew better than any living man the price of every
member and the intrigues of every borough. What he cared for
was not the control of affairs, but the distribution of patronage
and the work of corruption, and from this Pitt turned disdainfully
away. " Mr. Pitt does everything," wrote Horace Walpole, " and
the Duke gives everything. So long as they agree in this partition
they may do what they please." Out of the union of these two
strangely contrasted leaders, in fact, rose the greatest, as it was
the last, of the purely Whig administrations. But its real power
lay from beginning to end in Pitt himself. Poor as he was, for his
income was little more than two hundred a year, and springing as
he did from a family of no political importance, it was by sheer
dint of genius that the young cornet of horse, at whose youth and
inexperience Walpole had sneered, seized a power which the Whig
houses had ever since the Revolution kept jealously in their grasp.
His ambition had no petty aim. " I want to call England," he said
as he took office, " out of that enervate state in which twenty
thousand men from France can shake her." His call was soon
answered. He at once breathed his own lofty spirit into the country
he served, as he communicated something of his own grandeur to
the men who served him. " No man," said a soldier of the time,
" ever entered Mr. Pitt's closet who did not feel himself braver
when he came out than when he went in." Ill-combined as were
his earlier expeditions, many as were his failures, he roused a
temper in the nation at large which made ultimate defeat impossible.
" England has been a long time in labour," exclaimed Frederick
of Prussia as he recognised a greatness like his own, " but she has
at last brought forth a man."

It is this personal and solitary grandeur which strikes us most as
we look back to William Pitt. The tone of his speech and action

stands out in utter contrast with the tone of his time. In the mids
of a society critical, polite, indifferent, simple even to the affecta
tion of simplicity, witty and amusing but absolutely prosaic, cool o
heart and of head, sceptical of virtue and enthusiasm, sceptica
above all of itself, Pitt stood absolutely alone. The depth of hi
conviction, his passionate love for all that he deemed lofty and true
his fiery energy, his poetic imaginativeness, his theatrical airs an
rhetoric, his haughty self-assumption, his pompousness and extrava
gance, were not more puzzling to his contemporaries than th
confidence with which he appealed to the higher sentiments o
mankind, the scorn with which he turned from a corruption whic
had till then been the great engine of politics, the undoubting faith
which he felt in himself, in the grandeur of his aims, and in hi
power to carry them out. " I know that I can save the country,'
he said to the Duke of Devonshire on his entry into the Ministry
" and I know no other man can." The groundwork of Pitt's
character was an intense and passionate pride; but it was a pride
which kept him from stooping to the level of the men who had
so long held England in their hands. He was the first statesman
since the Restoration who set the example of a purely public spirit.
Keen as was his love of power, no man ever refused office so often,
or accepted it with so strict a regard to the principles he professed.
" I will not go to Court," he replied to an offer which was made
him, " if I may not bring the Constitution with me." For the
corruption about him he had nothing but disdain. He left to Newcastle the buying of seats and the purchase of members. At the
outset of his career Pelham appointed him to the most lucrative
office in his administration, that of Paymaster of the Forces; but
its profits were of an illicit kind, and poor as he was, Pitt refused
to accept one farthing beyond his salary. His pride never appeared
in loftier and nobler form than in his attitude towards the people
at large. No leader had ever a wider popularity than " the great
commoner," as Pitt was styled, but his air was always that of a
man who commands popularity, not that of one who seeks it. He
never bent to flatter popular prejudice. When mobs were roaring
themselves hoarse for " Wilkes and liberty," he denounced Wilkes
as a worthless profligate; and when all England went mad in its
hatred of the Scots, Pitt haughtily declared his esteem for a people
whose courage he had been the first to enlist on the side of loyalty.
His noble figure, his flashing eye, his majestic voice, the fire and
grandeur of his eloquence, gave him a sway over the House of
Commons far greater than any other Minister has possessed. He
could silence an opponent with a look of scorn, or hush the whole
House with a single word. But he never stooped to the arts by
which men form a political party, and at the height of his power
his personal following hardly numbered half a dozen members.

The
Great
Com-
moner
His real strength, indeed, lay not in Parliament but in the people
at large. His significant title of " the great commoner " marks a
political revolution. " It is the people who have sent me here,"

Pitt boasted with a haughty pride when the nobles of the Cabinet opposed his will. He was the first to see that the long political inactivity of the public mind had ceased, and that the progress of commerce and industry had produced a great middle class, which no longer found its representatives in the legislature. " You have taught me," said George the Second when Pitt sought to save Byng by appealing to the sentiment of Parliament, " to look for the voice of my people in other places than within the House of Commons." It was this unrepresented class which had forced him into power. During his struggle with Newcastle the greater towns backed him with the gift of their freedom and addresses of confidence. " For weeks," laughs Horace Walpole, " it rained gold boxes." London stood by him through good report and evil report, and the wealthiest of English merchants, Alderman Beckford, was proud to figure as his political lieutenant. The temper of Pitt indeed harmonized admirably with the temper of the commercial England which rallied round him, with its energy, its self-confidence, its pride, its patriotism, its honesty, its moral earnestness. The merchant and the trader were drawn by a natural attraction to the one statesman of their time whose aims were unselfish, whose hands were clean, whose life was pure and full of tender affection for wife and child. But there was a far deeper ground for their enthusiastic reverence and for the reverence which his country has borne Pitt ever since. He loved England with an intense and personal love. He believed in her power, her glory, her public virtue, till England learnt to believe in herself. Her triumphs were his triumphs, her defeats his defeats. Her dangers lifted him high above all thought of self or party-spirit. " Be one people," he cried to the factions who rose to bring about his fall: " forget everything but the public! I set you the example! " His glowing patriotism was the real spell by which he held England. Even the faults which chequered his character told for him with the middle classes. The Whig statesmen who preceded him had been men whose pride expressed itself in a marked simplicity and absence of pretence. Pitt was essentially an actor, dramatic in the cabinet, in the House, in his very office. He transacted business with his clerks in full dress. His letters to his family, genuine as his love for them was, are stilted and unnatural in tone. It was easy for the wits of his day to jest at his affectation, his pompous gait, the dramatic appearance which he made on great debates with his limbs swathed in flannel and his crutch by his side. Early in life Walpole sneered at him for bringing into the House of Commons " the gestures and emotions of the stage." But the classes to whom Pitt appealed were classes not easily offended by faults of taste, and saw nothing to laugh at in the statesman who was borne into the lobby amidst the tortures of the gout or carried into the House of Lords to breathe his last in a protest against national dishonour.

Above all Pitt wielded the strength of a resistless eloquence. The power of political speech had been revealed in the stormy debates of the Long Parliament, but it was cramped in its utterance by the legal and theological pedantry of the time. Pedantry was flung off by the age of the Revolution, but in the eloquence of Somers and his rivals we see ability rather than genius, knowledge, clearness of expression, precision of thought, the lucidity of the pleader or the man of business, rather than the passion of the orator. Of this clearness of statement Pitt had little or none. He was no ready debater like Walpole, no speaker of set speeches like Chesterfield. His set speeches were always his worst, for in these his want of taste, his love of effect, his trite quotations and extravagant metaphors came at once to the front. That with defects like these he stood far above every orator of his time was due above all to his profound conviction, to the earnestness and sincerity with which he spoke. " I must sit still," he whispered once to a friend, " for when once I am up everything that is in my mind comes out." But the reality of his eloquence was transfigured by a glow of passion which not only raised him high above the men of his own day but set him in the front rank among the orators of the world. The cool reasoning, the wit, the common sense of his age made way for a splendid audacity, a large and poetic imagination, a sympathy with popular emotion, a sustained grandeur, a lofty vehemence, a command over the whole range of human feeling. He passed without an effort from the most solemn appeal to the gayest raillery, from the keenest sarcasm to the tenderest pathos. Every word was driven home by the grand self-consciousness of the speaker. He spoke always as one having authority. He was, in fact, the first English orator whose words were a power, a power not over Parliament only but over the nation at large. Parliamentary reporting was as yet unknown, and it was only in detached phrases and half-remembered outbursts that the voice of Pitt reached beyond the walls of St. Stephen's. But it was especially in these sudden outbursts of inspiration, in these brief passionate appeals, that the power of his eloquence lay. The few broken words we have of him stir the same thrill in our day which they stirred in the men of his own.

But passionate as was Pitt's eloquence, it was the eloquence of a statesman, not of a rhetorician. Time has approved almost all his greater struggles, his defence of the liberty of the subject against arbitrary imprisonment under " general warrants," of the liberty of the press against Lord Mansfield, of the rights of constituencies against the House of Commons, of the constitutional rights of America against England itself. His foreign policy was directed to the preservation of Prussia, and Prussia has at last vindicated his foresight by the creation of Germany. We have adopted his plans for the direct government of India by the Crown, plans which when he proposed them were regarded as insane. Pitt was the first to recognize the liberal character of the Church of England, its " Calvinistic Creed and Popish Liturgy; " he was the first to sound the note of Parliamentary reform. One of his earliest measures shows the generosity and originality of his mind. He quieted 1742
to
1762 Scotland by employing its Jacobites in the service of their country and by raising Highland regiments among its clans. The selection of Wolfe and Amherst as generals showed his contempt for precedent and his inborn knowledge of men. There was little indeed in the military expeditions with which Pitt's Ministry opened to justify his fame. Money and blood were lavished on buccaneering descents upon the French coasts which did small damage to the enemy. But in Europe Pitt wisely limited himself to a secondary part. He recognized the genius of Frederick the Great, and resolved to give him a firm and energetic support. The Convention of Closter-Seven had almost reduced Frederick to despair. But the moment of Pitt's accession to power was marked on the King's part by the most brilliant display of military genius which the modern world had as yet seen. Two months after his repulse at Kolin he flung himself on a French army which advanced into the heart of Germany and annihilated it in the victory of Rossbach. Before another month had passed he hurried from the Saale to the Oder, and by a yet more signal victory at Leuthen cleared Silesia of the Austrians. But these prodigious efforts would have been useless but for the aid of Pitt. The English Minister poured subsidy upon subsidy into Frederick's exhausted treasury, while he refused to ratify the Convention of Closter-Seven, and followed the King's advice by setting the Prince of Brunswick at the head of the army on the Elbe.

The victory of Rossbach was destined to change the fortunes of Clive the world by bringing about the unity of Germany; but the year of Rossbach was the year of a victory hardly less important in the East. The genius and audacity of a merchant-clerk made a company of English traders the sovereigns of Bengal, and opened that wondrous career of conquest which has added the Indian peninsula, from Ceylon to the Himalayas, to the dominions of the British crown. The early intercourse of England with India gave little promise of the great fortunes which awaited it. It was not till the close of Elizabeth's reign, a century after Vasco de Gama had crept round the Cape of Good Hope and founded the Portuguese settlements on the Goa coast, that an East India Company was founded in London. The trade, profitable as it was, remained small in extent, and the three early factories of the Company were only gradually acquired during the century which followed. The first, that of Madras, consisted of but six fishermen's houses beneath Fort St. George; that of Bombay was ceded by the Portuguese as part of the dowry of Catherine of Braganza; while Fort William, with the mean village which has since grown into Calcutta, owes its origin to the reign of William the Third. Each of these forts was built simply for the protection of the Company's warehouses, and guarded by a few "sepahis," sepoys, or paid native soldiers; while the clerks and traders of each establishment were under the direction of a President and a Council. One of these clerks in the middle of the eighteenth century was Robert Clive, the son of a small proprietor near Market Drayton in Shropshire, an idle daredevil of a boy whom his friends had been glad to get rid of by packing him off in the Company's service as a writer to Madras. His early days there were days of wretchedness and despair. He was poor and cut off from his fellows by the haughty shyness of his temper, weary of desk-work, and haunted by home sickness. Twice he attempted suicide; and it was only on the failure of his second attempt that he flung down the pistol which baffled him with a conviction that he was reserved for higher things.

Dupleix   A change came at last in the shape of war and captivity. As soon as the war of the Austrian Succession broke out the superiority of the French in power and influence tempted them to expel the English from India. Labourdonnais, the governor of the French colony of the Mauritius, besieged Madras, and at a later time its clerks and merchants were carried prisoners to Pondicherry. Clive was among these captives, but he escaped in disguise, and returning to the settlement threw aside his clerkship for an ensign's commission in the force which the Company was busily raising. For the capture of Madras had not only established the repute of the French arms, but had roused Dupleix, the governor of Pondicherry, to conceive plans for the creation of a French empire in India. When the English merchants of Elizabeth's day brought their goods to Surat, all India, save the south, had just been brought for the first time under the rule of a single great power by the Mogul Emperors of the line of Akbar. But with the death of Aurungzebe, in the reign of Anne, the Mogul Empire fell fast into decay. A line of feudal princes raised themselves to independence in Rajpootana. The lieutenants of the Emperor founded separate sovereignties at Lucknow and Hyderabad, in the Carnatic, and in Bengal. The plain of the Upper Indus was occupied by a race of religious fanatics called the Sikhs. Persian and Affghan invaders crossed the Indus, and succeeded even in sacking Delhi, the capital of the Moguls. Clans of systematic plunderers, who were known under the name of Mahrattas, and who were in fact the natives whom conquest had long held in subjection, poured down from the highlands along the western coast, ravaged as far as Calcutta and Tanjore, and finally set up independent states at Poonah and Gwalior. Dupleix skilfully availed himself of the disorder around him. He offered his aid to the Emperor against the rebels and invaders who had reduced his power to a shadow; and it was in the Emperor's name that he meddled with the quarrels of the states of Central and Southern India, made himself virtually master of the court of Hyderabad, and seated a creature of his own on the throne of the Carnatic. Trichinopoly, the one town which held out against this Nabob of the Carnatic, was all but brought to surrender when Clive, in 1751, came forward with a daring scheme for its relief. With a few hundred English and sepoys he pushed through a thunderstorm to the surprise of Arcot, the Nabob's capital, enrenched himself in its enormous fort, and held it for fifty days **1742** gainst thousands of assailants. Moved by his gallantry, the **to** Mahrattas, who had never believed that Englishmen would fight **1762** efore, advanced and broke up the siege; but Clive was no sooner reed than he showed equal vigour in the field. At the head of raw ecruits who ran away at the first sound of a gun, and sepoys who aid themselves as soon as the cannon opened fire, he twice attacked nd defeated the French and their Indian allies, foiled every effort f Dupleix, and razed to the ground a pompous pillar which the French governor had set up in honour of his earlier victories.

Recalled by broken health to England, Clive returned at the **Plassey** utbreak of the Seven Years' War to win for England a greater rize than that which his victories had won for it in the supremacy f the Carnatic. He had only been a few months at Madras when a crime whose horror still lingers in English memories called him to Bengal. Bengal, the delta of the Ganges, was the richest and most ertile of all the provinces of India. Its rice, its sugar, its silk, and he produce of its looms, were famous in European markets. Its Viceroys, like their fellow lieutenants, had become practically ndependent of the Emperor, and had added to Bengal the pro-vinces of Orissa and Behar. Surajah Dowlah, the master of this vast domain, had long been jealous of the enterprise and wealth of he English traders; and, roused at this moment by the instigation f the French, he appeared before Fort William, seized its settlers, and thrust a hundred and fifty of them into a small prison called he Black Hole of Calcutta. The heat of an Indian summer did its work of death. The wretched prisoners trampled each other under foot in the madness of thirst, and in the morning only twenty-three remained alive. Clive sailed at the news with a thousand English-men and two thousand sepoys to wreak vengeance for the crime. He was no longer the boy-soldier of Arcot; and the tact and skill with which he met Surajah Dowlah in the negotiations by which the Viceroy strove to avert a conflict were sullied by the Oriental falsehood and treachery to which he stooped. But his courage remained unbroken. When the two armies faced each other on the plain of Plassey the odds were so great that on the very eve of the battle a council of war counselled retreat. Clive withdrew to a grove hard by, and after an hour's lonely musing gave the word to fight. Courage, in fact, was all that was needed. The fifty thousand foot and fourteen thousand horse who were seen covering the plain at daybreak on the 23rd of June, 1757, were soon thrown into confusion by the English guns, and broke in headlong rout before the English charge. The death of Surajah Dowlah enabled the Company to place a creature of its own on the throne of Bengal; but his rule soon became a nominal one. With the victory of Plassey began in fact the Empire of England in the East.

In Germany, the news of Rossbach called the French from the **Minden** Elbe back to the Rhine in the opening of 1758. Ferdinand of Bruns-wick, reinforced with twenty thousand English soldiers, held them

1742
to
1762

at bay during the summer, while Frederick, foiled in an attack o
Moravia, drove the Russians back on Poland in the battle c
Zorndorf. His defeat, however, by the Austrian General Daun a
Hochkirch, proved the first of a series of terrible misfortunes. Th
year 1759 marks the lowest point of Frederick's fortunes. A fres
advance of the Russian army forced the King to attack it a
Kunersdorf in August, and his repulse ended in the utter rout c
his army. For the moment all seemed lost, for even Berlin lay ope
to the conqueror. A few days later the surrender of Dresden gav
Saxony to the Austrians; and at the close of the year an attemp
upon them at Plauen was foiled with terrible loss. But ever
disaster was retrieved by the indomitable courage and tenacity c
the King, and winter found him as before master of Silesia and o
all Saxony save the ground which Daun's camp covered. The yea
which marked the lowest point of Frederick's fortunes was th
year of Pitt's greatest triumphs, the year of Minden and Quibero
and Quebec. France aimed both at a descent upon England an
the conquest of Hanover, and gathered a naval armament at Brest
while fifty thousand men under Contades and Broglie united o
the Weser. Ferdinand with less than forty thousand met the
(August 1) on the field of Minden. The French marched along th
Weser to the attack, with their flanks protected by that river an
a brook which ran into it, and with their cavalry, ten thousan
strong, massed in the centre. The six English regiments in Ferdi
nand's army fronted the French horse, and, mistaking the
general's order, marched at once upon them in line, regardless c
the batteries on their flank, and rolling back charge after charg
with volleys of musketry. In an hour the French centre was utterl
broken. "I have seen," said Contades, "what I never thought t
be possible—a single line of infantry break through three lines o
cavalry, ranked in order of battle, and tumble them to ruin!"
Nothing but the refusal of Lord George Sackville to complete th
victory by a charge of Ferdinand's horse saved the French fron
utter rout. As it was, their army again fell back broken o
Frankfort and the Rhine. The project of an invasion of Englanc
met with the same success. Eighteen thousand men lay ready t
embark on board the French fleet, when Admiral Hawke came i
sight of it on the 20th of November, at the mouth of Quiberon Bay
The sea was rolling high, and the coast where the French ships la
was so dangerous from its shoals and granite reefs that the pilo
remonstrated with the English admiral against his project o
attack. "You have done your duty in this remonstrance," Hawk
coolly replied; "now lay me alongside the French admiral." Tw
English ships were lost on the shoals, but the French fleet wa
ruined and the disgrace of Byng's retreat wiped away.

The Conquest of Canada

It was not in the Old World only that the year of Minden and
Quiberon brought glory to the arms of England. In Europe, Pit
had wisely limited his efforts to the support of Prussia, but acros
the Atlantic the field was wholly his own. The French dominior

n North America, which was originally confined to Cape Breton nd Canada, had been pushed by the activity of the Marquis of Iontcalm along the great chain of lakes towards the Ohio and the lississippi. Three strong forts, that of Duquesne on the Ohio, that f Niagara on the St. Lawrence, and that of Ticonderoga on Lake 'hamplain, supported by a chain of less important posts, threatened ɔ cut off the English colonies of the coast from any possibility of xtension over the prairies of the West. Montcalm was gifted with ngular powers of administration; he had succeeded in attaching he bulk of the Indian tribes from Canada as far as the Mississippi ɔ the cause of his nation, and the value of their aid had been hown in the rout of the British detachment which General braddock led against Fort Duquesne. But Pitt had no sooner urned his attention to American affairs than these desultory raids ere superseded by a large and comprehensive plan of attack. combined expedition under Amherst and Boscawen captured ouisburg in 1758, and reduced the colony of Cape Breton at the iouth of the St. Lawrence. The American militia supported the british troops in a vigorous campaign against the forts, and though Iontcalm was able to repulse General Abercromby from Ticon-eroga, a force from Philadelphia made itself master of Duquesne. 'he name of Pittsburg which was given to their new conquest still ommemorates the enthusiasm of the colonists for the great Iinister who first opened to them the West. The next year (1759) ıw the evacuation of Ticonderoga before the advance of Amherst, nd the capture of Fort Niagara after the defeat of an Indian force hich marched to its relief. But Pitt had resolved not merely to ɔil the ambition of Montcalm but to destroy the French rule in america altogether; and while Amherst was breaking through the ne of forts, an expedition under General Wolfe entered the St. awrence and anchored below Quebec. Pitt had discerned the enius and heroism which lay hidden beneath the awkward manner nd the occasional gasconade of the young soldier of thirty-three hom he chose for the crowning exploit of the war, but for a while is sagacity seemed to have failed. No efforts could draw Montcalm rom the long line of inaccessible cliffs which at this point borders he river, and for six weeks Wolfe saw his men wasting away in ıactivity while he himself lay prostrate with sickness and despair. ιt last his resolution was fixed, and in a long line of boats the army ropped down the St. Lawrence to a point at the base of the Heights f Abraham, where a narrow path had been discovered to the ummit. Not a voice broke the silence of the night save the voice f Wolfe himself, as he quietly repeated the stanzas of Gray's Elegy in a Country Churchyard," remarking as he closed, " I had ather be the author of that poem than take Quebec." But his ature was as brave as it was tender; he was the first to leap on hore and to scale the narrow path where no two men could go breast. His men followed, pulling themselves to the top by the elp of bushes and the crags, and at daybreak on the 12th of

**1742
to
1762**

September the whole army stood in orderly formation befor
Quebec. Wolfe headed a charge which broke the lines of Montcalm
but a ball pierced his breast in the moment of victory. " The
run," cried an officer who held the dying man in his arms—"
protest they run." Wolfe rallied to ask who they were that ran
and was told " the French." " Then," he murmured, " I di
happy! " The fall of Montcalm in the moment of his defea
completed the victory, and the submission of Canada put an en
to the dream of a French empire in America. In breaking throug
the line with which France had striven to check the westwar
advance of the English colonists Pitt had unconsciously change
the history of the world. His support of Frederick and of Prussi
was to lead in our own day to the creation of a United Germany
His conquest of Canada, by removing the enemy whose dread kni
the colonists to the mother country and by flinging open to thei
energies in the days to come the boundless plains of the West, lai
the foundation of the United States.

Section II.—The Independence of America, 1761—1785

[*Authorities.*—For the American question, see Lecky, " History o
England "; Fiske, " American Revolution," and the " Cambridg
Modern History," vol. vii. For the English history of the period, i
addition to works already mentioned, the correspondence of George II
with Lord North; the Grenville Papers; Burke's speeches and pamphlets
and the Letters of Junius. Erskine May, " Constitutional History,'
extends from 1760 onwards. For Warren Hastings, see Lyall's biography.

**History
and the
War**

England had never played so great a part in the history of man
kind as now. The year 1759 was a year of triumphs in every quarte
of the world. In September came the news of Minden, and of a
victory off Lagos. In October came tidings of the capture of Quebec
November brought word of the French defeat at Quiberon. " W
are forced to ask every morning what victory there is," laughe
Horace Walpole, " for fear of missing one." But it was not s
much in the number as in the importance of its triumphs that th
war stood and remains still without a rival. It is no exaggeratio
to say that three of its many victories determined for ages to com
the destinies of the world. With that of Rossbach began the re
creation of Germany, its intellectual supremacy over Europe, it
political union under the leadership of Prussia and its kings. Wit
that of Plassey the influence of Europe told for the first time sinc
the days of Alexander on the nations of the East. The world, i
Burke's gorgeous phrase, saw " one of the races of the north-eas
cast into the heart of Asia new manners, new doctrines, ne
institutions." With the triumph of Wolfe on the Heights o
Abraham began the history of the United States of America.

The progress of the American colonies from the time whe
the Puritan emigration added the four New England States

Massachusetts, New Hampshire, Connecticut, and Rhode Island, to those of Maryland and Virginia had been slow, but it had never ceased. Settlers still came, though in smaller numbers, and two new colonies south of Virginia received from Charles the Second their name of the Carolinas. The war with Holland transferred to British rule the district claimed by the Dutch from the Hudson to the inner Lakes, and the country was at once granted by Charles to his brother, and received from him the name of New York. Portions were soon broken off from this vast territory to form the colonies of New Jersey and Delaware. In 1682 a train of Quakers followed William Penn across the Delaware into the heart of the primæval forest, and became a colony which recalled its founder and the woodlands in which he planted it in its name of Pennsylvania. A long interval elapsed before a new settlement, which received its title of Georgia from the reigning sovereign, George the Second, was established by General Oglethorpe on the Savannah as a refuge for English debtors and for the persecuted Protestants of Germany. Slow as this progress seemed, the colonies were really growing fast in numbers and in wealth. Their population at the accession of George the Third was little less than a million and a half, a fourth of the population of the mother country. Their wealth had risen even faster than their numbers. Half a million of slaves were employed in tilling the rice-fields of Georgia, the indigo fields of the Carolinas, and the tobacco plantations of Virginia. New York and Pennsylvania grew rich from corn-harvests and the timber trade. But the distinction between the Northern and Southern colonies was more than an industrial one. In the Southern States the prevalence of slavery produced an aristocratic spirit and favoured the creation of large estates. Even the system of entails had been introduced among the wealthy planters of Virginia, where many of the older English families found representatives in houses such as those of Fairfax and Washington. Throughout New England, on the other hand, the characteristics of the Puritans, their piety, their intolerance, their simplicity of life, their love of equality and tendency to democratic institutions, remained unchanged. In education and political activity New England stood far ahead of its fellow colonies, for the settlement of the Puritans had been followed at once by the establishment of a system of local schools which is still the glory of America. " Every township," it was enacted, " after the Lord hath increased them to the number of fifty householders, shall appoint one to teach all children to write and read; and when any town shall increase to the number of a hundred families, they shall set up a grammar school."

Great, however, as these differences were, and great as was to be their influence on American history, they were little felt as yet. In the main features of their outer organization the whole of the colonies stood fairly at one. In religious and in civil matters alike all of them contrasted sharply with the England at home. Religious tolerance had been brought about by a medley of religious faiths

such as the world had never seen before. New England was sti
a Puritan stronghold. In Virginia the bulk of the settlers clung t
the Episcopalian Church. Roman Catholics formed a large par
of the population of Maryland. Pennsylvania was a State c
Quakers. Presbyterians and Baptists had fled from tests and per
secutions to colonize New Jersey. Lutherans and Moravians fror
Germany abounded among the settlers of Carolina and Georgia
In such a chaos of creeds religious persecution or a uniform Churcl
were equally impossible. There was the same real unity in the
political tendency and organization of the States as in the religious
Whether the temper of the colony was democratic, moderate, o
oligarchical, its form of government was pretty much the same
The original rights of the proprietor, the projector and grantee o
the earliest settlement, had in most cases either ceased to exis
or fallen into desuetude. The government of each colony lay in
House of Assembly elected by the people at large, with a Counci
sometimes elected, sometimes nominated by the Governor, and
a Governor either elected, or appointed by the Crown, with whose
appointment administrative interference on the part of the Govern
ment at home practically ended. The colonies were left by a happy
neglect to themselves. It was wittily said at a later day, that
" Mr. Grenville lost America because he read the American
despatches, which none of his predecessors ever did." There was
little room, indeed, for any interference within the limits of the
colonies. Their privileges were secured by royal charters. Their
Assemblies had the sole right of internal taxation, and exercised
it sparingly. Walpole, like Pitt afterwards, set roughly aside the
project for an American excise. " I have Old England set against
me," he said, " by this measure, and do you think I will have New
England too ? " Even in matters of trade the supremacy of the
mother country was far from being a galling one. There were some
small import duties, but they were evaded by a well-understood
system of smuggling. The restriction of trade with the colonies to
Great Britain was more than compensated by the commercia
privileges which the Americans enjoyed as British subjects. As
yet, therefore, there was nothing to break the good will which the
colonists felt towards the mother country, while the danger of
French aggression drew them closely to it. Populous as they had
become, the English settlements still lay mainly along the sea-
board of the Atlantic. Only a few exploring parties had penetrated
into the Alleghanies before the Seven Years' War; and Indian
tribes wandered unquestioned along the lakes. It was by his
success in winning over these tribes to an acknowledgment of the
supremacy of France that Montcalm was drawn to the project of
extending the French dominion over the broad plains of the Ohio
and the Missouri from Canada to the Mississippi, and of cutting
off the English colonies from all access to the West. The instinct
of the settlers taught them that in such a project lay the death-
blow of America's future greatness; the militia of the colonies

marched with Braddock to his fatal defeat, and shared with the troops of Amherst the capture of Duquesne. The name of " Pittsburg," which they gave to their prize, still recalls the gratitude of the colonists to the statesman whose genius had rolled away the danger which threatened their destinies.

But strong as the attachment of the colonists to the mother country seemed at this moment, there were keen politicians who saw in the very completeness of Pitt's triumph a danger to their future union. The presence of the French in Canada had thrown the colonies on the protection of Great Britain. With the conquest of Canada their need of this protection was removed. For the moment, however, all thought of distant result was lost in the nearer fortunes of the war. In Germany the steady support of Pitt alone enabled Frederick to hold out against the terrible exhaustion of his unequal struggle. His campaign of 1760 indeed was one of the grandest efforts of his genius. Foiled in an attempt on Dresden, he again saved Silesia by his victory of Liegnitz and hurled back an advance of Daun by a victory at Torgau; while Ferdinand of Brunswick held his ground as of old along the Weser. But even victories drained Frederick's strength. Men and money alike failed him. It was impossible for him to strike another great blow, and the ring of enemies again closed slowly round him. His one remaining hope lay in the firm support of Pitt, and triumphant as his policy had been, Pitt was tottering to his fall. The envy and resentment of his colleagues at his undisguised supremacy found an unexpected supporter in the young sovereign who mounted the throne on the death of his grandfather in 1760. For the first and last time, since the accession of the House of Hanover, England saw a king who was resolved to play a part in English politics; and the part which George the Third succeeded in playing was undoubtedly a memorable one. In ten years he reduced government to a shadow, and turned the loyalty of his subjects into disaffection. In twenty he had forced the colonies of America into revolt and independence, and brought England to the brink of ruin. Work such as this has sometimes been done by very great men, and often by very wicked and profligate men; but George was neither profligate nor great. He had a smaller mind than any English king before him save James the Second. He was wretchedly educated, and his natural taste was of the meanest sort. " Was there ever such stuff," he asked, " as Shakspere ? " Nor had he the capacity for using greater minds than his own by which some sovereigns have concealed their natural littleness. On the contrary, his only feeling towards great men was one of jealousy and hate. He longed for the time when " decrepitude or death " might put an end to Pitt, and even when death had freed him from " this trumpet of sedition," he denounced the proposal for a public monument as " an offensive measure to me personally." But dull and petty as his temper was, he was clear as to his purpose and obstinate in the pursuit of it. And his purpose was to rule.

"George," his mother, the Princess of Wales, had continually repeated to him in youth, "George, be king." He called himself always "a Whig of the Revolution," and he had no wish to undo the work which he believed the Revolution to have done. His wish was not to govern against law, but simply to govern, to be freed from the dictation of parties and ministers, to be in effect the first minister of the State. How utterly incompatible such a dream was with the Parliamentary constitution of the country as it had received its final form from Sunderland we have already seen, but George was resolved to carry out his dream. And in carrying it out he was aided by the circumstances of the time. The defeat of Charles Edward and the later degradation of his life had worn away the thin coating of Jacobitism which clung to the Tories. They were ready again to take part in politics, and in the accession of a king who unlike his two predecessors was no stranger but an Englishman, who had been born in England and spoke English, they found the opportunity they desired. Their withdrawal from public affairs had left them untouched by the progress of political ideas since the Revolution of 1688, and they returned to invest the new sovereign with all the reverence which they had bestowed on the Stuarts. A "King's party" was thus ready made to his hand; but George was able to strengthen it by a vigorous exertion of the power and influence which was still left to the Crown. All promotion in the Church, all advancement in the army, a great number of places in the civil administration and about the court, were still at the King's disposal. If this vast mass of patronage had been practically usurped by the ministers of his predecessors, it was resumed and firmly held by George the Third; and the character of the House of Commons made patronage, as we have seen, a powerful engine in its management. George had one of Walpole's weapons in his hands, and he used it with unscrupulous energy to break up the party which Walpole had held so long together. He saw that the Whigs were divided among themselves by the factious spirit which springs from a long hold of power, and that they were weakened by the rising contempt with which the country at large regarded the selfishness and corruption of its representatives. More than thirty years before, Gay had quizzed the leading statesmen of the day on the public stage under the guise of highwaymen and pickpockets. "It is difficult to determine," said the witty playwright, "whether the fine gentlemen imitate the gentlemen of the road, or the gentlemen of the road the fine gentlemen." And now that the "fine gentlemen" were represented by hoary jobbers such as Newcastle, the public contempt was fiercer than ever, and men turned sickened from the intrigues and corruption of party to the young sovereign who aired himself in the character which Bolinbroke had invented of a Patriot King.

The Peace of Paris

Had Pitt and Newcastle held together, supported as the one was by the commercial classes and public opinion, the other by the Whig families and the whole machinery of Parliamentary manage-ent, George must have struggled in vain. But the ministry was already disunited. The Whigs, attached to peace by the traditions of Walpole, dismayed at the enormous expenditure, and haughty with the pride of a ruling oligarchy, were in silent revolt against the war and the supremacy of the Great Commoner. It was against their will that Pitt rejected proposals of peace from France on the terms of a desertion of Prussia. In 1761 he urged a new war with pain. He had learnt the secret signature of a fresh family compact between the two Bourbon Courts of Spain and France, and he proposed to anticipate the blow by a seizure of the treasure fleet from the Indies, by occupying the Isthmus of Panama, and attacking the Spanish dominions in the New World. His colleagues shrank from plans so vast and daring: and Newcastle was spurred to revolt by the King and backed in it by the rest of the Whigs. It was in vain that Pitt enforced his threat of resignation by declaring himself responsible to "the people," or that the Londoners hung after his dismissal from office on his carriage wheels, hugged his footman, and even kissed his horses. The fall of the great statesman in October changed the whole look of European affairs. "Pitt disgraced," wrote a French philosopher,—"it is worth two victories to us!" Frederick, on the other hand, was almost driven to despair. George saw in the great statesman's fall nothing but an opening for peace. He quickly availed himself of the weakness and unpopularity in which the ministry found itself involved after Pitt's departure to drive the Duke of Newcastle from office by a series of studied mortifications, and to place the Marquis of Bute at its head. Bute was a mere court favourite, with the abilities of a gentleman usher, but he was willing to do the King's will, and the King's will was to end the war. Frederick, who still held his ground stubbornly against fate, was brought to the brink of ruin in the spring of 1762 by the withdrawal of the English subsidies. It was in fact only his wonderful resolution and the sudden change in the policy of Russia which followed on the death of his enemy the Czarina Elizabeth which enabled him to retire from the struggle in the Treaty of Hubertsberg, without the loss of an inch of territory. George and Lord Bute had already purchased peace at a very different price. With a shameless indifference to the national honour, they had even offered Silesia to Austria, and East Prussia to the Czarina, in return for a cessation of hostilities. Fortunately the issue of the strife with Spain saved England from such humiliation as this. Pitt's policy had been vindicated by a Spanish declaration of war three weeks after his fall; and the surrender of Cuba and the Philippines to a British fleet brought about the Peace of Paris in September 1763. England restored Martinique, the most important of her West Indian conquests, to France, and Cuba and the Philippines to Spain in return for the cession of Florida. Her real gains were in India and America. In the first the French abandoned all right to any military settlement: in the second they gave up Canada and Nova Scotia.

1761
to
1785
—
The
House
of Com-
mons

The anxiety which the young king showed for peace abroad sprang simply from his desire to begin the struggle for power at home. So long as the war lasted Pitt's return to office and the union of the Whigs under his guidance was an hourly danger. But with peace the King's hands were free. He could count on the dissensions of the Whigs, on the new-born loyalty of the Tories on the influence of the Crown patronage which he had taken into his own hands; but what he counted on most of all was the character of the House of Commons. At a time when it had become all-powerful in the State, when government hung simply on its will the House of Commons had ceased in any real and effective sense to represent the Commons at all. The changes in the distribution of seats which were called for by the natural shiftings of population and wealth since the days of Edward the First had been recognized as early as the Civil Wars; but the reforms of the Long Parliament were cancelled at the Restoration. From the time of Charles the Second to that of George the Third not a single effort had been made to meet the growing abuses of our parliamentary system Great towns like Manchester or Birmingham remained without member, while members still sat for boroughs which, like Old Sarum, had actually vanished from the face of the earth. The effort of the Tudor sovereigns to establish a Court party in the House by a profuse creation of boroughs, most of which were mere villages then in the hands of the Crown, had ended in the appropriation of these seats by the neighbouring landowners, who bought and sold them as they sold their own estates. Even in towns which had a real claim to representation, the narrowing of municipal privileges ever since the fourteenth century to a small part of the inhabitants, and in many cases the restriction of electoral rights to the members of the governing corporation, rendered their representation a mere name. The choice of such places hung simply on the purse or influence of politicians. Some were "the King's boroughs," others obediently returned nominees of the Ministry of the day, others were " close boroughs " in the hands of jobbers like the Duke of Newcastle, who at one time returned a third of all the borough members in the House. The counties and the great commercial towns could alone be said to exercise any real right of suffrage, though the enormous expense of contesting such constituencies practically left their representation in the hands of the great local families. But even in the counties the suffrage was ridiculously limited and unequal. Out of a population in fact of eight millions of English people, only a hundred and sixty thousand were electors at all.

How far such a House was from really representing English opinion we see from the fact that in the height of his popularity Pitt could hardly find a seat in it. When he did find one, it was at the hands of a great borough-jobber, Lord Clive. Purchase was the real means of entering Parliament. Seats were bought and sold in the open market at a price which rose to four thousand pounds nd we can hardly wonder that the younger Pitt cried indignantly t a later time, " This House is not the representative of the People f Great Britain. It is the representative of nominal boroughs, of uined and exterminated towns, of noble families, of wealthy ndividuals, of foreign potentates." The meanest motives naturally old on a body returned by such constituencies, cut off from the nfluence of public opinion by the secrecy of Parliamentary pro-ceedings, and yet invested with almost boundless authority. New-astle had made bribery and borough-jobbing the base of the power f the Whigs. George the Third seized it in his turn as the base of he power he purposed to give to the Crown. The royal revenue vas employed to buy seats and to buy votes. Day by day, George imself scrutinized the voting-list of the two Houses, and dis-ributed rewards and punishments as members voted according o his will or no. Promotion in the civil service, preferment in the hurch, rank in the army was reserved for " the King's friends." Pensions and court places were used to influence debates. Bribery vas employed on a scale never known before. Under Bute's ninistry an office was opened at the Treasury for the bribery of nembers, and twenty-five thousand pounds are said to have been pent in a single day.

The result of these measures was seen in the tone of the very Parliament which had till now bowed beneath the greatness of Pitt. n the teeth of his denunciations the Peace was approved by a najority of five to one. " Now indeed my son is king ! " cried the Princess Dowager. But the victory was far from being won yet. o long as the sentiment of the House of Commons had fairly epresented that of the nation at large, England had cared little or its abuses or its corruption. But the defeat of the Great Commoner disclosed the existence of a danger of which it had ever dreamed. The country found itself powerless in the face of body which wielded the supreme authority in its name, but which ad utterly ceased to be its representative. It looked on helplessly hile the King, by sheer dint of corruption, turned the House hich was the guardian of public rights into a means of governing t his will. Parliament was the constitutional expression of public pinion, and now public opinion was without the means of uttering self in Parliament. The natural result followed. The early years f George the Third were distinguished by a public discontent, by olitical agitation and disturbances, such as have never been nown since. Bute found himself the object of a detestation so udden and so universal in its outbreak as to force him to resign 1763. The King, as frightened as his minister, saw that the time ad not yet come for ruling by his own adherents alone, and ppealed for aid to Pitt. But though he had been betrayed by ewcastle and his followers, Pitt saw clearly that without the upport of the whole Whig party a minister would be, as Bute had een, a tool of the Crown; and he made the return of all its sections o office a condition of his own. George refused to comply with

Fall of Bute

terms which would have defeated his designs; and he was able to
save himself from submission by skilfully using the division which
was rending the Whig camp into two opposite forces. The bulk of
it, with Lord Rockingham and the Cavendishes at its head, leant
to Pitt and to the sympathy of the commercial classes. A smaller
part, under George Grenville and the Duke of Bedford, retained
the narrow and selfish temper of a mere oligarchy, in whom greed
of power overmastered every other feeling. In an evil hour George
threw himself on the support of the last.

Of what moment his choice had been he was soon to learn.
With Grenville's ministry began the political power of the Press
and the struggle with America. The opinion of the country no
sooner found itself unrepresented in Parliament than it sought an
outlet in the Press. We have already noted the early history of
English journalism, its rise under the Commonwealth, the censorship which fettered it, and the removal of this censorship after the
Revolution. Under the two first Georges, its progress was hindered
by the absence of great topics for discussion, the worthlessness of
its writers, and above all the political lethargy of the time. It was
in fact not till the accession of George the Third that the impulse
which Pitt had given to the national spirit and the rise of a keener
interest in politics raised the Press into a political power. The new
force of public opinion found in it a court of political appeal from
the House of Commons. The journals became mouthpieces for that
outburst of popular hatred which drove Lord Bute from office in the
teeth of his unbroken majority. The *North Briton*, a journal written
by John Wilkes, denounced the Peace with peculiar bitterness,
and ventured for the first time to attack a minister by name.
Wilkes was a worthless profligate, but he had a remarkable power
of enlisting popular sympathy on his side, and by a singular irony
of fortune he became the chief instrument in bringing about three
of the greatest advances which our constitution has ever made.
At a later time he woke the nation to a conviction of the need for
Parliamentary reform by his defence of the rights of constituencies
against the despotism of the House of Commons, and took the lead
in the struggle which put an end to the secrecy of Parliamentary
proceedings. The prosecution of his *North Briton* in 1764 first
established the right of the Press to discuss public affairs. Wilkes
was sent to prison on a " general warrant " from the Secretary of
State. The legality of such a mode of arbitrary arrest by an officer
of state on a warrant which did not name the person to be arrested
or specify the papers to be seized was at once questioned, and no
such warrant has ever been issued since. A writ of *habeas corpus*
freed Wilkes from prison, but he was soon prosecuted for libel, and
the House of Commons condemned the paper, which was still before
the civil courts, as a " false, scandalous, and seditious libel." The
House of Lords at the same time voted a pamphlet found among
Wilkes's papers to be blasphemous, and advised a prosecution.
Wilkes fled to France, and was soon expelled from the House of

Commons. But the assumption of an arbitrary judicial power by both Houses, and the system of terror which Grenville put in force against the Press by issuing two hundred injunctions against different journals, roused a storm of indignation throughout the country. Every street resounded with cries of "Wilkes and Liberty." Bold as he was, Grenville dared go no further; and six years later, the failure of the prosecution directed against an anonymous journalist named "Junius" for his Letter to the King established the right of the Press to criticize the conduct not of ministers or Parliament only, but of the sovereign himself.

The same recklessness which was shown by Grenville in his struggle with the Press was shown in his struggle with the American colonies. Pitt had waged war with characteristic profusion and defrayed its expenses by enormous loans. The public debt now stood at a hundred and forty millions, and the first work of the Grenville Ministry was to make provision for the new burthens the nation had incurred. As the burthen had been partly incurred in the defence of the American colonies, Grenville resolved that the colonies should bear their share of it. He raised the import duties at colonial ports. To deal with external commerce was generally held to be an unquestioned right of the mother country: and irritated as they were by these changes, the colonists submitted to them. A far heavier blow was dealt at their commerce by the rigid enforcement of the laws which restricted colonial trade to British ports, and the suppression of the illicit trade which had grown up with the Spanish settlements. The measure was a harsh and unwise one, but it was legal, and could only be resented by a general pledge to use no British manufactures. But the next scheme of the Minister, his proposal to introduce internal taxation within the bounds of the colony itself by reviving the scheme of an excise or stamp duty which Walpole's good sense had rejected, was met in another spirit. Taxation and representation, the colonists held, went hand in hand. America had no representatives in the British Parliament. The representatives of the colonists met in their own colonial Assemblies, and these were willing to grant supplies of a yet larger amount than a stamp-tax would produce. With this protest and offer they despatched Benjamin Franklin, who had risen from his position of a working printer in Philadelphia to high repute among scientific discoverers, as their agent to England. But his remonstrances only kindled Grenville's obstinacy, and the Stamp Act was passed in 1765. Franklin saw no other course for the colonies than submission, but submission was the last thing which the colonists dreamed of. The Northern and Southern States were drawn together by the new danger. The Assembly of Virginia was the first to formally deny the right of the British Parliament to meddle with internal taxation, and to demand the repeal of the Act. Massachusetts not only adopted the denial and the demand as its own, but proposed a Congress of delegates from all the colonial Assemblies to provide for common and united action. In

October 1765 this Congress met to repeat the protest and petition
of Virginia.

For the moment this unexpected danger seemed to raise English
politics out of the chaos of faction and intrigue into which they
were sinking. Not only had the Ministry incurred the hatred of the
people, but the arrogance of Grenville had earned the resentment
of the King. George again offered power to William Pitt. But Pitt
stood almost alone. The silence of Newcastle and the Rockingham
party while the war and his past policy was censured in Parliament
had estranged him from the only section of the Whigs which could
have acted with him: and the one friend who remained to him, his
brother-in-law, Lord Temple, refused to aid in an attempt to
construct a Cabinet. The King had no resource but to turn to the
Marquis of Rockingham and the Whig party which he headed, but
Rockingham had hardly taken office in July 1765 when the startling
news came from America that Congress had resolved on resistance.
Its resolution had been followed by action. No sooner had the
stamps for the new Excise arrived in Boston than they were seized
and held in custody by the magistrates of the town. The news at
once called Pitt to the front. As a Minister he had long since
rejected a similar scheme for taxing the colonies. He had been ill
and absent from Parliament when the Stamp Act was passed, but
he adopted to the full the constitutional claim of America. He
gloried in the resistance which was denounced in Parliament as
rebellion. "In my opinion," he said, "this kingdom has no right
to lay a tax on the colonies. . . . America is obstinate! America
is almost in open rebellion! Sir, I rejoice that America has resisted.
Three millions of people so dead to all the feelings of liberty as
voluntarily to submit to be slaves would have been fit instruments
to make slaves of the rest." His words determined the action of
the timid Ministry, and in spite of the resistance of the King and
the "King's friends" the Stamp Act was formally repealed in 1766.
But the doctrine he had laid down was as formally repudiated by
a Declaratory Act passed at the same time which asserted the
supreme power of Parliament over the colonies "in all cases
whatsoever."

From this moment the Ministry was unable to stand against the
general sense that the first man in the country should be its ruler.
Pitt's aim was still to unite the Whig party, and though forsaken
by Lord Temple, he succeeded to a great extent in the administration which he formed in the summer of 1766. Rockingham indeed
refused office, but the bulk of his fellow Ministers remained, and
they were reinforced by the few friends who clung to Pitt. In his
zeal to bring all parties together, even some of the Court party were
admitted to minor offices in the administration, a step which won
the warm approbation of the King as likely to destroy "all party
distinctions." Never had the hopes of a wise and noble government
been stronger, and never were they fated to be more signally foiled.
The life of the Ministry lay in Pitt, in his immense popularity, and

n the command which his eloquence gave him over the House of Commons. His acceptance of the Earldom of Chatham removed im to the House of Lords, and for a while ruined the confidence which his reputation for unselfishness had aided him to win. But ᵗ was from no vulgar ambition that Pitt laid down his title of the Great Commoner. It was the consciousness of failing strength which made him dread the storms of debate, and in a few months he dread became a certainty. A painful and overwhelming illness, he result of nervous disorganization, withdrew him from public ᵃffairs; and his withdrawal robbed his colleagues of all vigour or union. The plans which Chatham had set on foot for the better government of Ireland, the transfer of India from the Company ᵗo the Crown, and the formation of a Northern Alliance with Prussia and Russia to balance the Family Compact of the House ᵒf Bourbon, were suffered to drop. The one aim of the Ministry vas to exist. It sought strength by the readmission of George Grenville and the Bedford party to office, but this practical ᵃbandonment of the policy of Pitt was soon followed by the retire- ᵐent of his friends and of the chief of the Rockingham Whigs. A series of changes which it is needless to recount in detail left it practically a joint Ministry of the worst faction of the Whigs and of ᵗhe new party which had been slowly gathering strength under the ᵑame of the King's friends. In spite however of the worthlessness ᵃnd mediocrity of its members, this Ministry lasted under the successive guidance of the Duke of Grafton and Lord North for fourteen years, from 1768 to the close of the American war.

Its strength lay in the disorganization of the Whig party and the steady support of the King. George the Third had at last reached his aim. Pitt was discredited and removed for a time from the stage. The Whigs under Rockingham were fatally divided both from him and from the Bedford party. If the Bedfords were again in office it was on the condition of doing the King's will. Their Parliamentary support lay in the Tories and the "King's friends," who looked for direction to George himself. In the early days of the Ministry his influence was felt to be predominant. In its later and more dis- astrous days it was supreme, for Lord North, who became the head of the Ministry on Grafton's retirement in 1770, was the mere mouthpiece of the King. "Not only did he direct the Minister," a careful observer tells us, "in all important matters of foreign and domestic policy, but he instructed him as to the management of debates in Parliament, suggested what motions should be made or opposed, and how measures should be carried. He reserved for himself all the patronage, he arranged the whole cast of the administration, settled the relative place and pretensions of ministers of state, law officers, and members of the household, nominated and promoted the English and Scotch judges, appointed and translated bishops and deans, and dispensed other preferments in the Church. He disposed of military governments, regiments, and commissions, and himself ordered the marching of troops. He gave and refused titles, honours, and pensions." All this immense patronage was steadily used for the creation and maintenance of a party in both Houses of Parliament attached to the King himself; and its weight was seen in the dependence to which the new Ministry was reduced. George was in fact sole Minister during the eight years which followed; and the shame of the darkest hour of English history lies wholly at his door.

Again, as in 1763, the Government which he directed plunged at his instigation into a struggle with opinion at home and with the colonists of America. The attempt of the House of Commons to gag the Press and to transform itself into a supreme court of justice had been practically foiled. It now began the most daring attack ever made, by a body professing to be representative, on the rights of those whom it represented. In 1768 Wilkes returned from France and was elected member for Middlesex, a county the large number of whose voters made its choice a real expression of public opinion. The choice of Wilkes was in effect a public condemnation of the House of Commons. The Ministry shrank from a fresh struggle with the agitator, but the King was eager for the contest. " I think it highly expedient to apprise you," he wrote to Lord North, " that the expulsion of Mr. Wilkes appears to be very essential, and must be effected." The Ministers and the House of Commons bowed to his will. By his non-appearance in court when charged with libel Wilkes had become an outlaw, and he was now thrown into prison on his outlawry. Dangerous riots broke out in London and over the whole country; but the Government persevered. In 1769 the House of Commons expelled Wilkes as a libeller. He was at once re-elected by the shire of Middlesex. Violent and oppressive as the course of the House of Commons had been, it had as yet acted within its strict right, for no one questioned its possession of a right of expulsion. But the defiance of Middlesex led it now to go further. It resolved, " That Mr. Wilkes having been in this session of Parliament expelled the House, was and is incapable of being elected a member to serve in the present Parliament; " and it issued a writ for a fresh election. Middlesex answered this insolent claim to limit the free choice of a constituency by again returning Wilkes; and the House was driven by its anger to a fresh and more outrageous usurpation. It again expelled the member for Middlesex, and on his return for the third time by an immense majority, it voted that the candidate whom he had defeated, Colonel Luttrell, ought to have been returned, and was the legal representative of Middlesex. The Commons had not only limited at their own arbitrary discretion the free election of the constituency, but they had transferred its rights to themselves by seating Luttrell as member in defiance of the deliberate choice of Wilkes by the free-holders of Middlesex. The country at once rose indignantly against this violation of constitutional law. Wilkes was elected an Alderman of London; and the Mayor, Aldermen, and Livery petitioned the king to dissolve the Parliament. A remonstrance from London nd Westminster said boldly that "there is a time when it is learly demonstrable that men cease to be representatives. That ime is now arrived. The House of Commons do not represent the people." Junius, an anonymous writer, attacked the Government n letters, which, rancorous and unscrupulous as was their tone, gave a new power to the literature of the Press by their clearness and terseness of statement, the finish of their style, and the terrible rigour of their invective.

The storm, however, beat idly on the obstinacy of the King. Junius was prosecuted, and the petitions and remonstrances of London haughtily rejected. At the beginning of 1770 however a cessation of the disease which had long held him prostrate enabled Chatham to reappear in the House of Lords. He at once denounced the usurpations of the Commons, and brought in a bill to declare them illegal. But his genius made him the first to see that remedies of this sort were inadequate to meet evils which really sprang from the fact that the House of Commons no longer represented the people of England. He brought forward a plan for its reform by an ncrease of the county members. Further he could not go, for even n the proposals he made he stood almost alone. Even the Whigs under Lord Rockingham had no sympathy with Parliamentary reform. They shrank with haughty disdain from the popular agitation in which public opinion was forced to express itself, and which Chatham, while censuring its extravagance, deliberately encouraged. It is from the quarrels between Wilkes and the House of Commons that we may date the influence of public meetings on English politics. The gatherings of the Middlesex electors in his support were preludes to the great meetings of Yorkshire freeholders in which the question of Parliamentary reform rose into importance; and it was in the movement for reform, and the establishment of corresponding committees throughout the country for the purpose of promoting it, that the power of political agitation first made itself felt. Political societies and clubs took their part in the creation and organization of public opinion: and the spread of discussion, as well as the influence which now began to be exercised by the appearance of vast numbers of men in support of any political movement, proved that Parliament would soon have to reckon with the sentiments of the people at large.

But an agent far more effective than popular agitation was preparing to bring the force of public opinion to bear on Parliament itself. We have seen how much of the corruption of the House of Commons sprang from the secrecy of Parliamentary proceedings, but the secrecy was the harder to preserve as the nation woke to a greater interest in its own affairs. From the accession of the Georges imperfect reports of the more important discussions began to be published under the title of "The Senate of Lilliput," and with feigned names or simple initials to denote the speaker. Obtained by stealth and often merely recalled by memory, these reports were naturally inaccurate; and their inaccuracy was eagerly seized on as a pretext for enforcing the rules which guarded the secrecy of proceedings in Parliament. In 1771 the Commons issued a proclamation forbidding the publication of debates; and six printers who set it at defiance, were summoned to the bar of the House. One who refused to appear was arrested by its messenger; but the arrest at once brought the House into conflict with the magistrates of London. They set aside the proclamation as without legal force, released the printers, and sent the messenger to prison for an unlawful arrest. The House sent the Lord Mayor to the Tower, but the cheers of the crowds which followed him on his way told that public opinion was again with the Press, and the attempt to hinder its publication of Parliamentary proceedings dropped silently on his release at the next prorogation. Few changes of equal importance have been so quietly brought about. Not only was the responsibility of members to their constituents made constant and effective by the publication of their proceedings, but the nation itself was called in to assist in the deliberations of its representatives. A new and wider interest in its own affairs was roused in the people at large, and a new political education was given to it through the discussion of every subject of national importance in the Houses and the Press. Public opinion, as gathered up and represented on all its sides by the journals of the day, became a force in practical statesmanship, influenced the course of debates and controlled in a closer and more constant way than even Parliament itself had been able to do the actions of the Government. The importance of its new position gave a weight to the Press which it had never had before. The first great English journals date from this time. With the *Morning Chronicle*, the *Morning Post*, the *Morning Herald*, and the *Times*, all of which appeared in the interval between the opening years of the American War and the beginning of the war with the French Revolution, journalism took a new tone of responsibility and intelligence. The hacks of Grub Street were superseded by publicists of a high moral temper and literary excellence; and philosophers like Coleridge or statesmen like Canning turned to influence public opinion through the columns of the Press.

But as yet these influences were feebly felt, and George the Third was able to set Chatham's protests disdainfully aside, and to plunge into a contest far more disastrous for the fortunes of England. In all the wretched chaos of the last few years, what had galled him most had been the one noble act which averted a war between England and her colonies. To the King the Americans were already "rebels," and the great statesman whose eloquence had made their claims irresistible was a "trumpet of sedition." George deplored, in his correspondence with Lord North, the repeal of the Stamp Act. "All men feel," he wrote, "that the fatal compliance in 1766 has increased the pretensions of the Americans to absolute independence." In America itself the news of the repeal had been received with universal joy, and taken as a close of the strife. But on both sides there remained a pride and irritability which only wise handling could have allayed; and in the present state of English politics wise handling was impossible. No sooner had the illness of Lord Chatham removed him from any real share in public affairs than the wretched administration which still bore his name suspended the Assembly of New York on its refusal to provide quarters for English troops, and resolved to assert British sovereignty by levying import duties of trivial amount at American ports. The Assembly of Massachusetts was dissolved on a trifling quarrel with its Governor, and Boston was occupied for a time by British soldiers. The remonstrances of the Legislatures of Massachusetts and Virginia, however, coupled with a fall in the funds, warned the Ministers of the dangerous course on which they had entered; and in 1769 the troops were withdrawn, and all duties, save that on tea, abandoned. A series of petty quarrels went on in almost every colony between the popular Assemblies and the Governors appointed by the Crown, and the colonists persevered in their agreement to import nothing from the mother country. But for three years there was no prospect of serious strife. In America the influence of George Washington allayed the irritation of Virginia. Massachusetts contented itself with quarrelling with the Governor and refusing to buy tea so long as the duty was levied. In England, even Grenville, though approving the retention of the duty in question, abandoned all dream of further taxation. But the King was supreme, and the fixed purpose of the King was to seize on the first opportunity of undoing the "fatal compliance of 1766."

A trivial riot gave him the handle he wanted. He had insisted on the tea duty being retained when the rest were withdrawn, and in December 1773 the arrival of some English ships laden with tea kindled fresh irritation in Boston, where the non-importation agreement was strictly enforced. A mob in the disguise of Indians boarded the vessels and flung their contents into the sea. The outrage was deplored alike by the friends of America in England and by its own leading statesmen; and both Washington and Chatham were prepared to support the Government in its looked-for demand of redress. But the thought of the King was not of redress but of repression, and he set roughly aside the more conciliatory proposals of Lord North and his fellow-ministers. They had already rejected as "frivolous and vexatious" a petition of the Assembly of Massachusetts for the dismissal of two public officers whose letters home advised the withdrawal of free institutions from the colonies. They now seized on the riot as a pretext for rigorous measures. A bill introduced into Parliament in the beginning of 1774 punished Boston by closing its port against all commerce. Another punished the State of Massachusetts by withdrawing the liberties it had enjoyed ever since the Pilgrim Fathers landed on its soil. Its charter was altered. The choice of its Council was transferred from the people to the Crown, and the nomination of its judges was transferred to the Governor. In the Governor, too, by a provision more outrageous than even these was vested the right of sending all persons charged with a share in the late disturbances to England for trial. To enforce these measures of repression troops were sent to America, and General Gage, the commander-in-chief there, was appointed Governor of Massachusetts. The King's exultation at the prospect before him was unbounded. "The die," he wrote triumphantly to his Minister "is cast. The colonies must either triumph or submit." Four regiments would be enough to bring Americans to their senses. They would only be "lions while we are lambs." "If we take the resolute part," he decided solemnly, "they will undoubtedly be very meek." Unluckily, the blow at Massachusetts was received with anything but meekness. The jealousies between State and State were hushed by the sense that the liberties of all were in danger. If the British Parliament could cancel the charter of Massachusetts and ruin the trade of Boston, it could cancel the charter of every colony and ruin the trade of every port from the St. Lawrence to the Gulf of Mexico. All, therefore, adopted the cause of Massachusetts; and all their Legislatures, save that of Georgia, sent delegates to a Congress which assembled on the 4th of September at Philadelphia. Massachusetts took a yet bolder course. Not a citizen would act under the new laws. Its Assembly met in defiance of the Governor, called out the militia of the State, and provided arms and ammunition for it. But there was still room for reconciliation. The resolutions of the Congress had been moderate; for Virginia was the wealthiest and most influential among the States who sent delegates; and Virginia under Washington's guidance, though resolute to resist the new measures of the Government, still clung to the mother country. At home, the merchants of London and Bristol pleaded loudly for reconciliation; and in January 1775 Chatham again came forward to avert the strife he had once before succeeded in preventing. With characteristic grandeur of feeling he set aside all half-measures or proposals of compromise. "It is not cancelling a piece of parchment," he insisted, "that can win back America: you must respect her fears and her resentments." The bill which he introduced in concert with Franklin provided for the repeal of the late Acts and for the security of the colonial charters, abandoned the claim to taxation, and ordered the recall of the troops. A colonial Assembly was directed to assemble and provide means by which America might contribute towards the payment of the public debt.

The Independence of America

The contemptuous rejection of Chatham's measure began the great struggle which ended eight years later in the severance of the American Colonies from the British Crown. The Congress of delegates from the Colonial Legislatures at once voted measures for general defence, ordered the levy of an army, and set George Washington at its head. No nobler figure ever stood in the forefront of a nation's life. Washington was grave and courteous in

ddress; his manners were simple and unpretending; his silence
nd the serene calmness of his temper spoke of a perfect self-
ʜastery; but there was little in his outer bearing to reveal the
ʀandeur of soul which lifts his figure, with all the simple majesty
f an ancient statue, out of the smaller passions, the meaner
ᴍpulses of the world around him. What recommended him for
ommand as yet was simply his weight among his fellow land-
ᴡners of Virginia, and the experience of war which he had gained
ʏ service in Braddock's luckless expedition against Fort Duquesne.
t was only as the weary fight went on that the colonists learnt
ʈtle by little the greatness of their leader, his clear judgment, his
ɛroic endurance, his silence under difficulties, his calmness in the
ᴏur of danger or defeat, the patience with which he waited, the
ʋuickness and hardness with which he struck, the lofty and serene
ɛnse of duty that never swerved from its task through resentment
ʀ jealousy, that never through war or peace felt the touch of a
ʜeaner ambition, that knew no aim save that of guarding the
ʀeedom of his fellow countrymen, and no personal longing save
ʜat of returning to his own fireside when their freedom was secured.
t was almost unconsciously that men learnt to cling to Washington
ʀith a trust and faith such as few other men have won, and to
ɛgard him with a reverence which still hushes us in presence of
is memory. Even America hardly recognized his real grandeur till
ɛath set its seal on " the man first in war, first in peace, and first
ɪ the hearts of his fellow countrymen." Washington, more than
ʜy of his fellow colonists, represented the clinging of the Virginian
ɪndowners to the mother country, and his acceptance of the com-
ɪand proved that even the most moderate among them had no
ᴏpe now save in arms. The struggle opened with a skirmish
ɛtween a party of English troops and a detachment of militia
t Lexington, and in a few days twenty thousand colonists appeared
ɛfore Boston. The Congress reassembled, declared the States
ʜey represented " The United Colonies of America," and under-
ᴏok the work of government. Meanwhile ten thousand fresh
ʀoops landed at Boston; but the provincial militia seized the neck
f ground which joins it to the mainland, and though they were
ʀiven from the heights of Bunker's Hill which commanded the
ᴏwn, it was only after a desperate struggle in which their bravery
ut an end for ever to the taunts of cowardice which had been
ɛvelled against the colonists. " Are the Yankees cowards ? "
ʜouted the men of Massachusetts, as the first English attack
ᴏlled back baffled down the hill-side. But a far truer courage was
ʜown in the stubborn endurance with which sixteen thousand raw
ʜilitia-men, who gradually dwindled to ten, ill fed and ill armed,
ʀith but forty-five rounds of ammunition to each man, cooped up
ʜrough the winter, under Washington's command, a force of ten
ʜousand veterans in the lines of Boston till the spring of 1776 saw
ʜem withdraw from the city to New York, where the whole
ᴃritish army, largely reinforced by mercenaries from Germany,

was concentrated under General Howe. Meanwhile a raid of th
American General Arnold nearly drove the British troops from
Canada; and though his attempt broke down before Quebec, it
showed that all hope of reconciliation was over. The colonies of
the south, the last to join in the struggle, expelled their Governor
at the close of 1775. This decisive step was followed by the grea
act with which American history begins, the adoption on th
4th of July, 1776, by the delegates in Congress of the Declaration
of Independence. "We," ran its solemn words, "the representa
tives of the United States of America in Congress assembled
appealing to the Supreme Judge of the world for the rectitude of
our intentions, solemnly publish and declare that these United
Colonies are, and of right ought to be, Free and Independent
States."

The triumph of the colonies was soon followed by suffering an
defeat. Howe, an active general with a fine army at his back
cleared Long Island in August by a victory at Brooklyn; and
Washington, whose army was weakened by withdrawals and
defeat, and disheartened by the loyal tone of the State in which
it was encamped, was forced to evacuate New York and New
Jersey, and to fall back, first on the Hudson and then on the
Delaware. The Congress prepared to fly from Philadelphia, and a
general despair showed itself in cries of peace. But a well-managed
surprise at Trenton, and a daring march on the rear of Howe's
army at Princetown restored the spirits of Washington's men
and forced the English general in his turn to fall back on New
York. The spring of 1777 opened with a combined effort for the
suppression of the revolt. An army assembled in Canada under
General Burgoyne marched by way of the Lakes to seize the line
of the Hudson, and with help from the army at New York to cut
off New England from her sister provinces. Howe meanwhile sailed
up the Chesapeake, and marched on Philadelphia, the temporary
capital of the United States and the seat of the Congress. The
rout of his little army of seven thousand men at Brandywine
forced Washington to abandon Philadelphia, and after a bold but
unsuccessful attack on his victors at Germantown to retire into
winter quarters on the banks of the Schuylkill. The unconquerable
resolve with which he nerved his handful of beaten and half-
starved troops in their camp at Valley Forge to face Howe's army
through the winter is the noblest of Washington's triumphs. But
in the north the war had taken another colour. When Burgoyne
appeared on the Upper Hudson he found the road to Albany barred
by an American force under General Gates. The spirit of New
England, which had grown dull as the war rolled away from its
borders, quickened again at the news of invasion and of the outrages committed by the Indians whom Burgoyne employed among
his troops. Its militia hurried from town and homestead to the
camp; and after a fruitless attack on the American lines, Burgoyne
saw himself surrounded on the heights of Saratoga. On the 13th of

)ctober he was compelled to surrender. The news of this terrible alamity gave force to the words with which Chatham at the very ime of the surrender was pressing for peace. " You cannot conquer America," he cried when men were glorying in Howe's successes. " If I were an American as I am an Englishman, while a foreign roop was landed in my country, I never would lay down my arms, ,ever, never, never! " Then, in a burst of indignant eloquence he hundered against the use of the Indian and his scalping-knife s allies of England against her children. The proposals which]hatham brought forward might perhaps, in his hands, even yet ,ave brought America and the mother country together. His plan vas one of absolute conciliation, and of a federal union between he settlements and Great Britain which would have left the olonies absolutely their own masters in all matters of internal ,overnment and linked only by ties of affection and loyalty to the ;eneral body of the Empire. But it met with the same fate as his ,revious proposals. Its rejection was at once followed by the news f Saratoga, and by the yet more fatal news that the disaster had oused the Bourbon Courts to avenge the humiliation of the Seven ears' War. In February 1778 France concluded an alliance with he States, and that of Spain followed after a year's delay. Even n the minds of the Ministers themselves all hope of conquering America had disappeared. The King indeed was as obstinate for var as ever; and the country, stung by its great humiliation, sent ifteen thousand men to the ranks of the army. But even the King's nfluence broke down before the general despair. Lord North arried through Parliament bills which conceded to America all she ,ad originally claimed. The Duke of Richmond and a large number f the Whigs openly advocated the acknowledgment of American ndependence. If a hope still remained of retaining the friendship f the colonies and of baffling the efforts of France and Spain, it lay n Lord Chatham, and in spite of the King's resistance the voice of he whole country called him back to power. But on the eve of is return to office this last chance was shattered by the hand of leath. The day for which George the Third only two years before ,ad longed was come. Broken with age and disease, the Earl was ,orne to the House of Lords on the 7th of April, and uttered in a ew broken words his protest against the proposal to surrender America. " His Majesty," he murmured, " succeeded to an Empire ,s great in extent as its reputation was unsullied. Seventeen years ,go this people was the terror of the world." Then falling back in , swoon, he was borne home to die.

From the hour of Chatham's death England entered on a conflict **Progress** vith enemies whose circle gradually widened till she stood single- **of the** ,anded against the world. In 1778, France and Spain were leagued **War** vith America against her. Their joint fleet of sixty ships rode the nasters of the Channel, and threatened a descent on the English oast. But dead as Chatham was, his cry woke a new life in England. " Shall we fall prostrate," he exclaimed with his last

breath, " before the House of Bourbon ? " and the divisions whic
had broken the nation in its struggle with American libert
vanished at a threat of French invasion. The weakness of th
Ministry was compensated by the heroic energy of the nation itsel
For three years, from 1779 to 1782, General Elliot held agains
famine and bombardment the rock fortress of Gibraltar. Althoug
a quarrel over the right of search banded Holland and the Court
of the North in an armed neutrality against her, and added th
Dutch fleet to the number of her assailants, England held her ow
at sea. Even in America the fortune of the war seemed to turr
After Burgoyne's surrender the English generals had withdraw
from Pennsylvania, and bent all their efforts on the south wher
a strong Royalist party still existed. The capture of Charlesto
and the successes of Lord Cornwallis in 1780 were rendered fruitles
by the obstinate resistance of General Greene; but the States wer
weakened by bankruptcy and unnerved by hopes of aid fror
France. Meanwhile the losses of England in the West were all bu
compensated by new triumphs in the East.

England
and
India

Since the day of Plassey, India had been fast passing into th
hands of the merchant company whose traders but a few year
before held only three petty factories along its coast. The victor
which laid Bengal at the feet of Clive had been followed in 176
by a victory at Wandewash, in which Colonel Coote's defeat c
Lally, the French Governor of Pondicherry, established Britis
supremacy over Southern India. The work of organization ha
soon to follow on that of conquest; for the tyranny and corruptio
of the merchant-clerks who suddenly found themselves lifted int
rulers was fast ruining the province of Bengal; and although Cliv
had profited more than any other by the spoils of his victory, h
saw that the time had come when greed must give way to th
responsibilities of power. In 1765 he returned to India, and th
two years of his rule were in fact the most glorious years in his life
In the teeth of opposition from every clerk and of mutiny through
out the army, he put down the private trading of the Company'
servants and forbade their acceptance of gifts from the native
Clive set an example of disinterestedness by handing over to publi
uses a legacy which had been left him by the prince he had raise
to the throne of Bengal; and returned poorer than he went to fac
the storm his acts had roused among those who were intereste
in Indian abuses at home. His unsparing denunciations of th
misgovernment of Bengal at last stirred even Lord North t
interfere; and when the financial distress of the Company drov
it for aid to Government, the grant of aid was coupled wit
measures of administrative reform. The Regulation Act of 177
established a Governor-General and a Supreme Court of Judicatur
for all British possessions in India, prohibited judges and member
of Council from trading, forbade any receipt of presents fror
natives, and ordered that every act of the Directors should b
signified to the Government to be approved or disallowed. Th

ew interest which had been aroused in the subject of India was en in an investigation of the whole question of its administration y a Committee of the House of Commons. Clive's own early acts ere examined with unsparing severity. His bitter complaint in ie Lords that, Baron of Plassey as he was, he had been arraigned xe a sheep-stealer, failed to prevent the passing of resolutions hich censured the corruption and treachery of the early days of ritish rule in India. Here, however, the justice of the House opped. When his accusers passed from the censure of Indian isgovernment to the censure of Clive himself, the memory of his eat deeds won from the House of Commons a unanimous vote, That Robert Lord Clive did at the same time render great and eritorious services to his country."

By the Act of 1773 Warren Hastings was named Governor-eneral of the three presidencies. Hastings was sprung of a noble mily which had long fallen into decay, and poverty had driven im in boyhood to accept a writership in the Company's service. live, whose quick eye discerned his merits, drew him after Plassey ito political life; and the administrative ability he showed, during ie disturbed period which followed, raised him step by step to ie post of Governor of Bengal. No man could have been better tted to discharge the duties of the new office which the Govern-ient at home had created without a thought of its real greatness. astings was gifted with rare powers of organization and control. is first measure was to establish the direct rule of the Company ver Bengal by abolishing the government of its native princes, hich, though it had become nominal, hindered all plans for fective administration. The Nabob sank into a pensionary, and ie Company's new province was roughly but efficiently organized. ut of the clerks and traders about him Hastings formed that ody of public servants which still remains the noblest product of ur rule in India. The system of law and finance which he devised, asty and imperfect as it necessarily was, was far superior to any iat India had ever seen. Corruption he put down with as firm a and as Clive's, but he won the love of the new " civilians " as he on the love of the Hindoos. Although he raised the revenue of engal and was able to send home every year a surplus of half a iillion to the Company, he did this without laying a fresh burden n the natives or losing their good will. His government was guided y an intimate knowledge of and sympathy with the people. At a ime when their tongue was looked on simply as a medium of trade nd business, Hastings was skilled in the languages of India, he as versed in native customs, and familiar with native feeling. We an hardly wonder that his popularity with the Bengalees was such s no later ruler has ever attained, or that after a century of great vents Indian mothers still hush their infants with the name of Varren Hastings.

With Hastings began the conscious and deliberate purpose of ubjecting India to the British Crown. As yet, though English

1761
to
1785
—
India
in the
Ameri-
can War

influence was great in the south, Bengal alone was directly i
English hands. The policy of Warren Hastings looked forward t
a time when England should be absolute mistress of the whole o
Hindostan, from Ceylon to the Himalayas. For this he boun
native princes, as in Oude or Berar, by treaties and subsidie
crushed without scruple every state which like that of the Rohilla
seemed to afford a nucleus for resistance, and watched with incessan
jealousy the growth of powers even as distant as the Sikhs. Th
American war surprised him in the midst of vast schemes whic
were to be carried out by later Governors, and hurried him int
immediate action. The jealousy of France sought a counterpoise t
the power of Britain in that of the Mahrattas, freebooters of Hindo
blood whose tribes had for a century past carried their raids ove
India from the hills of the western coast, and founded sovereigntie
in Guzerat, Malwa, and Tanjore. All were bound by a slight tie o
subjection to the Mahratta chief who reigned at Poonah, and it wa
through this chieftain that the French envoys were able to set th
whole confederacy in motion against the English presidencies. Th
danger was met by Hastings with characteristic swiftness of resolve
His difficulties were great. For two years he had been rendere
powerless through the opposition of his Council; and when free
from this obstacle the Company pressed him incessantly for money
and the Crown more than once strove to recall him. His ow
general, Sir Eyre Coote, was miserly, capricious, and had to b
humoured like a child. Censures and complaints reached him wit
every mail. But his calm self-command never failed. No trace o
his embarrassments showed itself in his work. The war with th
Mahrattas was pressed with a tenacity of purpose which th
blunders of subordinates and the inefficiency of the soldiers he wa
forced to use never shook for a moment. Failure followed failure
and success had hardly been wrung from fortune when a new an
overwhelming danger threatened from the south. A militar
adventurer, Hyder Ali, had built up a compact and vigorou
empire out of the wreck of older principalities on the table-land o
Mysore. Tyrant as he was, no native rule was so just as Hyder's
no statesmanship so vigorous. He was quickwitted enough t
discern the real power of Britain, and only the wretched blunderin
of the Council of Madras forced him at last to the conclusion tha
war with the English was less dangerous than friendship with them
Old as he was, his generalship retained all its energy; and a dis
ciplined army, covered by a cloud of horse and backed by a trai
of artillery, poured down in 1780 on the plain of the Carnatic. Th
small British force which met him was driven into Madras, an
Madras itself was in danger. The news reached Hastings when h
was at last on the verge of triumph over the Mahrattas; but hi
triumph was instantly abandoned, a peace was patched up, an
every soldier hurried to Madras. The appearance of Eyre Coot
checked the progress of Hyder, and in 1781 the victory of Port
Novo hurled him back into the fastnesses of Mysore. India wa

he one quarter of the world where Britain lost nothing during the American war; and though the schemes of conquest which Hastings had formed were for the moment frustrated, the annexation of Benares, the extension of British dominions along the Ganges, the reduction of Oude to virtual dependence, the appearance of English armies in Central India, and the defeat of Hyder, laid the foundation of an Indian Empire which his genius was bold enough to foresee.

But while England triumphed in the East, the face of the war in America was changed by a terrible disaster. Foiled in an attempt in North Carolina by the refusal of his fellow general, Sir H. Clinton, to assist him, Lord Cornwallis fell back in 1781 on Virginia, and intrenched himself in the lines of York Town. A sudden march of Washington brought him to the front of the English troops at a moment when the French fleet held the sea, and the army of Cornwallis was driven by famine to a surrender as humiliating as that of Saratoga. The news fell like a thunderbolt on the wretched Minister who had till now suppressed at his master's order his own conviction of the uselessness of further bloodshed. Opening his arms and pacing wildly up and down his room, Lord North exclaimed "It is all over," and resigned. England in fact seemed on the brink of ruin. Even Ireland turned on her. A force of Protestant Volunteers which had been raised for the defence of the island, and had rapidly grown to a hundred thousand men, demanded the repeal of Poyning's Act and the recognition of the Irish House of Lords as a final Court of Appeal. The demand was in effect a claim of Irish independence; but there was no means of resisting it, for England was destitute of any force which she could oppose to the Volunteers. The hopes of her enemies rose high. Spain refused peace at any other price than the surrender of Gibraltar. France proposed that England should give up all her Indian conquests save Bengal. But at this moment the victories of Admiral Rodney, the greatest of English seamen save Nelson and Blake, saved the country from a dishonourable peace. He encountered the Spanish fleet off Cape St. Vincent, and only four of its vessels escaped to Cadiz. The triumphs of the French Admiral De Grasse called him to the West Indies, and on the 12th April, 1782, a manœuvre which he was the first to introduce broke his opponent's line and drove the French fleet, shattered, from the sea. The final repulse of the allied armament before Gibraltar in September ended the war. In November the Treaties of Paris and Versailles, while yielding nothing to France and only Minorca and Florida to Spain, acknowledged without reserve the Independence of America.

**1783
to
1789**

Section III.—The Second Pitt, 1783—1789

[*Authorities.*—To Lecky's " History of England " may be adde<
Stanhope's " Life of Pitt "; Trevelyan's " C. J. Fox "; the " Annua
Register "; and Prior's " Life of Burke," and Burke's own works. Fo
the slave trade, see the " Memoirs of Wilberforce," by his sons. For th
general condition of foreign affairs, see Sorel, " L'Europe et la Révolutio
Française," and the " Cambridge Modern History."]

**England
and the
World**

The larger and world-wide issues of the establishment of America
Independence lie beyond the scope of the present work, nor can w
dwell here on the political and social influence which America ha
exercised ever since on the mother country itself. What startle
men most at the time was the discovery that England was no
ruined by the loss of her colonies or by the completeness of he
defeat. She rose from it indeed stronger and greater than ever. Th
next ten years saw a display of industrial activity such as the worl
had never witnessed before. During the twenty which followed sh
wrestled almost single-handed against the energy of the Frenc
Revolution, as well as against the colossal force of Napoleoni
tyranny, and came out of the one struggle unconquered and out o
the other a conqueror. Never had England stood higher among th
nations of the old world than after Waterloo; but she was alread
conscious that her real greatness lay not in the old world but in th
new. From the moment of the Declaration of Independence i
mattered little whether England counted for less or more with th
nations around her. She was no longer a mere European power
no longer a mere rival of Germany or Russia or France. She wa
from that hour a mother of nations. In America she had begotte
a great people, and her emigrant ships were still to carry on th
movement of the Teutonic race from which she herself had sprung
Her work was to be colonization. Her settlers were to disput
Africa with the Kaffir and the Hottentot, to wrest New Zealan
from the Maori, to sow on the shores of Australia the seeds of grea
nations. And to these nations she was to give not only her bloo
and her speech, but the freedom which she had won. It is th
thought of this which flings its grandeur round the pettiest detail
of our story in the past. The history of France has little resul
beyond France itself. German or Italian history has no direct issu
outside the bounds of Germany or Italy. But England is only
small part of the outcome of English history. Its greater issues li
not within the narrow limits of the mother island, but in th
destinies of nations yet to be. The struggles of her patriots, th
wisdom of her statesmen, the steady love of liberty and law in he
people at large, were shaping in the past of our little island th
future of mankind.

**The
Rock-
ingham
Ministry**

At the time, however, when this work first became visible in th
severance of America, the wisdom of English statesmen seemed a
its lowest ebb. The fall of Lord North in March 1782 recalled th
Whigs to office; and though the Tories had now grown to a com

ct body of a hundred and fifty members, the Whigs still remained
perior to their rivals in numbers and ability as in distinctness of
litical aim. The return, too, of the Bedford section of their party,
 well as its steady opposition to the American war, had restored
uch of its early cohesion. But the return of this aristocratic and
ctious section only widened the breach which was slowly opening,
a questions such as that of Parliamentary reform, between the
ilk of the Whig party and the small fragment which remained true
 the more popular sympathies of Lord Chatham. Lord Shelburne
as owned as the head of the Chatham party, and it was reinforced
 this moment by the entry into Parliament of the second son of
s earliest leader. William Pitt had hardly reached his twenty-
cond year; but he left college with the learning of a ripe scholar,
d his ready and sonorous eloquence had been matured by the
aching of Chatham. " He will be one of the first men in Parlia-
ent," said a member to the Whig leader, Charles Fox, after Pitt's
st speech in the House of Commons. " He is so already," replied
ox. His figure, tall and spare, but without grace, showed even now
 every movement the pride which was written on the hard lines
 a countenance never lighted by a smile, a pride which broke out
 his cold and repulsive address, his invariable gravity of de-
eanour, and his habitual air of command. How great the qualities
ere which lay beneath this haughty exterior no one knew; nor
d any one guessed how soon this " boy," as his rivals mockingly
yled him, was to crush every opponent and to hold England at
s will. There was only a smile of wonder when he refused any of
ie minor offices which were offered him in the new Whig Adminis-
ation, which in spite of the King's reluctance was formed on the
ll of Lord North under the Marquis of Rockingham.

On Rockingham fell the duty of putting an end at any cost to the Econo-
ar. Ireland was satisfied by the repeal of the Act of George the mical
rst which declared the right of the Parliament of Great Britain Reform
 legislate for the Irish people; and negotiations were begun with
merica and its allies. But more important even than the work of
eace was that of putting an end to those abuses in the composition
 Parliament by which George the Third had been enabled to
lunge the country into war. A thorough reform of the House of
ommons was the only effectual means of doing this, and Pitt
rought forward a bill founded on his father's plans for that purpose.
ut the Whigs could not resolve on the sacrifice of property and
fluence which such a reform would involve. Pitt's bill was thrown
it; and in its stead the Ministry endeavoured to weaken the
eans of corrupt influence which the King had so unscrupulously
sed by disqualifying persons holding government contracts from
tting in Parliament, by depriving revenue officers of the elective
anchise (a measure which diminished the influence of the Crown
 seventy boroughs), and above all by a bill for the reduction of
ie civil establishment, of the pension list, and of the secret service
nd, which was introduced by Burke. These measures were to a

**1783
to
1789**

great extent effectual in diminishing the influence of the Crow
over Parliament, and they are memorable as marking the da
when the direct bribery of members absolutely ceased. They wer
absolutely inoperative in rendering the House of Commons real
representative of or responsible to the people of England. But th
jealousy which the mass of the Whigs entertained for the Chatha
section and its plans was more plainly shown on the death of Lor
Rockingham in July. Shelburne was no sooner called to the hea
of the Ministry than Fox with his immediate followers resigned
Pitt on the other hand accepted office as Chancellor of th
Exchequer.

The
Coali-
tion

The Shelburne Ministry only lasted long enough to conclude th
Peace of Paris; for in the opening of 1783 it was overthrown by th
most unscrupulous coalition known in our history, that of the Wh
followers of Fox with the Tories who still clung to Lord North
Secure in their Parliamentary majority, and heedless of the pow
of public opinion without the walls of the House of Commons, th
new Ministers entered boldly on a greater task than had as ye
taxed the constructive genius of English statesmen. To leave suc
a dominion as Warren Hastings had built up in India to the contr
of a mere company of traders was clearly impossible; and Fo
proposed to transfer the political government from the Directo
of the Company to a board of seven Commissioners. The appoin
ment of the seven was vested in the first instance in Parliamen
and afterwards in the Crown; their office was to be held for fiv
years, but they were removable on address from either Hou
of Parliament. The proposal was at once met with a storm
opposition. The scheme was an injudicious one; for the new Com
missioners would have been destitute of that practical knowledg
of India which belonged to the Company, while the want of an
immediate link between them and the actual Ministry of the Crow
would have prevented Parliament from exercising a real contr
over their acts. But these objections to the India Bill were hard
heard in the popular outcry against it. The merchant-class wa
galled by the blow levelled at the greatest merchant-body in th
realm: corporations trembled at the cancelling of a charter; th
King viewed the measure as a mere means of transferring th
patronage of India to the Whigs. With the nation at large the re
fault of the bill lay in the character of the Ministry which propose
it. The Whigs had a second time rejected Pitt's proposal of Parli
mentary reform; but their coalition with North showed that in a
unreformed Parliament the force of public opinion was unable
check the most shameless efforts of political faction. The power
the Crown had been diminished by the reforms of Lord Rockin
ham to the profit, not of the people, but of the borough-monge
who usurped its representation. To give the rule and patronage
India over to the existing House of Commons was to give a ne
and immense power to a body which misused in the grossest wa
the power it possessed. It was the sense of this popular feelin

which encouraged the King to exert his personal influence to defeat the measure in the Lords, and on its defeat to order his Ministers to deliver up the seals. In December 1783 Pitt accepted the post of First Lord of the Treasury; but his position would at once have been untenable had the country gone with its nominal representatives. He was defeated again and again by large majorities in the Commons; but the majorities dwindled as a shower of addresses from every quarter, from the Tory University of Oxford as from the Whig Corporation of London, proved that public opinion went with the Minister and not with the House. It was the general sense of this which justified Pitt in the firmness with which, in the teeth of addresses for his removal from office, he delayed the dissolution of Parliament for five months, and gained time for that ripening of opinion on which he counted for success. When the elections of 1784 came the struggle was at once at an end. The public feeling had become strong enough for the moment to break through the corrupt influences which generally made representation a farce. Every great constituency returned supporters to Pitt; of the majority which had defeated him in the Commons a hundred and sixty members were unseated; and only a fragment of the Whig party was saved by its command of nomination boroughs.

India owes to Pitt's triumph a form of government which remained unchanged to our own day. The India Bill which he introduced in 1784 preserved in appearance the political and commercial powers of the Directors, while establishing a Board of Control, formed from members of the Privy Council, for the approval or annulling of their acts. Practically, however, the powers of the Board of Directors were absorbed by a secret committee of three elected members of that body, to whom all the more important administrative functions had been reserved by the bill, while those of the Board of Control were virtually exercised by its President. As the President was in effect a new Secretary of State for the Indian Department, and became an important member of each Ministry, responsible like his fellow-members for his action to Parliament, the administration of India was thus made a part of the general system of the English Government; while the secret committee supplied the practical experience of Indian affairs in which the Minister might be deficient. But a far more important change than any which could be wrought by legislative measures took place at this time in the attitude of England itself towards its great dependency. The discussions over the rival India Bills created a sense of national responsibility for its good government. There was a general resolve that the security against injustice and misrule which was enjoyed by the poorest Englishman should be enjoyed by the poorest Hindoo; and this resolve expressed itself in 1786 in the trial of Warren Hastings. Hastings returned from India at the close of the war with the hope of rewards as great as those of Clive. He had saved all that Clive had gained. He had laid the foundation of a vast empire in the East. He had shown rare powers

**1783
to
1789**

of administration, and the foresight, courage, and temperance which mark the real rulers of men. But the wisdom and glory of his rule could not hide its terrible ruthlessness. To glut the ceaseless demands of the Company at home, to support his wars, to feed his diplomacy, he had needed money; and he took it wherever he could find it. He sold for a vast sum the services of British troops to crush the free tribes of the Rohillas. He wrung half a million by oppression from the Rajah of Benares. He extorted by torture and starvation more than a million from the Princesses of Oude. Nor was this all. He had retained his hold upon power by measures hardly less unscrupulous. At the opening of his career, when he was looked upon as helpless before his enemies in the Council, he had shown his power by using the forms of English law to bring Nuncomar, a native who chose the party opposed to him, to death as a forger. When Sir Elijah Impey, the first Chief Justice of Bengal, stood in the way of his plans, he bribed him into acquiescence by creating a fictitious and well-paid office in his favour. It was true that the hands of the Governor-General were clean, and that he had sought for power from no selfish motive, but from a well-grounded conviction that his possession of power was necessary for the preservation of India to the British Crown. But even Pitt shrank from justifying his acts when Burke, in words of passionate eloquence, moved his impeachment. The great trial lingered on for years, and in the long run Hastings secured an acquittal. But the end at which the impeachment aimed had really been won. The crimes which sullied the glory of Hastings have never been repeated by the worst of his successors. From that day to this the peasant of Bengal or of Mysore has enjoyed the same rights of justice and good government as are claimed by Englishmen.

**William
Pitt**

The refusal, in spite of pressure from the King, to shelter Hastings when he had once convinced himself that Hastings was unjust, marked the character of William Pitt. At the moment when the new Parliament came together after the overthrow of the Coalition the Minister of twenty-five seemed master of England as no Minister had been before. Even the King yielded to his sway, partly through gratitude for the triumph he had won for him over the Whigs, partly from a sense of the madness which was soon to strike him down. The Whigs were broken, unpopular, and without a policy. The Tories clung to the Minister who had " saved the King." All that the trading classes had loved in Chatham, his nobleness of temper, his consciousness of power, his patriotism, his sympathy with a wider world than the world within the Parliament-House, they saw in William Pitt. He had little indeed of the poetic and imaginative side of Chatham's genius, of his quick perception of what was just and what was possible, his far-reaching conceptions of national policy, his outlook into the future of the world. Pitt's flowing and sonorous commonplaces rang hollow beside the broken phrases which still make his father's eloquence a living thing to Englishmen. On the other hand he possessed some ualities in which Chatham was utterly wanting. His temper, though naturally ardent and sensitive, had been schooled in a proud self-command. His simplicity and good taste freed him from his other's ostentation and extravagance. Diffuse and commonplace s his speeches seem, they were adapted as much by their very ualities of diffuseness and commonplace, as by their lucidity and good sense, to the intelligence of the middle classes whom Pitt felt be his real audience. In his love of peace, his immense industry, is despatch of business, his skill in debate, his knowledge of nance, he recalled Sir Robert Walpole; but he had virtues which Walpole never possessed, and he was free from Walpole's worst efects. He was careless of personal gain. He was too proud to ile by corruption. His lofty self-esteem left no room for any ealousy of subordinates. He was generous in his appreciation of outhful merits; and the "boys" he gathered round him, such as anning and Lord Wellesley, rewarded his generosity by a devotion hich death left untouched. With Walpole's cynical inaction Pitt ad no sympathy whatever. His policy from the first was one of active reform, and he faced every one of the problems, financial, onstitutional, religious, from which Walpole had shrunk. Above ll he had none of Walpole's scorn of his fellow-men. The noblest eature in his mind was its wide humanity. His love for England as as deep and personal as his father's love, but of the sympathy ith English passion and English prejudice which had been at once is father's weakness and strength he had not a trace. When Fox unted him with forgetting Chatham's jealousy of France and his ith that she was the natural foe of England, Pitt answered nobly lat "to suppose any nation can be unalterably the enemy of nother is weak and childish." The temper of the time and the rger sympathy of man with man, which especially marks the ghteenth century as a turning-point in the history of the human ce, was everywhere bringing to the front a new order of states-en, such as Turgot and Joseph the Second, whose characteristics ere a love of mankind, and a belief that as the happiness of the dividual can only be secured by the general happiness of the mmunity to which he belongs, so the welfare of individual ations can only be secured by the general welfare of the world. these Pitt was one. But he rose high above the rest in the nsummate knowledge and the practical force which he brought the realization of his aims.

Pitt's strength lay in finance; and he came forward at a time English hen the growth of English wealth made a knowledge of finance Industry sential to a great Minister. The progress of the nation itself was onderful. Population more than doubled during the eighteenth ntury, and the advance of wealth was even greater than that of pulation. The war had added a hundred millions to the national ebt, but the burden was hardly felt. The loss of America only creased the commerce with that country. Industry began that eat career which was to make England the workshop of the world.

During the first half of the century the cotton trade, of which Manchester was the principal seat, had only risen from the value of twenty to that of forty thousand pounds; and the hand-loom retained the primitive shape which is still found in the hand-loom of India. But three successive inventions in ten years, that of the spinning-machine in 1768 by the barber Arkwright, of the spinning jenny in 1764 by the weaver Hargreaves, of the mule by the weaver Crompton in 1776, turned Lancashire into a hive of industry. At the accession of George the Third the whole linen trade of Scotland was of less value than the cloth trade of Yorkshire. Before the close of his reign Glasgow was fast rising into one of the trading capitals of the world. The potteries which Wedgewood established in 1763 and in which he availed himself of the genius of Flaxman, soon eclipsed those of Holland or France. Before twenty years had passed more than twenty thousand potters were employed in Staffordshire alone. This rapid growth of manufactures brought about a corresponding improvement in the means of communication throughout the country. Up to this time these had been of the rudest sort. The roads were for the most part so wretched that all cheap or rapid transit was impossible; and the cotton bales of Manchester were carried to Liverpool or Bristol on packhorses. One of the great works of this period was the covering England with a vast network of splendid highways. But roads alone could not meet the demands of the new commerce. The engineering genius of Brindley joined Manchester with its port of Liverpool in 1761 by a canal which crossed the Irwell on a lofty aqueduct; and the success of the experiment soon led to the universal introduction of water-carriage. Canals linked the Trent with the Mersey, the Thames with the Trent, the Forth with the Clyde. The cheapness of the new mode of transit as well as the great advance in engineering science brought about a development of English collieries which soon gave coal a great place among our exports. Its value as a means of producing mechanical force was revealed in the discovery by which Watt in 1765 transformed the Steam Engine from a mere toy into the most wonderful instrument which human industry has ever had at its command. The same energy was seen in the agricultural change which passed gradually over the country. Between the first and the last years of the eighteenth century a fourth part of England was reclaimed from waste and brought under tillage. At the Revolution of 1688 more than half the kingdom was believed to consist of moorland and forest and fen; and vast commons and wastes covered the greater part of England north of the Humber. But the numerous enclosure bills which began with the reign of George the Second and especially marked that of his successor changed the whole face of the country. Ten thousand square miles of untilled land have been added under their operation to the area of cultivation; while in the tilled land itself the production has been more than doubled by the advance of agriculture which began with the travels and treatises of Arthur Young, the introduction of the system of large farms by Mr. Coke of Norfolk, and the development of scientific tillage in the valleys of Lothian.

If books are to be measured by the effect which they have produced on the fortunes of mankind, the " Wealth of Nations " must rank among the greatest of books. Its author was Adam Smith, an Oxford scholar and a professor at Glasgow. Labour, he contended, was the one source of wealth, and it was by freedom of labour, by suffering the worker to pursue his own interest in his own way, that the public wealth would best be promoted. Any attempt to force labour into artificial channels, to shape by laws the course of commerce, to promote special branches of industry in particular countries, or to fix the character of the intercourse between one country and another, is not only a wrong to the worker or the merchant, but actually hurtful to the wealth of a state. The book was published in 1776, in the opening of the American war, and studied by Pitt during his career as an undergraduate at Cambridge. From that time he owned Adam Smith for his master. He had hardly become Minister before he took the principles of the ' Wealth of Nations " as the groundwork of his policy. The ten earlier years of his rule marked a new point of departure in English statesmanship. Pitt was the first English Minister who really grasped the part which industry was to play in promoting the welfare of the world. He was not only a peace Minister and a financier, as Walpole had been, but a statesman who saw that the best security for peace lay in the freedom and widening of commercial intercourse between nations; that public economy not only lessened the general burdens but left additional capital in the hands of industry; and that finance might be turned from a mere means of raising revenue into a powerful engine of political and social improvement.

That little was done by Pitt himself to carry these principles into effect was partly owing to the mass of ignorance and prejudice with which he had to contend, and still more to the sudden break of his plans through the French Revolution. His power rested above all on the trading classes, and these were still persuaded that wealth meant gold and silver, and that commerce was best furthered by jealous monopolies. It was only by patience and dexterity that the mob of merchants and country squires who backed him in the House of Commons could be brought to acquiesce in the changes he proposed. How small his power was when it struggled with the prejudices around him was seen in the failure of the first great measure he brought forward. The question of parliamentary reform had been mooted, as we have seen, during the American war. Chatham had advocated an increase of county members, who were then the most independent part of the Lower House. The Duke of Richmond talked of universal suffrage, equal electoral districts, and annual Parliaments. Wilkes anticipated the Reform Bill of a later time by proposing to disfranchise the rotten boroughs, and to give members in their stead to the counties and to the more populous and wealthy towns. William Pitt had made the question his own by bringing forward a motion for reform on his first entry into the House, and one of his first measures as Minister was to bring in a bill in 1785 which, while providing for the gradual extinction of all decayed boroughs, disfranchised thirty-six at once, and transferred their members to counties. He brought the King to abstain from opposition, and strove to buy off the borough-mongers, as the holders of rotten boroughs were called, by offering to compensate them for the seats they lost at their market-value. But the bulk of his own party joined the bulk of the Whigs in a steady resistance to the bill. The more glaring abuses, indeed, within Parliament itself, the abuses which stirred Chatham and Wilkes to action, had in great part disappeared. The bribery of members had ceased. Burke's Bill of Economical Reform had dealt a fatal blow at the influence which the King exercised by suppressing a host of useless offices, household appointments, judicial and diplomatic charges, which were maintained for the purpose of corruption. Above all, the recent triumph of public opinion had done much to diminish the sense of any real danger from the opposition which Parliament had shown till now to the voice of the nation. "Terribly disappointed and beat" as Wilberforce tells us Pitt was by the rejection of his measure, the temper of the House and of the people was too plain to be mistaken, and though his opinion remained unaltered, he never brought it forward again.

Pitt's
Finance

The failure of his constitutional reform was more than compensated by the triumphs of his finance. When he entered office public credit was at its lowest ebb. The debt had been doubled by the American war, yet large sums still remained unfunded, while the revenue was reduced by a vast system of smuggling which turned every coast-town into a nest of robbers. The deficiency was met for the moment by new taxes, but the time which was thus gained served to change the whole face of public affairs. The first of Pitt's financial measures—his revival of the plan for gradually paying off the debt by a sinking fund which Walpole had thrown aside—was undoubtedly an error; but it had a happy effect in restoring public confidence. He met the smuggler by a reduction of custom-duties which made his trade unprofitable. He revived Walpole's plan of an Excise. Meanwhile the public expenses were reduced, and commission after commission was appointed to introduce economy into every department of the public service. The rapid development of the national industry which we have already noted no doubt aided the success of these measures. Credit was restored. The smuggling trade was greatly reduced. In two years there was a surplus of a million, and though duty after duty was removed the revenue rose steadily with every remission of taxation. Meanwhile Pitt was showing the political value of the new finance. France was looked upon as England's natural enemy. Ireland, then as now, was England's difficulty. The tyrannous misgovernment under which she had groaned ever since the battle of the Boyne was producing its natural fruit; the miserable land was torn with political faction, religious feuds and peasant conspiracies; and so threatening had the attitude of the Protestant party which ruled it become during the American war that they had forced the English Parliament to relinquish its control over their Parliament in Dublin. Pitt saw that much at least of the misery and disloyalty of Ireland sprang from its poverty. The population had grown rapidly while culture remained stationary and commerce perished. And of this poverty much was the direct result of unjust law. Ireland was a grazing country, but to protect the interest of English graziers the import of its cattle into England was forbidden. To protect the interests of English clothiers and weavers, its manufactures were loaded with duties. To redress this wrong was the first financial effort of Pitt, and the bill which he introduced in 1785 did away with every obstacle to freedom of trade between England and Ireland. It was a measure which, as he held, would "draw what remained of the shattered empire together," and repair in part the loss of America by creating a loyal and prosperous Ireland; and though he struggled almost alone in face of a fierce opposition from the Whigs and the Manchester merchants, he dragged it through the English Parliament, only to see it flung aside by the Protestant faction under Grattan which then ruled the Parliament of Ireland. But the defeat only spurred him to a greater effort elsewhere; and his Treaty of Commerce with France in 1787 enabled the subjects of both countries to reside and travel in either without license or passport, did away with all prohibition of trade on either side, and reduced every import duty. But the spirit of humanity which breathed through these measures of commercial freedom soon took a larger scope. The trial of Warren Hastings was rousing England to a more vivid sympathy with the Hindoo; and in the year which followed the adoption of free trade with France the new philanthropy allied itself with the religious spirit created by the Wesleys in an attack on the Slave Trade. At the Peace of Utrecht the privilege of carrying negroes from the coast of Africa to sell them as labourers in the American colonies and the West Indian islands had been counted among the gains which England reaped from the war with Lewis; but the horrors and iniquity of the trade, the ruin and degradation of the native tribes which it brought about, and above all the oppression of the negro himself, were now felt widely and deeply. "After a conversation in the open air at the root of an old tree at Holwood, just above the steep descent into the vale of Keston," Pitt encouraged his friend William Wilberforce, whose position as the Parliamentary representative of the Evangelical party gave weight to his advocacy of such a cause, to bring in a bill for the abolition of the Slave Trade. In spite of Pitt's ardent support, the bill of 1788 fell before the opposition of the Liverpool slave-merchants and the general indifference of the House. But the great movement of which it formed a part was now passing on the other side of the Channel into a revolution which was to change the face of the world.

The Puritan resistance of the seventeenth century had in the end succeeded in checking, so far as England was concerned, the general tendency of the time to religious and political despotism. Since the Revolution of 1688 freedom of conscience and the people's right to govern itself through its representatives in Parliament had been practically established. Social equality had begun long before. Every man from the highest to the lowest was subject to, and protected by, the same law. The English aristocracy, though exercising a powerful influence on government, were possessed of few social privileges, and prevented from forming a separate class in the nation by the legal and social tradition which counted all save the eldest son of a noble house as commoners. No impassable line parted the gentry from the commercial classes, and these again possessed no privileges which could part them from the lower classes of the community. After a short struggle, public opinion the general sense of educated Englishmen, had established itself as the dominant element in English government. But in all the other great states of Europe the wars of religion had left only the name of freedom. Government tended to a pure despotism. Privilege was supreme in religion, in politics, in society. Society itself rested on a rigid division of classes from one another, which refused to the people at large any equal rights of justice or of industry. We have already seen how alien such a conception of national life was from the ideas which the wide diffusion of intelligence during the eighteenth century was spreading throughout Europe; and in almost every country some enlightened ruler endeavoured by administrative reforms in some sort to satisfy the sense of wrong which was felt around them. The attempts of sovereigns like Frederick the Great in Prussia and Joseph the Second in Austria and the Netherlands were rivalled by the effort of statesmen such as Turgot in France. It was in France indeed that the contrast between the actual state of society and the new ideas of public right was felt most keenly. Nowhere had the victory of the Crown been more complete. The aristocracy had been robbed of all share in public affairs; it enjoyed social privileges and exemption from any contribution to the public burdens without that sense of public duty which a governing class to some degree always possesses. Guilds and monopolies at once fettered the industry of the trader and the merchant and cut them off from the working classes, as the value attached to noble blood cut both off from the aristocracy.

If its political position indeed were compared with that of most of the countries round it, France stood high. Its government was less oppressive and more influenced by public opinion, its general wealth was larger and more evenly diffused, there was a better administration of justice, and greater security for public order. Poor as its peasantry seemed to English eyes they were far above he peasants of Germany or Spain. Its middle class was the ꭐuickest and most intelligent in Europe. Opinion under Lewis the ꞁifteenth was practically free, though powerless to influence the ꞁovernment of the country; and a literary class had sprung up ꞁhich devoted itself with wonderful brilliancy and activity to ꝑopularizing the ideas of social and political justice which it ꞁearned from English writers, and in the case of Montesquieu and ꞁoltaire from personal contact with English life. The moral conꞁeptions of the time, its love of mankind, its sense of human brotherꞁood, its hatred of oppression, its pity for the guilty and the poor, ꞁts longing after a higher and nobler standard of life and action, ꞁere expressed by a crowd of writers, and above all by Rousseau, ꞁith a fire and eloquence which carried them to the heart of the ꝑeople. Everywhere the new force of intelligence jostled roughly ꞁith the social forms with which it found itself in contact. The ꝑhilosopher denounced the tyranny of the priesthood. The peasant ꞁrumbled at the lord's right to judge him in his courts and to exact ꞁeudal services from him. The merchant was galled by the trading ꞁestrictions and the heavy taxation. The country gentry rebelled ꞁgainst their exclusion from public life and from the government ꞁf the country. Its powerlessness to bring about any change at ꞁome turned all the new energy into sympathy with a struggle ꞁgainst tyranny abroad. Public opinion forced France to ally itself ꞁith America in its contest for liberty, and French volunteers under ꞁhe Marquis de Lafayette joined Washington's army. But while ꞁhe war spread more widely throughout the nation the craving ꞁr freedom, it brought on the Government financial embarrassꞁent from which it could only free itself by an appeal to the ꞁountry at large. Lewis the Sixteenth resolved to summon the ꞁtates-General, which had not met since the time of Richelieu, and ꞁo appeal to the nobles to waive their immunity from taxation. ꞁIis resolve at once stirred into vigorous life every impulse and ꞁesire which had been seething in the minds of the people; and the ꞁtates-General no sooner met at Versailles in May 1789 than the ꞁabric of despotism and privilege began to crumble. A rising in ꞁ'aris destroyed the Bastille, and the capture of this fortress was ꞁaken for the sign of a new era of constitutional freedom for France ꞁnd for Europe. Everywhere men thrilled with a strange joy at ꞁhe tidings of its fall. "How much is this the greatest event that ꞁver happened in the world," Fox cried with a burst of enthusiasm; ꞁand how much the best!"

Pitt regarded the approach of France to sentiments of liberty ꞁhich had long been familiar to England with characteristic coolꞁess, but with no distrust. For the moment, indeed, his attention ꞁas distracted by an attack of madness which visited the King in ꞁ788, and by the claim of a right to the Regency which was at once ꞁdvanced by the Prince of Wales. The Prince belonged to the Whig ꞁarty; and Fox, who was travelling in Italy, hurried home to ꞁupport his claim in full belief that the Prince's Regency would be

Pitt and
Russia

**1783
to
1789**

followed by his own return to power. Pitt successfully resisted
on the constitutional ground that in such a case the right to choos
a temporary regent, under what limitations it would, lay wit
Parliament; and a bill which conferred the Regency on the Princ
in accordance with this view, was already passing the Houses whe
the recovery of the King put an end to the long dispute. Abroa
too, Pitt's difficulties were increasing. Russia had risen into grea
ness under Catherine the Second; and Catherine had resolved from
the first on the annexation of Poland, the expulsion of the Turk
from Europe, and the setting up of a Russian throne at Constant
nople. In her first aim she was baffled for the moment by Frederic
the Great. She had already made herself virtually mistress of th
whole of Poland, her armies occupied the kingdom, and she ha
seated a nominee of her own on its throne, when Frederick in unio
with the Emperor Joseph the Second forced her to admit German
to a share of the spoil. If the first Polish partition of 1773 brough
the Russian frontier westward to the upper waters of the Dwin
and the Dnieper, it gave Galicia to Maria Theresa, and West Prussi
to Frederick himself. Foiled in her first aim, she waited for th
realization of her second till the alliance between the two Germa
powers was at an end through the resistance of Prussia to Joseph
schemes for the annexation of Bavaria, and the death of Frederic
removed her most watchful foe. Then in 1788 Joseph and th
Empress joined hands for a partition of the Turkish Empire. Bu
Prussia was still watchful, and England was no longer fettered a
in 1773 by troubles with America. The friendship established b
Chatham between the two countries, which had been suspended b
Bute's treachery and all but destroyed during the Northern Leagu
of Neutral Powers, had been restored by Pitt through his co
operation with Frederick's successor in the restoration of the Dutc
Statholderate. Its political weight was now seen in the alliance of
England, Prussia, and Holland in 1789 for the preservation of th
Turkish Empire. A great European struggle seemed at hand; an
in such a struggle the sympathy and aid of France was of th
highest importance. But with the treaty the danger passed away
In the spring of 1790 Joseph died broken-hearted at the failure of
his plans and the revolt of the Netherlands against his innovations
and Austria practically withdrew from the war with the Turks.

Burke

Meanwhile in France things moved fast. By breaking down th
division between its separate orders the States-General became
National Assembly, and abolished the privileges of the provinci
parliaments, of the nobles, and the Church. In October the mo
of Paris marched on Versailles and forced both King and Assembl
to return with them to the capital; and a Constitution, hastily pu
together, was accepted by Lewis the Sixteenth in the stead of h
old despotic power. To Pitt, the tumult and disorder with whic
these great changes were wrought seemed transient matters. I
January 1790 he still believed that " the present convulsions i
France must sooner or later culminate in general harmony an

regular order," and that when her own freedom was established, "France would stand forth as one of the most brilliant powers of Europe." But the coolness and good-will with which Pitt looked on the Revolution was far from being universal in the nation at large. The cautious good sense of the bulk of Englishmen, their love of order and law, their distaste for violent changes and for abstract theories, as well as their reverence for the past, were fast rousing throughout the country a dislike of the revolutionary changes which were hurrying on across the Channel. That the dislike passed slowly into fear and hatred was due above all to the impassioned efforts of Edmund Burke. Forty years before, Burke had come to London as a poor and unknown Irish adventurer. The learning which made him at once the friend of Johnson and Reynolds, and the imaginative power which enabled him to give his learning a living shape, promised him a philosophical and literary career: but instinct drew Burke to politics; he became secretary to Lord Rockingham, and in 1765 entered Parliament under his patronage. His speeches on the Stamp Acts and the American War soon lifted him into fame. The heavy Quaker-like figure, the little wig, the round spectacles, the cumbrous roll of paper which loaded Burke's pocket, gave little promise of a great orator and less of the characteristics of his oratory,—its passionate ardour, its poetic fancy, its amazing prodigality of resources; the dazzling succession in which irony, pathos, invective, tenderness, the most brilliant word-pictures, the coolest argument followed each other. It was an eloquence indeed of a wholly new order in English experience. Walpole's clearness of statement, Chatham's appeals to emotion, were exchanged for the impassioned expression of a distinct philosophy of politics. "I have learned more from him than from all the books I ever read," Fox exclaimed with a burst of generous admiration. The philosophical cast of Burke's reasoning was unaccompanied by any philosophical coldness of tone or phrase. The groundwork indeed of his nature was poetic. His ideas, if conceived by the reason, took shape and colour from the splendour and fire of his imagination. A nation was to him a great living society, so complex in its relations, and whose institutions were so interwoven with glorious events in the past, that to touch it rudely was a sacrilege. Its constitution was no artificial scheme of government, but an exquisite balance of social forces which was in itself a natural outcome of its history and development. In the Revolution of 1688 Burke saw the fated close of a great æra of national progress which had moved on "from precedent to precedent." His temper was in this way conservative, but his conservatism sprang not from a love of inaction but from a sense of the value of social order, and from an imaginative reverence for all that existed. Every institution was hallowed to him by the clear insight with which he discerned its relations to the past and its subtle connexion with the social fabric around it. To touch even an anomaly seemed to Burke to be risking the ruin of a

1783
to
1789

complex structure of national order which it had cost centuries
to build up. " The equilibrium of the Constitution," he said, " has
something so delicate about it, that the least displacement may
destroy it." " It is a difficult and dangerous matter even to touch
so complicated a machine." Perhaps the readiest refutation of
such a theory was to be found in its influence on Burke's practical
dealing with politics. It left him hostile to all movement whatever.
He gave his passionate adhesion to the helpless inaction of the
Whigs. He made an idol of Lord Rockingham, an honest man, but
the weakest of party leaders. He strove to check the corruption of
Parliament by his bill for civil retrenchment, but he took the lead
in defeating all plans for its reform. Though he was the one man
in England who understood with Pitt the value of free industry,
he struggled bitterly against the young Minister's proposals to give
freedom to Irish trade, and against his Commercial Treaty with
France. His work seemed to be that of investing with a gorgeous
poetry the policy of timid content which the Whigs had inherited
from Sir Robert Walpole. The very intensity of his belief in the
natural development of a nation seemed to render him incapable
of understanding that any good could come from particular laws
or special reforms.

Nootka
Sound

It was easy to see in what way a temper such as this would be
stirred by the changes which were now going on in France. The fall
of the Bastille, which kindled enthusiasm in Fox, filled Burke with
distrust. " Whenever a separation is made between liberty and
justice," he wrote a few weeks later, " neither is safe." The night
of the fourth of August, when the privileges of every class were
abolished, filled him with horror. He saw, and rightly saw, in it
the critical moment which revealed the character of the Revolution,
and his part was taken at once. " The French," he cried in January
while Pitt was foretelling a glorious future for the new Constitution,
" the French have shown themselves the ablest architects of ruin
who have hitherto existed in the world. In a short space of time
they have pulled to the ground their army, their navy, their commerce, their arts and their manufactures." But in Parliament he
stood alone. The Whigs, though distrustfully, followed Fox in his
applause of the Revolution. The Tories, yet more distrustfully,
followed Pitt; and Pitt warmly expressed his sympathy with the
constitutional government which was ruling France. At this
moment indeed the revolutionary party gave a signal proof of its
friendship for England. Irritated by an English settlement at
Nootka Sound in California, Spain appealed to France for aid in
accordance with the Family Compact; and the French Ministry
with the constitutional party at its back resolved on a war as the
best means of checking the progress of the Revolution and restoring
the power of the Crown. The revolutionary party naturally opposed
this design; after a bitter struggle the right of declaring war, save
with the sanction of the Assembly, was taken from the King; and
all danger of hostilities passed away. " The French Government,"

Pitt asserted, "was bent on cultivating the most unbounded friendship for Great Britain," and he saw no reason in its revolutionary changes why Britain should not return the friendship of France. He saw that nothing but the joint action of France and England would in the end arrest the troubles of Eastern Europe. His intervention foiled for the moment a fresh effort of Prussia to rob Poland of Dantzic and Thorn. But though Russia was still pressing Turkey hard, a Russian war was so unpopular in England that a hostile vote in Parliament forced Pitt to discontinue his armaments; and a fresh union of Austria and Prussia, which promised at this juncture to bring about a close of the Turkish struggle, promised also a fresh attack on the independence of Poland.

But while Pitt was pleading for friendship between the two countries, Burke was resolved to make friendship impossible. In Parliament, as we have seen, he stood alone. He had long ceased, in fact, to have any hold over the House of Commons. The eloquence which had vied with that of Chatham during the discussions on the Stamp Act had become distasteful to the bulk of its members. The length of his speeches, the profound and philosophical character of his argument, the splendour and often the extravagance of his illustrations, his passionate earnestness, his want of temper and discretion, wearied and perplexed the squires and merchants about him. He was known at last as "the dinner-bell of the House," so rapidly did its benches thin at his rising. For a time his energies found scope in the impeachment of Hastings; and the grandeur of his appeals to the justice of England hushed detraction. But with the close of the impeachment his repute had again fallen; and the approach of old age, for he was now past sixty, seemed to counsel retirement from an assembly where he stood unpopular and alone. But age and disappointment and loneliness were all forgotten as Burke saw rising across the Channel the embodiment of all that he hated—a Revolution founded on scorn of the past, and threatening with ruin the whole social fabric which the past had reared; the ordered structure of classes and ranks crumbling before a doctrine of social equality; a state rudely demolished and reconstituted; a Church and a nobility swept away in a night. Against the enthusiasm of what he rightly saw to be a new political religion he resolved to rouse the enthusiasm of the old. He was at once a great orator and a great writer; and now that the House was deaf to his voice, he appealed to the country by his pen. The "Reflections on the French Revolution" which he published in October 1790, not only denounced the acts of rashness and violence which sullied the great change that France had wrought, but the very principles from which the change had sprung. Burke's deep sense of the grandeur of social order, of the value of that continuity in human affairs "without which men would become like flies in a summer," blinded him to all but the faith in mere rebellion and the yet sillier faith in mere novelty which disguised a real nobleness of aim and temper even in the most

*L 728

ardent of the revolutionists. He would see no abuses in the past,
now that it had fallen, or anything but the ruin of society in the
future. He preached a crusade against men whom he regarded as
the foes of religion and civilization, and called on the armies of
Europe to put down a Revolution whose principles threatened
every state with destruction.

The great obstacle to such a crusade was Pitt: and one of the
grandest outbursts of the " Reflections " closed with a bitter taunt
at the Minister. "The age of chivalry," Burke cried, "is gone;
that of sophisters, economists, and calculators has succeeded, and
the glory of Europe is extinguished for ever." But neither taunts
nor invective moved Pitt from his course. At the moment when the
" Reflections " appeared he gave a fresh assurance to France of his
resolve to have nothing to do with any crusade against the Revolution. "This country," he wrote, "means to persevere in the
neutrality hitherto scrupulously observed with respect to the
internal dissensions of France; and from which it will never depart
unless the conduct held there makes it indispensable as an act of
self-defence." So far indeed was he from sharing the reactionary
panic which was spreading around him that he chose this time for
supporting Fox in his Libel Act, a measure which, by transferring
the decision on what was libellous in any publication from the
judge to the jury, completed the freedom of the press; and himself
passed in 1791 a Bill which, though little noticed among the storms
of the time, was one of the noblest of his achievements. He boldly
put aside the dread which had been roused by the American war,
that the gift of self-government to our colonies would serve only as
a step towards their secession from the mother country, and established a House of Assembly and a Council in the two Canadas. "I
am convinced," said Fox, who gave the measure his hearty support,
" that the only method of retaining distant colonies with advantage
is to enable them to govern themselves; " and the policy of the one
statesman as well as the foresight of the other have been justified
by the later history of our dependencies. Nor had Burke better
success with his own party. Fox remained an ardent lover of the
Revolution, and answered a fresh attack of Burke upon it with
more than usual warmth. A close affection had bound till now the
two men together; but the fanaticism of Burke declared it at an
end. "There is no loss of friendship," Fox exclaimed, with a
sudden burst of tears. "There is!" Burke repeated. "I know the
price of my conduct. Our friendship is at an end." Within the
walls of Parliament, Burke stood utterly alone. His "Appeal from
the New to the Old Whigs," in June 1791, failed to detach a
follower from Fox. Pitt coldly counselled him rather to praise the
English Constitution than to rail at the French. "I have made
many enemies and few friends," Burke wrote sadly to the French
princes who had fled from their country and were gathering in arms
at Coblentz, " by the part I have taken." But the opinion of the
people was slowly drifting to his side. A sale of thirty thousand

copies showed that the "Reflections" echoed the general sentiment of Englishmen. The mood of England indeed at this moment was unfavourable to any fair appreciation of the Revolution across the Channel. Her temper was above all industrial. Men who were working hard and fast growing rich, who had the narrow and practical turn of men of business, looked angrily at its sudden disturbance of order, its restless and vague activity, its rhetorical appeals to human feeling, its abstract and often empty theories. In England it was a time of political content and social well-being, of steady economic progress, and of a powerful religious revival; and the insular want of imaginative interest in other races hindered men from seeing that every element of this content, of this order, of this peaceful and harmonious progress, of this reconciliation of society and religion, was wanting abroad. The general sympathy which the Revolution had at first attracted passed slowly into disgust at the violence of its legislative changes, the anarchy of the country, the bankruptcy of its treasury, and the growing power of the mob of Paris. Sympathy in fact was soon limited to a few groups of reformers who gathered in "Constitutional Clubs," and whose reckless language only furthered the national reaction. But in spite of Burke's appeals and the cries of the nobles who had fled from France and longed only to march against their country, Europe held back from war, and Pitt preserved his attitude of neutrality, though with a greater appearance of reserve.

So anxious, in fact, did the aspect of affairs in the East make Pitt for the restoration of tranquillity in France, that he foiled a plan which its emigrant nobles had formed for a descent on the French coast, and declared formally at Vienna that England would remain absolutely neutral should hostilities arise between France and the Emperor. But the Emperor was as anxious to avoid a French war as Pitt himself. Though Catherine, now her war with Turkey was over, wished to plunge the two German powers into a struggle with the Revolution which would leave her free to annex Poland single-handed, neither Leopold nor Prussia would tie their hands by such a contest. The flight of Lewis the Sixteenth from Paris in June 1791 brought Europe for a moment to the verge of war; but he was intercepted and brought back; and for a while the danger seemed to incline the revolutionists in France to greater moderation. Lewis too not only accepted the Constitution, but pleaded earnestly with the Emperor against any armed intervention as certain to bring ruin to his throne. In their conference at Pillnitz therefore, in August, Leopold and the King of Prussia contented themselves with a vague declaration inviting the European powers to co-operate in restoring a sound form of government in France, availed themselves of England's neutrality to refuse all military aid to the French princes, and dealt simply with the affairs of Poland. But the peace they desired soon became impossible. The Constitutional Royalists in France availed themselves of the irritation caused by the Declaration of Pillnitz to rouse again the cry for a war which,

Confer-
ence of
Pillnitz

as they hoped, would give strength to the throne. The Jacobins on the other hand, under the influence of the " Girondists," o deputies from the south of France, whose aim was a republic, and who saw in a great national struggle a means of overthrowing the monarchy, decided in spite of the opposition of Robespierre on a contest with the Emperor. Both parties united to demand the breaking up of an army which the emigrant princes had formed on the Rhine; and though Leopold assented to this demand, France declared war against his successor, Francis, in April 1792.

Pitt's
Struggle
for
Peace
Misled by their belief in a revolutionary enthusiasm in England the French Constitutionalists had hoped for her alliance in this war but though Pitt at once refused aid and stipulated that Holland must remain untouched, he promised neutrality even though Belgium should for a time be occupied by a French army. In the same temper he announced in 1792 a reduction of military forces and brought forward a Peace Budget which rested on a large remission of taxation. But peace grew hourly more impossible. The French revolutionists, in their eagerness to find an ally in their war, were striving by intrigues with the Constitutional Clubs to rouse the spirit in England which they had roused in France. The French ambassador, Chauvelin, boldly protested against a proclamation which denounced this seditious correspondence. Even Fox, at such a moment, declared that the discussion of Parliamentary reform was inexpedient. Meanwhile Burke was working hard, in writings whose extravagance of style was forgotten in their intensity of feeling, to spread alarm throughout Europe. He had from the first encouraged the emigrant princes to take arms, and sent his son to join them at Coblentz. " Be alarmists," he wrote to them, " diffuse terror!" But the royalist terror which he sowed had at last roused a revolutionary terror in France itself. At the threat of war against the Emperor the two German Courts had drawn together, and reluctantly abandoning all hope of peace with France gathered eighty thousand men under the Duke of Brunswick, and advanced slowly in August on the Meuse. France, though she had forced on the struggle, was really almost defenceless; her army in Belgium broke at the first shock of arms into shameful rout; and the panic, spreading from the army to the nation at large, took violent and horrible forms. At the first news of Brunswick's advance the mob of Paris broke into the Tuileries on the 10th of August; and on its demand Lewis, who had taken refuge in the Assembly, was suspended from his office and imprisoned in the Temple. From this moment the Revolution, if by the Revolution we mean the progress of France towards political, social, and religious freedom, was at an end. The populace of Paris, with the Commune of Paris at its head, imposed its will upon the Assembly and upon the nation. The only changes which France was for a long time to experience were changes of masters; but whether the Commune or the Directory or Buonaparte were its despot, the government was a simple despotism. And despotism, as ever

egan its work with bloodshed and terror. While General Dumouriez by boldness and adroit negotiations arrested the progress of the allies in the defiles of the Argonne, bodies of paid murderers butchered in September the royalist prisoners who crowded the gaols of Paris, with a view of influencing the elections to a new Convention which met to proclaim the abolition of royalty. The retreat of Brunswick's army, whose numbers had been reduced by disease till an advance on Paris became impossible, and a brilliant victory won by Dumouriez at Jemappes which laid the Netherlands at his feet, turned the panic of the French into a wild self-confidence. In November the Convention decreed that France offered the aid of her soldiers to all nations who would strive for freedom. " All Governments are our enemies," said its President; " all peoples are our allies." In the teeth of treaties signed only two years before, and without any pretext for war, the French Government resolved to attack Holland, and ordered its generals to enforce by arms the opening of the Scheldt.

To do this was to force England into war. Public opinion was pressing harder day by day upon Pitt. The horror of the massacres of September, the hideous despotism of the Parisian mob, had done more to estrange England than the Revolution than all the eloquence of Burke. But even while withdrawing our Minister from Paris on the imprisonment of the King, Pitt clung stubbornly to the hope of peace. He had hindered Holland from joining the coalition against France. His hope was to bring the war to an end through English mediation, and to " leave France, which I believe is the best way, to arrange its own internal affairs as it can." No hour of Pitt's life is so great as the hour when he stood alone in England, and refused to bow to the growing cry of the nation for war. Even the news of the September massacres could only force from him a hope that France might abstain from any war of conquest and escape from its social anarchy. In October the French agent in England reported that Pitt was about to recognize the Republic. At the opening of November he still pressed on Holland a steady neutrality. It was France, and not England, which at last wrenched from his grasp the peace to which he clung so desperately. The decree of the Convention and the attack on the Dutch left him no choice but war, for it was impossible for England to endure a French fleet at Antwerp, or to desert allies like the United Provinces. But even in December the news of the approaching partition of Poland nerved him to a last struggle for peace; he offered to aid Austria in acquiring Bavaria if she would make terms with France, and pledged himself to France to abstain from war if that power would cease from violating the independence of her neighbour states. But across the Channel his moderation was only taken for fear, while in England the general mourning which followed on the news of the French King's execution showed the growing ardour for the inevitable contest. Both sides now ceased from diplomatic communications, and in February 1793 France issued her Declaration of War.

France declares War on England

SECTION IV.—THE WAR WITH FRANCE, 1793—1815

[*Authorities.*—To those already mentioned there may be added the biographies of Castlereagh, Eldon, and Sidmouth; the " Memoirs " of Romilly; the Cornwallis Correspondence, and other similar works. For the general history of England, see Lecky, " History of Ireland "; Massey, " History of England during the Reign of George III. "; and May, " Constitutional History." Fortescue, " British Statesmen of the Great War," is very illuminating, and Toynbee, " Industrial Revolution," is a brilliant study of that event. For the Peninsular War, see Napier's " History," and the more recent history by Oman. For contemporary foreign history, Sorel, " L'Europe et la Révolution Française," and Rose, " Napoleon I." Complete bibliographies will be found in the " Cambridge Modern History."]

France and the Coalition

From the moment when France declared war against England Pitt's power was at an end. His pride, his immovable firmness, and the general confidence of the nation still kept him at the head of affairs; but from this moment he drifted along with a tide of popular feeling which he never fully understood. The very excellences of his character unfitted him for the conduct of a war. He was in fact a Peace Minister, forced into war by a panic and enthusiasm which he shared in a very small degree, and unaided by his father's gift of at once entering into the sympathies and passions around him, or of rousing passions and sympathies in return. Politically indeed his task at home became an easy one, for the nation was united by its longing to fight. Even the bulk of the Whigs, with the Duke of Portland, Lords Fitzwilliam and Spencer, and Mr. Wyndham at their head, deserted Fox when he remained firm in his love of France and of the Revolution, and gave their support to the ministry. Abroad all seemed at first to go ill for France. She was girt in by a ring of enemies: the Emperor, Prussia, Saxony, Sardinia, and Spain were leagued in arms against her, and their efforts were seconded by civil war. The peasants of Poitou and Brittany rose in revolt against the Revolutionary government. Marseilles and Lyons were driven into insurrection by the Jacobins, as the more violent leaders who had now seized the supreme power were called, and a great naval port, that of Toulon, not only hoisted the royalist flag, but admitted an English garrison within its walls. The French armies had already been driven back from Belgium and across the Rhine, when ten thousand English soldiers, under the Duke of York, joined the Austrians in Flanders in 1793. But the chance of crushing the Revolution was lost by the greed and incapacity of the allied powers. Russia, as Pitt had foreseen, was now free to carry out her schemes in the East; and Austria and Prussia turned from the vigorous prosecution of the French war to new attacks upon Poland. The allies frittered away in sieges the force which was ready for an advance into the heart of France until the revolt of the West and South was alike drowned in blood. Whatever were the crimes and violence

of the Jacobin leaders at this critical moment, France felt in spite
of them the value of the Revolution, and rallied enthusiastically
to its support. In 1794 the English were driven from Toulon by
a young artillery officer from Corsica, whose name was to become
famous, Napoleon Buonaparte; while a victory at Fleurus again
made the French masters of the Netherlands. At this moment, too,
the overthrow and death of their leader, Maximilian Robespierre,
brought about the downfall of the Jacobins, and a more moderate
government which succeeded, the government of the Directory,
united the whole people in the defence of the country. Victory
everywhere followed on the gigantic efforts with which France met
the coalition against it. Spain was forced to sue for peace, the
Sardinians were driven over the Alps, the provinces along the
Rhine were wrested from the Austrians, and the starving and un-
shod soldiers of the Republic threw back the English army from
the Waal and the Meuse and entered Amsterdam in triumph.

The victories of France broke up the confederacy which had
threatened it with destruction. Spain, Sweden, and Prussia hastened
to make peace with the French Republic. Pitt himself became
earnest for peace. He was indeed without means of efficiently
carrying on the war. The English army was small and without
military experience, while its leaders were utterly incapable. " We
have no General," wrote Lord Grenville, the Minister for Foreign
Affairs, " but some old woman in a red riband." Nor was weakness
and defeat Pitt's only ground for desiring the close of the war.
Inflexible and impassive as he seemed, he felt bitterly that the
contest was undoing all that he had done. The growth of the public
burdens was terrible. If England was without soldiers, she had
wealth, and Pitt was forced to turn her wealth into an engine of
war. He became the paymaster of the Coalition, and his subsidies
brought the allied armies into the field. Immense loans were raised
for this purpose and for a war expenditure at home which was as
useless as it was extravagant. The public debt rose by leaps and
bounds. Taxation, which had reached its lowest point under Pitt's
peace administration, mounted to a height undreamed of before.
The public suffering was increased by a general panic. Burke had
been only too successful in his resolve to " diffuse the terror." The
partisans of France and of republicanism in England were in reality
but a few handfuls of men, who played at gathering conventions
and at calling themselves citizens and patriots in childish imitation
of what was going on across the Channel. But the dread of Revolution soon passed beyond the bounds of reason. Even Pitt, though
still utterly untouched by the political reaction around him, was
shaken by the dream of social danger, and believed in the existence
of " thousands of bandits," who were ready to rise against the
throne, to murder every landlord, and to sack London. " Paine
is no fool," he said to his niece, who quoted to him the " Rights of
Man," in which that author had vindicated the principles of the
Revolution; " he is perhaps right; but if I did what he wants,

1793
to
1815

I should have thousands of bandits on my hands to-morrow, and London burnt." He shared the belief in a social danger with Parliament and with the nation at large. The Habeas Corpus Act was suspended, a bill against seditious assemblies restricted the liberty of public meeting, and a wider scope was given to the Statute of Treasons. Prosecution after prosecution was directed against the Press; the sermons of some dissenting ministers were indicted as seditious; and the conventions of sympathizers with France were roughly broken up. The worst excesses of the panic were witnessed in Scotland, where young Whigs, whose only offence was an advocacy of Parliamentary reform, were sentenced to transportation, and where a brutal judge openly expressed his regret that the practice of torture in seditious cases should have fallen into disuse. In England, however, the social panic soon passed away as suddenly as it had come. In 1794 three leaders of the Corresponding Society, a body which professed sympathy with France, Hardy, Thelwall, and Horne Tooke, were brought to trial on a charge of high treason; but their acquittal proved that the terror was over. Save for occasional riots, to which the poor were goaded by sheer want of bread, no social disturbance appeared in England through the twenty years of the war.

Progress
of the
War

But though failure abroad and panic and suffering at home made Pitt earnest to close the struggle with the Revolution, he stood almost alone in his longings for peace. The nation at large was still ardent for war, and its ardour was fired by Burke in his " Letters on a Regicide Peace," which denounced Pitt's attempt in 1796 to negotiate with France. Nor was France less ardent for war than England. Prussia had become a friend, and Spain an ally, in 1795. Her victories had roused hopes of wider conquests, and though General Moreau was foiled in a march on Vienna, the wonderful successes of Napoleon Buonaparte, who now took the command of the army of the Alps, laid Piedmont at her feet. The year 1797 saw Lombardy conquered in a single campaign; and Austria was forced to purchase peace in the treaty of Campo Formio by the cession of the Netherlands and Milanese to the French Republic. England was left without a single ally. Her credit had sunk to the lowest ebb, and the alarm of a French invasion brought about a suspension of cash payments on the part of the Bank, while a mutiny of the fleet which continued for three months was ended by humiliating concessions. It was in this darkest hour of the struggle that Burke passed away, protesting to the last against the peace which, in spite of his previous failure, Pitt tried in 1797 to negotiate at Lille. But the Minister's efforts were again foiled by the unquenched hatred of the two nations. A French threat of invasion put an end to the depression and disunion which had grown up in England. Credit revived, and in spite of the enormous taxation a public subscription poured two millions into the Treasury towards the expenses of the war. Great military and naval triumphs restored the confidence of the nation. In rejecting

tt's offers of peace the Directory had counted on a rising which
as looked for in Ireland, and on a war in India where Tippoo
hib, the successor of Hyder Ali in Mysore, had vowed to drive
e English from the south.   But in 1798 the Irish rising was
ushed in a defeat of the insurgents at Vinegar Hill; and Tippoo's
ath in the storm of his own capital, Seringapatam, only saved
m from witnessing the English conquest of Mysore.   A yet
eater success awaited the British flag at sea.   Throughout the war
ngland had maintained her naval supremacy, and the triumphs
her seamen were in strange contrast with her weakness on land.
t the outset of the contest the French fleet was defeated and
ippled by Lord Howe in a victory which bore the name of the day
n which it was won, June the 1st, 1794.   When Spain joined the
rench, her fleet was attacked in 1797 by Admiral Jervis off Cape
t. Vincent, and driven with terrible loss back to Cadiz.   When
olland was conquered by France, her navy was used by the con-
uerors to attack the English in the Channel with a view to a
escent on Ireland.   But the Dutch fleet from the Texel was met
y a fleet under Admiral Duncan, and almost annihilated in a
attle of Camperdown in 1797, an obstinate struggle which showed
he Hollanders still worthy of their old renown.   The next year saw
he crowning victory of the Nile.   After his successes in Italy
Napoleon Buonaparte had conceived the design of a conquest of
Egypt and Syria, a march upon Constantinople, and the subjection
f the Turkish Empire.   Only the first step in this vast project was
ated to be realized.   He landed in Egypt, and by a defeat of the
Mamelukes soon reduced that country to submission.   But the
hirteen men-of-war which had escorted his expedition were found
y Admiral Nelson in Aboukir Bay, moored close to the shore in a
ine guarded at either end by gun-boats and batteries.   Nelson
esolved to thrust his own ships between the French and the shore;
is flagship led the way; and after a terrible fight of twelve hours,
ine of the French vessels were captured and destroyed, two were
urnt, and five thousand French seamen were killed or made
risoners.

The battle of the Nile and the failure of Buonaparte in an **England**
nvasion of Syria aided Pitt to revive the coalition of the con- **alone in**
inental powers against France.   A union of the Russian and **the War**
Austrian armies drove the French back again across the Alps and
he Rhine.   Italy and the Rhineland were lost, and only the
enacity of General Massena held Switzerland for the Republic.
The part which England took in this struggle was an invasion of
Holland by a force under the Duke of York, which ended in
miserable failure; but an English captain, Sir Sidney Smith, foiled
Buonaparte's projects on Syria by his defence of Acre, and the
French General, despairing of further success, abandoned his army,
which surrendered at a later time to a British expedition, and
returned to Europe.   The confidence of Pitt in the success of the
Coalition for the first time blinded him to the opening for peace

that offered itself in the new position of French affairs which w
brought about by Buonaparte's return, by his overthrow of t
Directory, and his elevation to the office of First Consul of t
Republic. His offers of peace were no doubt intended simply
dissolve the Coalition, and gain breathing time for a new organiz
tion of France and a new attack on Europe; but their rejection
England was intemperate and unwise. The military genius of t
First Consul, however, soon reversed the hopes of the Allies.
1800 he crossed the St. Bernard, and by his victory at Maren
forced Austria to conclude a peace at Luneville which fixed t
frontiers of France at the Rhine, and established a Cisalpi
Republic, entirely dependent on her, in Lombardy. At the sam
time the surrender to England of the island of Malta, which ha
been taken from the Knights of St. John by a French fleet, an
had ever since been blockaded by English ships, stirred the resen
ment of the Czar Paul, who looked on himself as the patron of t
Knights; and at his instigation Sweden and Denmark join
Russia in a league of armed neutrality, and protested against t
right of search by which England prevented the importation
France in neutral vessels of materials which might be used in wa

But it was at this moment, when England stood once more alon
that Pitt won the greatest of his political triumphs in the union
Ireland with England. The history of Ireland, from its conque
by William the Third up to this time, is one which no Englishma
can recall without shame. Since the surrender of Limerick ever
Catholic Irishman, and there were five Catholics to every Protestan
had been treated as a stranger and a foreigner in his own countr
The House of Lords, the House of Commons, the right of voting f
representatives in Parliament, the magistracy, all corporate offic
in towns, all ranks in the army, the bench, the bar, the who
administration of government or justice, were closed again
Catholics. Few Catholic landowners had been left by the sweepin
confiscations which had followed the successive revolts of th
island, and oppressive laws forced even these few with scar
exceptions to profess Protestantism. Necessity, indeed, ha
brought about a practical toleration of their religion and the
worship; but in all social and political matters the native Catholic
in other words the immense majority of the people of Ireland, wer
simply hewers of wood and drawers of water to their Protestar
masters, who still looked on themselves as mere settlers, wh
boasted of their Scotch or English extraction, and who regarde
the name of "Irishman" as an insult. But small as was th
Protestant body, one half of it fared little better, as far as pow
was concerned, than the Catholics; for the Presbyterians, wh
formed the bulk of the Ulster settlers, were shut out by law from
all civil, military, and municipal offices. The administration an
justice of the country were thus kept rigidly in the hands c
members of the Established Church, a body which comprised abou
a twelfth of the population of the island; while its government wa

actically monopolised by a few great Protestant landowners. he rotten boroughs, which had originally been created to make he Irish Parliament dependent on the Crown, had by this time llen under the influence of the adjacent landlords; whose command of these made them masters of the House of Commons, while hey formed in person the House of Peers. To such a length had his system been carried that at the time of the Union more than xty seats were in the hands of three families alone,—that of Lord ownshire, of the Ponsonbys, and of the Beresfords. One half of he House of Commons, in fact, was returned by a small group of obles, who were recognized as " parliamentary undertakers," and ho undertook to "manage" Parliament on their own terms. rish politics were for these men a mere means of public plunder; hey were glutted with pensions, preferments, and bribes in hard ash in return for their services; they were the advisers of every ord-Lieutenant, and the practical governors of the country. The esult was what might have been expected; and for more than a entury Ireland was the worst governed country in Europe. That s government was not even worse than it was, was due to its onnection with England and the subordination of its Parliament o the English Privy Council. The Irish Parliament had no power f originating legislative or financial measures, and could only say " yes " or " no " to Acts submitted to it by the Privy Council in England. The English Parliament, too, claimed the right of binding Ireland as well as England by its enactments, and one of its tatutes transferred the appellate jurisdiction of the Irish Peerage o the English House of Lords. Galling as these restrictions were o the plundering aristocracy of Ireland, they formed a useful heck on its tyranny. But as if to compensate for the benefits of his protection, England did her best to annihilate Irish commerce nd to ruin Irish agriculture. Statutes passed by the jealousy of English landowners forbade the export of Irish cattle or sheep to English ports. The export of wool was forbidden, lest it might nterfere with the profits of English wool-growers. Poverty was hus added to the curse of misgovernment, and poverty deepened with the rapid growth of the native population, till famine turned he country into a hell.

The bitter lesson of the last conquest, however, long sufficed **Pitt and** o check all dreams of revolt among the natives, and the murders **Ireland** nd riots which sprang from time to time out of the general misery nd discontent were roughly repressed by the ruling class. When evolt threatened at last, the threat came from the ruling class tself. Some timid efforts made by the English Government at the ccession of George the Third to control its tyranny were answered by a refusal of money bills, and by a cry for the removal of the checks imposed on the independence of the Irish Parliament. But t was not till the American war that this cry became a political danger. The threat of a French invasion and the want of any regular force to oppose it compelled the Government to call on Ireland to

provide for its own defence, and forty thousand volunteers appeare
in arms in 1779. The force was wholly a Protestant one, com
manded by Protestant officers, and it was turned to account b
the Protestant aristocracy. Threats of an armed revolt backed th
eloquence of two Parliamentary leaders, Grattan and Flood, i
their demand of " Irish independence; " and the Volunteers bi
for the sympathy of the native Catholics, who looked with ir
difference on these quarrels of their masters, by claiming for the
a relaxation of the penal laws against the exercise of their religio
and of some of their most oppressive disabilities. So real was th
danger that England was forced to give way; and Lord Rocking
ham induced the British Parliament to abandon in 1782 the judicia
and legislative supremacy it had till then asserted over that c
Ireland. From this moment England and Ireland were simpl
held together by the fact that the sovereign of the one island wa
also the sovereign of the other. During the next eighteen year
Ireland was " independent; " but its independence was a mer
name for the uncontrolled rule of a few noble families. The victor
of the Volunteers had been won simply to the profit of the " under
takers," who returned the majority of members in the Irish Hous
of Commons, and themselves formed the Irish House of Lords. Th
suspension of any control or interference from England left Irelan
at these men's mercy, and they soon showed that they meant t
keep it for themselves. When the Catholics claimed admission t
the franchise or to equal civil rights as a reward for their aid in th
late struggle, their claim was rejected. A similar demand of th
Presbyterians, who had formed a good half of the Volunteers, fo
the removal of their disabilities was equally set aside. Eve
Grattan, when he pleaded for a reform which would make th
Parliament at least a fair representative of the Protestant Englishry
utterly failed. The ruling class found government too profitabl
to share it with other possessors. It was only by hard bribery tha
the English Government could secure their co-operation in th
simplest measures of administration. " If ever there was a countr
unfit to govern itself," said Lord Hutchinson, " it is Ireland. /
corrupt aristocracy, a ferocious commonalty, a distracted Govern
ment, a divided people! " The real character of this Parliamentar
rule was seen in the rejection of Pitt's offer of free trade. In Pitt'
eyes the danger of Ireland lay not so much in its factious aristocrac
as in the misery of the people they governed. Although the Irish
Catholics were held down by the brute force of their Protestan
rulers, he saw that their discontent was growing fast into rebellion
and that one secret of their discontent at any rate lay in Iris
poverty, a poverty increased if not originally brought about by
the jealous exclusion of Irish products from their natural markets
in England itself. One of his first commercial measures put an en
to this exclusion by a bill which established freedom of trade
between the two islands. But though he met successfully the fear
and jealousies of the English farmers and manufacturers, he wa

ꞏiled by the factious ignorance of the Irish landowners, and his ꞏll was rejected by the Irish Parliament. So utterly was he dis-ꞏuraged that only the outbreak of the Revolutionary struggle, ꞏd the efforts which France at once made to excite rebellion ꞏmongst the Irish Catholics, roused him to fresh measures of con-ꞏliation and good government. In 1792 he forced on the Irish ꞏarliament measures for the admission of Catholics to the electoral ꞏranchise, and to civil and military offices within the island, which ꞏromised to open a new era of religious liberty. But the promise ꞏame too late. The hope of conciliation was lost in the fast rising ꞏde of religious and social passion. An association of " United ꞏrishmen," begun among the Protestants of Ulster with a view ꞏf obtaining Parliamentary reform, drifted into a correspondence ꞏith France and projects and insurrection. The Catholic peasantry, ꞏrooding over their misery and their wrongs, were equally stirred ꞏy the news from France; and their discontent broke out in the ꞏutrages of " Defenders " and " Peep-o'-day Boys," who held the ꞏountry in terror. For a while, however, the Protestant landowners, ꞏanded together in " Orange Societies," held the country down by ꞏheer terror and bloodshed.

At last the smouldering discontent and disaffection burst into ꞏame. Ireland was in fact driven into rebellion by the lawless ꞏruelty of the Orange yeomanry and the English troops. In 1796 ꞏnd 1797 soldiers and yeomanry marched over the country tortur-ꞏng and scourging the " croppies," as the Irish insurgents were ꞏalled in derision from their short-cut hair, robbing, ravishing, and ꞏurdering. Their outrages were sanctioned by a Bill of Indemnity ꞏassed by the Irish Parliament; and protected for the future by ꞏn Insurrection Act and a suspension of the Habeas Corpus. Mean-ꞏhile the United Irishmen prepared for an insurrection, which was ꞏelayed by the failure of the French expeditions on which they ꞏounted for support, and above all by the victory of Camperdown. ꞏtrocities were answered by atrocities when the revolt at last broke ꞏut in 1798. Loyal Protestants were lashed and tortured in their ꞏurn, and every soldier taken was butchered without mercy. The ꞏebels however no sooner mustered fifteen thousand men strong ꞏn a camp on Vinegar Hill near Enniscorthy than the camp was ꞏtormed by the English troops, and the revolt utterly suppressed. ꞏhe suppression only just came in time to prevent greater disasters. ꞏ few weeks after the close of the rebellion a thousand French ꞏoldiers under General Humbert landed in Mayo, broke a force of ꞏhrice their number in a battle at Castlebar, and only surrendered ꞏvhen the Lord-Lieutenant, Lord Cornwallis, faced them with thirty ꞏhousand men. Lord Cornwallis, a wise and humane ruler, found ꞏnore difficulty in checking the reprisals of his troops and of the ꞏDrangemen than in stamping out the last embers of insurrection; ꞏout the hideous cruelty brought about one good result. Pitt's ꞏlisgust at " the bigoted fury of Irish Protestants " ended in a firm ꞏresolve to put an end to the farce of " Independence," which left

The Union

1793
to
1815

Ireland helpless in their hands. The political necessity for a unic of the two islands had already been brought home to every Engli statesman by the course of the Irish Parliament during the disput over the Regency; for, while England repelled the claims of th Prince of Wales to the Regency as of right, Ireland admitted ther As the only union left between the two peoples was their obedien to a common ruler, such an act might conceivably have ended their entire severance; and the sense of this danger secured welcome on this side of the Channel for Pitt's proposal to unite th two Parliaments. The opposition of the Irish boroughmongers wa naturally stubborn and determined. But with them it was a she question of gold; and the assent of the Irish Parliament was bough with a million in money, and with a liberal distribution of pensior and peerages to its members. Base and shameless as such mean were, Pitt may fairly plead that they were the only means by whic the bill for the Union could have been passed. As the matter wa finally arranged in June 1800, one hundred Irish members becan part of the House of Commons at Westminster, and twenty-eigh temporal with four spiritual peers, chosen for each Parliament b their fellows, took their seats in the House of Lords. Commerc between the two countries was freed from all restrictions, and a the trading privileges of the one were thrown open to the othe while taxation was proportionately distributed between the tw peoples.

Pitt
and the
Peerage

The lavish creation of peers which formed a part of the price pai for the Union of Ireland was only an instance of Pitt's deliberat policy in dealing with the peerage. If he had failed to reform th House of Commons, he was able to bring about a practical chang in our constitution by his reform of the House of Lords. Fe bodies have varied more in the number of their members. At th close of the Wars of the Roses the lay lords who remained numbere fifty-two; in Elizabeth's reign they numbered only sixty; th prodigal creations of the Stuarts raised them to one hundred an sixty-eight. At this point, however, they practically remaine stationary during the reigns of the first two Georges; and, as w have seen, only the dogged opposition of Walpole prevented Lor Stanhope from limiting the peerage to the number it had at tha time reached. Mischievous as such a measure would have bee it would at any rate have prevented the lavish creation of peerage on which George the Third relied in the early days of his reign a one of his means of breaking up the party government whic restrained him. But what was with the King a mere means c corruption became with Pitt a settled purpose of transferring th peerage from a narrow and exclusive caste into a large representa tion of the wealth of England. As he defined his aim, it was to us the House of Lords as a means of rewarding merit, to bring th peerage into closer relations with the landowning and opulen classes, and to render the Crown independent of factious com binations among the existing peers. While himself therefore dis

,inful of hereditary honours, he lavished them as no Minister had vished them before. In his first five years of rule he created fifty w peers. In two later years alone, 1796-7, he created thirty-five. y 1801 the peerages which were the price of the Union with eland had helped to raise his creations to one hundred and forty- ιe. So busily was his example followed by his successors that at e end of George the Third's reign the number of hereditary peers d become double what it was at his accession. Nor was the ange in the peerage merely one of numbers. The whole character the House of Lords was changed. Up to this time it had been a ιall assembly of great nobles, bound together by family or party ?s into a distinct power in the State. By pouring into it members the middle and commercial class, who formed the basis of his ∙litical power, small landowners, bankers, merchants, nabobs, my contractors, lawyers, soldiers and seamen, Pitt revolutionized e Upper House. It became the stronghold, not of blood, but of operty, the representative of the great estates and great fortunes ιich the vast increase of English wealth was building up. For e first time, too, in our history it became the distinctly con- rvative element in our constitution. The full import of Pitt's ιanges has still to be revealed, but in some ways their results ιve been very different from the end at which he aimed. The rger number of the peerage, though due to the will of the Crown, ιs practically freed the House from any influence which the Crown ιn exert by the distribution of honours. This change, since the wer of the Crown has been practically wielded by the House of ∙mmons, has rendered it far harder to reconcile the free action of ιe Lords with the regular working of constitutional government. ∣ the other hand, the larger number of its members has rendered ιe House more responsive to public opinion, when public opinion strongly pronounced; and the political tact which is inherent great aristocratic assemblies has hitherto prevented any collision ith the Lower House from being pushed to an irreconcileable ιarrel. Perhaps the most direct result of the change is seen in ιe undoubted popularity of the House of Lords with the mass of ιe people. The large number of its members, and the constant ∣ditions to them from almost every class of the community, has cured it as yet from the suspicion and ill will which in almost ∕ery other constitutional country has hampered the effective ∕rking of a second legislative chamber.

But the legislative union of the two countries was only part of ιe great plan which Pitt had conceived for the conciliation of eland. With the conclusion of the Union his projects of free trade �ɛtween the two countries, which had been defeated a few years ιck by the folly of the Irish Parliament, came quietly into play; ιd in spite of insufficient capital and social disturbance, the growth f the trade, shipping, and manufactures of Ireland has gone on ∕ithout a check from that time to this. The change which brought ∶eland directly under the common Parliament was followed too

Catholic Emancipation

by a gradual revision of its oppressive laws and an amendment
their administration; taxation was lightened, and a faint beginni
made of public instruction. But in Pitt's mind the great means
conciliation was the concession of religious equality. In proposi
to the English Parliament the union of the two countries he h
pointed out that, when thus joined to a Protestant country li
England, all danger of a Catholic supremacy in Ireland, shou
Catholic disabilities be removed, would be practically at an en
and had suggested that in such a case " an effectual and adequa
provision for the Catholic clergy " would be a security for th
loyalty.   His words gave strength to the hopes of " Cathol
Emancipation," or the removal of the civil disabilities of Catholic
which were held out by Lord Castlereagh in Ireland itself as mea
of hindering any opposition to the project of Union on the part
the Catholics.   It was agreed on all sides that their oppositic
would have secured its defeat; but no Catholic opposition show
itself.   After the passing of the bill, Pitt prepared to lay before t
Cabinet a measure which would have raised not only the Cathol
but the Dissenter to perfect equality of civil rights.   He propos
to remove all religious tests which limited the exercise of t
franchise, or were required for admission to Parliament, t
magistracy, the bar, municipal offices, or posts in the army or t
service of the State.   Political security was provided for by t
imposition, in the place of the Sacramental Test, of an oath
allegiance and of fidelity to the Constitution; while the loyalty
the Catholic and Dissenting clergy was secured by the grant
some provision to both by the State.   To conciliate the Churc
measures were added for strengthening its means of disciplin
and for increasing the stipends of its poorer ministers.   A con
mutation of tithes was to remove a constant source of quarrel i
Ireland between the episcopal clergy and the people.   The schem
was too large and statesmanlike to secure the immediate asser
of the Cabinet, and before that assent could be won the plan wa
communicated through the treachery of the Chancellor, Lor
Loughborough, to George the Third.   " I count any man m
personal enemy," the King broke out angrily to Dundas, " wh
proposes any such measure."   Pitt answered this outburst b
submitting his whole plan to the King.   " The political circun
stances under which the exclusive laws originated," he wrot
" arising either from the conflicting power of hostile and nearl
balanced sects, from the apprehension of a Popish Queen a
successor, a disputed succession and a foreign pretender, a divisio
in Europe between Catholic and Protestant Powers, are no longe
applicable to the present state of things."   But argument wa
wasted upon George the Third.   In spite of the decision of th
lawyers whom he consulted, the King held himself bound by hi
Coronation Oath to maintain the tests; and his bigotry agreed to
well with the religious hatred and political distrust of the Catholic
which still prevailed among the bulk of the English people not t

lake his decision fatal to the bill. Pitt however held firm to its
rinciple; he resigned in February 1801, and was succeeded by the
peaker of the House of Commons, Mr. Addington, a man as dull
nd bigoted as George himself.

Hardly a single member of the Addington Ministry could be
egarded as rising even to the second rank of political eminence,
ut their work was mainly one of peace. Although the debt had
isen from 244 millions to 520, the desire for peace sprang from no
ense of national exhaustion. On the contrary, wealth had never
ncreased so fast. Steam and canals, with the inventions of Ark-
right and Crompton, were producing their effect in a rapid
evelopment of trade and manufactures, and commerce found fresh
utlets in the colonies gained by the war; for the union of Holland
vith the French Republic had been followed by the seizure of the
Jape of Good Hope, of Ceylon, of Malacca, and of the Dutch
oossessions in the Spice Islands. Nor was there any ground for
lespondency in the aspect of the war itself. The Treaty of Lune-
rille, as we have seen, left England alone in the struggle against
France; while an armed neutrality of the Northern powers, with
he Czar Paul of Russia at its head, revived the claim that a
heutral flag should cover even contraband of war. But in 1800
he surrender of Malta to the English fleet gave it the mastery of
the Mediterranean; and General Abercromby, landing with a small
orce in Aboukir Bay, defeated on the 21st of March, 1801, the
French army that Buonaparte had left in Egypt, and which soon
ound itself forced to surrender in the Convention of Cairo. By
ts evacuation of Egypt, India was secured and Turkey saved from
sinking into a dependency of France. In April a British fleet
appeared before Copenhagen, and after a desperate struggle silenced
the Danish batteries, captured the bulk of the Danish ships, and
forced Denmark to withdraw from the Northern Coalition, which
was finally broken up by the death of the Czar. Both parties in
this gigantic struggle however were at last anxious for peace. On
the English side there was a general sense that the struggle with
the Revolution was in fact at an end. Not only had England held
its principles at bay, but the war had at last seated on the throne
of France a military despot who hated the principles of the Revolution even more than England did. So far as France herself was
concerned, the First Consul, Buonaparte, was eager at the moment
for a peace which would enable him to establish his power and to
crush the last sparks of freedom in the country of which he had
made himself in reality the absolute master.

After long negotiations the Peace of Amiens was concluded in
March, 1802, on terms of mutual restitution. France promised
to retire from Southern Italy, and to leave the new republics it had
established in the countries along its border to themselves. England
engaged to give up her newly conquered colonies save Ceylon, and
to replace the Knights of St. John in the isle of Malta. " It is a
peace which everybody is glad of and nobody is proud of," said a

1793
to
1815

witty critic; but there was a general sense of relief at the close o
the long struggle, and the new French ambassador was drawn i
triumph on his arrival through the streets of London. But th
Peace brought no rest to Buonaparte's ambition. It was soon plai
that England would have to bear the brunt of a new contest, bu
of a contest wholly different in kind from that which the Peace ha
put an end to. Whatever had been the errors of the Frenc
Revolutionists, even their worst attacks on the independence o
the nations around them had been veiled by a vague notion o
freeing the peoples whom they invaded from the yoke of thei
rulers. But the aim of Buonaparte was simply that of a vulga
conqueror. He was resolute to be master of the western world
and no notions of popular freedom or sense of national right eve
interfered with his resolve. The means at his command wer
immense. The political life of the Revolution had been cut shor
by his military despotism, but the new social vigour it had give
to France through the abolition of privileges and the creation o
a new middle class on the ruins of the clergy and the nobles stil
lived on. While the dissensions which tore France asunder wer
hushed by the policy of the First Consul, by his restoration of th
Church as a religious power, his recall of the exiles, and the econom
and wise administration which distinguished his rule, the centralize
system of government bequeathed by the Monarchy to the Revolu
tion and by the Revolution to Buonaparte enabled him easily t
seize this national vigour for the profit of his own despotism. Th
exhaustion of the brilliant hopes raised by the Revolution, th
craving for public order, the military enthusiasm and the impuls
of a new glory given by the wonderful victories France had won
made a Tyranny possible; and in the hands of Buonaparte thi
tyranny was supported by a secret police, by the suppression o
the press and of all freedom of opinion, and above all by the iro
will and immense ability of the First Consul himself. Once chose
Consul for life, he felt himself secure at home, and turned restlessl
to the work of outer aggression. The republics established on th
borders of France were brought into mere dependence on his wil
Piedmont and Parma were annexed to France; and a French arm
occupied Switzerland. The temperate protests of the Englis
Government were answered by demands for the expulsion of th
French exiles who had been living in England ever since th
Revolution, and for its surrender of Malta, which was retained ti
some security could be devised against a fresh seizure of the islan
by the French fleet. It was plain that a struggle was inevitable
and in May 1803 the armaments preparing in the French port
hastened the formal declaration of war.

Trafal-
gar

Whatever differences might have parted Whig from Tory in th
earlier war with the Revolution, all were at one in the war agains
the ambition of Buonaparte. England was now the one country
where freedom in any sense remained alive. " Every other monument of European liberty has perished," cried Sir James Mackintosh,

e of the most eminent of the Whig leaders. "That ancient fabric
hich had been gradually raised by the wisdom and virtue of our
refathers still stands; but it stands alone, and it stands among
ins!" With the fall of England despotism would have been
niversal throughout Europe; and it was at England that Buona‧
arte resolved to strike the first blow in his career of conquest.
Fifteen millions of people," he said, in allusion to the dispro‧
ortion between the population of England and France, "must
ve way to forty millions." His attempt to strike at the English
ower in India through the Mahrattas of the central provinces was
iled by their defeat at Assaye; but an invasion of England itself
as planned on a gigantic scale. A camp of one hundred thousand
en was formed at Boulogne, and a host of flat-bottomed boats
athered for their conveyance across the Channel. The peril of the
ation not only united all political parties but recalled Pitt to
ower. On the retirement of Addington in 1804, Pitt proposed to
clude Fox and the leading Whigs in his new Ministry, but he was
iled by the bigotry of the King; and the refusal of Lord Grenville
nd of Wyndham to take office without Fox, as well as the loss of
is post at a later time by his ablest supporter, Dundas, left Pitt
most alone. His health was broken and his appearance was
aggard and depressed; but he faced difficulty and danger with
he same courage as of old. The invasion seemed imminent when
apoleon, who had now assumed the title of Emperor, appeared in
he camp at Boulogne. "Let us be masters of the Channel for six
ours," he is reported to have said, "and we are masters of the
orld." A skilfully combined plan by which the British fleet would
ave been divided, while the whole French navy was concentrated
the Channel, was delayed by the death of the admiral destined
o execute it. But an alliance with Spain placed the Spanish fleet
t Napoleon's disposal in 1805, and he formed a fresh scheme for
s union with that of France, the crushing of the squadron under
ornwallis which blocked the ports of the Channel before Admiral
elson could come to its support, and a crossing of the vast arma‧
nent thus protected to the English shore. Three hundred thousand
olunteers mustered in England to meet the coming attack; but
itt trusted more to a new league which he had succeeded in form‧
ng on the Continent itself. The annexation of Genoa by Napoleon
ided him in his effort; and Russia, Austria, and Sweden joined in
n alliance to wrest Italy and the Low Countries from the grasp of
he French Emperor. Napoleon meanwhile swept the sea in vain
or a glimpse of the great armament whose assembly in the Channel
e had so skilfully planned. Admiral Villeneuve, uniting the
panish ships at Cadiz with his own squadron from Toulon, drew
elson in pursuit to the West Indies and then suddenly returning
o Cadiz hastened to unite with the French squadron at Brest and
rush the English fleet in the Channel. But a headlong pursuit
rought Nelson up with him ere the manœuvre was complete, and
he two fleets met on the 21st of October, 1805, off Cape Trafalgar.

"England," ran Nelson's famous signal, "expects every man t
do his duty;" and though he fell himself in the hour of victory
twenty French sail had struck their flag ere the day was done
"England has saved herself by her courage," Pitt said in wha
were destined to be his last public words: "she will save Europ
by her example!"　　But even before the victory of Trafalga
Napoleon had abandoned the dream of invading England to mee
the coalition in his rear; and swinging round his forces on th
Danube he forced an Austrian army to a shameful capitulation i
Ulm three days before his final naval defeat. From Ulm he marche
on Vienna, and crushed the combined armies of Austria and Russi
in the battle of Austerlitz. "Austerlitz," Wilberforce wrote in hi
diary, "killed Pitt." Though he was still but forty-seven, th
hollow voice and wasted frame of the great Minister had long tol
that death was near; and the blow to his hopes proved fatal
"Roll up that map," he said, pointing to a map of Europe whic
hung upon the wall; "it will not be wanted these ten years!"
Once only he rallied from stupor; and those who bent over hin
caught a faint murmur of "My country! How I leave my country!"
On the 23rd of January, 1806, he breathed his last; and was laic
in Westminster Abbey in the grave of Chatham. "What grave,"
exclaimed Lord Wellesley, "contains such a father and such a
son! What sepulchre embosoms the remains of so much humai
excellence and glory!"

The
Grenville
Ministry

So great was felt to be the loss that nothing but the union o
parties, which Pitt had in vain desired during his lifetime, coulc
fill up the gap left by his death. In the new Ministry Fox, with the
small body of popular Whigs who were bent on peace and interna
reform, united with the aristocratic Whigs under Lord Grenville
and with the Tories under Lord Sidmouth. All home questions, ir
fact, were subordinated to the need of saving Europe from the
ambition of France, and in the resolve to save Europe Fox was as
resolute as Pitt himself. His hopes of peace, indeed, were stronger
but they were foiled by the evasive answer which Napoleon gave
to his overtures, and by a new war which he undertook against
Prussia, the one power which seemed able to resist the arms of
France. By the fatal indecision of the Ministry Prussia was left
unaided till it was too late to aid her; and on the 14th of October,
1806, the decisive victory of Jena laid North Germany at Napoleon's
feet. Death had saved Fox only a month before from witnessing
the overthrow of his hopes; and his loss weakened the Grenville
Cabinet at the moment when one of its greatest errors opened a
new and more desperate struggle with France. By a violent
stretch of her rights as a combatant England declared the whole
coast occupied by France and its allies, from Dantzig to Trieste, to
be in a state of blockade. It was impossible to enforce such a
"paper blockade," even by the immense force at her disposal;
and Napoleon seized on the opportunity to retaliate by the entire
exclusion of British commerce from the Continent, an exclusion

vhich he trusted would end the war by the ruin it would bring on he English manufacturers. Decrees issued from Berlin and Milan rdered the seizure of all British exports and of vessels which had ouched at any British port. The result of these decrees would, he oped, prove the ruin of the carrying trade of Britain, which would ass into the hands of neutrals and especially of the Americans; nd it was to prevent this result that the Grenville Ministry issued)rders in Council in January 1807 by which neutral vessels voyaging o coasts subject to the blockade already declared were compelled n pain of seizure to touch previously at some British port. The erms of a yet wider struggle lay in these Orders; but the fall of he Grenville Ministry was due not so much to its reckless foreign olicy as to its wise and generous policy at home. Its greatest work, he abolition of the Slave Trade in February, was done in the teeth f a vigorous opposition from the Tories and the merchants of Liverpool; and the first indications of a desire to bring about Catholic Emancipation was met on the part of the King by the lemand of a pledge not to meddle with the question, and by the lismissal of the Ministry in March on their refusal to give it.

The dismissal of the Grenville Ministry broke up the union of **Canning** parties; and from this time to the end of the war England was wholly governed by the Tories. The nominal head of the Ministry which succeeded that of Lord Grenville was the Duke of Portland; ts guiding spirit was the Foreign Secretary, George Canning, a young and devoted adherent of Pitt, whose brilliant rhetoric gave him power over the House of Commons, while the vigour and oreadth of his mind gave a new energy and colour to the war. At no time had opposition to Napoleon seemed so hopeless. From Berlin the Emperor marched into the heart of Poland, and though checked in the winter by the Russian forces in the hard-fought oattle of Eylau, his victory of Friedland brought the Czar Alexander in the summer of 1807 to consent to the Peace of Tilsit. From foes the two Emperors of the West and the East became friends, and the hope of French aid in the conquest of Turkey drew Alexander to a close alliance with Napoleon. Russia not only enforced the Berlin decrees against British commerce, but forced Sweden, the one ally which England still retained on the Continent, to renounce her alliance. The Russian and Swedish fleets were thus placed at the service of France, and the two Emperors counted on securing the fleet of Denmark, and threatening by this union the maritime supremacy which formed England's real defence. The hope was foiled by the appearance off Elsinore in July 1807 of an expedition, promptly and secretly equipped by Canning, with a demand for the surrender of the Danish fleet into the hands of England, on pledge of its return at the close of the war. On the refusal of the Danes the demand was enforced by a bombardment of Copenhagen; and the whole Danish fleet with a vast mass of naval stores were carried to British ports. But whatever Canning did to check France at sea, he could do nothing to arrest her progress on land. Napoleon

1793
to
1815

was drunk with success. He was absolutely master of Weste
Europe, and its whole face changed as at an enchanter's touc
Prussia was occupied by French troops. Holland was changed in
a monarchy by a simple decree of the French Emperor, and i
crown bestowed on his brother Louis. Another brother, Jerom
became King of Westphalia, a new realm built up out of t
Electorates of Hesse Cassel and Hanover. A third brother, Josep
was made King of Naples; while the rest of Italy, and even Rom
itself, was annexed to the French Empire.

The Pen-
insular
War

As little opposition met Napoleon's first aggressions in th
Peninsula. In the Treaty of Fontainebleau (Oct. 1807) France an
Spain agreed to divide Portugal between them; and the reignir
House of Braganza fled helplessly from Lisbon to a refuge in Brazi
But the seizure of Portugal was only meant as a prelude to th
seizure of Spain. Charles the Fourth, whom a riot in his capital ha
driven to abdication, and his son Ferdinand the Seventh wer
drawn to Bayonne in May 1808 on pretext of an interview with th
Emperor, and forced to resign their claims to the Spanish crow
while the French army entered Madrid and proclaimed Josep
Buonaparte King of Spain. This infamous act of treachery wa
hardly completed when Spain rose as one man against the stranger
and desperate as the effort of its people seemed, the news of tl
rising was welcomed throughout England with a burst of enthu
siastic joy. "Hitherto," cried Sheridan, a leader of the Whi
opposition, "Buonaparte has contended with princes withou
dignity, numbers without ardour, or peoples without patriotisn
He has yet to learn what it is to combat a people who are animate
by one spirit against him." Tory and Whig alike held that "neve
had so happy an opportunity existed for Britain to strike a bo
stroke for the rescue of the world;" and Canning at once resolve
to change the system of desultory descents on colonies and suga
islands for a vigorous warfare in the Peninsula. Supplies were ser
to the Spanish insurgents with reckless profusion, and two sma
armies placed under the command of Sir John Moore and S
Arthur Wellesley for service in the Peninsula. In July 1808 th
surrender at Baylen of a French force which had invaded Andalusi
gave the first shock to the power of Napoleon, and the blow wa
followed by one almost as severe. Landing at the Mondego wit
fifteen thousand men, Sir Arthur Wellesley drove the French arm
of Portugal from the field of Vimiera, and forced it to surrender i
the Convention of Cintra on the 30th of August. In Spain itsel
the tide of success was soon roughly turned by the appearance c
Napoleon with an army of two hundred thousand men; and Moore
who had advanced from Lisbon to Salamanca to support th
Spanish armies, found them crushed on the Ebro, and was force
to fall hastily back on the coast. His force saved its honour in
battle before Corunna on the 16th of January, 1809, which enable
it to embark in safety; but elsewhere all seemed lost. The whole c
northern and central Spain was held by the French armies; an

en Zaragoza, which had once heroically repulsed them, submitted er a second desperate siege.

The landing of the wreck of Moore's army and the news of e Spanish defeats turned the temper of England from the wildest pe to the deepest despair; but Canning remained unmoved. On e day of the evacuation of Corunna he signed a treaty of alliance th the Spanish Junta at Cadiz; and the English force at Lisbon, ich had already prepared to leave Portugal, was reinforced with irteen thousand fresh troops and placed under the command of r Arthur Wellesley. " Portugal," Wellesley wrote coolly, " may defended against any force which the French can bring against " At this critical moment the best of the French troops with the nperor himself were drawn from the Peninsula to the Danube; r the Spanish rising had roused Austria as well as England to a newal of the struggle. When Marshal Soult therefore threatened sbon from the north, Wellesley marched boldly against him, ove him from Oporto in a disastrous retreat, and suddenly anging his line of operations pushed with twenty thousand men r Abrantes on Madrid. He was joined on the march by a Spanish rce of thirty thousand men; and a bloody action of two days th a French army of equal force at Talavera on the 27th of July, .09, restored the renown of English arms. The losses on both sides ere enormous, and the French fell back at the close of the struggle; at the fruits of the victory were lost by the sudden appearance of ault on the English line of advance, and Wellesley was forced to treat hastily on Badajoz. His failure was embittered by heavier sasters elsewhere. Austria was driven to sue for peace by apoleon's victory at Wagram; and a force of forty thousand nglish soldiers which had been despatched against Antwerp in uly returned home baffled after losing half its numbers in the arshes of Walcheren.

The failure at Walcheren brought about the fall of the Portland inistry. Canning attributed the disaster to the incompetence of ord Castlereagh, an Irish peer who after taking the chief part in inging about the union between England and Ireland had been ised by the Duke of Portland to the post of Secretary at War; and e quarrel between the two Ministers ended in a duel and in their signation of their offices (Sept. 1809). The Duke of Portland tired; and a new Ministry was formed out of the more Tory embers of the late administration under the guidance of Spencer erceval, an industrious mediocrity of the narrowest type; the arquis of Wellesley, a brother of the English general in Spain, ecoming Foreign Secretary. But if Perceval and his colleagues ossessed few of the higher qualities of statesmanship, they had 1e characteristic which in the actual position of English affairs as beyond all price. They were resolute to continue the war. 1 the nation at large the fit of enthusiasm had been followed by fit of despair; and the City of London even petitioned for a ithdrawal of the English forces from the Peninsula. Napoleon

seemed irresistible, and now that Austria was crushed and Englan
stood alone in opposition to him, the Emperor resolved to put a
end to the strife by a strict enforcement of the Continental Syste
and a vigorous prosecution of the war in Spain. Andalusia, th
one province which remained independent, was invaded in th
opening of 1810, and with the exception of Cadiz reduced to sul
mission. Marshal Massena with a fine army of eighty thousan
men marched upon Lisbon. Even Perceval abandoned all hope
preserving a hold on the Peninsula in face of these new effort
and threw on Wellesley, who had been raised to the peerage a
Lord Wellington after Talavera, the responsibility of resolving t
remain there. But the cool judgment and firm temper which di
tinguished Wellington enabled him to face a responsibility fro
which weaker men would have shrunk. " I conceive," he answere
" that the honour and interest of our country require that w
should hold our ground here as long as possible; and, please Go
I will maintain it as long as I can." By the addition of Portugue
troops who had been trained under British officers, his army wa
now raised to fifty thousand men; and though his inferiority i
force compelled him to look on while Massena reduced the fronti
fortresses of Ciudad Rodrigo and Almeida, he inflicted on him
heavy check at the heights of Busaco, and finally fell back i
October 1810 on three lines of defence which he had secretly co
structed at Torres Vedras, along a chain of mountain heigh
crowned with redoubts and bristling with cannon. The positic
was impregnable; and able and stubborn as Massena was he foun
himself forced after a month's fruitless efforts to fall back in
masterly retreat; but so terrible were the privations of the Frenc
army in passing again through the wasted country that it wa
only with forty thousand men that he reached Ciudad Rodrig
in the spring of 1811. Reinforced by fresh troops, Massena turne
fiercely to the relief of Almeida, which Wellington had besieged
but two days' bloody and obstinate fighting on the 5th of May, 181
failed to drive the English army from its position at Fuente
d'Onoro, and the Marshal fell back on Salamanca and relinquishe
his effort to drive Wellington from Portugal.

England
and
America

Great as was the effect of Torres Vedras in restoring the spirit
the English people and in reviving throughout Europe the hope
resistance to the tyranny of Napoleon, its immediate result wa
little save the deliverance of Portugal. The French remaine
masters of all Spain save Cadiz and the eastern provinces, and eve
the east coast was reduced in 1811 by the vigour of General Suche
An attempt of Wellington to retake Badajoz was foiled by th
co-operation of the army of the South under Marshal Soult wit
that of the North under Marshal Marmont; and a fruitless attac
on Almeida wasted the rest of the year. Not only was the Frenc
hold on Spain too strong to be shaken by the force at Wellington'
disposal, but the Continental System of Napoleon was beginnin
to involve England in dangers which he was far from having fore

een. His effort to exclude English exports from the Continent had
een foiled by the rise of a vast system of contraband trade, by
he evasions practised in the Prussian and Russian ports, and by
he rapid development of the carrying trade under neutral flags.
'he French army itself was clad in great coats made at Leeds, and
hod with shoes from Northampton. But if Napoleon's direct blow
t England had failed to bring about any serious results, the Orders
ı Council with which the Grenville Ministry had attempted to
revent the transfer of the carrying trade from English to neutral
hips, by compelling all vessels on their way to ports under blockade
ɔ touch at British harbours, had at once created serious embarrass-
ɪents with America. A year after the issue of these Orders America
ɛplied to both combatants by a Non-Intercourse Act (March 1808),
'hich suspended all trade between either France or England and
he United States. Napoleon adroitly met this measure by an offer
ɔ withdraw the restrictions he had imposed on neutral trade if
ᴀmerica compelled England to show equal respect to her flag; but
ɪo concession could be obtained from the Perceval Cabinet. The
ɪuarrel between the two countries was embittered by the assertion
ɪ England's side of a "right of search," which compelled American
essels to surrender any British subjects who formed part of their
ɾew and who were claimed as deserters from the English navy.
ɪ 1811 Napoleon fulfilled his pledge of removing all obstacles to
ᴀmerican trade, and America repealed the Non-Intercourse Act as
ᴀr as it related to France. But no corresponding concession could
e wrung from the English Government; though the closing of the
ᴀmerican ports inflicted a heavier blow on British commerce than
ny which the Orders could have aimed at preventing. During 1811
ɪdeed English exports were reduced by one-third of their whole
ɪmount. In America the irritation at last brought about a cry for
ɾar which, in spite of the resolute opposition of the New England
tates, forced Congress to raise an army of twenty-five thousand
ɪen, and to declare the impressment of seamen sailing under an
ᴀmerican flag to be piracy. England at last consented to withdraw
er Orders in Council, but the concession was made too late to
ɪvert a declaration of war on the part of the United States in
une, 1812.

The moment when America entered into the great struggle was a
ritical moment in the history of mankind. Six days after President
Iadison issued his declaration of war, Napoleon crossed the Niemen
ɪ his march to Moscow. Successful as his Continental System had
een in stirring up war between England and America, it had been
ɔ less successful in breaking the alliance which he had made with
he Emperor Alexander at Tilsit and in forcing on a contest with
ɾussia which was destined to be a fatal one. On the one hand,
ɪapoleon was irritated by the refusal of Russia to enforce strictly
he suspension of all trade with England, though such a suspension
ɾould have ruined the Russian landowners. On the other, the Czar
ᴀw with growing anxiety the advance of the French Empire which

Sala-
manca
and
Moscow

M 728

sprang from Napoleon's resolve to enforce his system by a seizur
of the northern coasts. In 1811 Holland, the Hanseatic towns, pa
of Westphalia, and the Duchy of Oldenburg were successivel
annexed, and the Duchy of Mecklenburg threatened with seizur
A peremptory demand on the part of France for the entire cessatio
of intercourse with England brought the quarrel to a head; an
preparations were made on both sides for a gigantic struggle. Th
best of the French soldiers were drawn from Spain to the frontie
of Poland; and Wellington, whose army had been raised to a forc
of forty thousand Englishmen and twenty thousand Portuguese
profited by the withdrawal to throw off his system of defence an
to assume an attitude of attack. Ciudad Rodrigo and Badajo
were taken by storm during the spring of 1812; and three day
before Napoleon crossed the Niemen (June 24) in his march o
Moscow, Wellington crossed the Agueda in a march on Salamanca
After a series of masterly movements on both sides, Marmont wit
the French army of the North attacked the English on the hills i
the neighbourhood of that town (July 22). While marching roun
the right of the English position, the French left wing was le
isolated; and with a sudden exclamation of " Marmont is lost!
Wellington flung on it the bulk of his force, crushed it, and drov
the whole army from the field. The loss on either side was nearl
equal, but failure had demoralized the French army; and i
retreat forced Joseph to leave Madrid, and Soult to evacuat
Andalusia and to concentrate the southern army on the easter
coast. While Napoleon was still pushing slowly over the vast plain
of Poland, Wellington made his entry into Madrid in August, an
began the siege of Burgos. The town however held out gallantl
for a month, till the advance of the two French armies, now co
centrated in the north and south of Spain, forced Wellingto
(Oct. 18) to a hasty retreat on the Portuguese frontier. A day lat
(Oct. 19) began the more fatal retreat of the Grand Army fro
Moscow. Victorious in the battle of Borodino, Napoleon ha
entered the older capital of Russia in triumph, and waited in
patiently to receive proposals of peace from the Czar, when a fir
kindled by its own inhabitants reduced the city to ashes. Th
French army was forced to fall back amidst the horrors of
Russian winter. Of the four hundred thousand combatants wh
formed the Grand Army at its first outset, only a few thousan
recrossed the Niemen in December.

Gallantly as Napoleon was still to struggle against the foes wh
sprang up around him, his ruin became certain from the hour whe
he fell back from Moscow. But a new English Ministry reaped th
glory of success in the long struggle with his ambition. A return c
the King's madness had made it necessary in the beginning of 181
to confer the Regency by Act of Parliament on the Prince of Wales
and the Whig sympathies of the Prince threatened the Perceva
Cabinet with dismissal. The insecurity of their position told on th
conduct of the war; for much of Wellington's apparent inactivit

during 1811 was really due to the hesitation and timidity of the Ministers at home. In May 1812 the assassination of Perceval by a maniac named Bellingham brought about the fall of his Ministry and fresh efforts to install the Whigs in office. But the attempt was as fruitless as ever, and the old Ministry was restored under the guidance of the Earl of Liverpool, a man of no great abilities, but temperate, well informed, and endowed with a singular gift of holding discordant colleagues together. But the death of Perceval marks more than a mere change of Ministry. From that moment the development of English life, which had been roughly arrested in 1792 by the reaction against the French Revolution, began again to take its natural course. The anti-revolutionary terror which Burke did so much to rouse had spent most of its force by the time of the Peace of Amiens; and though the country was unanimous in the after-struggle against the ambition of Buonaparte, the social distress which followed on the renewal of the war revived questions of internal reform which had been set aside ever since the outbreak of the French Revolution as Jacobinical. The natural relation of trade and commerce to the general wealth of the people at large was disturbed by the peculiar circumstances of the time. The war enriched the landowner, the capitalist, the manufacturer, the farmer; but it impoverished the poor. It is indeed from the fatal years which lie between the Peace of Amiens and Waterloo that we must date that war of classes, that social severance between rich and poor, between employers and employed, which still forms the great difficulty of English politics.

The increase of wealth was indeed enormous. England was sole mistress of the seas. The war had given her possession of the colonies of Spain, of Holland, and of France; and if her trade was checked for a time by the Berlin decrees, the efforts of Napoleon were soon rendered fruitless by the vast smuggling system which sprang up along the coast of North Germany. In spite of the far more serious blow which commerce received from the quarrel with America, English exports nearly doubled in the last fifteen years of the war. Manufactures profited by the great discoveries of Watt and Arkwright; and the consumption of raw cotton in the mills of Lancashire rose during the same period from fifty to a hundred millions of pounds. The vast accumulation of capital, as well as the constant recurrence of bad seasons at this time, told upon the land, and forced agriculture into a feverish and unhealthy prosperity. Wheat rose to famine prices, and the value of land rose in proportion with the price of wheat. Inclosures went on with prodigious rapidity; the income of every landowner was doubled, while the farmers were able to introduce improvements into the processes of agriculture which changed the whole face of the country. But if the increase of wealth was enormous, its distribution was partial. During the fifteen years which preceded Waterloo, the number of the population rose from ten to thirteen millions, and this rapid increase kept down the rate of wages, which would naturally have advanced in a corresponding degree with the increase in the national wealth. Even manufactures, though destined in the long run to benefit the labouring classes, seemed at first rather to depress them. One of the earliest results of the introduction of machinery was the ruin of a number of small trades which were carried on at home, and the pauperization of families who relied on them for support. In the winter of 1811 the terrible pressure of this transition from handicraft to machinery was seen in the Luddite, or machine-breaking, riots which broke out over the northern and midland counties; and which were only suppressed by military force. While labour was thus thrown out of its older grooves, and the rate of wages kept down at an artificially low figure by the rapid increase of population, the rise in the price of wheat, which brought wealth to the landowner and the farmer, brought famine and death to the poor, for England was cut off by the war from the vast corn-fields of the Continent or of America, which now-a-days redress from their abundance the results of a bad harvest. Scarcity was followed by a terrible pauperization of the labouring classes. The amount of the poor-rate rose fifty per cent.; and with the increase of poverty followed its inevitable result, the increase of crime.

Revival
of
Reform
The sense both of national glory and of national suffering told, however feebly, on the course of politics at home. Under the Perceval Ministry a blind opposition had been offered by the Government to every project of change or reform: but the terror-struck reaction against the French Revolution which this opposition strove to perpetuate was even then passing away. The publication of the *Edinburgh Review* in 1802 by a knot of young lawyers at Edinburgh, (Brougham, Jeffrey, Horner, and Mackintosh,) marked the revival of the policy of constitutional and administrative progress which had been reluctantly abandoned by William Pitt. Jeremy Bentham gave a new vigour to political speculation by his advocacy of the doctrine of Utility, and his definition of " the greatest happiness of the greatest number " as the aim of political action. In 1809 Sir Francis Burdett revived the question of Parliamentary Reform. Only fifteen members supported his motion; and a reference to the House of Commons, in a pamphlet which he subsequently published, as " a part of our fellow-subjects collected together by means which it is not necessary to describe " was met by his committal to the Tower, where he remained till the prorogation of the Parliament. A far greater effect was produced by the perseverance with which Canning pressed year by year the question of Catholic Emancipation. So long as Perceval lived both efforts at Reform were equally vain; but on the accession of Lord Liverpool to power the advancing strength of a more liberal sentiment in the nation was felt by the policy of " moderate concession " which was adopted by the new Ministry. Catholic Emancipation became an open question in the Cabinet itself, and was adopted in 1812 by a triumphant

majority in the House of Commons, though still rejected by the Lords.

From this moment, however, all questions of home politics were again thrown into the background by the absorbing interest of the war. In spite of the gigantic efforts which Napoleon made to repair the loss of the Grand Army, the spell which he had cast over Europe was broken by the retreat from Moscow. Prussia rose against him as the Russian army advanced across the Niemen, and the French were at once thrown back on the Elbe. In May 1813 Wellington again left Portugal with an army which had now risen to ninety thousand men; and overtaking the French forces in retreat at Vittoria inflicted on them a defeat (June 21) which drove them in utter rout across the Pyrenees. Madrid was at once evacuated; and Clauzel fell back from Zaragoza into France. The victory not only freed Spain from its invaders; it restored the spirit of the Allies at the darkest hour of their new fortunes. The genius of Napoleon rose to its height in his last campaigns. With a fresh army of two hundred thousand men whom he had gathered at Mainz he marched on the allied armies of Russia and Prussia in May, cleared Saxony by a victory over them at Lutzen, and threw them back on the Oder by a fresh victory at Bautzen. Disheartened by defeat, and by the neutral attitude which Austria still preserved, the two powers consented in June to an armistice, and negotiated for peace; but the loss of Spain and Wellington's advance on the Pyrenees gave a new vigour to their councils. The close of the armistice was followed by the union of Austria with the Allied Powers; and a terrible overthrow of Napoleon at Leipzig in October forced the French army to cross the Rhine. Meanwhile the sieges of San Sebastian and of Pampeluna, with the obstinate defence of Marshal Soult in the Pyrenees, held Wellington for a time at bay; and it was only in October that a victory on the Bidassoa enabled him to enter France and to force Soult from his entrenched camp before Bayonne. But the war was now hurrying to its close. On the last day of 1813 the allies crossed the Rhine, and in a month a third of France had passed without opposition into their hands. Soult, again defeated by Wellington at Orthez, fell back on Toulouse: and Bordeaux, then left uncovered, hardly waited the arrival of the English forces to hoist the white flag of the Bourbons. On the 10th of April, 1814, Wellington again attacked Soult at Toulouse in an obstinate and indecisive engagement; but though neither general knew it, the war was at that moment at an end. The wonderful struggle which Napoleon with a handful of men had maintained for two months against the overwhelming forces of the Allies closed with the surrender of Paris on the 31st of March; and the submission of the capital was at once followed by the abdication of the Emperor and the return of the Bourbons.

England's triumph over its great enemy was dashed by the more doubtful fortunes of the struggle which Napoleon had kindled across the Atlantic. The declaration of war by America in Jun 1812 seemed an act of sheer madness. The American navy consisted of a few frigates and sloops; its army was a mass of half-drilled and half-armed recruits; the States themselves were divided on the question of the war; and Connecticut with Massachusett refused to send either money or men. Three attempts to penetrate into Canada during the summer and autumn were repulsed with heavy loss. But these failures were more than redeemed by unexpected successes at sea. In two successive engagements between English and American frigates, the former were forced to strike their flag. The effect of these victories was out of all proportion to their real importance; for they were the first heavy blows which had been dealt at England's supremacy over the seas. In 1813 America followed up its naval triumphs by more vigorous efforts on land. Its forces cleared Lake Ontario, captured Toronto, destroyed the British flotilla on Lake Erie, and made themselves masters of Upper Canada. An attack on Lower Canada, however, was successfully beaten back; and a fresh advance of the British and Canadian forces in the heart of the winter again recovered the Upper Province. The reverse gave fresh strength to the party in the United States which had throughout been opposed to the war, and whose opposition to it had been embittered by the terrible distress brought about by the blockade and the ruin of American commerce. Cries of secession began to be heard, and Massachusetts took the bold step of appointing delegates to confer with delegates from the other New England States "on the subject of their grievances and common concerns." In 1814, however, the war was renewed with more vigour than ever. Upper Canada was again invaded, but the American army, after inflicting a severe defeat on the British forces in the battle of Chippewa in July, was itself defeated a few weeks after in an equally stubborn engagement, and thrown back on its own frontier. The fall of Napoleon now enabled the English Government to devote its whole strength to the struggle with an enemy which it had at last ceased to despise. General Ross, with a force of four thousand men, appeared in the Potomac, captured Washington, and before evacuating the city burnt its public buildings to the ground. Few more shameful acts are recorded in our history; and it was the more shameful in that it was done under strict orders from the Government at home. The raid upon Washington, however, was intended simply to strike terror into the American people; and the real stress of the war was thrown on two expeditions whose business was to penetrate into the States from the north and from the south. Both proved utter failures. A force of nine thousand Peninsular veterans which marched in September to the attack of Plattsburg on Lake Champlain was forced to fall back by the defeat of the English flotilla which accompanied it. A second force under General Packenham appeared in December at the mouth of the Mississippi and attacked New Orleans, but was repulsed by General Jackson with the loss of half its numbers. Peace, however, had already been concluded. The close of the French war removed the causes of the struggle, and the claims, whether of the English or of the Americans, were set aside in silence in the new treaty of 1814.

The close of the war with America freed England's hands at a moment when the reappearance of Napoleon at Paris called her to a new and final struggle with France. By treaty with the Allied Powers Napoleon had been suffered to retain a fragment of his former empire—the island of Elba off the coast of Tuscany; and from Elba he had looked on at the quarrels which sprang up between his conquerors as soon as they gathered at Vienna to complete the settlement of Europe. The most formidable of these quarrels arose from the claim of Prussia to annex Saxony and that of Russia to annex Poland; but their union for this purpose was met by a counter-league of England and Austria with their old enemy, France, whose ambassador, Talleyrand, laboured vigorously to bring the question to an issue by force of arms. At the moment, however, when a war between the two leagues seemed close at hand, Napoleon quitted Elba, landed on the 1st March, 1815, on the coast near Cannes, and, followed only by a thousand of his guards, marched over the mountains of Dauphiné upon Grenoble and Lyons. He counted, and counted justly, on the indifference of the country to its new Bourbon rulers, on the longing of the army for a fresh struggle which should restore its glory, and above all in the spell of his name over soldiers whom he had so often led to victory. In twenty days from his landing he reached the Tuileries unopposed, while Lewis the Eighteenth fled helplessly to Ghent. But whatever hopes he had drawn from the divisions of the Allied Powers were at once dispelled by their resolute action on the news of his descent upon France. Their strife was hushed and their old union restored by the consciousness of a common danger. A Declaration adopted instantly by all put Napoleon to the ban of Europe. " In breaking the convention which had established him in the island of Elba, Buonaparte has destroyed the sole legal title to which his political existence is attached. By reappearing in France with projects of trouble and overthrow he has not less deprived himself of the protection of the laws, and made it evident in the face of the universe that there can no longer be either peace or truce with him. The Powers, therefore, declare that Buonaparte has placed himself out of the pale of civil and social relations, and that as the general enemy and disturber of the world he is abandoned to public justice." An engagement to supply a million of men for the purposes of the war, and a recall of their armies to the Rhine, gave practical effect to the words of the Allies. England furnished subsidies to the amount of eleven millions to support these enormous hosts, and hastened to place an army on the frontier of the Netherlands. The best troops of the force which had been employed in the Peninsula, however, were still across the Atlantic; and of the eighty thousand men who gathered round Wellington only about a half were English-

men, the rest principally raw levies from Belgium and Hanover
The Duke's plan was to unite with the one hundred and fifty
thousand Prussians under Marshal Blucher who were advancing
on the Lower Rhine, and to enter France by Mons and Namur
while the forces of Austria and Russia closed in upon Paris by way
of Belfort and Elsass.

But Napoleon had thrown aside all thought of a merely defensive
war. By amazing efforts he had raised an army of two hundred and
fifty thousand men in the few months since his arrival in Paris
and in the opening of June one hundred and twenty thousand
Frenchmen were concentrated on the Sambre at Charleroi, while
Wellington's troops still lay in cantonments on the line of the
Scheldt from Ath to Nivelles, and Blucher's on that of the Meuse
from Nivelles to Liege. Both the allied armies hastened to unite
at Quatre Bras; but their junction was already impossible. Blucher
with eighty thousand men was himself attacked on the 16th by
Napoleon at Ligny, and after a desperate contest driven back with
terrible loss upon Wavre. On the same day Ney with twenty
thousand men, and an equal force under D'Erlon in reserve
appeared before Quatre Bras, where as yet only ten thousand
English and the same force of Belgian troops had been able to
assemble. The Belgians broke before the charges of the French
horse; but the dogged resistance of the English infantry gave time
for Wellington to bring up corps after corps, till at the close of the
day Ney saw himself heavily outnumbered, and withdrew baffled
from the field. About five thousand men had fallen on either side
in this fierce engagement: but heavy as was Wellington's loss, the
firmness of the English army had already done much to foil
Napoleon's effort at breaking through the line of the Allies.
Blucher's retreat, however, left the English flank uncovered; and
on the following day, while the Prussians were falling back on
Wavre, Wellington with nearly seventy thousand men—for his
army was now well in hand—withdrew in good order upon
Waterloo, followed by the mass of the French forces under the
Emperor himself. Napoleon had detached Marshal Grouchy with
thirty thousand men to hang upon the rear of the beaten Prussians,
while with a force of eighty thousand men he resolved to bring
Wellington to battle. On the morning of the 18th of June the two
armies faced one another on the field of Waterloo in front of the
forest of Soignies, on the high road to Brussels. Napoleon's one
fear had been that of a continued retreat. " I have them! " he
cried, as he saw the English line drawn up on a low rise of ground
which stretched across the high road from the château of Hougomont on its right to the farm and straggling village of La Haye
Sainte on its left. He had some grounds for his confidence of
success. On either side the forces numbered between seventy and
eighty thousand men: but the French were superior in guns and
cavalry, and a large part of Wellington's force consisted of Belgian
levies who broke and fled at the outset of the fight. A fierce attack

upon Hougomont opened the battle at eleven; but it was not till midday that the corps of D'Erlon advanced upon the centre near La Haye Sainte, which from that time bore the main brunt of the struggle. Never has greater courage, whether of attack or endurance, been shown on any field than was shown by both combatants at Waterloo. The columns of D'Erlon, repulsed by the English foot, were hurled back in disorder by a charge of the Scots Greys; but the victorious horsemen were crushed in their turn by the French cuirassiers, and the mass of the French cavalry, twelve thousand strong, flung itself in charge after charge on the English front, carrying the English guns and sweeping with desperate bravery round the unbroken squares whose fire thinned their ranks. With almost equal bravery the French columns of the centre again advanced, wrested at last the farm of La Haye Sainte from their opponents, and pushed on vigorously though in vain under Ney against the troops in its rear. Terrible as was the English loss—and many of his regiments were reduced to a mere handful of men—Wellington stubbornly held his ground while the Prussians, advancing, as they promised, from Wavre through deep and miry forest roads, were slowly gathering to his support, disregarding the attack on their rear by which Grouchy strove to hold them back from the field. At half-past four their advanced guard deployed at last from the woods; but the main body was still far behind, and Napoleon was still able to hold his ground against them till their increasing masses forced him to stake all on a desperate effort against the English front. The Imperial Guard—his only reserve, and which had as yet taken no part in the battle—was drawn up at even in two huge columns of attack. The first, with Ney himself at its head, swept all before it as it mounted the rise beside La Haye Sainte, on which the thin English line still held its ground, and all but touched the English front when its mass, torn by the terrible fire of musketry with which it was received, gave way before a charge from the English Guards. The second, three thousand strong, advanced with the same courage over the slope near Hougomont, only to be shattered and repulsed in the same way. At the moment when these masses, shattered but still unconquered, fell slowly and doggedly back down the fatal rise, the Prussians rushed forward some forty thousand strong on Napoleon's right, their guns swept the road to Charleroi, and Wellington seized the moment for a general advance. From that moment all was lost. Only the Old Guard stood firm in the wreck of the French army; and nothing but night and exhaustion checked the English in their pursuit of the broken masses who hurried from the field. The Prussian horse continued the chase through the night, and only forty thousand Frenchmen with some thirty guns recrossed the Sambre. Napoleon himself fled hurriedly to Paris, and his second abdication was followed by the triumphant entry of the English and Prussian armies into the French capital.

EPILOGUE

WITH the victory of Waterloo we reach a time within the memory of some now living, and the opening of a period of our history, the greatest indeed of all in real importance and interest, but perhaps too near to us as yet to admit of a cool and purely historical treatment. In a work such as the present at any rate it will be advisable to limit ourselves from this point to a brief summary of the more noteworthy events which have occurred in our political history since 1815.

The Peace The peace which closed the great war with Napoleon left Britain feverish and exhausted. Of her conquests at sea she retained only Malta, (whose former possessors, the Knights of St. John, had ceased to exist,) the Dutch colonies of Ceylon and the Cape of Good Hope, the French colony of Mauritius, and a few West India islands. On the other hand the pressure of the heavy taxation and of the debt, which now reached eight hundred millions, was embittered by the general distress of the country. The rapid development of English industry for a time ran ahead of the world's demands; the markets at home and abroad were glutted with unsaleable goods, and mills and manufactories were brought to a standstill. The scarcity caused by a series of bad harvests was intensified by the selfish legislation of the landowners in Parliament. Conscious that the prosperity of English agriculture was merely factitious, and rested on the high price of corn produced by the war, they prohibited by an Act passed in 1815 the introduction of foreign corn till wheat had reached famine prices. Society, too, was disturbed by the great changes of employment consequent on a sudden return to peace after twenty years of war, and by the disbanding of the immense forces employed at sea and on land. The movement against machinery which had been put down in 1812 revived in the formidable riots of the Luddites, and the distress of the rural poor brought about a rapid increase of crime. The steady opposition too of the Administration, in which Lord Castlereagh's influence was now supreme, to any project of political progress created a dangerous irritation which brought to the front men whose demand of a "radical reform" in English institutions won them the name of Radicals, and drove more violent agitators into treasonable disaffection and silly plots. In 1819 the breaking up by military force of a meeting at Manchester assembled for the purpose of advocating a reform in Parliament increased the unpopularity of the Government; and a plot of some desperate men with Arthur Thistlewood at their head for the assassination of the whole Ministry, which is known as the Cato Street Conspiracy (1820), threw light on the violent temper which

784

was springing up among its more extreme opponents. The death of George the Third in 1820, and the accession of his son the Prince Regent as George the Fourth, only added to the general disturbance of men's minds. The new King had long since forsaken his wife and privately charged her with infidelity; his first act on mounting the throne was to renew his accusations against her, and to lay before Parliament a bill for the dissolution of her marriage with him. The public agitation which followed on this step at last forced the Ministry to abandon the bill, but the shame of the royal family and the unpopularity of the King increased the general discontent of the country.

The real danger to public order, however, lay only in the blind Canning opposition to all political change which confused wise and moderate projects of reform with projects of revolution; and in 1822 the suicide of Lord Castlereagh, who had now become Marquis of Londonderry, and to whom this opposition was mainly due, put an end to the policy of mere resistance. Canning became Foreign Secretary in Castlereagh's place, and with Canning returned the earlier and progressive policy of William Pitt. Abroad, his first act was to break with the "Holy Alliance," as it called itself, which the continental courts had formed after the overthrow of Napoleon for the repression of revolutionary or liberal movements in their kingdoms, and whose despotic policy had driven Naples, Spain, and Portugal in 1820 into revolt. Canning asserted the principle of non-interference in the internal affairs of foreign states, a principle he enforced by sending troops in 1826 to defend Portugal from Spanish intervention, while he recognized the revolted colonies of Spain in South America and Mexico as independent states. At home his influence was seen in the new strength gained by the question of Catholic Emancipation, and in the passing of a bill for giving relief to Roman Catholics through the House of Commons in 1825. With the entry of his friend Mr. Huskisson into office in 1823 began a commercial policy which was founded on a conviction of the benefits derived from freedom of trade, and which brought about at a later time the repeal of the Corn Laws. The new drift of public policy produced a division among the Ministers which showed itself openly at Lord Liverpool's death in 1827. Canning became First Lord of the Treasury, but the Duke of Wellington, with the Chancellor, Lord Eldon, and the Home Secretary, Mr. Peel, refused to serve under him; and four months after the formation of Canning's Ministry it was broken up by his death. A temporary Ministry formed under Lord Goderich on Canning's principles was at once weakened by the position of foreign affairs. A revolt of the Greeks against Turkey had now lasted some years in spite of Canning's efforts to bring about peace, and the despatch of an Egyptian expedition with orders to devastate the Morea and carry off its inhabitants as slaves forced England, France, and Russia to interfere. In 1827 their united fleet under Admiral Codrington attacked and destroyed that of Egypt in the bay of Navarino; but the blow at Turkey was disapproved by English opinion, and the Ministry, already wanting in Parliamentary strength, was driven to resign (1828).

The formation of a purely Tory Ministry by the Duke of Wellington, with Mr. Peel for its principal support in the Commons, was generally looked on as a promise of utter resistance to all further progress. But the state of Ireland, where a "Catholic Association" formed by Daniel O'Connell maintained a growing agitation, had now reached a point when the English Ministry had to choose between concession and civil war. The Duke gave way, and brought in a bill which, like that designed by Pitt, admitted Roman Catholics to Parliament, and to all but a few of the highest posts, civil or military, in the service of the Crown. The passing of this bill in 1829 by the aid of the Whigs threw the Tory party into confusion; while the cry for Parliamentary Reform was suddenly revived with a strength it had never known before by a Revolution in France in 1830, which drove Charles the Tenth from the throne and called his cousin, Louis Philippe, the Duke of Orleans, to reign as a Constitutional King. William the Fourth, who succeeded to the crown on the death of his brother, George the Fourth, at this moment (1830) was favourable to the demand of Reform, but Wellington refused all concession. The refusal drove him from office; and for the first time after twenty years the Whigs saw themselves again in power under the leadership of Earl Grey. A bill for Parliamentary Reform, which took away the right of representation from fifty-six decayed or rotten boroughs, gave the 143 members it gained to counties or large towns which as yet sent no members to Parliament, established a £10 householder qualification for voters in boroughs, and extended the county franchise to leaseholders and copyholders, was laid before Parliament in 1831. On its defeat the Ministry appealed to the country. The new House of Commons at once passed the bill, and so terrible was the agitation produced by its rejection by the Lords, that on its subsequent reintroduction the Peers who opposed it withdrew and suffered it to become law (June 7, 1832). The Reformed Parliament which met in 1833 did much by the violence and inexperience of many of its new members, and especially by the conduct of O'Connell, to produce a feeling of reaction in the country. On the resignation of Lord Grey in 1834 the Ministry was reconstituted under the leadership of Viscount Melbourne; and though this administration was soon dismissed by the King, whose sympathies had now veered round to the Tories, and succeeded for a short time by a Ministry under Sir Robert Peel (Nov. 1834—April 1835), a general election again returned a Whig Parliament, and replaced Lord Melbourne in office. Weakened as it was by the growing change of political feeling throughout the country, no Ministry has ever wrought greater and more beneficial changes than the Whig Ministry under Lord Grey and Lord Melbourne during its ten years of rule from 1831 to 1841. In 1833 the system of slavery which still existed in the British colonies, though the Slave Trade was suppressed, was **1815** abolished at a cost of twenty millions; the commercial monopoly **to** of the East India Company was abolished, and the trade to the **1873** East thrown open to all merchants. In 1834 the growing evil of pauperism was checked by the enactment of a New Poor Law. In 1835 the Municipal Corporations Act restored to the inhabitants of towns those rights of self-government of which they had been deprived since the fourteenth century. 1836 saw the passing of the General Registration Act, while the constant quarrels over tithe were remedied by the Act for Tithe Commutation, and one of the grievances of Dissenters redressed by a measure which allowed civil marriage. A system of national education, begun in 1834 by a small annual grant towards the erection of schools, was developed in 1839 by the creation of a Committee of the Privy Council for educational purposes and by the steady increase of educational grants.

Great however as these measures were, the difficulties of the **Peel** Whig Ministry grew steadily year by year. Ireland, where O'Connell maintained an incessant agitation for the Repeal of the Union, could only be held down by Coercion Acts. In spite of the impulse given to trade by the system of steam communication which began with the opening of the Liverpool and Manchester Railway in 1830, the country still suffered from distress: and the discontent of the poorer classes gave rise in 1839 to riotous demands for " the People's Charter," including universal suffrage, vote by ballot, annual Parliaments, equal electoral districts, the abolition of all property qualification for members, and payment for their services. In Canada a quarrel between the two districts of Upper and Lower Canada was suffered through mismanagement to grow into a formidable revolt. The vigorous but meddlesome way in which Lord Palmerston, a disciple of Canning, carried out that statesman's foreign policy, supporting Donna Maria as sovereign in Portugal and Isabella as Queen in Spain against claimants of more absolutist tendencies by a Quadruple Alliance with France and the two countries of the Peninsula, and forcing Mehemet Ali, the Pacha of Egypt, to withdraw from an attack on Turkey by the bombardment of Acre in 1840, created general uneasiness; while the public conscience was wounded by a war with China in 1839 on its refusal to allow the smuggling of opium into its dominions. A more terrible blow was given to the Ministry by events in India; where the occupation of Cabul in 1839 ended two years later in a general revolt of the Affghans and in the loss of a British army in the Khyber Pass. The strength of the Government was restored for a time by the death of William the Fourth in 1837 and the accession of Victoria, the daughter of his brother Edward, Duke of Kent. With the accession of Queen Victoria ended the union of England and Hanover under the same sovereigns, the latter state passing to the next male heir, Ernest, Duke of Cumberland. But the Whig hold on the House of Commons passed steadily away, and a general election in 1841 gave their opponents, who now took the name of Conservatives, a majority of nearly a hundred members. The general confidence in Sir Robert Peel, who was placed at the head of the Ministry which followed that of Lord Melbourne, enabled him to deal vigorously with two of the difficulties which had most hampered his predecessors. The disorder of the public finances was repaired by the repeal of a host of oppressive and useless duties and by the imposition of an Income Tax. In Ireland O'Connell was charged with sedition and convicted, and though subsequently released from prison on appeal to the House of Lords, his influence received a shock from which it never recovered. Peace was made with China by a treaty which threw open some of its ports to traders of all nations; and in India the disaster of Cabul was avenged by an expedition under General Pollock which penetrated victoriously to the capital of that country in 1842. The shock, however, to the English power brought about fresh struggles for supremacy with the natives, and especially with the Sikhs, who were crushed for the time in three great battles at Moodkee, Ferozeshah, and Sobraon (1845 and 1846) and the province of Scinde annexed to the British dominions.

Free
Trade Successful as it proved itself abroad, the Conservative Government encountered unexpected difficulties at home. From the enactment of the Corn Laws in 1815 a dispute had constantly gone on between those who advocated these and similar measures as a protection to native industry and those who, viewing them as simply laying a tax on the consumer for the benefit of the producer, claimed entire freedom of trade with the world. In 1839 an Anti-Corn-Law League had been formed to enforce the views of the advocates of free trade; and it was in great measure the alarm of the farmers and landowners at its action which had induced them to give so vigorous a support to Sir Robert Peel. But though Peel entered office pledged to protective measures, his own mind was slowly veering round to a conviction of their inexpediency; and in 1846 the failure of the potato crop in Ireland and of the harvest in England forced him to introduce a bill for the repeal of the Corn Laws. The bill passed, but the resentment of his own party soon drove him from office; and he was succeeded by a Whig Ministry under Lord John Russell which remained in power till 1852. The first work of this Ministry was to carry out the policy of free trade into every department of British commerce; and from that time to this the maxim of the League, to " buy in the cheapest market and sell in the dearest," has been accepted as the law of our commercial policy. Other events were few. The general overthrow of the continental monarchs in the Revolution of 1848 found faint echoes in a feeble rising in Ireland under Smith O'Brien which was easily suppressed by a few policemen, and in a demonstration of the Chartists in London which passed off without further disturbance. A fresh war with the Sikhs in 1848 was closed by the victory of Goojerat and the annexation of the Punjaub in the following year.

1815
to
1873
—
Russian
and
Sepoy
Wars

The long peace which had been maintained between the European powers since the treaties of 1815 was now drawing to a close. In 1852 the Ministry of Lord John Russell was displaced by a short return of the Conservatives to power under Lord Derby; but a union of the Whigs with the Free Trade followers of Sir Robert Peel restored them to office at the close of 1852. Lord Aberdeen, the head of the new administration, was at once compelled to resist the attempts of Russia to force on Turkey a humiliating treaty; and in 1854 England allied herself with Louis Napoleon, who had declared himself Emperor of the French, to resist the invasion of the Danubian Principalities by a Russian army. The army was withdrawn; but in September the allied force landed on the shores of the Crimea, and after a victory at the river Alma undertook the siege of Sebastopol. The garrison however soon proved as strong as the besiegers, and as fresh Russian forces reached the Crimea the Allies found themselves besieged in their turn. An attack on the English position at Inkermann on November the 5th was repulsed with the aid of a French division; but winter proved more terrible than the Russian sword, and the English force wasted away with cold or disease. The public indignation at its sufferings forced the Aberdeen Ministry from office in the opening of 1855; and Lord Palmerston became Premier with a Ministry which included those members of the last administration who were held to be most in earnest in the prosecution of the war. After a siege of nearly a year the Allies at last became masters of Sebastopol in September, and Russia, spent with the strife, consented in 1856 to the Peace of Paris. The military reputation of England had fallen low during the struggle, and to this cause the mutiny of the native troops in Bengal, which quickly followed in 1857, may partly be attributed. Russian intrigues, Moslem fanaticism, resentment at the annexation of the kingdom of Oude by Lord Dalhousie, and a fanatical belief on the part of the Hindoos that the English Government had resolved to make them Christians by forcing them to lose their caste, have all been assigned as causes of an outbreak which still remains mysterious. A mutiny at Meerut in May 1857 was followed by the seizure of Delhi where the native king was enthroned as Emperor of Hindostan, by a fresh mutiny and massacre of the Europeans at Cawnpore, by the rising of Oude and the siege of the Residency at Lucknow. The number of English troops in India was small, and for the moment all Eastern and Central Hindostan seemed lost; but Madras, Bombay, and the Punjaub remained untouched, and the English in Bengal and Oude not only held their ground but marched upon Delhi, and in September took the town by storm. Two months later the arrival of reinforcements under Sir Colin Campbell relieved Lucknow, which had been saved till now by the heroic advance of Sir Henry Havelock with a handful of troops, and cleared Oude of the mutineers. The suppression of the revolt was followed by a change in the government of India, which was transferred in 1858 from the Company to the Crown; the Queen being formally proclaimed its sovereign, and the Governor-General becoming her Viceroy.

The credit which Lord Palmerston won during the struggle with Russia and the Sepoys was shaken by his conduct in proposing an alteration in the law respecting conspiracies in 1858, in consequence of an attempt to assassinate Napoleon the Third which was believed to have originated on English ground. The violent language of the French army brought about a movement for the enlistment of a Volunteer force, which soon reached a hundred and fifty thousand men; and so great was the irritation it caused that the bill, which was thought to have been introduced in deference to the demands of France, was rejected by the House of Commons. Lord Derby again became Prime Minister for a few months; but a fresh election in 1859 brought back Lord Palmerston, whose Ministry lasted till his death in 1865. At home his policy was one of pure inaction; and his whole energy was directed to the preservation of English neutrality in five great strifes which distracted not only Europe but the New World, a war between France and Austria in 1859 which ended in the creation of the kingdom of Italy, a civil war in America which began with the secession of the Southern States in 1861 and ended four years later in their subjugation, an insurrection of Poland in 1863, an attack of France upon Mexico, and of Austria and Prussia upon Denmark in 1864. The American war, by its interference with the supply of cotton, reduced Lancashire to distress; while the fitting out of piratical cruisers in English harbours in the name of the Southern Confederation gave America just grounds for an irritation which was only allayed at a far later time. Peace, however, was successfully preserved; and the policy of non-intervention was pursued after Lord Palmerston's death by his successor, Lord Russell, who remained neutral during the brief but decisive conflict between Prussia and Austria in 1866 which transferred to the former the headship of Germany.

With Lord Palmerston, however, passed away the policy of political inaction which distinguished his rule. Lord Russell had long striven to bring about a further reform of Parliament; and in 1866 he laid a bill for that purpose before the House of Commons, whose rejection was followed by the resignation of the Ministry. Lord Derby, who again became Prime Minister, with Mr. Disraeli as leader of the House of Commons, found himself however driven to introduce in 1867 a Reform Bill of a far more sweeping character than that which had failed in Lord Russell's hands. By this measure, which passed in August 1867, the borough franchise was extended to all ratepayers, as well as to lodgers occupying rooms of the annual value of £10; the county franchise was fixed at £12, thirty-three members were withdrawn from English boroughs, twenty-five of whom were transferred to English counties, and the rest assigned to Scotland and Ireland. Large numbers of the working classes were thus added to the constituencies; and the indirect effect of this great measure was at once seen in the vigorous policy of the Parliament which assembled after the new elections in 1868. Mr. Disraeli, who had become Prime Minister on the withdrawal of Lord Derby, retired quietly on finding that a Liberal majority of over one hundred members had been returned to the House of Commons; and his place was taken by Mr. Gladstone, at the head of a Ministry which for the first time included every section of the Liberal party. A succession of great measures proved the strength and energy of the new administration. Its first work was with Ireland, whose chronic discontent it endeavoured to remove by the disestablishment and disendowment of the Protestant Church in 1869, and by a Land Bill which established a sort of tenant-right in every part of the country in 1870. The claims of the Non-conformists were met in 1868 by the abolition of compulsory church-rates, and in 1871 by the abolition of all religious tests for admission to offices or degrees in the Universities. Important reforms were undertaken in the management of the navy; and a plan for the entire reorganization of the army was carried into effect after the system of promotion to its command by purchase had been put an end to. In 1870 the question of national education was furthered by a bill which provided for the establishment of School Boards in every district, and for their support by means of local rates. In 1872 a fresh step in Parliamentary reform was made by the passing of a measure which enabled the votes of electors to be given in secret by means of the ballot. The greatness and rapidity of these changes, however, produced so rapid a reaction in the minds of the constituencies that on the failure of his attempt to pass a bill for organizing the higher education of Ireland, Mr. Gladstone felt himself forced in 1874 to consult public opinion by a dissolution of Parliament; and the return of a Conservative majority of nearly seventy members was necessarily followed by his retirement from office, Mr. Disraeli again becoming First Minister of the Crown.

A POLITICAL AND SOCIAL SURVEY

From 1815–1914. By R. P. Farley

CHAPTER I

From Waterloo to the Reform Bill

1815–1832

[*Authorities.*—An immense amount of material, which shows no sign of slackening, has been accumulated for the study of the whole of the nineteenth century, especially its closing period. For 1815–1832 the student must consult the " Annual Register " and the " Parliamentary Debates " for particular events. The general history is to be found in Walpole's " History of England from the Conclusion of the Great War in 1815 "; J. A. L. Marriott's " England since Waterloo "; and Justin Macarthy's " Modern England before the Reform Bill (1810–1832)." These should be supplemented by Broderick and Fotheringham's " Political History of England (1801–1837)," and E. and A. G. Porritt's " Unreformed House of Commons," while Dicey's " Law and Public Opinion " is an invaluable commentary on the course of legislative evolution. Special aspects of the period are treated in Cunningham's " English Industry and Commerce "; Levi's " History of Commerce " and " Wages and Earnings of the Working Classes "; Arnold Toynbee's " Industrial Revolution "; the Reports of the Select Committees on Agriculture (1814, 1821 – 1822); Hasbach's " The History of the English Agricultural Labourer "; J. L. and B. Hammond's " The Village Labourer (1760–1832)"; and Cobbett's " Political Register " (the last three describe the condition of the labouring classes). S. and B. Webb's " Trade Unionism " and Hutchins' and Harrison's " Factory Legislation " deal with efforts for the amelioration of industrial conditions, whether in the shape of working-class organisation or of legislation. Much light is thrown upon the events between Waterloo and the Reform Bill in Greville's " Journals of the Reigns of George IV. and William IV." and J. W. Croker's " Correspondence and Diaries " (edited Jennings). The part played by particular leaders may be studied in Bagot's " George Canning and his Friends "; the " Private Papers of Sir Robert Peel " (edited C. S. Parker); Lord Dalling and E. Ashley's " Life of Viscount Palmerston "; Podmore's " Life of Robert Owen "; G. Wallas' " Life of Francis Place."]

By the overthrow of Napoleon in 1815, England brought peace to Europe and secured for herself the lordship of the seas and the commercial supremacy of the world at that time. But precisely during the period of struggle with despotism abroad, internal changes of the most profound character had taken place in England, changes which transformed an agricultural to a manufacturing country, and which, though bringing with them much that was good, created a series of domestic problems of the gravest and most far-reaching character, so far-reaching that at the end of the century many of them still remained unsolved. During the period from 1790 to 1812 the fortunate possessors of agricultural land found their rents increase, in some cases five-fold. But if the position of the tenant farmer was bad, owing to high rents and a heavy income tax, that of the labourer was infinitely worse. During the reign of George III. 3200 Enclosure Acts were passed

The Agrarian Revolution

d more than 6,000,000 acres were enclosed. It is true that
ore scientific methods of agriculture were introduced, but the
ttager was deprived of his little plot of land and garden and of
s common rights. Henceforth he had to depend entirely upon
e scanty wages of daily labour, frequently supplemented by
les from private charity or the poor rates. Professor Levi
lculates that from 1760 to 1813 wages rose 60 per cent., but
ainst this increase must be set off a rise of 130 per cent. in the
ice of wheat.[1] The supersession of small farms by large also
fected the labourer's budget. Formerly he was able to buy milk,
tter, and other necessaries in every parish in such quantity as
s exiguous means allowed. Now the large farmer carried his
mmodities to the towns, and was often unwilling to sell, even
his own labourers, the small quantities which alone the workmen
uld afford to buy at one time. The pernicious system introduced
y the Berkshire Justices of the Peace at Speenhamland on 6th
ay, 1795, was gradually adopted in almost every part of England,
d remained in general use until swept away by the Poor Law
eforms of 1834. The meeting of the Justices, though summoned
r the express purpose of calling upon employers to give wages
hich reached a subsistence level, had the fatal unwisdom to
cide that in cases where employers failed to do this they would
ake an allowance to every poor family in accordance with its
mbers. " When the gallon loaf of second flour, weighing 8 lbs.
. ozs., shall cost 1s., then every poor and industrious man shall
ve for his own support 3s. weekly, either produced by his own
his family's labour, or an allowance from the poor rates, and for
e support of his wife and every other of his family 1s. 6d. When
e gallon loaf shall cost 1s. 4d., then every poor and industrious
an shall have 4s. weekly for his own and 1s. 10d. for the support
every other of his family. And so in proportion as the price of
ead rises or falls (that is to say) 3 per cent. to the man and 1 per
nt. to every other of the family, on every penny which the loaf
ses above a shilling." The effect of this method, unfortunately so
on and so frequently to be imitated elsewhere, was disastrous,
d was a potent source of demoralisation both to the employer,
hom it relieved of the responsibility of paying subsistence wages,
d to the labourer, in whom it encouraged habits of thriftlessness.
ow the employer made use of the Speenhamland principle may
 inferred from the fact that in 1814 the amount expended on
or Law relief had reached the total of 12s. 8d. per head of the
pulation, whereas at the beginning of the reign of George III.
e figure stood at 3s. 7d. For the year ending March 31, 1818, the
nount was 13s. 9d. per head of population. The labourer, forcibly
vorced from his plot of land and demoralised by doles, only too
ten lost his sturdy independence. The economic reaction which
pervened on the close of war increased his distress and dis-
tisfaction. His grievances began to find articulate form in the

[1] " Large and Small Holdings," p. 11.

writings of William Cobbett, a consummate master of terse an
vigorous English, whose weekly " Political Register " strove t
teach the workmen of both town and country that a reform
Parliament would bring about a redress of their evils. Cobbet
the general accuracy of whose pictures of working-class life cann€
be questioned, thus describes [1] the conditions in his own distri€
in Sussex: " I have the good fortune to live in a part of the countr
where the labouring people are better off than in any part €
England I have seen. . . . (Indeed, until the last three year
very little distress was known here.) But now it has found us ou
and threatens to involve us in one general mass of misery. I coul
name numerous individuals who are actually become a sort €
skeletons. . . . I see scores of young men, framed by nature to b
athletic, rosy-cheeked, and bold. I see scores of young men forme
by nature to exhibit this appearance: I see them as thin as herring
dragging their feet after them, pale as a ceiling and sneakir
about like beggars."

The events of the generation immediately preceding the war, an
especially the policy of enclosures, had substituted for the peasal
with some vested rights in his village and some share in i
government the mere labourer, robbed of his status, stripped ≪
his common rights, broken in spirit. A contemporary pictur
sombre in its colours, is yet no unfair description of one aspect of
typical village. " Go to an ale-house kitchen of an old enclos€
country, and there you will see the origin of poverty and po€
rates. For whom are they to be sober ? For whom are they to save
For the parish ? If I am diligent shall I have leave to build
cottage ? If I am sober, shall I have land for a cow ? If I a≋
frugal, shall I have half an acre of potatoes ? You offer no motive
you have nothing but a parish officer and a workhouse ! Brir
me another pot——" [2]

During the war that rapid change which has come to be know
as " the industrial revolution " had transformed England fro≋
an agricultural to a manufacturing country. In 1769, the san
year in which Napoleon and Wellington were born, Watts patent€
his steam-engine. Hargreaves' invention of the spinning-jenr
(1770), Arkwright's of the " Water-frame " (1771), Crompton
of " the Mule," combining the principles of both the precedir
(1779), and Cartwright's of the power-loom (1785) destroyed tl
old domestic worker and substituted the method of productic
in factories. In the 15 years from 1788 to 1803 the cotton tra€
trebled itself. The employment of steam power in mills necessitate
the use of coal and made proximity to mines desirable. Hen€
manufacture tended to gravitate towards the great coal and ir€
fields of Yorkshire, Lancashire, Staffordshire, and South Wale
Simultaneously with the change in the cotton industry, ne

---

[1] " Political Register," August 10, 1816.
[2] " Annals of Agriculture," vol. xxxvi. p. 508, quoted in Hammond
" Village Labourer," p. 105.

ethods began to be applied to mining. And the greater demand
f coal in its turn brought about a revival and an enormous
crease of the trade in iron. The population of England in 1760
as under 8,000,000, but in 1821 it had risen to nearly 12,000,000,
nd the migration of the workers to the new manufacturing
istricts was no less remarkable than the extraordinary rise in
eir numbers. All through the war period the rate of industrial
roduction and the volume of exports went up by leaps and bounds.
1 1793 exports were valued at over £17,000,000, in 1815 they had
ounted up to £58,000,000. Nevertheless the manual workers
ffered grievously as the bulk of the profits went into the pockets
f capitalist manufacturers, every necessity of life was heavily
xed, the price of wheat, which in 1793 had been 49s. 3d. per
uarter, had risen to 106s. in 1810, while at the close of the war
ages rapidly fell. The conditions of the worker whether above
r under ground were such as we should have difficulty in believing
ere not the details set out for us in reliable contemporary records
nd Parliamentary or other official reports. To cope with the
ew demand for goods, factories were hastily erected without any
gard to the most elementary principles of sanitation, and even
ld barns, cart-houses, and out-buildings of all descriptions were
rbished up somehow and used as loom-shops. Men (and women,
ho began to be employed in large numbers) were worked unduly
ng hours and to the utmost limits of physical endurance. When
e wages of the men fell to starvation point they consented to
eir women entering the factories. The most horrifying feature
f the industrial life of this period was the treatment of children.
any manufacturers, when they wanted even cheaper labour than
as then available to them, obtained pauper children from the
orkhouses on the pretext of apprenticing them to the new
mployments which were springing up in such plenty. By an
dded refinement of cruelty it was sometimes arranged (in order
at the responsibility for imbeciles should be passed on a stage
rther) that the mill-owner should take one mentally deficient
hild to twenty presumably normal ones. Though nominally
pprenticed, these luckless infants were subjected to a veritable
avery; they were insufficiently clad, fed upon the cheapest food,
nd often employed sixteen hours out of the twenty-four. They
orked day and night in relays, sleeping in filthy beds which were
ever allowed to cool, for one batch succeeded another without
terval, and often without discrimination of sex. The majority
d not commence work till nine years of age, but cases were known
f children beginning at five. The few who after this brutal regi-
en had sufficient spirit left to wish to run away, or who were sus-
ected of such rebellious inclinations, had irons riveted to their
nkles and were compelled to work and sleep in them. Instances
ere recorded of women and girls being subjected to similar
eatment. An official report dating from 1833, when conditions
ad slightly improved, thus summarises some of the grosser evils

which the new methods of production, desirable in themselves, though grossly exploited for private profit, brought in their train: " We hear of children and young people in factories overworked and beaten as if they were slaves; of diseases and distortions only found in the manufacturing districts; of filthy, wretched homes where people huddle together like beasts; we hear of girls and women working underground in the dark recesses of the coalmines, dragging loads of coal in cars in places where no horses could go, and harnessed and crawling along the subterranean pathways like beasts of burden. Everywhere we find cruelty and oppression, and in many cases the workmen were but slaves, bound to fulfil their master's commands under fear of dismissal and starvation." These evils were aggravated at the close of the war by a falling off in the hitherto abnormal demand for manufactured goods, the colossal debt arising out of a protracted war, and, to crown all, a falling revenue. It is small wonder that political and social discontent became sharply vocal. To meet the agricultural dislocation and to calm the fears of the landed interest who dreaded foreign competition in food products, the first of

a series of Corn Laws was passed in 1815, which forbade the importation of foreign wheat until the home price had reached 80s. per quarter, of rye and pulse till the home price was 53s. of barley and oats till the price in the native market was 40s. and 20s. respectively. Meantime Cobbett and others strove to add fuel to the flames of unrest which had burst out not only in the agricultural but also in the manufacturing counties. In May, 1816, riots broke out in Norfolk, Suffolk, Huntingdon, and Cambridgeshire, and houses, barns, and ricks were set on fire by labourers who demanded more employment and better wages. Similarly the colliers of the Tyne-side, the ironworkers of Monmouthshire and Staffordshire, the juteworkers of Dundee, and the clothworkers of Wiltshire were also aflame with the spirit of revolt. Cobbett's " Political Register," the price of which he had reduced in August from 1s. 0½d. to 2d., was said by the end of the year to have reached a circulation, enormous for that time, of 50,000 copies per week and exercised a most potent influence among manual workers. He denounced violence and rioting and urged his readers to concentrate upon the demand for political reforms. On November 15,

1816, an abortive meeting of workmen in the Spa Fields, Bermondsey, to call attention to the miseries of the London working classes, was followed a week afterwards by a less violent and more authoritative protest in the shape of a formal address to the Prince Regent by the Corporation of London, who declared that " the distress and misery which for so many years has been progressively accumulating, has at length become insupportable; that the commercial, the manufacturing, and the agricultural interests are equally sinking under its irresistible pressure, and it has become impossible to find employment for a large mass of the population." The causes of the evil were said by this august body to be " rash and ruinous wars, unjustly commenced and pertina- ciously persisted in," and " the corrupt and inadequate state of the representation of the people in Parliament," and the remedies, to make " every practicable reduction in the public expenditure and restore to the people their just share and weight in the legislature."

The reports of secret committees, appointed in both Houses of Parliament to investigate the causes of the wide-spread agita- tion (as evinced by the rise of large numbers of political societies and the dissemination of the literature of a propaganda which demanded, for instance, universal suffrage and annual elections), caused the suspension of the Habeas Corpus Act for four months and the passing of further legislation to prevent seditious meetings. Further agitation in the North and the Midlands led to what was called the " March of the Blanketeers," because some thousands of workmen who took part in it, and who set out to march to London, each carried provisions and a blanket so as to be able to encamp by the way. In June of the same year another abortive rising took place in the Midlands under the leadership of a man named Brandreth, a pauper in receipt of parish relief, who suc- ceeded in inducing a band of about 500 men to march on Notting- ham. The attempt was instantly foiled by the yeomanry, the insurrectionists were scattered, and Brandreth with two other leaders was arrested and subsequently executed. For a time the agitation slackened and at the General Election of 1818, which was hotly contested, the majority remained with the Tories, though the Whigs gained about 30 votes. In the new House of Commons Sir Francis Burdett's motion urging reform of Parliament was de- feated by 153 to 58. In various parts of the country huge meetings to agitate for reform were held at Glasgow, Leeds, Stockport, and elsewhere. The disaffected workers and their sympathisers of Lancashire and Cheshire planned a great demonstration to be held at St. Peter's Field, Manchester. On the appointed day the demon- strators to the number of at least 60,000 marched to the place of meeting bearing the mottoes " Universal Suffrage," " Annual Parliaments," " Vote by Ballot," " No Corn Laws," and similar watchwords. As soon as the meeting began, the yeomanry, by order of the Manchester magistrates, charged with drawn swords into the crowd with the object of arresting Orator Hunt, the chair- man, and his supporters on the platform. In the *mêlée* which followed several people were trampled or sabred to death and some hundreds were injured. Hunt, Bamford, and others were arrested, and Hunt sentenced to imprisonment for two years and six months, Bamford and two others for twelve months. Although the Regent and the Government emphatically approved the con- duct of the magistrates, meetings to express sympathy with the demonstrators were held at Liverpool, Norwich, Westminster, Nottingham, Bristol, and York. Perhaps the most weighty protest came from the Common Council of London, which by 71 votes to 45 affirmed " the undoubted right of Englishmen to assemble together for the purpose of deliberating upon public grievances," and expressed the strongest disapproval of the action of the Manchester authorities.   An interesting by-product of Peterloo was Shelley's " Masque of Anarchy," with its stirring refrain:

> " Rise like lions after slumber
> In unvanquishable number.
> Shake your chains to earth, like dew,
> Which in sleep have fallen on you :
> Ye are many, they are few,"

which the poet, at the time absent in Italy, was moved to write when reports of the meeting and the conflict with the yeomanry reached him.

Notwithstanding the numerous expressions of sympathy with the promoters of the Manchester meeting, the Ministry, which summoned Parliament on November 23 to discuss the situation, determined not to give way to popular feeling and forced through, in spite of strong opposition from Lord Grey and other Whigs, the series of measures known as the " Six Acts."   The objects of these were: (1) to accelerate " the administration of justice in cases of misdemeanour," and to alter the procedure in such cases; (2) " to prevent the training of persons in the use of arms and the practice of military evolutions"; (3) to prevent and punish " blasphemous and seditious libels " (a second conviction for libel was to be punished with transportation); (4) " to authorise Justices of the Peace in certain disturbed counties to seize and detain arms "; (5) " to subject certain publications to the duties of stamps upon newspapers, and to make other regulations for restraining the abuses arising from the publication of blasphemous and seditious libels "; and (6) to prevent more effectually " seditious meetings and assemblies."

The long reign of George III. came to an end in 1820, to be succeeded by that of one who was not only not liked but not even respected by his subjects.   Princess Caroline of Brunswick had been married to the Regent in 1795, but had been separated from him by mutual consent after a very brief and unhappy married life, and had withdrawn to the Continent, where it was said that she led an irregular life.   She returned to England in 1820 to claim the rights and dignities of a Queen.   George IV. refused to acknowledge her, and Lord Liverpool, the Prime Minister, introduced a " Bill of Pains and Penalties " to deprive her of her title and to dissolve the marriage.   The Queen posed as an injured woman and had the vehement support outside Parliament of people of all ranks, especially the middle and labouring classes, and even the Army.   Whigs and Radicals, influenced as much by a desire to snatch a party advantage as by any more worthy motive, joined in championing the cause of the Queen. The bill was dropped, though it passed by a small majority, but
the Queen died in 1821.   The mutual support of the Whigs and

Radicals in the cause of the Queen persisted after her death and kept them associated in later efforts for political reform. In one of these, Lord John Russell in 1821 succeeded in carrying his bill for the disfranchisement of the corrupt borough of Grampound and the transference of its seats to the County of York.

The year 1822 was marked by the return of Canning to the Foreign Office in the room of Castlereagh. In many ways he carried on, though with more vigour and effectiveness, principles laid down by his predecessor, and especially two by which his own name is best known and which coloured, if they did not dominate, British foreign policy for generations afterwards: (1) the recognition of national independence, including the claims of new nations which had won their freedom; (2) non-interference in the internal policy of foreign states. He broke away from " the Holy Alliance," which in its inception was an attempt to Christianise international politics. In the words of the scheme drafted by the Czar in September, 1815, the rulers of Russia, Austria, and Prussia pledged themselves "agreeably to the words of Holy Scripture which commands all men to love as brothers, to remain united in the bonds of true and indissoluble brotherly love; always to assist one another; to govern their subjects as parents; to maintain religion, peace, and justice. They consider themselves but as members of one and the same Christian family commissioned by Providence to govern the branches of one family. They call on all powers who acknowledge similar principles to join this Holy Alliance." This lofty ideal unfortunately does not appear to have been translated into practice. Canning seems to have considered it impracticable at the time, if not an insincere pretence. As a matter of fact in practice it degenerated into a policy of maintaining absolutism and reaction in place and repressing movements in the direction of liberalism or revolution. In home politics, Huskisson's acceptance of the Presidency of the Board of Trade inaugurated a series of fiscal and commercial reforms based on the belief that "national prosperity would be most effectually promoted by an unrestrained competition not only between the capital and the industry of different classes in the same country, but also by extending that competition as much as possible to all other countries." Import duties were reduced, or at least made more uniform. Bounties on exports were abolished. The rigidity of the Navigation Laws was relaxed and by the Reciprocity Act power was given to the King in Council to conclude reciprocity treaties with our own colonies or with other countries. A rough summary of the results would estimate the reduction of taxes at 30 per cent. *ad valorem* on manufactured goods and at 10 per cent. on raw materials. Similarly restrictions on labour were removed, and by the Combination Act of 1824, which was carried, in the words of Francis Place, who with Hume had skilfully engineered its progress through Parliament, " almost without the notice of members within or newspapers without," trade unions, which at that time were unlawful associations, were made legal. Trade societies seemed to rise out of the ground in all directions immediately after the passage of the Act and many strikes occurred not unaccompanied by violence. A Sheffield newspaper called attention to the fact that " it is no longer a particular class of journeymen at some single point that have been reduced to commence a strike for an advance of wages, but almost the whole body of the mechanics in the kingdom are combined in the general resolution to impose terms on their employers." Another newspaper in the same town warned the local operatives that if they persisted in their demand for double their former wages for a week of only three days, the whole industry of the town would be ruined.[1] The result of these outbursts was the

passing in 1825 of a further Combination Act which reaffirmed the common law of conspiracy and conceded a limited right of combination, but, a most important fact in the history of the relations between capital and labour, for the first time explicitly established the right of " collective bargaining," usually regarded with disfavour by employers for fifty years to come, but later accepted by many, if not most, disinterested observers of its working as not only in the long run beneficial to employers as well as workmen, but also on the whole socially beneficent. One of the most curious examples of political prophecy was the statement of Place, to the extraordinarily alert intelligence of whom more than any one else the passing of these acts was due, that by the grant to workmen of liberty to combine combinations would " soon cease to exist! "

Ministry
of the
Duke of
Welling-
ton
1828
to
1830
The two years during which the Duke of Wellington was Prime Minister were marked by two important measures, the wisdom of which would now not be disputed, though they were hotly contested at the time. The Test and Corporation Acts, which compelled every holder of a public office, whether civil or military, to take the Sacrament according to the rites of the Church of England, were repealed and for the sacramental Test was substituted a simple declaration that the holder of an office would do nothing " to injure or subvert the Protestant Established Church." The

Catholic Emancipation Act marked the concluding and decisive battle in the long struggle for the political rights of Catholics. Pitt had meant to grant complete emancipation side by side with the Act of Union; Peel, Fox, Grattan, Plunket, Canning had striven for the principle, but it was the foundation of the Catholic Association by Daniel O'Connell in 1823 and his subsequent triumphant election in 1828 for the County of Clare against Fitzgerald which made the grant of this long-withheld measure inevitable. It contained various provisions designed as the framers of the Bill unwisely supposed to prevent the spread of Catholicism, but it permitted Roman Catholics to become eligible for all civil, military, Parliamentary, and municipal offices save those of Regent,

[1] Webb, " Trade Unionism," pp. 93, 94.

ord Lieutenant of Ireland, Lord Chancellor of England or Ireland, nd a very few others.

Unfortunately, this concession to justice and toleration was eutralised by a second Act in the same year, conceived in a short-ighted spirit of spleen and desire for revenge. The cause of atholic Emancipation had been carried to victory by the votes f the 40s. freeholders, but by the new Act the qualification for a ote in an Irish county was fixed at £10 and the electorate at a troke reduced from 200,000 to 26,000.

In 1830 George IV. died unregretted on June 26 and on November 16 the Ministry of Wellington and Peel resigned. Wellington, otwithstanding the growing demand for political reform, declined have anything to do with the question. Peel, if he was at variance with the Whigs on the subject of changes in Parliamentary epresentation, will be remembered for many salutary changes uring his tenure of the Home Office (1822–27, 1828–30). He eformed the criminal code (especially by drastically reducing the wo hundred offences for which capital punishment could be flicted) and criminal procedure; swept away some of the grosser nomalies of the Marriage Laws; systematised the constitution and unctions of juries; improved the condition of the gaols; and stablished in London a new police force.

The question of the moment was parliamentary reform. The uccess of movements for popular government in France and elgium added impetus to the efforts of British Whigs and Radicals, hose demands became more insistent. In England there were umerous outbreaks of disaffection among labourers in Kent, ussex, Surrey, Dorsetshire, Gloucestershire, Hampshire, Wiltshire, xfordshire, who demanded higher wages, and in many cases red stacks, ricks, and barns, and broke up threshing machines. onsiderable damage was done by the rioters to property, but ttle or none to persons. The demands of the labourers that their ages, which usually stood at 9s. or 10s. a week and in extreme ases at not more than 6s., should be raised to 2s. 6d. a day met ith a considerable amount of sympathy from other classes. The pecial correspondent of the "Times" (November 17) describing he outbreak in Sussex, where the revolt was more widely spread, etter organised, and more successful than in any other part of he country, gives a description of the methods of the labourers, hich might equally have been applied to the risings in other arts of the country. "Divested of its objectionable character, as dangerous precedent, the conduct of the peasantry has been dmirable. There is no ground for concluding that there has been ny extensive concert amongst them. Each parish, generally peaking, has risen *per se ;* in many places their proceedings have een managed with astonishing coolness and regularity; there as been little of the ordinary effervescence displayed on similar ccasions: a deputation of two or more of the latter produce a ritten statement, well drawn up, which the farmers are required

1815 to 1832

William IV. 1830 to 1837

1830

"The Last Labourers' Revolt."

**1815
to
1832**

to sign; the spokesman, sometimes a Dissenting or Methodist teacher, fulfils his office with great propriety and temper. When disorder has occurred, it has arisen from dislike to some obnoxious clergyman, or tithe man, or assistant overseer, who has been trundled out of the parish in a wheel-barrow, or drawn in triumph in a load of ballast by a dozen old women. The farmers universally agreed to the demands they made: that is, they were not man enough to refuse requests which they could not demonstrate to be unreasonable in themselves, and which were urged by three hundred or four hundred men after a barn or two had been fired, and each farmer had an incendiary letter addressed to him in his pocket." [1] Nevertheless, special Commissions at Winchester, Salisbury, Dorchester, Reading, Aylesbury, appointed to try the rioters for offences which in most cases amounted to nothing more serious than " seditious assembly," and at worst to offences against property which involved no loss of life, condemned about 450 men, some to death, many to transportation for life, and the remainder to long terms of imprisonment.

**The
need for
Parlia-
mentary
Reform**

Had the agitation for political reform, however, been merely the outburst of disaffected labourers it would have been doomed to failure at that time. But it had long been evident that a system which (in England and Wales) had undergone no change since 1688 was inadequate for the needs of an age which had entered upon an agrarian and an industrial revolution. In the " unreformed House of Commons " the counties were represented by two members each, the boroughs returned to Parliament men elected on a chaotic and indefensible variety of franchise and an equally chaotic and indefensible distribution of seats. Of 203 parliamentary boroughs with two members each there were 62 where only the hereditary " freemen " could vote; in 59 (the so-called " scot and lot ") the electors were those who paid church and poor rates or " potwallopers " (a name applied to another variety of boroughs), *i.e.*, persons who (1) had a hearth of their own where they could boil a pot and (2) were not in receipt of poor relief; 39 where only the owners or occupiers of certain houses known " ancient tenements " had the right of franchise. Some of these places, like Old Sarum or Bramber, were barely discoverable on the map, while large and growing centres of industry like Manchester, Birmingham, and Leeds had no independent representation at all. Worse still, as Erskine May pointed out, not more than a third of the members of the House of Commons had entered as " the free choice even of the limited bodies of electors then entrusted with the franchise." The demand for reform now reached a point where it could no longer be delayed or denied, as the results of the labours, extending over a generation, of many hands. To this demand contributed the reasoned politics of Bentham, Hume, and the two Mills; the fiery invective and terse vigour of Cobbett; the restless energy and astute manipulation of Francis

[1] Quoted in Hammond's " Village Labourer," pp. 247, 248.

1815
to
1832
—
1831
Earl
Grey's
Ministry

lace; the determination of the commercial classes in general to ave a share of political power. Earl Grey's Whig Ministry of 831 was sure of powerful backing when, as its first legislative ask, it set about drafting proposals for reform. The Bill presented Parliament disfranchised 60 boroughs, and deprived 47 others f one member each, while it gave members to counties or large owns hitherto unrepresented. The voting qualification was also rastically altered and simplified. In the counties, to the old 40s. eeholders were added copyholders and £50 tenants. In the oroughs the old freeholders retained the right of suffrage and to heir number were added householders with a £10 property quali- cation. As the Bill passed the second reading by a majority of nly one, the Ministry appealed to the country and received the riumphant mandate of a majority of over 100. The Bill, substan- ally unaltered, was immediately re-introduced, and though it assed its second reading by a majority of 136 was thrown out by he House of Lords by a majority of 41. This action was imme- iately followed by demonstrations of protest, sometimes accom- anied with violence. At Birmingham a meeting, said to have een attended by 150,000 persons, was held and resolutions were arried affirming that no taxes should be paid until the Bill was assed. At Nottingham the Castle was burnt down, at Bristol the ansion House and Bishop's Palace were set on fire. When the ouse of Commons met again in December a third Reform Bill assed its second reading by a majority of 162, but in the following ay the House of Lords carried an important amendment against by a majority of 35. The Cabinet thereupon advised the King create as many peers as would ensure the passing of the Bill ndamentally unaltered, but as he was opposed to this step, the inistry offered and he accepted their resignation. After a period eleven days, during which the King appealed to Lord Lyndhurst, anners-Sutton, and finally to the Duke of Wellington to form a inistry, and in various places throughout the country preparation as made for armed rebellion, the King, on the advice of the Duke Wellington, recalled Earl Grey, to whom he granted permission to create such a number of Peers as will be sufficient to ensure e passing of the Reform Bill, first calling up Peers' eldest sons." his rendered further opposition to the Bill fruitless. In its final rm its main clauses provided that 56 boroughs with two members ach should be disfranchised; 30 should lose one member each. f the 143 seats thus to be disposed of, to keep the total number 658, 65 were given to English and Welsh counties; 22 English oroughs received two members each, 21 one member each; 8 hers were given to Scotland and 5 to Ireland. The voting ualification in the counties was assigned to the old 40s. freeholders lus copyholders, long-lease holders, and tenants at will paying rent of not less than £50 a year; in the boroughs to resident eemen in corporate towns and to all £10 householders.

The main significance of the Act was that for the first time it brought into being a representative House. It transferred the political centre of gravity from the old landed aristocracy to the middle and commercial classes and gave Protestant Dissenters real political influence. It satisfied neither the philosophic Radicals who wished for something more systematic and logical, nor the working classes, who saw few of their number added to the electorate by it, but it left the door open for further change and it swept away many intolerable abuses.

CHAPTER II

FROM THE REFORM BILL TO THE EDUCATION ACT OF 1870

1832–1870

[*Authorities.*—The " Annual Register," the " Parliamentary Debates," and the files of the " Times " must be constantly studied. Good detailed histories are Walpole's " History "; Herbert Paul's " Modern England "; the " Cambridge Modern History " (vol. xi.); Marriott's " England since Waterloo "; and Justin Macarthy's " Modern England from the Reform Bill to 1898 "; Low and Sandar's " Political History of England (1837–1901) "; Rose's " Development of the European Nations." Dicey's " Law and Public Opinion " and Dickinson's " Development of Parliament in the Nineteenth Century " are most informing and instructive. Special aspects of the period are treated in Cunningham's " Growth of English Industry and Commerce "; the Reports of the Factory Commissions of 1833 and 1842 and of the Poor Law Commission of 1834; Engel's " The Condition of the Working Classes in England in 1844 "; Hutchins' " The Health Agitation (1834–1848)"; B. Webb's " The Co-operative Movement." Literature has supplied pictures of the national life which are also of historical value. Disraeli's novels; Mrs. Gaskell's " Mary Barton "; Kingsley's " Yeast " and " Alton Locke "; Carlyle's " Chartism," " Past and Present," and " Sartor Resartus " are full not merely of interesting but instructive material. The biographical literature dealing with this period is of the highest importance. Queen Victoria's " Letters " (edited by Lord Esher and A. C. Benson); Greville's " Journals "; Croker's " Correspondence and Diaries " (edited Jennings); the " Memorials of Roundell Palmer, Earl of Selborne "; the biographies of Palmerston (Lord Dalling and E. Ashley), Granville (Lord Fitzgerald), Lord George Bentinck (Disraeli), Lord Shaftesbury (E. Hodder), Macaulay (Sir G. Trevelyan), Disraeli (W. Sichel: Monypenny), Gladstone (Morley), Cobden (Morley), John Bright (Trevelyan), Robert Owen (Podmore), and Samuel Smiles' " Lives of the Engineers " give most vivid and also historically valuable accounts of the surging life of the time. Special information about Ireland may be found in the Report of the Devon Commission (1845), Bryce's " Two Centuries of Irish History "; O'Connor Morris's " Ireland from 1798 to 1898 "; O'Brien's " Fifty Years of Concession to Ireland "; R. T. Ball's " The Reformed Church in Ireland "; and Brady's " The English State Church in Ireland." On the subject of India Sir A. Lyall's " British Dominion in India "; Earl Roberts' " Forty-one Years in India "; and Sir J. Outram's " History of the Mutiny " may be consulted; while for Canada Lord Durham's Report (edited Lucas) and Egerton and Grant's " Evolution of Canadian Self-Government " are for the ordinary reader perhaps the most useful. Graham Balfour's " Educational Systems of Great Britain and Ireland " is quite the best compendious account of public education in the British Islands.]

THE reformed Parliament immediately set about the task of making up arrears in legislation. Up to 1833 the work of secular education for the children of the poor in England and Wales fell mainly upon two voluntary societies, the National Society for Promoting the Education of the Poor in the Principles of the

Established Church and the British and Foreign School Society, which was mainly supported by Nonconformists. On August 17, 1833, the House of Commons voted a sum of £20,000 " for purposes of education," and this amount was handed over to the Treasury to be used for the erection of schoolhouses in Great Britain subject to the condition that half the cost should be met by voluntary contributions. Hume voted against the grant on the ground that other moneys were available for the purpose, while Cobbett maintained that it was an attempt " to force education on the country— a French, a Doctrinaire plan," the sole result of which would be " to increase the number of schoolmasters and mistresses, that new race of idlers." To the same year belongs also Lord Althorp's Factory Act, which was the culmination of the " Ten Hours " Agitation, in which the most prominent figures were Richard Oastler, Michael Sadler, and Lord Shaftesbury among Tories, and Fielden, Hindley, and Brotherton among Liberals and Radicals. In 1830 Oastler had written a series of letters to the " Leeds Mercury " and the " Leeds Intelligencer," entitled " Slavery in Yorkshire," in which he denounced the factory system, and demanded a ten-hours' day for all workers under twenty-one years of age. These letters were the beginning of a vigorous demand, which gathered momentum as it went, and finally was embodied in the Act mentioned, which was carried through under the Parliamentary leadership of Lord Shaftesbury. The new law prohibited work between 8.30 p.m. and 5.30 a.m. to all under 18 employed " in or about any cotton, woollen, worsted, hemp, flax, tow, linen, or silk mill "; work for more than 12 hours a day or 69 a week for persons under 18, and all work by children under nine years of age except in silk mills. The most important provision of the Act was the appointment of paid inspectors, empowered to enter at will any factories at work, to examine the children, or to subpœna witnesses, to make binding rules and regulations, and to enforce school attendance. In 1833 Fowell Buxton, Clarkson, Wilberforce, and Zachary Macaulay reaped the fruits of the painful efforts of many years when the government passed an Act for the " abolition of slavery throughout the British Colonies." Slavery, it was decided, should come to an end on August 1, 1834, but all children under six years of age were to be set free at once and all unborn children were to be born free. The planters were to receive a compensation of £20,000,000. If the high hopes of the supporters of the movement which culminated in the passing of this Act were not completely fulfilled, at least it was a stroke of disinterested self-sacrifice which is a proud memory of the British race. Freedom received a further extension in 1833, when Quakers, Moravians, and Separatists were allowed to enter the House of Commons and to substitute an affirmation for an oath. The growth of a new feeling of refinement was shown in the passing of an Act (carried in 1833 and two years afterwards extended to the whole country) which made it illegal " to drive any ox or cattle, or to bait any bull, bear, badger,

1832 to 1870
___
1833
Beginnings of public education

Factory Legislation

Emancipation of the Slaves

or other animal, or to fight cocks, within 5 miles of Temple Bar."

1834 is a landmark in the social history of England in its way perhaps as important as 1832. In that year the Commission of inquiry appointed by Lord Grey's Government in 1832 reported and the Poor Law Amendment Act was passed. The Report, which in its main features was the work of the laborious and penetrating intellect of Edwin Chadwick, one of the Commissioners, described conditions of demoralisation, filth, and maladministration which, outside an official document, would have been almost incredible. The expenditure on poor relief, which in 1802 stood at £4,000,000, had risen in 1818 to £7,870,000 or an average of 13s. 8d. per head of population. The vicious Speenhamland system of allowances to supplement wages had proved a direct stimulus to underpayment and sweating on the one hand, to sluggishness and thriftlessness on the other. Poor relief (until 1834) was a matter of local administration, carried on by the Justices of the Peace, without direction or interference from the centre. The new Act, which followed close upon the publication of the Report of the Commission and adopted its main recommendations, was carried almost unanimously in both Houses of Parliament. It established central control and put administration in the hands of a body of three Poor Law Commissioners. It made the union, instead of the parish, the unit of local administration. It provided that all owners and occupiers of rateable property should be represented (by votes for the Boards of Guardians) and that representation should be in proportion to taxable capacity. The general principle of relief was that " the situation of the person receiving relief should not on the whole be made really or apparently so eligible as the situation of the independent labourer of the lowest class,' or, as it was expressed in a grimmer and slightly different form by the Assistant Commissioner in his address to the labouring classes of the county of Kent, " the hanger-on ought not to be raised higher than him on whom he hangs." Perhaps this principle was an echo of Bentham who wrote in 1831, " Maintenance at the expense of others should not be made more desirable than self-maintenance.' The first Board to which Chadwick was appointed as secretary met with vigorous opposition. Disraeli called Chadwick " this monster in human shape " and Cobbett was no less outspoken, while the "Times" thundered against " the three Pashas of Somerset House, or the Pinch-Pauper Triumvirate." Nevertheless, the Act stemmed the rising tide of demoralisation and will be remembered for its introduction of the principle of centralisation (useful at the time and circumstances), for the " less-eligibility " standard and for the appointment of permanent paid officials presumably trained for the special work of relief.

The working classes, however, were learning the lesson of self help and beginning to combine in large and powerful associations and even to federate these in larger combinations. In the year

3 attempts were made to form a " General Union of all Trades,"
' General Union of the Productive Classes," and in 1834 a
rand National Consolidated Trades Union." " Within a few
ks the Union appears to have been joined by at least half a
ion members, including tens of thousands of farm labourers
women. The extension of new lodges in previously unorgan-
l trades and districts was enormous. Numerous missionary
egates, duly equipped with all the paraphernalia required for
mystic initiation rites, perambulated the country; and a
itive mania for Trade Unionism set in. In December, 1833, we
told that ' scarcely a branch of trade exists in the West of
tland that is not now in a state of union.' The ' Times ' reports
t two delegates who went to Hull enrolled in one evening a
usand men of various trades. At Exeter the two delegates were
ed by the police, and found to be furnished with ' two wooden
s, two large cutlasses, two masks, and two white garments or
es, a large figure of Death with the dart and hourglass, a Bible
l Testament.' Shop assistants on the one hand, and journey-
n chimney-sweeps on the other, were swept into the vortex.
e cabinet-makers of Belfast insisted on joining ' the Trades
ion, or Friendly Society, which had for its object the unity of
cabinet-makers in the three kingdoms.' We hear of ' Plough-
n's Unions ' as far off as Perthshire, and of a ' Shearman's
ion ' at Dundee. And the then rural character of the metro-
itan suburbs is quaintly brought home to us by the announce-
nt of a union of the ' agricultural and other labourers ' of
nsington, Walham Green, Fulham, and Hammersmith. Nor
re the women neglected. ' The Grand Lodge of Operative
nnet Makers ' vies in activity with the miscellaneous ' Grand
dge of the Women of Great Britain and Ireland,' and the
odge of Female Tailors' asks indignantly whether the ' Tailors'
der ' is really going to prohibit women from making waist-
ats. Whether the Grand National Consolidated Trades Union
s responsible for the Lodges of ' Female Gardeners ' and
ncient Virgins,' who afterwards distinguished themselves in
e riotous demand for an eight-hours' day at Oldham, is not
ar." [1]

The Parliament of 1835 was responsible for an important measure Munici-
ich laid the foundation for progress in the development of pal Cor-
vns, the government of which had more and more passed into poration
e hands of corrupt oligarchies, who either elected themselves or Act
re elected by persons or interests whose behests they had to
ey. The Report of a Commission of Inquiry appointed in 1833
vealed a shocking condition of bribery, misappropriation, and
smanagement with a hopeless absence of any attempt on the
rt of the corporations to apply themselves to local government,
eir proper task. The Commissioners reported that " there pre-
ils among the great majority of the incorporated towns a

1832
to
1870

general, and in our opinion a just, dissatisfaction with th
municipal institutions; a distrust of the self-elected munici
councils, whose powers are subject to no popular control, a
whose acts and proceedings, being secret, are unchecked by
influence of public opinion; a distrust of the municipal mag
tracy; a discontent under the burthens of local taxation, wh
revenues which ought to be applied to the public advant:
are sometimes wastefully bestowed upon individuals, sometin
squandered for objects injurious to the character and morals of
people . . . the existing municipal corporations neither poss
nor deserve the confidence or respect " of His Majesty's subjec
and " a thorough reform must be effected before they beco
useful and efficient instruments of local government." The n
Act vested the government in councillors, elected by the burgess
who in their turn elected mayor and aldermen and with th
appointed and had control of all municipal servants. Upon t
body of elected persons were devolved the usual duties of lo
administration and the power to raise and expend funds for pul
purposes, under the safeguard of an independent audit. Anoti
clause, which applied to the provinces and not to London, provic
that members should sit in groups of three or six for wards, in
which the boroughs were divided, and one-third of the memb
for each ward should retire each year.

Victoria
1837
to
1901

With the death of William IV. in 1837 and the accession
Queen Victoria the personal rule of the sovereign came to an e
and constitutional monarchy, in any real sense of the term, beg
The young Princess who succeeded to the throne had been carefu
trained in habits of order, industry, and considerateness for oth
combined with independence. Her first Minister, Melbourne,
whose advice she placed great reliance, guided her in the way th
led to constitutionalism. Disorder and the clamour for repeal
Ireland, rebellion in Canada, the growing strength of the Chart
and similar movements in England made the circumstances of l
accession difficult. In Canada the people of both the Upper a
Lower Provinces were dissatisfied with their Executives, which
Pitt's Act of 1791 were separate, and were jealous of each oth
for the Upper Province was peopled mainly by British, the Lov
by French settlers. In Lower Canada the representative assem
decided to refuse supplies, and the French party under the lead
ship of Papineau raised the standard of rebellion and receiv
some support from the other province. The Home Government

1838

1838 decided to suspend temporarily the Constitution of Lov
Canada and to send out Lord Durham as High Commission
with full powers to deal with the rebellion and to recast the consti
tion of both provinces. The Report which appeared under

1839
Lord
Dur-
ham's
Report

name in 1839 is an historic document, wherein were formulat
principles that were adopted in the following year in the case
Canada and later in all the more important British colonies.
recommended that as far as possible Canada should be govern

the colonists themselves without interference from the Imperial
vernment and that all officers of the Canadian administration,
ept the Governor and his secretary, must be responsible to the
islature of the two provinces. The Act of Union passed in 1840
ted Ontario and Quebec, and provided for a bi-cameral Parlia-
nt, a Legislative Council nominated by the crown, and an elected
use of Representatives. Lord Durham's mission was marred
incredible tactlessness, but the Report which bears his name
queathed to the nation fundamental principles which ever
ce have been the foundation, and indeed explain the success,
ur colonial policy.

The dissatisfaction of the working classes of England with the
ults of the Reform Act of 1832 was the prime cause of the
vement known as Chartism, led by Lovett of the London
orking Men's Association, who believed in constitutional
thods, and by Feargus O'Connor, who, sometimes at least,
vocated a policy of violence. Lovett, at the suggestion of Francis
ice, drafted, with the authority of the London Working Men's
sociation, a programme of reforms upon which the workpeople
re to be asked to concentrate as an irreducible minimum, to be
manded forthwith and to be used as a lever for remedying indus-
al evils such as low wages and unsatisfactory conditions of
our. This programme, upon which O'Connell bestowed the
me of Charter, whence the movement came to be known as
artism, had six points: annual parliaments, manhood suffrage,
te by ballot, abolition of the property qualification for members
parliament, payment of members, equal electoral districts.
is programme, which at the time caused much alarm in staid
litical dovecotes, was anything but new. But now for the first
ne life seemed to be breathed into it and it spread like wildfire.
fortunately the physical force wing of the movement became
dominant, and the House of Commons refused even to consider
uge petition, embodying five of the points contained in it, and
ned by nearly two million names.

The year 1839, however, brought with it two measures, the
ects of which upon the great mass of the people, if not immediately
servable, were immense in their ultimate results. A new com-
ttee of the Privy Council was appointed to supervise elementary
ucation, the grant in aid was raised from £20,000 to £30,000, and
pectors were appointed. Rowland Hill, who had convinced himself
at the high charges for the delivery of letters were unjustifiable
d from the merely commercial point of view unwise, worked out
omprehensive scheme in which he proposed that letters should
despatched more frequently and more speedily and that there
uld be a uniform charge of one penny the half-ounce within the
ited Kingdom. Though the Post Office authorities at first
posed, the commercial classes strongly supported the scheme,
ich the government adopted and placed on the statute book.
e results are too obvious to require comment.

1832
to
1870
—
Union of
Ontario
and
Quebec

Chartism

1839

Penny
Postage

Other influences at this time were introducing fundament
changes in the lives of the people. The application of steam power
locomotion, due to George Stephenson, the self-educated mechani
who at eighteen years of age had not learnt to read and who
belief in the potentialities of steam made staid and unrece
tive people think he was beside himself, was now beginnir
to be firmly established. The Stockton and Darlington Rai
way, which on the advice of its engineer, George Stephenson, ha
applied for parliamentary powers to use steam, was opened on Se
tember 27, 1825. Yet the " Annual Register " for that year, suc
was the blindness of the official mind, did not even mention it.

The event had at the time a merely local importance, an
though some London newspapers published brief accounts
it a week after the opening took place, neither those who believe
in the new invention nor the good people who supposed that
speed of a couple of dozen miles an hour was an impious inte
ference with the designs of Providence realised that for Englan
something had occurred more noteworthy than the passing of th
Reform Act, and for both the New World and the Old, somethin
more important than the battle of Waterloo. No change intr
duced into England in the nineteenth century was received wit
such doubts and fears, none was so immediately and consistentl
a gain to the whole population. The application of steam to ir
dustry made transport more reliable, more punctual, and mor
frequent; stimulated industry and invention in every depart
ment; created, by the curious paradox which makes labou
saving devices bring in their train an increased demand for labou
an immensely larger number of avenues of employment; enable
factories and workshops to be established over a wider area o
country, and increased the mobility of labour; more profoundl
important still, by cheapening and speeding up the means o
communication, it facilitated human intercourse not only fro
town to town, but from country to country. The changes brough
about by the railway in England, where distances were short
were amazing, but not so amazing as in the case of the Unite
States, where railways not only made a highway between th
East and the Middle West, but opened up the Far West. Now
adays the mention of a Cape to Cairo railway or a Trans-Siberia
line from the Far East to Petrograd no longer provokes wonder
The later effects of the application of steam to transit by land o
sea have been the possibility of rapid transference not only o
goods, raw or manufactured, but of perishable food products ove
long distances; the specialisation of industry and the division o
labour; the introduction of large scale industry, followed by th
rise of the joint-stock company system and the development o
banking and credit; and the possibility of linking up and develop
ing the several parts of a world-wide empire.[1]

[1] The reader will see at a glance the importance of this point by con
sulting the Map of the World facing p. 838.

The annual expenditure on railways, which until 1844 had not been more than £5,000,000, rose to £185,000,000 in 1844-6. In 1840 the Railway Regulation Act was passed, which empowered the Board of Trade in the interests of public safety to inspect railways before they were opened. The Cheap Trains Act of 1844 provided that every line must run a train each way daily at a speed of not less than 12 miles an hour and at a charge to passengers, who must be carried in covered waggons, of not more than one penny a mile. An important clause of this Act, which, curious to relate, has been left sterile, though it might have been made fruitful to the advantage of commerce, industry, agriculture, and the travelling public in general, laid down the principle that future railways, the profits of which exceeded 10 per cent., might be bought out by the state at twenty-five years' purchase of " the annual divisible profits, estimated on the average of the three next preceding years." 1832 to 1870 — Development of Railways

The opening of a co-operative store by the Rochdale Pioneers in 1844 was the seed-plot of movements destined to have profound effects not only on the labouring classes of England, but on the Continent of Europe, where the ideas of British co-operators were adopted and in some instances applied with greater success. Co-operation was not a new idea in 1844, but from that date it began to be an effective force. The purposes of the society included, besides the establishment of a store for the sale of provisions, " the building, purchasing, or erecting a number of houses, in which those members, desiring to assist each other in improving their domestic and social condition, may reside; " the manufacture of articles, or purchase or rent of land, in order to employ members who were out of work or under-paid; and further, " that as soon as practicable this society shall proceed to arrange the powers of production, distribution, education, and government; or, in other words, to establish a self-supporting home colony of united interests, or assist other societies in establishing such colonies." The society, which began its career at the " Auld Weyvur's Shop " in Toad Street, had at its inception 28 members, with a duly appointed secretary, a cashier (responsible for a turnover of £2 per week), and a treasurer, who had to administer an accumulated capital of £28. The original members were Chartists, Trade Unionists, or Owenite Socialists, but their aims were identical with those propounded nearly a generation earlier by Robert Owen. Co-operation

The removal of taxes by Peel's great Budget of 1842, though it had produced some improvement, had not availed to produce satisfactory amelioration in the condition of the working classes. Walpole [1] declared that in 1842 " one person in every eleven was a pauper, and one person in every five hundred was committed for trial." In Ireland conditions were worse and were aggravated

---

[1] " History of England," v. p. 503.

1832
to
1870

1845
Failure
of Potato
Crop in
Ireland

by the failure in 1845 of the potato crop, the staple food of the Irish peasantry. Disraeli's picture [1] of the state of the country at that time was literally true. "It was said by the Royal Commission over which Lord Devon presided, that the Irish people were the worst housed, the worst fed, and the worst clothed of any in Europe. They live in mud cabins littered upon straw; their food consists of dry potatoes, of which they are often obliged to stint themselves to one spare meal. Sometimes a herring or a little milk may afford them a pleasing variety, but sometimes also they are driven to seaweed and to wild herbs. Dwelling in hovels and feeding upon roots, they are clothed in rags. Those were the ordinary circumstances of Ireland, and to such a state of affairs famine was now added with all its attendant horrors, pestilence and death. In the southern and western parts of the country the population was decimated; 10,000 persons at the meeting of Parliament had died in the Union of Skibbereen, which numbered 100,000 souls." It might be added that the total population of Ireland, which stood at 8,175,124 at the census of 1841, had in 1851 fallen to 6,552,385, and that the decrease in population, though not with such fatal rapidity, continued till the end of the century with undiminished and appalling regularity.

The failure of the potato crop in Ireland convinced Peel that the only way to meet the need of the labouring classes not only in Ireland, but in Great Britain, for cheaper food was "the total and absolute repeal for ever of all duties on all articles of subsistence." In his speech on the Address to the Throne at the January Parliament of 1846 he declared that he had been converted to the principle of Free Trade, and on May 15 he carried the third reading of his Act for the Repeal of the Corn Law by a majority of 98 against the Protectionists led by Disraeli and Lord George Bentinck. In 1836 an Anti-Corn Law Association had been started in London by Grote, Molesworth, Joseph Hume, and Roebuck, and a similar society in Manchester in 1838, the parent of the Anti-Corn Law League, of which the moving spirit was Richard Cobden, powerfully assisted by Bright, W. J. Fox, and other brilliant lieutenants. It is true that the driving-power of this movement, whether in eloquence or organising capacity, was supplied in the main by cotton manufacturers who were fighting in a sense for their own interests, but it is no less true that they were fighting for the interests of the whole working population of the British islands. Moreover they were profoundly right in their main contentions that the manufacturer must have cheaper raw materials, the farmer cheaper seed, and the whole population cheaper means of subsistence. Even if their dream that unrestricted freedom of trade between nations would tend to produce friendly relations has hardly been justified by subsequent events, at least it was a noble dream, which brought no shame to the heads that conceived it.

[1] "Life of Lord George Bentinck."

The movement for the improvement of industrial conditions, **1832** and especially in the direction of shortening excessive hours of **to** labour, made a perceptible advance by the passing of the Ten **1870** Hours Act (1847), introduced into the House of Commons by Mr. **1847** Fielden, though the credit for it must in the main be given to Lord **The Ten** Shaftesbury, the noble-hearted peer who in season and out of **Hours** season, in face of prejudice and opposition even from those who **Act** might have been expected to assist him, gave himself with single-minded devotion to the cause of the poor and oppressed. The Act, which is valuable not so much for its immediate application as because it gave Parliamentary sanction to a principle afterwards to be widely developed and extended, limited the hours of labour for women and children in textile factories to ten hours. It is curious to find that Bright, assuredly a sincere friend of the people, spoke of the Act as "one of the worst measures ever passed in the shape of an Act of the legislature," and Cooke Taylor, another Free Trader, said of it, "a remedy (for industrial dislocation) has been proposed, which has no parallel in the annals of quackery." When in the same year Lord John Russell proposed to defray **Element-** from taxes one-third of the money required for elementary teach- **ary Edu-** ing, Bright, Roebuck, and other Radicals strongly opposed the **cation** scheme on the ground that education was not a State concern. Macaulay, however, in one of his finest speeches, maintained that not the policeman or the judge, but the schoolmaster, was the sure guardian of life and property, and the measure was triumphantly carried by a huge majority.

Public sanitation may be said to have begun with the establish- **1848** ment of the "General Board of Health" in 1848, a body created as **Begin-** an outcome of the Report issued in 1845 by a Royal Commission **nings of** appointed to inquire into the Health of Towns and Populous **Public** Places. The Report declared that, out of 50 towns studied, scarcely **Sanita-** one had drainage that could be pronounced good; in seven it was **tion** indifferent, and in forty-two decidedly bad, especially in the poor quarters. The Board, which in several respects took as a model the Poor Law Board of 1834, was composed of Lord Shaftesbury, Lord Morpeth, Edwin Chadwick, and Dr. Southwood Smith, able, sincere, disinterested, and determined men, who cared nothing for the clamours of party politics. Chadwick had been sent to the Board with the avowed hope "that he would now keep quiet." Alas! for the fulfilment of this hope he seems to have been even more energetic, determined, and deadly in his criticisms than he had been on the Poor Law Commission. Although the Board of Health came to an end in 1854 and was replaced by a new Board with a paid President sitting in the House, it was while it lasted a kind of accusing witness against filth and insanitation with their attendant evils of disease and aggravated poverty.

A pathetic interest attaches to the Great Exhibition of 1851, **1851** initiated and carried to a striking success by the Prince Consort. **The** The promoters of the enterprise believed that it would not only **Great** **Exhibi-** **tion**

benefit trade and industry, but "bring in the universal peace."
The next 60 years were to show that not thus alone was the demon
of war to be exorcised. The high hopes which inspired the Great
Exhibition were only too speedily to be frustrated by a series

of wars, in the first of which, the Crimean, we were deeply
involved.

The complex details of the campaign which began in 1854 and
ended (superficially speaking) with the Peace of Paris in 1856,
cannot here be set down, but it is well to recall the causes which
brought about the war, and the terms to which the nations engaged
in it agreed at the conclusion of peace. By a treaty, dating from
1740, France had obtained from Turkey the custody of the sacred
places in and about Jerusalem, whither the pious of both Greek
and Latin Churches made pilgrimage. For more than 100 years
France had neglected her duty to care for these shrines, and
members of the Greek Church had tended and kept them in repair.
In May, 1850, Louis Napoleon, supported by Austria, Spain, and
other Catholic countries, reasserted the treaty rights of France,
and, after prolonged negotiation, the Porte in substance conceded
his demand, whereupon Russia immediately entered an energetic
protest. In March, 1853, the Czar Nicholas sent Prince Menschikoff
on a special mission to Constantinople to demand full satisfaction
about the holy places and an acknowledgment by the Sultan of
the Czar's protectorate over all orthodox subjects in Turkish
territory. In April Lord Stratford de Redcliffe, the British representative at Constantinople, persuaded the Porte to admit Russia's
first claim but to refuse the second. On July 21 a Russian army
occupied the Principalities of Moldavia and Wallachia. In October
the Sultan, on the suggestion of Lord Stratford, called upon Russia
to evacuate the Principalities within fifteen days, and followed
up the demand with a declaration of war on October 23. On
November 30 the Russian Black Sea fleet annihilated a Turkish
squadron in the Bay of Sinope, and the British cabinet thereafter
decided that in consequence of this act the allied fleets of England
and France must enter the Black Sea. On February 27 Great
Britain presented an ultimatum to Russia demanding complete
evacuation of the Principalities by the 30th April, and as the Czar
refused to reply, the western Powers declared war on March 27
and 28.

As Austria and Prussia were not prepared to bring active,
but only diplomatic, pressure to bear upon Russia, England and
France were left to bear the burden of war alone, and the campaign proper began when the allied armies landed in the Crimea on
September 14. The personal bravery and endurance of the troops
were shown at the battles of the Alma, Balaclava, and Inkerman;
during the terrible winter of 1854-55, and at Sebastopol and Kars.
Misfortune, as in the loss of the transport steamer "The Prince,"
was aggravated by gross and incredible mismanagement both
in the transport and commissariat departments. England alone

lost 23,000 men and about £80,000,000 in one of the least credit-able wars in which she has ever been engaged. Students of human nature and of human wisdom (or unwisdom) will notice that whereas while it lasted the war was most popular with the majority of people in England, the public opinion of two generations later almost unanimously endorses the dictum of the great statesman who tersely summed up the situation in the words, " England put her money on the wrong horse."

The one thing in the history of the war which later times have endorsed without qualification is the work of Miss Florence Nightingale and her band of trained nurses, who not only in-augurated a new profession, but, incidentally, opened another door for the entry of women into public life.

By the terms of the Treaty of Paris (March 30, 1856) the Sublime Porte, on the invitation of the six Powers, who pledged themselves severally and collectively to guarantee the independence and territorial integrity of the Ottoman Empire and repudiated the right to interfere either separately or collectively in its internal affairs, was formally admitted " to participate in the public law and concert of Europe." The Black Sea was neutralised and with the river Danube was declared open to the mercantile navigation of all nations. Russia renounced her claim to an exclusive pro-tectorate over the Principalities of Moldavia and Wallachia, which were granted complete independence under the suzerainty of the Porte. The Powers collectively guaranteed the liberties of the Principalities and of Serbia. The Sultan on his part made a formal undertaking to place his Christian on an equality with his Mussul-man subjects.

By the Declaration of Paris, to which the Powers also sub-scribed, it was agreed to abolish privateering and to lay down as established principles of naval warfare that, except in the case of contraband, (1) a neutral flag was to cover enemy goods; (2) and that neutral merchandise could not be seized under an enemy flag, and further that a blockade could not be declared unless it was backed by an adequate naval force.

How indecisive was the situation created by the Treaty of Paris the next twenty years were to tell. The Crimean War was not only directly responsible for a huge loss of men and money, but indirectly it brought about that state of unstable equilibrium from which sprang the Franco-Austrian War of 1859, the Prusso-Danish of 1864, the Austro-Prussian of 1866, the Franco-German of 1870, the Russo-Turkish of 1878, and these in their turn created a condi-tion of yet more unstable equilibrium with consequences in 1912 and 1914 the ultimate results of which no man as yet can foresee.[1]

When Lord Dalhousie left India in 1856, and made way for Lord Canning, he was convinced that the native army was loyal to the British rule. But others, who had served England in India, Sir Charles Napier and Sir Henry Lawrence, had uttered words of

The Indian Mutiny 1857

[1] For Crimean War see " Cambridge Modern History," vol. xi. ch. xi.

warning which were disregarded. For thirty years before 1857 mutinies of greater or less magnitude had taken place, but had been officially hushed up. The annexation of the Punjab and of Oude, the growing belief that it was the aim of British rule to uproot the native religion and caste, the reports spread from mouth to mouth of England's military weakness as displayed in the Crimea, Persia, Afghanistan, and the Punjab—all these were elements contributing to a spirit of unrest concealed beneath apparent impassivity, but ready at the slightest touch to break out into overt acts. Cartridges for the new Enfield rifle, distributed to the native troops in 1853, were said—and in this case rumour was *not* a lying jade— to be smeared with the fat of cows and pigs. As to load the new rifle it was necessary to bite the cartridge, the act meant sacrilege to the Hindus and pollution to the Mohammedans. The gross tactlessness of allowing cartridges prepared in this way to be issued for use was aggravated by an official denial that they had been so prepared, and the feeling spread that a deliberate attempt was being made to set at nought the most sacred native beliefs. An outbreak at Meerut, where the whole native regiment mutinied, destroyed the European quarters, and butchered every European man, woman, and child, was followed by the march of the mutineers to Delhi, where the old Mogul King was proclaimed Emperor of India, the Christian churches desecrated, and the European inhabitants, chiefly women, massacred. The recapture of Delhi by the British was not sufficient to turn the tide of war. The horrors of the mutiny at Cawnpore exceeded those of Delhi; other massacres hardly less repulsive took place at Jhansi and in Bengal, the North-West Provinces, and Oude, and the Residency at Lucknow was besieged. Not indeed until January, 1859, were the mutineers, as an organised force, defeated by the efforts of Havelock, Outram, Nicholson, and Sir Colin Campbell.

The mutiny had made it clear that India could no longer be administered by a commercial company, and by an Act passed in 1858 the Queen was proclaimed Sovereign, with the Governor-General as Viceroy, the territories of the Company were taken over by the Crown, and the administration was entrusted to a Secretary of State, supported by a Council of fifteen members, nine of whom were required to have resided recently for ten years in India. The terms of the Queen's Proclamation, issued on November 1 (the wording was due to Lord Derby, who at the Queen's request drafted the document), show the spirit in which it was proposed to discharge these new responsibilities. "It is our royal will and pleasure that no one shall in any wise suffer for his opinions, or be disquieted by reason of his religious faith or observance. We will show to all alike the equal and impartial protection of the law, and we do strictly charge and enjoin those who may be in authority under us that they abstain from all interference with the religious belief or worship of any of our subjects on pain of our highest displeasure. It is our further will

East
India
Company's
territories
taken
over by
the
Crown
1858

that, so far as may be, our subjects of whatever class or creed be fully and freely admitted to any offices the duties of which they may be qualified by their education, abilities, and integrity duly to discharge."

The year 1858 at last crowned with success efforts extending over a quarter of a century to secure the admission of the Jews to Parliament. An Act was passed empowering either House to alter by resolution the form of oath to be taken by its members. The Commons used the opportunity afforded by the Act to pass a resolution that the words " on the true faith of a Christian " might be omitted by Jews, and Baron Rothschild, who for ten years had been one of the members for the City of London, took his seat. In the same session, chiefly through the persistence of Mr. Locke King, the property qualification for members of Parliament was abolished.

The years 1859 to 1866 are of surpassing interest to the student of the history of nations. To them belong Italy's successful struggle for national unity, under the leadership of Garibaldi, Mazzini, and Cavour, in which the sympathies of the mass of Englishmen were with Italy; the American Civil War, in which the workers of the North of England, though they suffered cruelly by it, warmly espoused the cause of the Northern States; and the Prusso-Danish War of 1864, in which popular feeling in England was on the side of the Danes, while the Government stood aside, though interest as well as honour should have led them to throw their weight into the scales against Prussia. Palmerston, writing in 1863, expressed his deliberate opinion that at the bottom of the German design was " the dream of a German fleet and the wish to get Kiel as a German seaport." He went on to add that any attempt to violate the rights and independence of Denmark would bring England to her aid. Bismarck, however, had taken the measure of both the French Emperor and the British statesman, Denmark was left to herself, and from the military point of view ignominiously defeated.

The struggles, a mingled record of success and failure, of the British working classes were not only widening their political sympathies, but increasing their initiative and skill in affairs. The propaganda and practical experiments of Robert Owen had impressed not only the intelligent working classes, but many of the ablest and most sincere among non-manual workers. The tiny seed planted by the Rochdale Pioneers had spread widely and surely. In November, 1863, the Co-operative Wholesale Society, a federation of 45 societies, was established at Manchester. Beginning with a capital of 1400 £5 shares the Society grew rapidly, and besides its business of selling, undertook manufacturing, transport, banking, insurance, and other activities by the end of the century when its annual turnover was to be estimated in many millions of pounds. The question of Parliamentary reform, so far as Parliament was concerned, had long lain dormant.

But inasmuch as out of 5,300,000 adult males in England and Wales, only 900,000 had the vote and great urban populations increasing in numbers and self-consciousness were springing up, it was obvious that some changes would have to be made.

Gladstone's Reform Bill of 1866 proposed to make the qualification for the boroughs £7 and for the counties £14, and to enfranchise lodgers, compound householders, and Savings Banks depositors who had had £50 continuously to their credit for at least two years. The Ministry were defeated and tendered their resignation. As Prussia, or rather Bismarck, had just engineered another war (against Austria) and the European situation was fraught with peril, the Queen was averse to accepting the proffered resignation, but Lord Russell persisted and Lord Derby was asked to form a ministry. This was the signal for a great popular demand for an extension of the Parliamentary franchise. Huge demonstrations were held at Trafalgar Square and in Hyde Park, in Manchester, Birmingham, Leeds, Glasgow, and many other towns. Disraeli, as leader of the House of Commons, introduced a bill of much wider scope than that which the House had rejected twelve months before. Nevertheless Parliament took the step which Lord Derby called " taking a leap in the dark," and Carlyle, with a profusion of dyspeptic epithet, denounced as " Shooting Niagara." By the new Act every householder paying rates, and having resided for one year, lodgers occupying rooms of the annual rental of £10, and in the counties all with a rating qualification of £12 were admitted to the franchise. J. S. Mill, supported by John Bright and Henry Fawcett, introduced an amendment in favour of women suffrage, which was thrown out by 196 to 73; other amendments embodying Mr. Hare's scheme of proportional representation met with some sympathy, but had to be withdrawn. The effect of the Act was to put on the register over 1,000,000 voters, while Gladstone's bill of the year before would not have added half the number.

The British North America Act of 1867 put an end to the friction between the two provinces of Canada by a wise compromise which allowed them local liberty, and initiated the first experiment in federalism under a constitutional monarch. The new Constitution for Canada established by the Act was expressly modelled upon that of the United Kingdom. The executive was vested in the Sovereign of the United Kingdom, represented in the Dominion by a Governor-General, who had command of the armed forces and the right to appoint or discharge the Lieutenant-Governors of the Provinces. The Legislature was to be composed of the Sovereign, the Senate of 87 members nominated for life by the Governor-General on the advice of his responsible ministers, and a House of Commons of 181 members. Similarly in each province there were to be a Lieutenant-Governor, appointed by the Governor-General, and an Executive Council. In Quebec, Nova Scotia, and New Brunswick the Legislature was

nposed of two Houses, but of only one in Ontario. Provision
s inserted in the Act for the admission of other colonies beside
)se mentioned to the Dominion. The importance of this measure
s little understood at the time. Most English people thought it
s a mere stepping-stone to complete independence. Bright,
leed, thought the alternatives were independence or annexation
the States, and even Disraeli with all his marvellous shrewdness
d imagination had not, or at least did not say that he had, begun
perceive the significance of such a policy in establishing the
ndations of Empire.

The appointment in 1867 of a Royal Commission of Inquiry
o the work and legal position of Trade Unions may be traced
two causes. Trade Unions, increasing in numbers and in wealth,
d now become of national importance, and had aroused the
stility of many employers, who began to unite in powerful
inter-associations. The employees resorted to the weapon of
strike, the masters retaliated with the lock-out. Some outrages,
particular one at Sheffield, where the Saw-Grinders' Union was
ved to have instigated the exploding of a can of gunpowder in
house of a workman who had deserted the union and was
rking for a firm against whom they had struck, could un-
ibtedly be traced to trade-union agency. Employers demanded
t the criminal acts of trade-unionists should be investigated.
e unions demanded an opportunity of clearing themselves of
allegations made against them. Moreover, it had become clear
them that they must obtain legal protection for the large
umulated funds by means of which they discharged their
ictions. By the Act of 1825, trade unions, as such, were no longer
gal associations, but they had as yet no legal status and could
t take proceedings as corporate entities, even if, for example, they
sired to take action against a defaulting secretary or treasurer.

In 1868 Gladstone carried a Bill for the abolition of compulsory
urch Rates, which removed a legitimate grievance of English
nconformists; and in 1869 swept away a yet more intolerable
d indefensible anomaly by the Act for the Disestablishment and
rtial Disendowment of the English Church in Ireland. This
urch, than which no body of people ever did less to justify a
vileged position, was a purely exotic growth. Episcopalians were
s than one in eight of the whole population, and in 199 parishes
t of 2428 this form of Christianity was wholly unrepresented.[1]
t the revenues of this minority of 700,000 people (in 1868)
iounted to £614,000 a year. By the Act of 1869 the Irish Church
s disestablished and its connection with the English Church
minated. The four Irish bishops who had hitherto sat in the
use of Lords were deprived of their seats. All beneficed clergy
re to retain their places and their net income for life, or commute
for a life annuity and resign their charges. The grant to the
tholic College of Maynooth and the *Regium Donum* (to Presby-

Dises-
tablish-
ment of
English
Church
in Ire-
land

[1] Brady, " English State Church in Ireland," p. 159.

1870
to
1914

terian ministers) were commuted on an equitable if not libe
basis. The Act has been an immense boon to the Disestablish
Church, which being driven to rely upon itself and not on t
insecure foundation of indefensible privilege has done more use
work in the fifty years during which it has been on a footing
equality than in all its previous history.

CHAPTER III

From the Education Act to Outbreak of European W.

1870-1914

[*Authorities.*—An immense amount of material for this period l
been accumulated, but much more remains, still to be made access
and to be sifted for general readers, in official papers, in the records
numerous organisations, and in private diaries. The following is
brief selection: The " Cambridge Modern History " (vol. xii.); Pa
" Modern England "; Macarthy's " History of our own Times "; Ro
" Development of the European Nations "; Marriott's " England si
Waterloo " and " English Political Institutions "; Low and Sand
" Political History of England (1837-1901) "; R. H. Gretton's " Mod
History of England (1880-1910) "; Bright's " History of Engl
(1880-1901)." Irish questions may be studied in Paul Dubois' " C
temporary Ireland "; O'Connor Morris' " Ireland from 1798 to 1898
Plunkett's " Ireland in the New Century " and " New Ireland "; and
the Reports of the Bessborough (1881) and Parnell (1890) Commissic
On the subject of Egypt, Lord Cromer's " Modern Egypt " and Colvi
" The Making of Modern Egypt "; and for South Africa, Lucas' " So
Africa "; Fitzpatrick's " The Transvaal from Within." Cook's " 1
Rights and Wrongs of the Transvaal War "; De Wet's " Three Ye
War "; V. Markham's " South Africa, Past and Present," should be c
sulted. The biographies of Queen Victoria (Lee) and King Edward V
(Lee), of Beaconsfield (Sichel: Monypenny), the Duke of Devons
(Holland), Gladstone (Morley), John Bright (G. M. Trevelyan), L
Randolph Churchill (W. S. Churchill), Parnell (O'Brien) are indispensa
Working-class conditions and efforts to improve them are described
A. L. Bowley's " Wages in the Nineteenth Century "; C. Booth's " I
and Labour of the People of London "; Rowntree's " Poverty "; Gen
Booth's " In Darkest London "; S. and B. Webb's " Trade Unionis
and " Industrial Democracy." The most recent and most authoritat
general statement of the condition of the very poor in the British Isla
is the Report of the Poor Law Commission, 1909. The annual volun
of the Co-operative Wholesale Society and the files of papers like
" Labour Leader," " Justice," " The Clarion," are a valuable index
movements of opinion among the organised working classes.]

THE Reform Act of 1867 brought one political era to an e
and introduced another. Until 1832 political power in Gr
Britain had largely resided in the landed aristocracy; during t
period between the two great Reform Bills (1832 and 1867) t
centre of gravity had passed to the commercial and manufactur
classes. Henceforth the bounds of freedom and responsibility w
to be extended to include the manual working population, w
whose interests much of the legislation of the next 40 years was
be concerned. In 1870 Gladstone, having dealt with one Irish di
culty, attacked another, but one much more thorny and comp
cated, the question of Irish land tenure. Ireland was seething w
discontent, and Fenian outrages in England brought home to t
average man the depth of feeling which Irish grievances, whet
genuine or merely fictitious, had engendered. Irish difficulties w

Land
Reform
in
Ireland
1870

gland have always sprung from the fact that English rule in
eland in its earlier stages, and until well on in the nineteenth
ntury, was an attempt to Anglicise a people whose national
nius and traditions, for good or ill, were essentially different
om those of their conquerors. The Report of the Devon Com-
ssion of 1845 made it clear for the first time that a serious
rarian problem existed in Ireland, due to the fact that by age-
ng tradition the Irish tenant believed himself to have customary
hts in the land which he rented. The same commission recorded
e fact that in Ireland improvements were made by the tenant,
d not, as in England, by the landlord; that the landlords, when
provements were made, raised the rent; and that the feeling of
itation at this barefaced injustice led to crime. The effect of the
Encumbered Estates Act " of 1849 was to introduce a new set of
ndlords, who looked upon their estates as a mere commercial
eculation out of which they extorted as much profit as possible.
rdwell's Act of 1860 laid down the principle, well meant, but
tirely irrelevant to the facts of the case, that " the relation
tween landlord and tenant shall be deemed to be founded on the
press or implied contract of the parties and not upon tenure or
rvice." Gladstone, who until he began to prepare his Bill had
t studied the subject, had the assistance of J. S. Mill and many
her distinguished authorities. Mill thought the only plan was to
y out the landlords, but this was felt to be too bold a step for
70, and the Bill after being severely mauled in both Houses
ssed and received the Royal assent. The main provisions of the
t secured to the tenant compensation (1) in the case of being
icted for any other cause than non-payment of rent and (2) for
exhausted improvements made by himself or his predecessor.
e Ulster tenant-right and similar customs were given legal
nction and something was done to facilitate purchase. Though
is was very far from being a settlement of the question, it was at
ast a great advance. Unfortunately for some time before the
ogress of the Bill through Parliament, and especially while it
as being discussed, there had been a recrudescence of agrarian
ime in Ireland, incalculably mischievous from every point of view.
quell these Acts of violence the Government carried through
e Peace Preservation Act which forbade the use of firearms
districts proclaimed by the Lord-Lieutenant, and the possession
arms under any circumstances without a licence. The police
ere empowered (1) to enter dwelling-houses in search of arms or
evidence to prove the authorship of threatening letters, and
) to arrest any persons wandering about at night under suspicious
rcumstances. In cases where it was supposed to be impossible
secure a conviction, power was given to change the venue of a
ial. So far as Irish history is concerned, 1870 was also remarkable
r the beginning of the " Home Rule " movement by the forma-
n, under the leadership of Isaac Butt, of the " Home Government
ssociation of Ireland." This Society, which in 1873 was renamed

the " Home Rule League," was an organisation established 1
secure by constitutional means an Irish Parliament meeting i
Ireland to legislate for and to regulate all internal affairs (finan
included), leaving Imperial questions to be dealt with by th
Imperial Government. It is curious in view of later events to not
that no one attacked the new movement more bitterly tha
Gladstone.

Much more important for England than an Irish Land Act o
the birth of a new Irish propaganda was the Education Act o
1870, for which Mr. W. E. Forster was mainly responsible, an
which laid the foundation of modern English elementary educatio
England's neglect of popular education could only be describe
as scandalous. Other European countries, even some much weake
in material resources, were far in advance of England, whe
educational progress was hampered by stupid people who professe
to believe that education was not the business of the State and b
sectarians of one camp or another who were more concerned t
defend their own vested interests than to have the rising genera
tion educated. Forster on the other hand, whose sincerity has nev
been questioned, was possessed by a single-minded desire " t
cover the country with good schools." His Act embodied thre
principles new to English public education: the compulsor
attendance of children at school, a representative local authority
and a compulsory local rate. The whole of England for the pu
poses of the Act was divided into school districts, in towns th
municipal borough being the unit and in the country the civ
parish. Where accommodation for elementary scholars wa
insufficient, School Boards, in the boroughs chosen by the Tow
Council, and in the country by the Vestry, would be electe
charged with the duty of providing elementary education an
empowered to levy a rate for the purpose. The expenses of th
Board Schools were to be borne in equal proportions by the Stat
the local rate, and the parents of the scholars. Free schools migh
be established in very poor districts, and in any district the fee
of very poor parents might be paid by the Board. An importan
point was left to the discretion of the local authority, whether i
their district education should be made compulsory, and by th
famous Cowper-Temple Clause, which the Government accepte
as an amendment, it was provided that no catechism or othe
distinctive denominational formulary should be taught in an
Board School, and that no voluntary school should receive assist
ance from the rates. In November the first School Board fo
London was elected by ballot, and a woman, Dr. Elisabet
Garrett, headed the poll.

The spirit of reform was not confined to the sphere of educatio
in this *annus mirabilis* of legislative activity. It even whiske
away some of the cobwebs of the military system, the most costly
least efficient, and least enlightened of all the activities of th
British Government. During Cardwell's tenure of office as Secre

tary of State for War he reorganised (or rather organised) the business of his office under three departments, under the control of the Commander-in-Chief, the Surveyor-General of the Ordnance, and the Financial Secretary. All three were to be under the control of the Secretary of State, whereas previously the Commander-in-Chief could dispense patronage and exercise other powers without consulting the Secretary of State. As regards the Army, Cardwell considered, but rejected, the Prussian idea of compulsory service, and contented himself with the attempt to make our small voluntary Army efficient. By royal warrant the practice of purchasing commissions, and subsequent promotion in the Army, was abolished, and in the Army Enlistment Act the short-service system and permanent reserve were established. In 1872, though reducing the Army estimates by more than a million, he increased the number of soldiers at home by withdrawals from the Colonies. Another change, an immense advance on what preceded it, was the system of " linked " battalions. The country was divided into territorial districts, each of which was to raise a regiment of the line, consisting of two battalions, one serving at home and one abroad, while the militia and the volunteers were to be grouped under the same Lieutenant-Colonel.

To 1870 belongs also another long-delayed change in public administration. Until the middle of the nineteenth century Government Service appointments were regarded by a large section of society as existing merely to provide avenues of employment for their sons. From 1854 candidates for the Civil Service of India had to submit to competitive examination. An Order in Council of June 7, 1870, gave effect to proposals which, in the main, had been made by Sir Charles Trevelyan and Sir Stafford Northcote as early as 1853. By the new Order all public offices, except those in the Foreign Office and Diplomatic Service, were only obtainable after open and competitive examination. *Admission to Civil Service*

Another anomaly was swept away by the Act of 1871, which abolished all theological tests for professors, tutors, fellows, and scholars, a reservation being made in the case of college headships, clerical fellowships, and of theological chairs and degrees in divinity. By this means Oxford and Cambridge were started on the way to becoming what they were not then, representative of all forms of faith in the country. Still some time was to elapse before it could be said that university life was a mirror of all classes in the nation. *Abolition of Theological Tests*

Vote by ballot, of which there had been some advocates as long before as 1780 and at intervals ever since, was at last put upon the statute book in 1872. Many were opposed to it on the high ground that the vote is a trust and that the world should see how it was used. As in the case of most changes that have been brought about by struggle, its results have not been so pernicious as its opponents maintained they would be, nor so beneficial as its advocates believed. The man who wishes to do so can still *Ballot Act* find means to bribe and to intimidate without coming within the four corners of the law.

The Board of Health to which Edwin Chadwick had been appointed in 1848 came to an end in 1854, chiefly because of the unbending zeal of Chadwick and his collaborators for an efficient Health Administration. Chadwick was retired on pension, in other words cashiered, just at the time when he was at the zenith of his usefulness in the war against dirt and disease. It became clear to the more thoughtful minds that these twin evil spirits could only be driven out by carefully conceived efforts and by the joint endeavours of public and private agencies. A Royal Commission on the subject (1869) recommended (1) that a strong central authority should supervise the administration of all laws relating to public health and (2) that the charge of local public health administration should be entrusted to the municipalities. These recommendations, as has been the fate of many Royal Commissions, were for the time shelved, but in 1872, when Disraeli was developing the creed of the new Toryism in a series of speeches, he inscribed upon his banner, besides the maintenance of the Constitution and the Empire, the war-cry *Sanitas sanitatum omnia sanitas*. The Public Health Act of 1875 established a system of local health administration and codified the duties thus to be imposed on the municipalities. The charge of public health was handed over to the Poor Law Board without fitting it to assume these new and onerous duties or introducing any change, save to alter its name to the "Local Government Board." Nevertheless, the Act is important as it explicitly recognised that the care of the public health is a national responsibility.

In 1871 the Trade Union Act for the first time gave legal recognition to trade societies, but the Criminal Law Amendment Act put further restraint upon the means (strikes, picketing, etc.) by which they endeavoured to enforce their demands. This was the signal for four years' determined agitation on the part of the organised workers who attained their desires by Mr. Cross' Trade Union Act of 1875. This measure brought to a close what is perhaps the most important period in trade-union history. It enacted that "an agreement or combination by two or more persons to do or procure to be done any act in contemplation or furtherance of a trade dispute between employers and workmen shall not be indictable as a conspiracy if such act committed by one person would not be punishable as a crime." Peaceful picketing was permitted, but certain kinds of intimidation likely to be used by trade unionists were forbidden under heavy penalties. Lastly, trade unions were legally protected as regards their funds.

Samuel Plimsoll, member for Derby, had for some years devoted himself to the task of securing protection for British seamen by putting an end to the system which allowed them to go to sea in over-loaded and often over-insured ships. He was so far successful that the then President of the Board of Trade, Sir Charles Adderley, introduced a Merchant Shipping Bill, which would have given some protection to seamen. When Disraeli announced that the Bill would be postponed, Plimsoll's indignation could not control itself and he burst forth in a torrent of language which was quite unparliamentary, but entirely true and justifiable. Moreover, to the great scandal of lovers of precedent, he had volleyed forth his wrath not from his usual seat but from the middle of the floor. As a result he was suspended for a week, when he apologised for the irregularity of his outburst, but refused to withdraw the charges he had made. During the week, however, public opinion emphatically endorsed his condemnation of "the villains who send men to death and destruction," the Government passed as a temporary measure the Unseaworthy Ships Act, and in the following year the Merchant Shipping Bill empowered the Board of Trade to detain ships, but left with the owners the responsibility of fixing a loadline for each voyage.

In 1875 Disraeli, on the suggestion of Greenwood, the brilliant editor of the "Pall Mall Gazette," bought from the Khedive, who wished to dispose of them and probably would have done so to France had not Disraeli acted with promptness, his shares in the Suez Canal. This stroke, though opposed by some of Disraeli's colleagues, appealed to the imagination of most Englishmen both in Parliament and out of it. Its author recommended it as an act of far-seeing imperial policy, not as a financial speculation. From the point of view of our position in the East, its effects have been far-reaching; as an investment it has been extremely profitable, for shares which were bought for £4,000,000 are worth £30,000,000 and produce a dividend of 25 per cent. on the purchase money. Purchase of Suez Canal Shares 1875

Another felicitous stroke by the same hand, which appealed no less to the imagination of the mass of Englishmen, was the Royal Titles Bill of 1876, by which the Queen was in future to be named Empress of India.

Lord Sandon, Vice-President of the Education Committee in Disraeli's Ministry, carried in 1876 an Act of great importance in the history of elementary education. This measure carried to a further stage the principle of compulsion. It enacted that "it shall be the duty of the parent of every child to cause such child to receive efficient elementary instruction in reading, writing, and arithmetic, and if such parent fail to perform such duty he shall be liable to such orders and penalties as are provided by the Act." In cases of poverty school fees might be obtained by parents from the Poor Law Guardians instead of from the School Boards, without incurring the stigma of pauperism. No child might be employed at all under the age of ten, and no child between the ages of ten and fourteen without a certificate of having passed the Fourth Standard. To enforce attendance School Attendance Committees were set up in every district in England and Wales where no School Boards existed. Compulsory Education 1876

By the Sand River Convention of 1852, as a result of which

the Transvaal Republic came into existence as an independent state, the British Government conceded "to the emigrant farmers beyond the Vaal River the right to manage their own affairs, and to govern themselves without any interference on the part of Her Majesty's Government." This agreement, however, was subject to two important qualifications, that the Republic was to be open to all comers and that slavery was neither to be practised nor permitted. Sir George Grey, the far-seeing administrator under whose *régime* (1854–1861) Natal was granted an elected Legislature, was in favour of some form of federation and advocated this view in a State paper submitted to the Home Government in 1858. It is noteworthy that at this period the Orange River Boers were in favour of union or alliance on a federal basis with Cape Colony. By the South African Federation Bill of 1877 the Transvaal was annexed and the Boers promised autonomy under the British Crown. While the Bill was in progress through the House, two independent members, Mr. Leonard Courtney, as he then was, and Professor Fawcett, vigorously opposed the policy of annexation on the ground that it would lead to trouble later, and maintained with equal vigour that South Africa was not yet ripe for federalism. These criticisms fell on deaf ears, but time has amply justified them.

As has already been pointed out, the Crimean War had brought no permanent settlement of questions in the Near East. Turkey had done nothing to improve the lot of the Christians within her borders, as she had undertaken to do by the terms of the Treaty of Paris. The administration of her finances was no less unsatisfactory and in October, 1875, the Sultan informed his creditors that he was unable to pay the interest on the debt. When the Sultan appeared unable to quell a revolt in Bosnia and Herzegovina, which had lasted for five months, the Emperors of Germany, Austria-Hungary, and Russia communicated to Great Britain, France, and Italy, through Count Andrassy, the Austro-Hungarian Chancellor, a Note which laid down what, in the opinion of Russia and the Central Empires, ought to be the policy of Europe towards Turkey. The Porte should be required to carry out the promised reforms, to establish complete religious liberty, to abolish taxfarming, to guarantee that the taxes levied in Bosnia and Herzegovina should be applied for the benefit of those provinces, to introduce peasant ownership among the agrarian population, and to appoint a commission, half of whose members should be Christian and half Mussulman, to see that these reforms were carried out. The British Government endorsed the policy of the Note and the
Sultan in January, 1876, consented to all its demands except that with regard to the application of the taxes.

The insurrection, however, spread and the area of revolt was increased by the rising of the Bulgarians, upon whom the Turks inflicted the most savage and incredible barbarities. The French and German Consuls at Salonica were massacred by a mob of ammedans. The Austrian, Russian, and German Chancellors at Berlin (May 11) and drew up a peremptory memorandum, ch demanded an immediate armistice of two months and the triation during this interval of refugees from Bosnia and zegovina. France and Italy accepted the memorandum, but land declined on the ground that she had not been consulted that in any case the plan suggested would not succeed. On 30 the Sultan was deposed and he was found dead on June 4. Princes of Serbia and Montenegro declared war against Turkey. orts of atrocities committed by Bashi-Bazouks in Bulgaria an to reach England, and Lord Derby, the Foreign Minister, ugh the British Ambassador at the Porte, demanded from the an immediate and adequate reparation. By this time indigna- in England had reached a high pitch, but it was roused to ie by Gladstone's pamphlet " The Bulgarian Horrors and the stion of the East," which was circulated far and wide. This t is popularly remembered for its demand that the British ernment, " which has been working in one direction, shall work he other, and shall apply all its vigour to concur with the other tes of Europe in obtaining the extinction of the Turkish Execu- power in Bulgaria. Let the Turks now carry away their abuses he only possible manner, namely, by carrying off themselves. ir Zaptiehs and their Mudirs, their Bimbashis and their Yuz- nis, their Kaimakams and their Pashas, one and all, bag and gage, shall, I hope, clear out from the province they have)lated and profaned." On April 24 Russia declared war against key, and when the Russian Army reached Adrianople in uary (1878) it became clear that the Turks would have to come erms. By the Treaty of San Stefano, 1878, Montenegro, Serbia, . Roumania were to be recognised as independent of Turkey; reforms promised in Bosnia, Herzegovina, and Armenia were)e carried out; Russia was to have Batoum, Kars, and other itory in Asia; Bulgaria was to be constituted an autonomous icipality with a Christian Government and a national militia, xtend from the Danube to the Ægean, and nearly as far south Adrianople and Salonica. Great Britain insisted that the Treaty uld be submitted to a European Congress, which was held at lin on June 8 and was attended by Lord Beaconsfield and Lord isbury. Why these distinguished men should have taken the ible to cross to Berlin is not obvious to the plain intelli- ce, seeing that Lord Salisbury had already (on May 30) ied a secret convention with Count Schouvaloff, and a secret ity had also been concluded with the Porte, by which England lertook to defend Turkey's Asiatic possessions and Turkey eed to introduce reforms satisfactory to England in Syria, Asia ior, and Armenia. By the Treaty of Berlin, which was signed July 13, the terms of the Treaty of San Stefano were confirmed h certain vital exceptions. Bulgaria was to consist of a narrow ct of land between the Danube and the Balkans and to have

Russia's
Declara-
tion of
War,
April 24,
1877

1870
to
1914

autonomy under the suzerainty of Turkey.   The area to the so
of Bulgaria, Eastern Rumelia, was to be restored to the Sult
and was to be administered by a Christian governor approved
the Powers.   Bosnia and Herzegovina were to be occupied
Austria.   This treaty was the cause of friction and misundersta
ing with Russia for nearly thirty years and it is highly questi
able if the policy of keeping the Turk in Europe has been justi
by results.

The
Trans-
vaal

1879

1880

1881

The policy of annexation of the Transvaal was in the high
degree unsatisfactory to the Boer leaders, who persistently p
tested against it.   The grant of a Crown Colony Constitution
1879, after Sir Garnet Wolseley assumed the duties of H
Commissioner, disappointed expectations, which had been arou
by Shepstone's promise of self-government.   Gladstone's Gove
ment, which came into power in 1880, laid down the principle t
under no circumstances could the Queen's authority in the Tra
vaal be relinquished.   On December 16, Kruger, Pretorius, a
Joubert proclaimed at Heidelberg a Boer Republic.   A Brit
detachment was cut up at Brunkerspruit.   Sir George Colley w
checked at Laing's Nek and at Ingogo and heavily defeated
Majuba Hill (February 26, 1881).   Sir Frederick Roberts, w
had been sent to South Africa, was recalled from Cape Town a d
after his arrival.   While he was on the way Sir Evelyn Wood h
come to terms with the Boers at the Convention of Preto
(March 23) by which the Boers were granted autonomy under t
suzerainty of the Queen, but the foreign relations of the count
were to be under British control and there was to be a Brit
Resident at Pretoria for the protection of natives.   The vacillati
policy of the British in this and other matters that appertained
South Africa increased the difficulties naturally inherent in t
situation and the Convention of Pretoria no more settled t
South African question than the Treaty of Berlin solved the pro
lems of the Near East.

1880
Compul-
sory
Educa-
tion

Less exciting but not unimportant problems were being handl
if not solved, nearer home.   In 1880, on the initiative of M
Mundella, the son of an Italian refugee, who, by his own exertio
had risen from the workshop to the position of a Minister of t
Crown, the provisions for compulsory attendance at elementa
schools were strengthened by a new Act which made it obligato
on all School Boards and School Attendance Committees to pa
by-laws under the Act of 1870 instead of waiting for a requisiti
from their parish.   Further security was added to the position

Em
ployers'
Liability
Act,
1881

the workman by the Employers' Liability Act of 1881, though
did not wholly remove the grievance at which it was aimed.   Sin
1837 it had been the decision of the Law Courts by what came
be known as the doctrine of "common employment," that thou
an employer was liable to strangers for an accident caused by
servants, he was not liable to one servant for an accident broug
about by the carelessness of another.   If an explosion at a mi

ld be traced to a miner, people at the pit-head who were
ared by the accident could sue the mineowner, though other
aers could not. The Act modified, but did not abolish, the
trine of "common employment."

Gladstone had been returned to power in 1880 on his indictment
the whole Disraelian policy. But there were breakers ahead
his own party, even if Disraeli had passed away and the system
which he had stood seemed ignominiously beaten from the
d. Charles Bradlaugh, a militant atheist, who had been returned Bradlaugh
and Affir-
mation
member for Northampton, asked to be allowed to make an
rmation instead of taking the Parliamentary Oath, which
plied religious belief. Select Committees decided that he could
ther make affirmation nor take the oath in its usual form. The
e was taken to the Courts, which decided against him and
clared his seat vacant. He was re-elected four times by North-
apton. Finally, after the election of 1885, Mr. Speaker Peel
clared that he knew of no reason why Bradlaugh, whom North-
apton had chosen for the fourth time, should not take his seat.
the passing of the Affirmation Act of 1888 freedom was given
scrupulous consciences to affirm instead of taking the more
ual oath.

The Bradlaugh case, which excited the most protracted and
olent discussion both in Parliament and the country, was the
st difficulty which beset Gladstone's Government. Others of a
ore serious kind were speedily to arise. Ireland had for long been
ething with disturbance. Evictions on the one hand, ceaseless Unrest
in
Ireland
itation and outbreaks of lawlessness on the other, made the task
governing the country an unenviable one. Isaac Butt's Home
ule Party was not led with sufficient vigour to make it formid-
le, and it was not till Parnell, a leader of extraordinary tenacity,
ill, and power, assumed the chief place, that the Irish Party in
arliament began to make itself felt. The fact that 2590 agrarian 1880
atrages were reported in 1880 drove the Cabinet to ask Parlia-
ent that the Irish Executive should be equipped with still more
ringent methods of repressing turbulence, and the first of many
ercion Acts was passed, only after the fiercest discussion and
ost dogged obstruction on the part of members of the Land
eague in the House of Commons. In the same year Gladstone
mself introduced a Land Act which gave to the Irish tenant free
le, fixity of tenure, and the right to have a fair rent fixed for a
eriod of 15 years by a judicial tribunal. The Act, however, did
ot go far enough to satisfy Parnell and his followers in the House;
Ireland the number of agrarian outrages increased rather than
iminished, and Parnell himself was arrested and lodged in Kil-
ainham Gaol. Parnell and other leaders who had been arrested
ere subsequently set free; the Government were understood to
e willing to deal sympathetically with the case of 100,000 small
enants who were unable to take advantage of the Land Act
ecause they were in arrears with their rents; the agitation for

1870
to
1914

1882
Phœnix
Park
Murders

the time at least died down, and it seemed as if a brighter day
mutual understanding between Great Britain and Ireland h
begun. The new Viceroy, Lord Spencer, with Lord Freder
Cavendish, the Chief Secretary, made a state entry into Dub
on May 6. On the same evening Mr. Burke, the Under-Secreta
and Lord Frederick Cavendish, who were walking through Phœ
Park to the Viceregal Lodge, were stabbed to death by a gang
men who called themselves the Invincibles. The assassins h
been lying in wait for Mr. Burke (they had on a former occasi
waited for Mr. Forster, who by a mere accident due to an unp
meditated change in his travelling arrangements had escap
them), but as Lord Frederick went to the assistance of his colleag
he met the same fate. This dastardly act naturally aroused t
utmost detestation, and many in Great Britain who were turni
towards a policy of conciliation hardened their hearts. At We
minster the Nationalists had acquired the use of a new weapon
offence, the organised obstruction of debate, which was carried
such a pitch of efficiency that the House had to spend the autu
session of 1882 revising its rules of procedure.

Egyptian
adminis-
tration

British responsibilities were soon to be increased in Egy
which Russia had twice offered to England, and Bismarck at t
Berlin Conference had suggested to England that she should ta
over, an opening which curiously enough Disraeli declined. T
Khedive, who had sold his shares in the Suez Canal to Disrae
had, by his tyranny and extravagance before and after that tin
brought the country to the verge of ruin. In 1879 the Sultan w
persuaded by the Powers to bring about the abdication of t
Khedive, who was succeeded by his son Tewfik, a well-intention
but invertebrate person incapable of coping with the disconte
then rife in the army and in the country at large. On September
the Khedive found himself forced to give way to the demands of
large force, led by Arabi, which surrounded him in his palac
England and France, in a joint Note, promised their support
Tewfik in the restoration of order, but France afterwards withdre
when a rising at Alexandria, and subsequent bombardment of t
town by the British, made it clear that drastic steps would have
be taken. A British army under Sir Garnet Wolseley was sent

Tel-el
Kebir

Egypt ; Arabi, after being totally defeated at Tel-el-Kebir, o
September 13, 1882, was captured and sentenced to death, bu
finally banished to Ceylon. The British army was left in occupa
tion until, but only until, order should finally be restored. Thi
however, meant that the British Government now had on the
hands the responsibility of Egypt which they had previousl
declined.

But events following the fall of Arabi were little calculated t
serve the restoration of order in Egypt. The Arabs of the Souda
a territory also included in the dominions of the Khedive, ha
been grievously oppressed by their Egyptian masters, and whe
Muhammed Ahmad, who professed to be the Mahdi or Messiah o

WORLD

ON MERCATOR'S PROJECTION

British Possessions in 1814

British Possessions in 1914

377

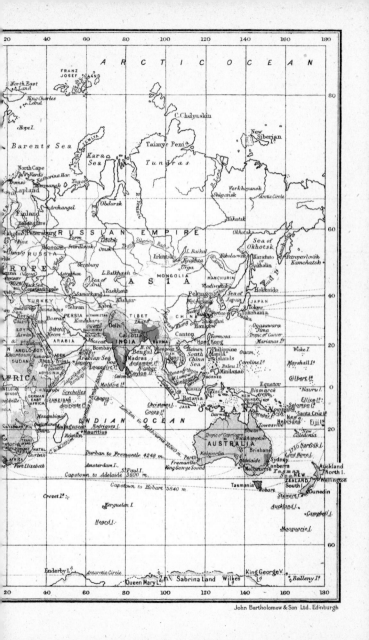

John Bartholomew & Son Ltd. Edinburgh

1870
to
1914

promise, rose in revolt, the Soudanese promptly joined him,
with their aid he captured El Obeid and Kordofan. In
ember, 1883, General Hicks was sent by the Khedive to
nquer the Soudan with a force which proved to be wholly
fficient, and which met with utter disaster at Shekan. On
uary 18, 1884, General Gordon was sent to Khartoum to
rt on the situation. He soon found himself besieged by the
di and his followers there. Inexcusable delays in sending
orcements to him from home took place, and it was not till
ust that Lord Wolseley left England to lead an expedition
he Nile. But through the inability of the Gladstone Cabinet
ake up its mind, he had not been despatched soon enough,
on January 26 the Mahdi attacked Khartoum and Gordon

1885
Fall of
Khar-
toum
and
death of
Gordon

Though the Government were formally censured by the
s and only just escaped censure in the Commons for their
re to support Gordon, they decided to abandon the Soudan
h of Wady Halfa, and owing to Gladstone's personal influence,
h was sufficiently powerful to overbear strong Parliamentary
sition, the British force was withdrawn in 1885. In 1896,
Egyptian army, having in the meantime been reorganised by
erals Kitchener and Grenfell, the Khedive resolved on an
mpt to recapture the Soudan. General Kitchener was
inted to the command of the Nile expedition with this object,
by 1898 with the victory of Omdurman accomplished the task.

Parlia-
mentary
Reform
1884

1884 the Government took up again the question of Parlia-
tary reform and committed themselves to a further extension
he franchise. The Bill which they introduced passed the
mons, but was rejected by the Lords, and an embittered con-
ersy between the Houses was brought to an end by the personal
vention of the Sovereign, who, acting as peace-maker, brought
wo sets of disputants together. In the upshot the Conserva-
leaders accepted the Franchise Bill, and a Redistribution Bill
passed. The result of these two measures was to assimilate
county to the borough franchise; to merge in the county areas
ughs with less than a population of 15,000, and to deprive of
member two-member constituencies with a population of less
50,000; and to divide the whole country into single-member
tituencies, with the exception of certain universities and
ty-two towns which retained two members each. The sum
was to add about 2,000,000 electors to the register.

Home
Rule
1886

e return of 86 Irish Home Rulers at the first election
wing the new franchise completed Gladstone's conversion
ome Rule, to which he had for some time been leaning, and
h some of the most distinguished Liberals, Mr. John Morley,
Bryce, and Sir Charles Dilke, had been consistently advocat-
Gladstone introduced his first Home Rule Bill in 1886, and as
ndant, a Land Bill. The opposition to these measures, which
ded Lord Hartington, Chamberlain, Bright, and many other
inent Liberals, was triumphant. Gladstone appealed to the

country and was overwhelmingly defeated.   Salisbury, w.
specific for the Irish malady was twenty years of resolute gov
ment, became the head of a Conservative administration,
Mr. Arthur Balfour, who became Chief Secretary for Irel.
proceeded to administer the remedy prescribed by his Chief.
series of articles published in the " Times," entitled " Parnel
and Crime," sought to bring home to Nationalist leaders
responsibility for recent and increased outbursts of lawlessnes
Ireland.   Parnell asked for a Select Committee to investigate
charges brought against his colleagues and himself.   This req
was refused, but a year afterwards the Government appointe
Commission of three judges to investigate the whole activitie

Parnell-ism and Crime

the Nationalist Movement.   A facsimile letter, said to be
Parnell, which condoned the Phœnix Park murders, and w
had been published by the " Times," was proved to be a clu
forgery of an out-at-heel journalist, Richard Pigott, who confe
his crime, but shot himself at Madrid before the police could a
him.   The Report of the Commission, which was presented
February 13, 1890, declared that the respondents collectively
not members of a conspiracy to secure the absolute independ
of Ireland, but that some of them had conspired to impoverish
Irish landlords and expel them from the country, and had inc
to intimidation which indirectly, if not directly, led to crime.
the moment it seemed as if Parnell had cleared himself of the m
charges against him, but shortly afterwards there was a violen
vulsion of feeling when he made no attempt to defend himse
the divorce courts against the charge of adulterous relations
Mrs. O'Shea.   The Roman Catholic Bishops, the majority of his
followers, Gladstone, and most people in England felt tha
ought to retire from the leadership of his party.   He fought fier
to maintain his position, but wore himself out in a futile e
which was terminated by his death in 1891 at the early age o

The Queen's Jubilee 1887

If the condition of Ireland in 1887 was unsatisfactory t
parties concerned, new ties were being woven for other par
the Empire.   The celebration of the Queen's Jubilee in that
showed not only the profound respect and affection which
Sovereign had won, but proved that the monarchy had now bec
for the vast majority of her subjects the centre and rallying
of the Empire.   At home the principle of self-government rece

Local Government

further extension in 1888 by the establishment of elective co
and district councils, consisting partly of Councillors dir
elected by the ratepayers for a term of three years, and pa
of Aldermen co-opted by the Councillors.   Something was
to remedy one of the greatest national shortcomings—the

Education

of adequate technical instruction—by the Act of 1899, w
authorised County or Borough Councils to supply or aid in sup
ing technical and manual instruction.   The new interest in
care of the young both inside and outside of school was evince
an important measure passed in the same year, introduced

ate member, Mr. Mundella. The Prevention of Cruelty to
dren Act prohibited the employment of children under ten,
made it a misdemeanour to neglect or ill-treat them. The
spread Dock Strike of the same year, led to success by Mr.
Tillett, Mr. Tom Mann, and Mr. John Burns, and supported
arge numbers of disinterested clergymen, journalists, ship-
ers, and philanthropists, had two important results. The
ral public, which in this case almost universally sympathised
the 75,000 dockers on strike, realised, as most of them had
done before, that the whole fabric of commerce and industry
d on a foundation of ill-paid labour. The second effect was to
confidence to the trade unionists and to increase their numbers
n extent hitherto unknown, and no longer to be waved aside
he irresponsible demands of self-seeking demagogues. The
servative Administration has the credit of passing in 1890 the
sing of the Working Classes Act, by which local authori-
were empowered to buy up insanitary areas and demolish
itary buildings, to let out land to contractors on condition
uilding dwellings for the poor, and to sell to private persons
buildings thus erected.

f great importance also were the educational changes intro-
d by Sir William Hart Dyke, Minister of Education in Lord
bury's Government. In 1890 it was made possible to establish
ing continuation schools, and the vicious system of " payment
esults " was abandoned for a block grant, based on average
ndances. In 1891, largely by the efforts of Mr. Chamberlain,
had included it in his " unauthorised programme " of 1885,
had never abandoned it, free education in the elementary
ols of England and Wales became the law of the land. Mr.
hews carried a measure for the improvement of factories
workshops, which limited the hours of women's labour to
ve a day, with an hour and a half for meals, and forbade
gether the employment of children under eleven in any work-
or factory.

r. Balfour, though during his tenure of office as Chief Secre-
for Ireland he had rigorously carried on a *régime* of re-
sion exemplified in the Crimes Act, did not confine himself
ly to a policy of coercion. In 1890 he won great popularity
the poorest peasants in the poverty-stricken West of Ireland,
her he had gone to see the condition of the people for himself,
by setting up in 1891 the Congested Districts Board. That in
land also at the very heart of the Empire there was a plague-
of dire poverty was shown by the publication in 1891 of
Darkest England and the Way Out," by General Booth,
der and head of the Salvation Army. The publication of
Charles Booth's monumental " Life and Labour of the People
ondon " (begun in 1889 and concluded in 1903), embodying
unbiassed conclusions of an army of skilled investigators,
lutionised the whole method of approach to the problem of

1870 to 1914

poverty. The innumerable questions arising out of the condi
of the masses were being sympathetically investigated and
cussed, and remedies were gradually being found. In 1892
Mundella established at the Board of Trade a Labour Dep
ment, the business of which was, by the aid of corresponden
every large town and by other means, to collect, sift, and pu
statistics concerning labour. The new Department was for
ate in beginning its course under the leadership of a very
statistician, Mr. Giffen, and with Mr. Burnett, who had be
manual worker, as its chief Labour Correspondent. At the H
Office Mr. Asquith made another useful and important depar
by the appointment of women factory inspectors.

Gladstone's Fourth Ministry

The election of 1892 was a grievous disappointment to Glads
who was returned to power with a majority of but 40. His se
Home Rule Bill, introduced in February, 1893, differed from
first in retaining at Westminster only 80 members from Irel
but with permission to vote only on Irish questions. This mea
passed the Commons, but was thrown out in the Lords
majority of 419 to 41. Immediately afterwards the Govern
carried their Parish Councils Bill, which introduced the elec
principle into District and Parish Government. Early in the
1894 Gladstone, who was now eighty-five years of age and de
an interval of quiet before the end came, resigned the premier
His last speech in the House of Commons was a declaration
the grave differences between the Lords and the popular H

Lord Rosebery Premier

must " go forward to an issue." Lord Rosebery succeeded G
stone as premier and Sir William Harcourt became Leade
the House of Commons. The Budget which the latter introd
in 1894 is one of the landmarks of national finance. In it
Chancellor applied the graduation principle to the duties
succession and made the legacy duty identical on real and pers
estate. The death duties were vigorously criticised at the t
but no political party since 1894 has proposed to abolish t
and they are now a means of revenue adopted by all section
the House.

Lord Salisbury's Third Ministry

The Ministry resigned in consequence of being defeated
snatch vote, and the Unionists at the ensuing election ha
majority of 132, whereupon Lord Salisbury formed his third
ministration, in which several prominent Liberal-Unionists,
Duke of Devonshire, Lord Lansdowne, Mr. Chamberlain,
others, held posts. Largely owing to the influence of Mr. Cham

Workmen's Compensation Act, 1897

lain, the Government carried the Workmen's Compensation
which made employers liable for compensation even though t
workmen had been guilty of " contributory negligence " and
had not. The Act was at first confined to mines, factories,
ways, quarries, docks, and engineering sheds, but in 1900 it wa
tended to cover the case of agricultural labourers. In 1898 the L
Government Act substituted in Ireland popularly elected cou
for grand juries. A Department of Agriculture and other indust

and Technical Instruction in Ireland was established in 1899 on lines suggested by Sir Horace Plunkett, the foremost agricultural reformer of his time, who became its first head. Unfortunately, the year 1899 was to close with the outbreak of a war that was to bring us little glory. The discovery of gold in the Transvaal in 1886 led to the influx into South Africa of a class of colonists whose presence was resented by the Boer farmers. The "Uitlanders" demanded political rights suited to their economic importance. The Boer Government, led by Oom Paul Kruger, refused to grant their demands. On January 1, 1896, Dr. Jameson, the Administrator of the British South Africa Company, which had been incorporated by Royal Charter ten years before, raided Transvaal territory with a force of 600 armed men. Jameson was heavily defeated and he and his fellow-raiders were handed over to the British Government. This abortive expedition increased the friction between the Boers and the "Uitlanders." A Committee of the House of Commons was appointed to inquire into the circumstances leading up to the raid, but as no punishment was inflicted on Cecil Rhodes, who knew that it was planned, the Boers became filled with the idea that some scheme, not without the knowledge of the home authorities, was in preparation to deprive them of their independence. Sir Alfred Milner, who was appointed High Commissioner in 1897, speedily declared himself emphatically on the side of the Uitlanders. A conference at Bloemfontein in May, 1899, between President Kruger and Sir Alfred Milner proved abortive and on October 10 the two South African Republics declared war against us. Until the opening months of 1900 the campaign went disastrously for us, but the appointment of Lord Roberts as commander-in-chief with Lord Kitchener as his second in command brought victory to British arms, and the two republics were annexed by the peace of Vereeniging in 1902. The war, which was not a little due to tactless diplomacy in both England and South Africa, was grossly bungled when it started, but it had the salutary effect of showing England her military weakness, and it did something to bring to an end the reign of red-tape at the War Office.

In 1901 the blameless and laborious life of Queen Victoria came to an end. Her frankness and truthfulness, her observance of constitutional limitations, her intense devotion to duty, the purity and simplicity of her private life, brought about the paradox that in an increasingly democratic age the popularity of the Crown towards the close of her reign was greater than it had ever been in its history, so far as the majority of her subjects were concerned. This popularity, if anything, tended to increase in the hands of her immediate successor.

At the General Election of 1900 the Conservatives had appealed for a patriotic vote to enable them to bring the war to a satisfactory conclusion on the understanding that problems of domestic controversy would not be raised in the new Parliament. Never-

1870
to
1914
—
War in
South
Africa
1899
to
1902

Death of
Queen
Victoria
and ac-
cession
of
Edward
VII.

theless, highly controversial issues were raised by the Education Bill of 1902 which abolished School Boards, transferred the control of elementary education to County and Town Councils, and made the local rates available for "voluntary," *i.e.*, denominational schools. The Nonconformists were displeased because in these schools the head teacher must belong to the denomination, though the secular education given in them was under the control of the public authority. The Act, however, though it left Nonconformists with a sense of grievance, was a distinct advance towards complete public control of elementary education. In the domain of Foreign Affairs Lord Lansdowne achieved a great personal success by his treaty of alliance with Japan, also to be assigned to 1902. In Ireland a conference held under the presidency of Lord Dunraven to consider the difficulties of the Irish agrarian question formulated a scheme which in principle was afterwards embodied in Mr. George Wyndham's Land Act of 1903, which bought out the Irish landlords, on the security of the British Treasury, leaving the tenant to pay off the purchase money in $68\frac{1}{2}$ years by annual instalments less in amount than his rent had been.

Under Mr. Balfour's *régime* the Army was reorganised in the light of the experience of the South African War. The office of Commander-in-Chief was abolished and the control of the Army handed over to the Army Council, over which the Secretary for War was to preside. Another measure of the highest importance, though its work is obviously not of a nature to be described in detail for public information, was due to Mr. Balfour's personal suggestion, the appointment of a Committee of Imperial Defence, over which the Prime Minister for the time being was to preside.

In 1903 Mr. Chamberlain, after his return from South Africa, advocated Colonial Preference as a means of welding together the several parts of the Empire. As he was unable to carry the Cabinet with him, though Mr. Balfour went so far as to accept "retaliation," he resigned his place in the Government to leave himself free to carry on a campaign in the country. The schism thus created, joined to the unpopularity of certain measures like the introduction of Chinese coolie labour into the Transvaal mines, so weakened the Government that Mr. Balfour resigned office in November,

1905, and Sir Henry Campbell-Bannerman undertook to form a Ministry. The ensuing election of 1906 resulted in an utter rout of the Unionist party, due not so much to the conversion of the electorate to Radicalism, as to a widespread feeling that the South African War, if it could not have been avoided, was grossly mismanaged in its earlier stages; to the determination of the industrial parts of the country not to abandon Free Trade, which at least gave them cheap food, for the alleged benefits of Protection; to the dissatisfaction of Nonconformists with the Education Act of 1902; and to the unpopularity among the organised workers of Chinese labour and of the Taff Vale judgment, which deprived Trades Unions of the position which they supposed themselves to have. The most remarkable feature of the 1906 election was the return to Parliament of an organised Labour party. The House of Commons had long had Labour members, who, with the exception of Mr. Keir Hardie, usually voted with Liberals, but the formation in 1893 of the Independent Labour Party definitely pledged to Socialism, and in 1900 of the Labour Representation Committee, a fusion of the Socialist and Trade Union movements, had made possible the return of a number of members pledged to act independently of the two older parties. The new Parliament proceeded to prohibit the further introduction of Chinese labour into the Transvaal mines; to confer self-government upon the Transvaal and Orange River Colony (which with the Cape and Natal became in 1909 the South African Union); to reverse the Taff Vale judgment, by the Trades Disputes Act; and to authorise contributions from the rates for the feeding of necessitous school children. Sir Henry Campbell-Bannerman resigned the Premiership on the ground of ill-health in 1908, and Mr. Asquith, who succeeded him, carried on vigorously the policy of making up arrears in social legislation. Old Age Pensions, which had been advocated by Tom Paine and by others after him, but which first had been made a serious issue by Mr. Charles Booth in 1892 in his " Pauperism, a Picture, and the Endowment of Old Age, an Argument," were put on the statute book in 1908. The Poor Law Commission, appointed by Mr. Balfour in 1905, presented in 1909 a Report, which was not only a masterpiece of literary skill and arrangement, but the most important document of its kind which had appeared for over 100 years. Indeed it is probably no exaggeration to say that never in its history has the nation had at its disposal for the purposes of a public inquiry such a combination of disinterestedness, administrative capacity, wide experience, and knowledge of the subject investigated. All the more striking, therefore, are the words with which the majority section of the Commission conclude their Report: " It is very unpleasant to record that notwithstanding our assumed moral and material progress, and notwithstanding the enormous expenditure, amounting to nearly sixty millions a year, upon poor relief, education, and public health, we still have a vast army of persons quartered upon us unable to support themselves, and an army which in numbers has recently shown signs of increase rather than decrease . . . the statistical review of the expense incurred and of the results attained by it prove that something in our social organisation is seriously wrong, and that whatever may be the evils, they are not of such a nature as to be improved or removed by the mere signing of cheques or the outpouring of public funds." The Minority Report, a brilliant literary document, afterwards separately reprinted by its authors and widely circulated, was still more strongly condemnatory of the Poor Law, but the wonder was not that the two sections of the Commission differed so widely,

1870
to
1914
—
The
Labour
Party

Social
Legislation

Old Age
Pensions
1908

Report
of Poor
Law
Commission,
1909

but that they agreed so much as to the causes of poverty and, to a surprising extent, as to the remedies to be applied.

A Bill to establish a University for Irish Catholics and an important Town Planning Act were carried in 1909, but the Government's most ambitious scheme, a Licensing Bill, was rejected by the Lords, just as in 1906 the Upper House had introduced such changes in the Education Bill that the Government, being unable to accept them, withdrew the Bill. The rejection of the Licensing Bill caused Mr. Asquith immediately to declare that henceforth the veto of the House of Lords must be the dominant issue of politics. Mr. Lloyd George's Budget of 1909, which embodied a scheme of land taxes highly unpalatable to the Lords, increased the friction between the two Houses, and Mr. Asquith determined to submit the questions of the Veto and the Budget to the decision of the country. At the subsequent election in January, 1910, the Liberals were returned to power, though with a greatly diminished majority. The 1909 Budget was sent back to the Lords, and the Government formulated their policy, which would have abolished the Lords' Veto on finance, limited the veto on other measures to two years, and reduced the duration of Parliament from seven to five years. The Lords, at the suggestion of Lord Rosebery, agreed to resolutions which admitted that a peerage should not of itself entitle its holder to a seat in the Upper House. In the middle of these hostilities King Edward VII. died, amid manifestations of sorrow, not only from all classes and parties in the Empire, but from other countries where he was hardly less popular than in his own. As it was felt that it would have been indecent to continue an embittered controversy while the grave had hardly closed upon a beloved Monarch, the leaders of the Conservative and Liberal parties entered into a Conference which considered not only the question of the veto, but some other controversial themes. As the Conference proved abortive, Parliament was dissolved, and appeal made to the country on the single issue of the Lords' Veto, with the result that in December, 1910, the verdict of January was confirmed. This mandate was translated into law by the Parliament Act of 1911. Two important measures, due to the party led by Mr. Asquith, may be mentioned not so much because of their particular application as because they are symptomatic of a complete change in public opinion with regard to social and industrial questions. Mr. Winston Churchill's Trade Boards Act of 1909 prescribed a standard wage for a class of workers who, until the passing of the Act, had been shamelessly sweated, and the later insurance scheme of Mr. Lloyd George adopted a general principle already in active use in some continental countries, especially Germany, and relieved a large number of industrial workers of the graver risks of sickness and disability. This measure also is not in principle objected to by any party, though there is very great divergence as to detail and method.

Death of
King
Edward
VII. and
Accession of
King
George
V.

Trade
Boards
Act,
1909
Insurance Act,
1911

The Home Rule Bill, which Mr. Asquith introduced in the House of Commons on April 11, 1911, proposed to confer on Ireland the government through a Senate and a House of Commons of her own internal affairs, with the exception of the Irish Land Purchase Scheme, Old Age Pensions, National Insurance, the Royal Irish Constabulary, and the Post Office Savings Bank, which were to be reserved as Imperial services. The army and navy, treaties, and other Imperial subjects would be outside of the jurisdiction of the Irish Parliament, which would not be permitted to establish or endow any religion, or to impose disabilities for religious belief. The Lord Lieutenant could withhold his consent to bills passed by the Irish Parliament, and the Imperial Legislature could nullify or amend any Irish Act. This measure, which evoked the most heated controversy in both Houses of Parliament, and the threat of armed violence in Ulster, the Protestant part of which desired to be excluded from the operation of the Act, became law, under the Parliament Act, on September 17, 1914. On the same day, and also under the Parliament Act, the Bill to disestablish the Welsh Church reached the Statute Book. The danger of civil war in Ireland, the rancour of party controversy, the continued manifestations of industrial unrest melted away and left a united nation and empire to face the greater peril of the European War.

1870 to 1914

Home Rule for Ireland

Welsh Disestablishment

A bird's-eye view of the century from 1815 to 1915 reveals the most profound changes in every activity of the national life. In religion, if there is less church-going at the end of this period than at some other epochs, there is more real religion. The evil spirit of sectarianism is being slowly but surely driven out. Anglicanism and Nonconformity are not so much rivals as fellow-workers in the same field. Catholicism is learning from Protestantism, which is mellowed by the lessons that the oldest Christian community has to teach. Judaism now takes its place on a footing of equality as one of the religious forces of a great free community. Above all, in practically every Protestant religious community, the battle of free inquiry has been won and tradition must give way to the claims of truth and of the inspirations of our own day. Religious tests at the Universities, in Parliament, and elsewhere in public life are gone or going.

The Monarchy, which in the time of George IV. had deservedly fallen into disrepute, in the Victorian epoch won not only profound respect, but warm affection. Victoria and her Consort, each " wearing the white flower of a blameless life," won a securer place than falls to the autocrat and the absolutist, though observant of constitutional restrictions, ever growing in a country with a democratic tradition. Republicanism is not a living issue, and the monarchy is, for most British subjects, the silken thread that binds the Empire together. The aristocracy, which in 1815 consisted of the hereditary owners of land, has received large infusions of those whose wealth has been won in the fields of commerce or industry,

and of some who had served at least their party if not the commonwealth. More and more it was becoming clear to them that " the
chivalry of this age is the performance of public duty." The war
of 1914 showed that they have lost none of the older chivalry
of arms. Political power passed from the landed aristocracy to
the commercial classes, and is now passing to the intelligent
manual workers. England, which in the days of Waterloo was an
agricultural country, has at the end of the century become a
manufacturing and trading nation. The tale of exports and
imports has mounted up, but the clamant need of commerce and
industry is the application of science not only to means of production, but to methods of distribution. Whether England is to keep
her commercial supremacy depends not on her attitude to the
question of tariffs, but upon her willingness (or unwillingness) to
submit all who are carrying on the operations of commerce,
whether as leaders or manual workers, to thorough scientific
and technical training as her greatest commercial rivals, Germany
and the United States, have done. Agriculture, also, in England
is sorely in need of the application of " brains," for though it
is true that the best English farming is as good as any to be
found elsewhere, the average when compared with countries like
Holland, Denmark, Belgium, for example, is depressing. In
general the educational outlook in England has features which are
sadly unsatisfactory. Scotland, Wales, and even Ireland respect
and love education for its own sake. In England it cannot yet be
said that the people, as a whole, believe sufficiently in education
to be willing to pay for it. It is not merely that we are behind the
great nations, but the educational average of poor and geographic-
ally small nations like the Scandinavian countries, Holland,
Denmark, Switzerland, ought to bring shame to any candid
English traveller who has sufficient intimacy with those countries
to form a judgment. This and " the condition of the people "
question are the two most serious problems bequeathed by the
nineteenth century to the twentieth. Notwithstanding the
colossal increase in the sum total of the national wealth, it is still
true, in 1915 as in 1815, that we have not yet learnt to distribute
material wealth equitably, though we have immeasurably increased its production. The Report of the Poor Law Commission
of 1909, the investigations of the Rt. Hon. Charles Booth, and
numerous other disinterested inquirers, have proved indisput-
ably that an enormous proportion of the manual workers, whether
of the towns or of the country, a proportion frequently extending to one-third of the total population in given areas, is endeavouring to live upon a wage insufficient even for decent
physical maintenance. The hopeful elements in the situation are
that this maldistribution of wealth is common to other industrial
countries, though it is worst in the British Islands and the United
States, and that, so far as ourselves are concerned, great numbers
of the ablest and most disinterested men and women in all classes

f the community and of every shade of religious and political
belief are devoting themselves to the scientific study of social and
industrial questions, and to the practical experiments by which
alone solutions will be found. The lamentable war of 1914, the
greatest catastrophe that has ever befallen the human race, has
proved that throughout the British Islands as in the Colonies there
is no widespread or deep-seated deterioration, either physical or
moral; that the spirit of dogged resistance to tyranny and the
ineradicable love of justice are still present in the children of a
race which, though its history has been stained by many blunders
and not a few crimes, has yet attained to a greater measure of
freedom combined with security than any other State has known.

CHAPTER IV

A SUMMARY OF EVENTS, 1914–1950

Section I.—The First World War, 1914–1918

[*Authorities.*—Sir Winston Churchill, " The World Crisis," 4 vols.
1923–1929); Sir J. E. Edmonds, " Official History of the Great War,"
vols. (1928, etc.); Sir C. P. Lucas, " The Empire at War," 3 vols.
1921, etc.).]

Declarations of War

1914. Austria-Hungary on Serbia, 28 July; Germany on Russia,
1 Aug.; Germany on France, 3 Aug.; Britain on Germany,
4 Aug.; Germany on Belgium, 4 Aug.; Montenegro on Austria-
Hungary, 7 Aug.; France on Austria-Hungary, 10 Aug.;
Britain on Austria-Hungary, 12 Aug.; Japan on Germany,
23 Aug.; Britain on Turkey, 5 Nov.
1915. Italy on Austria, 23 May; Italy on Turkey, 20 Aug.;
Britain on Bulgaria, 15 Oct.; France on Bulgaria, 16 Oct.;
Italy on Bulgaria, 19 Oct.
1916. Albania on Austria, 11 Jan.; Germany on Portugal, 9
Mar.; Rumania on Austria, 27 Aug.; Italy on Germany, 28
Aug.; Germany on Rumania, 28 Aug.; Turkey on Rumania,
30 Aug.; Bulgaria on Rumania, 1 Sept.
1917. U.S.A. on Germany, 6 April; Cuba on Germany, 7 April;
Austria on U.S.A., 8 April; Bulgaria on U.S.A., 9 April;
Panama on Germany, 10 April; Siam on Central Empires,
22 July; China on Germany, 14 Aug.; China on Austria, 11
Sept.; Brazil on Germany, 26 Oct.

Military Events

France and Flanders :
1914. German invasion of Belgium begun, 4 Aug.; Brussels
entered, 20 Aug.; Namur captured, 23 Aug.; Antwerp taken,

9 Oct. Bs.: Mons, 23–4 Aug.; Le Cateau, 26 Aug.; Marne, 7–10 Sept.; Aisne, 12–15 Sept.; Ypres, 19 Oct.–22 Nov.

1915. Bs.: Neuve-Chapelle, 10–13 Mar.; Ypres, 22 April–25 May (first German attack with gas, 22 April); Festubert, 15–25 May; Loos, 25 Sept.–8 Oct.

1916. Bs.: Verdun, begun 21 Feb. (Douaumont, 25 Feb. and 24 Oct.); Somme, 1 July–18 Nov. (Beaumont-Hamel, 13 Nov.); Verdun, 15 Dec.; Ancre, 13–18 Nov.

1917. German retreat to Hindenburg Line, 14 Mar.–5 April. Bs.: Arras, 9 April–4 May (Vimy Ridge, 9–14 April; Scarpe, 9–14, 23–4 April, 3–4 May); Chemin des Dames, 5 May; Bullecourt, 3–17 May; Messines, 7–14 June; Ypres, 31 July–10 Nov. (Passchendaele, 12 Oct., 26 Oct.–10 Nov.); Verdun, 20 Aug.; Cambrai, 20 Nov.–3 Dec.

1918. Bs: Somme, 21 Mar.–5 April; Lys, 9–29 April (Kemmel Ridge, 17–19 April); Aisne, 27 May–6 June; Marne, 18 July; Ourcq, 23 July–2 Aug.; Amiens, 8–11 Aug.; Bapaume, 21–31 Aug.; Somme, 21 Aug.–3 Sept.; Arras, 26 Aug.–3 Sept. (Drocourt-Quéant, 2–3 Sept.); Sainte-Mihiel, 12 Sept.; Hindenburg Line, 12 Sept.–9 Oct. (Épéhy, 18 Sept.; Cambrai, 8–9 Oct.); Ypres, 28 Sept.–2 Oct.; Selle River, 17–25 Oct.; Valenciennes, 1 Nov.; Sambre, 4 Nov.

Prussia—Poland—Russia—Austria-Hungary :

1914. Bs.: Tannenberg, 26–9 Aug.; Lemberg, 31 Aug.–2 Sept.; Augustovo, 1–4 Oct.; for Warsaw, 15–20 Oct., 18 Nov.–28 Dec.; Lodz, 1–5 Dec.

1915. Przemysl surrendered to Russians, 22 Mar.; recaptured, 3 June; Lemberg retaken, 22 June; third b. for Warsaw, 19 July; Warsaw evacuated by Russians, 5 Aug.; Kovno stormed, 7 Aug.; b. of Brest-Litovsk, 26 Aug.; b. of Tarnopol, 7–8 Sept.; Vilna taken by Germans, 17 Sept.

1916. B. of Lake Narotch, Mar.–April; Russian offensive in Ukraine, 4 June; in E. Galicia, 8 June; near Baronovitchi, 13 June; near Brody, 15 July.

1917. Russian offensive at Brzezany, 1 July; b. of Halicz, 10 July, 23 July; fall of Riga, 3 Sept.

1918. Odessa occupied by Germans, 13 Mar.

Rumania :

1916. Invasion of Transylvania, 28 Aug.; Silistria taken by Bulgarians, 12 Sept.; Constanza taken by Bulgarians, 22 Oct.; Bukarest occupied by Germans, 7 Dec.

1917. Evacuation of the Dobrudja, 8 Jan.; Galatz evacuated, 11 Jan.

Dardanelles :

1915. Landing at Cape Helles, 25–6 April; bs. for Krithia, 28 April, 6–8 May, 4 June; Anzac bs., 25 April–30 June; landing

The First World War 843

at Suvla, 6-15 Aug.; Suvla bs., 6-21 Aug. (Sari-Bair, 6-10
Aug.). Evacuation of Dardanelles declared, 8 Dec.
1916. Evacuation completed, 8 Jan.

Italy :

1915. First b. of the Isonzo, 2-29 July.
1916. B. of Trentino, 14 May-16 June; b. of Gorizia, 6-14 Aug.
1917. Italian offensive on Isonzo, 14 May-10 June; Italian
attack between Tolmino and sea, 19 Aug.; b. of Caporetto,
24 Oct.-18 Nov.
1918. B. of Piave, 15-23 June, 26 Oct.; b. of Vittoria Veneto,
24 Oct.-4 Nov.

Balkans :

1915. Allied landing at Salonika, 5 Oct.; fall of Üsküb, 22 Oct.;
b. of Kachanik, 4 Nov.; fall of Monastir, 2 Dec.
1916. Cettinje taken, 1-3 Jan.; Durazzo taken, 24 Feb.;
Monastir retaken, 23 Nov.
1917. B. of Doiran, 24-5 April, 8-9 May.
1918. B. of the Vardar, 15-25 Sept.; b. of Doiran, 18-19 Sept.;
Üsküb retaken, 30 Sept.

Egypt, Palestine, and Arabia :

Operations against the Senussi, Nov. 1915-Feb. 1917; b. of
Rumani, 4-5 Aug. 1916; bs. of Gaza, 26 Mar.-7 Nov. 1917;
capture of Jerusalem, 7-9 Dec. 1917; of Jericho, 19-21 Feb.
1918; b. of Megiddo, 19-25 Sept. 1918; Arab rising against
Turks began, 7 June; Mecca taken, 10 June.

Mesopotamia—Persia :

1915. B. of Kut, 28 Sept.; b. of Ctesiphon, 22-4 Nov.
1916. Kermanchah taken by Russians, 26 Feb.; B. of Sanna-i-
Yat, 6-22 April.
1917. British occupied Bagdad, 11 Mar.; Samaria, 19 Sept.;
Ramadi taken, 28 Sept.; b. of Sherghat, 30 Oct.

Africa :

E. Africa. Tanga operations, Nov. 1914; surrender of Mafia Is.,
12 Jan. 1915; Tanga occup., 7 July 1916; Dar-es-Salaam
surrendered, 4 Sept. 1916; final surrender, 25 Nov. 1918.
S.-W. Africa. Luderitzbucht occupied, 18 Sept. 1914; occupation
of Windhoek, 12 May 1915; German capitulation, 9 July 1915.
Cameroons. Capture of Duala, 26 Sept. 1914; of Mora, 8 Sept.
1916.
Togoland. Lome captured, 8 Aug. 1914.
S. Africa. Rebellion began, 15 Sept. 1914; surrender at Reitz,
4 Dec. 1914.

Caucasus :

Erzerum taken, Feb. 1916, retaken, Mar. 1918; Trebizond taken,
April 1916, retaken, Mar. 1918; Erzingan taken, July 1916,

retaken, Mar. 1918; Batum occupied, April 1918; Bak~
evacuated by British, 14 Sept. 1918.

N. Russia—Siberia :

Kem occupied, 7 June 1918; Irkutsk occupied by Czecho
slovakians, July 1918; Dukhovskaya, 23 Aug. 1918; Archange
occupied, 1 Aug. 1918; Troitsa, 10 Aug. 1919; British evacua
tion, 27 Sept. 1919.

NAVAL EVENTS

1914. *Goeben* and *Breslau* reach Turkey, 11 Aug.; blockade o
Kiaochow, 27 Aug.; b. of Heligoland Bight, 28 Aug.; siege o
Tsingtao, 23 Sept.–5 Nov.; H.M.S.s *Aboukir, Hogue,* anc
Cressy torpedoed, 22 Sept.; b. of Coronel (Adm. Cradock'~
squadron lost), 1 Nov.; Kiaochow surrendered, 7 Nov.
German cruiser *Emden* destroyed, 9 Nov.; b. of Falkland Is
(Spee's squadron sunk), 8 Dec.; Germans bombard Yorkshir~
coastal towns, 16 Dec.; seaplane raid on Cuxhaven, 25 Dec.

1915. B. of Dogger Bank, 24 Jan.; German submarine blockad~
of Britain opened, 18 Feb.; British attack on Dardanelle~
forts, 19 Feb.; again, 4–7 Mar.; German cruiser *Dresden* sunk
14 Mar.; *Lusitania* torpedoed, 7 May; *Königsberg* destroyed ir
Rufiji river, 11 July.

1916. Germans bombard Lowestoft, 25 April; b. of Jutland, 3]
May; H.M.S. *Hampshire* with Kitchener aboard mined of
Orkneys, 5 June; Allies bombard Athens, 1 Sept.; blockad~
of Greece, 19 Sept.

1917. Suffolk coast bombarded, 26 Jan.; Germans begin un
restricted submarine warfare, 1 Feb.; H.M.S.s *Swift* and *Brok~*
figure in a destroyer action in the Channel, 23 April; Rams
gate shelled, 27 April; first U.S. destroyers arrive, 3 May;
British naval success in Kattegat, 2 Nov.

1918. Germans bombard Yarmouth, 14 Jan.; British blocking
attack on Zeebrugge and Ostend, 22–3 April; another on
Ostend, 9–10 May; German naval meeting at Kiel, 10 Nov.;
Allied fleet passed through Dardanelles, 12 Nov.; German
fleet surrenders, 21 Nov.

ARMISTICES AND TREATIES

Armistices: Central Powers—Russia, 29 Nov. 1917; Rumania
—Central Powers, 7 Dec. 1917; Central Powers—Ukraine, 9
Feb. 1918; Allies—Bulgaria, 29 Sept. 1918; Allies—Turkey,
30 Oct. 1918; Allies—Austria-Hungary, 3 Nov. 1918; Allies—
Germany, 11 Nov. 1918.

Peace Treaties: Brest-Litovsk, between Russia and Germany,
2 Mar. 1918; preliminary peace between Rumania and Central
Powers, Buftea, 5 Mar. 1918; ratified, 7 May 1918; annulled at

Versailles, 1919. Versailles, signed by the Allies and Germany, 29 June 1919; ratified in Paris, 10 Jan. 1920. Saint-
Germain, between Allies and Austria, signed, 10 Sept. 1919;
ratified in Paris, 16 July 1920. Trianon, between Allies and
Hungary, signed, 4 June 1920. Neuilly, between Allies and
Bulgaria, signed, 27 Nov. 1919; ratified in Paris, 9 Aug. 1920.
Sèvres, between Allies and Turkey, signed, 10 Aug. 1920
(never ratified). Lausanne, between Allies and Turkey,
signed, 24 July 1923; ratified, autumn 1923.

NOTE.—The following section is adapted from Douglas Jerrold's
England: Past, Present, and Future " (1950), by kind permission
f the author.

SECTION II.—1918–1939

[*Authorities.*—" Documents on British Foreign Policy, 1919–1939 "
ed. E. L. Woodward and R. Butler); D. C. Somervell, " British Politics
ince 1902 " (1950); H. Kohn, " The Twentieth Century " (1950).]

IN December 1918 Mr. Lloyd George, at the head of the National
Coalition which perhaps too loudly claimed to have won the war,
appealed to the country for a mandate to win the peace. The
appeal was made to an electorate just increased from under seven
millions in 1914 to over twenty millions. The vast new electorate
could clearly no longer be regarded as the masters. Its members
insensibly became the clients of the rival political caucuses. As
the customer is always right, flattery, after 1918, displaced argument as the chief political weapon. It was in the new spirit that
Mr. Lloyd George proposed to celebrate the victory of 1918 by
making Britain a land fit for heroes to live in. The new electorate
responded with alacrity to the new blarney, and returned "the
wealthiest, the least intelligent, and the least representative House
of Commons since Waterloo." The chief reason for this unbalancing
of historic political forces was the suddenness of the reaction from
the deep-seated pessimism general throughout the country until
only a few weeks before the armistice.

As the election campaign proceeded, ministers were stampeded
by public pressure, as they conceived it, into all kinds of vindictive
pledges and impossible promises about living conditions. Whether
the men who made these promises were ignorant or deceitful must
remain a matter of opinion, but the fact remained that, with the
end of the war, the whole political and economic fabric of Europe
had collapsed. Anarchy, unemployment, and starvation were rife
and the effects of the disaster would not, and could not, be confined to the territories and peoples of our late enemies, nor should
men of any political experience have imagined otherwise.

The lasting evil of the First World War arose from its character as a " civil war " within the framework of the old European order, and its really damaging effects were, as with all civil wars, moral. The citizens of all the Western European countries after 1918 suffered a loss of faith. They no longer believed in the mission and destiny of their traditional civilization and were therefore disinclined to effort or sacrifice. The result, once the boom was over, was a feverish search for security, for indemnities, for reparations, for a system of organization through which the nations of post-war Europe could secure, at someone else's expense, the benefits which they had come to claim as a right and had ceased to regard as the rewards of prudence, virtue, and thrift. It was the error both of " Homes for Heroes " and " Organization for Peace," those two slogans which echoed through England from 1918 to 1931, that these desirable things were to be supplied to all who needed them by third parties—to the working man by the State, to the British people by the League of Nations. The same attitude of nerveless optimism was responsible for the grotesque and impossible demands made on Germany for reparations by all the signatories to the Treaty of Versailles. No one had the courage to place any limit to the day-dreams which kept them from contemplating the hard realities of a world at once tired, impoverished, and discontented.

The basic evils of the inter-war international situation had, however, been written into the peace treaties and the League of Nations Covenant, and, once these were confirmed as the foundation of the public law of Europe, there was little or nothing to be done, within their framework, which could remedy a situation fraught with danger from the very first. The first of these evils was the substitution for the long-established principle of nationality of a narrow racialism. The second evil was the failure—rendered all the more disastrous by the ill-chosen racial basis of the new order—to make the League of Nations an effective agent of peaceful change. For both these evils the liberal belief in the natural wisdom and virtue of man was at bottom responsible. The theory was, in fact, plain nonsense, flying in the face of every lesson of history, to say nothing of every precept of Christian teaching.

The frontiers of the new Poland, obviously the most vulnerable of all the new states, were strategically indefensible. The Austro-Hungarian Empire was split up into a number of states, none of which was economically viable. The Baltic republics existed from the very start purely by grace of Russia. Germany was left intentionally without a frontier, with her territory cut in two by the Polish Corridor, with a large group of her population on the wrong side of the Czechoslovakian frontier, and crippled by an undisclosed liability for reparations. By rendering Germany permanently unstable politically, we destroyed the possibility of peace for the rest of Europe. We also placed the whole world on the horns of a dilemma. By the balkanization of Southern and Eastern Europe we created a situation in which a stable regime, if it ever arose in Germany, would find no effective barrier to German expansion either south or east. If, on the other hand, Germany remained disorganised, discontented, and impoverished, there could be no effective European recovery. Meanwhile, the French frontier remained as vulnerable in 1919 as it had been four years before.

It was inevitable, after the temporary boom of 1919–20, that we, as the one great free-trade country, should be the principal sufferers from the world chaos. By February, 1921, the unemployed were over a million and before the end of the year they had reached the staggering total of 2,038,000. The public temper was not rendered more sympathetic to Mr. Lloyd George's administration by the conduct of affairs in Ireland where the Sinn Fein rebellion had come to a head in 1920 and the British Government had taken the desperate decision to engage themselves in a guerrilla warfare with the rebels. Nor was Ireland the only storm centre in the British Empire. There was widespread unrest in India, and the British Government had thought it necessary to introduce a sweeping measure of constitutional reform which, since it conceded the form and withheld the substance of self-government, weakened our authority without adding either to our prestige or our popularity.

The lack of realism with which Mr. Lloyd George had approached the British economic problem was reflected also in his approach to what became for some years the central problem of Anglo-French relations with Germany, the problem of reparations. In December 1920 the Brussels Conference fixed the total of reparations due from Germany at £12,412,000,000 to be paid within forty-two years. This absurdity prejudiced the whole course of the relations between Germany and the western powers. The sequel was a steady depreciation of the German mark, which had fallen to nearly 12,000 to the £ in October, 1922. The world was suffering for the first, but not, unfortunately, for the last, time from the conduct of its affairs by men eminently capable of conducting them if only they had known the purpose for which they were doing so. As it was, we were only re-creating an angry and aggressive Germany.

That was the sum, as the British people saw it at the time, and as history has seen it since, of Mr. Lloyd George's Western European policies. His Irish policy had already ended, as Lord Carson bluntly observed in the House of Lords, in his "surrender at the point of a revolver." His reconstruction policy had ended with 2,000,000 unemployed. In August, 1922, his pro-Greek policy, which had given Smyrna for five years to our rather unwilling allies, also collapsed. The Turks, led by Mustapha Kemal, drove the Greeks out of Asia Minor and invaded the neutral zone of the

Dardanelles.   And so we come to October, 1922, a month which notably foreshadowed the shape of things to come but also registered a great and pregnant change in the existing balance of forces in Europe.

In October, 1922, three things happened.   Our French-Italian allies deserted us at Chanak;[1] the dominions also refused to support our stand against Mustapha Kemal, with whom we were forced to negotiate and almost immediately to make peace on his own terms. In this nadir of Britain's fortunes, Mr. Lloyd George was driven from office by the rising indignation of the Conservative party. At the same time the last of the historic succession of Turkish sultans was driven from his throne and Turkey became the second of the dictatorships which were soon to dominate Europe.   The third of the dictators was close at his heels.   On October 31 the King of Italy called on Mussolini, who had just arrived in Rome at the head of his Fascist militia, to form a government.   The rise to supreme power of these two men of limitless energy, audacity, and ambition was contemporaneous with the appointment as Prime Minister of Great Britain of a dying man, Mr. Andrew Bonar Law.   He succeeded to an unpleasant heritage but secured the suffrage of the British people on his programme of tranquillity. Mr. Lloyd George, after having for six years enjoyed greater personal power than probably any other statesman in our history, fell from office, never to return.

With Mr. Bonar Law, the Conservatives returned to power as well as public office for the first time since 1905.   They were at once confronted with the issue of unemployment, a problem which was to dominate the political scene for a generation to come.

Unemployment reached its first peak under Mr. Lloyd George and as the direct, if not intended, result of the deflation of 1920–21 which crippled our export trade.   Deflation, however, coincided with the end of the sellers' market which inevitably followed the war, and it is wrong to suppose that a wiser monetary policy would have done more than mitigate unemployment, which was due to a number of different causes perfectly well known to students of elementary economics.

Mr. Bonar Law had resigned after a few months of office and was succeeded by Mr. Stanley Baldwin, who showed his independence and his intention to rule when he committed himself, in defiance of Mr. Bonar Law's pledges, to the introduction of a protective tariff.   He did so, it is said, without realizing that in the circumstances the decision made it necessary for him to ask for a dissolution and seek a mandate for the new policy.   As we know, the two free-trade parties, the Liberal party superficially reunited under Mr. Asquith, and the Labour party now under Mr. Ramsay Macdonald, won a decisive victory over Mr. Baldwin at the election of December, 1923.   In the new Parliament these

[1] Where the British and Turkish forces faced each other.

parties combined to defeat the Conservative Government, and Mr.
Ramsay Macdonald became the first Labour Prime Minister.
After a few uneasy months his Government was defeated by a
combination of Conservatives and Liberals, and at the ensuing
election in October, 1924, Mr. Baldwin won a great victory. He
had, however, pledged himself not to introduce a protective tariff,
on the ground that the country had voted against it less than a
year before at an election held on this specific issue.

There was, indeed, lurking in Mr. Baldwin's decision of 1924 the
germ of a new and dangerous constitutional doctrine, derived
beyond a doubt from the fear of the vast new electorate, that the
duty of government is to reflect the majority opinion, and that the
proper course before an election is to put forward the programme
which contains the largest measure of prudence and common sense
consistent with a reasonable chance of obtaining a majority.
Such a doctrine implies that the electorate can confer a "mandate"
and that a government has not only the right but the duty to act
upon it. This highly contentious doctrine in turn tends to transform the House of Commons from a sovereign assembly into an
assembly of delegates and to reduce the cabinet from the high
estate of Ministers of the Crown to the lowly rank of the hired
servants of a caucus. We shall see that this view of the constitution and of the relationship between the king's ministers and the
electorate was to gain ground and lead the country into grave
difficulties in 1931 and again in 1935.

The fear of the electorate was due mainly to the fact that just
when, for the first time in British parliamentary history since the
reign of Queen Anne, really fundamental issues divided the
Government from the Opposition, British statesmen had to face an
immense new electorate of twenty millions without the party
machinery necessary to bring the real issues home to the nation
as a whole. The first of these issues, in 1925, was Socialism itself,
the second the Socialists' approach to the pressing international
problems.

The fundamental difference in regard to Socialism needs no
elaboration. Socialism can be, as Mr. Ramsay Macdonald wished
it to be, introduced gradually, but each step is by its nature
irreversible. It is, therefore, none the less a revolutionary measure
for being introduced by stages. The fundamental differences
between the British left- and right-wing parties over foreign policy
between the wars were more subtle. They were violently felt and
experienced and their existence was one of the contributory causes
of the disasters of 1938 and 1939, but it is exceedingly difficult to
define their causes in general terms. Perhaps one difference can
be fairly suggested by quoting Mr. Ramsay Macdonald's statement
to the fifth assembly of the League in 1924: "Our interests for
peace are far greater than our interests in creating a machinery of
defence; a machinery of defence is easy to create, but beware lest

in creating it you destroy the chances of peace." If that doctrine meant only that the object of a defence machinery is the preservation of peace, no one could have objected to it. But it was held to imply, and no doubt did, a belief to which not even the most Liberal-minded Conservative could ever subscribe, that the existence of a formula for negotiations and arbitration rendered national armaments superfluous. Another and equally fundamental difference lay in the attitude of the two parties to Russia, in particular, and to the revolution in general. Long before 1925 the British Government had abandoned all idea of intervening in Russia's internal affairs, but revolution *per se* represented to the Conservatives a dangerous solvent of international order and economic recovery, and they accordingly viewed Russia from the outset with much of the distrust with which the whole Western world views her to-day.

It is against the background of these fundamental differences of creed and temperament rather than under the influence of the more fashionable polemical views of the inherent vices of Conservatives or Labour-Socialists that we should consider the political history of the period from 1925 to our own times. January, 1925, marks fairly clearly the end of the immediate post-war confusion. By that date there was at least a marked improvement in the general political and economic situation in Europe. The reparations problem had been partially solved by the Dawes scheme; the German currency was on the way to being re-established (albeit at the cost of the ruin of the German middle classes for which the world was to pay very dearly); the eastern frontiers were at last more or less stabilised; a treaty had been signed with a stable government in Turkey; the French had withdrawn from the Ruhr which they had occupied on the plea of a default by the Germans over reparations in January, 1923 (during their occupation the mark had fallen to 15,000,000 to the £); there were faints signs of a revival of international trade. The debate at Geneva between the apostles of sanctions and the apostles of disarmament was, however, still in progress; the French were the champions of a new draft instrument, the Geneva protocol, which proposed in effect a system of guarantees, backed by sanctions, for the enforcement of the unchanged provisions of the different peace treaties; the British dominions, members of the League of Nations in their own right, refused to support such a system and Mr. Baldwin's government were thus forced, almost as soon as they had taken office, to decide against the protocol. Without some international guarantees the French would not disarm; without disarmament Germany's rearmament could not be indefinitely forbidden. So the problem presented itself to all parties in Britain in 1925.

The world was now, for the first time, face to face with the real defect of the 1918 settlement. The succession states to the Austro-Hungarian Empire were so economically weak and so strategically indefensible that a rearmed Germany would dominate the Central European plain. It was, however, plainly incompatible with the ideals of the League to keep Germany permanently in tutelage to the military forces of their late enemies. Mr. Baldwin and the new British Foreign Secretary, Mr. Austen Chamberlain, found an imagined solution in the Locarno Treaties whereby Belgium, France, and Germany were to be guaranteed against aggression from one another by Great Britain and Italy, and as a reward for such an engagement voluntarily entered into, Germany was to be admitted to the League of Nations and to join in the disarmament negotiations as a free and equal party. The Locarno Treaties were signed in London amid great rejoicing, but what was much more significant than the guarantees offered to France and Belgium (for that was really the sum of the matter) by Great Britain and Italy was the tacit refusal of either country to guarantee the other territorial provisions of the peace treaties. If there had been a general will to disarmament, Locarno might, indeed, have been the starting point of a return to peaceful conditions, but disarmament was, in fact, a futile conception on a continent dominated in the east by Russia. Germany, Italy, Poland, and Czechoslovakia were not going, in the circumstances, to disarm voluntarily and there was no machinery for coercion, nor any will to coerce. In Great Britain alone disarmament proceeded steadily, but this only served to increase the nervousness of France while exciting the hopes of the enemies of the treaties elsewhere. It would be wrong to condemn the Locarno Treaties. They created a far more friendly atmosphere in Western Europe and, had any statesman of the period been in a position to profit by it, history would no doubt note these treaties as a memorable step towards the re-establishment of peace. The diplomacy of the twenties and thirties was, however, as sterile and irrelevant as the violent controversies to which it gave rise and which still influence political tempers all over the world.

Mr. Baldwin's approach to the domestic problems of Great Britain was, fortunately, rather firmer than his handling of foreign policy. Having abandoned, as we have seen, protection and imperial preference he proceeded, very deliberately, to lay, with the assistance of Mr. Neville Chamberlain and Mr. Winston Churchill, the firm foundations of the welfare state. Time had, by 1925, ended the old differences which had given Britain for so long a rigid two-party system. What was in question, as the Conservative party of those days saw it, was how the private enterprise system, necessary in its judgment to a non self-supporting country which can only live by selling its products at competitive prices in the world's markets, could be made acceptable in an unlimited democracy. The answer, it seemed clear, was to be found by accepting as public responsibilities, and thus, in effect, as a first charge on private enterprise, full statutory provision for old age, sickness, widowhood, and unemployment. The decision in 1926 to introduce widows' and contributory old age pensions was not a hurried remedy for an emergency, but a deliberate act of policy, and one from which there could be no withdrawal. Here was something permanent and revolutionary.

The State was here put forward as the normal paymaster to whom all were to look for maintenance in widowhood (which comes to the majority of women) and in old age, which comes to all. The State was no longer to be the occasional intervener in times of stress and strain and the reliever of dire poverty, but the habitual and actually compulsory channel to which, in many of the normal eventualities of life, all people without distinction of means, class, and occupation would look for financial assistance.

Unfortunately, the Acts dealing with widows' and old age pensions were also noteworthy in a less creditable way. They marked the low-water mark of post-war finance. These Acts made vast promises, and conferred on future generations burdens vastly greater than those which would be borne by the first beneficiaries from the scheme.

To this ambitious scheme were added Mr. Neville Chamberlain's important Housing Act, which in effect solved the housing shortage in the inter-war period, and his still more important Local Government Act of 1929, which paved the way for the final abolition of the Poor Law and for the creation in its place of the Public Assistance Board, which in the hey-day of Mr. Attlee's Socialist and full employment administration was still paying out over £60,000,000 a year to over 1,200,000 in the relief of destitution.

It is fair to say that, as a matter of history, the pattern of the social system under which we live to-day is the creation not of Mr. Attlee, nor even of Mr. Churchill, but of the 1925 Conservative administration. Whether the path on which they set our feet was the right one or no, we have been unable to leave it, and most subsequent legislation has been within the framework of the social legislation of the twenties and thirties.

In 1929 Mr. Baldwin's government went to the country and was decisively rejected by the new electorate which returned 287 Labour members, 261 Conservatives, and 59 Liberals.

It is generally said that the cause of the defeat was the failure of Mr. Baldwin and his lieutenants to solve the problem of unemployment. That is quite unhistorical. By 1929 there was no unemployment problem. There was the terrible problem of the distressed areas, created by the permanent shrinkage of demand for our textiles, shipbuilding, coal, and iron and steel. The problem which Mr. Baldwin so notably failed to solve was solved partly by time and partly by circumstance. Since 1945, governments have sought to remedy it by encouraging new industries in the affected areas. It was then a problem which could only be solved by the migration of labour and by time. The young people moved out of the distressed areas; the older people in the course of time died. In 1929, however, there seemed to Mr. Baldwin to be no hope of a quick solution and he said so. It was Mr. Baldwin's candour, not his callousness, which lost him the election.

Mr. Ransay Macdonald had nothing to offer in place of Mr. Baldwin's policy. He could, and did, spend more money, but the huge anti-Socialist majority made it impossible to nationalize our industries, and it is merely unhistorical to suppose that the Socialist Government had any policy of its own to cure the sickness of the distressed areas or to support our export trade in face of the increasingly adverse conditions which marked the years 1929 to 1932. We shall pull through, said Mr. Baldwin rather ruefully, and lost the election. We shall go from strength to strength, said Mr. Ramsay Macdonald, and led the country into the public bankruptcy of 1931.

There is no mystery whatever about the origins or nature of that crisis as far as it concerns this country. It had nothing to do with reparations, war debts, or the maldistribution of gold. It was the direct result of a prolonged failure of British costs to follow the trend of world prices, and their failure was reflected in the over-valuation of the £ sterling. What the Socialists did between 1929 and 1931 was to place the last straws on the back of an already enfeebled camel. Directly political confidence in the integrity of British governmental finance weakened, the long-feared flight from the £ became a fact. The immediate causes of the crisis were some foolish loans to Germany, and Mr. Snowden's reckless budgeting in March 1930 and his still more improvident arrangements for 1931–2. These mistakes greatly intensified foreign anxiety and, by further weakening Government credit at home, added to the overhead costs of industry just at the time when world prices were near their worst.

It was now that the train of events was set in motion that ultimately led to the outbreak of the Second World War. In the early 1930's Britain was in the throes of a financial crisis. France was hopelessly divided and incapable of producing any stable government. Those who say that we had only to overthrow Hitler by military force in 1933 (when Germany left the League) to relieve Europe for ever from the threat of another world war, forget that relations between Italy and France were strained almost to breaking point, that we could not even get into Germany, let alone fight there, without French co-operation, and that public opinion in both countries was unprepared for war and disinclined to effort. Even, however, if the effort had been made and Hitler had been driven from office, the world would have continued to face the central problem of rewriting the peace treaties, or not rewriting them, in the same mood as before and not in the mood of 1938 or 1939. It was on allied disarmament, not on rearmament, that such enthusiasm as there was in those uneasy days was centred, and the peaceful gesture, not the mailed fist, was the only fashionable prescription for the world's ills.

In this spirit a provisional armament agreement was actually reached with Germany in 1932. The initiative had come from Dr. Brüning's tottering government. But Germany by then was on the verge of revolution. For the delays which wrecked any hope of a settlement of the armaments issue with Germany in 1930 and 1931 the blame must be laid chiefly on France, but there was a lack of statesmanship everywhere, for which no creed or party bears sole blame.

Early in 1932 the Disarmament Conference opened at Geneva. By that time Mr. Ramsay Macdonald had formed the first National Government. The conference opened to the accompaniment of the Japanese guns bombarding Shanghai. Though few realized it, the post-1918 peace years were over for ever. Two months later the Nazis, in the spring elections, gained control of Prussia.

Dr. Brüning, immediately he learned the results of the Prussian elections, hurried to Geneva with a concrete proposal for limited German rearmament. He secured the agreement of Great Britain, but the French representative, M. Tardieu, was not at Geneva; a general election was in progress in France. Chance, again, was playing the hand. When he was summoned to discuss the Geneva proposals, he was dissuaded by his ambassador in Berlin, who assured him that Dr. Brüning was about to fall from office and that a lasting and more favourable agreement could be secured from his successor. M. Tardieu fell into the trap. That was the end of the Weimar republic, and it sealed the fate of parliamentary democracy on the Continent for a generation. On January 30, 1933, Hitler became Chancellor of the German Reich.

The result was devastating for the Disarmament Conference, which became a public farce. The powerlessness of the League, in face of the divisions of the great powers, roused the dormant energies of Russia, Japan, and Germany to a realization of their opportunities. Russian penetration in Turkestan and Mongolia was quiet, and little notice was taken of it. If we had lost the Nelson touch, we had at least preserved his blind eye. The overt blow to the peace organization was struck by Japan in 1933, when she invaded Manchuria and refused to account to the League for her action. As usual, Great Britain had no policy.

China was the first victim of the fatal League doctrine of non-intervention; once the great powers disinterested themselves in her growing anarchy, Japanese intervention was inevitable. The attempt of the League to condition and limit it, after years of inaction, was doomed to failure. If the powers were too idle, too callous, or too poor to make that relatively small military effort that would have been necessary to save China from herself, it is folly to suppose that they would or could have dispatched the two

illion men who would have been necessary to challenge the
trongest military power in Asia.

The impotence of the League in this matter was quickly noted
y France. It was obvious that the support of the League, even
, unanimous verdict of the League Council, was at best a mere
liplomatic asset. It provided no element of security against an
pen breach of the Versailles Treaty of Germany. The immediate
onsequence was the breakdown of the Disarmament Conference
nd the withdrawal of Germany from the League.

It needed only one more blow to the League's prestige in Europe
efore Germany formally fulfilled France's expectations and
lenounced the Versailles Treaty openly and without even the
ormality of consultation. This last blow was provided by the
esults of the Saar Plebiscite on January 17, 1935.

The population of the Saar was of mixed race, enjoying free
nstitutions. It had, by a stroke of good fortune, escaped the
nonstrous political tyrannies which a ruthless political gangster
vas imposing on Germany. They were also enjoying marked
conomic advantages under the League's *régime*. British, Swedish,
nd Italian officials supervised the polling stations, and the polling
ists and stations were so arranged that by no human possibility
ould it become known how towns, districts, or individuals had
voted. The result was a vote for National Socialism so overwhelming that it actually exceeded the majority which Hitler had
obtained in Germany under conditions of his own choosing, on the
issue of disarmament, on which his opponents felt almost as
strongly as his supporters. We had intervened at last in the
European theatre, only to mount guard over the formal and
enthusiastic obsequies of the system to which we had pinned
our faith.

For the second time since 1918—the first time had been at
Chanak—the statesmen of the democracies learned that men of
strong will and ruthless determination will triumph over the best
intentions of irresolute committee men.

The European situation deteriorated rapidly after the Saar
Plebiscite and Hitler's denunciation of the disarmament clauses
of the Versailles Treaty in the spring of 1935. Nevertheless, the
British Government, through Mr. Ramsay Macdonald and Sir John
Simon, made a last effort to ride the storm. Immediately after
Hitler's introduction of conscription, they created the so-called
Stresa Front. Mr. Ramsay Macdonald was harking back to his
original policy and determined on a last effort to keep Italy by the
side of Great Britain and France. With a friendly Italian Army
on the Brenner, Germany's designs on Austria could be checked,
if not checkmated. The enigmatic M. Laval in France was of the
same mind, and was prepared at the eleventh hour (or so it was
believed) to make substantial concessions to Italy. The Stresa
policy collapsed on the issue of Abyssinia. The Franco-Italian

Agreement was signed but not ratified. The Stresa agreemen
between Great Britain, Italy, and France became a dead letter.

We shall probably never know how it came about that n
reference was made to Abyssinia at the Stresa meeting betwee
Mussolini, Mr. Ramsay Macdonald, and Sir John Simon. Th
Italians had brought their colonial experts to discuss the matte
which was not only ripe for discussion but capable of settlemen
The question became later impossible of settlement by reason c
the Italian aggression, but in its origin and essence it was not s
The methods of the Government at Addis Ababa at that date ha
been denounced much more severely by the British than by th
Italians. Further, there had been trouble for some years on th
Sudan-Abyssinia frontier as well as on the Eritrea border. Finally
the ultimate need for some agreement between Great Britair
Italy, and Egypt on the future of Abyssinia had been recognize
as long ago as 1906, when Italy's special interests in the regio
had been accepted by Britain and France in one of the secret clause
of the agreements made at Algeciras.

The year 1935 was the prelude to revolution. The next yea
saw the first Popular Front Government in France and the Spanis
Civil War, while the pro-English, pro-League sentiment in Ital
was overwhelmed by the patriotic excitements which accompanie
the Abyssinian campaign. The British Government had, indeed
seen late and dimly the writing on the wall, and in March 193
(three days before Hitler reintroduced conscription) they ha
issued the first feeble call to the nation to rearm. Unfortunatel
for the peace of the world, the faint voice of the first White Pape
on rearmament had been drowned by the strident noise of the Peac
Ballot, which in the summer of 1935 disclosed, or appeared t
disclose, an immense majority in Great Britain in favour of th
League policy just when the League prestige in Europe was at it
lowest.

Only from Great Britain and France was there any effectiv
withholding of supplies. On these two powers fell the whol
burden of Italy's hostility. Soon after the general election o
October, 1935, we tried to repair the greatest diplomatic blunde
committed by this country since the days of James I by formulating
proposals with France for a compromise settlement. The Frenc
Government was tottering to its fall, but Mr. Baldwin's governmen
had just received a fresh and clear mandate from the electorat
and decided, for once, to take a bold initiative. The result wa
the famous Hoare-Laval proposal. This proposal, if put forward
privately, might have been acceptable to both belligerents, woul
have given Italy a great diplomatic success but would have preserved a measure of sovereignty to the Abyssinians. Instead, it
was made in good faith by a government determined above all to
save the face of the League. The plan was therefore published to
the world, and at once condemned by the left-wing press in France

d the whole of the press in Great Britain and the United States.
ost of the neutrals were sceptical; Russia was frankly hostile.
ae plan was withdrawn in a panic, almost before it had been
jected by both belligerents on very different grounds. Italy
w in the disunion of the League forces the chance of a complete
ctory. Abyssinia was so utterly misled by the outcry against
e concessions proposed to be given to Italy as to think that the
orld would, if need be, rally actively to her side. Mr. Baldwin
st his nerve; Sir Samuel Hoare resigned; Haile Selassie lost
s throne and the world drifted on to the catastrophe which was
ow, humanly speaking, unavoidable.

While Great Britain was licking her wounds, Hitler, on March 7,
936, staged the second of his coups and marched into the Rhine-
nd.

This, if *Realpolitik* had been our game, was the moment for firm
tion against Germany. Germany's bluff was audacious. Not
ven the German General Staff expected it to succeed. But France
as weak and irresolute and British public opinion in a state of
onfusion. Germany was allowed to secure her flank and so
repare for the annexation of Austria.

The same fatal confusion of opinion was to paralyse our
iplomacy over Austria and over the Sudeten Germans in
zechoslovakia.

In March, 1938, while the Spanish Civil War was at its height
nd relations between Britain, France, and Russia were very
rained, Hitler invaded Austria.

This stroke was the direct consequence of the British Govern-
ent's ineffective support of Abyssinia and the French Govern-
ent's futile support of the revolutionary side in the Spanish Civil
Var. Hitler saw Great Britain involved for the hundredth time in
sterile policy of reluctant acquiescence in illegalities which were
o open as to be flagrant. The annexation of Austria would only
e another illegality, and we should, he argued, undoubtedly
cquiesce in that also.

The significance of the Austrian *coup* was military, not political.
By annexing Austria Hitler turned the line of the Czechoslovakian
efences. The unique military inexperience of the British and
rench political leaders at that time was perhaps responsible for
he failure to appreciate this, and when the Czechoslovakian crisis
eveloped almost immediately afterwards, hardly any one seemed
o be aware that the much-vaunted Czechoslovakian defences
vere, after the annexation of Austria, about as much use as the
Maginot Line after the collapse of the front in northern France.

In May, 1937, Mr. Baldwin had resigned, and had been succeeded
by Mr. Neville Chamberlain. Mr. Baldwin bequeathed to his
uccessor a divided country, a navy, army, and air force wholly
nadequate to our responsibilities, and a prestige in Europe vastly
liminished by diplomatic defeats. George VI., second son of

George V., was now king: his elder brother had earlier succeed
to the throne as Edward VIII. on George V.'s death in January, 193
He abdicated later the same year, to marry Mrs. Ernest Simpso
an American whose two previous marriages had ended in divor
and he then took the title of Duke of Windsor.

Only one major change in domestic policy had marked the s
years of the Macdonald-Baldwin national governments, but th
was a revolutionary one. A revenue tariff had been introduc
immediately following on the general election of 1931, but in 193
following on the Ottawa Conference, a complex system of imperi
preference was introduced, and at the same time a great measu
of protection was afforded to British agriculture by a wide varie
of measures, including not only protective duties, but quota
subsidies, controlled marketing, and guaranteed prices. The
decisions marked a definite step on the road to a planned econom
They reflected the first realization that the old Liberal econom
order could not survive unchanged in a world where politic
considerations were driving nation after nation towards se
sufficiency, buttressed by bilateral trade agreements, and wher
simultaneously, the State was expected to guarantee to all i
citizens minimum standards of living. The now much less infl
ential Liberal party remained unconverted either to planning or
tariffs, but after 1932 the tariff issue ceased to be controversi
among the people at large, and the fact that the Liberals henc
forward were committed to reversing the only wholly successf
measures introduced by any party since 1929, condemned th
Liberal party to progressive and rapid decline as a political forc
until the late 1950's.

The effect of the protective tariff, the empire preferences, an
the measures for the relief of British agriculture were marked
unemployment had fallen to the 1929 figure; wages and saving
had risen and the cost of living fallen; industrial production an
housing had substantially increased.

In the course of this slow upward climb from bankruptcy t
solvency, but when progress was still slow and there was a lon
way to go, there had been the general election of 1935, when
according to his own subsequent admission, Mr. Baldwin did no
tell the full truth to the country about the need for rearmamen
and when, perhaps for that very reason, he obtained a surprisingl
large majority. It remains doubtful whether Mr. Baldwin'
decision had any real effect on the subsequent situation. Had h
asked for a mandate for rearmament on a great scale he woul
probably have lost the election, but had he won it, it is unlikely tha
war could have been averted. The trouble with Mr. Ramsay
Macdonald and Mr. Baldwin was not that their foreign policy wa
wrong but that they had no policy. Precisely the same indictmen
lies against that of Mr. Baldwin's opponents both on the right and
on the left. Our foreign policy failed in the thirties for precisely

e same reason that it had failed in the twenties.   We never made
our minds what it was we wanted and therefore we never
epared ourselves to get it.

With the advent of Mr. Neville Chamberlain to power in 1937
e drift towards war continued.   Mr. Chamberlain was a man of
r greater decision of character than Mr. Baldwin, but he had,
om the start, a hopeless hand to play, and he was a man who
as tragically disinclined to take advice.   Nevertheless, it would
wrong to suppose that there were many real chances still open
hich were lost.   These chances had been lost at Versailles, at
eneva in 1932, and at Stresa, if we are thinking of diplomatic
oportunities, and in 1933 and 1936, if we are thinking of oppor-
nities for an easy military victory.

Although Mr. Chamberlain is primarily remembered as an
appeaser," British rearmament proceeded on an ever-increasing
ale during his first year of office; income-tax was raised to provide
e necessary revenues.   At last the British public was taking
riously the danger about which Winston Churchill had been
arning it, all in vain, for several years past.   But the German pace
rearmament continued to draw ahead of the British effort.   The
reats to world peace grew rapidly more imminent and more
oecific in 1938, and the year was marked by successive crises.   On
ch occasion, though war was averted, its inevitability became
ore apparent.   Hitler assumed command of all the armed forces
f the Reich, and clearly indicated that henceforth Germany would
ly on her military strength to solve her "grievances."

The arrogant claims of the German Government to the Czech
udetenlands, in September, 1938, seemed bound to trigger off world
onflict, for France had guaranteed Czech integrity, and, as Britain
tood pledged for the ultimate security of France, she too was
nmediately involved.   Chamberlain, now 70 years of age, resolved
o make an unprecedented personal effort to avert the catastrophe.
'ravelling by air for the first time in his life, he visited Hitler at
3erchtesgarten, and followed this up by two further flights to
iermany to secure the acceptance of a plan agreed upon with
'rance, which, in effect, forced Czechoslovakia to strip herself of
.er fortified frontier-territories and rendered her defenceless, in the
upposed cause of world peace.   At the Munich Conference, Mr.
'hamberlain signed with Hitler a declaration pledging their two
ountries to seek peaceful means of settling any future differences
etween them.   Mr. Chamberlain sincerely believed that he had
' brought back peace in our time"; and he received a tumultuous
velcome when he returned to England.   But most informed
bservers, in Britain and elsewhere, justifiably regarded the
leclaration on Hitler's part as worthless and hypocritical and the
vhole transaction as a shameful betrayal of Czechoslovakia.

Mr. Chamberlain clung to his course of substituting the method
f discussion for that of force even when Hitler overran the rest of

Czechoslovakia, but on March 31, 1939, in the face of rumours
German designs on Poland, he announced that Britain would su
port Poland if the latter were attacked.   When Italy subsequent
occupied Albania, he declared that Britain would support Ruman
and Greece, should their sovereignty be threatened.   These pledg
marked the end of "appeasement"—a policy which had had ove
whelming popular support at the time but which has since be
bitterly criticized by every shade of political opinion.   The gover
ment introduced limited conscription.   In July, 1939, the Germ
threat to Danzig and the flagrant violations of Polish rights the
made it obvious that conflict was imminent.   The nation ha
however, now become thoroughly inured to the prospect of wa
and it was recognized that Nazi methods were incompatible wi
any settled order in Europe.   Germany invaded Poland o
September 1, 1939; on September 3, Britain and France declar
war on her.

The principal military and political events of the Second Wor
War are listed chronologically in the next section.   The Brita
which emerged from the struggle in 1945 was to be very differe
from the Britain of 1939.   As had been the case twenty-five yea
earlier, war considerably accelerated basic social changes which ha
been taking place very gradually during the years of peace: but th
time the changes were, in some ways, even more radical in natur
By 1939 Britain had fully accepted the idea of the State's ultima
responsibility towards its less fortunate members: governme
policy on pensions, unemployment benefits, and housing indicate
this.   Despite the hardships of the depression, and considerab
remaining inequalities of wealth and opportunity between differe
sections of the population, class distinctions were already far weak
than they had been at the end of the First World War, and th
chances of individual advancement on merit much greater.   Durin
the Second World War, economic pressures swung the wag
structure sharply in favour of the working class as a whole, whi
State intervention became an accepted part of the life of ever
member of the community, and not merely of the unfortunate
and by 1945 the principle of the "Welfare State" was acknow
leged, in practice at least, by both major British political parties.

SECTION III.—THE SECOND WORLD WAR, 1939–1945

[*Authorities.*—Sir Winston Churchill, "The Second World War" (1948, c.); Sir W. M. James, "The British Navies in the Second World War" 948); D. Richards and H. St. G. Saunders, "A Preliminary History the Royal Air Force," 2 vols. (1949).]

1939. Germany invades Poland, 1 Sept.; Britain, New Zealand, Australia, and France declare war on Germany, 3 Sept.; Canada and S. Africa declare war: Gen. Smuts becomes Premier of S. Africa, 4 Sept.; Russia invades Poland, 17 Sept.; Poland partitioned between Germany and Russia, 28 Sept.; *Royal Oak* sunk in Scapa Flow, 14 Oct.; Anglo-Turkish pact, 19 Oct.; U.S.A. "Cash and Carry Act" repeals the arms embargo, 4 Nov.; Russia invades Finland, 30 Nov.; b. of the River Plate, 13 Dec.; *Admiral Graf Spee* scuttled, 17 Dec.

1940. Russo-Finnish Peace, 12 Mar.; Reynaud French Premier, 20 Mar.; Germans attack Denmark and Norway, 9 April; Germans invade the Low Countries, 10 May; Churchill forms coalition govt., 10 May; Dutch army surrenders and German victory at Sedan, 15 May; Belgian army surrenders, 28 May; Dunkirk evacuation, 30 May–3 June; British evacuate Norway and Italy declares war on Allies, 10 June; Spain seizes Tangier and Germans enter Paris, 14 June; French reject British offer of union and Pétain becomes Premier, 16 June; French surrender, 22 June; Russians seize Bessarabia from Rumania, 28 June; Rumania denounces Anglo-French guarantee, 1 July: British disable the French fleet in N. Africa at Oran, 3 July; Italians invade the Sudan, 4 July; Vichy breaks off relations with Britain, 5 July; Britain closes Burma road, 18 July; Lithuania annexed by U.S.S.R., 3 Aug.; Italians invade British Somaliland, 4 Aug.; U.S.S.R. annexes Estonia and Latvia, 5 Aug.; b. of Britain, 8 Aug.–6 Sept.; Vienna award dismembers Rumania, 30 Aug.; British obtain 50 destroyers from U.S.A. in return for bases in W. Indies, 2 Sept.; beginning of the London blitz, 7–8 Sept.; Italians invade Egypt, 13 Sept.; British attack on Dakar fails, 25 Sept.; the "New Order" Pact (Germany, Italy, Japan), 27 Sept.; Germans occupy Rumania, 7 Oct.; Italy attacks Greece, 28 Oct.; Italian fleet severely damaged by British air attack at Taranto, 11 Nov.; blitz on Coventry, 14 Nov.; Wavell opens victorious offensive against Italians in N. Africa, 8 Dec. (till 8 Feb., 1941).

1941. Italian forces placed under German control, 20 Jan.; Germans occupy Bulgaria, 9 Feb.; Britain breaks off relations with Rumania, 10 Feb.; British capture Mogadishu, 26 Feb.; Bulgaria joins Axis, 1 Mar.; U.S.A. Lend-Lease Act becomes law, 11 Mar.; Rommel's counter-attack in Libya begins, 24 Mar.; Gen. Simovic overthrows pro-Axis govt. in Yugoslavia,

27 Mar.; British naval victory over Italians at C. Matapan
28 Mar.; Rashid Ali's pro-Axis revolt in Iraq, 3 April; British
capture Addis Ababa, 5 April; Germans invade Yugoslavia
and Greece, 6 April; Germans capture Sollum, 26 April
Athens, 27 April; Hess flies to Scotland, 10 May; Italian
surrender at Amba Alagi, 19 May; German conquest of Crete
19 May–1 June; H.M.S. *Hood* sunk, 24 May; *Bismarck* sunk
27 May; British and French occupy Syria, 8 June–14 July
Germany invades U.S.S.R., 22 June; U.S.A. occupies Iceland
7 July; British and Russians occupy Persia, 25 Aug.–1 Sept.
Reza, Shah of Persia, forced to abdicate, 16 Sept.; Germans
reach Leningrad, 4 Sept.; capture Kiev, 19 Sept.; second
British offensive in Libya, 18 Nov.; final Italian surrender in
Ethiopia at Gondar, 27 Nov.; Three-Power Conference at
Moscow, 29 Nov.; Japanese attack Pearl Harbour, 7 Dec.
Japanese occupy Siam and invade Malaya, 8 Dec.; H.M.S.
Prince of Wales and *Repulse* sunk, 10 Dec.; Japanese take
Guam and Axis declare war on U.S.A., 11 Dec.; Hitler takes
immediate command of German army, 19 Dec.; Japanese take
Wake I., 23 Dec.; Hong Kong, 25 Dec.

1942. United Nations Pact at Washington, 1 Jan.; Japanese take
Manila, 2 Jan.; Japanese naval victory in Macassar Straits
23–25 Jan.; Japanese invade Burma, 8 Feb.; capture Singa-
pore, 15 Feb.; Rangoon, 9 Mar.; Java, 10 Mar.; American
raid on Tokio, 18 April; fall of Corregidor, 6 May; Japanese
naval victory in the Coral Sea, 7–11 May; second German
offensive in Libya opens, 12 May; first 1,000-bomber raid (on
Cologne) 30 May; b. of Midway, 3–6 June; Japanese attack
Aleutians, 3 June; Gen. Eisenhower C.-in-C. U.S. forces
European theatre, 25 May; Germans reach El Alamein, 1 July
Germans take Sebastopol, 2 July; Americans attack Guadal-
canal, 7 Aug.; British raid on Dieppe, 14 Aug.; Germans take
Stalingrad, 5 Sept.; Russian counter-offensive at Stalingrad
begins, 27 Sept.; British victory at Alamein, 23 Oct.–3 Nov.
allied landing in N. Africa, 8 Nov.; Germans occupy Vichy
France, 11–12 Nov.; French fleet scuttled at Toulon, 27 Nov.
Germans driven from Agheila, 13 Dec.; Russian victory at
Kotelnikovo, 29 Dec.

1943. Casablanca Conference, 14–26 Jan.; British take Tripoli
23 Jan.; Russians take Voronezh, 25 Jan.; final German
surrender in Stalingrad, 2 Feb.; Gen. Eisenhower allied C.-in-C
N. Africa, 6 Feb.; Russians take Kursk, 8 Feb.; Americans
finally clear Guadalcanal, 9 Feb.; b. of the Bismarck Sea
1–3 Mar.; b. of the Mareth, 21–29 Mar.; Allies take Tunis
7 May; Axis surrender in N. Africa, 13 May; Allies take
Pantelleria, 11 June; Allies conquer Sicily, 9 July–7 Aug.
Mussolini resigns, 25 July; Russians take Orel, 4 Aug.
Kharkov, 23 Aug.; Mountbatten becomes allied C.-in-C. S.E

Asia, 25 Aug.; Allies land in Italy and Italy surrenders, 3 Sept.;
allied landing at Salerno, 9 Sept.; Russians take Bryansk,
17 Sept.; Smolensk, 25 Sept.; Kiev, 6 Nov.; Americans
capture Tarawa, 21–25 Nov.; Cairo Conference, 22–26 Nov.;
Teheran Conference, 26 Nov.–2 Dec.; U.S.A. and Britain give
aid to Tito, 20 Dec.

1944. Ciano executed, 11 Jan.; Russian offensive in Leningrad
area begins, 15 Jan.; allied landings at Nettuno and Anzio,
22 Jan.; Americans capture Kwajalein, 1–6 Feb.; b. of Cassino,
1 Feb.–18 May; Japanese defeat in Manipur, 13 Mar.–30 June;
Russians reach Polish and Rumanian frontiers, 2 April;
capture Sebastopol, 9 May; Allies enter Rome, 4 June; allied
landings in Normandy, 6 June; flying bomb attacks on
London begin, 15 June; break-through at St. Lô, 27 July;
Polish rising in Warsaw begins, 1 Aug.; b. of the Falaise gap,
7–23 Aug.; allied landings in S. of France, 15 Aug.; Allies
capture Paris, 25 Aug.; Brussels, 3 Sept.; Americans take Palau
Is., 15 Sept.–13 Oct.; Russians invade Hungary, 6 Oct.; b. of
Arnhem, 17–26 Oct.; decisive Japanese naval defeat in
Philippine Sea, 23–25 Oct.; armistice with Bulgaria, 28 Oct.;
British land on Walcheren, 1 Nov.; last German offensive in
the Ardennes, 16–22 Dec.; Hungary changes sides, 30 Dec.

1945. Russians take Warsaw, 11 Jan.; Russians take Budapest,
13 Feb.; Turkey declares war on Germany and Japan, 23
Feb.; Americans cross the Rhine at Remagen, 7 Mar.; Russians
denounce the neutrality pact with Japan, 5 April; Pres.
Roosevelt dies, 12 April; Russians occupy Vienna, 13 April,
and reach Berlin, 21 April; Russians and Americans meet
near Torgau, 26 April; Mussolini shot, and German pleni-
potentiaries in Italy sign terms of surrender, 29 April; Berlin
surrenders and armistice in Italy effective, 2 May; German
forces in N.W. Europe surrender, 5 May; all German forces
surrender, 7 May; Americans capture Okinawa, 21 June;
atomic bomb on Hiroshima, 6 Aug.; Russia attacks Japan,
8 Aug.; atomic bomb on Nagasaki, 9 Aug.; Japan surrenders,
14 Aug.; Japanese forces in China surrender, 9 Sept.; in
S.E. Asia, 12 Sept.

SECTION IV.—1945–1960

AT THE end of the Second World War it soon became evident that
Britain had undergone a peaceful social revolution during the preceding six years. In addition, her position as a world power had
changed fundamentally. In 1940 Britain had "stood alone"
against the might of a Germany which effectively dominated the

rest of Europe. After 1945 she recognized her interdependence with the United States of America and with the non-Communist nations on the Continent in any future struggle, and this recognition was to be expressed in her membership of the North Atlantic Treaty Organization, established in 1948, whose members co-operated in their joint defence. The Britain of 1945 was a debtor-nation impoverished by war, and bereft of many of her former sources of colonial wealth; yet in her struggle to regain her solvency and her place as one of the great trading nations of the world, she still placed stringent conditions on the economic links she was prepared to forge with Europe. The year 1959 thus saw the emergence of two economic blocs in Western Europe—the "Inner Six" and the "Outer Seven": the first, dominated by Gaullist France and Adenauer's Federal Germany; the second by Britain. This fact was not without potential dangers for the future. The military and material leadership of the West had passed to the United States of America. Britain's influence diminished in the Middle East, in particular; rising Arab nationalism was "anti-Imperialist," and the Suez fiasco in 1956 and the republican *coup* in Iraq in 1958 really marked the end of Britain's effective authority in the area. Conversely, British policy towards what had been her pre-1939 Empire was generally enlightened and progressive: India, Pakistan, and Ceylon became self-governing dominions within the Commonwealth in 1946, and Malaya and Ghana in 1958, and all maintained close and affectionate relations with Britain. Considerable efforts were made to achieve constitutional progress and racial harmony in Britain's other African territories, though here success was not uniform: in 1960, Mr. Macmillan, on a visit to South Africa, declared Britain unable to accept Nationalist South Africa's policy of *apartheid*.

After 1945 the European countries liberated from Germany by the Soviet armies rapidly succumbed to Communism. The "iron curtain" of the Red Army divided Communist from non-Communist Europe, and split Germany into two ideologically opposed states. Relations between East and West deteriorated rapidly. The episode of the "Berlin blockade" in 1948 seemed, for a time, on the verge of leading to open hostilities; but the uneasy state of "cold war" remained, tension lessening a little after Stalin's death in 1953, increasing in 1956 after the Russians' bloody suppression of an anti-Communist revolution in Hungary, and subsequently subsiding in face of Mr. Khruschev's apparent willingness to discuss some at least of the issues at stake with the United States and Britain. Throughout the period, the tense world situation forced Britain to maintain extremely heavy expenditure on defence, and she also pursued her own experiments in the field of nuclear warfare. In the Far East the rise of Communist China first became really obvious to Western eyes in 1950, when the Korean war broke out. America took the initiative in countering Communist aggression in South Korea with armed force, and Britain supported er, sending troops to join the United Nations' army there. Unlike he United States, however, Britain recognized the Communist egime as the legal government of China.

In 1945 a General Election resulted in a sweeping Labour victory: r the first time, a British Labour government had a clear working najority. Labour's proposed programme of social reform had learly attracted large numbers of uncommitted young voters. ttlee became Prime Minister, and the next five years saw the nactment of a vast amount of social legislation and nationalization. he previous government had already passed an important Education Act (1944): the Labour Government carried through weeping legislation dealing, among other things, with social insurnce and legal aid, and set up the National Health Service. During ts period of office, coal-mines, railways, gas and electricity underakings, air-lines, road haulage, and iron and steel were nationalized, nd the power of the House of Lords further curtailed. This proramme involved heavy taxation, and the government's belief in a ' planned economy " was expressed in numerous controls, notably n such spheres as building, etc. The continuing austerity of 3ritish life, several years after the end of the war, for which governnent policy was at least partially responsible, soon began to evoke nuch popular discontent. At the General Election in 1950 the ,abour majority was cut from 186 to 8; the following year, there vas a serious economic crisis, and Attlee again went to the country. The result was a Conservative victory, and Winston Churchill once nore became Prime Minister. The Conservatives accepted most of heir predecessors' legislation, but repealed the Acts nationalizing ron and steel and road transport. They also abolished many of he controls used by Labour.

The sudden death of George VI. in 1952 brought to the throne the irst Queen-Regnant Britain had had for more than half a century. The coronation of Queen Elizabeth II. took place with full ceremony n 1953. By 1955 " austerity" Britain had largely disappeared. Rationing had ended, industry was booming, and the housing hortage, acute since 1945, was easing. Churchill, now over eighty rears of age, resigned, to be succeeded as Premier by Anthony Eden, and in the General Election that followed the Conservatives ncreased their majority. But by 1956 the situation was less stable. Jnemployment began to rise: inflationary pressures reasserted hemselves. In July, Britain relinquished her Suez Canal bases. 'n October, Franco-British intervention in an armed dispute etween Israel and Egypt, in the form of a military landing at Port Said, caused a serious, though only temporary, rift between Britain and the United States, and damaged British prestige immeasurably hroughout the Middle East. In Britain itself, public opinion was leeply divided on the issue. Early in 1957 Eden resigned and etired from politics for health reasons, and Harold Macmillan became Prime Minister. During the year the Bank Rate was raised

to 7 per cent (the highest since 1920). The Rent Act freed larg
numbers of properties from long-standing rent restrictions, and i
passing this measure the government incurred considerabl
unpopularity. However, by the time the next General Electio
took place, in 1959, economic stability had been regained. Th
country as a whole was prosperous; save in a few particula
industries (e.g. cotton) unemployment had fallen; consumer good
were plentiful. Once again the Conservatives returned to powe
with a majority still bigger than before. Never before had
British political party had such a succession of election victorie
with its majority progressively increasing from Parliament t
Parliament.

This period of British history has already been criticized in som
quarters for its apparently overriding preoccupation with materia
concerns. Certainly it was a period in which high wages, scientifi
progress, and industrial expansion combined to make many of th
material perquisites of modern civilization—television sets, car
refrigerators, holidays abroad, etc.—available to vastly large
sections of the population than ever before. Poverty had not bee
eliminated, but its boundaries had shrunk drastically. The Labou
party in 1959 became suddenly aware that many people whom i
had regarded as its traditional supporters now had what might b
termed a "middle-class" standard of living, and that their politica
attitude had modified accordingly. It was forced to set about
reappraisal of its own ideas on basic issues. In addition, the Trad
Union movement was becoming discredited in the eyes of man
citizens owing to its failure to control its more extreme members
The "unofficial strike" was a familiar feature of the domestic scen
1945–60. Many observers noted a decline in the status of th
individual *per se*: public and private monopolies, the "closed shop
policy of some of the unions, and, above all, the tremendous increas
in the State's authority to intervene in the affairs of all its citizen
tended to restrict the individual's freedom. This tendency was no
confined to Britain: it existed throughout the Western world, an
the "existentialist" literature of post-war France and the "angr
young man" of English letters of the 1950's can be interpreted a
literary expressions of resentment against it. On the other hand
charity was dispensed on a larger scale than ever before, albeit b
the State machine, while catastrophes such as the disastrous coasta
floods of 1953 and the Hungarian revolution of 1956 evoked a mos
generous financial reaction from all sections of the British public
However, despite the social benefits provided by the Welfare State
despite the increasing opportunities for leisure produced by im
proved health, shorter working hours, and higher wages, and despit
the greater educational opportunities available to all, moral prob
lems remained, and even grew more pressing. The decline ir
religious observance, evident since the end of the First World War
showed few concrete signs of being arrested. A consistently hig

te of divorce and crime, the prevalence of prostitution in the big
ties, sporadic outbreaks of intolerance towards racial minorities,
d an acknowledged "'teen-age problem" were some of the signs
at indicated that material progress was ultimately of little value
the right spiritual and moral bases were missing.

Index